Struggles for Representation

African American Documentary Film and Video

EDITED BY
Phyllis R. Klotman
AND
Janet K. Cutler

Indiana University Press

BLOOMINGTON AND INDIANAPOLIS

This book is a publication of

Indiana University Press
601 North Morton Street
Bloomington, IN 47404-3797 USA

http://www.indiana.edu/~iupress

Telephone orders   800-842-6796
Fax orders   812-855-7931
Orders by e-mail   iuporder@indiana.edu

The paper used in this publication meets the minimum requirements of American National Standard for Information Sciences—Permanence of Paper for Printed Library Materials, ANSI Z39.48-1984.

MANUFACTURED IN THE UNITED STATES OF AMERICA

Library of Congress Cataloging-in-Publication Data

Struggles for representation : African American documentary film and video /
    edited by Phyllis R. Klotman and Janet K. Cutler.
        p.   cm.
    Filmography: p.
    Includes bibliographical references (p.   ) and index.
        ISBN 0-253-33595-7 (alk. paper). — ISBN 0-253-21347-9 (pbk. : alk. paper)
        1. Afro-Americans in motion pictures. 2. Documentary films—United
States—History and criticism. I. Klotman, Phyllis Rauch. II. Cutler,
Janet K.
    PN1995.9.N4S77   1999
    070.1'8—dc21   99-29890

1 2 3 4 5 04 03 02 01 00 99

and video to every stage of the project's development. The book could not have been completed without his participation. Robert Klotman provided invaluable advice about collaborative enterprises and the intricacies of publishing. We appreciate his steadfast support, and his help with the myriad details of the project.

Katya McElfresh worked tirelessly as the primary research assistant for the book and coordinated the acquisition of photographs and permissions. Her attention to detail, her artful management of the photo log, and her cheerful perseverance proved invaluable to the project. Paul Max McElfresh also supported the day-to-day work on this project, contributing his considerable computer skills and sense of humor to the enterprise.

We are particularly indebted to those who read various parts of the manuscript and offered useful suggestions. Rima Shore provided expert editorial advice and guidance that made possible the completion of the book. James Nash lent his skillful attention to detail and clarity of language; he and Teri Gatto generously helped to excerpt the considerable mass of interview material. Paul Arthur offered ongoing encouragement, made helpful interventions and insightful suggestions, and served as a constant model of scholarly energy and intellectual engagement.

As photo researcher on the project, Jim Supanick discovered useful images and designed captions for the book. We are grateful to him and to the following individuals and institutions for production stills: the Associated Press, Camille Billops and James Hatch (Hatch–Billops Collection), St. Clair Bourne (Chamba Mediaworks Film Library), Pearl Bowser (African Diaspora Images), Brown Brothers, Simon Chaput, Joanne Grant, William Greaves (William Greaves Productions), Thomas Allen Harris, Velma Green Hopkins, Pamela Jennings, Philip Mallory Jones, the Massachusetts Historical Society, William Miles (Miles Educational Film Productions, Inc.), Third World Newsreel, the University of Chicago Library, Video Data Bank, and Reginald Woolery.

We thank Aimee Hall and Elizabeth Underhill who researched, reconciled conflicting information, and entered the data for the Bibliography, Filmography, and Index of Film / Videomakers. For their assistance in word processing parts of the manuscript and their computer expertise, we thank Karen Frane, Linda Jean, and Monique Threat. We would also like to acknowledge Thomas Cripps, Fred McElroy, Marlene Provizer, and John Williams, who provided useful advice along the way. Among those who were supportive and helpful throughout the process, we owe special thanks to Amy Gilman Srebnick for sharing her knowledge and experience with publishing matters.

ACKNOWLEDGMENTS

Because this book is a collaborative project, there are many people and institutions to thank for their assistance. The National Endowment for the Humanities provided generous multi-year support of the research and writing that made this book possible. In particular, we wish to express our appreciation to NEH program officers George Lucas and Elizabeth Arndt, who shepherded this project through its application, planning, and implementation stages.

In conceptualizing the project and defining its scope, we talked with scholars and film/videomakers across the country. We are grateful to Manthia Diawara, William Greaves, Louis Massiah, Marlon Riggs, and Roy Thomas for their early counsel; to the chapter authors for their dedication to the project and their contributions to its development; and to the many film/videomakers who graciously consented to be interviewed for the book and whose ideas helped shape its direction.

In researching the book, we benefited from the expertise of staff at a number of institutions: Madeline Matz of the Library of Congress and James Murray of the Schomburg Center for Research in Black Culture were especially helpful in locating materials for the project. Films, videotapes, and secondary research materials were provided for study at the Donnell Media Center of the New York Public Library, Electronic Arts Intermix, the Film Study Center of The Museum of Modern Art, the Performing Arts Library of the New York Public Library, Women Make Movies, and Third World Newsreel. The Black Film Center/Archive was the primary resource for this book, providing film and video texts, interview transcripts, and additional source materials to the editors and other chapter authors.

We wish to express our thanks to our institutions—Indiana University and Montclair State University—for their support of the project. Joan Catapano of Indiana University Press has been enthusiastic about the book from the beginning; we are grateful to her and to the readers of the manuscript, whose suggestions for revision were extremely useful.

This book created something of a cottage industry, involving the dedicated help of our family, friends, and colleagues. We owe a special debt of gratitude to Sam McElfresh, who contributed his expertise in grant-writing, his critical skills, and his formidable knowledge of film

10. Black High-Tech Documents   ERIKA MUHAMMAD   298

11. The "I" Narrator in Black Diaspora Documentary
MANTHIA DIAWARA   315

Interviews with Filmmakers / 329
Filmography / 395
Film/Videomaker Index / 441
Bibliography / 457
Contributors / 471
Index / 473

CONTENTS

Acknowledgments / ix

Introduction   JANET K. CUTLER AND PHYLLIS R. KLOTMAN / xiii

1. Pioneers of Black Documentary Film
PEARL BOWSER   1

2. Military Rites and Wrongs: African Americans in
the U.S. Armed Forces   PHYLLIS R. KLOTMAN   34

3. Documenting Social Issues: *Black Journal,* 1968–1970
TOMMY LEE LOTT   71

4. *Eyes on the Prize:* Reclaiming Black Images, Culture,
and History   ELIZABETH AMELIA HADLEY   99

5. Paths of Enlightenment: Heroes, Rebels, and Thinkers
CLYDE TAYLOR   122

6. Rewritten on Film: Documenting the Artist
JANET K. CUTLER   151

7. Uptown Where We Belong: Space, Captivity, and the
Documentary of Black Community
MARK FREDERICK BAKER AND HOUSTON A. BAKER, JR.   211

8. Discourses of Family in Black Documentary Film
VALERIE SMITH   250

9. Springing Tired Chains: Experimental Film and Video
PAUL ARTHUR   268

This book is dedicated to

Henry Hampton, 1940–1998

Carlton Moss, 1909–1997

Marlon Riggs, 1957–1994

Jacqueline Shearer, 1946–1993

Finally, we would like to acknowledge each other. As anyone who has edited a collection of essays knows, the challenges of coordinating the work of many contributors can sometimes be daunting, especially when all of the research and writing involves original work. And while many people regarded our mother–daughter collaboration with some degree of skepticism, the project genuinely benefited from it. *Struggles for Representation* gave us an opportunity to bring together our expertise in African American studies and cinema studies and provided an occasion to enjoy each other's abilities as researchers, writers, editors, and administrators. We recommend it to others.

Introduction

Struggles for Representation

African American Documentary Film and Video

JANET K. CUTLER AND PHYLLIS R. KLOTMAN

Since the mid-1970s, African American cinema has generated both popular attention and scholarly study, with a significant body of writing
focused on the narrative works of Charles Burnett, Julie Dash, Warrington and Reginald Hudlin, Albert and Allen Hughes, Spike Lee, Kasi
Lemmons, John Singleton, and others. The creative work that has occasioned this interest continues a tradition of narrative filmmaking begun in the 1910s by George P. and Noble Johnson and Oscar Micheaux,
whose pioneering efforts to portray cinematically the aspirations and
oppression of their people helped to shape today's black fiction film.

While the latest round of critical assessment has focused on black
narrative film, African American documentary has been largely neglected. Scholars and critics have yet to consider fully the groundbreaking body of nonfiction productions that offer privileged views
of American life. These rich and varied works in film, video, and new
electronic media convey vast stores of knowledge and experience. Although most documentary cannot hope to match fiction film's mass appeal, it is unrivaled in its ability to portray searing, indelible impres-
sions of black life, including concrete views of significant events and
moving portraits of charismatic individuals. There is no equivalent for
footage of that moment when hundreds of civil rights protestors, crossing the Edmund Pettus Bridge in Selma on their way to Montgomery, were attacked by mounted police and state troopers, or when the
caskets of some of the murdered Attica inmates were carried through
their neighborhoods. Documentary's power and pleasure are immediate, unique, and sometimes overwhelming: it provides the sights and

sounds of Malcolm X delivering an electrifying speech to a New York City audience, Betty Carter performing a heart-wrenching song in a crowded university auditorium, and Langston Hughes strolling on a beach in Senegal.

In addition, documentary film/video production—which requires relatively modest financial resources and invites a range of formats from shorts to mini-series—offers possibilities for politicized, experimental work not often available in the arena of commercial fiction film. With access to channels of community exhibition and with institutions committed to funding and distribution, documentary has provided a home for risk-taking and controversy, creating opportunities for the best efforts of socially engaged and aesthetically innovative film/videomakers.

Struggles for Representation is the first volume devoted to an examination of the more than 300 nonfiction works by more than 150 African American film/videomakers that constitute the burgeoning African American documentary tradition. The book explores the extraordinary scope of these aesthetic and social documents in eleven original essays, each solicited specifically for this project, accompanied by a filmography, bibliography, and excerpted interviews with film/videomakers. Taken together, this original research and writing charts a previously undiscovered territory: documentaries that examine the aesthetic, economic, historical, political, and social forces that shape the lives of black Americans, as seen from their perspectives.

While African American documentaries span the century, the lineage of these works may be traced back even further. Indeed, the struggle to "document" an alternative vision of black life has been an aspect of virtually every black cultural form—oral and written, fiction and nonfiction—from spirituals and the blues to black folktales, novels, and newspapers. African American documentary can be seen as an extension of this expressive tradition, and especially as a modern-day inheritor of the slave narrative: nonfiction writings that document and authenticate the experience of slavery from the perspective of former slaves. Originating in the eighteenth century with Briton Hammon's *Narrative* (1760) and ending with Harriet Jacobs's *Incidents in the Life of a Slave Girl* (1861), these texts include *The Life and Adventures of Olaudah Equiano; or Gustavus Vassa, the African*, William Wells Brown's account of his life under the "peculiar institution," and the remarkable autobiographical narratives of Frederick Douglass. Slavery's countless supporters and apologists were challenged by those accounts, and by the printed word of freemen like David Walker, whose *Appeal* (1829)[1] shook the foundations of slavery by exhorting those in bondage to free themselves.

Like the slave narratives, African American documentaries construct black experience from inside the culture. Just as autobiographical story-telling served as a means for former slaves to recount the conditions of their own existence, documentary films and videos create opportunities for African Americans to define a sense of self and of place in their own voices. The slave narratives establish a record of human experience that counters fragmentary historical records; in the same way, documentary films and videos fill in for the absence of conventional historical documents and create alternative narratives of contemporary black life. The need to convey one's own reality, resisting definitions imposed by the dominant culture, is an important theme in both the slave narratives and black documentary film and video, as is the desire to be an agent of one's own destiny, to achieve freedom and full participation in society. Like their literary counterparts, African American documentaries offer testimony to the power of lived experience.[2]

African American documentary practice begins with the silent era film *A Day at Tuskegee* (1910) and continues into the 1910s and 1920s with scores of short subjects exhibited in "race theaters" and at community meeting places. However, little footage survives from the early decades of the century. The body of documentary work available for viewing today begins with a number of seminal social-issue films and short subjects produced during and immediately after World War II: William Alexander's *All American News* series (beginning in 1943), Carlton Moss's *The Negro Soldier* (1944), and William Alexander and Biddy Wood's *By-Line Newsreel* series (beginning in 1946).

Contemporary African American documentary has its origins in the 1960s with the groundbreaking *Black Journal*, the first nationally broadcast television series designed to present issues of concern to the black community. *Black Journal* launched today's black documentary movement: its executive producer William Greaves defined the goals for socially engaged black documentary production and influenced a number of filmmakers who got their start with that series, among them Madeline Anderson, St. Clair Bourne, Charles Hobson, and Stan Lathan. It was Greaves who laid out the "three-point dictum" that articulated *Black Journal*'s approach to documentary: define black reality, pointing to a problem or a struggle; explain how and why the situation evolved; and most importantly, suggest a way out. St. Clair Bourne describes Greaves's emphasis on solutions: "If you didn't do this, then you were really derelict in your duty. . . . It did not have to be *the* way out, but you had to show people trying to attempt to resolve the difference. . . . We could actually get inside and show a direction out."[3]

African American documentary continues into the present with innovative, autobiographical studies like Marlon Riggs's *Tongues Untied* (1989), Marco Williams's *In Search of Our Fathers* (1991), and Camille Billops and James Hatch's *Finding Christa* (1991). These more personal works by a new generation of film/videomakers, which began in the 1980s, extend the tradition of African American documentary while consciously diverging from documentary practices of the past. A number of these more experimental documentaries are hybrid works that juxtapose disparate materials and approaches, while others are interactive, "high-tech" documents, such as Pamela Jennings's CD-ROM *Solitaire: dream journal* (1996).

From its beginnings, African American documentary has addressed a broad spectrum of concerns and employed diverse narrative and cinematic strategies. African American documentary production encompasses the full range of moving image media, from modest independently produced films and videotapes to ambitious theatrically released films and prime-time public television programs. This book acknowledges that the history of African American documentary is a history of participation in both film/video and television, with many media artists moving freely between forms, and using a variety of film and video formats.

If a single strand unites all of this work, it is the "struggle for representation" that characterizes virtually every effort—an urgent desire to convey black life in ways that counter the relatively uninformed and often distorted representations of mass media film and television productions. Documentary filmmaker William Greaves describes his response to witnessing demeaning depictions of African Americans in mainstream cinema:

> I became progressively aware of stereotyping, the way in which the motion picture was used to misrepresent the black American. . . . I decided that what I ought to do is become a filmmaker, so that I could combine . . . my interests in certain types of educational materials—social issues films and films that in one way or another impacted on the social fabric of a country.[4]

St. Clair Bourne's decision to become a documentarian was triggered by his reaction to television coverage of the social upheavals of the 1960s:

> I saw the representation, misrepresentation and confusion of the civil rights movement in the major media by white male spokespeople who attempted

to tell white America what those people were doing, and usually what they said was wrong, or distorted, for their own psychic needs. And I knew I had a better handle on that.[5]

For these filmmakers and others, documentary is the most compelling mode with which to present an alternative, more authentic narrative of black experience and an effective critique of mainstream discourse.

Of course, representation is not a simple matter. As scholars and critics have pointed out, there is no single truth of a community, nor is there an unmediated relationship between film/video and reality. Even if documentary carries the cultural valence of authenticity, cinematic reality is shaped by each filmmaker's personal vision, the film-making process, and the institutions of funding, production, and exhibition through which these works find their audiences. Although many film/videomakers embrace "the real" as a way of expressing their own truths, it is important to recognize that "realism" is a style influenced by the demands of genre, just as "truth" is both a personal and collective construct influenced by political and historical factors.

Nonetheless, in the face of a history of exclusion and misrepresentation, many African American film/videomakers have adopted the documentary mode to assert their view of reality. Documentary's identification with realism as a social signifier and its non-commercial status have made it a welcome site for challenging the authority of mainstream American history and culture. Despite the skepticism of film theorists, many African American film/videomakers embrace the documentary mode as an opportunity to be direct and truthful. In fact, for these documentarians and their audiences, "non-commercial" signals "authenticity": that assumption is part of the rhetorical structure of the works. Thus, many socially and politically committed film/videomakers view documentary as a tool with which to interrogate and reinvent history; their works fill gaps, correct errors, and expose distortions in order to provide counter-narratives of African American experience.

Although current documentary theory challenges idealist notions of documentary expression, African American documentaries have long been identified with struggles for social and political empowerment. There are crucial connections between documentary, the historical world, and present conditions—connections to real people and events, to pressing social problems and political issues. Documentary begins with evidence from reality, but interprets that evidence, using film/video techniques to shape and structure material. These strategies are not always visible to audiences, who often view documentaries as "windows on the world," believing in an unmediated relationship between film and reality.

The struggle for representation occurs on more than one front. First, there is the struggle to be seen. African American documentaries, while frequently made with black audiences in mind, represent a culture which remains largely invisible to all but African Americans themselves; as social documents, these works promote cultural awareness on many levels. As Charles Hobson explains, "I was interested in [producing] programs or subject matter about the black experience that whites in general, whites and some blacks, didn't get from reading the white press and that was really documenting them. . . . Making film, that's what I tried to do."[6] There is also the struggle for expression. Film/videomakers must adopt idioms and rhetorical devices best suited to representing black experience in creative ways; as aesthetic documents, African American documentaries view reality though diverse lenses—for example, didactic educational modes, *cinéma vérité*, and first person narrative—to articulate a range of issues seldom explored in mainstream nonfiction works.

In addition, documentary production involves the struggle to solicit funding, secure distribution, and obtain exhibition venues. Many African American documentarians adopt conventional formats in order to get work made and shown. Still others discover modes more expressive of their own experience and that of their subjects. These more experimental works not only break with conventions of documentary practice, they consciously resist traditional modes. Carroll Blue explains the dilemma: "For the PBS audience I'd pretty much try to stay within the guidelines as much as possible. Because I know it won't even get on the air if it doesn't have a high-quality look to it, and if it doesn't have a certain format. I really stay within those guidelines. However, personally, I'm beginning to make video poems with little things I'm doing on my own, that have nothing to do with my work in 16mm."[7]

Finally, for most African American documentarians, representation is a burning political and social struggle. In the interview material, William Greaves suggests, "A lot of the documentary film movement—filmmaking from a black perspective—are films that are weapons in the struggle for freedom, for equality, for liberation and self-expression, and all those human rights. . . . These films tend to agitate in the tradition of Frederick Douglass. . . . They're activist, advocacy-oriented productions."[8] Other film/videomakers, including Michelle Parkerson, respect documentary "as a political tool";[9] Alonzo Crawford talks about the power of film "to raise social consciousness" and describing one production says, "we went to war, and . . . we used the camera."[10]

Carlton Moss speaks urgently about the need for film and video to portray the racist conditions of American society: "It's impossible for black films to express the black experience without relating to the oppression that blacks have been under, that's within the experience. And if you don't deal with that, then you don't have a story that reflects the life."[11]

Thus, the title of this book refers to these struggles: to make black life visible; to define black personal and collective identity in ways that counter mass media representations; to find appropriate, expressive film/video language; to gain access to and control of the means of production; to reach an audience; to create effective social and political works.

In the context of this book, the terms "black American" and "African American" are used interchangeably to denote Americans of African descent. Because film and television are collaborative media, documentaries are called "African American" when an African American—either as the producer, director, or writer—determined the vision of the work. Although this definition is somewhat arbitrary, it is designed to accommodate the complexities of the "crediting" process, including the different roles that exist on different film and television projects, and the fact that the creative contributions of African Americans have not always been adequately acknowledged.

This study of documentaries by African Americans emphasizes the ties between the makers and their subjects. Rather than using documentary as a form of visual anthropology that investigates "the other," African American documentarians tend to express an identification with their subjects and a sense of shared concerns. Thus, the impulse to explore "the other" is virtually absent from African American documentary, as is the anthropological gaze of so much mainstream nonfiction work. Instead of defining antinomies between the outsider film/videomaker and the insider subject, as one finds in pioneering documentarian Robert Flaherty's *Nanook of the North*, for example, African American documentaries illuminate communal values and subjectivities. By focusing on films about African Americans made by African Americans, *Struggles for Representation* calls attention to the reciprocal relationship between creative agents and their subjects.

"Documentary" is treated as an expansive term that can incorporate a range of historical and personal materials and, in contrast to "nonfiction," has power and significance for African Americans whose experience was, for so long, undocumented and negated. Certainly one of the longstanding "struggles" this book addresses is the struggle over the definition of documentary. Works considered in this book encompass a range of subjects and forms: didactic "activist journalism" designed to explicate otherwise unpublicized issues and prompt social/political action; television series that take innovative approaches to the documentation of social issues and movements; film/video portraits of African American artists and leaders; personal documentaries that link the lives of individual African Americans to broader social issues; documentaries that demonstrate connections between the work by film/videomakers of color in the U.S. and other parts of the world; and works exploiting new technologies that increase African Americans' access to international audiences. Although docudrama, fictional bio-pics, and other forms of realist inscription are not included here, the book does suggest that documentary is a wider term than commonly assumed. By defining the field in a broad way, the book acknowledges the competing and contesting definitions of documentary that characterize this body of work.

In fact, a great deal of contemporary theory has been about breaking down the traditional distinctions between documentary and narrative. Scholars like Michael Renov seek to expose "the truth about nonfiction," pointing to the formal strategies it shares with fiction and raising questions about documentary's special claim to representing reality.[12] Documentary theoretician Bill Nichols raises a related issue, the shifting standards of realism, in his very useful 1994 *Blurred Boundaries: Questions of Meaning in Contemporary Culture:* "the definition of nonfiction, documentary, or even historiography remains highly elusive, and strongly debated. Claims of authenticity butt up against evidence of story telling; claims of objectivity confront signs of dramatic intensification; claims that what we see belongs to the historical world of actual occurrences come up against indications that the act of representation shaped and determined the event in fundamental ways."[13]

Questions about the illusory boundaries between fiction and nonfiction are embodied in the works of African American film/videomakers who merge documentary and narrative modes, producing documentary-influenced narratives grounded in everyday life and nonfiction films of extraordinary poetic power. A number of today's film/videomakers doubt that conventional realism is more authentic than personal and subjective expression, while theorists question the adequacy of critical analysis based on the "correction" model. As film scholars Ella Shohat and Robert Stam suggest in *Unthinking Eurocentrism:* "While these 'stereotypes and distortions' analyses pose legitimate questions about social plausibility and mimetic accuracy, about negative and positive images, they are often premised on an exclusive allegiance to an esthetic of verisimilitude. An obsession with 'realism' casts the question as simply one of 'errors' and 'distortions' as if the 'truth' of a community were unproblematic, transparent, and easily accessible, and 'lies' about that community easily unmasked."[14]

The works explored in this book engage fundamental questions about documentary theory and the representation of race, reflecting tensions between various modes and practices, and shifts in the way black experience has been portrayed in different historical periods. Cultural critic Kobena Mercer points out that while black film / videomakers may assert the advantage of offering their unique perspective on black experience, there are pitfalls in assuming one voice can speak for many: "although it is always necessary to document and validate the authority of experience ('who feels it, knows it'), the selection of *who* is given the right to speak may also exclude others. . . . Not only does this reduce the diversity of black opinion and experiences to a single perspective assumed to be 'typical,' it may reinforce the tokenistic idea that a single film can be regarded as 'representative of every black person's perception of reality.'"[15]

Media artist and theoretician Trinh T. Minh-ha also warns that while film / videomakers may work from "inside the community," their situation is often complex:

> The question is . . . not that of merely "correcting" the images whites have of non-whites, not of reacting to the colonial territorial mind by simply reversing the situation and setting up an opposition that at best will hold up a mirror to the Master's activities and preoccupation. . . . For there can hardly be such a thing as an essential inside that can be homogeneously represented by all insiders; an authentic insider in here, an absolute reality out there, or an uncorrupted representative who cannot be questioned by another uncorrupted representative.[16]

Henry Louis Gates addresses some of the "burden of representation" in *Thirteen Ways of Looking at a Black Man:* "Each, in his own way, rages against the dread requirement to *represent;* against the demands of 'authenticity.' . . . Somehow the choice is always between alternate inauthenticities, competing impostures. Another approach toward the question: How does it feel to be a paradox?"[17]

So much current academic debate has focused on the complexity of documentary representation in recent, personal and experimental film / video work, that it is easy to overlook the large body of historically specific African American documentary designed to shed light on social issues. In that regard, film scholar Noël Carroll's writing offers a helpful reminder. For example, he argues that the fact that documentaries are structured by individuals does not preclude their conforming to accepted standards of evidence, argument and even objectivity: "Though objectivity is not equivalent to truth, the two are related in an important way. In any given field of research or argument, there are patterns of reasoning, routines for assessing evidence, means of weighing the comparative significance of different kinds of evidence, and the standards for observations, experimentation and for the use of primary and secondary sources that are shared by practitioners in the field."[18] In a more recent essay, Carroll insists that there is nothing about nonfiction film, including the selectivity involved in the filmmaking process, that makes it inherently different from or more biased than nonfiction writing in science, history, or journalism. Carroll takes on the postmodernist inclination to deconstruct nonfiction: "refuting what I take to be the overly facile skepticism about the possibility of making motion pictures that are genuinely in the service of knowledge."[19]

Carroll's analysis is useful since so many black documentaries make claims to knowledge, information, and truth. Even when documentary film/videomakers abandon conventional methods of argument in favor of more subjective strategies, they assert the authenticity of their work, celebrating its divergence from the language of traditional authority. Thus, it is important to distinguish between the documentary filmmaker's sense of mission, the audience's reception to the work, and the critic's analysis of documentary in the wider frame of film history and theory.

Interviews conducted for this book suggest that, whatever the differences in subject and style of individual works, there is an intensely idealist, social activist thrust to African American documentary. Film/videomakers from Carlton Moss to Marlon Riggs express a strong sense of obligation to community, a need to bear witness to the lives of ordinary people, and a commitment to do work that honors black life. Influenced by socially engaged family members, community-based institutions like the Federal Theater, and current events—from the civil rights movement of the 1960s to the AIDS crisis of the 1980s/1990s—these film/videomakers see documentary as a way to make vital contributions to their communities. They have a sense that their work offers an opportunity for black people to say what they don't normally say and be heard by people who don't normally hear their concerns.

The documentarians interviewed for this book assert the power of filming African American life, sensing that something extraordinary can happen when black people are afforded the chance to speak and be seen. More than one film/videomaker talks about the opportunities created by low-cost video equipment to turn cameras on elders and record alternative narratives. As Ayoka Chenzira notes:

I looked at *Schindler's List* . . . and the film reminded me of how much we'd lost in black culture. There were few people who put our pictures under floorboards to hide them; there were few recorders going up to the slave and saying "How do you feel on this cotton picking day?" . . . so you don't really have the visual information that would allow you to organize and to have the world be sympathetic to your cause because the things that the world is used to seeing, the evidence, does not exist. . . . I think it is critical that people document. I am so happy that the cost of videocameras keeps going down and I am hoping that more people will just pick up a camera and turn it on their grandmother, turn it on their grandfather . . . to really begin to consciously think about all the holes that we have, again because so much of the history is in the oral tradition and because we need the proof.[20]

If there is a desire among these documentarians to construct counter-narratives of black experience, there is a further concern that those narratives be inclusive. Marlon Riggs's work redresses the historical absence of depictions of black gay life: "I was just so sick of images, of words, of history being written in which I was constantly written out."[21] In recounting the making of *Eyes on the Prize*, Jacqueline Shearer points out, "I was the only black woman producer. Also because of having grown up poor, I would always be the voice calling for gender and class issues, in addition to race. You know they always intertwine."[22]

The interviews also convey a shared conviction that film and video are tools for social and political change, regardless of whether the speakers are classical documentarians who value scholarly studies, practitioners of *cinéma vérité* who advocate a more engaged, direct relationship with their documentary subjects, or vanguard film/videomakers whose more personal works seek to extend the possibilities of documentary practice. The impulse to historicize is articulated by filmmakers Jacqueline Shearer and William Miles, both of whom describe coming upon boxes of archival material that no one has looked at for years and embarking on huge projects involving lengthy research and extensive fundraising in an attempt to "take all that information and put it on the screen."[23] Another impulse—to employ the relatively mobile technology of *cinéma vérité* to create intimate portraits of subjects who speak for themselves—is celebrated by film/videomakers who are suspicious of the "authority" of voiceover narration and other techniques of traditional documentary. Finally, the impulse to celebrate subjectivity and to experiment with hybrid forms is enthusiastically endorsed by a number of the film/videomakers, including Michelle Parkerson:

This time in the early nineties is really exciting in documentary for me. Look at Marlon Riggs's work, Camille Billops's work, to name a few that are innovating format. Our preconceptions and our pretensions about documentary are all being messed with, and that's wonderful. The current generation of documentary filmmakers is meshing documentary, performance, autobiography, narration, stock footage compilation, all of it in various combinations that give the meaning, the message of the film, the documentary, more impact.[24]

Another thread that runs though the interviews is the suspicion with which African American documentarians view the mainstream culture's valuing of "objectivity" in nonfiction work. For many, "objectivity" is a term used by the dominant culture to define its version of reality. Ayoka Chenzira explains, "Nothing is objective. Narrative pieces aren't, and certainly documentary isn't. Not even *60 Minutes* is objective. Everything is quite skillfully shaped and some people shape better than others, but they're not objective in any way."[25] Gil Noble takes a similar position, and goes on to assert the journalist's responsibility to express a particular point of view: "we live in a subjective world, in an unfair world, in a world that's laden with bias, so I think the few of us that make documentaries who are of color should really go out of our way to tell our story."[26]

Jacqueline Shearer opposes the idea of "objectivity" to a desire to be a vehicle for "higher truths"; in her view, "all films are constructions, including documentaries. So, this myth of objectivity is so ridiculous that I can't believe it takes hold as much as it does. I like to think that I don't tell lies, but that's different from claiming to be objective, and that's different from saying that the world that I construct in my film is reality."[27] One documentarian who strove to present a balanced perspective and reach a wide audience was Henry Hampton, who not only made the controversial decision to pair black and white producers on each segment of the *Eyes on the Prize* series in order to tell "the full story"[28] of the civil rights and black power movements, but also insisted on giving voice to a variety of the participants.

The film/videomakers interviewed for this book express a range of viewpoints just as their body of work spans a range of media—"high-tech" digital media, avant-garde films and videos, television series and mini-series, and conventional educational works. It is also true that many of these film/videomakers work in both narrative and documentary, in more than one format, and in more than one style. One of the filmmakers, Abiyi Ford, says, "deep down I truly do not believe in the dichotomy between documentary and fiction." Having employed both video and film, Ford says, "In the end, it's not a question of one medium over the other, but rather a question of the specific task before you."[29]

The diversity of cinematic modes adopted by African American film / videomakers is echoed by the variety of approaches employed by chapter authors—scholars in the fields of African American studies and cinema studies—to survey this material. Several examine works which share a common thematic focus—those that "document the family," "document the artist," or "document leaders." These chapters tend to be inclusive, describing and analyzing many works, only a few of which have previously enjoyed critical attention. Others explore the evolution and impact of historically important television series—*Black Journal* and *Eyes on the Prize*. And still others develop a theoretical framework of analysis applicable to a broad range of documentaries.

Despite these differences in critical approach, certain motifs recur throughout the book. For instance, a number of authors question what it means to speak for one's self and for one's community. They explore the ways that documentary can serve both individual and collective interests, defining black identity in ways that are both personal and communitarian, constructing alternative narratives of black experience while advocating social and political change. Since there is no single, unchanging black community, the "burden of representation" involves varying viewpoints, differing degrees of objectivity and subjectivity, and competing facts and fictions. Negotiating this terrain raises fundamental questions: What are the personal and public standards of evidence? What constitutes a socially and politically responsible construction of history? What are the social and political uses of documentary? *Struggles for Representation* examines the way in which cultural perceptions of documentary are mediated by politics, historical moment, changing terms of cinema language, and the institutions of nonfiction production and distribution.

This study also addresses the complex relationship between the film / videomaker, the documentary subject, and the audience, as well as the ways in which such relationships affect choices regarding mode of address. Authors explore the degree to which African American documentary is genuinely intended for and speaks to black audiences: the ways in which black documentary can be viewed as populist art or as a tool for social change and political reform. Related to this is the question of spectatorship—the way audiences position themselves in relationship to documentary. At stake are the social and political uses of documentary and the impact of documentary on audiences.

In addition, *Struggles for Representation* examines the question of what it means to represent black experience in different modes—the degree of commitment to traditional realism demanded by certain audiences, and the extent to which oppositional aesthetic practices are problematic. A number of authors point to recurring elements of black documentary aesthetics: an emphasis on performance as a mode of expression and opposition, an interest in exploiting the possibilities of first-person narration, a creative insistence on capturing the speech/voice of documentary subjects, the significant role of music as an agent for change. Authors examine the consequences of fragmentary archival material for black documentary practice and the relationship between available technology and historical representation, tracing the efforts made by African Americans to document their experience and the economic, social, aesthetic, and historical factors that propel their work. They explore the impetus behind such productions, while examining the strategies employed to communicate and authenticate African American concerns. And they examine the ways in which media shape and are shaped by history and culture.

In the opening chapter, Pearl Bowser charts early efforts to document black experience on film. She shows how the field of still photography provided a training ground for documentarians, producing portraits of black people and images of their lives that became source materials for later films and videos. Bowser's chapter has a broad scope. While providing lively accounts of important early filmmakers and films, it also digs into underlying issues: the conditions and circumstances in which the pioneers of African American nonfiction films worked; the marketing, distribution, exhibition, and reception of their work; and the challenges of early cinema scholarship. This chapter provides an important historical backdrop for the rest of the book.

Bowser's essay establishes that military service by black Americans was an important and frequent subject of early documentaries. Phyllis R. Klotman pursues this theme into the present, exploring how contemporary African American documentarians interrogate the received history of the United States military establishment. In every major U.S. war, African Americans have linked their service abroad to their struggle for freedom and equality at home. Klotman's chapter focuses on filmmakers Jacqueline Shearer and William Miles, whose works rely primarily on the oral histories of compelling witnesses to counteract the often scanty and incomplete records of the contributions of African Americans in the Civil War as well as World Wars I and II.

Two chapters highlight historical landmarks in African American documentary production. Tommy Lee Lott examines the influential *Black Journal* series (1968–1971), the first broadcast news program to focus exclusively on African American concerns. Lott places *Black Journal* in the context of the political and social upheaval of the 1960s, particularly the Kerner Commission's report which implicated the mass media in the social alienation and political frustration that sparked uprisings in black communities. *Black Journal* was founded to respond to the needs of black audiences to see African American people, history, and achievements validated as an integral part of the American experience. Under William Greaves's leadership, *Black Journal* provided opportunities for a generation of black documentarians, while the "Black Journal Workshop" offered instruction in film production for black technicians. Lott's chapter focuses on the larger political debate that surrounded *Black Journal,* including debates within the black community. The central question Lott addresses is: What form can viable, alternative black media take?

Elizabeth Amelia Hadley analyzes the groundbreaking public television series, *Eyes on the Prize,* Parts I and II (1986, 1987), that traces the course of the civil rights and black power movements using historical footage and music from the period. In her chapter on this 14-episode series, Hadley draws on interviews she conducted with producer Henry Hampton and other members of the Blackside production team, illuminates the artistic and technical conceptualization of the project, and explores Hampton's view of what the responsible treatment of history looks like. The role of public television has been crucial—particularly its commitment to "minority programming"—and Hadley discusses some of the personnel considerations, as well as the economic, social, and political factors, that made PBS an important venue for black film and video.

The following two chapters focus on exemplary individuals. Clyde Taylor's chapter deals with nonfiction films that chronicle the lives of African American leaders. He describes a number of these biographies in detail, showing how the filmmaker's vision, as well as the requirements of white-controlled distribution outlets, affect the conceptualization and tone of the work, especially the use of historical commentary. In particular, he describes the "PBS-ification" of black documentary—a process which he says simplifies and flattens history in order to target a young audience. Taylor calls for adult, fully nuanced accounts of black leadership. "Black world enlightenment," he asserts, "cannot be kept running on a strict diet of disarming sweetness and light." Taylor also locates these nonfiction films in the ideological setting of contemporary African American studies.

Janet K. Cutler's study of more than fifty documentaries about artists working in various media shows how these films and videos celebrate extraordinary lives and works while challenging assumptions about the function of art and the role of the artist. Depicting the processes and products of artistic creation (in the performing, visual, literary, and media arts), these documentaries address the way art serves as a means for self-definition and collective expression, recoding black images and representing the multiplicity of black experience. Black art is shown to function as an extension of black communities and to act as a social/political weapon. Like the artist-subjects to whom they lend visibility, the film/videomakers in this study also engage in a process of reclaiming black history and providing alternative narratives of black experience. Cutler's chapter focuses particular attention on the achievements of St. Clair Bourne and Michelle Parkerson, but also considers works by women who pay homage to their mentors, documentaries that survey an art form, and works that document performances.

Several chapters take up the subject of border crossings and aesthetic hybrids. Mark Frederick Baker and Houston A. Baker, Jr. proceed from the premise that black history is largely undocumented and therefore requires alternative methods of archiving and historiography, as well as the creation of new forms. They make a case for expanding the definition of black documentary to encompass both traditional nonfiction films and certain narrative films. In their view, "black documentary" refers to work that deals "with the situation of African personhood in America in its myriad transmutations," and calls attention to the forces that "brought about and sustain African American oppression." As well, the term "black community"—minus the article—"signifies the imagined and 'alternatively documented' cultural, material, intellectual and spiritual life and history of Africans and their descendants in the United States." In contrast, "*the* black community" is a concept designed to confine and entrap; it suggests spatial and creative constriction. The films juxtaposed in this chapter are used to explore space and captivity, while illustrating diverse approaches to representing black experience.

Valerie Smith examines the way film/videomakers Camille Billops and James Hatch, Marco Williams, Thomas Allen Harris, and June Cross position themselves in relationship to discourses of the family. These documentarians question underlying assumptions about the nature of families—both black and white. Smith identifies the desire to destabilize and defamiliarize conventional notions of the family as central to the strategies of these media artists. Their works undermine a number of myths: the ideal nuclear family, the pathological black family, the heteronormative family, the respectable white family.

Paul Arthur's chapter examines the growing body of experimental films/videos that document the subjective concerns of African American media artists. Arthur argues that there are various points of intersection with the avant-garde, while acknowledging significant points of divergence. For example, he identifies the shared interest in historical retrieval and reliance on recycled materials (found footage) as forms of ideological criticism. At the same time, he shows that the hostility of black artists toward mass media representation is necessarily different from the position of the avant-garde, resulting not just from alienation but from subjugation. In his description and analysis of individual works, Arthur distinguishes the thematic and formal elements of black experimentation from those of other non-mainstream works. Finally, Arthur traces some of the obstacles to black participation in the avant-garde, as well as recent calls for greater inclusion of non-white perspectives. In this process, he "shows how black experimentation has claimed a place within prevailing channels of avant-garde funding, distribution, and exhibition."

Erika Muhammad's chapter looks toward future ways that black artists can employ what she calls "black high-tech documents"—interactive media, the Internet, and high-tech digital forms—to re-work images of identity, race, and nationhood. Rather than seeing blacks as victims of technology, Muhammad instead offers an overview of where African Americans stand in relation to new technology, and especially to its use in expanding notions of community. Muhammad cites Pamela Jennings, Philip Mallory Jones, and Reginald Woolery as examples of artists who engage new media in creative and progressive ways. She examines how their works resist the traditional manipulation of black images in mainstream culture and provide fresh readings of African diaspora life.

While *Struggles for Representation* is devoted primarily to an exploration of African American documentary, several chapters touch on connections between works produced in the United States and those produced in the rest of the diaspora. African American documentaries like other Afro-diasporic works have much to say about links to Africa, the impact of slavery and colonization, patterns of displacement, migration and settlement, and the issue of race throughout the Americas, the Caribbean, and Europe. In *Cinemas of the Black Diaspora: Diversity, Dependence, and Oppositionality*, Michael Martin credits a number of film critics—Tommy Lott, Clyde Taylor, Ella Shohat, and Robert Stam—with formulations of black film practice that emphasize "political orientation and transnational features"[30]; this global approach embraces minority work within the First World as part of an expanding definition of Third World practice. Haile Gerima is one of many film/videomakers who emphasize the political/social perspective that unites black diasporic work: "Our films have to contribute, to be a part of social change. Society has to be confronted, challenged, within the cultural parameters."[31] For these reasons, Manthia Diawara's essay concludes this study, providing an international perspective on black documentary's thematic concerns and representational strategies.

Manthia Diawara's chapter places African American documentary in the context of diasporic works by John Akomfrah, Louis Massiah, and Raoul Peck. Diawara argues that the first-person point of view enables these directors to build and validate their own identity through the identities of the subjects of their films. Employing devices such as irony, realism and allegory, such film/videomakers demonstrate the significance of their subjects to present conditions in the world. In Diawara's view, these media artists have reshaped the documentary genre in their attempt to reconcile identity politics with the universal message of modernity. "It is possible to define the first-person narrative in diasporic cinema as the filmmaker's revisionist construction of history in which the narrator is as central to the film as the film's diasporic subject." Diawara notes that Massiah's biography of W. E. B. Du Bois goes a step further than the others by employing multiple points of view, filtering the filmmaker's concerns through the perspective of four narrators.

While much of the book is necessarily descriptive and identified with the content of the films and the aspirations of the filmmakers, *Struggles for Representation* also engages current controversies in documentary theory. Several chapter authors examine works that blur the line between traditional documentary and other film/video genres. Mark Frederick Baker and Houston A. Baker, Jr. question the boundary between documentary and certain narrative films like Allen Hughes and Albert Hughes's *Menace II Society* (1993); they celebrate the degree to which "black documentary successfully resists traditional disciplinary imperatives and moves out of shadows to act. . . . Emergent forms provide representative voice for uptown longings for a black good life in America." Paul Arthur's provocative essay makes the case for a connection between the avant-garde and documentary, analyzing experimental works like William Greaves's *Symbiopsychotaxiplasm: Take One* (1971); Erika Muhammad examines new works in digital media and video that extend the documentary impulse. Rather than viewing African American documentary in the context of conventional realism and "low-tech" production, both Arthur and Muhammad argue for connections between black documentary and experimental modes.

The book touches on historical controversies as well: Phyllis R. Klotman's chapter analyzes the maelstrom surrounding William Miles's *Liberators* (1992), a film which has been both praised for calling attention to the role of blacks in World War II and attacked as factually inaccurate. The level of invective heaped on *Liberators* speaks to much wider questions—not just truth and authenticity in documentary, but also the history of black–Jewish relations at a particular moment in New York City politics, and the issue of who gets to tell what story. Read together, chapters by Tommy Lee Lott, Elizabeth Amelia Hadley, and

Clyde Taylor present very different perspectives on the role of public television in the history of black documentary. Clyde Taylor is particularly critical of the way public television has sacrificed sophisticated analysis to accommodate white sensitivities.

While the chapter authors were given particular topics to research and explore, all were encouraged to develop a focus that best reflected their expertise and interest. No single theoretical perspective underpins this study; rather, the book benefits from the diverse methodologies of its multidisciplinary authors. This is especially true when a single work is treated by more than one scholar, and that is why chapter authors were encouraged to analyze the same work in different contexts. Film/videomakers such as St. Clair Bourne, William Greaves, and William Miles are discussed in more than one chapter in order to account for their extensive bodies of work and to show how their documentaries can be viewed in different critical frameworks. On the other hand, documentaries not covered by chapter authors are cited in the filmography; examples are significant, long-running news and information television series *Like It Is*, *Say Brother*, and *Tony Brown's Journal*, which have regularly featured short documentary studies.

In actively striving to incorporate diverse critical perspectives that reflect the broad scope of the work at hand, *Struggles for Representation* includes a variety of powerful voices: the critical, theoretical, and historiographical voices of the chapter authors; the film/videomakers' voices, available in the excerpted interview material; archival voices, as represented by the extensive bibliography and filmography. Together these voices illuminate crucial areas of African American documentary theory and practice.

Certainly, this study could have employed different organizational strategies. However, the book was designed to reflect central issues in black American documentary: the definition of leadership, community, and family; the role of blacks in the military and the arts; the portrayal of important social, historical moments; and the depiction of subjective concerns. These categories invite analysis of a wide range of film/video materials and engage issues of gender, sexual orientation, and class in ways that are inclusive. Thus, the chapter topics address contested arenas in social policy and public discourse and call attention to the variety and scope of African American documentary.

It may be that in the next generation of scholarship, it will be less necessary to "chart the territory," but the central task of this study is to lay out what has been done in the field of African American documentary and to suggest productive approaches to that material. Rather than evaluate the degree to which the goals of these documentarians are realized, the book articulates the film/videomakers' views, describes their work and provides information about the circumstances under which works were produced. That approach is informed by the extensive interviews conducted in the course of researching this book, many of which appear in excerpted form in the book's appendix and are available for study as full transcripts at Indiana University's Black Film Center/Archive in Bloomington, Indiana.

It is the purpose of this book to instate the African American documentary tradition: to invite audiences to experience black documentary and to encourage teacher/scholars to include these works in their classes and research. The interview materials, filmography, and bibliography are designed to aid those interested in researching and teaching black documentary. Many of the chapter authors have already begun to expand their research, developing course materials, articles, and books. This is particularly gratifying, since so many of the documentaries considered in this volume have yet to be fully studied or appreciated.

Struggles for Representation constitutes an initial attempt to trace the emerging and diverse African American documentary film/video movement, addressing a void in the current scholarship, which has tended to concentrate either on black fiction film or on mainstream nonfiction film. In so doing, this book acknowledges the importance of exploring the intersection of two central cinema studies discourses—documentary on the one hand, race and ethnicity on the other. The success of this study will hinge on the extent to which it brings much-deserved recognition to the achievements of African American documentary film/videomakers and inspires others to extend the work begun here.

NOTES

1. The full name of this text is *Walker's Appeal, in Four Articles Together With a Preamble, to The Coloured Citizens of the World, But in Particular, and Very Expressly To Those of the United States of America, Written in Boston, State of Massachusetts, September 28, 1829.*

2. It may be possible to see the African griot as an even earlier antecedent of today's black documentarian, as a number of authors in this volume, including Mark Baker and Houston Baker, suggest. Manthia Diawara is among those who have explored various aspects of the relationship between this oral narrative tradition and contemporary film and video forms, for example in "Oral Literature and African Film: Narratology in *Wend Kunni*," in *Questions of Third Cinema*, ed. Jim Pines and Paul Willemen (London: British Film Institute, 1989).

3. Interview with St. Clair Bourne, conducted by Phyllis Klotman, 1992.

4. Interview with William Greaves, conducted by Klotman and Janet Cutler, 1991.

5. Bourne interview.

6. Interview with Charles Hobson, conducted by Klotman and Cutler, 1995.

7. Interview with Carroll Blue, conducted by Klotman, 1992.

8. Greaves interview.

9. Interview with Michelle Parkerson, conducted by Klotman, 1992.

10. Interview with Alonzo Crawford, conducted by Klotman, 1992.

11. Interview with Carlton Moss, conducted by Klotman, 1992.

12. Michael Renov, "Introduction: The Truth about Non-Fiction," in *Theorizing Documentary* (New York: Routledge, 1993), 1–3.

13. Bill Nichols, *Blurred Boundaries: Questions of Meaning in Contemporary Culture* (Bloomington: Indiana University Press, 1994), ix–x. Nichols goes on to describe "the innovative nature of recent nonfiction film and video that confounds fact and fiction, documentary and the avant-garde" (p. xi).

14. Ella Shohat and Robert Stam, *Unthinking Eurocentrism: Multiculturalism and the Media* (New York: Routledge, 1994), 178.

15. Kobena Mercer, "Diaspora Culture and the Dialogic Imagination: the Aesthetics of Black Independent Film in Britain," in *Blackframes: Critical Perspectives in Black Independent Cinema*, ed. Mbye Cham and Claire Andrade-Watkins (Cambridge: MIT Press, 1988), 53.

16. Trinh T. Minh-ha, "Outside In Inside Out," in *Questions of Third Cinema*, 144, 146.

17. Henry Louis Gates, *Thirteen Ways of Looking at a Black Man* (New York: Random House, 1997), xvii, xix.

18. Noël Carroll, "From Real to Reel: Entangled in Nonfiction Film," *1983 Philosophical Exchange*, 14 (1983): 15.

19. Carroll, "Nonfiction Film and Postmodernist Skepticism," in *Post-Theory: Reconstructing Film Studies*, ed. David Bordwell and Noël Carroll (Madison: University of Wisconsin Press, 1966), 285.

20. Interview with Ayoka Chenzira, conducted by Klotman and Cutler, 1994.

21. Interview with Marlon Riggs, conducted by Klotman, 1990.

22. Interview with Jacqueline Shearer, conducted by Klotman and Cutler, 1992.

23. Interview with William Miles, conducted by Klotman and Cutler, 1992.

24. Parkerson interview.

25. Chenzira interview

26. Interview with Gil Noble, conducted by Cutler, 1997.

27. Interview with Shearer.

28. Interview with Henry Hampton, conducted by Elizabeth Amelia Hadley, 1997.

29. Interview with Abiyi Ford, conducted by Klotman, 1993.

30. Michael T. Martin, "Framing the 'Black' in Black Diasporic Cinema," in *Cinemas of the Black Diaspora: Diversity, Dependence, and Oppositionality*, ed. Michael T. Martin (Detroit: Wayne State University Press, 1995), 3.

31. Interview with Haile Gerima, conducted by Klotman, 1993.

Struggles for Representation

1

Pioneers of Black Documentary Film

PEARL BOWSER

The first half of this century witnessed the mass exodus of African Americans from the south.[1] Lured by stories of educational opportunities and employment, individuals, families, and sometimes whole groups abandoned their homes, leaving the fields of the deep south for the Promised Land—the industrial areas up-south and farther north.[2] Communities and individuals whose lives had occupied the margins of American life and history emerged abruptly at the center of changes that would resonate throughout the nation, crossing the color line and unraveling a once-sturdy web of segregation, disenfranchisement, and intimidation.

The dispersion of blacks among the growing metropolises of Detroit, Philadelphia, Chicago, New York, Indianapolis energized these cities, and spurred the growth of a black middle class. Despite rigid segregation and an oppressive legal environment, a similar transformation occurred in southern cities like Memphis, Tennessee, and Jackson, Mississippi, that drew black migrants from more rural areas. In all of these places, a new class of wage earners clamored for services, and African American entrepreneurs and investors helped to fill this demand, erecting apartment buildings, establishing banks, hotels, and insurance companies. They established newspapers and schools; they designed and built churches, theaters, and movie houses.

THE CONTRIBUTIONS OF BLACK PHOTOGRAPHERS

The great migration brought in its wake affirming stories of ordinary and extraordinary lives, captured by black artists in a variety of media. As early as 1900, black photographers documented their communities in the act of self-transformation and renewal. Working in the field and in their studios, these men and women chronicled growth and change in individual lives and in the lives of their communities, at once personalizing and historicizing the great social and economic changes that were taking place.

A study of the black documentary rightfully begins with these community photographers. They created portraits of shopkeepers in their places of business; laborers, skilled and unskilled, digging the subways or paving the streets; artists and entertainers; participants in all areas of community life. They recorded the parades, celebrations, and other activities of the churches and schools, clubs and other community institutions. In thousands of photographs, they captured moments in family histories that graced the walls in the homes of field hands and merchants, domestics and professionals.

Today many of these portraits and life scenes, preserved in libraries, museums, and private collections, are testimonials to the desire to establish one's own identity and, by extension, a group identity. The images speak to us knowingly of a particular time and culture, and constitute a vital part of the historical record of that culture. Indeed, some images will stand as the primary text for lost segments of that history.

The work and careers of these black photographers constitute an important chapter in the history of African American documentary film production. Like the first film documentaries, their photographs were signifiers of uplift and achievement, images that reflected the dreams and ambitions of their subjects. Indeed, among the subjects were some who were determined to record their dreams: a family poses in the front yard of their own home; a woman frames two portraits of herself side by side, one in a maid's uniform, the other in satin and lace.[3]

The contributions of black photographers to early cinema have long been unrecognized. Most accounts would have us believe the craft and technology of photography and cinema were created exclusively for and by whites. The guiding assumption has been that the face behind the camera was naturally white and male. Only in the last decade has this assumption been re-examined by such scholars as Deborah Willis-Thomas, whose seminal research project, Black Photographers, 1840–1940: An Illustrated Bio-bibliography, was published in 1985, and Jeanne Moutoussamy-Ashe's Viewfinders: Black Women Photographers, one of the first studies to document the history of black women photographers, appeared in 1986.

Primary sources from as early as 1900 tell the story.[4] The history of black photography follows a trail of entrepreneurs through local business directories and census listings, proceedings of National Negro

Business League meetings, archives of the War Department and foreign governments, diary and journal entries by black writers, and personal scrapbooks.

Census data, for example, confirm that African Americans, although few in number, were among the ranks of the nation's professional photographers in the century's early decades. In 1910, the year of the first census, blacks made up about 11 percent of the total population, but accounted for just over 1 percent of professional photographers. Where occupational records were kept, 404 blacks were listed as photographers.[5] By 1920 the number of black professional photographers had increased to 608, including 101 women.[6] Because occupational data were not consistently collected or kept, these figures certainly underestimate the actual number of black photographers, but serve to document their existence.

The names and experiences behind these numbers are occasionally preserved in newspaper ads and local business directories that listed photographic services and occasionally offered information on the photographer's background or training. Some who opened studios on Main Street or in the heart of the community were self-taught; others, such as Peter P. Jones in Chicago and Jennie Toussaint Welcome in New York, were highly trained in art and photography and well educated in other disciplines as well. Elise Forrest Harleston and her husband opened the Harleston Studio in Charleston in the early 1920s. Elise Harleston had taken graduate courses in photography at Tuskegee Institute under C. M. Battey, distinguished photo-documentarian and head of the Institute's photography department.

STILL PHOTOGRAPHY AND
EARLY FILM DOCUMENTARIES

The histories of black photography and documentary overlap in two ways. First, still photographs taken in the century's early decades have enriched black documentaries. Images created by James Van Der Zee (1886–1983), the celebrated recorder of 50 years of Harlem history, are familiar icons of the 1920s and 1930s seen in many contemporary documentaries.

Second, among black photographers were individuals who ventured into motion pictures as a natural extension of their craft. Some continued to earn their living as still photographers, but occasionally made use of the movie camera to capture events of special interest in their communities, shooting the live action of a game in the Negro Baseball League; a state fair; civic happenings in an all-black town; an annual gathering of the National Negro Business League; or the ever-popular traditional marching bands of the Elks, Shriners, or Mummers. They documented black communities marking the fiftieth anniversary of the Emancipation Proclamation, and celebrating fifty years of freedom. Such images were a part of the visual records passed from generation to generation, from community to community.

One photographer who took up the art of the motion picture was Addison N. Scurlock (1883–1964). Scurlock ran a successful business in Washington, D.C., for more than half a century, beginning in 1911. His photographs were published in the three major black literary publications of the 1920s: *The Messenger,* founded by A. Philip Randolph; *The Crisis,* edited by W. E. B. Du Bois; and *Opportunity Magazine,* edited by Charles S. Johnson. In the latter part of his career he produced weekly newsreels focusing on social and political events involving members of Washington, D.C.'s, black middle class; these were shown weekly in several neighborhood theaters.[7]

Another pioneer of early black cinema was photographer Arthur Laidler Macbeth, who opened his first studio in Charleston and was later listed in the directories of Norfolk (1909) and Baltimore (1910) as a commercial photographer. Macbeth invented Macbeth's Day Light Projection Screen for the purpose of showing stereopticon and movies in daylight.[8] He studied photography under German, French and American artists and chemists, and opened his Charleston studio in 1886. He won medals and diplomas at the South Carolina Fair (1890), the Cotton State Exposition in Atlanta (1895), and the South Carolina Interstate and West Indian Exposition in Charleston (1902). He was also a member of the Photographers Association of America.

In New York there was the husband-and-wife team of Jennie Louise Toussaint Welcome (sister of the now-famous photographer James Van Der Zee) and Ernest Toussaint Welcome. In addition to their studio work, both were actively engaged in making motion pictures at some point in their careers. The work of these early photographers and filmmakers celebrated community life and, although fragmented and incomplete, is a part of the public record vital to the retelling of African American history.

BLACK DOCUMENTARIES OF THE SILENT ERA

Newspaper accounts, diary entries, and other such sources are even more vital to the history of black film documentary than black still photography. So little footage remains from these early films produced by African Americans that the history is fragmented; information about the people who took part in these productions is incomplete. However, the emergence of narrative films by and about African Americans—known as race films—provided a measure of opportunity, creating a training ground for still photographers who wanted to make the transition to cinematic photography.

We know, from advertisements, accounts, and occasional reviews in the black press, that one- and three-reel films were screened for public audiences in the early decades of the century. References to these early works generally identify them only by title and length, giving little sense of their form or structure. To what extent did these early works adhere to, or advance, evolving conventions of the film documentary? In the absence of actual footage, it is difficult to know. However, the few on-screen images that remain do offer a view of the American experience that is often obscured or left out of local histories: ordinary citizens, people of little renown, whose stories are rarely reflected in the modern interpretive texts that purport to represent the African American experience.

Community events filmed on location, such as parades, conventions or special celebrations, provided the texts for early newsreels and documentary short subjects. Carlton Moss, documentary filmmaker and educator, referred to these unedited, unrehearsed moments lifted from life as "actualities," adding that early filmmakers "shot whatever they saw—because it was moving."[9] The recorded moments ranged from commonplace doings to moments of pomp and ceremony.

The rudiments of story emerged out of activities or events that sparked recognition or pride: people at church; students at work on a black college campus; black soldiers training or going off to war. Early footage captures baseball games and boxing matches; social clubs; gatherings of the Negro club women's movement; a black state fair; conferences; and the activities of prominent political and cultural figures. More than a few African American film companies produced short subjects depicting blacks in the workplace, particularly in government jobs. They showed the first black postal worker, for example, officials of an all-black incorporated town, or blacks serving in the armed forces. The subject matter of these documentaries was often unplanned and spontaneous with an apparent local focus, but they reflected shared areas of interest and experience for a wider audience of African Americans hungry for their own image.

Some documentaries called attention to the progress and pride of ordinary citizens. Two such films were screened at the State Theater in Chicago: *A Day in the Magic City,* described by a reviewer as "an extraordinary picture of colored people of Birmingham, Alabama," and a screen story entitled *Youth Pride and Achievement of Colored People of Atlanta, Georgia.* In these films, communities celebrated themselves and told their own stories. The State Theater promoted these films as "a new type of production—featuring the progress and pride of colored people in motion pictures."[10]

Movie houses that catered to African Americans—race theaters—provided ready audiences for these natural scenes of black life. In the beginning there were no formal distribution networks for documentaries aimed at the African American spectator. Some prints were sold outright, while others followed a prescribed distribution circuit of towns and cities mapped out by showmen[11] or the filmmakers themselves. Often they served as fillers in mixed programs of vaudeville and film. Many of the companies responsible for short subjects also produced comedies and later dramatic pieces.

Sometimes comic or dramatic skits were incorporated into the short subject, adding a story line to the captured moments of community life. These embellishments helped to create a mirror through which the audience might view itself as participants in their own culture and contributors to the larger tapestry of American life.

Advertisements suggest that the typical program shown in race theaters of this period might include newsreels, several short subjects (documentaries), and the ever-popular Western serials.[12] But the arrival in town of a black film of any length was treated as an occasion; the film was often featured prominently on the marquee, and ads were placed in the local paper by the theater owner or the production company.

When they added local flavor to the fare at race movie houses, short subjects proved to be highly effective marketing tools. Owners of race theaters in rural towns along the Delta commonly offered prizes and used a variety of gimmicks to increase their box office, but images of the patrons proved to be the most powerful draw. In Ruell, Mississippi, for example, one theater owner would film patrons gathered in front of his establishment on a Saturday, capturing images of country people who had come to town for a little relaxation. He exploited the vanity of his subjects, promising to display their images, larger than life, on the silver screen the following week. This form of advertisement became a common and effective way to ensure repeat business. Footage from his camera in the Jackson, Mississippi, archives reveals a group of people in front of his theater, including a black teenager carrying a white baby on her hip. Ironically, the theater marquee in the background announces an Oscar Micheaux movie called *God's Step Children*.[13]

While geared to small towns, the practice spread to urban theaters as well. In Chicago, the Magic Motion Picture Company ran an ad in the *Chicago Defender* announcing something new for Chicago and its citizens—a "Picture Making Exhibition and Grand Ball." The copy read,

"Have you seen the movie picture cameraman in your neighborhood? Well He Got a Picture of You and it will be shown at this moving picture exhibition and hall so don't miss coming and seeing it."[14] The pictures were to be shown at the 8th Regiment Armory—the same space where in 1919, Oscar Micheaux had shown his first feature, *The Homesteader*— the longest black film of that time.

The subjects of black shorts were both entertaining and educational, connecting the lives of people in disparate communities to larger events. Many of the documentaries and newsreels shown in commercial venues were also used in educational programs run by churches, schools, lodges, and other community organizations at the forefront of the race consciousness movement.

Among early black documentaries were race movies promoting and documenting economic and political movements and organizations, such as Booker T. Washington's National Negro Business League (NNBL) and Marcus Garvey's United Negro Improvement Association (UNIA). Washington commissioned and inspired the first black documentary, which is discussed below. The UNIA not only published its own newspaper, *The Negro World*, but also established its own film company to publicize the movement and its leader, who proclaimed himself "The Provisional President of Africa." Garvey carried his message of Negro improvement into black communities across 38 states, attracting thousands of new members along the way. Photographer James Van Der Zee, among others, made portraits of Garvey's elite guard in dress uniform with their families. He recorded the August, 1920 parade of fifty thousand Garveyites on Harlem's wide boulevard, and covered UNIA conventions and rallies.

African American camera operators working for the UNIA film company captured movement activities on film, including the "Garvey fleet"—a ship of the "Black Star Line" with its black captain Hugh Mulzac and crew—steaming up the Hudson. Purchased with money raised by Garvey's followers, the ship promoted the return of blacks to their African homeland and publicized commerce between the Garvey movement and Africa.

As chroniclers of their people's culture, life styles, hopes, and dreams, African American photographers and filmmakers—amateur and professional alike—reinforced the sense that they were presenting slices of reality in moving pictures by giving their work such prosaic titles as *A Day with the Tenth Cavalry* or *A Day in Birmingham, The Magic City*. The kinds of everyday, untold stories that black photographers across the nation had been documenting in their communities and in their studios were now subjects for films.

RESEARCHING EARLY BLACK DOCUMENTARIES

Most if not all of these early films are lost to us. Our knowledge of them comes largely from newspapers of the time—information mentioned in reviews and ads; buried in the stories of veteran reporters such as D. Irland Thomas of the *Chicago Defender* or St. Clair S. Bourne of the *Amsterdam News;* or wedged between announcements from J. A. Jackson's rolltop desk in *Billboard* and the *Defender;* or noted in unsigned columns and stories in the *Indianapolis Freeman, New York Age, Norfolk Journal and Guide* or other newspapers and magazines of the period.

These sources are not sufficient, however, to allow us to gauge the audiences that these films reached, or their impact on various communities. The films were not advertised or reviewed every time they played in a theater or became part of a larger program. More often than not, the producer was his or her own distributor, and made films available not only to commercial theaters, but also to lodge halls, neighborhood churches, and club groups. Sometimes the films found their way into the baggage of individual showmen who took to the road with projection equipment. These showmen brought a personal style of presentation and an eclectic mix of programs to whatever public space could be found in small towns in the deep south that lacked movie theaters but had an enthusiasm for the "picture show."[15]

Other documentaries were never intended for public viewing, but nevertheless figure in the history of black filmmaking. These include promotional and training films made by businesses in the first half of this century. For example, the Walker Manufacturing Company of Indianapolis, Indiana, produced its own films showing the development and production of an array of beauty and hair products and promoting the "Walker System of Beauty." Long before the age of television, Madame C. J. Walker's products, and the beauty culture she developed, were being marketed as far away as South Africa. The company used films to train women in beauty techniques (how to apply makeup, care of the skin, hair styles, etc.) and to prepare them to go into business for themselves.

The sections that follow describe these films and filmmakers, placing them in historical context. Perhaps the best known of these was the film that is generally considered the first black documentary—*A Day at Tuskegee.*

THE FIRST BLACK DOCUMENTARY

The silent era produced a host of newsreels and short subjects, but none was as widely seen or as influential as *A Day at Tuskegee.* The moving force behind this project was Booker T. Washington, the first president of Tuskegee Institute in Alabama.

A passionate advocate of industrial education for Negroes, and a fiery orator, Washington attracted the support of many wealthy and powerful white businessmen and politicians, including former President Theodore Roosevelt. Welcoming his accommodationist views, many of these individuals provided the financial support that helped Washington to pursue his long-range goal of an economically self-reliant and independent black workforce. In 1900, he established the National Negro Business League to foster his program and to encourage, by example and shared information, the growth of black enterprises. Annual meetings, located in a different region each year, encouraged new black enterprises around the country. Indeed, one such meeting held during an NNBL convention was filmed and screened for the general public at a nearby theater. This experiment proved successful, and was repeated at other NNBL conventions. While informational, such films were also objects of race pride; they permitted the general audience to take part in events at the NNBL convention meeting that was taking place in their town. At the same time, they promoted participants' individual businesses by associating them with the larger national organization wherever the film was screened.

Recognizing the persuasive power of film, Booker T. Washington commissioned George W. Broome to make a short film about Tuskegee Institute that would help to promote his industrial education program. This project resulted in *A Day at Tuskegee*. Broome and a group of NNBL businessmen in Boston formed a production company, and shot the film on the Institute's 2,400-acre grounds and in buildings erected with student labor.

In December, 1909, a private screening in Boston exhibited some 43 scenes shot at the Alabama school, depicting the industrial education of young men and women. Emmett J. Scott, Dr. Washington's assistant at Tuskegee, attended the screening at the Crescent Theater and commented favorably on the film. A reporter for the *Defender* promised to make every effort to bring the film to Chicago and noted, "Booker T. was way ahead of the game. . . . [The film] will show our would-be leaders what makes Booker T. so great."[16]

The film opened at a public meeting in New York's Carnegie Hall on January 24, 1910. The press reported that an audience of two thousand (black and white) attended the meeting, which was chaired by New York's former mayor, Seth Low. Speakers included President Finley of City College, Dr. B. F. Riley of Alabama, and Dr. Booker T. Washington.

Producer George W. Broome had previously spoken at an NNBL meeting about the importance of the motion picture as an instrument of communication capable of delivering information to African American communities a thousand miles away. The black press reviewing the film reported, "People could see what the school was doing and what an industrial education, as Booker T. Washington conceives it, means." The *New York Age* maintained that critics of Tuskegee have usually been "those who know the least about it." The Broome company announced its intention to produce similar films showing the progress of the Negro along industrial lines for Shaw Institute in North Carolina, Hampton Institute in Virginia, and Fisk Institute in Tennessee.[17]

Washington's industrial education program did not escape criticism, however. Two factions emerged in the debate over the development of trade schools. One group of black intellectuals and educators, including W. E. B. Du Bois, put the education of black professionals at the top of their agenda. Du Bois was the author of *The Souls of Black Folk*—an essay collection that was to shape the course of the emerging civil rights movement, and one of Washington's staunchest critics. Du Bois believed that it was essential to develop leadership among young men and women through a college education steeped in the arts, sciences, history, and literature; he asserted that the realization of full citizenship would be hastened through the development of an intellectual elite—or "Talented Tenth." On the other side of the debate was the powerful machine built by Washington at Tuskegee with the backing of northern industrialists and southern segregationists. Washington described his critics as "artificial" men—"graduates of New England colleges" who did not represent the masses of black people.[18] His comments did not name, but referred to, not only Du Bois, but also Monroe Trotter, publisher of the *Guardian*.

Washington was confident that he not only had the total support of blacks, but would also be listened to by whites in high places. But his access to the White House and his association with white industrialists sparked controversy when President Theodore Roosevelt disastrously mishandled two key events: the Brownsville raid of 1905 and the brutal outbreak of violence against blacks in Atlanta in 1906. In the first case, Roosevelt summarily and unfairly discharged and disgraced the famous black 25th Texas Regiment, which had taken part in the charge up San Juan Hill.[19] In the second, the president belatedly ordered the use of federal troops to quell the mob.

In the aftermath of these events, the rock-solid support Washington had enjoyed showed signs of erosion. He weathered the storm, however, and over the next decade Tuskegee Institute became the focus of a number of films shown in churches, schools, and theaters. These films helped to shape the public discourse of the day concerning Washington's accommodationist views and Du Bois's more progressive stance on education and leadership. Long after his death in 1915, Booker T. Washington's industrial education program, his bootstrap approach, and identification with the greater mass of the working class proved to have seductive power. His image and his influence have pervaded popular culture through portraits, statuary, and film; his name has become synonymous with self-reliance (a bootstrap approach to the progress of the race) and African American entrepreneurship.

The images that filled *A Day at Tuskegee* became symbols of what could be achieved: not only the stately buildings that graced the campus, but also the images of students at work in the classroom and in the fields. By 1915 the school was not only a monument to its founder, but also a symbol of progress and race pride. Films about Tuskegee and the controversial educational experiment continued to have an audience as late as 1923.[20]

What role did Washington play in making *A Day at Tuskegee* beyond commissioning the Broome company? Was he in a position to suggest or encourage black camera operators to participate in the project? Press reports indicate only that Washington's assistant, Emmett J. Scott, attended the preview screening of the film prior to the New York public event. There appears to be no mention of anyone else from the Institute staff taking part in the project. Some years earlier, Tuskegee students had participated in a "parade of 100 wagons" exhibiting the various activities of the school before a reviewing stand occupied by former President Theodore Roosevelt and his party. The documentation on film of the school's vocational studies program was indeed a novel idea in 1909—a time when print dominated communication.[21] Washington apparently recognized that film could be not only a powerful educational tool, but also an effective fund-raising instrument, and he used it when he approached white industrialists and educators in the north for support. On January 10, the *New York Age* provided a detailed description of the film's content and named George Broome as the manager, but provided no other credits. Three years later *A Day at Tuskegee* was picked up by another company, the Anderson Watkins Film Company.[22]

A final word about *A Day at Tuskegee*.[23] While Booker T. Washington launched this project, others deserve credit for the production itself, and for the technical quality of the film. But who these individuals were remains a mystery, in spite of the attention the film enjoyed in the black press. Tuskegee certainly had a professional photographer on staff.

THE PETER P. JONES PHOTOPLAY LTD.

The Peter P. Jones Photoplay Ltd. was one of the few early race companies with an identified professional camera operator. Jones scripted, shot, and edited his own films. He began his career as a photographer in 1900 in a small studio on State Street capturing images of Chicago's African American community, including portraits of leading figures in sports, the arts, and business. He was also commissioned to photograph buildings designed by African American architects, in particular Chicago's black churches. In 1914, with the backing of South American investors, Jones established the Peter P. Jones Photoplay Ltd. to make short films focusing on the black community. The company's first production, reported in the *Chicago Defender*, recorded a Shriners parade in Chicago:

> The march of the Mystic Shriners Sunday is to be perpetuated in moving pictures and incidentally Jones, former State Street photographer again comes into the limelight in this new scientific fad. He was the operator of the machine and strange to say it was set up in front of the first place on State Street that he did his photographic work. This is the first moving picture ever taken of the Shriners and marks the beginning of a series [on] our marching organizations and other features of race life that will encourage and uplift.[24]

The Freeman: A National Illustrated Colored Newspaper in Indianapolis, praised Jones's work for setting new standards for race pictures, noting that in addition to his work in motion pictures, he was a prize-winning commercial photographer and colorist, and a member of the American Photographers Association. *The Freeman* also reported that Jones's productions would be shown in Brazil and other South American countries before opening in the United States. No records of such screenings exist; we do know, however, that the films Jones created with South American backing were shown in the United States in 1914.

An ad for *The Dawn of Truth*, a Peter P. Jones Photoplay production, listed titled sections that incorporated the company's earlier films in a "movie spectacle."[25] The program contained scenes from the *Lincoln Jubilee* (Chicago, August–September, 1915), including *Gorgeous Elks Parade; Historic National Baptist Convention* (two reels); *Negro Soldiers Fighting for Uncle Sam* (three reels); *Progress of the Negro: Facts from Farm, Factory, and Fireside; Tuskegee and Its Builder; Mound Bayou, MS: A Negro City Built by a Former Slave; Prime Factors in the Re-birth of a Nation.* This complex grid of images was produced, directed, and edited by Jones. The final documentary contained footage acquired from the War Department and other agencies, a compilation of materials from Jones's earlier films, newsreel footage (probably from his own camera), and added interludes of drama and comedy. The program also included scenes of other cities' celebrations of the Half Century Anniversary

Exposition and the Lincoln Jubilee. Under the headline, "Featuring Negro Progress in Moving Pictures," one reviewer referred to scenes of troops embarking for Cuba (*On to Cuba*) followed by

> a pleasing little drama which was supposed to have been enacted on that soil. In this playlet were included all the little turns known to the moving picture art. . . . The colonel's daughter, "Lucy," the captain who courted her and the major who failed in his suit was realistic leaving an impression on the memory owing to the faithfulness to the ways of men. It is a rare thing to see one of the race, depicted by the race, as a rascal or a scoundrel. As the story goes Major Duplex was that, because worsted in his love by Captain Smith, who wins "Miss Lucy." The plot was clean cut, holding through in spite of the spirit of war that enveloped all. One gets a real war glimpse with all of its possible horror.[26]

The heading of Jones's ad for the program—"1865 to 1915" framed by broken slave chains and shackles—cites the fiftieth anniversary of freedom from slavery. A review appearing in the *Freeman* describes Peter P. Jones as an artist whose photographs have been exhibited at galleries at home and abroad, and refers specifically to Jones's long-time relationship with the Victor George Galleries. The reviewer was particularly impressed with one segment of the film:

> Beyond all of this almost matchless experience is the grand work which was thrown on the screen to the view of the curious throngs. As for things that stand for the real and enduring, and the monumental growth of the race perhaps, the splendid buildings and spacious well-kept grounds of Tuskegee are the most inspiring. One thinks of all this as the ingenuity of a member of the race and occupied by the race. Nothing like these scenes have been seen here before. The art triumph of the presentation is decidedly the 8th Regiment scene . . . where the troops are being reviewed by Governor Dunne of Illinois, Col. Dennison and his staff of officers. Here the artist and his subjects seem to have been at their best. The most exacting military martinet and the purest art critic would have been convinced and satisfied.[27]

This description suggests that footage from Jones's 1914 documentary, *For the Honor of the 8th Illinois Regiment* was incorporated into *The Dawn of Truth*. It is quite possible that Jones recycled scenes from this documentary as well as footage of a number of other events that he had filmed earlier. But more importantly, Jones's title, *Rebirth of a Nation*, appearing in the ad as part of the special program, embodied the spirit of the African American celebration of fifty years of freedom and achievement since Lincoln's signing of the Emancipation Proclamation. That anniversary was widely celebrated and Jones's "movie spectacle," according to the reviewer, included documentation of these festivities in other cities. The reviewer commented:

> The management of the production speaks of it as re-birth of a nation, some-what in answer to that orgy of contempt and reflection known as the "Birth of a Nation." These pictures are the true birth of a nation as it concerns the Negro race. They tell the story of the ascent from life's hovel to where the Negroes fused and became one with other people in the great melting pot of the nation. They do not show the ugly past: it is known well enough. The victories are the subject, leaving it to the dead past to bury the dead.[28]

In the absence of the actual film, we can only speculate about how Jones may have handled the making of *The Dawn of Truth*. Many questions remain. Did the audience see the program as one long documentary or as a series of short pieces tied together under a single title? Did Jones draw upon footage from earlier films to create an entirely new piece, or did he assemble earlier shorts as chapters of a longer work? The former appears more likely, based on Jones's years of experience as a studio photographer and photo documentarian, his considerable darkroom and editing skills, and his experiments with natural light in architectural photographs. The lengthy review that ran in *The Freeman* following the Washington Theater screening in Indianapolis, alludes to the quality of Jones's images: "The fine art of making motion pictures has not been confined to a special people. This fact was proven when the splendid pictures by the Peter P. Jones Film Company of Chicago were shown at the Washington Theater."[29]

Today, much more is known about Jones's career and his artistry with both still and motion picture cameras than about most of his contemporaries in the field. His photographs frequently appeared in newspaper ads, and the *Chicago Defender* followed his career, running stories about his projects. He was lauded for his portraits of famous people (Booker T. Washington, Henry O. Tanner, Bert Williams, Henry Bannerchek, Ada Overton Walker, and others), and reproductions of these works were marketed by William Foster, an African American producer and distributor. His portraits of well known actresses and performers such as Anita Bush, founder of the Lafayette Players, were used in ads for various black businesses promoting hair products, cosmetics, and personal instruction.[30] Jones clearly saw his work as a celebration of black life and an homage to black identity. His company was founded to film the first in a series of marching organizations and others germane to the African American community.

Jones seems to have had few competitors—at least in Chicago, where he spent the better part of his professional career from 1908 to

1922. To be sure, there were other African American commercial photographers producing films or at least working as camera operators during this period. Several photographs survive showing camera operators with the tools of their trade: one is a portrait of Arthur Bedou, who had himself photographed walking with his camera in the center of a crowd; another is Richard Samuel Roberts's photograph entitled "Man with a Movie Camera."[31] But there is little mention of these professionals in the press.

Jones was already well known in the field and had recently released his third film, a short comedy called *The Slacker*, when he went to work for the Selznick Film Laboratories in 1917. He quickly gained a reputation as the industry's most skilled still photographer. He was praised in the company paper for the quality of his photographs and his work as a colorist, and for his shrewd selection of scenes to be photographed and used on lobby cards advertising a film.[32]

OTHER EARLY PRODUCTION COMPANIES

During the silent era, the number of venues open to producers of race movies was severely limited. Nevertheless, over time a number of commercial African American production companies came into being. In addition to Peter P. Jones Photoplay Ltd., there were Foster Photoplay Company (1913), Afro-American Film Company, Haynes Photoplay (1914), Lincoln Motion Picture Company (1916), Whipper's Reel Negro News (1921), Dunbar Films, Monumental Pictures Corporation (1921) organized solely for the production of newsreels, Turpin Film Company, and others. Each produced one or more newsreels or documentaries as well as short narratives, and each developed its own strategies for dealing with the tough challenge of promoting and distributing its work.

While we know that these companies were in business in the 1910s and 1920s, relatively little is known about their personnel, production process, or technical capacities. This is one of the frustrating facts of life for scholars of early black cinema: there tend to be few details available about a production or its crew unless the information happened to be included in a release, review, or newspaper ad of the time. For films which are known to have been made, but for which no copies remain, production details are particularly elusive. Fortunately, some records were kept. For example, George P. Johnson, general manager of the Lincoln Motion Picture Company, kept extensive clipping files on his company's productions and on the race movies of other producers. (This collection is now housed at the University of California at Los

Angeles.) However, Lincoln used the same white camera operator, Harry Grant, on all of its films from 1916 until it ceased production in 1922; Johnson did not record the names of technical staff (such as camera operators) working for other companies.[33]

Among the first black companies to produce or distribute shorts subjects was the Afro-American Film Company. Based in New York City, the company announced plans to produce films recording the activities of prominent Negro leaders. In 1913, it produced coverage of a regional meeting, convened in Philadelphia, of the National Negro Business League (NNBL), the organization Washington helped to establish in 1900. In 1914, it filmed the regional NNBL meeting in Muskogee, Oklahoma, and in the same year, it produced scenes of the incorporated all-black town of Boley, Oklahoma.[34]

At the same time, other companies were also documenting life in black communities. The Haynes Company filmed the Odd Fellows convention in Boston in 1914, and in 1916 it documented notable Negro enterprises that were developing in the eastern part of the country. The Foster Photoplay Company, run by William Foster, a producer of short comedies, also produced at least one newsreel, *YWCA Parade*, which was shown along with his comedies *The Pullman Porter* and *The Butler* in 1913.[35] He also attempted to establish himself as a distributor, listing Peter P. Jones's documentary *For the Honor of the 8th . . . ,*[36] and briefly handled sales of photographs, suitable for framing, of well known figures such as Booker. T. Washington and Paul Laurence Dunbar. Other companies in various parts of the nation were filming blacks at work in fields and factories, the proceedings of conventions, activities of local dignitaries, or the work of renowned figures such as Marcus Garvey and the United Negro Improvement Association.[37] Since much of this work has been lost, we can only speculate about the aesthetic that these artist/photographers brought to the film documents they created.

WORLD WAR I AND THE POST-WAR YEARS

Black soldiers in battle was a dominant theme of documentaries and newsreels, as well race movies, during the silent era. While the press may not have had camera operators in the trenches or on the battlefield, there were writers who shared their personal stories with black newspapers, and news of the states' black regiments was eagerly followed in the papers. The *Chicago Defender*, the *Pittsburgh Courier*, papers with national black readership, more than likely had journalists in the field. In *This Is Our War* (1945), Carl Murphy writes that, "*The Afro-American* sent none of its writers abroad to cover World War I. As a weekly newspaper with its influence then limited mainly to Baltimore, it depended altogether on letters from service men abroad, on occasional interviews with returned soldiers and on War Department handouts."[38] There were some efforts to document blacks' contributions to the war effort on film. In 1916, for example, Jennie Louise and Ernest Toussaint Welcome made *Doing Their Bit* (1916), a twelve-part series shown in two-reel segments focusing on "the military and economic role played by all races in the War of Nations both 'Over Here' and 'Over There.'" But the most memorable documentary efforts of the World War I era focused on an earlier generation of black soldiers, recalling their exploits in Cuba and Mexico.

Heroic black soldiers were also the subject of a lithograph by Jennie Louise Toussaint Welcome and Ernest Toussaint Welcome. The lithograph, displayed in many black homes, depicted members of the 369th Colored Infantry fighting the Germans in hand-to-hand combat in a French forest. The soldiers' faces were painted from photographs—a common practice that avoided long studio sessions, and each soldier was identified by name. The 369th and the 371st regiments were awarded the Croix de Guerre, and individual soldiers were cited for bravery.

In 1914, Peter P. Jones Photoplay Ltd., the era's most prominent producer of documentaries, made a three-reel film called *For the Honor of the Fighting 8th Illinois Regiment*, which included scenes of the 8th Illinois in dress parade; being reviewed by the governor; marching in Cuba during the Spanish-American War; being attacked and later repulsing the enemy on a bridge in Cuba with a thousand soldiers engaging in battle; taking a block house on San Juan Hill; firing cannons; and the victory celebration."[39] By combining newsreel footage of the 8th Illinois in battle with his own footage of their triumphal return, Jones created an historical record that directly addressed the black spectator. This documentary did not survive, and one can only imagine the historical and cultural insights it might have provided.

Two years later, in 1916, Jones's company produced *The Colored Soldiers Fighting in Mexico*, which also featured the 8th Illinois Regiment. Soldiers in training and battle—this period's recurring theme—brought home to audiences African Americans' contributions to the nation's security and their role in its history.

One of the most successful films of the military genre, and the first to garner national exposure in the decade of World War I, was Lincoln Motion Pictures' dramatic re-enactment of the Negro soldiers of the Tenth Cavalry at the battle of Carrizal along the U.S.–Mexican border. *Trooper of Company K* (1916) was a story of individual acts of heroism that caught the attention of the general public and was seen by both black and white audiences, according to the production company's general manager, George P. Johnson.[40]

Trooper might be considered an early "docudrama." It owed much of its popularity to its re-creation of the historic battle and the heroism of troopers in the face of the enemy's superior firing power with the Gatling gun. The Lincoln Motion Picture Company restaged the battle with a cast of three hundred, including former Ninth and Tenth Cavalry troopers and Mexican cowboys. The film's most affecting moment, which created a momentary bond between the races, depicted the rescue of the Tenth Cavalry's white commanding officer. Lobby cards and posters for the film showed the unknown trooper of Company K (played by Noble Johnson) carrying the wounded officer to safety.

Lincoln Motion Pictures invested in multiple prints to meet exhibitors' demands, but the film's initial success was not sustained. *Trooper of Company K* could not match the enduring popularity of the 1910 documentary, *A Day at Tuskegee*. The George Broome documentary or some version of it was still in distribution as late as 1922. Like most early black documentaries, *Trooper* was forgotten; once they had completed their initial run, they were ignored by critics and other journalists, and disappeared from advertisements.

Several factors may have contributed to the demise of these early documentaries: the lack of distribution outlets; the small number of commercial venues; and limited advertising budgets. It is also possible that the films had a longer life as educational material, and were shown in schools and local clubs. They may have been exhibited by showmen in small theaters which changed their programs on a daily basis and rarely advertised specific titles in the papers.

In the years following World War I, black documentarians continued to pursue military themes, focusing on black soldiers' heroism in Europe. Initially, the U.S. government encouraged this effort. The Frederick Douglass Film Company produced the documentary *Heroic Negro Soldiers of the World War* (1919), showing black regiments as they trained for war, embarked for overseas, fought in battle, and triumphantly returned home. The *New York Age* printed a glowing review of the film and its producers, praising the quality of the screen images, saying:

> There is no doubt about this being the best and most attractive motion picture made of the Negro soldier in the World War. The company is owned and controlled by Negroes, whose aim is to present the better side of Negro life, and to use the screen as a means of bringing about a better feeling between the races. In most pictures the Negro only appears in menial po-

sitions or in a degrading role, but the Frederick Douglass Film Company shows the race at its best. Dr. W. S. Smith, the director, has given much time and study to photographing the negro and has become an expert in making the features clear and distinct under all conditions. This picture measures up to the standards of motion picture requirements, and is a credit to Dr. Smith's ability as a director.[41]

One might be led, from the description in the *Age*, to believe that Dr. Smith was the camera operator as well as director. It was important for the audience to be able to identify their loved ones, and the critic for the *Age* took pains to inform the audience of the director's sensitivity and skill in representing on screen the physical appearance of the Negro.

In 1921, the Lincoln Motion Pictures Company produced *A Day with the Tenth Cavalry at Fort Huachaca, Arizona* (1921), a one-reel pictorial of 33 scenes showing the black cavalry training at the fort. For black audiences, such scenes sustained public memory of African Americans' loyalty and patriotism, and inspired them to continue to press for the rights of citizenship. After 1922, *A Day with the Tenth Cavalry* attracted little attention in the press. The use of such images in race propaganda or efforts to resurrect and recycle footage of blacks in the military seemed to wane.

In the years after World War I, the political climate had become more contentious. Racial tensions ran high in 1919, as reports of lynchings made front-page headlines in the black press. Films of heroism and sacrifice in battle, shown not only in theaters, but also in community churches and lodge halls, helped to strengthen African American resolve to fight against the prejudice, hatred, and oppression they faced at home. At the same time, images of heroic black soldiers taking up arms to defend their homes, neighbors, or towns, and defeating the enemy in hand-to-hand combat, challenged notions of racial inferiority and threatened white domination. It was becoming all too clear that these black documentaries, which had initially been accepted as an effort to stir patriotism against a foreign enemy, were also capable of uniting blacks in the struggle for democracy at home. Images of heroism were a great source of pride, and each individual act of valor in the war to "make the world safe for democracy" held the promise of victory at home.

"THE MAN BEHIND THE MOVIE SHORTS"

By the mid-1920s, race movies were on the decline. They had always been undercapitalized, but now fewer venues and smaller profits plagued the field's veterans and made the enterprise less attractive for newcomers. In the years that preceded the advent of sound and the collapse of the stock market, Hollywood was actively developing theater chains and squeezing out the smaller independent movie houses. In that atmosphere there were fewer and fewer new black production companies, and among the veterans in the field only Oscar Micheaux successfully negotiated the transition into the era of sound. As sound took over the next decade, the market for short films focusing on black music was dominated by Hollywood and by white independent filmmakers. It was against this backdrop that a talented young cameraman, Edward Lewis, ventured forth with a novel idea—an all-sports African American newsreel.

An article in the *Amsterdam News,* under the headline "The Man behind the Movie Shorts," profiled 26-year-old Edward Lewis, producer of two popular series that were making the rounds nationally: *The Colored Champions of Sports* and *Colored America on Parade.* The article described Lewis as "the youngest motion picture producer in America and the only one who does his own camera work and script writing."[42] In 1938, Lewis purchased his own movie camera and left a promising career as photographer for the *New York Daily News* to start over as an independent filmmaker.

As an experienced news photographer Lewis knew how to tell a story with pictures, and in 1938, he set out to create a series of documentary shorts joined by a common theme. This series, *Life in Harlem,* followed a day in the lives of Harlem residents. Working as a one-man production company—scripting, shooting, and editing his own material—Lewis produced twelve documentary shorts in 1939 which were released by Million Dollar Productions.

Lewis followed up with a second series that capitalized on the popularity of African American sports figures. His *Colored Champions of Sports* brought to the screens of neighborhood theaters the players most viewers had only read about in the entertainment sections of black newspapers. Shown in ten-minute segments along with regular programs, the series featured World Heavyweight Champion Joe Louis at his training camp or socializing in the community; Josh Gibson of the Grays, the heaviest-hitting catcher in the colored league; Smokey Joe Williams, one of the oldest and best pitchers in colored baseball; and boxer Henry Armstrong, who held both the lightweight and welterweight titles.[43]

Sitting in their local movie houses, audiences could watch the Black Yankees play, or witness young athletes representing the U.S. abroad at Olympic competitions. Segments on athletes like track star Jesse Owens or Negro League pitcher Satchel Paige could be seen at the Loew's Theaters in Harlem, for example, and often these short pieces were as big an attraction (if not bigger) than the Hollywood features sharing the marquee.

Despite his substantial accomplishments, Edward Lewis never achieved prominence as a filmmaker. While he was well known in Harlem for his documentaries, audiences outside New York City seldom knew his name or realized that he was African American. The expense of producing his documentaries made his operation unprofitable. The value to black audiences of the short films he made far exceeded the small monetary returns the filmmaker realized in his all too brief career.

Lewis was not the only journalist to contribute to documentary filmmaking. For example, veteran reporter St. Clair T. Bourne was often called upon to write a script for one of Lewis's *Colored Champion of Sports* reels or for William Alexander's *All American Newsreels*. A versatile writer, Bourne reported on both domestic and international news, sports, and entertainment. He contributed film reviews and wrote for the society pages. Bourne says that black reporters had to be ready for anything: they could expect to be sent by an editor to Washington one week to cover the activities of a half-dozen federal agencies, and then to the deep south the next week to report on segregation, jobs, race relations, or other issues of the day. Such broad experience made journalists like Bourne a valuable asset for independent filmmakers like Lewis, who were always short staffed and strapped for funds.[44]

In the years leading up to World War II, a number of other black filmmakers were devoting themselves to producing newsreels and documentaries. In the 1930s, Gordon Parks was beginning to shape a career in photography. A high school dropout from Kansas, Parks was a self-taught, multi-talented artist who developed his craft in the field, first as a commercial photographer and then as a cinema photographer. With the advent of war, Gordon Parks and his contemporaries, Carlton Moss and William Alexander, seized the opportunity to broaden their experience as cameramen and journalists in the military, and to bring to public attention black participation in the war effort at every level. They wanted to bring home the sacrifices made by blacks despite the bigotry and oppression they experienced at home.

This goal proved very difficult for Parks to pursue. African American pilots and their segregated units were assigned to escort the big bombers making raids on German strongholds in World War II. The black pilot's job was to divert anti-aircraft guns and enemy fighter planes from the bombers. The government was not eager to publicize this strategy, or the success of the African American pilots—this was an issue of racism, not military secrets. When documentaries appeared recently about the "Tuskegee Airmen," they ended a half-century of suppression of images of these men in combat. For the most part, war correspondents representing the black press had to rely on interviews conducted on the ground and handouts provided by the government. Papers with small circulations had to make use of letters from returning soldiers or interviews that took place stateside.[45] Images of black troops in combat were systematically suppressed, edited out of mainstream media in the U.S.

Gordon Parks set out to document the experience of the black airmen. Although he held the rank of first lieutenant in the Office of War Information (OWI), his efforts to carry out an assignment to follow the 332nd fighter pilots into action were thwarted. The experience ended in bitter disappointment, and his formidable skills as a photo-documentarian went unrealized.

Parks went on to become a fashion photographer and photojournalist for *Life* magazine and the first African American producer, director, writer, and composer to make his mark in Hollywood. (He filled all of these roles in his first feature film, *The Learning Tree*, 1969.) *Diary of a Harlem Family*, a 20-minute short made for television in 1968, was Parks's first film documentary and sought to give poverty in America a human face. Parks spent the winter months of 1968 getting to know the family and winning their trust by talking to them about what he was trying to do. The project grew out of a photo essay entitled *Flavio* that Parks had previously published in *Life*. *Flavio* depicted poverty in São Paulo, Brazil, by telling the story of a teenage boy who tries to hold his family together in the face of poverty, illiteracy, and unemployment. It also showed individuals and communities reaching out to help the boy and his family. The strong emotional impact that *Flavio* had on the magazine's large readership moved Parks to undertake *Diary of a Harlem Family*, this time capturing the family's experience on film. Another documentary made nearly two decades later, *Moments without Proper Names* (1987), brought to the screen a brilliant visualization of the filmmaker's life—his travels, the films he produced, and the people he knew. Covering nearly 40 years, the film is impressionistic and lyrical, employing Parks's artistry not only as a filmmaker, but also as a photographer, writer, and musician.

Near the end of World War II, Parks's contemporaries, Carlton Moss and William Alexander, were more successful in their wartime filmmaking efforts. Moss's *The Negro Soldier* (1944) and Alexander's *A Call to Duty* (1946), depicting blacks in the navy, were part of the war effort to boost civilian morale and patriotism. Both films resurrected the theme of black soldiers' heroism, as earlier documentaries had done in the World War I era.

THE NEGRO SOLDIER

Carlton Moss (1909–1997)[46] was born in Newark, New Jersey. As a young man he toured with the theater company of Morgan College, one of the first black colleges to organize a touring drama group. As a member of the Federal Theater Project in Harlem, he wrote, directed, and acted on stage. His original play, *Prelude to Swing*, had been performed by the Harlem Federal Theater. Moss also staged plays and pageants at the 135th Street YMCA, and wrote scripts for his own NBC radio show. He made his film debut in two Oscar Micheaux feature films, *The Phantom of Kenwood* (1927) and *Harlem after Midnight* (1934).

During World War II, the War Department's Information and Education Division needed a scriptwriter for a special project on Negro troops. The first script, written by Marc Connelly, the playwright known for *Green Pastures*, was rejected as too stereotypical. An approach that had worked on stage as folksy fable appealing to a white audience would not help stir patriotic passion in black viewers. The War Department realized that they needed a black writer, and Moss's name was put

Still from Carlton Moss's *The Negro Soldier*.
Courtesy of African Diaspora Images.

forth by Vincente Minnelli. But to get the assignment, Moss had to be okayed by a white Southerner in the agency. The officer asked him one question: "Where you from boy?" Moss replied, "North Carolina—Sir." He was bending the truth a bit, but it worked; by the code of southern paternalism, he was "one of our Negroes," which meant he would know his place.

Moss was designated a special consultant to the Office of War Information. He was neither a draftee nor a volunteer, yet he was on the front lines of battle in France, attached to the film unit assigned to shoot *The Negro Soldier* on location. On one occasion Moss was spotted by Ollie Stewart, war correspondent for *The Afro-American*, accompanying Brig. General Benjamin O. Davis, the military's highest ranking black officer and the first African American to hold that position. The General was in France to observe the action, and spent part of his time with the special pictorial unit that was filming colored troops.[47]

As a civilian on the front, Moss proved something of an embarrassment for the Army. It was customary, during the war, to induct whites in the entertainment industry and the media (actors, photographers, and journalists) into the special services, where they would automatically be awarded the rank of officer. Moss remained a civilian because the military simply did not know what to do with him. They had already filled their quota of black officers. Chaplains, doctors, and dentists could hold the rank of first lieutenant but Carlton was none of the above. Officials in Harlem's local draft board tried to pressure the Army into giving Moss the rank he was due as an artist, but to no avail.

Moss's final script was accepted by the War Department—except for the title. Moss had taken his title, *Colored Men to Arms!*, from a Frederick Douglass speech. Lest it be interpreted as a call to arms against white people, the title was changed to *The Negro Soldier*. Although the new title sounded more bland, the film's narrative and images offered a strong, historically accurate account of black soldiers' participation in every conflict that involved American soldiers, including the Civil War.

After a selected panel of viewers backed Moss's contention that the film should be seen by white audiences as well as black, a national public relations campaign was organized. General Davis was flown to Hollywood for a round of social functions to help gather support from the Hollywood community. The result was endorsements, personal appearances by movie stars such as Judy Garland, and expressions of support from other public-spirited individuals. The press and radio were effectively used to publicize the film's premiere. All of this brought national attention to Moss's personal mission—offering a lesson in history by telling the story of black Americans' courage and contribu-

Filmmaker William Alexander.
Courtesy of African Diaspora Images.

tions, and making it available to large audiences on the silver screen. The film toured the country and traveled abroad.

Moss returned to Europe to produce a sequel to *The Negro Soldier* entitled *Teamwork* (1946). He subsequently produced a number of other documentaries based on historical figures and events, including *Two Centuries of Black American Art, House on Cedar Hill: Frederick Douglass,* and *The Gift of Black Folk* (1978). Moss also taught film production for eight years at Fisk, and cinema studies at the University of California at Irvine.

THE FILMS OF WILLIAM ALEXANDER

The early pioneers of the black documentary, like George Broome and Peter P. Jones, were dedicated men with a mission. They were motivated by the desire to break new ground, to burst through the color line, and in the process to make names for themselves. Others continued in their footsteps in the decades that followed. Oscar Micheaux (1884–1951) certainly had their pioneering spirit and commitment to individualism. A producer, writer, and director, Micheaux was determined to go it alone right up to the end of his 30-year career.

While Micheaux is credited with being the most prolific black feature filmmaker of his time, William H. Alexander has an equally strong claim as producer of documentaries. Compared with Micheaux, Alexander kept a lower profile. He tended to be a team player who surrounded himself with top professionals—the best talent he could find. For example, Alexander engaged working journalists to write scripts for some of his projects. Veteran reporter St. Clair T. Bourne wrote and narrated scripts for a number of his documentaries.[48] Alexander was always on the lookout for ways to improve the quality of his productions, and would seize any opportunity that would help meet his goals. In 1973 a Paramount Pictures press biography described Alexander as the "consummate producer" and offered this account of his career: "For more than a quarter of a century, Colorado-born William Alexander has been roaming the world performing minor miracles of communication through filmmaking. . . . A man of boundless energy, close associates have known him as a daring self starter, full of original ideas, with the aggressiveness to set the domino theory in motion and effect its ultimate results."[49]

Alexander grew up in Colorado, where he attended Greeley High School and Colorado State College of Education before spending several years studying at Chicago State University. He moved to Washington, D.C., where he ran a radio show interviewing blacks in government and generally covering the social life of the African American middle class in the nation's capital.

Like Moss, Alexander's career was deeply affected by his work with the Office of War Information during World War II. Headed by Elmer Davis, OWI played a key role in boosting Negro morale around the country through press releases sent out to black newspapers. Planning and carrying out this effort was the work of a group of men sometimes known as the "Black Brain Trust" who fed the black press with stories and pictures. In addition to Alexander, information specialist and chief of the black press section, the group included William Bryant, an organization analyst attached to the Bureau of Intelligence, and Charles Austen, staff cartoonist.

Recognizing the power of film, Alexander's group at OWI went beyond the print media and formed a production company. In an interview given after the war, Alexander explained it this way:

We were very concerned about the morale of "minority groups"—whatever that meant. They worked in war industries, but when people went to the cinema, it looked like a white man's war. We formed the All American Newsreel Company and used to take OSS film crews and shoot stuff all over the world. One of the most interesting stories was on Willa Brown Coffee, the second black woman aviator (Bessie Coleman was the first). She trained all the instructors for the black 99th Pursuit Squadron at her Coffee School of Aeronautics outside Chicago. Although the releases were made in a government agency, the documentaries were privately filmed. Two of our shorts were on blacks in the Army and Navy: *The Highest Tradition,* narrated by Fredric March, and *Call to Duty,* narrated by Walter Huston.[50]

The All American Newsreel Company, under Alexander's direction, produced more than 250 newsreels. This collection has survived, and was recently purchased from a private collector by the Columbia Broadcasting System (CBS).

After the war, in 1945, Alexander moved to New York taking with him a wealth of experience and contacts acquired in his work for OWI. There he established the Associated Film Producers of Negro Motion Pictures, Inc., and started producing short musical films and features for theatrical release. Like Edward Lewis, Alexander leased these shorts

Anna Mae Winborn *(left)* and filmmaker William
Alexander on the set of *The Sweethearts of Rhythm.*
Courtesy of African Diaspora Images.

to theaters. He then found a new market for his work, taking three-to-five minute performance segments from the shorts and selling them as soundies that played in coin-operated jukeboxes in restaurants, bars, and cafes.

These short performance pieces had very simple stories or plot lines. They were cheap to produce and easy to sell, according to Haryette Miller Barton, Alexander's production assistant and one of the few African American women working in the film industry behind the camera. She explains:

> Mr. Alexander's shorts were sometimes made just to give a group of musicians work, making up the story as they went along or using the lyrics of a song for plot. Sometimes we shot in donated spaces—a barber shop after hours or on a Sunday. But for top performers like Billy Eckstine and his band, the Sweet Hearts of Rhythm, and Dizzy Gillespie's band, we worked with larger budgets, in a studio with a hired union (usually white) crew. Soundies and shorts were quick, easy to set up, and required little or no costuming. The plus was . . . they helped to pay the rent and salaries.[51]

In 1950 Alexander moved to London and established the Blue Nile Production Company. With London as his base he traveled to Africa where he produced a series of documentaries for and about the newly independent countries of the Sub-Sahara. These films, many commissioned by individual states, reflected life after independence and were used for public relations purposes and to record the historic changes that were taking place.

Alexander's films reflected life in the newly emerging African nations. The documentaries were used by individual states for public relations purposes and to record the historic changes that were taking place. He often worked with heads of state, and in two cases took on an official capacity: Alexander became the official film producer for the Republic of Liberia, and subsequently served in the same post for the government of Ethiopia. The documentaries produced by Alexander in these capacities received critical acclaim around the world. *The Village of Hope*, about a leper colony in Liberia, won a prize for the Best Short Film at the 1964 Cannes Film Festival. At the Venice Film Festival the following year, Alexander won a prize for his *Portrait of Ethiopia*, and in 1967 he received the United Nations Award at the International Festival in Madrid for *Wealth in Wood*.

Alexander spent nearly 18 years working in Africa and Europe. Relatively little of the work he produced during the African period has surfaced so far. The scope of his work is well documented, however.

Alexander filmed some of the first conferences of the Organization of African States. He helped bring television equipment to Liberia and Ethiopia, and assisted in developing TV programming in those countries. He received awards or decorations from heads of states in all of the 22 countries where he worked, including Liberia, Ethiopia, the Sudan, Morocco, the United Arab Republic, Zaire, Kenya, Senegal, Ghana, Algeria, Malagasy, Dahomey, Togo, Malawi, Sierra Leone, Tanzania, Zambia, French Congo, the Ivory Coast, Guinea, and the General African Republic. (His work was also recognized by the government of Singapore.)[52]

The films Alexander produced between the mid-1950s and 1973 constitute a sizeable body of work. Despite the awards he received abroad, his contribution as filmmaker and visionary at a critical juncture in Africa's history has yet to be fully acknowledged at home. Scholars have yet to address key questions about his work. What contributions did his documentaries make to each nation's development? How was his perspective and approach influenced by the heads of state who hired him, including such leaders and thinkers as Sékou Touré, Julius Nyerere, Jomo Kenyatta, Gamal Abdul Nasser, and Léopold Senghor? Answers to some of these questions must await the recovery of Alexander's historically important footage of the African independence movements, shot inside the former colonies. This footage would provide an invaluable resource for historians and film scholars alike.

BRIDGING THE GENERATIONS

Alexander remained active into the early 1970s, when he undertook an ambitious project to produce a film version of William Bradford Huie's novel, *The Klansman*. He acquired the screen rights to the novel and then, according to the Paramount Pictures press biography, traveled more than 300,000 miles to acquire financial backing ($4.5 million), engage a top director and crew, and attract a cast that included Richard Burton, Lee Marvin, O. J. Simpson, and Lola Falana. His expansive filmmaking career bridged a gap between the first generation of black documentary filmmakers that had all but disappeared by the 1950s, and a new generation of more strident, independent voices that emerged in the 1960s and helped to shape and record the civil rights struggle.

In the tradition of Peter P. Jones, Jennie Toussaint Welcome, Addison N. Scurlock, and other pioneers of black documentary filmmaking, these new chroniclers of African American history and culture used film to capture events as they were happening, and to empower their community by offering a deeper, stronger sense of its own identity and history, and ultimately to effect change. Their call to action helped to break the iron circle of segregation, racism, and containment, and to bring about a new era of race consciousness and renewal. While the media brought film clips and sound bites of the revolution in the streets to a national audience, African American filmmakers challenged viewers with a fuller, more textured sense of black culture and history, providing a context for the scenes of protest that were appearing more and more often on the evening news.

Today, as one generation reaches out to the next, the list of African American filmmakers is steadily growing. Foremost among them is William Greaves, who became executive producer of the public affairs program *Black Journal* in 1969. Greaves's work in network television created crucial new outlets for black documentarians. He helped to usher in a new era of filmmaking not only through his own work, but also through his efforts to mentor and support other filmmakers. William Miles, Louis Massiah, St. Clair Bourne, Julie Dash, Stan Lathan, Michelle Parkerson, Yvonne Smith, Stanley Nelson, Carroll Parrott Blue, Gil Noble, Henry Hampton, Charles Hobson, S. Pearl Sharp, Carol Munday Lawrence, Orlando Bagwell, Ayoka Chenzira, and (the late) Jackie Shearer and Toni Cade Bambara—these documentarians, and many others, are helping to light our way into the next century.

Looking ahead, many challenges await not only filmmakers, but also film historians. Many questions remain unanswered. Photographers' contributions in the century's early decades have yet to be fully explored.[53] The recovery of information about individual photographers and filmmakers may help to expand and clarify what is known about early motion picture technology. And more filmmakers need to be rescued from anonymity: what names might we attach to footage of African American soldiers in battle during the First World War? Or in Cuba during the Spanish American War?[54] A great deal of footage remains to be found. Many early filmmaking efforts are no doubt lost forever, but the whereabouts of later films are more puzzling. Where, for example, are the missing documentaries of William Alexander?

To be sure, current documentary techniques and approaches are light years away from those of the early pioneers, but for the most part, today's black filmmakers share the commitments of their forerunners: recording the highs and lows of ordinary folk, as well as extraordinary moments in black history and culture as seen from within. From the 1910 Tuskegee footage to Jones's marching bands and regiments to Alexander's newsreels, to today's commentaries—each has contributed to bringing to life the great canvas of African American experience.

NOTES

1. Nicholas Lemann, *The Promised Land: The Great Black Migration and How It Changed America* (New York: Knopf, 1991).
2. Ibid.
3. Thomas L. Johnson and Philip C. Dunn, eds., *A True Likeness: The Black South of Richard Samuel Roberts, 1920–1936* (Columbia, S.C.: Bruccoli Clark; and Chapel Hill, N.C.: Algonquin Books of Chapel Hill, 1986), 107.
4. See *Negro History Week*, February 10, 1935, 15.
5. The 1910 census listed 3,257 white photographers.
6. Jeanne Moutoussamy-Ashe, *Viewfinders: Black Women Photographers* (New York: Dodd, Mead, 1986).
7. Deborah Willis-Thomas, *Black Photographers, 1894–1940: An Illustrated Bio-bibliography* (New York: Garland, 1985), 15.
8. A magic lantern, especially one with two projectors arranged so as to produce dissolving views. Did Macbeth sell or rent his invention to showmen? Or filmmakers? Did he use it himself to project his own creations or the work of other photographers? Research on inventors is beyond the scope of this paper, but it should be noted that race and politics played a strong role in who could register for a patent. Even if an inventor managed to get a patent, information about his or her product could be buried in the offices of the government agency. In 1900, Henry E. Baker, Assistant Examiner of the U.S. Patent Office, published four volumes, *The Colored Inventor: A Record of Fifty Years*, which included drawings and plans submitted to the agency. See *Chicago Defender*, August 2, 1919. At a church in Brooklyn returning chaplain Arthur E. Rankin showed 35 stereopticon slides and three reels of a film on black troops in France.
9. Carlton Moss interview conducted by Pearl Bowser, 1987; Carlton Moss interview for *Midnight Ramble*, conducted by Pearl Bowser and Saundra Sharp 1991.
10. *Chicago Whip*, July 16, 1921.
11. Sherman H. Dudley, Robert T. Motts, and others contributed to the development of a circuit of theaters for black vaudeville and films. Sherman Dudley owned several theaters which were part of the substructure already in place for race movies. Showmen with packaged material worked the churches and lodge halls and set up tent shows. Before 1910, C. E. Hawk was exhibiting footage of the famous black Ninth Cavalry in the Inaugural Parade being applauded by President Theodore Roosevelt. The Ninth Cavalry served in Cuba under Roosevelt during the Spanish American War. Who shot the footage? Where did Hawk purchase this and other films he traveled with? Were black camera operators among the groups of freelance photographers selling to distributors or showmen before 1910? These are among the questions that remain unanswered.
12. Noble Johnson, African American actor and founder of Lincoln Motion Pictures, played in one such serial, *Bulls Eye*, produced by the Lubin Company. The black press advertised this serial as if Johnson were the star instead of white actor Eddie Polo. Johnson was under contract with the Lubin Company and ultimately had to choose between his own company and a steady job with a Hollywood studio. He chose Hollywood and a career that rewarded him with more than one hundred character roles in mainstream cinema.
13. Footage in the Jackson Mississippi Archives about 1940. The theater marquee displayed the race movie *God's Step Children*, an Oscar Micheaux film.

14. *Chicago Defender,* September 22, 1923.

15. *Deep South Showman Versie Lee Lawrence: A Reflection Book* (New York: Carlton Press, 1962). Henry Sampson in *Blacks in Black and White,* p. 2, cites touring black companies and showmen before 1910 exhibiting films for black audiences in schools, parks, and churches, including C. E. Hawk's *Electrical Display of Life Motion Pictures* (1905) and Royston's *Chicago Moving Picture Show* (as early as 1899).

16. *Chicago Defender,* December 31, 1910.

17. Ibid.

18. David Levering Lewis, *W. E. B. Du Bois: Biography of a Race, 1868–1919* (New York: Henry Holt and Company, 1993), 301.

19. The Brownsville raid occurred in 1905 when a group of black soldiers was accused of starting a gunfight and "shooting up" the town. Soldiers in the famous black 25th Texas Regiment, though innocent, were summarily discharged by order of President Theodore Roosevelt, without a trial or court martial. This was the same regiment that had fought with Roosevelt in Cuba in the taking of San Juan Hill. Now, by his order, its members were disgraced and discharged from the military without pay or benefits. The President, who had claimed to be a friend of the Negro and Washington, refused to rescind the order even though he knew the regiment was innocent. Roosevelt's popularity among African American voters was further eroded after the bloody riot in Atlanta in 1906. Federal troops had been sent in by Roosevelt's order.

20. *Booker T. Washington's Great Industrial School at Tuskegee, Alabama,* shown on February 3, 1910 (*New York Age*); *A Trip to Tuskegee* (*New York Age,* August 11, 1910); *A Tuskegee Pilgrimage* (Reol Productions, 1922); *Tuskegee Finds a Way Out* (Crusader Films, 1923).

21. *New York Age,* January 10, 1910.

22. Henry T. Sampson, *Blacks in Black and White: A Source Book on Black Films* (Metuchen, N.J.: Scarecrow Press, 1995), 584.

23. A personal note about *A Day at Tuskegee.* Reflecting on the history of the black documentary, seemingly small and prosaic in its beginnings, the author is struck by the tenacity of details so familiar they seem like only yesterday—a part of my immediate experience and not incidents nearly a century old. In the early 1970s, I was invited to Tuskegee Institute by the South Carolina Arts Council. At that time, there were still hints of the architectural grandeur described in reviews of the film.

24. *Chicago Defender,* May 1914.

25. *The Freeman, an Illustrated Colored Newspaper,* April 1, 1916. Jones probably designed this ad himself. The ad indicates the *Dawn of Truth* had been a part of the special movie spectacle in 1915, the year before this announcement of the availability of the film for bookings. It is also conceivable, based on the dates in the ad, that in 1914 the films were shown first abroad in South America and Brazil. Sampson refers to this as newsreel coverage of the August 21–September 16, 1915, celebration.

26. Ibid.

27. Ibid.

28. Ibid.

29. Ibid.

30. Anita Bush starred in two black silent Westerns: *The Crimson Skull* (1921) and *The Bull-Dogger* (1923). She is credited with founding one of the first African American dramatic stock companies, The Anita Bush Stock Company, in 1915, which included such notable actors as Dooley Wilson, Charles Gilpin, Andrew Bishop, and Carlotta Freeman.

31. See photographs of unknown camera operators in Johnson and Dunn, *A True Likeness*, 90; and on the set of an outdoor stage on Wisconsin-Ebony Pictures promotional/stock offering material, George P. Johnson Collection.

32. Sampson, *Blacks in Black and White*, 184.

33. Harry Grant, the George P. Johnson Collection, University of California Archives, Los Angeles.

34. Sampson, *Blacks in Black and White*.

35. *Chicago Defender*, July 26, 1913.

36. Ibid.

37. *The Negro News Reel*, 1923, produced by William Herman, *The Negro Rice Farmer*, 1921. Dunbar Film and Theatrical Company documentary: Negroes at work in the rice fields in Louisiana.

38. *This Is Our War: Selected Stories of Six War Correspondents—Six Who Were Sent Overseas by the Afro-American Newspapers* (Baltimore, Washington, Philadelphia, Richmond, and Newark: The Afro-American Company, 1945). Introduction by Carl Murphy (Baltimore: The Afro-American Company, December 15, 1944), 7.

39. Sampson, *Blacks in Black and White*, 588.

40. George P. Johnson interview conducted by Pearl Bowser, Los Angeles, 1969.

41. *New York Age*, May 24, 1919.

42. *Afro-American*, March 1939.

43. Handbill for Loew's Victoria and Loew's 116th Street theater, January 5–9, 1938.

44. St. Clair T. Bourne telephone interview conducted by Pearl Bowser, September 11, 1997.

45. *This Is Our War*, 7.

46. Carlton Moss interview conducted by Pearl Bowser, May 1987.

47. *This Is Our War*, 28.

48. St. Clair T. Bourne telephone interview.

49. *By Line*, biography of William Alexander.

50. Newspaper article provided by Harryette Miller Barton, undated.

51. Harryette Miller Barton interview conducted by Pearl Bowser, 1990.

52. Based on an interview conducted by William Greaves with William Alexander a week before Alexander's death on November 20, 1991. William Greaves starred in Alexander's *The Fight Never Ends* (1947) and *Souls of Sin* (1949).

53. Examples of unanswered questions include: Who might have used Macbeth's daylight screen? What year was it invented? Did showmen such as Royston, Hawks, or Professor A. A. Moncret, who were exhibiting moving pictures before 1910, show their programs in parks as well as churches and schools?

54. Henry Sampson attributes images from the war in Cuba to Lubin Ceneographs, which a black company, Royston's Chicago Moving Picture Show, included in its tour of Virginia's black churches, schools, etc. See Sampson, *Blacks in Black and White*, 2nd ed., 2.

2

Military Rites and Wrongs

African Americans in the U.S. Armed Forces

PHYLLIS R. KLOTMAN

> MEN OF COLOR TO ARMS! NOW OR NEVER.
> BETTER TO DIE FREE THAN TO LIVE SLAVE.
>
> —FREDERICK DOUGLASS
>
> THEY LOOK LIKE MEN . . . THEY LOOK LIKE MEN . . .
> THEY LOOK LIKE MEN OF WAR.
>
> —THE ENLISTED SOLDIERS

African Americans have attempted in a number of ways to achieve the rights of full citizenship, including the right to bear arms in the service of their country. Nonetheless, what has been recognized as patriotic duty for white citizens has been looked upon with circumspection if not outright hostility when black Americans have volunteered for military service that would place lethal weapons in their hands. "In the early history of New England, blacks could not serve in the militias as combatants. . . . the black military hero Peter Salem had to beg his master's permission to serve during the American Revolution."[1] In every subsequent conflict blacks have demonstrated their patriotism by enlisting (or attempting to enlist) in every branch of the armed services, regardless of the military's official policy of segregation and the ubiquitous presence of discrimination. They have performed exemplary service, often without official acknowledgment of their presence or their contributions. Although disappointed again and again, African Americans have assumed that their service abroad would lead to freedom and equality at home. This chapter looks at the works of African American documentarians who have chosen to contest the history that has made African Americans in arms invisible Americans by providing a powerful record of their achievements.

DO YOU KNOW IT? JACQUELINE SHEARER

Although Massachusetts was a hotbed of abolitionist activity before the Civil War, contradictions in that New England state abound: it was, in 1641, the first American colony to recognize the legality of slavery as an institution. And yet, it was in Boston that the first northern black regiment was raised: the Massachusetts 54th Colored Infantry.[2] In 1991 Jacqueline Shearer brought her considerable talents to the production of a documentary on the Massachusetts 54th. Neither white nor male, Shearer may have seemed an unlikely filmmaker for this topic. Yet she grew up in Columbia Point, Dorchester, Massachusetts (she was bused to school in South Boston because there was no school in Columbia Point),[3] graduated with a degree in history from Brandeis University, and already had an impressive record at Blackside in Boston, co-producing two segments of *Eyes on the Prize II*, when she was approached by *American Experience*. In an interview in 1992, she was candid about her reaction to the idea: "I said I don't want to do that, but I'd love to do something on Reconstruction. Well, that didn't fit their menu for whatever reason, but it makes me want to go back and find the Reconstruction story that I want to tell. It's such an incredible period!"[4] *American Experience* wasn't wrong; she was the right person to make *The Massachusetts 54th Colored Infantry*. The tragedy is that her untimely death from cancer in 1993 meant that we would never see her vision of Reconstruction, that important post-Civil War period in American history.

In February of 1865, after the fall of Charleston, South Carolina (to which the Massachusetts 54th contributed), Martin Delaney, the first black major commissioned in the United States Army, importuned the Port Royal ex-slaves in Charleston with these words: "Do you know that if it was not for the black man this war never would have been brought to a close with success to the union and the liberty of your race if it had not been for the Negro. I want you to understand that. Do you know it? Do you know it? Do you know it?"[5] They are the words selected by Shearer (and spoken by Laurence Fishburne as Delaney) to underscore the political as well as military accomplishments of the men of the 54th. Delaney was not content to make it known that black soldiers, including his son and the sons of Frederick Douglass, had fought valiantly in the service of the Union; he wanted acknowledgment that they

Henry Steward,
Massachusetts 54th Colored Infantry.
Courtesy of Massachusetts Historical Society.

had fought to put an end to slavery forever. He wanted not just those listeners but the world to know that black men were the agents of their delivery; as the narrator (Morgan Freeman) says, they "had fought for the right to fight and they had won; they had fought for freedom and they had won."

What makes *The Massachusetts 54th* so effective is its clearly articulated political perspective: Shearer doesn't simply make this documentary a tribute to the gallant men of the regiment; she places their fight on the field and off in the context of the larger political battle to change the focus of the war from an economic and political struggle between white men of the North and white men of the South to a war against slavery. It is no accident that the first on-camera speaker who is *not* a descendant of one of the soldiers is Byron Rushing, an African American Massachusetts legislator who says, "Before emancipation this was a war between groups of white people, white people in the North and white people in the South." Throughout the film the motives of the political establishment, with Lincoln as its chief spokesman, and those of the abolitionists, passionately articulated by Frederick Douglass (the voice of Carl Lumbly) are contrasted. Shearer works with parallel sequences, dramatizing arguments for and against emancipation by focusing on the photographic images of the "combatants" and building to the climactic moment when news of the Emancipation Proclamation is finally received in Boston on January 1, 1863.

Unlike the feature film *Glory* (1989) which preceded it, Shearer's documentary does not make the battle of Fort Wagner the centerpiece of the film.[6] She uses the traditional tools of the documentarian—archival footage, photographs, cartoons, quotations from historic texts, letters, and diaries (some of which she discovered herself), and interviews with experts as well as with descendants of the men of the 54th—to tell both the personal and political story of the fight for freedom and dignity. In fact, the most compelling moments come from the off-the-field battles of the men and their families—the struggle for economic equity: When the men enlisted, they were offered "equal pay and equal treatment in every respect save one: blacks would not be commissioned as officers" (voice-over narrator). The pay was stipulated as $13, plus a $3.50 clothes allowance; however, on June 30, 1863, their first payday, the black soldiers were offered $10 and at the same time were required to pay $3 for their clothes. They refused the offer: "Too many of our comrades' bones lie bleaching near the walls of Fort Wagner to subtract even one cent from our hard earned pay. As men who have fought to feed and clothe and keep warm, we must say that $10 by the greatest government in the world is an unjust distinction to men who have only a black skin to merit it."

Technically their act constituted mutiny, but even their white officer, Colonel Robert Gould Shaw, supported their action. They and their families suffered because of their principled stand. A descendant of Steven Swayle, one of the soldiers, describes on-camera the desperate straits of Swayle's wife and children, who were sent to the poorhouse because they received no money from him. It wasn't until August of 1864, months after their courageous but costly attack on Fort Wagner, that the men drew their first *equitable* pay; their protest had resulted in Congressional action. But it was too late for those who had died at Fort Wagner.

The men's refusal to accept secondary status with regard to their pay is dramatized in one scene in *Glory*, but the linear narrative drives toward the bloody charge on the barricades at Fort Wagner;[7] the focus is on the development of Shaw (Matthew Broderick) as an officer and leader of (black) men and the voice-overs are mainly from his letters.[8] *Glory* perpetuates the misconception that the black volunteers, with rare exceptions, were unable to read or write.[9] Yet we know early on in *The Massachusetts 54th* that Delaney's son, Douglass's sons Charles and Lewis Hayden, and Sojourner Truth's grandson James Caldwell—all of whom were literate—fought with the regiment; and that dockworkers,[10] farmers, sailors, carpenters, masons, house servants, *free* men with all different levels of education volunteered from the small free black community in Boston. James Gooding, who had been a sailor, wrote poems; the letters he wrote as a member of the 54th were published in a column in his hometown newspaper. Thomas Ampey was killed in the assault on Fort Wagner, but his brother Isom wrote eloquent letters home to Indiana, the state from which they had been recruited. After that battle, Lewis Hayden Douglass (voice of Blair Underwood) wrote to his fiancée: "This regiment has established its reputation as a fighting regiment. Not a man flinched though it was a trying time. How I got out of that fight alive I cannot tell, but I am here. My dear girl, I hope again to see you. I must bid you farewell should I be killed. Remember, if I die, I die in a good cause. I wish we had 100,000 colored troops. We would put an end to this war."

Ultimately 178,975 African Americans served in the Grand Army of the Republic. The 54th's casualties were nearly 50 percent—yet no black regiment was invited to participate when the victorious army passed in "grand review" in Washington, D.C., at the end of the war in spite of the fact that African Americans accounted for 10 percent of the men then under arms.

MUSIC AS METAPHOR

Hark! Listen to the trumpeters,
They call for volunteers;
On Zion's bright and flow'ry mount,
Behold the officers.
They look like men.
They look like men.
They look like men of war.
All arm'd and dress'd in uniform,
They look like men of war.
—The Enlisted Soldiers

Shearer's selection of music in the *Massachusetts 54th Colored Infantry* is as artful as it was in the segments of *Eyes on the Prize II*, which she co-produced.[11] "We did the music research and got the pieces and had a music consultant from Wooster, Ohio, a woman who knew a lot about 19th century black music, make selections for us. And then we got two choirs, one from Howard University and one from U Mass, Amherst, both led by choir directors who knew a lot about 19th century black musical styles, to perform the pieces." The hymn, "The Enlisted Soldiers," frames the film. Performed by the Howard University Choir under the direction of J. Weldon Norris (who arranged it),[12] "The Enlisted Soldiers" sets the film's solemn yet magisterial tone, as well as the theme; it repeats as the credits roll. These men whose images the camera sets to music are *volunteers* in a war, not to preserve a Union that endorsed slavery, but to deal a death blow to slavery itself. The emphasis throughout the film is on their commitment to that cause despite the risks they faced and the conditions they endured. For example, if captured, they were tortured or put to death, never offered in prisoner exchange: "Any Negro taken in federal uniform will be summarily put to death," read a Confederate Congress proclamation.

When the choir later sings "We are coming, Father Abraham," the message is clear that Lincoln needs them to win the war. As Douglass admonished: "This is no time to fight with one hand when both are needed. This is no time to fight only with your white hand and allow your black hand to remain tied." *The Massachusetts 54th* shows how black men in the south, slave and free, also joined the struggle. Some, like Robert Smalls, were ingenious. A slave with navigating experience, he, with nine others, stole *The Planter*, a rebel gun boat, out of Charleston harbor and turned it over to the Union forces. "I thought *The Planter* might be of some use to Uncle Abe," he said.

WOMEN AND THE FAMILY

The Massachusetts 54th demonstrates the effect of the war on the families of the soldiers, the hardships suffered by wives and children, but it also considers how they coped. Historian James Horton discusses the women's ability to survive by working even longer hours than they usually did and coming together as a community to support each other. Unlike *Glory*, Shearer's film also makes clear that abolitionists were not all white and male. Charlotte Forten was among the New England teachers who went South to teach the Port Royal slaves in what was known as the "Port Royal Experiment" It was an experiment to prove that emancipation would work, that ex-slaves, such as those 10,000 abandoned by their masters, could learn to become self-sufficient. Forten was a staunch, assertive abolitionist who "craved anti-slavery food continually," and the story of her activism and her commitment to the cause is part of the seldom-told history of African American women.

Instead of the bloody and violent scenes of the Fort Wagner debacle that end *Glory*, *The Massachusetts 54th* continues with the story of the regiment that, in spite of tremendous losses, went on to engage in other battles, including the conflict at Olustee, Florida, and the siege of Charleston. The 54th was one of the first regiments to enter the city after the "Citadel of the South" finally fell. The documentary ends with an image of the family, focusing in close up on the photograph of a soldier reunited with his wife and children, accompanied by "When Johnny Comes Marching Home."

Shearer's documentary was well received. Commenting in the *St. Louis Post-Dispatch* on the tenuous financial future of public television, Eric Mink included *The Massachusetts 54th Colored Infantry* in his list of *quality* public television films of 1991. In recommending the documentary, Zan Stewart of the *Los Angeles Times* pointed out that "the highly informative, well-detailed program goes far beyond the specific unit, which assembled in Boston in 1863. . . . It also describes, with remarkably clear archival photographs, etchings from the period, interviews and narration by actor Morgan Freeman, the racial climate of the United States prior to, and after, the regiment's inception."[13]

Shearer came to film through the study of history and because of a strong political motivation: "When I think of my own background in documentary—Boston Newsreel, part of a national new left organization, in the 1960s and 1970s—it has very much to do with film as a political tool and with my being politically motivated because I didn't learn film in school. I liked the notion of . . . learning it by doing it."[14] In all her work she brought the issues of race, gender, and class powerfully to the screen.

CHALLENGING THE RECORD: WILLIAM MILES

"I HAVE ALWAYS LOOKED FOR SITUATIONS WHERE THERE IS AN IMBALANCE,
SOMETHING IMPORTANT MISSING FROM THE HISTORICAL RECORD."[15]

William Miles, who also learned by doing, is one of the filmmakers, along with Madeline Anderson and William Greaves, whom Jacqueline Shearer credited with having a profound impact on her. His *Men of Bronze* (1977) became a model for documentaries that put African Americans back into military history. His struggle to represent them on screen from *their* perspective began in the sixties.

Men of Bronze opens and closes with a parade—a highly successful structuring device. The marchers are proud African American soldiers, "sons and grandsons of the old New York Infantry, the Harlem Hell-

Private Melville "Doc" Miller.
Still from William Miles's *Men of Bronze*.
Miles Educational Film Production.

fighters who became famous in France as the 369th, the old Rattlesnake Regiment." (Miles himself served in the 369th for 21 years, beginning in 1948.) Reaction shots of the crowd reveal the warm reception of the spectators with whom the film audience identifies. But there is much more to the "men of bronze" than a parade up Fifth Avenue. The camera cuts to the flag, an icon of both patriotic and ironic dimensions, focusing in close up on a black father and his young son. This is their day.

Eventually the camera comes to rest on the face of Melville T. Miller, a veteran of the 369th Infantry Regiment who enlisted to fight in World War I when he was just 16 years old. It will be his story, that of Frederick Williams, another African American veteran, and Hamilton Fish, a white captain who, like Robert Gould Shaw of Massachusetts, was assigned to a "colored" regiment. They will tell the story of the 369th, which began as the 15th New York National Guard, the first black American combat troops to fight on French soil. Archival footage and photographs fill in the factual details, tracing the discrimination against

African Americans in the military back to the Spanish American war. State military law made no provisions for black men, even veterans of that conflict, to join the New York National Guard. Legislation was passed in 1913 to amend the law, but it was not until June, 1916 that the governor finally appointed William Hayward, a white colonel in the National Guard and Public Services Commissioner of New York City, to recruit a "colored" regiment.

Over these historic images is the authoritative and resonant voice of Adolph Caesar, the film's narrator,[16] but Miles never lets the narration overshadow the recollections of the three men, Williams, Miller, and Fish. It is their oral narrative that makes the film memorable. The two enlisted men, Williams and Miller, are completely different in personality: Williams, who was wounded and unable to return with the other men to homecoming fanfare, grimly recalls the injuries of racism. At home the men had to train ignominiously with broomsticks—they weren't allowed guns; at home and abroad they were met with hostility from their own countrymen and were confined to the role of stevedores (labor troops) until they were finally assigned to the Fourth French Army.

At age 93, Williams is extremely articulate. His story tells of a civilian life that embodies the experiences of thousands of African Americans who sought a better life in the North during the early part of the century—the period known as the Great Migration. Miller, at 75, is the "baby": he tells with great glee how he was able to enlist at sixteen because the examining doctor falsified papers that "pushed up my age to nineteen and a half."[17] Former congressman Hamilton Fish is 87 at the time of the filming. He recounts the threats against the men by an Alabama Regiment with guns and ammunition ("We thought the war would start in America"), recalling matter-of-factly how the situation was defused when the Alabamans learned that the men of the 15th New York had munitions. Fish told his battalion: "'If attacked fight back, if fired upon, fire back.' We were able to persuade the Alabama regiment it wouldn't be worthwhile to attack." Miles's respect for these men who volunteered in a war "to save the world for democracy" is apparent. They served in a racially segregated army which assumed that they were not real fighting men.

Thwarted as was the Massachusetts 54th, the 369th was finally offered the opportunity to fight with the French. Colonel Hayward had gone to Paris to advocate for his men, who had been trained to fight, not to stevedore. The War Department refused to mix white and black troops, but the British and the French, who had been fighting since 1914, had lost thousands of men and needed replacements in the front lines.

When Hayward returned he asked the men: "Do you want to be steve-dores or do you want to fight?" Melville Miller says that the men an-swered with one voice. By the time they reached the Argonne Forest, three more black regiments were fighting with the French; 3,925 were killed and wounded. Recalling how the 369th marched victoriously into Alsace-Lorraine, with famous musician James Reese Europe leading "the best band in the U.S. Army," Miller exults: "That day we were proud to be Americans, proud to be black and proud to be in the New York Infantry." They had spent 191 days on the front line: "We had not lost a foot of ground or a prisoner. Every man in our outfit was given the Croix de Guerre by the French Government."

The soundtrack features the original music of the 369th band as the regiment, led by Lieutenant Europe, parades up Fifth Avenue on their return to New York, and it lends great power to the footage. Miller says: "That was one day there wasn't the slightest bit of prejudice in New York City." The camera supports that, freezing on the frame of a white soldier shaking the hand of Henry Johnson, one of the regiment's heroes. However, the reluctance of Congress to appropriate funds to build a monument to those left behind belies that rosy picture, for it took ten years before the monument was finally erected in France, in 1937. Even then it avoided specific recognition of African Americans with the generic inscription "To the men who died here." Albert Veyrenc, former French commander, conveys (through a translator) the sentiments of the French soldiers with whom the 369th fought: "We felt a great deal of respect for these men who had come 10,000 kilometers to save our country, but who also risked staying behind in the trenches where we lost so many soldiers, so many men. All my gratitude to our black friends of 1918." Miles's respect for these veterans is reflected in the way he listens to their story, especially his willingness to allow time for silences between the words of Frederick Williams. Miles explained his strategy: "I always said to myself, no one can tell your story, so each individual that I have on camera, I figured, well, their experience is the thing that I want people to hear. It's not mine. So I stay out of their way. It seems as if when you hear it from the person that really lived that life, it has more meaning than if you come up with a script."[18]

Men of Bronze allows these courageous men the dignity they were so often denied even as they fought for "America, the Beautiful," sung soulfully as a finale by Ray Charles. It's voiced over the images of marching men and the flags of their regiment and their country.

Men of Bronze was first seen at the New York Film Festival in 1977 and aired on national public television later that year. Kudos came from fellow documentarian William Greaves in a review written by him and

Dharathula H. Millender for *Film News:* "It has verve, it has élan, it has *music*"; in *Film Library Quarterly* Juanita R. Howard called attention to its "esthetic and technical symmetry"; and *Variety* praised it for its balance and objectivity: "In short, an excellent film."[19] In 1978 it was awarded an American Film Festival Red Ribbon, a CINE Golden Eagle, and an American Association of Local History Award of Merit.

Miles never intended to spend his filmmaking career documenting the contributions of African Americans to the military. After devoting 12 years to the making *of Men of Bronze,* he wanted to move on to other important aspects of black history and achievement; however, he was importuned by a number of black veterans: "I started getting these phone calls from guys in the Navy, the Marine Corps, Air Force guys, saying 'hey, man, how come you don't do our story?'"[20] Hence, *The Different Drummer: Blacks in the Military*, a three-part series for television which was completed in 1983, produced by Miles Educational Film Productions, Inc. for WNET/Channel 13.

404 Army Service Band, Signal Corps. Still from William Miles's
The Different Drummer: Blacks in the Military.
National Archives.

The Different Drummer has all of the drawbacks as well as the virtues of historical surveys. Each segment opens with the same visuals, music and on-screen "prologue" showing how inclusive the series will be:

From Bunker Hill
To the Battle of New Orleans
At Shiloh and Antietam
From the Marne River
To the Rhine River
To the Yalu in Korea
Through all the offensives
of Vietnam
The Black American
Has been a presence
In all of America's Wars
Sometimes as the Stranger
The Outsider
The Different Drummer

Instead of concentrating in depth on one branch of the service, or one period, *The Different Drummer* organizes a vast amount of material under the following topics: Part I. "The Unknown Soldier," Part II. "The Troops: Black American Troops in Modern Combat," and Part III. "From Gold Bars to Silver Stars." The first, which might well have been called "The Invisible Soldier," surveys African American participation in all of the country's armed struggles from colonial times to the present—from Bunker Hill to Vietnam (the Gulf War had not yet been engaged). The second, the only one with a female narrator, looks at the various services African American men *and women* have performed in those conflicts in the Army, Navy, Air Force, Marines, and Merchant Marines, from the most menial to the most combative and dangerous. The third introduces 76 high-ranking black officers, and discusses the little known facts of their existence. What unites the series is the nagging persistence of racism, the devaluation of African Americans in spite of their demonstrable ability and patriotism, the resistance to their participation in every period and every service unless the country was in peril. For his work on this series, Miles received the 1984 CEBA Award for Excellence and the D. Parke Gibson Award in Journalism.

LIBERATORS: RECONSTRUCTING HISTORY

It was in the process of making *The Different Drummer* that Miles first heard about the 761st Tank Battalion that fought in World War II. No film record had ever been made of their experiences or even of their existence. Miles shot some footage of the men of the 761st who wanted their story told, and documented their return to Europe for a reunion with some of the families they had met during the war, but he couldn't incorporate all of that into *Drummer*. It was footage he had never used.

Production still from William Miles and Nina Rosenblum's *Liberators:*
Fighting on Two Fronts in World War II. From left: Benjamin Bender,
E. G. McConnell, Leonard "Smitty" Smith, Kevin Keating.
Copyright Simon Chaput.

Then, in 1985 he happened on a letter to the editor in *The New York Times*
by a man who "wanted to set the record straight." Benjamin Bender was
a holocaust survivor; he had been imprisoned in Buchenwald, one of
the infamous death camps, and he was contesting a claim that several
hundred inmates, "resistance fighters," had overwhelmed the guards
40 hours before the American Third Army arrived:

> I was liberated at the Nazi concentration camp of Buchenwald on April
> 11, 1945. For me it was a glorious day, full of sunshine, an instant awakening
> of life after long darkness.
> The recollections are still vivid—black soldiers of the Third Army, tall
> and strong, crying like babies, carrying the emaciated bodies of the liberated
> prisoners.
> The survivors of Buchenwald owe their lives to the American people
> and not to the "resistance fighters." The short resistance uprising took place
> hours before the Americans entered Buchenwald. The German SS guards,
> sensing the approaching defeat, escaped en masse on bikes, on horses or
> just running. Credit for liberation belongs totally and unequivocally to the
> American people, and not to cheap propaganda trying to erase the shame-
> ful memories.[21]

Miles persuaded a reluctant Bender to tell his experiences on camera. It was Bender's description of his liberation that brought Miles to see a connection between the survivor's story and that of the African Americans who had fought so effectively with Patton's Third Army in the Battle of the Bulge—men of the 761st Tank Battalion and the 183rd Engineers. Had they been left out of the official record as liberators, as they were so often as soldiers? Miles remembered that someone from the 761st had said his tank went into a concentration camp.[22] It was this perceived connection that finally moved Miles to bring the story of African Americans as both skillful fighters and compassionate human beings to the screen. He invited Nina Rosenblum, another documentary filmmaker, to co-produce and the concept of *Liberators: Fighting on Two Fronts in World War II* (1992) began to take shape.

Liberators is a profoundly affecting film. Miles relied primarily on oral history, a strategy he had used successfully in a number of films, but most effectively in *Men of Bronze*. His experience gathering information about the heroism of the 369th Infantry Regiment in World War I had taught him to be wary of official records, which are often flawed or incomplete. *Liberators* tells two stories: one of Holocaust survival and the other of bravery under fire; of horror and humanitarianism; of genocide and racism. Told primarily from the point of view of survivors and some of the men who helped to liberate them, the film opens in the present at the site of one of Germany's most infamous concentration camps.

Benjamin Bender is an arresting presence: although his experience is individuated by his narrative, it also speaks to all survivors. When he takes two soldiers of the 761st, Leonard "Smitty" Smith and E. G. McConnell, through the "iron gate of Hell," Buchenwald becomes every concentration camp; we all descend into that inferno and do not emerge until the end of the film—a celebration of thanksgiving. But the men of the 761st and the 183rd have their own story to tell of patriotism and prejudice, of racism made in America but acted out on two fronts. The narrative alternates between these two stories of twentieth century sin and redemption. Although the voice-over narration (by Denzel Washington and Louis Gossett, Jr.) fills in the necessary historical background to the visuals, it is the presence of the witnesses to the drama that gives *Liberators* its power.

Using a garish Nazi poster of a caricatured black saxophonist— "savage" face, huge earring, exaggerated lips—outlandishly dressed and wearing an oversized boutonniere with a Star of David superimposed on it (captioned *Entartete Musik: Degenerate Music*), *Liberators* effectively links Hitler's most despised. It was the Jews, Hitler claimed, who brought Negroes into the Rhineland for the purpose of bastardizing the white race. The poster is a startling visual representation of racism and anti-semitism. Leon Bass links blacks and Jews in a dramatic description of his experiences with American racism and Nazi barbarism. A retired high school principal and a member of the 183rd Combat Engineers, Bass is a major on-screen speaker. His address to an audience at Temple Israel in New Rochelle, New York stands in counterpoint to the on-screen recollections of the tankers, mainly Smith and McConnell, William McBurney, Preston McNeil, Johnny Stevens. Most memorable are the scenes showing the return of a group of 761st veterans, with their wives, to a village near Liège for a reunion with the family who billeted the men during the war; and the reunion in New York 47 years after liberation of 30 survivors and 40 African American soldiers who helped to liberate them. When *Liberators* was shown on *The American Experience*, on November 11, 1992 (Veterans Day), it captured the imagination of audiences (3.7 million) and reviewers. John J. O'Connor in *The New York Times* called it "a remarkably illuminating documentary"; Tony Scott wrote in the cryptic prose of *Variety: "This is a fine docu"*;[23] the International Documentary Association honored it for "outstanding documentary achievement"; it received an Oscar nomination; and Kareem Abdul-Jabbar with Laurel Entertainment optioned the book, written by Lou Potter with William Miles and Nina Rosenblum (which Jesse Jackson was to recommend be read by every child in the public schools), for a feature film.

CONTROVERSY:
THE UNMAKING OF *LIBERATORS*

It is unlikely that Bill Miles and co-producer Nina Rosenblum set out to create a *cause célèbre*, but unlike Miles's other excursions into unofficial or unrecorded history, *Liberators* immediately struck a responsive chord. Not only was a new chapter in military history being written on the screen, but it seemed an occasion to repair strained relationships between blacks and Jews and to reaffirm bonds established during the civil rights era. On December 17, a month after the film's initial airing, a special screening took place at the Apollo Theater in Harlem, arranged by Percy Sutton, Bill Lynch from then-mayor David Dinkins's office, and a representative of Time Warner. It was attended by 1,200 luminaries; Congressman Charles Rangel and Peggy Tishman, former President of the Jewish Community Relations Council, shared the podium. Speakers included, among others, Mayor Dinkins, District Attorney Robert Morganthau of Manhattan, Jesse Jackson and Elie Wiesel (on video). Betty Shabazz, the widow of Malcolm X, was intro-

William Miles and Nina Rosenblum, producers of
Liberators: Fighting on Two Fronts in World War II,
on location during filming.
Copyright. Simon Chaput.

duced from the audience. The presentations and screening were followed by a special *Neighbor-to-Neighbor* program, moderated by Charlie Rose, which was broadcast on cable. The underlying theme of the evening was "healing"—reconciliation between blacks and Jews whose relationship had been at a particularly low ebb since the Crown Heights debacle. [24] Many saw it as a political maneuver to bolster Dinkins's ill-fated re-election bid. The particular political and racial situation in New York may well have played a role in intensifying the attack that was to come—a sometimes virulent assault on the film and its makers. According to writer Lou Potter, politics "took the controversy up to the next level." [25]

The controversy over the film took hold even before it was aired on national television. The film's detractors charged that it was historically inaccurate and misleading, and that African Americans had not liberated concentration camps. Charges and countercharges began to appear in the media—primarily in New York—from various sources. Veterans groups especially expressed concern about the dangers of misattribution and Holocaust revisionism. Members of the Sixth Armored Division, as well as other veterans, began a letter-writing campaign to public television stations around the country, as well as to WNET/13 and WGBH/Boston, after the film was broadcast. Many threatened to stop their contributions to public television if *Liberators* was not withdrawn. They contended that if the history of the liberation of the concentration camps is altered in any way—even to include additional information—it will fuel revisionism, and those who maintain that there was no Holocaust will be well served.

In letters to me, a veteran of the Sixth Armored Division stated unequivocally that the "U.S. Sixth Armored Div., 9th Armored Infantry Bn. were the first and *only* troops in Buchenwald on April 11, 1945 and part of the 12th"; another veteran insisted that the 42nd Infantry Division and the 45th Infantry Division "are the Liberating Troops of Dachau, 29 April 1945." Yet, in a list of liberating units certified by the U.S. Army's Center of Military History in Washington, D.C., other troops also appear. For example, the 80th Infantry Division was also credited with being at Buchenwald on April 12, 1945; that unit had official documents to prove its presence within 48 hours of the first soldier's arrival, thereby meeting the criteria set by the center. In addition to the 42nd and the 45th Infantry Divisions, the 20th Armored was also present at Dachau on April 29, 1945, and is therefore certified as a liberating unit.[26]

Gail Frey Borden, author of the novel *Seven Six One* (1991), wrote a fifteen-page letter to journalists at four national publications, including the *Washington Post* and the *New York Times*, and to Herbert Mitgang of the Author's Guild, on January 24, 1993, detailing his research on the 761st. Borden expressed concern that the reputation of the battalion would be sullied: "I worry that the facts of the 761st's outstanding record . . . might be questioned if *Liberators'* central thesis is permitted to become accepted fact, and is then shown to be based upon what appears to be, at best, a foundation of questionable scholarship and shaky assertions."

Borden bases part of his argument on information from Jon Bridgman's *The End of the Holocaust: The Liberation of the Camps*, which names the units that liberated Buchenwald and Dachau: "elements of the 4th Armored Division first reached Buchenwald, and the 2nd Battalion of the 222nd Infantry Regiment first entered Dachau." However, he adds that Douglas Kelling, in *The Liberation of the Nazi Concentration Camps 1945, Eyewitness Accounts of the Liberators*, identifies the 45th and 42nd Infantry Divisions as the ones which liberated Dachau. These two statements are not consistent. Nor do they correlate with the list of divisions certified by the Center of Military History mentioned above, which credits the 4th Armored Division as the liberating unit of Ohrdruf, a Buchenwald *subcamp*, not Buchenwald itself;[27] and identifies the 6th Armored Division and the 80th Infantry Division as the liberating units of

Buchenwald. To reiterate, the 42nd and the 45th Infantry Divisions are listed as liberating units of Dachau, but so also is the 20th Armored. It is not surprising that discrepancies with regard to the official historical record appear—that is one of the points made in *Liberators*.

It is not clear when the trouble began, nor exactly when E. G. McConnell decided to change his story about Buchenwald. Christopher Ruddy, a conservative journalist[28] charged that the film was an "unholy hoax"; his article appeared in the *New York Guardian, Long Island Newsday*, the *New Republic* and the *Jewish Forward*. Researcher Asa Gordon lists a plethora of other attacks on the film by citing their hostile headlines: "The Liberators: Trendy politics, dubious history," *New York Post*, February 3, 1993; "The Exaggerators," the *New Republic*, Feb. 8, 1993; "Concocting History," *New York Post*, February 6, 1993; "WWII Documentary on Black GIs Pulled," *Washington Post*, February 13, 1993; "Doubts Mar PBS Film of Black Army Unit," *New York Times*, March 1, 1993; "Massaging History / How Presumably Good Intentions Turned a Poignant World War II Documentary into a Fantasy of Black–Jewish Healing."[29]

Kenneth Stern, Program Specialist on Anti-Semitism and Extremism of the American Jewish Committee, decided to investigate the charges himself. He issued *"Liberators:* A Background Report," February 10, 1993, that sought "to explore the historical accuracy of the film. It should also be understood that there is no claim here that either the survivors or the veterans of the 761st have lied about their recollections, nor that their recollections are unreliable. . . . the problems are more complex." In regard to the 183rd he writes that "those who challenge whether the 183rd was a 'liberating' unit miss the point. The unit was there when it counted, in the first few days, helping helpless souls— true liberators in the second, less technical but equally humane meaning of the term."

Stern spoke with producers Miles and Rosenblum, some of the veterans and survivors, and with an archivist at the U.S. Holocaust Memorial Museum, Dr. Robert Kesting. Although his report addresses the difficulty of reconciling "inconsistent memories," Stern is insistent that "the film has serious factual flaws that go well beyond what can be written off as 'artistic license'" and that "the film and book make claims that are, at the most generous, negligently sloppy."

PBS issued a response to questions raised about the film, addressing particular charges and affirming Thirteen / WNET, WGBH and the *American Experience*'s "absolute confidence in the veracity of this outstanding film." Then, on February 11, 1993, they temporarily withdrew the film and in March an "Independent Review Team" was formed. It was headed by documentary filmmaker Morton Silverstein, assisted by

Diane Wilson, a researcher and producer, and Nancy Ramsey, a free-lance reporter and writer. Their thirteen-page report, "An Examination of *Liberators: Fighting on Two Fronts in World War II*,"[30] is dated August 19, 1993; Thirteen/WNET released a five-page statement regarding the committee's findings on September 7th. The press release included a statement of WNET's intention regarding *Liberators:* "Thirteen/WNET has advised the filmmakers of the review team's findings and of Thirteen/WNET's decision not to present the documentary again on public television until the errors in the film are rectified." Thirteen/WNET requested that it be removed from the film's production credits for non-broadcast distribution "because the documentary does not meet Thirteen's standards of accuracy."

The review had concluded that the film's account of the liberation of Dachau and Buchenwald was seriously flawed. It "could not substantiate the presence of the 761st Tank Battalion at Buchenwald on its day of liberation, April 11, 1945, nor during the 48 hour period . . . criteria set forth by the U.S. Army Center of Military History." It also found a number of "less egregious" errors. For example, veteran Paul Parks's unit is identified as the 183rd Engineer Combat Battalion, while he was actually in the 365th; the narrator in the Bastogne sequence incorrectly identifies the Bastogne-Marche highway as the Brussels-Bastogne highway; the juxtaposition of some still photographs and narration misidentifies Dachau, Buchenwald, and Gardelegen, a lesser known concentration camp.[31] The review did find evidence of the 761st at Gunskirchen Lager and of the 183rd at Dachau, although not within 48 hours of the first unit's entrance.

Members of the review team consulted with eight "archival sources" and spoke with veterans and survivors of the three camps mentioned in the film: Buchenwald, Dachau, and Gunskirchen Lager. Bender says that he spoke with Silverstein by telephone for nine hours, as well as with Ramsey. Yet he is mentioned in only two sentences in the report. On page 7: "Survivor Benjamin Bender recalls seeing Black soldiers at his liberation"; and on page 8: "It is possible, then, that Bender and other Buchenwald survivors who remember seeing Black soldiers on the first day of liberation do so because their day of liberation may have been after the 11th." Yet Bender is adamant that he was released from the hospital on April 11th after 11 A.M., and he saw black soldiers enter the camp that afternoon. As additional proof he cites the photograph shot on April 11th by William Scott and recorded in Scott's diary that day.

A 22-year-old African American reconnaissance sergeant, photographer, and part-time historian in S–2 (Intelligence), Scott was with the 183rd Combat Engineers. He is interviewed in *Liberators* and three of his photographs are used in the film. One is a hideous record of Nazi atrocities; it shows five black soldiers, one of whom was Scott's friend Leon Bass, two white soldiers, and two inmates outside of an incinerator/crematorium building at Buchenwald. Bender explained: "When this picture was taken, I wasn't present, but on the day of the 12th in the morning, I was exploring the crematorium. Buchenwald was clean. So the black forces couldn't have come on the 12th, 13th or 14th and taken the pictures. They were present on April 11, 1945."[32]

Scott, who died in March 1992, before *Liberators* was aired, had been speaking to student, synagogue, and church groups about his concentration camp experience long before he appeared in *Liberators*. In fact, he gathered together a number of the pictures he took at Buchenwald and published them in 1989 in a pamphlet entitled "World War II Veteran Remembers the Horror of the Holocaust." The cover has a telling sentence: "I remember the day—clear and sunny—riding in a convoy into Eisenach, Germany, *11 April 1945* [my emphasis], as World War II was ending; and, a Third Army courier delivering a message to us to continue on to a concentration camp (Buchenwald), 10 or more miles further east, near Weimar." In 1981 Scott and his friend Bass participated in a gathering of liberators and survivors at the State Department in Washington. In 1991, President George Bush appointed Scott to the United States Holocaust Memorial Council.[33]

Miles and Rosenblum responded on March 5, 1993, to Kenneth Stern's report and on September 7th to the Silverstein report and the findings of WNET:

> We do not feel that WNET has conducted an independent assessment of the program. We stand by the testimony of the liberators and survivors who have given substantive oral testimony. We support the report's conclusion that African-American soldiers played a critical role in the liberation. *Liberators: Fighting on Two Fronts in World War II* has been widely recognized nationally and internationally for its contribution to the subject and we continue to object to PBS censorship. We feel it is dangerous to limit historical inquiry, especially in light of recent revelations concerning the role of black troops in the military. A continuation of this dialogue is counter productive and only serves to denigrate the courageous concentration camp survivors and their heroic liberators.[34]

Writers on the *Liberators* project, Daniel Allentuck and Lou Potter, wrote letters defending the film, the witnesses, and the integrity of their work.[35]

THE 761ST TANK BATTALION

When I was a child in Alamo School in Galveston, Texas, Santa Ana was the villain and Sam Houston the hero. Texas was born in 1836 and "The Eyes of Texas" were always upon us. Wars and soldiers were a part of our study of history in our segregated junior and senior high schools. Heroes were white and black people were primarily contented slaves or invisible. Documentary films were not a part of school instruction, but *The March of Time*, along with radio, informed us that the country was preparing for war. Young men came to Texas from all over the country for basic training in segregated units. If Carlton Moss's *The Negro Soldier* (1944) was screened in Galveston, it would probably have been at one of the segregated theaters. As war entered our lives, we learned about great white military leaders: Eisenhower, Bradley, MacArthur, Patton. It is General Patton who, ironically, came to stand for the hopes and aspirations of those invisible soldiers whose stories never made it to the textbooks, the airwaves, or the screen. To fully understand how this segregated battalion, the first of its kind in the U.S. military, became the subject of a feature-length documentary a bit of history is in order. We need to appreciate its relationship to the Army in general, and Patton in particular, and its depiction by witnesses to the liberation of the camps.

The first black tank battalion in the United States Army was inaugurated in 1942. Its soldiers trained at Camp Claiborne in Louisiana and Camp Hood in Texas where they were treated to southern-style racism. The battalion was finally sent overseas in 1944 and was assigned to Patton's Third Army. Every account of their first encounter with the enemy in Morville-les-Vic, France, includes a speech by General Patton (November 2, 1944), who was in the habit of giving his men a pep talk before they went into battle. Trezzvant W. Anderson, African American combat journalist,[36] recorded Patton's words to the 761st in his history of the battalion which was published in Germany in 1945: "Men, you're the first Negro tankers to ever fight in the American Army. I would never have asked for you if you weren't good. I have nothing but the best in my Army. I don't care what color you are, as long as you go up there and kill those Kraut sonsabitches. Everyone has their eyes on you and is expecting great things from you. Most of all, your race is looking forward to you. Don't let them down, and, damn you, don't let me down!"[37] In his autobiography, *War As I Knew It*, Patton confirmed the talk (dating it October 31st), but gave no account of what he'd said. However, he did give his assessment of the men: "On the thirty-first, I inspected and made a talk to the 761st Tank Battalion. A good many of the lieutenants and some of the captains had been my sergeants in the 9th and 10th Cavalry. Individually they were good soldiers, but I expressed my belief at that time, and have never found the necessity of changing it, that a colored soldier cannot think fast enough to fight in armor."[38] It was not the only derogatory comment Patton made about black troops, in spite of the fact that these men distinguished themselves, and the Armed Services, in the Third Army under his command.[39] Nevertheless, he remained an icon to the men of the 761st—the military man par excellence, "The Old Man" for whom they would risk their lives.

When Captain John Long,[40] commander, "B" Company of the 761st, was interviewed for the book *The Invisible Soldier: The Experience of the Black Soldier in World War II,* he reiterated the Patton speech but added two choice Patton sentences: "If you want me you can always find me in the lead tank. They say it's patriotic to die for your country, well let's see how many patriots we can make out of those German motherfuckers."[41] The men of the 761st did make a number of German "patriots," but were rarely given the recognition they had reason to expect for their efforts, perhaps because the 761st, as Long describes their function, "was a detached and self-sustained unit up for grabs by anyone who needed it in the 3rd Army." They spearheaded a number of Patton's advances into enemy territory. Long counters Ulysses Lee's version of the battle of Morville written for the government document *The Employment of Negro Troops,*[42] which credits a number of white officers with leading the battalion to victory:

> The victory of Morville-les-Vic belongs to the enlisted men and the junior officers of the 761st; they just happen to be black. The two white senior officers of our unit [Lee] credits with Morville-les-Vic didn't have a goddamn thing to do with our victory. . . . Lieutenant Colonel Bates, our commanding officer, . . . was shot in the ass the night before and had to be evacuated. They never found out whether or not he was accidentally shot by an American soldier or hit by sniper fire. The next man in command, Major Wingo, the morning of the attack, turned his tank around and went hell-bent in the opposite direction. He just plain chickened and that s.o.b. was evacuated for combat fatigue. Hell, we hadn't even been in battle yet.

WITNESSES[43]

> AS IN MANY ORAL HISTORY REMINISCENCES, THE CENTRAL MOMENTS
> OF SUCH EXPERIENCES TEND TO BE INERADICABLE MEMORIES,
> ALTHOUGH DETAILS AT THE EDGES MAY GROW FUZZY.
> THIS ONLY EMPHASIZES THE IMPORTANCE OF MULTIPLE WITNESSES.
>
> —ERIK BARNOUW[44]

Captain Long's attitude toward the Germans changed after he and his men *liberated* (his word) their first concentration camp:

> Have you ever seen a stack of bones with the skin stretched over it? At the camp you could not tell the young from the old. When we busted the gate the

inmates just staggered out with no purpose or direction until they saw a dead horse recently struck by a shell. . . . They tottered over to that dead carcass and threw themselves upon it, eating raw flesh. We cut ourselves back to one-third rations and left all of the food we could at the camp. There was just one thing wrong, we later learned our food killed many of them.

From this incident on Jerry was no longer an impersonal foe. The Germans were monsters! I have never found any way to find an excuse for them or any man who would do to people what I saw when we opened the gate to that camp and two others. We had just mopped them up before but we stomped the shit out of them after the camps.[45]

This interview, published in 1975, may be the first *written* record of the 761st as a liberating unit. Although Long does not say which camps he and his men liberated, he is clear about the experience. And yet there is apparently no validation in the morning reports (the "daily history" of a unit) or after-action reports to indicate that his unit took part in the liberation of Nazi victims.

Leonard "Smitty" Smith and E. G. McConnell, both of Company C, have as prominent a role in *Liberators* as Melville Miller and Frederick Williams have in *Men of Bronze*. Childhood friends who met again in the Army, they are witnesses in the film to Benjamin Bender's poignant recollections of Nazi brutality at Buchenwald, as well as to the exploits of the 761st, but they have become distinctly different witnesses in the controversy.

Smith has never wavered in his recollections of going into a concentration camp (the captain of the unit to which his tank was attached told the men it was Dachau). McConnell, on the other hand, said—after the film's release—that he was never at Buchenwald until he went with Miles and Rosenblum to shoot the film. However, McConnell met with survivors and other veterans in a reunion in midtown Manhattan in October 1991. George James reported in the *New York Times* a meeting with McConnell and Bender in that same month where the two men "remembered together": "E. G. McConnell, a soldier in the all-black 761st Tank Battalion, found a sudden insight in the misery of Buchenwald. Like many of his black colleagues, the young soldier from Jamaica, Queens, had gone into combat fired by the anger over racial indignities suffered in his own country and at the hands of his white comrades in arms. Looking at the end result of hatred, at its barely living survivors, he saw himself." McConnell was also quoted in *The Palm Beach Post*, February 18, 1992: "'My country tis of thee, sweet land of bigotry' was the common feeling among black soldiers . . . [but] the soldiers knew they were a part of history when they marched into the concentration camps and broke into tears at the sight of emaciated prisoners." In addition, he made presentations at such places as the Jewish Museum, and was interviewed on a number of occasions. At a Holocaust memorial service at East Northport Jewish Center, he told the interviewer Don Crawford: "I was really astounded that a man could do this to another man. You couldn't tell the young from the old, the bodies lined up head to foot. . . . They were string beans, just wasted."[46]

McConnell attributes his belated repudiation of the film in part to the lack of supportive information in the morning and after-action reports, as do the organizations which petitioned successfully to have their divisions certified as liberating units.[47] Smith points to the fact that not everything went into those reports and gives the example of "rape call"—the ignominious order that allowed German women to pick from African American troops but not from white troops, anyone they thought had violated them.

Corporal Horace Evans of "B" Company referred to a comparable experience: "I was called out of my tent at least a dozen times with other black soldiers to stand in line to let some German girl look us over to see if we had raped her the previous night." Captain Gates, black commander of "A" company, was outraged that surveys were made in every area where there were Negro soldiers. When he was ordered to have his men stand in formation for rape call, he said, "I don't have my men fall out for anything like that."[48]

Trezzvant Anderson is clear on the issue of "complete and accurate reporting":

[The 761st Tank Battalion] received scant attention in histories of some of the infantry divisions with which it worked. . . . The 761st was mentioned *twice* by name, in the history of the 26th Division. And in the 103rd Division's "REPORT AFTER ACTION," published this year, our M-4 General Sherman tanks, were frequently pictured and referred to as "614th Tank Destroyers." This is the story of the 761st *Tank Battalion*, not a "towed" tank destroyer battalion, but a *Tank Battalion*, which fought and fought, and earned its place in the sun, by the sheer weight of its relentless drive, push and might, and by the sweat of the brows of dusky Negro soldiers, who . . . gave their blood and their lives on the field of battle, ASKING NOTHING, but HOPING that their sacrifices would not go unheeded and un-noticed, . . . and that their record would go down in history, as a contribution to the winning of World War II. . . .[49]

Benjamin Bender was the first survivor to point out, in the letter to the *New York Times* which first drew Miles's attention, that at least some of the claims of self-styled "liberators" were specious. He has never wavered from his original statements about seeing black soldiers at

Buchenwald on April 11, 1945. He painfully relived his concentration camp experience before the camera, returning to Germany in spite of misgivings, after being importuned by Miles and Rosenblum. After the attacks on *Liberators*, he wrote letters to the newspapers, to the War Department and to President Clinton, in addition to speaking for hours to the Thirteen/WNET review team.

Although Buchenwald survivor Alex Gross did not have a prominent role in *Liberators*, he did appear in the reunion scene. He and William Scott had met in 1979 when they both responded to an invitation from Fred W. Crawford at Emory University. Crawford was attempting to locate veterans who had witnessed the Holocaust. In 1980 WAGA-TV taped and aired a session with Gross, Scott, and Crawford. Attacks on the credibility of the Holocaust prompted the Georgia Holocaust Commission to embark on an aggressive educational program in that state. Scott's pamphlet includes a picture of the two men (and the director of community relations, Atlanta Jewish Federation) at the 1981 Holocaust Memorial Services in Atlanta. Gross said that "he and one of his brothers were at Buchenwald when Scott's unit arrived and that he may be in the photo in this pamphlet of those leaving the camp." Their relationship existed long before *Liberators* and continued until Scott's death on March 7, 1992.[50] On April 11, 1995, Gross joined Leon Bass and Asa Gordon, William Scott's cousin, for a presentation at the United States Holocaust Memorial Museum in Washington, D.C.

In a report of his trip to Buchenwald in 1989, Henry Kamm wrote in the *New York Times* that East Germany made a national memorial of the camp, but the memorial doesn't "commemorate the victims for what they were, and it denies to the United States recognition for having liberated Buchenwald." In a legend created after the fact, he says, "Buchenwald was 'selbstbefreit' or 'self-liberated.'" In a telephone interview with Kamm, Elie Wiesel, the Nobel Prize-winning author, who was liberated at Buchenwald, gave a different account: "The most moving moment of my life was the day the Americans arrived, a few hours after the SS had fled, It was the morning of April 11. . . . I will always remember with love a big black soldier. He was crying like a child— all the pain in the world and all the rage. Everyone who was there that day will forever feel a sentiment of gratitude to the American soldiers who liberated us."[51]

Gunther Jacobs, a survivor who spent three and a half years of his life in Buchenwald and other Nazi concentration camps, told Jeff Bradley, *Denver Post* critic-at-large: "The first black people I ever saw in my life were the black soldiers who liberated us on April 11, 1945." The article reports that Jacobs had never been able to speak about what happened at Buchenwald, but that he wanted to speak out now "on behalf of his black liberators" whom he had never thanked. Jacobs, 17 years old at the time, remembers the black soldiers "coming to the camp with half-tracks and armored personnel carriers. About a half-dozen vehicles. These black GIs came out and gazed at us—we were very malnourished and dehydrated and I was hardly able to walk."[52] It is not clear whether Jacobs was responding to the attacks on *Liberators*. In any case, there seems to be no reason why he would fabricate such a story; he had not appeared in the film and had no apparent reason to defend it.

An international lawyer and native of Bialystok, Poland, Samuel Pisar survived Nazi concentration camps for four years. In 1979, he published his memoirs, *Of Blood and Hope*, which begin with an encomium to Joe Louis: "We were ecstatic my classmates and I, when we heard in 1938 that the black boxer Joe Louis had knocked out the Nazi Max Schmeling for the heavyweight championship of the world. So much for the 'Master Race.'" In the first three chapters he describes being thrown into the chaos and horror of the Nazi takeover of Bialystok, the murder of his father, mother and sister—the collapse of his world. Surviving for four horrific years (1941–1945) in labor and concentration camps in Poland and Germany, he was finally rescued in the vicinity of Dachau where the fleeing Germans had marched him and thousands of others to certain death. In the confusion of the German retreat before advancing Allied soldiers, Pisar and several of his friends escaped, but suddenly encountered a huge tank which they assumed to be German until Samuel realized that instead of a swastika the tank bore a five-pointed white star:

> With a wild roar . . . I leaped to the ground, and ran toward the tank. The German machine guns opened up again. The tank fired twice. Then all was quiet. I was still running. I was in front of the tank, waving my arms. The hatch opened. A big black man climbed out, swearing unintelligibly at me. Recalling the only English I knew, those words my mother had sighed while dreaming of our deliverance, I fell at the black man's feet, threw my arms around his legs and yelled at the top of my lungs: 'God Bless America!' With an unmistakable gesture, the American motioned me to get up and lifted me in through the hatch. In a few minutes, all of us were free.[53]

Pisar appeared on the *Dick Cavett Show* shortly after the publication of his memoirs and touched the studio audience with his rendition of the story of his rescue by a "colored" American soldier who emerged from a tank that was still in the thick of battle *near Dachau*.

On May 7, 1995, Pisar briefly recounted the same story of his experiences in the death camps and his dramatic rescue by a black American tanker in the *Washington Post*, "Escape from Dachau: My Own Private V-E Day." The article was taken from the keynote address he gave the next day at the U.S. Holocaust Memorial Museum in Washington.

More than a decade before the production of *Liberators,* as well as three and a half years after its release, Pisar described his liberation in the same way. Did he *invent* his story long before several 761st soldiers claimed that they were there? If it was not physically possible for 761st tanks to be deployed in the vicinity of Dachau, as several officers of the battalion have attested, who was that African American tanker? Even though Pisar was young and had no personal contact with Americans, he knew who Joe Louis was and would hardly have made a mistake about race. What's more he claimed to have recognized the soldier, Bill Ellington, and personally thanked Ellington's widow at the Olympic Games in Atlanta. Yet his daughter, after attending a screening of *Liberators* at Harvard University, attacked the veracity of the film in the *Forward* (February 12, 1993), claiming that the effect was to give credibility to Holocaust revisionists: "The fear among many here is that inaccuracy, especially regarding a topic so sensitive as the Holocaust, might fuel revisionism and add support to those who claim the Holocaust never happened."

Holocaust deniers will feed on anything. But if the rules of recognition—only divisions can be designated as "liberating units"—prevail, then segregated battalions, regiments, companies, individuals are swallowed up and denied credit for one of the most humane acts performed by soldiers during World War II. Edward J. Drea's article, cited in note #28, includes an important point about smaller units: "Given the great number of U.S. Army units involved in the advance across Germany and the great number of camps, many were freed by small units subordinate to a division. . . . Thus an infantry regiment of division X might find itself *temporarily attached* [my emphasis] to an armored battalion of division Y as they pushed across the Third Reich." For that reason, they decided to credit only the "parent division."[54] Drea's statement about temporarily attached units reinforces the comments of a number of the men in both the 761st battalion and the 183rd regiment. Corporal Evans, "B" Company, 761st, was particularly bitter: "Overseas we were known as a bastard outfit. It meant we didn't belong to any group permanently; we fought with any outfit that needed us. . . . It was definitely a ploy to keep from committing us together as a battalion as much as possible; whole units get credit while a few isolated tanks, no matter whether they saved the day or not, are overlooked."[55]

The culture of segregation in the armed forces was responsible for the retention of long-held attitudes about the ability of African Americans to measure up to the challenges of war. If their often menial assignments were judged to be fit for second-class citizen/soldiers, why would their exemplary performance of those or much more meaningful tasks be worthy of recognition? Hollywood's *Patton* included one role for the fine African American actor James Edwards—Patton's valet. It should be clear that the level of criticism and outrage occasioned by *Liberators* was due to complex historical and political factors—to attitudes and relationships—reaching far beyond the film itself. Regardless of its strengths and weaknesses *Liberators* provides a multiconscious view of World War II; it puts black soldiers back into the field of battle and into the concentration camps that some of them helped to liberate.

Responding to *Liberators*, film scholar/critic Annette Insdorf wrote in the *Washington Post:* "In 1993, we don't seem to be in danger of forgetting the Holocaust. But we are in danger of forgetting that all films —even documentaries—have a point of view, and that truth will always be partial." Insdorf added that *Liberators* is "certainly not the first—and probably won't be the last—Holocaust film to provoke heated discussion about the sanctity of the subject and the limitations not only of individual memory but of official records."[56]

If film theory offers useful insight into the way documentary presents a structured point of view, then critical race theory may provide a larger context for understanding the way that differing views of reality have contributed to the *Liberators* controversy. Critical race theory has emerged out of the desire of minority scholars in legal studies to construct an alternative way of explaining racial issues. In an attempt to attack racial subordination, some have developed a multiconsciousness analysis of phenomena that rejects efforts to harmonize diverse understandings. In fact, some scholars question whether objective reality matters when institutional structures, including the justice system, are designed to reflect the values of the dominant culture, ignoring or suppressing the perspectives of minorities.

Multiconsciousness analysis focuses on differences, not commonalities, in comprehending a given phenomenon. It posits competing versions of reality in part because our understanding of reality is based on different underlying assumptions and different belief systems.[57] Many critical race theorists "consider that a principal obstacle to racial reform is majoritarian mindset—the bundle of presuppositions, *received wisdoms*, and shared cultural understandings persons in the dominant group bring to discussions of race. To analyze and challenge these power-laden beliefs, some writers employ counterstories, parables, chronicles, and anecdotes aimed at revealing their contingency, cruelty, and self-serving nature."[58]

The controversy surrounding *Liberators* may invite analysis based on critical race theory that can help us understand the difficulties of reconciling such different views of reality. It is important to remember that, whatever its successes and failures, *Liberators* as a counterstory of World War II provides the privileged view of black soldiers and Jewish survivors themselves—one that should not be disregarded. The intense debate over truth and factual accuracy may tell us a lot about institutional and alternative ways of constructing history, but should not overwhelm the legitimate values of the film.

LEGACY

A new generation of African American documentary filmmakers may well inherit Miles's mantle. One candidate is Jerald Harkness who founded Visionary Productions in Indianapolis in June 1993. Following advice from his mentor Christopher Duffy, President and CEO of Wabash Valley Broadcasting, he embarked on a project to make a documentary on the first black Marines—mentioned briefly in *The Different Drummer*—who trained in North Carolina at Montford Point, a base built especially for the segregated training of "Negro" troops during World War II. When the Marines finally allowed black volunteers to enlist, they set limits on how many could join and what jobs they could do. One thing was clear: no African American would be allowed to give orders to whites.

The Men of Montford Point: The First Black Marines[59] documents the story of the first African Americans to break the color barrier in the Marine Corps. A white marine who served during the Korean conflict, Duffy broached the idea to Harkness who researched it with Nora Hiatt, producer-writer on the project. They started working in April of 1996 and began production in June. Most of the interviews were shot in Kansas City at the Montford Point Annual Convention; the rest in October at Montford Point in Jacksonville, North Carolina. George Hobbs, a black Marine with thirty years of service, acted as consultant. Harkness relies primarily on archival footage and on-screen interviews of the veterans of this token unit. Most speak candidly about why they left the Marines; the few who stayed tell why.

The themes that run through *The Men of Montford Point* echo those that emerged in all of the films discussed in this chapter: the struggle of African Americans to serve their country; the indignities suffered at the hands of civilians and military personnel alike; and the lack of recognition of their contributions.[60]

In *The Alchemy of Race and Rights* Patricia Williams articulates what so many African Americans in the U.S. Armed Forces painfully described for the documentarians who turned the cameras on their experience: "I wonder when I and the millions of other people of color who have done great and noble things or creative and scientific things —when our achievements will become generalizations about our race and seen as contributions to the larger culture, rather than exceptions to the rule."[61]

NOTES

1. Alton Hornsby, Jr., *The Black Almanac* (Woodbury, N.Y.: Barron's Educational Series, 1972), xii.

2. Boston is also the site of the monument to Robert Gould Shaw and the 54th, erected in 1897. According to Christine Temin, the "initial design for the memorial was an equestrian statue of Shaw period—no black soldiers. That was fine with [H. H.] Richardson [architect of Trinity Church and Boston's cultural czar] and [Augustus] Saint-Gaudens [the artist], but not with Shaw's family, who insisted that the men their son had commanded be included" ("Boston's Conscience Turns 100," *Boston Globe*, May 25, 1997, N1). Nonetheless, the statute is still known as the Robert Gould Shaw Memorial and the centennial celebration included a screening of *Glory*, not Shearer's documentary.

3. Taken from the tribute to Jackie Shearer published in Independent Television Service's *Buzzword* 2, no. 2 (Winter 1994): 2.

4. Jacqueline Shearer interview conducted by Phyllis Klotman and Janet Cutler, June 29, 1992.

5. In the BBC docudrama, *A Son of Africa: The Slave Narrative of Oloudah Equiano* (1995), Stuart Hall makes an important point about agency: "The historiography of the abolitionist movement itself has kind of written out the agency of Blacks themselves. It is as if abolition was really a gift by liberal and reforming whites to the enslaved peoples and not one in which slaves themselves played an active part." Shearer's film emphasizes the agency of slaves and former slaves in behalf of their own freedom, as does the narrator of William Miles's *The Different Drummer*, discussed later in this chapter, who says after numerous on-screen examples of their fight for freedom: "It is naive at best to even suggest that Abraham Lincoln, with a stroke of a pen, freed the slaves."

6. Jacqueline Shearer may not have intended to call into question the historical accuracy of the film *Glory*, produced by Freddie Fields; however, the fact that the feature film exists makes the comparison inevitable. Fields may have thought *Glory* needed a special marketing strategy to make a profit on his investment ("about $18,000,000," he responded to Dan Rather's question) since he agreed to have CBS's *48 Hours* crew at the Jekyll Island shoot. The resultant "making of . . ." film is distributed by Carousel Film and Video as *48 Hours: Lights, Camera, War* (1989). The best thing about that film is its showcasing of

black stuntmen. Tri-Star Pictures, Inc. issued a *Glory* Collector's Edition in 1991: *Glory* plus *The True Story of Glory Continues*, "A Documentary of the 54th Regiment That Inspired the Oscar-Winning film *Glory*," narrated, like Shearer's film, by Morgan Freeman. The 54th turned out to be a real commodity.

7. Nothing in that staged battle is quite as horrific as Eli Biddle's description of his experience on the parapets. Pieces of burning flesh from the dying soldiers in front would fly onto the men behind them. When the men tried to pull it off, their flesh would come with it. Their sergeant instructed them: "Don't touch it—let it dry."

8. The film's major virtue is its cadre of fine African American actors: Morgan Freeman as the natural leader of men, John "Pops" Rawlins; Denzel Washington in his Oscar-winning performance as "Trip," the one radical in the regiment; Andre Braugher as the only intellectual, Thomas Searles, who believed his status in Shaw's family (he and Robert were boyhood friends) would transcend the rigidity of Army and racial hierarchy.

9. The men in *Glory* appear to be much like those Colonel Thomas Higginson commanded and wrote about in his diary on December 11, 1862—the First South Carolina volunteers, the first slave regiment in the U.S. Army. Instead of a single educated soldier reading to the men, Higginson describes a camp laundress from a nearby plantation sitting in the firelight, in the center of a circle of men: "Sometimes the woman is reading slow monosyllables out of a primer, a feat which always commands all ears. Learning, to these men, is magic of the first magnitude, and the impressive syllables . . . command a respectful audience." *Army Life in a Black Regiment*, edited and abridged by Genevieve S. Gray (New York: Grosset and Dunlap, 1970), 19.

10. William Carney, a dockworker, was the first African American to win the Congressional Medal of Honor: "When Sgt. William Carney grabbed the regimental flags from the hands of the dying standard-bearer . . . he ran through a hail of fire." Wounded three times, Carney finally staggered into the field hospital, proud that the "dear old flag" had never touched the ground. Keith White, "*Glory* Short on Truth," Gannett News Service, January 19, 1990, Lexis-Nexis Universe.

11. In answer to a question about her film "signature," Shearer said: "I think music is my signature. I've . . . gotten a lot of favorable comments on the soundtrack in *The Massachusetts 54th* for the *American Experience* series. The *American Experience* people were a little worried that I wasn't going to do a score, that I wanted to do the same thing I did with *Eyes* instead of doing wall-to-wall stuff. But I did do wall-to-wall stuff and the music was actually good. I mean, we liked it in the editing room; it wasn't just historically accurate, it was fun to play around with" (Shearer interview).

12. I am indebted to Professor Norris for furnishing me a copy of his arrangement of "The Enlisted Soldiers."

13. Eric Mink, "Public TV: Quality Now, Problems Later," September 22, 1991, p. 9G; Zan Stewart, "'Colored Infantry' Views Race in 1860s," October 14, 1991, Calendar; Part F; 11.

14. Shearer interview.

15. Interview with Phyllis Klotman and Janet Cutler, 1992.

16. Coincidentally, Caesar would, in 1984, win an Oscar nomination for the best actor in a supporting role as Army non-commissioned officer Sgt. Waters in *A Soldier's Story*.

17. Miles confided that every time he would find one of the 369th veterans who served in World War I, he (Miles) "became a jinx," because by the time he got the money together to shoot the film, he would call up to confirm and be

told, "he just passed." Interview with William Miles, conducted by Janet Cutler and Phyllis Klotman, New York City, June 30, 1992.

18. Ibid.

19. The *Film News* article appeared in the Spring 1980 issue, 36; Howard's article is in the "Film Reviews" section of *Film Library Quarterly* 12, no. 4 (1979): 44–46; the *Variety* review by Land appeared in the September 28, 1977, issue, 22.

20. Miles interview.

21. Benjamin Bender's letter was published in the Late City Final Edition, Section A; Page 18, Column 4 of the *New York Times*, April 22, 1985.

22. Charles Baillou reported this comment in his article "PBS' documentary, 'Liberators,' portrays history of Blacks in WWII," *New York Amsterdam News*, November 14, 1992, 1.

23. "Review/Television: America's Black Army and a Dual War Front," *New York Times*, November 11, 1992, C 24; *Variety* 349, no. 3 (November 9, 1992): 66 (1).

24. Although New York had its own media feeding frenzy (Jesse Jackson's earlier remark characterizing the city as "Hymietown," for which he later apologized; Professor Jeffries's charges about Jews in the slave trade and the "Jewish Mafia" in Hollywood; and Jeffries's colleague Michael Levin at City College espousing his theory of black intellectual inferiority), the Crown Heights incident in Brooklyn was certainly in the national news. The violence in Crown Heights which exacerbated the tensions between blacks and Jews occurred on August 19, 1991, a few months before the airing of *Liberators:* It was "triggered . . . when one of the cars in a three-car procession carrying the Lubavitcher Hasidic rebbe, the spiritual leader of the sect, ran a red light and swerved onto the sidewalk, striking and killing Gavin Cato, a 7-year old black boy from Guyana and injuring his sister" (*Plain Dealer*, October 26, 1995, 5E). Rumors that a Hasidic ambulance crew failed to help the children set off hours of rioting, and Yankel Rosenbaum, an Australian Hasidic scholar, was stabbed to death. The uncontrolled violence lasted for three days. The driver of the car was not indicted; Lemrick Nelson, Jr., the young man who was arrested for the murder of Rosenbaum, was acquitted, but both Mayor Dinkins and Police Commissioner Lee P. Brown were strongly criticized by the Jewish community for their alleged mishandling of the crisis. They were also charged in a lawsuit by Orthodox Jewish groups with neglecting to protect them against attacks by black demonstrators, but in 1997 a federal judge ruled that they could not be "personally liable for actions taken by the city during the 1991 racial unrest in the Crown Heights Section of Brooklyn" (*Houston Chronicle*, August 23, 1997, Section E, 25), much too late to help Dinkins's political career, but not too late for Lee Brown who was later successful in his bid for mayor of Houston.

25. Lou Potter interview conducted by Phyllis Klotman, July 18, 1997.

26. Col. James B. Moncrief, Jr., USA-Retired, "PBS–Buchenwald Caper," *Super Sixer,* the Sixth Armored Division newsletter, undated (Moncrief also used the occasion to suggest that members advise their congressmen to reduce by 50 percent the funding for the Corporation for Public Broadcasting); Milton Harrison letter, August 21, 1997; Melvin Rappaport letter, July 12, 1997; the list, updated in January 1997, was sent to me on November 24, 1997, by Steven Luckert, Curator of the Permanent Exhibition of the United States Holocaust Memorial Museum. Perhaps these veterans are unaware that the process of certification is, according to Luckert, an ongoing one. Edward J. Drea, chief of the Research and Analysis Division, U.S. Army Center of Military History, published an article explaining the rationale for recognition of divisions that liberated concentration camps: "to honor the officers and men of the liberating

divisions and . . . to remember the victims of Nazi tyranny." Since the U.S. Holocaust Memorial Museum would open in 1993, that was considered the appropriate time. Drea explained the process: petitioning by division associations or division veterans; verification of the data submitted by researching the division records held at the National Archives' Washington National Records Center (Suitland, Maryland); and reliance on *primary* sources. Neither oral history nor testimony would be sufficient, nor would secondary accounts or unit histories unless they could be verified by official records. And yet, for the sake of expediency—flags for the first ten divisions had to be ready in time for the April ceremony—"Center historians *had to rely* [my emphasis] on secondary sources to verify the unit list." The Center and the Council agreed at that time not to limit recognition to the first divisions to reach a camp, but to also include "follow-on" divisions that entered the same camp, or camp complex, within 48 hours of the initial division. "Recognizing the Liberators: U.S. Army Divisions Enter the Concentration Camps," *Army History: The Professional Bulletin of Army History*, PB–20–93–1, no. 24 (Fall/Winter 1992/1993): 1, 4–5.

27. According to Sgt. Edward Donald of "B" Company, the 761st had after three days of steady fighting "punched a hole through the Siegfried Line" so that the 4th Armored Division could push through to Germany. Patton then diverted the 761st north to stop the Germans in the Ardennes Forest. Cpl. Horace Evans, also of "B" Company, pointed out that "the 4th Armored received all the credit for the breakthrough on the Siegfried Line, and we did the work. The 761st did not even receive an honorable mention." Mary Penick Motley, ed., *The Invisible Soldier: The Experience of the Black Soldier, World War II* (Detroit: Wayne State University Press, 1975), 155–56.

28. According to Anthony Lewis in the *New York Times*, Ruddy is "one of the leading promoters of the notion that Mr. [Vincent] Foster was murdered" (December 29, 1997, A17).

29. "*Liberators* under Fire (A documentary wounded by friendly fire)," a 10-page paper, is available at http://members.aol.com/dignews/underfire.htm.

30. I am indebted to Colby Kelly of Thirteen/WNET for the final report prepared for Thirteen/WNET by Morton Silverstein. In her letter to me of September 8, 1997, Kelly referred to the "internal review of the *Liberators*"; the press release calls it an "internal review by an independent team." When I asked Silverstein to clarify that point, he referred me to the legal counsel at WNET (telephone conversation, December 30, 1997).

31. Historian Clement Alexander Price has written a critique of both *Liberators* and *Men of Bronze*, faulting them for "factual errors," and, while acknowledging that "the world of traditional historiography has never been immune to using memory as the basis for fact," contends that the "world of historical movie documentation . . . is far more susceptible to error because it seeks not so much to render an accurate account of the past as to reintroduce us to feelings about the past"; ergo, "films like *Men of Bronze* and *Liberators* should especially serve a larger public need for scholarly objectivity to compete with historical passion." "Black Soldiers in Two World Wars: 'Men of Bronze' (1980) and 'Liberators' (1992)" was first published in *Historical Journal of Film, Radio and Television* 14, no. 4 (1994): 467–74. It was followed by "Clement Price, 'Liberators' and Truth in History: A Comment," by historian Daniel J. Leab, which compliments Price's "reasoned and unemotional" argument and explores some of the same terrain as the Stern and Silverstein reports, although he was not given access to the latter. These two articles were published in essentially the same form, but with slightly changed titles, in *World War II: Film and*

History, ed. John Whiteclay Chambers II and David Culbert (New York: Oxford University Press, 1996), although unless the reader checks the notes to the second article, it's not clear that they were published elsewhere. In both versions of Price's article *Men of Bronze* is incorrectly dated: 1980, instead of 1977. Leab's article refers to producer Nina "Rosenbaum" several times, but the producer's name is corrected in the version published by Oxford.

32. Benjamin Bender, Sara Bender, and Leonard "Smitty" Smith, interview conducted by Phyllis Klotman, June 1, 1997. I am indebted to the Benders and Leonard Smith for their willingness to share their personal collections and correspondence with me.

33. A copy of Scott's pamphlet, describing and picturing what he saw at Buchenwald, is in the Black Film Center / Archive and is available to researchers. Scott's first cousin, Asa Gordon, an aerospace engineer at the Godard Space Flight Center, who founded the Douglass Institute of Government, an educational "think tank" in Washington, D.C., has set up an institute web site, URL: http://members.aol.com/digasa/dig.htm. Articles on the *Liberators* controversy are available through a link to *"Liberators* under Fire—the Web Site/ Research and Analysis" or directly at http://members.aol.com/dignews/ liberate.htm, including speeches Gordon has given on the subject. He has also put the entire Scott pamphlet ("World War II Veteran Remembers the Holocaust"), including pictures, on the Web. Gordon called my attention to an article in *USA Today* in which documentary filmmaker Ken Burns defended the accuracy of his *Baseball* series against charges by ESPN's Keith Olbermann that there were 89 errors in the first five episodes. Burns said the same thing had been said about the *Civil War* series, comments he called "nitpicks" (September 26, 1994, 3D). However, as Gordon pointed out, those films were not taken off the air. He has continuously campaigned to have *Liberators* aired again nationally (telephone interview conducted by Phyllis Klotman, August 20, 1997).

34. Rosenblum continues to feel strongly that the attacks were racist and politically motivated—"New York politics really added fuel to it. . . . The controversy was different outside of New York"—and extended beyond *Liberators* to nationally supported funding agencies like the National Endowment for the Humanities and the Corporation for Public Broadcasting. She also pointed out that *Liberators* is still in distribution (see Filmography) and still being shown; and that veterans and survivors, Smith and Bender, Bass and Robert Waisman (who identified Bass through the B'nai B'rith newsletter) continue to speak together about their experiences at various community functions. Nina Rosenblum Interview conducted by Phyllis Klotman, March 27, 1997.

35. Allentuck and Potter, "To the Editor," *Newsday,* January 7, 1993; Allentuck, "Official WWII History Doesn't Tell All," February 9, 1993; Rosenblum and Miles, "The Filmmakers' Response to Kenneth Stern's report to the American Jewish Committee, March 5, 1993; Rosenblum and Miles, "To ID readers," *International Documentary,* March 1993, 11.

36. Trezzvant W. Anderson was with the 761st three times while they were in Europe: "being the last to visit them in November 1944, and the first to see them again in 1945, after six months of darkness had covered their whereabouts." Perhaps the fact that he didn't get back to the battalion until May explains why he didn't include in his book any of the concentration camp experiences that Captain Long later reported to Mary Penick Motley. In the conclusion he writes about the neglect of black units: "Covered by a fog of obscurity, there were 32 different Negro COMBAT UNITS in service on the Western Front and in Italy. VERY FEW, VERY, VERY FEW of these were visited

by Correspondents. One came for two days, the other for a day and a half. . . .
No glamorous accounts of their stirring deeds emblazoned the front pages of
the newspapers" even though the 761st was on the front lines for 183 days.
Come Out Fighting: The Epic Tale of the 761st Tank Battalion, 1942–1945 (Tiesendorf,
Germany: Salzburger Druckerei und Verlag, 1945), 125.

37. Anderson, 21.

38. George S. Patton, Jr., *War As I Knew It* (Boston: Houghton Mifflin, 1947),
159–60.

39. Patton was even more negative in his assessment of Jews. In his
biography of the general, *Patton: A Study in Command* (New York: Charles
Scribner, 1974), 237, H. Essame quotes this section from Patton's diary: "Everyone believes that the displaced person is a human being, which he is not, and
this applies particularly to the Jews who are lower than animals. Either the
displaced persons never had a sense of decency or else they lost it during their
period of internment by the Germans. My personal opinion is that no people
could have sunk to the level of degradation these have reached in the short
space of four years." Lou Potter also quotes Patton's words in the book,
Liberators: Fighting on Two Fronts in World War II (New York: Harcourt Brace
Jovanovich, 1992), 221.

40. John Long and Ivan Harrison were the first two black lieutenants in the
United States Tank Corps. A soldier who rose from the ranks, Long was a cook
at Fort Knox, Kentucky, when he was accepted for Officer Candidate School
(OCS). Motley, 151.

41. Ibid., 152.

42. Lee, *United States Army in World War II, Special Studies: The Employment
of Negro Troops* (Washington, D.C.: Office of the Chief of Military History,
United States Army, 1966), 662–66. Lee does however confirm that Lt. Colonel
Bates was wounded and evacuated from the field the first day of the attack,
November 7, 1944; he was hospitalized until mid-February 1945. Lee, 663.

43. This section is a random sampling of witnesses, both veterans and
survivors; not all of whom appeared in *Liberators*. Some responded to the
reunion invitation extended by the filmmakers and Thirteen/WNET where
most of the interviews were shot.

44. Barnouw, "In Defense of *Liberators*," Letter to *International Documentary*,
April 1993, 5.

45. Motley, 155.

46. "Nazi Survivors Reunite with Black Liberators," October 7, 1991, B1;
News 12, Long Island, New York. (Videotapes of live interviews with veterans
and survivors; reunions, celebrations, presentations, meetings connected with
the development of *Liberators* and the subsequent controversy; as well as
outtakes, were made available by Rosenblum and Miles through Miles Educational Film Productions, Inc. They are accessible for research and study at the
Black Film Center/Archive, Afro-American Studies Department, Indiana University.) In answer to my question: Did you say you had gone to some of the
camps?" E. G. McConnell responded, "I didn't say Dachau or Buchenwald.
Only once, I did mistakenly, I stated that, before I found out positively"
(telephone interview, August 14, 1997).

47. In March 1993, McConnell told Stephen J. Dubner that he had phoned
the mayor's office before the Apollo event, because he thought as a "Black man
[it was his] duty to warn Mayor Dinkins and Jesse Jackson about this thing," but
they "treated him like [he] was some kind of a kook" (*New York*, March 8, 1993,
51). Several officers of the 761st, Lt. Colonel Bates and Captains Charles Gates

and David Williams (author of a novel about the 761st, *Eleanor Roosevelt's Niggers*) have also denied that any of the men of the 761st were involved in the liberation of Buchenwald or Dachau. They did not mention Gunskirchen Lager.

48. Smith interview; Motley, 160; Studs Terkel, *The Good War: An Oral History of World War Two* (New York: Pantheon Books, 1984), 268.

49. Anderson, 127. He also lists, the number of awards the men received (eleven Silver Star medals, sixty-nine Bronze Star medals with four clusters; three Certificates of Merit; 296 Purple Hearts, with eight Clusters—a total of 391 battle awards), but he couldn't have known that it would take thirty-three years for the 761st to receive the Presidential Unit Citation (January 24, 1978, signed by President Jimmy Carter). Gates told Terkel: "We had discovered that at least twelve other units to which we had been attached had received Presidential Unit Citations. About eighteen had received the French Croix de Guerre. How easy it has been all through the years to conceal the history of the Negro Soldier." Terkel, 268. Borden questions why the 761st didn't include anything about liberating camps in their record when they petitioned for the Presidential Unit Citation (Borden letter). More appropriate questions would be: Were unit citations given for anything other than battle records? How many other units had to wait thirty-three years to be recognized?

50. Gross gave one of the eulogies at Scott's funeral, and Scott's widow told me that he often called her husband "his angel" (telephone interview, December 30, 1997). In "The Filmmakers' Response to Kenneth Stern's report to the American Jewish Committee" March 5, 1993, Miles and Rosenblum included a reference to Gross: "To this day, Alex Gross adheres to his recollection that he saw a black soldier emerge from 'the first American tank that approached my part of the camp'. (See the attached letter of Alex Gross to THE NEW REPUBLIC, to date unpublished)." Sylvia Wygoda of the Georgia Holocaust Commission has prepared a traveling exhibit entitled: "William A. Scott III: Witness to the Holocaust—World War II" as a part of the commission's ongoing education program. They continue to show *Liberators* on their programs (telephone interview, January 9, 1997).

51. Kamm, "No Mention of Jews at Buchenwald," *New York Times*, March 25, 1989, Section 1, 8:1.

52. Bradley, "Black Troops First to Reach Death Camp," *Denver Post*, March 7, 1993.

53. Samuel Pisar, *Of Blood and Hope* (Boston: Little, Brown and Company, 1979), 27, 91.

54. Drea, 2–3.

55. Motley, 163.

56. Annette Insdorf, "Truths Lost in the Night and Fog," *Washington Post*, September 26, 1993, G4.

57. Patricia J. Williams's *The Alchemy of Race and Rights* (Cambridge: Harvard University Press, 1991) is especially useful to an understanding of critical race theory.

58. Richard Delgado and Jean Stefancic, "#461 Critical Race Theory: An Annotated Bibliography," *Virginia Law Review*, March 1995, 1. The bibliography is an impressive list of work on critical race theory by legal scholars Derrick Bell, Kevin Brown, Kimberle Crenshaw, Lani Guinier, and others.

59. Aired once on WNDY-TV, Indianapolis, *The Men of Montford Point* (in its 90-minute format) was favorably reviewed by Steve Hall in the *Indianapolis Star*, February 18, 1997. Harkness considers it a work in progress and would like to cut the film to one hour (Jerald Harkness telephone interviews, conducted by

Phyllis Klotman, November 20 and 27, 1997). Steve Crump of Charlotte, North Carolina, has also taken up the cause of African Americans in the military. *Airmen and Adversity* (1998), a documentary which he produced, directed and narrated for WTVI, Charlotte public television, is the story of the "Tuskegee Airmen," African Americans who enlisted in the Air Force during World War II. Veterans on camera relate their struggle to become an integral part of the Air Force. A segregated unit, they were assigned to escort bombers piloted by whites; in 200 missions they never lost a bomber. Like the men of the 761st, they had to endure discrimination—the daily insults of segregation, not the least of which was seeing Nazi POWs being allowed access to all of the camp facilities which they were denied.

60. Black troops during World War II were especially offended by the differential treatment they and prisoners of war were given: German and Italian prisoners were allowed to use facilities, like the PX, to "fraternize" with white women (in North Carolina and in England). African Americans, whether Marines, tankers, or infantrymen, were not. They were especially outraged when a German officer was given a full military funeral.

61. Williams, 113.

3

Documenting Social Issues
Black Journal, *1968–1970*

TOMMY LEE LOTT

Few would disagree with the claim that, until recently, the history of the representation of African Americans by the mass media has been a one of distorted images. Commentators have noted the effects of the systematic omission of a black presence in both print and electronic media. In the case of television the result has been a vacuum filled with over-determined negative and counter-negative portrayals.[1] Some of the best accounts of the social and political function of mass media are framed by this truism, although it mostly conceals, rather than explains, an historically significant moment when a less mediated black voice briefly gained a foothold in network television.[2] Many younger generation television viewers watch weekly programs such as those hosted by Tony Brown on PBS, Jesse Jackson on CNN, and Julian Bond on syndicated stations, often with very little awareness that a voice for the black community was absent from network television until as recently as 1968. I want to halt the growth of this social amnesia by considering the extent to which the changing complexion of television since the late 1960s is a reflection within the industry of changes wrought by the civil rights movement.[3]

In its report on the 1967 urban riots the Kerner Commission cited the coverage of black community issues by a white-oriented mass media as a factor that influenced the rebellions. The commission's recommendations regarding media practices were shaped largely by the belief that, through the presentation of a more wholesome image of African Americans, mass media could be used as a means of preventing future uprisings. One important response to the Kerner Commission's mandate to change the white orientation of the mass media's coverage of the black community was the corporate-backed initiative by network television producers to present the views of the black community to white America. This initiative aimed to include more black people in a wide variety of television programs—advertisements as well as entertainment and news broadcasts.[4] Although a representation of black people *by black people* that placed the struggle for social justice in the forefront was never presented on commercial television, there was a brief interlude in the late 1960s when the figure of the black militant was evident in prime time programs.[5] The caricature of black power advocates on television news, however, served to delegitimate the goals of the more radical components of the civil rights movement.

Black Journal was a monthly news magazine program produced by a group of black filmmakers who, in the program's initial two years, endeavored to carry out the Kerner Commission's mandate by self-consciously constructing an alternative black cinema within a format provided by non-commercial television. Discussions of black cinema rarely include reference to any of the short documentary films that were produced for *Black Journal*.[6] It is of no small significance, however, that, by direct contrast with the feature films produced by black filmmakers working outside of Hollywood in the early 1970s—films that were viewed largely by participants in museum events, film festivals, or college courses, the short documentary films that had been produced a few years earlier for *Black Journal* were shown monthly for several years to a mass television audience. This market-distribution aspect of black film practice has important implications for black film theory. In particular it requires a re-examination of the question, "What form must a viable alternative black cinema take?" I explore some of the implications of this question with regard to the use of television by black filmmakers. I focus on the manner in which the ambivalent concerns expressed in the Kerner Commission report were aesthetically negotiated by the producers of *Black Journal*.

THE KERNER COMMISSION MANDATE

When President Johnson asked the Kerner Commission to investigate the effect of mass media on the 1967 riots he had an obvious concern with the performance of the press and broadcasters specifically with regard to their potentially inflammatory coverage of looting and violence.[7] The commission's response, however, was to give the President's question a much broader policy orientation. In its report the commission expressed a more general concern with the overall treatment in the mass media of race relations and issues concerning the black community. Indeed, the argument was advanced that the widespread distrust of news by black people was well justified given their exclusion from the industry. The report cited the fact that, in the white-oriented mass media, there was no voice for the concerns of the black urban masses, many of whom had engaged in the 1967 riots. It was further pointed out that, by failing to present an image of black people in all walks of life in America, the mass media had reinforced the African American's sense of exclusion from the mainstream. The commission concluded that this image of African Americans in the mass media added to the social alienation and political frustration that had led to rioting.

The Kerner Commission's recommendation recognized two objectives for the mass media. On the one hand there was the need of the white audience to know about black urban life and the concerns of the black community, while on the other hand there was the need of the black audience to see black people validated as a viable part of mainstream America. President Johnson's concern with news media coverage of the 1967 riots as perhaps an inflammatory cause was transformed by the commission into a much broader concern with the long-term effects of institutionalized racism in the mass media on the perpetuation of mainstream America's denial of the needs and aspirations of black people. Rather than focus entirely on President Johnson's worry about the impact of inflammatory television images and news reports of violence and looting on further rioting, the commission instead emphasized the systematic exclusion of black people from the mass media's image of America as a more important influence on the social disorder of 1967. News media had failed "to communicate to both their black and white audiences a sense of the problems America faces and the sources of potential solutions . . . the Negro's burning sense of grievance."[8] The Kerner Commission's mandate was twofold: to communicate to the majority white audience "a sense of the degradation, misery, and hopelessness of living in the ghetto" and to show "understanding or appreciation of . . . a sense of Negro culture, thought, or history."[9]

One of the underlying assumptions of this mandate was that a voice for the black urban communities that rioted must be represented in the mass media if the barriers to desegregation are to be removed. This mission of providing a voice for the black community was taken on by the producers of Black Journal. The program began as a one-time PBS special on the black community, with the aim of examining the social conditions that had produced the riots. In the brief eighteen-month period following the assassination of Martin Luther King, Jr., television executives were under pressure from regulatory agencies to include views that represented black America. It is useful to situate *Black Journal* in the general context of related television programs on commercial television to fully appreciate the producers' endeavor to provide a voice for the black struggle.

Between 1960 and 1968 there were over two dozen television series with black stars, co-stars, or continuing supporting black characters.[10] From 1963 through the summer of 1968 there were over three dozen documentaries on topics related to African Americans.[11] These programs, of course, were spawned by the image of black activists in earlier television news reports of the civil rights movement. Clearly it would be a mistake to claim that there was an absence of black people on television prior to the 1967 urban uprisings. The position taken by the Kerner Commission, however, was consistent with the fact that black people *appeared* on television. The Commission's claim was that, despite this rapid increase in the amount of television programming devoted to African Americans, the white-oriented bias of mainstream media had remained relatively unchanged. What was in question was the quality of the news media's coverage of the black community in particular, as well as their general representation of race relations. According to the report, in some cases issues of relevance to the black community were not covered at all, while in most cases they were presented only from a white viewpoint. It was exactly this bias, or at least the black community's perception of such a bias, that the Kerner Commission's mandate aimed to rectify.

Given their overriding concern with the prevention of future riots, the Commission's move to de-center the President's initial question regarding the role of television in promoting further rioting was quite significant, especially since this shift of focus occurred in the changing socio-political context of the late 1960s. Earlier civil rights leaders, who had appealed to the conscience of the white mainstream through the practice of non-violent demonstrations, had been quite effective in using the news media to gain publicity, albeit distorted, for their cause.[12] The Kerner Commission could not ignore the potential for advocates of black power in an era of urban rebellion to do likewise. The report carefully pointed out that the inflammatory live television coverage of the 1965 Watts riots by helicopter had already led network executives to agree that television would never again present a live telecast of civil disorder. Noting that news broadcasters for the most part had adopted what was known as the Chicago code, that is, a self-imposed moratorium on news reporting of a riot until "the situation is under control," the report also pointed out that the effectiveness of this code had been questioned in the case of the Detroit riot. Industry dissatisfaction with the Chicago code stemmed from the somewhat paradoxical demand on news broadcasters to provide television coverage of a riot without promoting it.

This dilemma also accompanies the endeavor by news media to satisfy the need of white America to know what so-called black militants have to say. The exploitation of negative images of black power advocates on commercial television contrasted sharply with the representation of the black power movement on *Black Journal*. My discussion will focus on the program's coverage of international affairs, the Black Panther Party, black student activism, unions and labor strikes, community empowerment and its treatment of a selection of various subjects pertaining to black culture and history. The question of how well *Black Journal* represented the black struggle will be shown to demand at once an account of the program's sense of both politics and aesthetics.

INVENTING THE CONTEMPORARY
AFRICAN AMERICAN DOCUMENTARY FILM

When the program first aired in June, 1968 the executive producer was listed as Alvin Perlmutter, but by September of that year the black staff had rebelled over the issue of control and Perlmutter was replaced by William Greaves. There was little noticeable difference in the program's news magazine format, but decisions regarding content were affected in several important ways. To insure the development of programs that would resonate with the black community, Greaves adopted an approach to decision-making using the black barbershop as the prime measure of social significance. A strong criterion for selecting a topic to be covered on the program was whether it was an issue that would be routinely discussed in a barbershop.[13] In addition to acquiring greater liberty to select topics that would be of interest to a black audience, the black takeover also created a situation in which the filmmakers were at liberty to express themselves artistically. Greaves encouraged his group of young black filmmakers to take full advantage of this artistic freedom. Undoubtedly, the program's visual energy was stimulated by an awareness in the group that this was a once in a lifetime opportunity.

The technical accomplishment of the program is a matter of record. After receiving a nomination for an Emmy the first year, the program won this award the following year. Much of the technical training was provided by a special school set up to train minorities, many of whom went on to become apprentices on one of the four or five crews that were constantly shooting in the New York area. The establishment of a privately funded training and apprenticeship program to facilitate the entry of minorities into the television industry was an important feature of the Kerner Commission's recommendation.[14] With *Black Journal* as a flagship for various local television shows, such as *Say Brother* in Boston and *Like It Is* in New York, the hope was that its impact on the industry would be a geometric increase in programming at the local level.[15]

When asked in a recent interview whether there was an African American tradition in documentary filmmaking, Greaves expressed the belief that this tradition began with *Black Journal*. While this may not be accurate film history, Greaves's claim is warranted by the fact that, upon his return to New York in the early 1960s, he was unable to find any other black documentary filmmakers with whom he could build a network.[16] At that time there were no film schools admitting black students. The earlier black independents had all but disappeared in the wake of desegregation, which had a negative impact on many black theaters. Just as Melvin Van Peebles later would have to go to France to acquire his filmmaking skill, Greaves relinquished his earlier career as an actor to venture to Canada to learn to make films. He quickly became an apprentice working on films produced under the auspice of Canada's National Film Board. The National Film Board had been set up by John Grierson on the principle that documentary filmmaking has a social function. In addition to filmmaking technique, Greaves was trained to view filmmaking as an educational tool that could be a force for social change. Before leaving the Film Board Greaves had worked on eighty or more films. He returned to America with a well-developed *cinéma vérité* style that has had a lasting influence on the post-1960s generation of black documentary filmmakers.[17]

The program's genesis in the riots following King's assassination accounts for the producer's strong identification with the black power movement. Many of the black nationalist codes of the late 1960s were employed to frame the content of each program. For example, the theme music used African conga drums, the two co-hosts often wore dashikis and one co-host, Lou Potter, opened and closed each program with salutations in Swahili. More importantly, however, white authority figures were represented from a black perspective. The novelty of this repositioning of the spectator challenged the traditional representation of blacks and whites on television. As noted by commentators, the inversion of the image of white over black functioned largely to re-code a television convention, a move designed to expose the nature of mainstream television.[18]

The influence of black nationalism also was evident in the frequent appearances by Charles Hamilton (Columbia University political scientist and co-author, with Stokely Carmichael, of the 1960s classic, *Black Power*). Instead of the militant activism of Stokely Carmichael, the black power ideology was presented in the person of a more genteel intellectual. In one clip Hamilton was shown lecturing in the classroom, in other segments he was employed as a panelist and a commentator on electoral politics. With the air of an Ivy League college professor, he offered sharp criticism of the policies advocated by both northern liberals and southern conservatives. Given the well-known tensions in the civil rights movement, as well as in the black community, between black nationalists and Marxist organizations, it is somewhat odd that Hamilton never mentioned the Panthers' Marxist ideology in his analysis of their plight.[19] While in this case such a lapse is negligible, it is worth noting that the glaring absence of a Marxist perspective in the framing of certain labor issues threatened to subvert the program's overall commitment to a black nationalist perspective. Despite this shortcoming, the hundred or so film sequences produced during the first two years of *Black Journal* were significantly different from other 1960s television documentaries on black life in America.

Television journalism rarely attempted to provide much more than an exposé for the white audience, whereas Greaves, as executive producer, was conscious of the educational function of documentary filmmaking for a black television audience and instead aimed to show black audiences possible solutions to their problems.[20] Shortly after leaving *Black Journal*, Greaves expressed this philosophy in an article he wrote for the *New York Times*: "In short, the search for candor, for honesty, and truth-rather than hypocrisy and self-delusion-must become a basic component of television programing.... On such a foundation the Black producer of today and tomorrow will most likely build his programming. For him, the mass media will be an agency for improving mass mental health and social reform, will be a catharsis, a means of purifying the emotional and spiritual life of this country.[21]" Greaves likened the black television producer to the jazz musician. The programs he produced for *Black Journal* were meant to be liberating in the sense that "jazz for the Afro-American has been a means of liberating the human spirit."[22] He saw himself as a change agent, but only in the sense that television can be used to educate and to foster mental health.[23]

The artistic freedom that stemmed from black control, along with an aesthetic of liberation that was modeled after jazz, were strong influences on Greaves's cadre of young filmmakers. He trained and sent film crews to countries as far away as Vietnam and Ethiopia. In contrast to the rugged individualism of his own background making race-neutral films for the National Film Board in Canada, the group of black film-makers working on *Black Journal* gained their experience by working *collectively* on films about black people for a black television audience. Under Greaves's leadership *Black Journal* gave birth to a new generation of black documentary filmmakers.[24]

Black Journal production crew at work on Harlem street.
From left: Shawn Walker, Leroy McLucas, Tony Batten,
William Greaves, Kent Garrett, St. Clair Bourne.
Photo courtesy of William Greaves Productions.

SAFETY VALVE OR ELECTRONIC STIMULUS FOR THE BLACK REVOLUTION

Nineteen sixty-eight, the year *Black Journal* first aired, continued to be extremely turbulent. In its first six months the program covered a wide variety of political issues including Huey Newton's imprisonment; school decentralization; the assassination of Martin Luther King Jr.; the Poor Peoples' Campaign; the CORE convention held that summer in Columbus, Ohio; the civil war in Biafra; the liberation struggle in Mozambique; the role of universities in the slums of cities such as New York, Chicago, and Philadelphia; the growth of a Louisiana cooperative; and police–community relations. The programs aired in the following year continued along the same lines with coverage of international af-

fairs, student activism, black police, labor and union issues, school decentralization, and community control. Although the black nationalist
frame of the program exerted a strong influence on the representation
of these issues, there were several noteworthy episodes in which issues
regarding labor, class, and gender were raised that were difficult to view
strictly along nationalist lines.

The Kerner commission's desire to give voice to the black community, along with the accompanying worry about the promotion of violence, were both manifested in *Black Journal*'s use of the panel format. In
some cases the panels seem to have served as a safety valve—in others,
as a potential catalyst for violence. The December 1968 broadcast featured two panel discussions focusing on some of the major events of the
year. Organized around roughly similar topics, with each co-host as
moderator, the entire program was composed of a series of jump cuts
between the panels, interspersed with documentary film clips devoted
to issues raised by the panelists.[25]

On one of the panels Kathleen Cleaver (at that time Communications Secretary for the Black Panther Party) dominated with a forcefully
stated justification of the role of violence in the struggle for black social
justice. She was placed in a face-off situation with civil rights leader
Andrew Young, a staunch defender of non-violence and electoral politics. After Cleaver's initial statement that black political power must
come from the barrel of a gun, film clips of a wide range of black people giving their opinion regarding the political function of violence
were shown to both panels. In one clip Cleaver's statement that young
black people were responding to the Black Panther Party's revolutionary stance was illustrated by a cut to a young black man in a small town
in Alabama who explained how the black community there had brought
an end to Klan activity and gained the respect of local whites by shooting back in self-defense at night riders. In another clip, Professor Charles Hamilton was shown giving a lecture in which he proclaimed that
violence is very healthy for society. A visually stunning moment was
captured when a middle-aged black man calmly pointed out, "We are in
a position where we can hurt the white man, and we are going to hurt
him. He knows we are going to hurt him and he is scared to death. And
that's good too. It is time to fight." The ensuing discussion by both
panels aimed to reflect a diversity of views by the panelists (as well as
the black leaders and "people on the street" in the film clips) regarding
the relative merits of seeking social change from within the system, in
contrast with seeking to overthrow the system altogether.

There was only one defender (historian Richard Moore) of the goals
of the civil rights movement on the other panel, which was dominated

by radical intellectuals.[26] The consensus of this second panel was that the Poor Peoples' Campaign was a clear indication that the electoral process had failed. Their call to move outside the system to overthrow it, an implicit endorsement of Cleaver's call to armed struggle, led the moderator, Bill Greaves (in an effort to restore balance) to ask the group whatever happened to the conservative voice. In the light of the group's rather lame response he surmised out loud that there had been a "death of the public Uncle Tom." Somewhat ironically, it was not this group of radicals, but the other more diverse panel (which, in fact, had a more conservative balance) that displayed a greater potential to provide what Cleaver referred to as "the electronic stimulus for revolution." Cleaver clarified the implication of this slogan with a further claim that, "Today black people are in a position to have instantaneous information about what's going on and are in a position to react to that."[27] In response to Cleaver's advocacy of violence, Alexander Allen (Eastern Regional Director of the Urban League) attempted to argue for an alternative by suggesting a way to appeal to the self-interest of whites. When he admitted that the resort to armed confrontation by black people is "certainly a possibility, and that violence has even erupted in some places," Cleaver interrupted his commentary with the correction that black armed struggle was "in progress," a construction he reluctantly accepted for didactic purposes. Needless to say, Allen's subsequent appeal to coalition politics was overridden by Cleaver's more powerful oratory. From the standpoint of mainstream America, some of her remarks surely must have seemed tantamount to a declaration of guerrilla warfare by the Black Panther Party.

The safety valve function of the panel format dovetails with Greaves's educational orientation to the representation of social and political issues. He hosted a segment dealing with the armed clashes between police and the Panthers and the Panthers' allegation that the police were engaged in an effort to destroy them. Greaves explained the reaction of the black community in a voice-over of documentary footage showing a group of black people being led through the home of murdered Chicago Panther Party member Fred Hampton by a spokesperson for the Panthers. This short segment was followed immediately by an interview with Masai Hewitt (Minister of Education) regarding the police assault as a lead-in to the panel discussion.[28] It is regrettable that Hewitt was unable to live up to the high standard of oratory that television viewers had come to expect from Panther spokespersons. (Hewitt was not at liberty to share pertinent details of the police raid on Panther leaders, because of the legal charges against other party members connected with the murder.) But since the consensus of the panel was that there was indeed a national conspiracy by law enforcement to destroy the Panthers, his disjointed comments were needless.

The moral high ground held by Hewitt and the Panthers was completely undermined by a bright young representative from the Afro-American Patrolman's League, Renault Robinson, who stole the show by insisting that since the wanton killing of black men by white policemen occurs on a regular basis there is no reason to focus on the death of Fred Hampton, simply because he was well-known. Robinson caught the ear of the other panelists by proposing a solution to police brutality that involved developing stronger ties between community organizations and black police organizations such as the one he represented. Hamilton, who earlier had spoken against the call for an investigation into the Fred Hampton murder (which he deemed a sure cover-up by the FBI and the Justice Department), intervened to reiterate a virtue of Robinson's proposal regarding community control. Both Hamilton and Robinson pointed out how this idea was consistent with one of the demands of the Black Panther Party's ten-point program. With Hamilton's endorsement of Robinson's proposal having the effect of shifting the attention toward a possible solution of police brutality, the moderator's initial question regarding the role of black policemen in the murderous assault was completely evaded. Indeed, the moderator (Lou House) was totally unprepared for the take-over of this panel by Robinson, who, after criticizing the Panthers' lack of community support, offered a justification of the shooting of Fred Hampton that challenged the veracity of the documentary segment in which the narrator claimed there was broad-based outrage in the black community.

The befuddled reaction of the panelists to Robinson's attempt to champion the Panthers' demand for more black police strikingly parallels the black community's well-known ambivalence toward black policemen.[29] Ironically, it was not a desire to alleviate racist police brutality that created a need for an increase in black policemen (especially undercover agents), but rather it was the threat to law enforcement posed by so-called black militants such as the Panthers. In an earlier segment, dubbed by the narrator, *Men Caught in the Middle*, the questionable role of black policemen had already been explored.[30] The film's expository narration allowed black policemen to comment on the racial politics involved in carrying out their duties and the dilemma this sometimes created. For example, in response to an off-camera question, one policeman stated flatly that he would not shoot a looter. Through a series of quick cuts, many of dark urban street scenes, accented by the sharp dissonant sounds of the Eric Dolphy orchestration of John Coltrane's *Africa*, this smartly fashioned piece juxtaposed statements by various rank and file police officers with critical comments from black people on the street—a sort of staged dialogue in which black policemen were given the opportunity to respond to the concerns of the black community. By means of a masterful application of *vérité* technique (hand held camera, rapid and seemingly unpredictable editing, and cut-away shots to the environment—decaying buildings, garbage cans, etc.) the narrator argues for a better understanding of the black policeman's split loyalties, sympathetically portraying him as a valuable (but often not valued) member of the community.

Although Garrett's *Men Caught in the Middle* was produced two years earlier and was much more polished for mass consumption, it nonetheless displayed an uncanny aesthetic resemblance to Michael Gray's popular underground documentary, *The Murder of Fred Hampton* (1971). I draw this comparison to suggest that the politics of representation cannot be resolved merely through the use of a *vérité* aesthetic.[31] These films show how, in one case, a *vérité* style served to exoticize the Panthers and, in the other, it was used to humanize black policemen— who, lest we forget, were hired largely to contain the growing militancy represented by the Panthers.[32] Nonetheless it was refreshing to see in Garrett's documentary a black police official part with his white counterpart and express support for a civilian review board to oversee police practices. The difficulty of bringing this about, even with the election of a black mayor, was highlighted in a later news report regarding a recall election initiated by a group of whites who opposed Cleveland Mayor Carl Stokes's reorganization of the police department. From the standpoint of innovative technique, Garrett's segment on the black policeman, along with some of the segments on the Panthers, were among *Black Journal*'s most engaging documentaries.

THE NATIONALIST–MARXIST DEBATE

In an era of political repression, the role of both black police and black elected officials in solving the problem of police brutality was complicated by class, as well as by race. It is somewhat unfortunate that issues related to class were not raised more explicitly in some of the episodes.[33] The appeal of the Panthers to legions of black male youth certainly crossed class lines on the issue of police brutality, but the fundamental concern of the Black Panther Party was always with (as Kathleen Cleaver maintained) America's systematic violence against the black *poor*. The Panthers' advocacy of violence as a legitimate mode of self-defense had become the dominant element of their image in mainstream media. Even after airing Kathleen Cleaver's invocation of

Huey Newton's definition of black power as "twenty million black people armed to the gills," in subsequent programs devoted to the Panthers, to their credit, the producers of *Black Journal* instead focused on the question of political repression.[34] The producers were well aware, however, that by the late 1960s the rejection of nonviolence as a strategy for social change had become an important aspect of the black power movement. They elected to present the Panthers, along with urban riots, as indicative of a higher level of militancy in black communities.

As evidenced by their elementary school in Oakland and their breakfast programs in several major cities, the Panthers advocated economic self-reliance along with armed resistance. Often panelists and other spokespersons appearing on *Black Journal* showed interest in the question of violence, but usually as a matter of strategy, and hardly ever without some attention to economic concerns. When historian Richard Moore explained, in the midst of a panel discussion, that the aim of King's Poor Peoples' Campaign was to begin a new phase of the struggle, one that focused on poverty, he was shouted down by several panelists. In response to Moore's suggestion one panelist argued that racism and not poverty is the problem, pointing out that King and many other blacks involved in the civil rights movement were not poor. Another panelist asked whether the notion of a mass movement to end poverty only existed in King's mind, or whether it was a genuine people's movement.[35] In their zest to denounce King's strategy of nonviolence these panelists were unable to acknowledge the change in objectives undergone by the movement since the passage of civil rights legislation.[36] They attributed little significance to King's involvement, at the time of his death, in a labor strike. Instead they preferred to interpret the violent eruptions that followed his assassination as a sign that the illusion of racial equality he had fostered had disappeared. But riots were not the only response to King's assassination. His assassination drew thousands of demonstrators to a march in Memphis, which resulted in a labor agreement with the city's black garbage workers' union. This important outcome was completely overlooked in the panel's debate over whether the march on Washington organized by King's followers was a failure. Other programs with segments dealing with labor issues were especially prone to display similar nationalist leanings.

In an episode that reported the success of a black cooperative in Louisiana, a black priest (Father Albert McKnight) explains how, through a *collective* endeavor, the black community had gone about setting up various business enterprises. Labeled a communist, he was also involved in a political battle with local white businessmen who were using the state's power structure to close down their operations.

Southern white racism provided the backdrop for one of television's most empowering images of the strength of the black community. In a humble (but articulate) voice Father McKnight outlined the various stages of development of the Southern Consumers' Cooperative, citing some of the obstacles they faced and indicating the steps they had taken to overcome them. The poor black people shown in the film were not striving to join the Fortune 500. They were presented as simply trying to earn a living. The principle of self-reliance embedded in this image had little to do with the notion of black capitalism espoused, for instance, by Lincoln Lynch (executive vice-president of the New York Urban Coalition) in a *Black Journal* editorial immediately following the election of Richard Nixon. In a subsequent report the ill fate of a similar endeavor by the East Georgia Farmer's Cooperative was cited. The cutoff of funds by the Office of Economic Opportunity for a manufacturing venture organized by the Southern Rural Action Project was offered as a reason to believe that, under Nixon, there were fewer opportunities in the deep south for blacks to enter the manufacturing industry.

Black Journal's coverage of unions and labor activities focused almost exclusively on the issue of racial discrimination. This positioning of race over economic issues was understandable in certain cases such as the voting down of unionization by black workers in the Avondale Shipyards in New Orleans, or the strike to gain unionization by black hospital workers in Charleston, North Carolina. *Black Journal*'s racialized treatment of the issues involved in these cases errs more on the side of excess, namely, by inadequate consideration of the broader context. Racial prejudice easily explains discrimination against black workers. Even so, the anti-unionization stance of the deep South was never limited to black workers. Moreover, racism within white-controlled unions was as much a problem for black workers in the North as was the racial barrier blacks faced in seeking to gain recognition of their all-black unions in the South.

The issue of white hegemony in union leadership was examined in an episode on the New York City Transit Union. Although 70 percent of the transit workers were black or Latino, 75 percent of those elected to the union's decision-making positions were whites. This systematic exclusion led black and Latino workers to seek to organize an independent union. Their protest was presented as a manifestation of the black militant labor movement, despite the fact that television audiences could readily see that the issue of racial discrimination in this case was not limited to black workers. The nationalist slant obfuscated the fact that a coalition of black and Latino workers had organized to improve their common plight.

One glaring instance of the ideological limitations of the program's treatment of unions and racism was its coverage of the United Federation of Teachers strike in New York City's Ocean Hill–Brownsville school district. The dispute was between the largely white teacher's union and black administrators over the issue of community control. The producers of this segment let pass the question of whether community control in the North would be detrimental to future efforts to unionize black labor in the South, given its similarity with the claim of states' rights by segregationists. On a different occasion this point was raised in a commentary by Charles Hamilton as a campaign issue on which Nixon had been inconsistent. It was not considered, however, in connection with the demand for community control in Ocean Hill–Brownsville. Community control was equated with black power. Within the allotted space of the documentary the narrator's attention turned immediately from Ocean Hill–Brownsville to another New York City school that had already won the battle for community control. The voice-over exclaimed that the success of the latter school is proof that community control can be a sound educational concept. Community control was touted as "a way to change a system that has psychologically neglected our children for decades." The narrator's use of "our" has to refer to more than the 65 percent black population at Ocean Hill–Brownsville. In fulfilling its commitment to giving the black community a voice, the producers were led to frame the issues in terms of a power struggle between the black community and the white teacher's union. But this racialized account elided the involvement of the Latino community, who constituted 30 percent of the students at Ocean Hill–Brownsville.

The UFT strike in Ocean Hill–Brownsville reflected a classic dispute between black nationalism and Marxism over the goals and direction of the civil rights movement. If, as many had claimed, the passage of civil rights legislation marked an end to legalized racial discrimination, the next level of engagement for black activism would be around issues of poverty. The Poor Peoples' Campaign was meant to be an extension of the earlier phase of the civil rights movement. King's followers had envisioned a mass movement based on an interracial coalition that included labor unions.[37] Alongside this development there were also the advocates of black power who denied the need for black participation in any such coalitions. Although Greaves's educational orientation permitted a plurality of voices to speak on labor issues, often Marxist concerns regarding class were silenced in favor of views expressed by a more dominant nationalist voice.

In his memoirs James Forman recalls that he and Malcolm X drew equally loud applause when they debated.[38] With debates of this sort between Marxists and black nationalists seeping into the black power movement, these opposing ideologies vied for attention on *Black Journal*. Through interviews and comments by various Panther spokespersons such as Kathleen Cleaver and Bobby Seale, black television audiences were in a position to learn surreptitiously how the principles of self-defense Malcolm X had popularized were incorporated by the Panthers into the Marxist ideology of Mao Tse-tung. Under Huey Newton's leadership the notion of black power was broadened to include a global perspective. *Black Journal* aired an interview filmed while Newton was still in prison in which he assimilated the black struggle in America to other Third World resistance movements. This image of the Panthers as a counterpart to other liberation groups was sustained, perhaps inadvertently, by the moderator's update of the ill-fated Panther leadership. His listing of events provided a forceful statement of the impact of systematic political repression: Newton's ongoing status as a political prisoner, the murder of Bobby Hutton and Fred Hampton by police, the incarceration of Bobby Seale and the exile of Eldridge Cleaver. Various activists, intellectuals, and panelists, also expressed Marxist ideas, although in a manner far less explicit than the Panther spokespersons, or represented by film clips that drew leftist commentary from a wide variety of community representatives. In a clip inserted into a sequence on King's assassination, civil rights activist John Singleton explained King's gradual shift toward a more radical view on Vietnam and nonviolence. Often these brief moments were enough to convey the basic logic of black revolutionary thought in America.

The alignment of the Panthers with other liberation struggles highlighted the international scope of *Black Journal*. When interviews with Stokely Carmichael (former prime minister) and Eldridge Cleaver (minister of information) conducted at the Pan African Cultural Festival in Algiers (1969) were broadcast, the producers capitalized on both the strictly journalistic value of showing these interviews on American television at the height of the political repression of the Panthers as well as the propagandistic value of bringing the festival itself to the attention of the American public. The festival provided a non-Western setting for an African American dialogue with Arabs from North Africa as well as other Africans. The interview of Cleaver by a group of Algerian students situated the African American struggle in an international context. Further signs of a Marxist perspective appear in other sequences, such as the intensely moving photo essay, *And We Still Survive*, in which the voice of a male blues singer moans "Have you ever been mistreated? Then you know what I'm talking about" over still shots of Vietnamese villagers. The photo of an elderly black male protester carrying a poster that read "No Vietnamese ever called me nigger" made the analogy explicit. This sequence was structured to evoke in black spectators a cross-racial identification with the colonial status of Third World people, a sentiment that was expressed by some of the black soldiers in a later episode on Vietnam.

African affairs were approached by the producers of *Black Journal* from a variety of standpoints. In addition to reports on the struggle for liberation in Mozambique, the civil war in Biafra, the post-colonial development of the East African countries of Kenya and Tanzania, and the resistance movement in South Africa, there were also segments on African history, art, music, and dance, and the study of ancient African civilizations. Each segment was interesting in its own right, but in later broadcasts some were re-played together to allow an entire program to focus on African or African American culture. In July 1969 the program featured a repeat of outstanding segments devoted to African American culture from the series's first year. Many of the segments on art and music aimed to be straightforwardly educational regarding African retentions and the African origin of African American culture. Support for the thesis that the principles governing African dance are exhibited in the defiant spirit of African American dance was both authoritatively explained by a dance instructor, as well as brilliantly displayed in a dance-poetry sequence shot by St. Clair Bourne in the rubble of an abandoned building.

Some of the segments on culture, however, were less edifying in this regard. Leon Bibb's discussion of children's games seemed to harp on regional differences but never considers African origins. The African authority on African art from the Washington, D.C., museum speaks at length about the influence of African art on European sculpture, but never relates African art to African American practices. Despite these minor (but sometimes annoying) oversights the program's black nationalist orientation was well served by the documentaries on art and culture.

AFFIRMING BLACK CULTURE AND BLACK IDENTITY

Just as the notion of decolonization was of primary importance to national liberation movements, the idea of controlling community institutions to pursue self-determination was a central issue in the black power phase of the struggle. In addition to the program's own endeavor to educate television audiences regarding African history and culture, *Black Journal* supported the demand for community control of schools.

Post-production on *Black Journal*.
From left: William Greaves, Kent Garrett, Madeline Anderson.
Photo courtesy of William Greaves Productions.

One of the educational objectives of community control was to change the Eurocentric curriculum that excluded black history and culture. The activism that developed in the late 1960s around educational issues was not confined to schools in the black community. High schools and colleges were also sites for the struggle to change the curriculum. On one program devoted to black student activism there was a panel discussion with representatives from six black student organizations in high schools from different regions. On other programs there were documentary segments devoted to the problems faced by black students at both black and white colleges. In the North and South, black high school and college students were shown making similar demands for black studies.

Black student activism on college campuses also exerted a strong influence on black athletes. A panel devoted to the black athlete featured two sports celebrities not known for their political advocacy of radical causes: baseball great Jackie Robinson, who strongly endorsed the protest actions of Tommy Smith and John Carlos at the 1968 Olympics, and tennis champion Arthur Ashe, who spoke against allowing South Africa to participate in the Davis Cup tournament. Contextualized to display the continuity of the social problems facing the black athlete with those faced by other black students, the black athlete's right to engage in political protest was examined in a segment on fourteen black football players at the University of Wyoming who were dismissed from the team when they wore black armbands to protest against the racial policies of Brigham Young University. In an approach to investigative journalism later made familiar by *60 Minutes* and *Frontline*, *Black Journal*'s coverage of the black athlete relentlessly sought to expose institutionalized racism in both the college and professional sports industry.

A clear instance of *Black Journal*'s function as alternative media can be seen in the program's treatment of an incident at Cornell University involving black students with guns. The narrator, William Greaves, introduced the report by pointing out that photographs of black students carrying guns had been widely publicized in mainstream media, and that leading news outlets had circulated the story that a radical group of black student protesters had threatened violence at Cornell University. To control the damage done by this misleading rumor, *Black Journal* employed the voice of a black woman narrator to dramatically recite the transcript of a statement by the assistant dean of students at Cornell (also a black woman). With deliberately slow pacing, the authoritative voice of the narrator recounts the events that had led to the black student demonstration, quietly pointing out that there was no threat of violence initiated by the black students. Instead, we are told that they were carrying guns only to defend themselves against threats of violence by white fraternities. The image of militancy and violence was diffused by the use of still photographs, supplemented with a noticeable absence of the ambient sounds that typically code the volatility of mass demonstrations. Unlike the kinetic footage of the famous gun-carrying demonstration by the Panthers on the steps of the California State Legislature, the static visual presentation of the Cornell University incident was designed to accord with Dean Joseph's attempt to characterize the incident along the lines of a panty raid. The issues that led to the threat of a violent confrontation between black and white students were overshadowed somewhat by the aesthetics of a montage that was used to diffuse the potential impact of the image of black student militants with guns. Perhaps incidents such as the shooting of Panther Party members John Huggins and Bunchy Carter by members of a rival nationalist group earlier the same year at the University of California at Los Angeles had caused the producers to hesitate to show anything inflammatory about black students with guns on a college campus.

The impact on television audiences of the energy transmitted through visual images of live events, such as Bourne's treatment of black student protest, was not easy to match with staged events. Yet the appearance of musicians, dancers, and poets to perform their work on the program was remarkably high-spirited. Some segments featured complete songs performed by artists such as John Lee Hooker and Roberta Flack. In almost every case the appearance of the artist on the program was accompanied by some kind of cultural education. The program's educational function was also well served by relaxing some of the emerging conventions governing the news magazine format. As I have already noted, panel discussions were treated as documentary footage subject to being edited and integrated with other clips. Even on programs which featured more extended autobiographical interviews with black cultural and political icons such as Nina Simone and Betty Shabazz, biographical tributes to historical figures such as Paul Robeson and A. Philip Randolph, or profiles of black elected officials such as Julian Bond, Leroy Johnson and Charles Evers, there was an attempt to interweave the various segments under a rubric of broader social and political themes.

The segment on the Cornell University incident that aired in May 1969, for instance, was preceded by Madeline Anderson's documentary of Malcolm X giving his famous house slave/field slave speech to a group of students in Selma shortly before his death. Malcolm X's concluding remarks regarding self-defense—that if the Federal Government is unwilling to rip off the hoods of the Ku Klux Klan, then "we will rip them off ourselves," were a direct lead-in for the segment on the Cornell University incident. With the general theme of militant black student activism as its structuring principle, the program paid homage to Malcolm X's birthday by invoking his legacy to frame its representation of black student protest. In the segment on the black youth movement in the South, St. Clair Bourne effectively used direct address by the students to tell a story involving a series of current events as they were occurring. Through vivid images of the students engaged in struggle, the scenes were edited to empower black spectators.

Bourne treats the story of black student activism as something composed of more than the occurrence of a series of events. Not that the events in this case were not compelling. For example, the demand for an Afro-American studies program at Duke University involved a student takeover of the administration building, followed by a police action and the University's rejection of the proposed program. Interspersed with cuts to students involved in community activities at nearby St. Augustine College and Shaw University, Bourne's focus was always on the agency of the black students, rather than the actions of the police, or administrators. Indeed, the events themselves were represented by means of the thoughts and deeds of the black students, many of whom were shown collectively engaged in social action. The segment closes with a rousing speech by the faculty advisor, Howard Fuller, to a large gathering of black students at Duke, announcing the opening of Malcolm X Liberation University. The crowd was shown responding to this announcement as though they had been told of a victory. In keeping with the black power movement's emphasis on autonomy and self-reliance, the nationalist orientation of the program was validated as the producers of this segment embraced a shining moment. The cold reality is that Malcolm X Liberation University did not provide a viable alternative. In this case, *Black Journal* seems to have fulfilled the Kerner Commission's mandate to give the black community a voice in mass media, but without much impact on institutional change.

BLACK JOURNAL'S INFLUENCE ON CONTEMPORARY BLACK FILMMAKING

By providing information omitted by mass media, a lot of the films on black history, art, culture and politics broadcast by *Black Journal* were meant to be corrective. The Kerner report cast the problem in terms of the harm to race relations caused by the hegemony of the white-oriented mass media. No single one-hour monthly television program could be expected to serve as a remedy for the distorted image of black people in mass media, yet through innovative adaptations of the news magazine format the producers of *Black Journal* pioneered the recoding of the black image in television journalism. The standard for representing black people and black culture set by their films, whether directly or indirectly, has had a lasting influence on successive generations of black documentary filmmakers.

This fact has not been widely recognized by black film scholars. In his discussion of black documentary filmmaking in the 1960s James Miller states that "radical Black films in the era of the assassination of Martin Luther King, the publication of *Soul on Ice* and riots throughout the country were made by radical white filmmakers."[39] This statement entails a misguided view of black filmmaking. Miller seems to ignore the work of filmmakers at *Black Journal* on the assumption that no films appearing on a television program can count as radical black filmmaking. This bias against television prevents his appreciation of films produced for *Black Journal*. Unlike the films on the Panthers that were distributed by Marxist groups such as San Francisco Newsreel and Third Word Newsreel, *Black Journal* was responsible for representing the entire spectrum of political ideologies among those in the black community who were involved in the movement for social justice, not only the radical elements.

Black filmmaking as a politicized cultural practice can only be understood from the standpoint of a specific historical context. In this relational sense then we can understand the initial call for black power as a radical move by frustrated civil rights workers. Given the ever-changing circumstances under which the black struggle has evolved, there is no reason to suppose that civil rights activists such as Stokely Carmichael, James Foreman and Willie Ricks in the South were any less radical than Panther Party members such as Eldridge Cleaver, Fred Hampton and Huey Newton in Chicago and Oakland. Moreover, the call for radical change was not voiced only by these spokespersons, but encompassed a broad spectrum of political activity by a wide variety of black people. For example, even on topics such as religion and the church, a range of theological and political perspectives were represented on *Black Journal*. Whether it was Reverend Clegg presenting an interpretation of Christ as a black revolutionary, Elijah Muhammad advocating self-help, or Father Albert McKnight explaining the politics of running a people's cooperative, there were radical voices on the program—even at times a Marxist voice, albeit submerged among a plurality of contending perspectives.

Miller's bias against including documentaries that appeared on *Black Journal* on his list of radical black films accords with a prevailing tendency among black film scholars to view radical black filmmaking as something that can occur only outside of the domain of the Hollywood industry. Many critics believe that independent black cinema is by definition a film practice that stands outside of the control of the mass market imperatives that govern Hollywood conventions. This dichotomy between Hollywood and independent black cinema posits a false paradigm of black filmmaking practice. At a conference on independent black filmmaking held at Ohio University in the spring of 1980, the subject of blaxploitation and its relation to independent black filmmaking was discussed by film critic Pearl Bowser and three black filmmakers, St. Clair Bourne, Haile Gerima, and Melvin Van Peebles.[40] The diversity of filmmaking practices represented by this group is an indication of the inadequacy of monolithic models of black filmmaking, whether independent or otherwise.[41]

Each of these three filmmakers has operated as a radical, but in quite different contexts. St. Clair Bourne came to work on *Black Journal* fresh from a night in jail for participating in student demonstrations at Columbia University, and was instrumental in the staff rebellion that resulted in African Americans gaining control of the production of the program. Haile Gerima was a film student at UCLA in the Third Cinema program founded by Teshome Gabriel.[42] Gerima has made several documentaries, but is better known for his Third Cinema style in films such as *Bush Mama, Ashes and Embers,* and *Sankofa.* Melvin Van Peebles has worked both in and out of Hollywood. He inadvertently fathered the blaxploitation era with his independently produced *Sweet Sweetback's Baadasssss Song,* released in 1971. At the Ohio University conference Haile Gerima's openly oppositional stance against Hollywood was criticized by Melvin Van Peebles as ineffective politics. The point of Van Peebles's criticism must be well taken, for he expressed a valid concern with the fact that the political message of independents never reaches a black audience. Van Peebles's more subversive approach can be understood as an attempt to address the problem of distribution. St. Clair Bourne's work on *Black Journal* can also be understood in terms of this problem.

The eleven black members of the original *Black Journal* staff who engaged in the "palace revolt" over the issue of editorial control were not a group of radical filmmakers who conspired to take over WNET, yet the idea of a network news magazine program produced by, for and about African Americans required a walkout that resulted in congressional intervention and negotiations with PBS executives.[43] Charles Hobson, who became the spokesman for the group during the negotiations, had come to *Black Journal* from a local television program, *Inside Bedford-Stuyvesant.* This community program was one of the earliest produced by, for, and about African Americans. Hobson left *Black Journal* after producing only a few segments in order to return to local programming as the producer of *Like It Is.* Madeline Anderson, who was also a producer and editor on the program, brought her extensive production background working with her own company, as well as experience as an assistant editor and assistant director on Shirley Clarke's *The Cool World.* She had been on staff at WNET since 1964, long before joining *Black Journal.* When she left *Black Journal* in 1969 she continued to produce films for clients as varied as the hospital workers' union, Local 1199, Children's Television Workshop, and Howard University Television.

The urban riots following the assassination of Martin Luther King, Jr. created a window of opportunity for a very creative and technically accomplished group of black filmmakers to function as the "electronic voice of the movement."[44] Their legacy can be witnessed in the work of documentary filmmakers that followed. Alonzo Sleigh's chronicle of the political struggle of Boston's black community that culminated in

Mel King's candidacy for mayor, Bill Hansard's very sensitive treatment of Huey Newton focusing on children in the elementary school founded by the Panthers, Carol Lawrence's historical documentaries on the black west and the Cotton Club, Michelle Parkerson's lively tribute to Betty Carter, and Marlon Riggs's critical examination of homophobia in the black community are but a few examples of the work of filmmakers influenced by *Black Journal*.

In a set of reflections on the impact of *Black Journal* on future generations, St. Clair Bourne pointed out that the second generation of black producers of television documentaries attempted to correct some of the unavoidable limitations of his generation.[45] For example, *Black Journal* graduate Tony Batten hosted a PBS program called *Interface* which concentrated on cultural interaction between ethnic groups. This was a step away from the first generation's flaw of addressing African Americans about issues related only to black people. Another program that followed in the footsteps of *Black Journal* was the "hard news" program, *Black Perspective on the News*, which lacked a cultural component but spoke to black people about issues that were not connected to African Americans. The next step, according to Bourne, would be a program that featured African Americans as participants in the mainstream talking about any issue. This would bring an interpretation of issues based on the black experience to bear on phenomena affecting everyone. This developmental aspect of the legacy of *Black Journal* has been undertaken by independent black filmmakers such as Henry Hampton and Carroll Blue. Blue was part of a group of filmmakers who worked with Hampton on *Eyes on the Prize*, but she has since moved to Southern California where she is currently working on a documentary film funded by the J. Paul Getty Foundation. In a fashion similar to the pioneering endeavor of William Greaves, Madeline Anderson, and Charles Hobson, all of whom have independently produced educational films for various media outlets, Hampton's company, Blackside, Inc., has also produced training films for the Census Bureau as well as a documentary series on the Great Depression for PBS. By overcoming the limitations of the earlier generation, the television documentaries produced by Hampton's film company reflect a broadening of the values represented on *Black Journal*.

When we consider the implications for independent black filmmaking practices, the success of *Black Journal* during its initial two-year run is filled with irony. National Educational Television provided a venue for *Black Journal* to carry out several functions of independent black cinema. First, and most importantly, it provided politically motivated black filmmakers access to a larger segment of the black audience. Secondly, because of the non-commercial nature of NET many of the segments on the program were explicitly designed to educate black viewers. Thirdly, by presenting an alternative aesthetic it set a new standard for the representation of black people on television. A paradox of independent black cinema is that the black audience for which it was created is the least likely to see the films. Through NET, a non-commercial branch of the most commercial mass medium, the filmmakers at *Black Journal* accomplished what has since eluded the 1970s independent movement—they found a black audience for their films.

NOTES

1. For a discussion of this systematic omission in pre-1970s television, see Michael R. Winston, "Racial Consciousness and the Evolution of Mass Communications in the United States," *Daedalus*, 3, 4 (Fall 1982): 171–82. For a quite different account of the politics of representation in post-1970s television see Herman Gray, *Watching Race: Television and the Struggle for "Blackness"* (Minneapolis: University of Minnesota Press, 1995).

2. See Jannette L. Dates and William Barlow, *Split Image: African Americans in the Mass Media* (Washington, D.C.: Howard University Press, 1990), 304–308.

3. In his book *Blacks and White TV* (Chicago: Nelson-Hall, 1983), J. Fred MacDonald raises this issue.

4. MacDonald refers to lengthy meetings between government officials and network executives to develop a plan to devote more coverage to black problems (ibid., 139).

5. MacDonald points out that the black protagonist of the 1968–1969 television series *The Outcasts* was a precursor to the "self-sufficient, virile, and threatening" protagonist in *Sweetback* (ibid., 126).

6. See Mark Reid, *Redefining Black Cinema* (Berkeley: University of California Press, 1993), for a text guilty of this omission. For a discussion of *Black Journal* in the context of black independent filmmaking see Clyde Taylor, "Black Films in Search of a Home," *Freedomways*, 4th Quarter (1983): 226–33; "The L.A. Rebellion: A Turning Point in Black Cinema," *The New American Filmmakers Series*, circular 26 (New York: Whitney Museum of American Art, January 3–19, 1986), and James Snead, *White Screens, Black Images: Hollywood on the Dark Side* (New York: Routledge, 1994), 116.

7. See MacDonald, 134–35. According to Mankiewicz and Sweidlow, "Studies indicate that many looters and potential looters watched television for status reports, and then used what they saw to plan their strategy." From "Race: Making and Unmaking a Revolution," in *Remote Control: Television and the Manipulation of American Life*, ed. Frank ManKiewicz and Joel L. Sweidlow (New York: Times Books, 1978), 122. (It should be noted that these authors also take the rather extreme position that, "had it not been for television; it [the civil rights movement] would not have occurred at all.") The Kerner Commission acknowledged that television was an influence in some cases, but chose to downplay its significance.

8. *Report of the National Advisory Commission on Civil Disorders* (New York: Bantam Books, 1968), 366.

9. *Report*, 383.

10. See MacDonald, 108–10. According to Mankiewicz and Sweidlow, the portrayal of blacks on television in the 1960s was in either stereotyped roles, subordinate roles, or law enforcement roles, "Race: Making and Unmaking a Revolution," 95.

11. MacDonald, 137–44.

12. Charles V. Hamilton, "Blacks and Mass Media," in *Issues and Trends in Afro-American Journalism*, ed. James S. Tinney and Justine J. Rector (Washington, D.C.: University Press of America, 1980), 225.

13. It is worth noting in connection with the barbershop model, that the weekly staff meetings included women such as Madeline Anderson, Angela Fontanez and Hazel Bright. See the William Greaves interview by James Hatch in *Artist and Influence* 9 (1990): 68.

14. The *Black Journal* Film School was funded by the Ford Foundation, the Carnegie Endowment, and the Corporation for Public Broadcasting.

15. MacDonald lists an additional eight such local black-oriented news magazine shows (*Blacks in White TV,* 210–11). William Greaves was involved in organizing a conference of over forty-five African Americans employed in public broadcasting. Held in Racine, Wisconsin, in 1969, it was funded by the Johnson Foundation, the Kellogg Foundation, and the Corporation for Public Broadcasting. The purpose of the conference was to create a national coalition that would deal collectively with the issues and problems confronting black producers. The group met only sporadically and by 1971 was no longer functioning. See Dates and Barlow, *Split Image,* 307.

16. Not much has been written on early documentaries by black filmmakers such as William Alexander and Biddy Wood. For a discussion of earlier black documentaries such as *The Negro Soldier,* see Thomas Cripps, *Making Movies Black* (New York: Oxford University Press, 1994).

17. In an interview with Lilian Jimenez, Greaves compares his first experimental feature film, *Symbiopsychotaxiplasm: Take One* (1968), to the work of Jean-Luc Godard and Robert Altman. He also had written and directed a 30-minute documentary, *Emergency Ward* (1958), for the Canadian Film Board, a film that, in some ways, presaged Fred Wiseman's *Hospital* (1968).

18. Adam Knee and Charles Musser, "William Greaves, Documentary Filmmaking, and the African American Experience" *Film Quarterly* 45, no. 3 (Spring 1992): 19.

19. Hamilton provides an extended discussion of the Black Panthers in his anthology *The Black Experience in American Politics* (New York: Capricorn Books, 1993), 212–43.

20. St. Clair Bourne described the program's editorial policy as follows: "In our editorial meetings, Greaves laid out the editorial guidelines that came to distinguish and unify our content. *Black Journal,* he stated, should "1. define the Black reality of any potential film situation. 2. identify the causes of any problems in that situation, and 3. document attempts to resolve those problems, whether successful or not." St. Clair Bourne "Bright Moments," *Independent Film and Video Monthly* 11, no. 4 (May 1988): 12.

21. William Greaves, "'100 Madison Avenues Will Be of No Help,'" *New York Times,* Sunday, August 9, 1970, 13.

22. Ibid.

23. Greaves discussed the idea of using television to set up encounter

groups between black militants and white racists, a proposal which suggests a middle ground from which he viewed both as too extreme.

24. Stan Lathan, Kent Garrett, Madeline Anderson, Horace Jenkins, Jimmy MacDonald, William Gladdis, Leroy McLucas, Osborn Smith, Babatunde Horatio Jones, and St. Clair Bourne were all mentored by Greaves.

25. The panels were composed of authors LeRoi Jones and Claude Brown; civil rights leaders Andrew Young, Bill Strickland, and Alexander Allen; editors Robert Johnson and Dan Watts; community activist Kathleen Cleaver; actor-author Julian Mayfield; and historian Richard Moore.

26. Claude Brown, Dan Watts, and Julian Mayfield.

27. "TV Electronic Stimulus for Black Revolution," *Athens* (Ohio) *Messenger,* December 27, 1968, 4.

28. The panel was composed of Masai Hewitt, Minister of Information, Chicago Black Panther Party; Charles Hamilton, Professor, Columbia University; James Finney, NAACP Legal Defense Fund; Renault Robinson, President of the Afro-American Patrolmen League; and Lincoln Lynch, Vice President of the New York Urban Coalition.

29. A clip was shown in which a Panther representative states this demand before a street crowd.

30. This segment was shown on the program that aired November 4, 1968.

31. I am indebted to Ruby Rich's comments in the exhibition flyer for the film series Documentary Matters, San Francisco Museum of Modern Art, 1994.

32. James Miller claims that *The Murder of Fred Hampton* and *Black Panther* contributed to the "spectacularization" of the Panthers. "Chained to Devil Pictures," in *The Year Left 2,* ed. Mike Davis, Manning Marable, Fred Pfeil, and Michael Sprinker (London: Verso, 1987), 133.

33. It should be noted here that Greaves had produced an earlier documentary for PBS (*Still a Brother: Inside the Negro Middle Class,* 1968) that critically examines the identity and consciousness of the black middle class.

34. There were at least a half-dozen segments on the Panthers broadcast between June 1968 and June 1970, including interviews with Eldridge Cleaver in exile and Huey Newton in prison.

35. Bill Strickland, former director of the Northern Student Movement, and Dan Watts, editor of the *Liberator,* respectively.

36. For an account of this change see Bayard Rustin, *Strategies for Freedom* (New York: Columbia University Press, 1976).

37. *The Making of Black Revolutionaries* (Washington, D.C.: Open Hand Publishing, 1985). See also Rustin's remarks regarding his debate with Malcolm X in *Down the Line.*

38. Ibid.

39. Miller, "Chained to Devil Pictures," 129.

40. "*Sweet Sweetback's Baaadasssss Song* and the Development of the Contemporary Black Film Movement," in *Black Cinema Aesthetics,* ed. Gladstone L. Yearwood (Athens, Ohio: Ohio University Center for Afro-American Studies, 1982), 53–66.

41. See Mark Reid's *Redefining Black Cinema* for a monolithic concept of independent black filmmaking. Ed Guerrero concedes more and presents a view of contemporary black cinema in terms of hybrid practices involving the overlap, and growing interdependence, of activity in the independent and commercial sphere. *Framing Blackness* (Philadelphia: Temple University Press, 1993). But even Clyde Taylor who includes the work of filmmakers at *Black Journal* in his account of the historical development of independent black cin-

ema, seems conciliatory when, with reference to *Black Journal,* he claims, "But even these revisionist documentarians understood the vital role of dramatic narrative for the full expression of black cinematic possibilities" (Taylor, "The L.A. Rebellion," 1).

42. See the account given by Ntongela Masilela, "The Los Angeles School of Black Filmmakers," in *Black American Cinema,* ed. Manthia Diawara (New York: Routledge, 1993), 107–17.

43. Interview with Charles Hobson by Phyllis R. Klotman and Janet K. Cutler, March 3, 1995, New York City.

44. *The Independent,* May 1988, 11.

45. St. Clair Bourne, "The African American Image in American Cinema," *The Black Scholar* 21, no. 2 (1990): 12–19.

4

Eyes on the Prize

Reclaimimg Black Images, Culture, and History

ELIZABETH AMELIA HADLEY

Days after "Bloody Sunday," the Rev. Martin Luther King Jr.
leads protestors across Edmund Pettus Bridge, March 1965.
AP/WIDE WORLD.

On Sunday, March 7, 1965, six hundred civil rights protesters were beaten and terrorized by state troopers and mounted police as they crossed the Edmund Pettus Bridge in Selma, Alabama, on their way to the state capital to press their demand for voting rights. Television cameras captured the violent scene and stunned the nation.[1] In the aftermath of the confrontation on Pettus Bridge, three white Unitarian ministers—who were among the hundreds of clergy who heeded Martin Luther King's call to join the Selma march—were attacked as they left a soul-food restaurant in Selma. One of them, 38-year-old James Reeb, was struck on the head with a club and died two days later.

From the White House, President Johnson told the nation that what happened in Selma was an "American tragedy." Reeb's murder galvanized civil rights advocates all over the country, including many Unitarians who headed for Selma. On Sunday, March 21st, thousands of demonstrators crossed the Pettus Bridge, determined to complete the 54-mile journey to Montgomery.

Among them was Henry Hampton, a 25-year-old black man from Saint Louis who had dropped out of medical school and was working for the Unitarian church as information director. The journey to Selma was Hampton's first visit to the Deep South, and it changed his life. Although he had no experience in filmmaking, he began conceptualizing a film documenting the civil rights struggle, which he thought of as the second American Revolution. He set about learning everything he could about film production, and in the process he developed his own techniques and strategies.[2] Three years later, Hampton founded an independent film company, Blackside, Inc., with the intention of bringing social history to a wide audience by means of film and television. To this endeavor, he brought the sensibility and commitments of a community activist. He launched Blackside in an era framed by the Black Arts Movement, which reflected the view of W. E. B. Du Bois that art should be for the people, by the people, and accessible to the people.

In the 1970s, Hampton launched a multi-year project to chronicle the civil rights movement and to capture the drama and spirit of black Americans' struggle for equity and inclusion in mainstream America. He was determined to convey not only facts and events, not only opinions and decisions, but also the rage and suffering, courage and confusion, felt by participants on all sides of the historic struggle. He sought to capture human feeling, and to record the faces and names, and the experiences, of anonymous heroes of the civil rights struggle.

The result was *Eyes on the Prize: America's Civil Rights Years, 1954–1965.* This six-part series, which premiered on public television in January 1987, attracted an audience of 40 million people, garnered numerous awards,[3] and became the most successful documentary program aired on Public Broadcasting System (PBS). It was followed by a sequel, *Eyes on the Prize II: America at the Racial Crossroads, 1965–1985,* narrated by Julian Bond. These landmark series tell the stories of the Civil Rights and Black Power movements through historical film footage and music. They became crucial educational vehicles for a "Sesame Street" generation of adults who could absorb and comprehend history better through multimedia formats than through print. *Eyes on the Prize* is now required viewing for students at many universities and colleges across the nation, and is often incorporated into high school curricula as well.

Hampton's method was to allow proponents and opponents of the civil rights struggle to speak for themselves. Using vintage film footage integrated with the rich musical heritage of African Americans, he gave voice to the voiceless. Rather than relying on the traditional format of public affairs programming—talking (white) heads interpreting historical events—Hampton rolled documentary film footage in which Blacks and whites voice grievances from their diverse viewpoints. The resulting programs elicit compassion for the oppressed, insight into the driving forces behind the actions of advocates and adversaries, and outrage at the systemic oppression meted out by mainstream America. They recall media strategies employed by Dr. Martin Luther King Jr. to depict, sympathetically, acts of civil disobedience, attracting a large and diverse population of viewers to the ranks of the civil rights movement.

Blackside's promotional materials characterize the series this way:

> *Eyes on the Prize* chronicles the civil rights years through the individual stories of people compelled by a meeting of conscience and circumstance to play a role in history. These are the stories of blacks and whites, of civil rights organizers from the South and the North, of government officials at all levels, of Southerners who fought to maintain a way of life they had cherished since Reconstruction and of blacks who were determined to make America live up to its promise of equality. Some played their parts and faded back into obscurity; others became household names in the America of the time and permanent figures on the pages of history.

Despite a relatively inexperienced production team, the technical level of the programs is very high. As one reviewer commented, "This is no easy achievement, considering the variety of film and still photographs that had to be successfully combined. The editing is smoothly done and the camera work on many of the interviews is excellent."[4] Meredith Woods, now a noted producer, recalls her early days at Blackside when, as "an unpaid intern . . . who found a home for the next eight years, [she] learned solid values as a filmmaker and a human being—respecting your witnesses, trusting your story and its dramatic structure, and having faith in your audience."[5] Woods says that Blackside's work sessions and the way they were conducted by Henry Hampton inspired her. She was struck by "the way in which he led those discussions, encouraged the teams not to defend their choices, but to listen—to figure out a way to be true to the past and make a good movie." Having seen many executive producers in action, Woods concludes that Henry Hampton was one of the extraordinary ones who consistently gave young talent a chance. There is a truism that you can judge a person by the company he keeps. Well, Henry is an executive producer who has chosen to collaborate with strong, independent-minded producers. Some of the finest documentary filmmakers of our time have worked for Blackside. Henry takes risks and he's not afraid of challenges.[6]

The challenges were not only aesthetic and historical, but also economic. To chronicle the civil rights movement, Hampton first had to raise money—a task that remained problematic throughout the production process. The first major break came in 1976, when Hampton responded to a request for proposals issued by CAP Cities Communica-

Rosa Parks being fingerprinted after her February 22, 1956,
arrest in Montgomery, Alabama.
AP/WIDE WORLD.

tion/ABC—then an independent distributor that had announced an intention to encourage and distribute more "minority" programming. The proposal submitted by Hampton envisioned a three-hour documentary. When the project was funded, Hampton began with a staff of two: his longtime collaborator and writer Steve Fayer, and movement activist Judy Richardson, who had gained strong communications, interviewing, and fact-finding skills while working closely with Julian Bond in the Student Nonviolent Coordinating Committee (SNCC). Richardson was content advisor and researcher for *Eyes on the Prize I*; Series Associate Producer for *Eyes on the Prize II*; and is currently education director for the Civil Rights Project, Inc. and for Blackside, Inc. The project gradually expanded, and long before "diversity" became politically correct, Hampton gathered a team of writers, researchers, producers, and editors (most with little experience as documentarians) that included blacks and whites, women and men.

COMMITMENT TO DIVERSITY

"We had great battles about *Eyes*," Hampton said, explaining his determination to use what he referred to as "mixed teams," and to portray the civil rights struggle from a broad spectrum of viewpoints. In an interview conducted for this chapter, Judy Richardson recalls, "Henry's idea was to have a black person and a white person on every team. He felt that it balanced it out. . . . From the start of the production you had these two lenses through which the film was being produced." These "salt and pepper" teams were assembled deliberately and consistently. Producer Orlando Bagwell, an African American who had worked as a cameraman for public television, was teamed with white associate producer Prudence Arndt. Senior producer Judith Vecchione, a white documentarian, collaborated with African American associate producer Llewellyn Smith. A third team had co-producers of equal standing: James De Vinney, a white producer who had worked at WQED, and Callie Crossley, an African American broadcaster for WGBH who had specialized in health issues.

Not everyone involved with the project supported this approach. Noting that as many as 150 people, including diverse scholars, were invited to the rough-cut screenings to critique each segment, Judy Richardson comments: "I would not have found a problem with an all-black staff. I really would not have. . . . As long as you have a lot of different inputs and you have the academic grounding and you're sending the scripts out at various stages to the scholars, then what a statement it would have been to have an all-black team to have done an amazing, wonderful segment. Because of the racism in this country, what is often said is: 'Oh, one of the reasons it's good is because it had that other piece.'"[7] Others criticized Hampton's approach because its intense focus on black/white teamwork neglected other perspectives, including those of Latinos and Asian Americans.[8]

While not unsympathetic to his critics, Hampton insisted on integrating the production unit. "We have to see the full story," he asserted, including the experience of "some people there who were caught in the event." The determination to tell the whole story also prompted Blackside to invest considerable money and time in research. "We wanted good history," said Hampton in a 1997 interview.[9]

But good history, in Hampton's view, is "messy history." He often expressed the view that while audiences tend to want neat stories with clear conclusions, documentaries must help them "understand that going through messy history may take a little more energy, a little more effort and a little more risk."[10]

"That's a big thing with Henry," said Judy Richardson in a 1997 interview. "You cannot tell people what to think. His thing is about testimony against interest so that you always have the other point of view. I have argued with him, but he's right about that. People have to feel that you are giving the other side their fair due, giving them their say. I have been finally convinced of this."

Hampton said that the responsible treatment of serious history is of greatest importance in the creation of a documentary. He stressed the need to ensure accuracy in retelling history. Anchoring history in context strengthens any documentary, he observed, but if even a single story proves to be false, the audience's trust evaporates. For this reason, he has placed great emphasis on checking the stories told in a film against genuine archival footage and against scholars' research and participants' recollections.[11] He made a conscious effort to gather the views and recollections of the movement's opponents, including dedicated segregationists. For example, Hampton interviewed the head of the Jackson, Mississippi, White Citizens Council. In interview after interview, Hampton's colleagues have praised the "integrity, fairness and honesty" that marked every stage of his career.

The effort to reflect more than one viewpoint was not lost on reviewers, who praised the series for its refusal to sentimentalize the civil rights movement, to lionize its leaders, to overlook dissension within the movement, or to focus exclusively on the achievements of black leaders. As one reviewer noted in *American Heritage*, "defeated white opponents are heard from along with the civil rights workers who overcame and outwitted them. Nor does [the series] ignore the genuine contribution made by white participants, whose simple presence in a demonstration often drew special lightning from enraged mobs. It does not flinch, either, from the conflicts over tactics and clashes of generation and personality that inevitably made the movement's task more difficult."[12]

Hampton's production team focused on the roles of ordinary people in history. *Eyes on the Prize* also sharpened the focus on the contributions of women to the civil rights struggle, and documented the strong presence of parents and children. The commitment to diversity went beyond race and gender, however. The project drew on the expertise of activists and academics; seasoned media professionals and individuals with no background in film. As Judy Richardson explains, "Blackside begins every series with what we call 'school,' and it is a scholar session. For *Eyes I*, it was about seven to ten days and we did it over at the Kennedy Library. You not only had the scholars who had written about the period, but you also had the people who participated in the event."[13]

EYES ON THE PRIZE AND PUBLIC TELEVISION

Hampton also drew upon the work of the documentarians who preceded him. Early, primitive documentaries were meant to disseminate information. The earliest form was the travel film, designated by the French as *documentaire*. Among speakers of English, John Grierson is credited with the first usage of the term documentary, which he introduced in 1926 to describe "the creative treatment of actuality."[14]

While the earliest documentaries were reportage of newsworthy events for film audiences, television was the most important outlet for African American documentary. In the years following World War II, television became the leading sponsor of documentaries. Public television, although historically as reluctant as its commercial counterparts to give black people and their projects entree into their domain, became the primary venue for African American documentarians. Public television's support of black documentarians responded, at least in part, to strong pressure from the Federal Communications Commission (FCC) for a steady flow of public affairs programming, including programming that addressed the experience and concerns of African Americans.

The pressure exerted by the FCC did not occur in a vacuum. Just as political activists protested, picketed, sat-in, and boycotted to win inclusion of blacks in mainstream American institutions, so too did community activists fight for the inclusion of African Americans in the media. Throughout the early 1970s, community activists tenaciously challenged their local television networks and public television stations and lobbied in Washington, D.C., for the inclusion of programming germane to black Americans. An array of associations assailed television management's commitment to affirmative action as spurious and their programming as racist, including the National Black Media Coalition, Black Effort for Soul in Television, Black Citizens for Media Access, the People's Communication Commission, Black Broadcasting Coalition, Blacks Concerned for Justice and Equality in the Media, and Black Citizens for Fair Media. These organizations galvanized their communities nationwide to fight for changes in the media, including the hiring of African American personnel, an increase in representative programming, and the positive representation of blacks on screen.[15]

Say Brother is one of public television's (WGBH/Channel 2) enduring local programs that continues to meet these demands. The first production aired July 15, 1968, "in the form of a series by the people, for the people, about the people."[16] The program has now almost 500 segments to its credit. Given its diverse format of drama, and politics germane to the black community, this award-winning[17] program may have been the catalyst for black documentaries on PBS. The program has been produced by such notables as Ray Richardson, Jim Boyd, John Slade, Topper Carew, Marita Rivero, Barbara Barrow-Murray, and Calvin A. Lindsay, Jr. Guided by this stellar group of producers, the series has expanded to cover global, multicultural, religious, political, and other issues not exclusively germane to black people.

The introduction of works by black documentarians to the Public Broadcasting System was made possible through the influence of three African Americans who gained key positions in the public communications arena over three decades. All three brought to their assignments a history of social and political activism.

President Nixon appointed Dr. Benjamin L. Hooks, attorney and minister, to the Federal Communications Commission (FCC) in 1972. He was the first African American commissioner selected to this bipartisan regulatory agency since its establishment in 1934. A civil rights activist, Hooks was a minister in the African Methodist Episcopal Church and in 1977 became executive director of the National Association for the Advancement of Colored People (NAACP), the nation's oldest civil rights organization. He was appointed to the FCC two years after Whitney Young of the National Urban League declared that black people would have to establish their own production houses and produce their own programming in order to achieve equitable representation and positive programming; and four years after the National Advisory Commission on Civil Disorders (the Kerner Commission) concluded that "the world that television and newspapers offer to their black audience is almost totally white, in both appearance and attitude."

The Blackside Productions crew interviews Muhammad Ali;
production still from *Eyes on the Prize*.
Copyright 1989 Blackside, Inc.

Hooks's appointment at this time reflected the political climate of an era during which black Americans were seeking inclusion in all American institutions. Many had lost patience with the "go slow" policy of the civil rights movement and the U.S. government after the assassination of Dr. Martin Luther King in 1968. They began to demand representation in American institutions nationally with "all deliberate speed." Among African Americans, there were some who questioned Hooks's selection to the FCC, contesting his media knowledge or challenging his approach. His adversaries believed that he would serve the FCC as a mute token. Hooks doubtless surprised these critics by championing civil and women's rights in the communication industry throughout his tenure on the commission and establishing a formidable record. According to Jannette L. Dates, Hooks and his allies deserve acknowledgment for the shifts in FCC policy achieved during his tenure:

> during the 1970s the FCC denied renewals of licenses to stations that were more blatantly discriminatory toward minorities, held minority ownership conferences, and made available tax certificates and distress sales to increase the involvement of African Americans and other minorities in decision-making positions and as owners of broadcasting facilities.
>
> Public television was a particular concern to Hooks. He made his support of public broadcasting conditional upon the recognition by public broad-

casters that they had underserved wide areas of the population. He accused public broadcasters of "arrogance" and of concentrating their efforts on the cultured, white cosmopolitans to the neglect of the less fortunate minorities. ... In 1975, he urged that the congressional oversight committee establish a PBS accountability committee to submit semiannual reports on minority programming and employment.[18]

For more than a decade, Hooks remained the sole African American with significant decision-making power in the realm of public communications. Not until 1989 after *Eyes on the Prize* had premiered was Jennifer Lawson, former film professor and civil rights worker, appointed First Executive Vice President for National Programming and Public Services for PBS in November 1990. Bruce Christensen, then president of PBS, explained why this position was created by Lawson. "What we wanted was a Solomon. ... Someone with extraordinary political skills as well as program judgment. And someone who was willing to take the heat." Lawson was a former member of SNCC; as field representative for the National Council of Negro Women, she had worked with Fannie Lou Hamer. She had also worked in Tanzania in Africa assisting in uniting Africans and African Americans interested in the arts. Lawson was responsible for acquiring, commissioning, distributing, and promoting the programs PBS provided to its 340 member stations nationwide.[19]

This human infrastructure was reinforced, in the 1990s, with the appointment of Donald L. Marbury as director of the Television Program Fund of the Corporation for Public Broadcasting. Marbury had been a community activist in his hometown, Pittsburgh, where he emerged during the 1970s as executive producer of *Black Horizons*, the first weekly black cultural program on a PBS station. (This distinction is usually accorded to *Black Journal*; however, while *Black Horizons* was broadcast locally, *Black Journal* had a national audience.) Marbury assumed responsibility for managing a $45 million television program fund which supported major series such as *Frontline*.

Hooks, Lawson, and Marbury have advanced the cause of black documentarians by using their positions to affect policy, programming, and funding decisions. They have created a setting in which black documentarians can work and succeed.

Eyes on the Prize owes a more direct debt to the black filmmakers who pioneered documentary programming. Indeed, among PBS documentarians, filmmakers were in the vanguard. By the time Henry Hampton emerged on the scene in the late 1980s with *Eyes on the Prize*, filmmakers and activists such as William Greaves and a number of his protégés had paved the way. Many of these pioneers had trained in other fields.

Greaves, for example, had been an actor and worked in Canada before becoming executive producer of *Black Journal* at New York City's public broadcasting station, WNET, in 1969. His appointment was announced only after black staff vehemently opposed white leadership of this black public affairs program. He quickly established a high standard for the program's content and production; that same year, Greaves won an Emmy for excellence in public affairs television.

Under Greaves's influence, WNET became a breeding ground for young black filmmakers. A number of his staff became independent media producers and directors; some of their films later debuted on PBS. The following are some of the documentarians who were mentored by Greaves:

- Kathleen Collins, who worked at WNET from 1967 to 1974 as a film editor for *American Dream Machine*, *Black Journal*, and *The 51st State*. She went on to produce and direct three feature films. Collins also worked on films for USIA, the BBC, Craven Films, Bill Jersey Productions, John Carter Associations and William Greaves Productions. She died in 1988 at age 46.

- St. Clair Bourne, whose television documentary *Let the Church Say Amen* (1973), according to James Snead, "set new standards for films of its kind."[20]

- Madeline Anderson, the first black woman producer at National Educational Television (NET). She worked with *Black Journal* and later directed for *Sesame Street* and the *Electric Company*.

- Jacqueline Shearer, the producer/director of *The Massachusetts 54th Colored Infantry* (1991), a segment of PBS's *The American Experience*. Shearer also produced two segments of *Eyes on the Prize II:* "The Keys to the Kingdom" and "The Promised Land" (1989). She died in 1993 at age 46.

- Tony Brown, who in 1977 became the producer of *Black Journal*, which is now known as *Tony Brown's Journal*.

Greaves himself was known as a filmmaker whose credits include *Still a Brother: Inside the Negro Middle Class* (1968), *From These Roots* (1974), and *Ida B. Wells: A Passion for Justice* (1989). These films embody his social and political commitments and his view of African American experience inside and outside black communities. His films are informative, practicing advocacy without didacticism. They seek to fuse three types of filmmaking which Greaves delineated in an interview with James Murray: (1) the Hollywood film, which "fulfills the Hollywood establishment's commercial requirements"; (2) the public service documentary, "ranging from the public affairs films on television to sponsored films for various institutions—some of them educational, some with social welfare objectives, some for government"; and (3) the independent film, created by "the independent cat who is out there. He's got himself four, five thousand dollars as a grant to make a film, or he's begged, borrowed, and stolen enough money from relatives to go out and do his thing."[21]

THE ROLE OF MUSIC IN *EYES ON THE PRIZE*

Henry Hampton was a documentarian of the third type. He drew upon the experiences of the black filmmakers and producers who preceded him; at the same time, he learned from documentary projects by white filmmakers who shared his commitment to telling big stories. In particular, he modeled his series on *Vietnam: A Television History*, which had made extensive use of archival footage, juxtaposing this vintage footage with contemporary interviews of participants.[22]

Hampton also recruited a key contributor to the *Vietnam* series to work on *Eyes on the Prize*. The senior producer for *Eyes*, Judith Vecchione, set the same high standards for research and fact-checking that had characterized her work on *Vietnam*. Each piece of archival footage had to be presented in context, accurately and appropriately. Every statement made by an interviewee (or interviewer) was subjected to a rigorous fact-checking process. According to Judy Richardson, "if you turn over any script that has come out of Blackside, you see on the back verification with at least two academic sources of anything that might be in question."[23]

In one important respect, however, Hampton and his team departed from the *Vietnam* model. Whereas the *Vietnam* documentarians had rejected the use of music in order to stress the project's calm, unemotional tone and its objectivity, *Eyes on the Prize* made extensive use of song to lend emotional power as well as authenticity to the movements and events it chronicled.

The decision to make music a key element in the series reflected the conviction of historian, composer, and vocalist Bernice Johnson Reagon, music consultant/researcher for *Eyes on the Prize I*, and ethnomusicologist Portia Maultsby, music consultant/researcher for *Eyes on the Prize II*, that music had been an integral part of the civil rights struggle and the Black Power movement. Indeed, the series title derived from the freedom song that included these lyrics:

I know one thing we did right
Was the day we started to fight.
Keep your eyes on the prize,
Hold on, hold on.

Alice Wine, who in 1956 became one of the first graduates of the voter education schools on Johns Island, South Carolina, adapted these lyrics to the melody of the traditional "Keep Your Hand on the Plow."[24] This song served as an anthem for the series, and underscored the importance of music to the movement. Bernice Johnson Reagon produced the theme music. Reagon had been one of the Freedom Singers, a chorus established by SNCC in 1962, that traveled nationwide providing inspiration and raising money for the civil rights movement. The other original Freedom Singers were Rutha Mae Harris, Charles Neblett, Chico Neblett, and Cordell Hull Reagon. Reagon recalls in particular the protests in Albany, Georgia that lasted from 1961 to 1965: "One of the things that kept people fighting all that time was music. Albany was a deeply spiritual community and its music transformed not only the singer, but the movement as well."[25]

Indeed, when Bernice Johnson Reagon was asked to contribute to the series, she was distressed that the musical element was being considered only after the series had already been in production for several months. According to Judy Richardson, who made the call, her initial response was: "You don't need to be doing this as if it's an afterthought. You're already in production. This [music] is such an integral part of the movement that it has to be the bedrock of whatever you're producing." Reagon was ultimately persuaded that only a scholar and musician who had been part of the movement could advise the production staff on the selection of music for the series. She declined to work on *Eyes II*, however, noting that the 1970s and 1980s were "not my period." Reagon recommended Portia Maultsby, who became a key music consultant for *Eyes II*.

One measure of the powerful role played by music in the civil rights movement was the authorities' efforts to silence it. Reagon has remarked that, "Singing is different than talking, because no matter what [the police] do, they would have to kill me to stop me from singing. . . . Sometimes they would plead and say, 'Please stop singing.'"[26]

Freedom Rider James Farmer also describes the authorities' attempts to stop activists from singing. He recalls singing in prison. "As a way of keeping our spirits up, we sang freedom songs. The prison officials wanted us to stop singing, because they were afraid our spirit would become contagious and other prisoners would become Freedom

Riders as a result of our singing. They said, 'If you don't stop singing, we'll take away your mattresses.'"[27] The men agreed that the confiscation of their mattresses was a metaphor for the theft of their souls, and they began singing "Ain't Gonna Let Nobody Turn Me Round." They lost their mattresses.

Coretta Scott King has also reflected on the inspirational impact of song during the mass meetings of the civil rights movement:

> There were songs interspersed.... They would end, of course, after Martin's message, with a song and a prayer, a benediction and prayer. And everyone would go home feeling good and inspired and ready to go back the next morning to a long day of hard work. But I think they could take it a little better, really—even the work that had been difficult became easier. It was something about that experience that gave all of us so much hope and inspiration, and the more we got into [the singing], the more we had the feeling that something could be done about the situation, that we could change it.[28]

With the assistance of Reagon and Maultsby, Hampton incorporated music into the documentaries in a way that recounts the history of blacks in America. The music in the series emphasizes and comments on the activities displayed on-screen, while illustrating the import of music in the civil rights struggle. The melodies, rhythms, and lyrics tell the story of how music has functioned as a balm and a bond, consoling and mobilizing people and contributing to African American survival. "I've always understood that music is a very important part of social history," said the late Jacqueline Shearer, documentarian and one of the producers on *Eyes II*.[29] Portia Maultsby praised Shearer as one of the producers who was very knowledgeable about black music and its importance to black lifestyles. Maultsby said that, "[Shearer] did her own [music], that's why I could really say when I saw hers, I couldn't have done it better. . . . *The Keys to the Kingdom* and *The Promised Land* were really good, I would've made pretty much the same choices that she made."[30]

The producers drew upon several genres of music, including spirituals, gospel, rhythm and blues, and a genre inspired by the civil rights movement—the protest song. *Eyes II* added salsa and disco, recalling the music that many danced to in the 1970s and 1980s at block parties and in discotheques. Artists such as Mahalia Jackson, James Brown, Jimi Hendrix, Aretha Franklin, Sweet Honey in the Rock, Curtis Mayfield, Bob Dylan, and many others were incorporated into the series. The music, like the documentary footage and interviews, suited Hampton's technique: it speaks for itself.

Music became an increasingly intrinsic element in both *Eyes on the Prize* series as the production process continued. It was used in various ways: to create continuity throughout the 14 one-hour programs that constituted the two series; to reproduce the musical experience that was part of the civil rights and black power movements; and to lend drama, irony or poignancy to a particular segment. *Eyes II*, for example, opens with Dinah Washington's rendition of "Blue Skies." Her haunting performance accompanies a still photograph of a mother and daughter sitting in a bleak stairwell. As the song continues, the camera zooms in on the headline of a newspaper the mother is sharing with her child, declaring the end of segregation.

In another sequence of *Eyes II*, the refusal by Atlanta mayor Maynard Jackson to build an airport unless construction crews were integrated is accompanied by the Afro-Latin instrumental by War, entitled "Why Can't We Live Together?" Subsequent footage of the airport's opening in 1980 is accompanied by Kool and the Gang's "Celebration," as the narrator reports that the $700 million facility opened on time, within budget, and with an interracial construction crew.

This kind of musical commentary runs throughout the series. Aretha Franklin's wailing rhythm-and-blues question, "If I had a dollar and you had a dime, I wonder could I borrow yours as easily as you could mine?" accompanies a still photograph of white and black poverty-stricken mothers and children. In another segment, Marvin Gaye's "What's Going On?" laments, "Mother, mother, there's too many of you crying/Brother, brother, brother there's far too many of you dying" under closing credits as the caskets of some of the 39 murdered Attica inmates are borne on the shoulders of friends and family through their neighborhood.

White artists are also represented in the documentaries, sometimes with ironic intent. Bob Dylan's "The Times They Are a-Changin'" introduces the black student movement at Howard University. Treatments of the student movement usually credit and focus on white students; the placement of Dylan's music at this point serves as counterpoint to the black campus protest, and resonates W. E. B. Du Bois's statement, in *The Souls of Black Folk* (1903), that "one ever feels his twoness." In this segment, black students at the historically black college include, among their demands, public acknowledgment by the administration of its commitment to the black community and its recognition that Howard University is a black university. These students, the sons and daughters of early civil rights protesters, tend to be middle-class and privileged, but embrace the legacy of activism and protest music by singing, as they shut down the campus, "Gonna lay down my shufflin' shoes, ain't gonna shuffle no more" to the tune of "Down by the Riverside."

Footage recounting the refusal of Cassius Clay, a conscientious objector, to participate in the Vietnam War, his embrace of Islam and his

Bobby Seale *(left)* and the Rev. Jesse Jackson confer at the
National Black Political Convention in Gary, Indiana, March 12, 1972.
AP/WIDE WORLD.

transformation into Muhammad Ali, is underscored by "Tell It Like It Is," the popular slow-drag song danced to by teens during red-and-blue-light parties. The song includes the line "Let your conscience be your guide." Stripped of his heavyweight title by the U.S. government, the boxer continued to speak out against the war. Curtis Mayfield's gentle falsetto in "Keep On Pushing" glides Ali through his proclamation that he has lost nothing, but that he has "gained a peace of mind and a peace of heart."

Maultsby detailed the complex process of selecting music:

> First of all I felt that music should not be incidental to the scene nor should music dominate the scene—but in fact music should support the scene. Now what do I mean by support? Music from a theoretical perspective in African American culture represents a translation of life, moods,

feelings, thoughts, ideals, ideas, world views. Music is a translation of those things. Therefore, the songs I selected had to correspond in one of those ways in that it is serving as a translation. So I was guided by the content— for example, secular settings, religious settings, a civil rights activity or work activity. I was also guided by region—it would be inappropriate to play some up tempo piece that's really reflective of a northern environment for a southern scene. And then also, I was influenced by the time period. I didn't want to have music for example, we can talk about a rural setting in the south in 1950 or 1960 which would be slightly different in terms of tone, attitudes, people, concerns—slightly different from that same rural scene in 1930. So for 1930 I might have used a strict rural blues piece. But over time in some rural areas—you know in some of the scenes that I was dealing with in the film you could clearly see some phase of development—you know from the thirties. Therefore, I considered a musical style that reflected that development whether it be in terms of attitudes not necessarily economically, but attitudes, styles—are people wearing the same clothing? What is the music that they're listening to? Are they workers, teenagers? Are we seeing a lot of teenagers, young adults, older people—all of that played a role in my selecting particular musical examples to translate those things.

Maultsby not only views music as a form of translation of the visuals, but she considers the "world view one's ideas about certain things—an individual's philosophy—whether representative of a group or of an individual." This process is exemplified in her choices of music accompanying the funerals of a Black Panther and of Malcolm X. She was mindful that Christian music would have been inappropriate to both. Maultsby explains that

> the Panthers in L.A., for example, did not believe in a lot of Christian ideology—so it would have been inappropriate even though they had a traditional funeral in that it took place in a church—but the whole Christian ideal did not follow—did not accompany what they were thinking—what their beliefs were at that time. Therefore, I did not use a gospel piece, that would have been appropriate for some other setting—but, instead, I chose a kind of bluesy, style guitar—I took the sample from a Sly Stone vocal tune, but it was perfect and the producers really liked it. I knew I could not play any type of gospel.[31]

In discussing her choice of music for Malcolm X's funeral, Maultsby remarked that there were so many funerals during the era that she actually ran out of music to incorporate in the film.

> Malcolm X, you know, he was a Muslim—so, you can't play a hymn in a gospel style or any kind of African American type of religious music. I

remember working with the producer in choosing—we really debated on that issue because for Malcolm X there were two kinds of funerals—Ossie Davis is narrating that part in an interview where he is describing the ways of the funeral in a Muslim setting versus the Christian. So initially we thought about following the general Muslim tradition—then all of sudden you have to make that switch within the Christian context—so what really kind of neutralized all of that, was again—what's going to be the appropriate music? Muslims frankly do not use music. I mean you have two concepts—either using effects of the far East—Islamic type effects—but when they are not dealing with music within their traditional service, then that's inappropriate. So then, we had to arrive at a degree of neutral there—so we ended up using a jazz-based instrumental—and see what a lot of people don't understand is that a lot of jazz musicians were very much inspired by religious principles—whether they're Muslim or Christians—that's irrelevant.

Maultsby's descriptions of her selection process reflect her belief that music is essential to black life. Maultsby's approach is indicative of the interdisciplinary nature of African American Studies. Her choices of music for the film are informed by her educational background in African American Studies with an emphasis on history, and the study of African and Islamic African history.

Not all of the producers realized the importance of music, however; Maultsby relates an incident which still disappoints her when she watches the segment *A Nation of Law? 1968–1971*, produced and written by Terry Kay Rockefeller and Louis Massiah, but directed by Thomas Ott. Maultsby wanted the dissonant chords of Jimi Hendrix's guitar to underscore the visual and internal discordance of the Attica rebellion, the storming of the prison by police, and the explosion of gas bombs dropped from aerial helicopters. When Louis Massiah left the project for another assignment, the new director chose not to use music at all. Maultsby was not consulted. She recalls:

That show was perhaps the one that I was most disappointed with in terms of how the music was cut—given what I submitted and that was no fault of the original producer. Louis Massiah liked what I had originally submitted, but he left the show before the final version was done, he had another commitment. But nevertheless, that show was so full of action, you know the guns, whatever they were dropping—the bombs—the airplanes and all of the sirens. I mean you just heard all of this in the footage and I chose music that would translate that into sound to sustain the sounds, to support the sounds and help give support to the environment, the atmosphere that you could already see in the film from the fires and even the riots in the cities. I mean it was already there and I chose a number of sound effects that would

just support that kind of action. I didn't try to vocalize or impose anything on it.

Maultsby attributes this decision not to use music to the German approach to documentary filmmaking which does not support the use
of music. If used at all, it is incidental. This approach conflicted with
Maultsby's concept of the place of music in African American culture.
Although she praises the idea of working with a multicultural filmmaking staff, she maintains that

> they must share a particular vision about the group that's being represented
> or a vision and an understanding of traditions and practices that are central
> to that group that must be captured in the filmmaking process. And some-
> times that defies standard practices about filmmaking, particularly if those
> practices are based on a specific school of thought about filmmaking. That's
> completely outside of the culture we are addressing. That is why it is so
> important to have cultural traditions of *whoever* is being represented guide
> some of the decisions that are being made.

Maultsby indicates that the cultural exchange that occurred as she
worked with several producers was a positive experience.

> As an ethnomusicologist, and one without formal training in the art of film-
> making, I was not bound by tradition, rules, and notions about a docu-
> mentary film—which would include the use of music. But, I brought to that
> art form a notion about music and culture and how it translated through
> various pieces. In this case I was guided by traditional practices of the cul-
> ture that is represented in the film. And those guidelines will change and
> vary with another culture—if another culture were represented in the film.
> I think then I brought and helped broaden the perspective on documentary
> filmmaking by having a different background from the others. At the same
> time, I learned from them, you know which again, helped me express what
> I wanted to do from an ethnomusical perspective.

EPILOGUE

The tradition of on-screen advocacy continues. All of the filmmakers
discussed in this chapter, and many of their protégés, have taken on the
formidable challenge of sharing the stories of black Americans' history in the United States. They have embraced traditional documentary
film techniques while at the same time augmenting this art form. Integral to their storytelling has been the reclamation of black images; powerful efforts to achieve equity in the telling of the stories; and incorporation, as a basic element of the documentary, of the music created by the

people whose stories are being told. Portia Maultsby indicates the importance of music in her declaration "that music is an integral part of African American life. It is part and parcel of what black people do . . . whether there is music present all the time or not—we are operating out of the musical, rhythmic system."[32] Their stories are told within the cultural context of black American homes, churches, communities, and in the socio-political arenas of mainstream America.

Several of the films that premiered on PBS adhere to this principle:

In 1983, Michelle Parkerson introduced the *a cappella* singers led by Bernice Johnson Reagon in a one-hour tribute entitled, *Gotta Make This Journey: Sweet Honey in the Rock* (1983).

In his 1989 film *Ida B. Wells: A Passion for Justice*, William Greaves incorporated performances by Sweet Honey in the Rock. Greaves made extensive use of photographic stills, but the narrative storytelling and the music engage viewer interest.

In 1995, Louis Massiah, a producer for *Eyes on the Prize II* and director of Scribe Video Center, made the film *W. E. B. Du Bois: A Biography in Four Voices.* The life of this seminal thinker, who traversed many disciplines and countries for almost a century, is recounted from the vantage points of four scholar / artists who interacted with him during his lifetime: the late Toni Cade Bambara, author, scriptwriter, filmmaker teacher and critic; Amiri Baraka, poet, playwright, essayist, activist, novelist, and editor; Wesley Brown writer, and Thulani Davis, author of *1959*, a novel focusing on a civil rights sit-in. Their words capture the development and maturation of Du Bois's complex ideas and ideologies. Massiah incorporated into his film the music of Sweet Honey in the Rock, as well as photographic stills, interviews, and modern-day technology of computer animation. Regarding Blackside as a training ground, Massiah states, "Both the material and the sense of privilege that comes from working at Blackside have made it one of the great 20th century destinations for independent filmmakers."

Derrick Evans, eighth-grade teacher and college lecturer on U.S. and civil rights history, credits his experience at Blackside for his choosing to become a teacher. "I had always loved history for its own sake, but working in an environment so rich with vision and purpose helped me clarify what I should do with it." Lillian Benson, an editor on *Eyes on the Prize II* and *The Great Depression*, continued to edit documentaries in Los Angeles for the Arts & Entertainment Channel. Lulie Hadad, who credits Hampton for her first break in film, was a production assistant and later an associate producer on *The Great Depression* and *America's War on Poverty.* [33]

Hampton's dogged struggle to produce *Eyes on the Prize* is the stuff of legend. Massiah describes his work experience with Hampton: "To mix Hollywood biblical metaphors, I have this image of Henry Hampton, Moses-like, carrying the sacred tablets containing the lessons of the Civil Rights movement to a nation that had been seduced by the golden calf of the Reagan era." Valerie Linson, production secretary on *Eyes on the Prize II* was associate producer for *W. E. B. Du Bois: A Biography in Four Voices* and WNET's *America on Wheels.*

The films produced by these (and other) black documentarians reclaim and give weight to African American experience as a substantial component of American history. As these histories were aired nationwide, they strengthened the Public Broadcasting System's commitment to serving and reflecting the "public." While they both found PBS to be their major outlet, Henry Hampton went one step further than Greaves. Greaves remained within the confines of an existing station while forming a training ground for young filmmakers; Hampton took the next step, establishing a new institution which continues to develop young filmmakers; convene community outreach meetings with students, parents and educators; and produce complementary publications for his productions that are used in educational institutions for students of all ages. He has defined the essence of and provided a paradigm for the role of "public historian."

The work of these two documentarians, and their production teams, paved the way for a new generation of filmmakers including: Marlon Riggs, who issued powerful, on-screen challenges to homophobia and intragroup racism in the black community; Julie Dash, who told the story of a matrilineal family living in the Geechee Islands decades after slavery; Jacqueline Shearer, who made a poignant film telling the story of the Massachusetts 54th Colored Infantry Regiment; and numerous other filmmakers who are reclaiming black images and recounting black experience on public television, previously an all-white forum. Louis Massiah recalls how PBS senior vice president Jennifer Lawson, while visiting Blackside, "reminded us that like WNET in the late 1960's and the fabled UCLA film program of the 1970's, the nexus created by Blackside would have an important impact on the American filmmaking and television community for years to come."[34] *Eyes on the Prize,* and the people who produced it, helped to provide a new paradigm for telling and teaching a painful but liberating and celebratory history to the people, with an integrity and compassion that can only serve to unify the nation as we move into a new millennium.

NOTES

1. Juan Williams, *Eyes on the Prize: America's Civil Rights Years, 1954–1965* (New York: Penguin, 1987), 269.

2. Press release by Heinz on the occasion of the selection of Henry Hampton as recipient of a 1996 Heinz Award in Arts and Humanities. See the web site http://www.awards.heinz.org/hampton.html.

3. Blackside is the recipient of the A. I. duPont–Columbia University Gold and Silver Baton, the George Foster Peabody Award, seven Emmys, an Academy Award nomination, the National Association of Black Journalists Award of Excellence, the American Film and Video Festival "Best of Festival," the International Documentary Association Award, the Chicago International Film Festival Gold Hugo, the National Educational Film Festival Gold Apple and "Best of Festival," the San Francisco International Film Festival "Best of Category," the Organization of American Historians' "Erik Barnouw Award," the Television Critics Association "Best Program," the Cine Golden Eagle, the Houston International Film Festival Grand, Gold and Silver, and the National Education Association Award.

4. Robert Pearce, "*Eyes on the Prize II: America at the Racial Crossroads, 1965–1985.*" *ABC-CLIO Video Rating Guide for Libraries,* 1995. Available on the Web at: http://www.lib.berkeley.edu/MRC/Eyes on the Prize.html.

5. Meredith Woods. "Blackside Memories," toast to Henry Hampton, November 23, 1996. Author's personal papers,1, 4.

6. Ibid., 3.

7. Interview with Judy Richardson, conducted by Elizabeth Hadley, Boston, Massachusetts, June 18, 1997.

8. Karen Everhart Bedford, "'Messy History': The Hardest Work," *Current,* July 13, 1993. Available on the Web at http://www.current.org/hi3l 3.html.

9. Interview with Henry Hampton, conducted by Elizabeth Hadley, Cambridge, Massachusetts, June 26, 1997.

10. Bedford, "Messy History."

11. Nick Rheinwald, "Filmmaker Discusses Accuracy in Documentaries," *Tufts Daily,* March 5, 1997.

12. Geoffrey C. Ward, "Up by the Bootstraps from Slavery," *American Heritage,* December 1986, 12.

13. Richardson interview.

14. Ephraim Katz, *The Film Encyclopedia: The Most Comprehensive Encyclopedia of World Cinema in a Single Volume* (New York: Harper and Row, 1979), 348.

15. J. Fred MacDonald, *Blacks and White: Afro-Americans in Television since 1948* (Chicago: Nelson-Hall Publishers, 1983), 205.

16. Tonia Collins Brown. "WGBH 'Say Brother' Celebrating 25 Years," *Reunion,* November 1993, 5.

17. *Say Brother* is the recipient of more than ten New England Emmy Awards, the Massachusetts Broadcasters Award and of a special recognition Award from the Board of Governors of the regional chapter of the National Academy of Television Arts and Sciences (NATAS).

18. Janette L. Dates, "Public Television: Statement of Commissioner Benjamin L. Hooks, Hearings" (Washington, D.C.: U.S. Government Printing Office, 10 April 1975), in *Split Image: African Americans in the Mass Media,* ed. Jannette L. Dates and William Barlow (Washington, D.C.: Howard University Press, 1990), 316.

19. Dorothy Ehrhart-Morrison, *No Mountain High Enough: Secrets of Successful African American Women* (Berkeley: Conari Press, 1997), 15–16; "The Wisdom of Ms. Solomon," *Time*, December 10, 1990, 76.

20. James Snead, *White Screens, Black Images: Hollywood from the Dark Side* (New York: Routledge, 1994), 116.

21. James Murray, *To Find an Image* (New York: Bobbs-Merrill, 1973), 92.

22. Harvard Sitkoff, Review of *Eyes on the Prize, Film & History*, May 1987, 43.

23. Richardson interview.

24. Guy and Candie Carawan, ed. and comp,. *Sing for Freedom: The Story of the Civil Rights Movement through Its Songs* (Bethlehem, Pa.: Sing Out Corp., 1990), 111.

25. Bernice Johnson Reagon, quoted in Juan Williams, *Eyes on the Prize: America's Civil Rights Years, 1954–1965* (New York: Penguin, 1987), 176–77.

26. Henry Hampton and Steve Fayer, *Voices of Freedom: An Oral History of the Civil Rights Movement from the 1950s through the 1980s* (New York: Bantam Books, 1990), 108.

27. Ibid., 94–95.

28. Ibid., 30.

29. Phyllis R. Klotman and Janet K. Cutler, *Black Film Review* 8, no. 12: 32.

30. Interview with Portia K. Maultsby, conducted by Elizabeth Hadley, Boston, Massachusetts, August 8, 1997.

31. Ibid.

32. Ibid.

33. Lillian Benson, "Eyes on the Prize as a Teaching Tool," Program Notes of the Boston Film/Video Foundation on the occasion of awarding Henry Hampton the 1996 Vision Award.

34. Louis Massiah, "Henry's Gift," Program Notes of the Boston Film/Video Foundation on the occasion of awarding Henry Hampton the 1996 Vision Award.

5

Paths of Enlightenment
Heroes, Rebels, and Thinkers

CLYDE TAYLOR

> THROUGHOUT HISTORY, THE POWERS OF SINGLE BLACK MEN
> FLASH HERE AND THERE LIKE FALLING STARS, AND DIE SOMETIMES
> BEFORE THE WORLD HAS RIGHTLY GAUGED THEIR BRIGHTNESS.
>
> —W. E. B. DU BOIS

In 1903 W. E. B. Du Bois wrote, "To the real question, How does it feel to be a problem? I answer seldom a word." But the question would not go away, for as he noted in almost the same breath, "The problem of the twentieth century is the problem of the color line." Let it be clear: the equation Blacks = Problem is one of the bonus stigmata of racism. As racism persists from one century to the next, popular discourse "blames" the object of race intolerance for the unpleasantness associated with racial friction. The hosts of racial socio-pathology are left free of any such reductive equation, and are even upheld as models of human identity.

Black documentarians have had to deal with this question, one way or another, throughout the century. What was it about their situation in the 1990s that made them begin to focus on extraordinary individuals as subjects? Why was it we suddenly saw feature-length nonfiction films about Du Bois, John Henrik Clarke, Aimé Césaire, and Frantz Fanon, and one-hour documentaries about Ida B. Wells, Patrice Lumumba, A. Philip Randolph, Audre Lorde, and Richard Wright? The available pattern suggests that the pronounced themes and strategies in black documentaries in one period or another demonstrate an intellectual response to a specific call from history, and to the current challenges of filmmaking possibility.

We can find some hints of patterns in earlier documentary filmmaking by and about black Americans. Granting Carlton Moss his deserved role as pioneer "modern" black documentarian, *The Negro Soldier* looks like an extension of its nonfictional cinematic times—something like a grand newsreel, a *Life* magazine feature given animation on the screen. The representation of black people that Moss inherited from the New Deal struggle against the Depression bears the traces of the two-dimensional sociology popular in that era. Nonfictional imagery of black people tended toward sober, government-approved imagery of farmers and workers, with overalls much in evidence, demonstrating their presence in the fabric of American "democracy," a much-used term in those days. The "voice of God" narration offered didactic instruction that black people had a place in the complex social undertakings facing the nation. Moss's film honored the commitment to approved national propaganda, including the wartime ideology of the "common front," emphasizing brotherhood against fascism. As in most such films in those days, we don't get many chances to hear the voices of its subjects. But Moss brought a degree of poetry to his screen image by inventing the device of a Negro preacher, played by Moss himself, as a pulpit narrator. And the sweep of his montage and elevated images approached epic grandeur.

A new era in black nonfiction cinema arrived in 1964 when Madeline Anderson completed *Integration Report #1*, ending a long drought in socially significant black filmmaking of any kind. Both the title and the style of this film set the pace in documentary filmmaking for years to come, making Anderson the Rosa Parks of black screen independence. In most of the nonfiction portrayals of the 1960s, we get THE NEGRO AS A PROBLEM. That is, the films cannot help reverberating the concerns and attitudes of the headlines and television news coverage of the civil rights era. The nation would not be denied its problem-probing during its latest crisis of color and race. Thus many documentarians, sometimes black, rushed to give the nation an answer to the question Du Bois refused to address. Gordon Parks's documentary *Diary of a Harlem Family* (1968) took cameras and lights into the hovel of a poor black family, where Parks stood over them retailing their abjection as a delicacy for civic-minded voyeurism.

The creation of the Public Broadcasting System (PBS) program *Black Journal* in the late 1960s got black documentary up off the floor again and moving toward the level of Moss's pace-setter. *Black Journal* introduced a national black perspective from which to look at events and issues. Three decades have passed between then and now. What explains the turn, during that time span, to longer, sometimes feature-length, documentaries about major black leaders? What was cause and what effect? What was produced by slow evolution and what came from sudden spurts and twists in the historical flow?

An important background to the "leadership" documentaries was the rise of the latest "new wave" of black-directed Hollywood movies, starting with the breakthroughs of Spike Lee and Robert Townsend. William Greaves, the dean of black documentary directors, answered my question at a conference on black cinema at Yale: Yes, black documentary was being pushed into the shadows by the fascination with feature films about black people, often graced with black stars. It looked, in the late 1980s, as though the campaign waged by black independent cinema against Hollywood for the license on blackness had been cut off at the knees, with the fiction-making part of that struggle defecting to Hollywood. We might read Warrington Hudlin's transformation from the director of the *vérité* documentary *Street Corner Stories* (1977) to the Hollywood producer of *House Party* (1990) and *Boomerang* (1992) as symptomatic of this shift.

It would be tempting in this context to set up dueling oppositions between fictional and documentary films about the same eminent figures. What happens if we set *The Great White Hope* (1970) beside *Jack Johnson*, the documentary made at almost the same time as the Hollywood feature? And surely there was some muttering about comparing Spike Lee's Hollywood epic *Malcolm X* with the three-hour documentary made by Blackside Inc. with the same name and focus. But for now, the results of such heavily laden discussions are uncertain.

For the documentarian of the late 1980s, new competition from black Hollywood only raised the ante on a fight that had never been easy in the first place. It had always been a struggle to say something real about black life, against the fictions, myths, stereotypes, misconceptions, and lies magnified in the fantasy factory that was then exploding with special effects and dazzling technologies. I found myself edging toward the thought that as "independent cinema" became steadily commercialized, aestheticized, and robbed of its social "whip," as Toni Cade Bambara might say, documentary was becoming one of the last refuges of sane, truly independent examination of social reality. Granted, documentaries were also shaped and manipulated by individual, politicized personalities. But at least something actual about people's lives was usually high on the agenda; grandiose special effects were foresworn, and in the realm of pornographic appeal, documentaries made no effort to compete. In short, documentaries now began to stand out in a space of public interest and debate where seriousness was not deemed offensive. So with higher stakes, socially serious black directors began to take on more ambitious projects.

There were other pressures, too. The Reaganite retrenchment in funding for public television drove all directors aiming for PBS toward "classic," high-profile subjects. Specific public television venues set bland, big-picture agendas, entitling their series *Great Americans, Great Performances, American Experience*. Other locations on an expanding cable-television horizon took a similar, mainstream approach. During one week in April 1997, for instance, the *New York Times* television guide selected 38 documentaries for its highlight sidebar, of which 12, slightly less than one-third, were biographies. The one biography of an African American, *A Litany for Survival: The Life and Work of Audre Lorde*, shared billing with genre pieces like *General John J. Pershing* on the History channel and *Annette Funicello* and *John Dillinger: Public Enemy Number 1* on A&E. The non-biographical films highlighted by the *Times* included profiles of sharks and salmon, and much material for war buffs. Black documentarians who might have pointed toward grassroots figures or themes now realized their chances for funding and exhibition would improve if they focused on indisputably great black Americans. The fact that their projects were ambitious did not phase the funders: these directors had attained, after many years of experience, a level of respect that made their proposals credible.

People will ask, "What is black about black documentary?"—as they ask about every creative enterprise launched by African Americans. The question is reasonable but less important than the attention it receives.[1] Sometimes the question is prompted by others: Is there such a thing as blackness as a cultural reality that need preoccupy us? Do we not make a mistake by essentializing blackness? But behind these questions is yet another wishful one: If we pretend to be color-blind long enough, won't blackness just disappear as a problem agitating the body politic? Looking for a particular definition of black documentary many decades after the development of many lines of nonfictional filmmaking is like asking, what new did Jackie Robinson bring to baseball? Didn't he swing a bat made of ash wood, just like all the other players? Didn't he run with two legs and throw with one arm? Was he ever able to convince an umpire to let him have four strikes? Some analysts of the game will insist that Robinson did in fact bring a new style to the game, a new excitement, a new flair, particularly to base-running. But the questioner would sidestep the historical significance of Robinson's introduction to the majors. The search for the distinctively black element in black documentary, in other words, may focus too quickly on style, technique, and manner. And such a focus may reflect (already) a bias toward form in Eurocentric cinema studies. It would be too simple to argue that the substance of these nonfiction films is more important than their form and vice versa.

We should let the original sense of the term *document*, at the heart of "documentary," reverberate in our minds. If a historian discovers important evidence establishing facts and truths about the past, should we inquire about the aesthetic excitement or lack of same in the evidence? Isn't the aestheticizing of documentary a diversion from the original mission of the genre, or one might argue of motion pictures in general, since they were invented with the aim of transmitting business information, and soon thereafter, of educating the public? The significance of black documentaries, including those about the lives of leaders, must be located not within aesthetic discourse but within the critique of discourse and the critique of representation generally. This means that it is not sufficient to study black documentaries alongside "white" and other non–African American documentaries, but within a discursive field that encompasses all forms of information: print biographies, feature films, black commercial and independent cinema, world cinema, as well as the conditions of the movie business.

For these reasons, it makes sense to step around the idea that only documentaries made by blacks constitute "black documentary." Nevertheless, such black-directed works must form the core of any defined group, since they respond most readily to the criterion of appealing to an authenticating community made up of African Americans. To this core, I would add selected white-directed documentaries that settle comfortably in this universe of discourse and work for that authenticating community much like films produced by black filmmakers. I have in mind films like *Jack Johnson* (1970) and *A. Philip Randolph* (1972).

This de-emphasis on the director's identity turns around the strategy sometimes used to define fictional black films, where authorship looms more heavily. I am arguing for a definition rooted in historical discourse, first of all, and secondly in the assumption that in some instances the personality of the biographical subject will outweigh that of the filmmaker. Muhammad Ali, I contend, is the *auteur* of *When We Were Kings* (1997).

The imperative to document black life and culture survived its 1960s and 1970s origins in the efforts of William Greaves, St. Clair Bourne, and

Jackie Shearer, among others, but in later decades acquired new urgency. By 1990, black people were more likely to turn up in mass media as psychotic killers, gang-bangers, welfare cheats, intimidating rappers, oversexed athletes, self-minstrelizing comics, and lethal drug pushers than as responsible citizens, diplomats or busy professionals. Illustrious black figures might easily have appealed to documentarians as an offset to the mass media fascination with black people as social basket cases, once again as PROBLEMS. By looking at the bold and the brilliant, the tough and the leaderly, such films restore agency to the narrative of black life. These figures bring "the good news" about being black. And they model possibility and achievement for communities starved for a good example. But they do more. They personify for the fascinated viewer an intimate acquaintance with vital passages of American history that might otherwise have been zapped from the television screen.

All important black expression carries the burden of changing the world's mind, upending received wisdom, reformulating knowledge— not only a body of material, but the very categories through which we know or don't know. There is an imperative to represent the nature of black existence with a new, free-standing urgency and vitality. The most valid forms of expression will burn and erase synapses clogged with stereotypical thinking, sclerotic Occidentalisms, and backward social mythologies, even while they are being replaced with beings unanticipated by the conventional spectator's consciousness. This is a value that biographical films can carry beyond the impress of social-problem or cultural-celebration documentaries.

One biographical film, made some decades ago, in which these fundamental issues reverberate and solutions emerge is *Paul Robeson: The Tallest Tree in Our Forest* (1977). Robeson's life, like Martin Luther King's, Malcolm X's, and W. E. B. Du Bois's, has been presented nonfictionally in multiple works. But this one, written and directed by Gil Noble, is the longest, best-informed and most authoritative. Robeson's life resonates interestingly on the question that Du Bois articulated, the issue of being equated with a PROBLEM. Some black people have responded to this equation by trying to be exemplary instead. This has doubtless led to a good deal of stiff-backed pomposity. But another effect has been the ontological challenge of locating a balanced black personality, undistorted either by racism or by the vain need to be above racism. The confirming being-in-the-world of blacks, refuting notions of dehumanization as well as of successful inferiorization, has been manifested in black cultural expression. But Robeson's career, well demonstrated in

Noble's film biography, absorbed the challenge of representing blacks through cultural production and at the same time lifted that level of representation to the political sphere.

Robeson was our first great stage performer who was at the same time a major political advocate. The undercurrent of minstrelsy in black entertainment was interrupted during Robeson's time and career. Curiously, Gertrude Stein, after meeting Robeson, pontificated that "the Negro suffers from nothingness." The remark at least can boast of eccentric originality when faced with this Princetonian valedictorian, All-American football player, and versatile athlete, lawyer, great singer, dominating stage actor, and incandescent screen persona, who was on his way toward learning more than twenty languages. One suspects that Stein misinterpreted the roundness of Robeson's personality, his amplitude and regal serenity, as lacking the edge and idiosyncrasy that Europeans often confuse with psychological depth. Robeson's ideological positioning has much to teach us today for its extraordinary balance between his humanism, embracing a global, racial, and ethnic inclusiveness on the one hand, and his persistent affirmation of respect and personal solidarity with all African cultures. In an era that can only see enforced, ersatz racial "color-blindness" as a solution to racial discord, Robeson's alternative example is of increased value. More aptly than Stein, one commentator in the Noble documentary views Robeson as an example for humanity, a model of what it might better become.

Like most of these rebels, thinkers, leaders, and heroes, Robeson was ahead of his time. Like them, he challenged his survivors, including documentarians and other cultural workers, to catch up with him. *The Tallest Tree in Our Forest* ends with a quote from Othello with which Robeson liked to sum up his own situation. "Speak of me as I am. Nothing extenuate. Nor set down aught in malice. Then must you speak of one that loved full wisely but too well." (As was his practice, Robeson has changed the wording of the original, that reads "not wisely.")

But Robeson's memory has perhaps been too jealously guarded by his survivors, who insist on extenuation. As the shelf of heroic documentaries becomes full, succeeding generations will be moved to reinterpret the past from their own sense of need, and that should allow more nuanced perspectives on great individuals. The Gil Noble documentary deals with Robeson's marriage to Eslanda Cardoza Goode with coy silence, spending about three minutes on photos of the couple accompanied by romantic music, but nary a word from her or about her feelings, her interactions with Robeson, or the sometimes tempestuous relations between them. There are also, for instance, stories and essays inside the Robeson iconography waiting to get out. One of these is the struggle within Robeson's performative personas to represent blackness vividly and with dignity, since he was sometimes drawn toward over-the-top impersonations of colorful blackness schooled in the theater of white amusement. This is of course a theme that extends beyond Robeson to ambiguous representations by others, such as Oscar Micheaux, Louis Armstrong, or Miles Davis. But this theme needs to be addressed, perhaps with Robeson in the foreground and these others providing contextualization, or vice versa.

Gil Noble is responsible for another important film about a leader of the Black Enlightenment, *Dr. Martin Luther King, Jr.: An Amazing Grace* (1978). Before the examination of black documentary is finished, a close look at this film is called for. This is not the most polished filmwork imaginable. But it works almost because of a certain practicality that goes beneath the artfulness of the documentarian working as a well-paid professional for an institution demanding broadcast quality and other straitjacketing requirements.

Noble's treatment of high points in King's career was made as a special presentation for his weekly television show, *Like It Is*, and as such may be thought of as an inheritor of the impetus of *Black Journal*. But with assists from Robert Van Lierop and Susan Robeson, among others, Noble achieves a crafty synthesis. The genius of this film is its simplicity. It makes no claim to cover the life and/or significance of Martin Luther King, nor to assess the civil rights movement. Instead, what it presents is a close-up of the man in action, or more precisely, in speech. It opens with King making a speech in which he reviews some of the crucial moments of the anti-segregation movement, with cutaways to those events, and to his part in them. After a slight introduction from Gil Noble on camera, there is no narration. But this is no affectation, since King's own eloquence replaces any need for narrative account. Jesse Jackson's brief commentary is the only interview I remember.

Maybe lack of funds explains the absence of a battery of talking heads delivering their summations, but such a handicap would turn out to be good fortune. Without the usual documentary dressings, we get a very close self-portrait of the man and his struggle, including most of his famous speeches. The viewer probably knows the rudiments of the history King is representing, which is easily dispensed with in favor of the immediacy of the man. The personhood of King comes through keenly, the inter-subjectivity that is rare in black representation, the sense of something personal and intimate being at stake. One might call it the existential King: Martin Luther King as lived experience. Getting to know him more intimately, we feel his death and loss more personally. His demise is announced quietly with the familiar tableau of his lieutenants on the balcony of the motel, their arms aiming at the point from which the fatal shot came.

II

The range of biographical documentaries appearing at the close of this century invites a long glance backward. The lights by which people of African descent live now were nearly dimmed a century ago. Then, at the dawn of the cinematic era, the blighted scene of black American existence went through a time that came to be called "the nadir," easily translated as "the pits." In popular caricature and minstrelization, as well as in serious Euro-American scholarship, the image of black people was routinely framed in scorn, ridicule, and contempt.

At the same time, there were countervailing assertions from black and white individuals, and from some institutions, of the humanity and dignity, and even the originality and genius, of black people. The young black intellectual W. E. B. Du Bois struggled to give definition to the obscure self-consciousness of his world in his pathbreaking book *The Souls of Black Folk* (1903). With such beginnings, the twentieth century has been a period of enlightenment. This social and intellectual transformation differs mightily from the European enlightenment of the eighteenth century, sometimes as a counter movement to its rationalizations of slavery and European imperialism. Through the most tortuous process, black people accumulated the knowledge and experience by which they could find their way into an upright posture to face the future.

This enlightenment was by no means a single-tribe event. It was part of a world-wide arousal among non-European people, signaled variously by the victory of the Ethiopians over an Italian army at the Battle of Adowa in 1896 and by the victory of the Japanese over the Russians in 1905. A significant moment in this growing self-awareness among people of African descent was the Pan-African Congress of 1900 in London. This was also a time of modernization movements around the world modeled on the Western example, but destined to confront Western domination within new competition and challenges. The many political, military, and cultural revolutions among people of color through the century have virtually ended colonialism and apartheid and made racism transparent as a socio-pathological affliction.

This counter-enlightenment has the historical role of amending the tribalistic limitations of the Euro-enlightenment of the eighteenth century. To speak of a "second enlightenment" is misleading, for that leads to the false notion that the Western movement of ideas that takes that name was the first and only one in history, when in fact such breakthroughs of clarity in the effort to reach a higher human consciousness have occurred many times over, in ancient Egypt, China, India, West Africa. The failure to account for these dynamic accelerations of human thought is only one more instance of the narcissism of Western knowledge—which makes a counter-enlightenment necessary. But only bigots of the classical Western canon of knowledge deny that the most significant *aufklarung* in this century's social knowledge has been made in redress and often at the expense of the chauvinistic wisdom of the monopolistic Occidental academy, mainly by non-Western intellectuals and cultural activists.

The trail of this counter-enlightenment can be tracked by the footsteps of several luminous personalities. The scope and ambition of some of the films that recount their lives suggest a growing confidence among black independents to handle larger themes and more historically imposing figures. Many black Hollywood storytellers who deal in fiction and drama dream of projecting the lives of Pushkin or Toussaint L'Ouverture. For documentary film directors, finishing mammoth projects on W. E. B. Du Bois and Aimé Césaire are comparable dreams—dreams that, fortunately, Louis Massiah and Euzhan Palcy have realized. These are joined by recent bio-docs on Richard Wright, John Henrik Clarke, Audre Lorde, Frantz Fanon, Oscar Micheaux, Patrice Lumumba, Malcolm X, and A. Philip Randolph. To these might be added slightly older films on Paul Robeson, Booker T. Washington, Lorraine Hansberry, Alice Walker, James Baldwin, Ella Baker, Leon Damas, Langston Hughes, Thelonious Monk, Amiri Baraka, Billie Holiday, James Van Der Zee, Marcus Garvey, Jack Johnson, and Madame C. J. Walker. (William Greaves is at work on a film biography of Ralph Bunche.)

The democratic impulses of most of these individuals place them in opposition to cults of personality or the great-man-on-horseback theory of history. Nevertheless, the unfolding of the black world enlightenment, like any enlightenment, has been mobilized by the work and personal force of many extraordinary individuals. There has certainly been a crucial groundswell of struggle among everyday African people demanding historical change over this period, but the transformations of consciousness could not have taken place without the agitations and articulations of knowledgeable and insightful individuals who gathered and circulated information about resistance against oppression in other parts of the black world, concretized issues of resistance and arguments against inferiorization, and devised original and often brilliant re-interpretations of historical experiences and social change strategies. The essential contribution of these major illuminators is underscored by the persistence with which dominant world power has assassinated, framed, jailed, defamed and/or exiled them, usually in the obscurantist interest of white supremacy.

The illuminating path of one such personality is followed in Louis Massiah's *W. E. B. Du Bois: A Biography in Four Voices* (1995). The spiritual reawakening that pulsed through the world of African people from Johannesburg to Houston in the 1890s, coming after the darkness of slavery and in the teeth of colonialism also animated a representative figure of this new black consciousness. W. E. B. Du Bois persistently sliced a path for others to follow as historical scholar, pioneering sociologist, political activist and one of the founders of the NAACP, editor of *Crisis* magazine, poet, novelist, champion of Pan-Africanism. In his pivotal book *The Souls of Black Folk* (1903), Du Bois laid the foundation for an Afro-modern grasp of history, culture, and spirituality. From that point on, as this grand documentary portrait establishes, Du Bois stood at the intersection of black people's struggles and the shifting tides of the century.

Virtually every African American artist and intellectual is indebted to the example presented by Du Bois. Fittingly, this documentary portrait is told from the point of view of four literary heirs to the DuBoisean tradition, three novelists, and one poet/activist. Together, they narrate and observe the century of Du Bois's effort to master his times in the interest of a more civilized world. Formally, the strengths of this portrait are located in its book-like approach to its subject. Each of the four "readers" of Du Bois's life narrates a chapter in a chronological sequence that shows overlaps between Du Bois's life and the history of his times. The film segments flow like chapters: Part One: *Black Folk in the New Century* (1895–1915), narrated by Wesley Brown; Part Two: *The Crisis and the New Negro* (1919–1929), narrated by Thulani Davis; Part Three: *A Second Reconstruction?* (1934–1948), told by Toni Cade Bambara; and Part Four: *Color & Democracy: Colonies and Peace* (1949–1963), told by Amiri Baraka.

The book-like organization of this film succeeds because the central strand of Du Bois's life—struggle for democracy—threaded through so many permutations holds the story together. Were one to want to portray the grandeur of the black American twentieth century, exalting its struggle to the level of nobility and high dedication, this film about Du Bois might support that desire. It is so capacious with information, perspectives, crises, radical departures, and resourceful solutions that one needs to return to turn its "pages" repeatedly. It is in many ways the

Still from William Greaves's
Ida B. Wells: A Passion For Justice.
Courtesy of the Department
of Special Collections, the
University of Chicago Library.

most complex, politically reflective film in this tradition—a classic of filmic Africana.

Louis Massiah's portrait of Du Bois could be indebted to William Greaves's *Ida B. Wells: A Passion for Justice* (1989). Ida B. Wells was one of the great "muckraking" journalists of the turn of the century, although her name is seldom mentioned with those of Upton Sinclair, Jacob Riis, or Jack London. Born into slavery in Holly Springs, Mississippi, Ida B. Wells was also a newspaper editor, social activist, and suffragist. She was also the indefatigable chronicler and denouncer of the national evil of race lynching, unmatched in her leadership in the crusade against these atrocities of an apartheid era. It is said that by the end of the nineteenth century, her stature among black people was equal to that of Booker T. Washington and W. E. B. Du Bois.

In watching this film, the difference between biographical documentaries about the living and the dead becomes apparent, almost to the point of defining the two as different genres. The first loss is the ability to put the subject on camera, to speak for self in the context of the film.

In the case of Wells, who died in 1931, there are apparently few surviving contemporaries whose interviews might inform her career. But even in the mode of the archival film, which such a post-mortem recollection must become, whatever materials survived Wells must have been skimpy. To overcome these limitations, Greaves had Toni Morrison read from Wells's autobiographical works, on and off camera, and used Al Freeman (the accomplished actor who played Elijah Muhammad in Spike Lee's *Malcolm X*) as narrator. In this way he brought uncommon voices to the film, and in the case of Morrison, a personality comparable in stature and commitment to Wells herself.

Toni Morrison *(left)* and William Greaves on
the set of *Ida B. Wells: A Passion for Justice*.
Photo courtesy of William Greaves Productions.

Understand, we are talking about one of the leading American women activists of her time, and clearly one of the outstanding black radicals of her era. Yet because she was a woman, full appreciation of the scope of her work and the force of her personality continues to elude mass recognition. The film does not manage to overcome a burden of disbelief imposed on such a woman, that she might naturally, and not as a freak, confront all the orders of her society—political, moral, administrative—with the gusto, spice, and steely determination of the classical hero, as opposed to remaining in the kitchen, or the garden—in her place. But the way Wells's gender impedes biographical felicity is a problem that extends to most female figures of significance, black or white, at the hands of male or female biographers and filmmakers.

Ultimately, this "lack" is a product of imperial, patriarchal knowledge, which wants to place non-whites and women in the role of expendable, bit players. The representation of all women suffers from a kind of duplexing. The level of significance granted to their lives and activities remains in a downstairs mode, framed in what can be called the little context. By contrast the affairs of men receive treatment within the big context, as an upstairs forum. The little context includes child-rearing, marriage, maintenance of community rituals, and children's education. The big context involves history, knowledge, and the governance of society. Remarkable women shuttle between the two frames of reference, and are treated consequently as not true insiders of the big picture. The level of value given to the lives they live and the world they influence is "petite," minority. There are many issues to be pursued around this kind of discrimination. One is the exclusion of women from the big picture, for many more need to be acknowledged there. Another issue is the reordered valuation of the "little" context.[2] The global neo-enlightenment to which black artists, heroes, rebels, and thinkers contribute has yet to find ways to overcome this dilution of unprivileged historical presences.

Among the falling stars who seem to pass before the world's eyes and disappear before being fully recognized are extraordinary black women like Wells. Fortunately, two of these figures have been given visual texture in documentary films—*Fundi: The Story of Ella Baker* (1981) and *Two Dollars and a Dream: Madame C. J. Walker* (1988). *Fundi*, the Swahili word for "teacher," applies roundly to Ella Baker. "Without Ella Baker there would be no Student Nonviolent Coordinating Committee," argued James Forman, the executive secretary of the risk-taking civil rights organization. Ella Baker was the inspirational, educational, and executive agent-of-the-moment for the pivotal organizations of the movement to end segregation in the United States during the 1960s. As in so many movements to advance the position of black Americans, it was black women like Ella Baker who tended to the details in the Southern Christian Leadership Conference, in the background behind better known personalities like Martin Luther King. Among her contributions is advancing the concept of the "invisible organizer," the

Still from Joanne Grant's *Fundi: The Story of Ella Baker*. First Run Features, 153 Waverly Place, NY, NY 10003. Southern Conference Educational Fund Photo.

facilitator who helps a community define their problems and find their own solutions for themselves. This analytical study, directed by Joanne Grant, also airs dissents and conflicts within the civil rights movement. Despite these tensions, the contribution of Ella Baker to what may be the most heroic moment in the nation's history since World War II stands out clearly. Until fuller explorations are made, her story forms a token of the crucial and overlooked contributions of black women to black liberation in every phase of enlightenment.

Madame C. J. Walker's is a different kind of story, highlighting another type of leadership. Stanley Nelson brings this almost legendary entrepreneur out of historical shadows. A poor child, Walker fulfilled her dream of revolutionizing beauty concepts and treatments for African American women, and in the process became the first self-made woman millionaire in American history.

But a question can be raised about all three of these films: do they surrender too easily to the limitations of their form? For *Ida B. Wells* falls short of its potential, despite the fine array of talent involved, including the direction of William Greaves, the most prolific and honored black documentarian perhaps of all time. Freeman's narration and Morrison's readings impose a distant respectability that becomes an anodyne to the feelings the real Ida B. must have aroused. The elements of her story are exciting enough. But as rendered here, the feeling is one of polite deference. Wells becomes a laminated icon, a talisman to be caressed for good luck in contemporary times. Such memorializing biographies of great leaders condescend by suggesting that we have nothing to learn from them except as pious examples.

The costliest loss is one of perspective. In these films it is dutifully expected that the figure will be located within a historical framework. In this particular kind of PBS format (the film was made for the *American Experience* series), the formula calls for stock and archival footage to be laid in among the few photos of the principal subject with appropriate historical contextualizing, sometimes from an on-camera historian—in this case, the estimable Paula Giddings, among others. But the appeal to journalistic even-handedness puts the commentators under wraps. The fairness doctrine of the recent decades, proffering equal time to all political candidates, has bled its influence into PBS documentaries. The demands of this genre are also heavily influenced by the need to shield the defensive sensibilities of white viewers, the majority public whose response can make or break a successful public television reception, and perhaps also call down the wrath of right-wing congressmen.

The subtle censorship effected by the PBS system constrains the films' possibilities. Its energies become constricted. The introduction of historical footage and commentary easily falls into a predictable rhythm, sometimes turning that material into perfunctory illustration. It serves as educational framing, a setting for the triumphs of the hero of the moment. What is needed is analysis and wider vision than is commonly available. In the case of Ida B. Wells this historical treatment stays close to the biographical vest. The well-informed viewer knows that Wells was a vital part of the Afro-enlightenment, but the film does not add to or deepen that knowledge. The anecdotes that demonstrate her courage and wit are neither thematized nor historicized beyond the reach of the comfortable frame of reference of the majority white television viewer.

Such constraints are not limited to biographical films about women, as we can see in looking at *Malcolm X: Make It Plain*, the Blackside feature-length documentary. Under the leadership of Henry Hampton until his death in 1998, Blackside Inc. credibly lays claim to the most singular triumph in black documentary, perhaps in all of black independent film-making,—the two *Eyes on the Prize* series. The tight, jour-

Malcolm X *(left)* and Muhammad Ali outside the
Trans-Lux Newsreel Theatre, March 1, 1964, after a
screening of films on Ali's title fight with Sonny Liston.
AP/WIDE WORLD

nalistic-objective, anecdotal approach works wonderfully in the *Eyes* series, for several reasons. The talking heads are mostly eyewitnesses to the marvelous stories they tell, not historians reciting rehearsed lines. The stories are incredible yet drenched in still-vivid detail. The narrative flow rises unbroken to pulsing climaxes. The *Eyes* films are in fact suspenseful action documentaries, and squeeze the emotional potential out of their subject and their construction. And the solicitude for white audience, the consideration for their need to be enlightened, is well-placed.

But Blackside's *Malcolm X*, like *Ida B. Wells*, flattens its subjects within an admiring neutrality. What Malcolm X meant to America and the world is more tellingly embodied in some of the many shorter documentaries made over the years, including *Malcolm X: Struggle for Freedom; Malcolm X: Nationalist or Humanist*, directed by Madeline Anderson for *Black Journal;* or even the Malcolm X episode in *Eyes on the Prize.* For all the criticisms leveled at Spike Lee's bio-pic, the notion that the much-awaited Blackside feature would clinch the superior value of documentary over Hollywood or black Hollywood was squelched on its appearance. If PBS gatekeepers had been holding their breath for fear that the Blackside documentary might arouse passions and high-placed criticisms, they might have sighed comfortably when the film was finally and uneventfully aired on television.

On serious reconsideration, comparing fictional features with documentaries may not always be meaningful. There maybe more value in comparing documentaries made under more independent circumstances with those made under state sponsorship, or with others made during different historical and political climates. Some of William Greaves's most powerful nonfictional films, such as *From These Roots* (1974), *Still a Brother* (1968), and *Nation Time* (1973), were made closer to the liberationist impulse of the 1960s and 1970s, at a time when the influence of PBS funding was less cautionary. (Greaves's work in progress on Ralph Bunche, parts of which I have previewed, promises to be a major contribution to the canon of enlightenment nonfictional films.)

The tender sensitivities that these semi-official gatekeepers take pains to protect have been summed up by a hip hop generation in the tee shirt logo, "Fear of a Black Planet." But the black world enlightenment would have been better served had the film let Malcolm be Malcolm. Malcolm's dramatic intervention into history would probably come over more powerfully through an uninterrupted one-hour compilation from his speeches and newsreels. Similarly, the wider meaning of Ida B. Wells and her life might have been better served had Toni Morrison been let loose to comment freely and analyze her significance, rather than held down to the role of Sunday School reader of text. (There are some marvelous moments in *Ida B. Wells* where Morrison, in her on-screen readings, projects her own celebratory enthusiasm for Wells and her exploits.)

The limitations I speak of come mainly through this concern for white audience and its sensitivities. This is all the more problematic, since for public television it is a narrower commodity than white audience for Hollywood or theatrical cinema—more upscale and institutionally oriented, more political and politically influential, and apparently more worrisome in the minds of film producers. The tone and tenor of most documentaries is heavily influenced by their sponsors, the people who pay the piper or greenlight the project. The motives of these sponsors is inevitably ideological in the widest sense: they hope to influence how people think. A documentary's intellectual influence can easily be more intense than that of a fictional film. Because the argument of the box office can overrule ideological considerations, a bio-pic like Lee's *Malcolm X* or a historical movie like John Singleton's *Rosewood* can be more daring and infectious than a PBS boilerplate documentary on black leaders, through their effective use of narrative to achieve historical vision, and most of all, through their enlistment of passion and committed storytelling. Fiction films have the advantages of emotion dramatized. Documentaries should not be satisfied with show-and-tell animated slide shows, but should give us some of the rhetorical distillation and analytical complexity that is beyond the fictional movie.

These limitations on state-sponsored documentaries are not explained away by the fact that the subject of a nonfiction film may be dead and the charisma of her presence on screen no longer available. By comparison, some powerful resonances arise from African and diasporan black documentaries made under similar circumstances. Raoul Peck's *Lumumba: Death of a Prophet*, while not successful on all counts, brings passion, pain and poetry to the evocation of a lost leader, even though the film crew was stopped from visiting the Congo.

Manthia Diawara has distinguished between those black biographical documentaries that manifest inter-subjective qualities like passion, intimacy, poetry, and those that assume an historical-objective posture. One might contrast in this way Euzhan Palcy's *Aimé Césaire: A Voice for History* (1994) with *W. E. B. Du Bois: A Biography in Four Voices* (1996). Significant nonfictional films from outside the U.S. take more regular advantage of the affective dimensions of cinema, as witnessed by *Afrique, Je Te Plumerai* (1992) by Jean-Marie Teno of Cameroon, *Allah Tantou* (1991) by David Achkar of Guinea, or more dramatically by black British documentarians such as John Akomfrah, Maureen Blackwood, Menelik Shabazz, and Isaac Julien. Wherever one finds nonfiction films that are memorable for their passion or unique vision, the enabling circumstance is usually a *filmmaker* who has been funded and given artistic license, rather than the subject and its timeliness or topical interest. (The excesses that can emerge from this more subjective license are exhibited in Julien's *Frantz Fanon: Black Skin, White Mask* [1995], whose narrative line is sometimes hijacked toward the gender and racial definition of Julien's amorous ideals.)

This is not meant to divert appreciation from solid historical reference works like *Ida B. Wells* or *Malcolm X: Make it Plain* (1995). The notion that committed, risk-taking, passionate documentaries cannot be found among American and black American documentaries is misleading. Examples abound, such as William Cayton's *Jack Johnson (1970)*, William Greaves's *Symbiopsychotaxiplasm: Take One* (1971), St. Clair Bourne's

In Motion: Amiri Baraka (1982), Haile Gerima's *The Wilmington 10–USA 10,000* (1978), Marlon Riggs's *Tongues Untied* (1989), Portia Cobb's *No Justice, No Peace!* (1994), and the works of Camille Billops, Tony Cokes, and many others. Nor are such questions useful mainly as issues of art or aesthetics. Passion, intensity, analytical commitment, and historical coloration become desiderata only as means to a higher end than aesthetic appreciation.

The question is, how do these films and their strategies advance the enlightenment brightened by these historical figures? Are the films able to stand profitably outside the notoriously cramped cognitive range of white audience reference—in a space where these personalities are fully at home. If they had not been able to bring a new perspective to the possibilities of their times instead of rehearsing the official story, we would not now find them compelling personalities. So it should not be too much to ask of films made about them that they do not rope them back inside conventional, mundane perspective.

This imperative gains force from a look at St. Clair Bourne's *John Henrik Clarke: A Great and Mighty Walk*. Clarke was an artist (short story writer), rebel, hero, and thinker, but on a less momentous scale than Malcolm X, whom he knew and exchanged ideas with, or King, Du Bois, Wells, Robeson, and others whom he wrote about as a radical historian. The aged and blind Clarke sits and talks throughout most of the film, supported by historical and stock footage. Clarke emerged as a king among Harlem "street historians," self-taught and partisan in his proselytizing for a redemptive interpretation of the black and African past. Interestingly, either through the passage of time or the mellowing of his views, his freely voiced opinions carry little of the quasi-occult enthusiasm into which this school of Afro-nationalist history can easily lapse. But what distinguishes Clarke as a historian is not innovative methodology, unparalleled research, the eloquence of his writing, or the depth of his insight. Clarke is remarkable for the range and intensity he brings to recovering the broad sweep of the whole of the African and Afro-diasporic past, from ancient times to the present.

A Great and Mighty Walk has its share of storytelling felicities, some fine anecdotes from Clarke, magnificent footage, some up-tempo editing in the vein of MTV, and smart organization of materials. But what makes it a modest revelation is the uncensored bite of Clarke's opinions and the élan with which he distributes them. As a historical expert in the typical PBS documentary about black Americans, Clarke's contributions would likely end up on the cutting room floor. Only Carlton Moss comes close to Clarke's political candor. Clarke bypasses the role of impartial commentator for the duty of the griot, the keeper of a people's collective memory. It is his fervent, prophetic commitment that lets us turn from this film to other documentaries where concern for the tastes of white audience is more delicately served and see what is missing. I have mentioned the value a film might have with Malcolm X's words and images presented without a narrator's interpretation. Such a scenario, amplified by supporting footage, is close to what you get in John Henrik Clarke.

The Clarke film helps sharpen the notion of "independence." There are several varieties of independence associated with American cinema, each connected to a particular "mode of production" and each one defined by particular predications, whether the desire to project erotic, artistic, political, socially subversive, or avant-garde images that the major production houses of Hollywood will not support. In the case of black cinema, fictional or documentary, independence necessarily involves the expression of themes and attitudes that would otherwise remain repressed in a culture where the views of the black minority, particularly those that smack of self-determination, are heavily filtered or blocked. *A Great and Mighty Walk* stands out as a film that PBS would not have likely funded. (I doubt if any but a few at PBS would have known who Clarke was.) Its more potent independence of mind owes much to its independent financing by movie star Wesley Snipes, its executive producer. St. Clair Bourne's film on Clarke is independent in the field of black documentary in much the same way that Gerima's *Sankofa* is an independent black feature movie, not beholden to the usual institutional gatekeepers and therefore able to say whatever is on its mind.

These qualities of independence do not rely on black direction. The very bracing *Jack Johnson*, directed by William Cayton, scores time and again with powerful imagery, striking archival footage, a gutsy narration by Brock Peters, and a crackling, high-energy sound track by Miles Davis. It is not just boxing that links this film with *When We Were Kings* (1997), the saga of Muhammad Ali and George Foreman fighting in what was then Zaire. Both films triumph by unleashing the stinging verbal jabs and high jinks of their irrepressible central figures. What is also impressive about *Jack Johnson* is the way the film achieves intersubjectivity, the sense that the subject of the film is present in his pulsing, sweating, exigent humanity. In contrast with Brock Peters's almost over-the-top vocalization of Johnson's words, the standardized, "broadcast voice" narration of the prototypical PBS documentary "libraries" its subjects. One film carries on an oral tradition with the twang of the field and the funk of the street; the other is a bookish memorialization, elevating the subject to a safe, approvable distance, where the audience is put on notice that this black person was someone to respect. PBS documentary style imposed on black subjects comes across like the Negro spirituals sung after getting a college education and classical training.

The lost possibilities of deeper analysis can be illustrated once again through the Ida B. Wells documentary. Wells boldly protested against the virtual exclusion of black people from the World Columbian Exposition in Chicago in 1893. But this protest falls within a context that deserves more attention than it gets. Around the turn of the century, large-scale international expositions and congresses were vehicles for the further diminishment or reconstitution of the black popular image. Wells's protest of the Chicago Exposition was one significant moment in an ongoing set of shifting, contradictory initiatives. In an era when minstrel-coon imagery of blacks was rife, there were also other contesting representations and efforts, such as the Pan-African Congress in London in 1900, in which Wells was very much interested. In the same year, the Exposition Universelle in Paris mounted an impressive "American Negro Exhibit." How were these events influenced by Wells's protest activities, or reflective of the struggle for enlightenment that she and thousands of other educated black people around the world were waging? Wells's activities need to be put in a context at least this embracing, before they can provoke the analytical energy that would offer a significant reward.

Some responsibility for this analytic energy, or its lack, must fall on black independent documentarians. The PBS type of nonfiction film tends to recruit historians as experts after the film's design is complete, to illustrate a point that the film is already committed to making. The reason often given for the late, limited use of historians is stylistic: the need to diversify the sources of verbal information, avoiding overuse of off-screen narrators. This kind of consideration often takes precedence over the goal of making an original and provocative contribution to knowledge. The historian becomes a substitute narrator, not a source of thought and interpretation. Filmmakers often seem to regard "too much" thought and interpretation as barriers to getting the film made.

One notable exception is the "school" that Blackside holds before producing a major documentary series—an intensive series of panels and discussions lasting three or more days, during which a wide variety of respected thinkers, artists, and scholars address key themes. More often, historians' knowledge is badly or insufficiently used. In the genre of biographical documentary that wins support from the National Endowment for the Humanities, National Endowment for the Arts, and PBS, a historian is asked to recite an anecdote showing that our hero acted bravely, and is then whisked off-screen until another anecdote is needed. The allusion to Sunday school accurately conveys both the emphasis on simplified moral lessons typical of this approach, and the satisfaction with a juvenile level of audience response.

The documentary format theoretically allows a rich, original treatment of an historical subject. Scholars and other interested persons can turn up again and again, providing perceptions and insights that are not available elsewhere. Too often, however, the filmmaker is satisfied with a video re-enactment of some of the better-known moments of the subject's biography, abbreviating and reducing, rather than augmenting, what is known. The films that transcend these limitations often do so because their subjects have spoken with such irrepressible energy in the past that the filmmaker can hardly contain their analytical drive, or because the filmmaker has the courage to let the subject have his or her say. This happens in *When We Were Kings:* Muhammad Ali mesmerizes the camera while riffing crisp apothegms of black consciousness; that film also gives voice to risk-taking interpreters, like Norman Mailer and his quirky, dubious propositions.

In a future, less-repressed era of documentary filmmaking, historians, film historians, and film directors will take another lesson from Robeson, repudiating the curious and debilitating separation between culture and politics in the interpretation of history. Black historical documentaries have sometimes missed great opportunities by restricting their commentators to sound but cautious academicians, neglecting the many wonderful black students of culture—intellects who are astute interpreters of black history and experienced performers when faced with a camera. Orlando Bagwell's decision to include Bernice Johnson Reagon in *New Worlds, New Forms* helps explain the flair and dramatic energy that characterize this enriching documentary on black dance but so often elude other documentaries on black culture. Other examples include the incisive cultural and historical interpretations made by novelist Toni Cade Bambara in *Midnight Ramble,* the documentary about Oscar Micheaux and the early race movie industry, and the poetry and verve of Harry Belafonte's on-screen commentaries in *Paul Robeson: The Tallest Tree in Our Forest.*

III

I return to the pivotal question: how do these films and strategies advance the enlightenment that these great historical figures helped to shape? How can we find a ground-zero position from which their relative contributions can be assessed? I propose to locate that ground zero in the situation of the DuBoisean center—the hypothetical space occupied by the dominant sector of African American social-political consciousness.

The DuBoiseans are not all of the same political convictions; that is, they are not equally anti-establishment, left, or movement-oriented. This breadth of perspectives was also a feature of Du Bois's many incarnations, as early socialist, modified nationalist, social democrat, and member of the Communist Party. What the DuBoisean center shares today are some persisting features like belief in rational inquiry and analysis addressing social problems; the conviction that movement politics are important for advancing black American development; the need for continuing education of both black and white Americans about the inequities and oppression of the current state of the nation; a self-determining posture, short of separatism, in relation to American hegemony; a commitment to revising historical distortions of the black past; an internationalism that challenges American exceptionalism; and for most DuBoiseans, an involvement with Africa and the Diaspora through a rational, sometimes spiritual pan-Africanism.

We can further identify the DuBoisean element through historical positioning. Contemporary DuBoiseans are heirs to the intellectuals and activists who resisted Booker T. Washington and his advocacy of accommodationism, patient assimilationism, and the smothering of black militancy. Du Bois's other great personal ideological struggle was with Marcus Garvey, but we must remember Du Bois's realization in later years that he and Garvey were closer than he understood at the time. Nevertheless, DuBoiseans today maintain a distance from that legacy of Garveyism that evolved into the apocalyptic separatism of Louis Farrakhan and the Nation of Islam. It bears repeating that this configuration does not reflect rigidly disciplined allegiances. Many DuBoiseans find common ground with both of these alternative positions, with the self-help ideals of both Washington and Elijah Muhammad, and with pragmatic elements in both these camps.

The center occupied by DuBoisean thought and example is made up of varied roles and practices. One core group of DuBoiseans is black academics, whose social value is best seen in this context. Apart from their role in inflecting public policy through institutional planning and legislative politics, they also play the role of historical timekeepers for the contemporary moment. They have a lot to say about whether the black population is going to accept an argument that a development is good or bad. Over the last half-century, black academics have predominantly followed DuBoisean models, awakened to that example by the civil rights and black power eras; recently, we are also seeing a growing black academic neo-conservatism informed by the thinking of Booker T. Washington. While not as influential among the black population, these neo-conservative academics achieve high-profile visibility and éclat in white American institutions that fear surrendering group power to blacks.

How do these historical movements and influences relate to black documentary? In its embrace of the notion that black people in America deserve a better destiny than becoming interchangeable with white Americans, the DuBoisean center is consistent with an independent black cinema. It recognizes that the triumph of black documentary is the construction of a canon of filmic literature that forms the nucleus of a viable black history on screen. The viewer who observes this body of films carefully would have the beginnings of a fundamental education about black public life in the twentieth century. The DuBoisean center has helped to create a demand for this kind of liberating knowledge, as well as a supply—by creating a context in which the filmmakers' consciousness and commitment could develop.

What happens next? The further fulfillment of this consciousness rests in the hands of the DuBoisean core, but today its perspective is showing signs of confusion, enervation, and possible exhaustion. A continuing backlash against the struggles of the 1960s has slowed its forward thrust. In the 1990s, it has been gagged and muffled, if not silenced, by a powerful white American consensus against any forms of black solidarity. Its adherents continue to work toward their historical goals, but their efforts are repressed or ignored. They are framed in the media as historically backward-looking; or placed in the shadows of Louis Farrakhan's Islamic fundamentalist nationalism; or cited as negative examples in contrast to the assimilationist appeals of Henry Louis Gates, Anthony Appiah, Albert Murray, Stanley Crouch, or outright black conservatives. Considering the eager support lavished on its ideological adversaries like Clarence Thomas, perhaps DuBoisean ideology has done well simply to march in place. But this relative stagnation may prove to be a missed opportunity of costly historical significance.

In this socio-political environment, black documentarians focusing on the biographies of great leaders deserve respect for getting very timely films completed. The value of these films is even greater when seen as buttresses against the tide pulling for the erasure of black identity. As South African writer Don Mattera says, "We must fight against this thing that tells us we should forget."

At the same time, as a group, black documentarians—most of whom are of various DuBoisean persuasions—have not always escaped the muting that has been imposed on liberative American thought. This muting reflects the damaging interference of the system in which they work. We can see in several of their works the "PBS-ification" of black representation. The imperative of the black world enlightenment that they serve demands that they continue to resist this stranglehold on expression. They must find better ways, while working within that system, to assert that concern about expanding the knowledge base of white audiences does not require acceptance of simple-minded ideology of racial assimilation. They must continue to assault banal arguments that rest on a Disneyland notion of color-blindness. They must fend off the continual appeal from PBS-type gatekeepers to turn every black film into an exercise for juveniles. And finally, they must overcome the institutionalized white liberal dogma that all racial problems in America can be erased through more "education" for black people.

We are approaching a point of assessment from which new beginnings can be anticipated and gauged. We are running out of top ten black leaders for first-time nonfiction treatment. It may also be time to assemble a scholarly racial memory about what has been done and to appreciate what needs to be done next. Now that over two decades have passed since the making of *Paul Robeson: The Tallest Tree in Our Forest*, we can anticipate that each generation will have to reinterpret its heroic past for itself. We can hope that the next cycle of films on major figures will not need to repeat the same homilies. Now that the Afro-heroic pantheon is nearly complete, it may be time for more specific, searching inquiries.

Realistic interpretation of black leadership in nonfiction films must incorporate some of the darker sides of their experience, providing the chiaroscuro that sharpens the representation of that experience. Black world enlightenment cannot be kept running on a strict diet of disarming sweetness and light. For the Euro-enlightenment of the eighteenth century, the campaign of rational thought was forged in opposition to the superstition and backwardness of the clergy, and the institutions and mentalities it dominated. The Afro-enlightenment must continue to make its way in opposition to the myth that Euro-enlightenment rationality spells the imminent end of racial oppression. The forces of repression organized against black people in the twentieth century have been far more potent and vicious than the few familiar still photos of lynchings indicate. The heft of an imaginary file labeled "The U.S. Government vs. Black Americans," which might include documents secured through the Freedom of Information Act and information about COINTELPRO, is but a fragment of the knowledge that cannot be excluded in a well-informed range of film documentaries. Of course, digging into this pile will also disclose the many instances when black leaders surreptitiously and under duress compromised with oppressive institutional power.

John Henrik Clarke: A Great and Mighty Walk gets some of its adrenaline from the way it makes its way through some of these darker passages. This film is unusual in making the slightest acknowledgment of what Arthur Jafa calls the "abject sublime" of black life, and the paradoxes it poses for understanding the shooting stars of brilliant black leadership: the historical opacity of most black people; the psychological and moral corruption among leaders and many followers alike; the role of race-traitors; the fawning performances for sadistic white subject positions; the silly consumerism; the inane waste of social and political resources; the slowness to understand the challenge before them and to mount a massive response. Spike Lee has been criticized for the length and detail given to Malcolm X's early life as a petty thief, hustler, and apprentice pimp. But he was only following Malcolm's own conviction, dramatized in his autobiography, of the necessity of facing squarely the condition of black people that must be changed.

Can we anticipate a wider vision in black leader films? The St. Clair Bourne film on John Henrik Clarke suggests what black documentary might have to offer once it joins other media of black expression and moves beyond defensiveness, beyond politically correct optimism, beyond positive imagism and PBS Novocain anesthesia. There is surely ground to be gained by employing a wider range of more freely expressive commentators in these films. Perhaps we can expect a post–morale-building phase of work, films that might include commentaries from Louis Farrakhan and Clarence Thomas, Molefi Asante and Henry Louis Gates. This broader perspective would generate adult black documentaries—what might be called "adultumentaries."

But documentary biographies of black leaders cannot change dramatically until the leaders themselves forge new paths. Perhaps it is time to exchange some of today's strategies and tactics for more powerful, persuasive ones. This question arises at a time when the DuBoisean center is demonstrating insecurity, confusion, and apathy. At a recent panel discussion at the Schomburg Museum in Harlem, Harry Belafonte spoke to the unproductive situation of black American social-political development. After evoking W. E. B. Du Bois and Paul Robeson as his two principal mentors, Belafonte lamented the lack of political force and commitment among those who would be leaders, including black elected officials, and the frequent willingness to settle for personal gain. "Everybody has carved out their little corner. There are pockets of us who speak together about common concerns, but most of us are missing our own boat."[3] Such apathy places a greater prize on the films that rise above it with clarity, force, and emotion.

Herein lies the dilemma: the DuBoisean center has temporarily lost its capacity to make itself a problem for the reactionary forces that impede its enlightenment projects. In this climate it is necessary to acknowledge the film professionals who have gone beyond the daring implied by being a documentary filmmaker and have taken on the tougher choices. Almost all of their subjects went through at least one period of public contempt and were shunned even by their friends, yet persisted without the hope of immediate reward. And it may be symptomatic of the honorable need to remain a problem that some of the best films in this genre have been made by directors who were either ejected or rejected from projects organized by Blackside Inc. or the PBS system, or who left voluntarily because of their fidelity to the tradition of telling the truth and encompassing the perspectives of black intelligence.

Long ago, Harold Cruse warned against allowing a separation among issues of culture, politics, and economics. Some of the losses from isolating cultural from political documentary expression have already been seen. We need to add economics to the mix of predicaments that must be addressed. The boat that black documentarians are currently missing is the need to diminish or offset economic dependence on state and institutional support. In the absence of a frightening, explosive climate in the streets or a guilt-based sense of obligation on the part of white liberals, black filmmaking must either find new sources of funding or new means of leveraging funds from familiar sources. Surely the reactionary national climate bears responsibility for the silencing of DuBoisean thought. But DuBoiseans have themselves to blame for their passive acceptance of the situation.[4]

Du Bois opened this century by posing the question: "How does it feel to be a problem?" The time will come when we can put that question to rest and celebrate the success of the black world enlightenment. But a century of struggle has not achieved that sweet moment. It may take another century to make this question incomprehensible. This may be the time to insist on remaining a problem that refuses to disappear into white-bread anonymity as a figment of a color-blind social fantasy. The refusal to evade the problems created by racism and imperialism, or to accept blame for their results, has been a defining characteristic of black world enlightenment, and of its brilliant leaders.

NOTES

This essay has its origins in two film series I have programmed, titled "Paths of Enlightenment: Artists, Heroes, Rebels and Thinkers," for Project

Black Cinema's annual festival in Sarasota, Florida, in September 1996 and, by the same title, at the Brooklyn Museum, February 1997. This essay expands the program notes for those exhibitions. I have left out the "Artist" dimension of the essay since it is otherwise covered in this collection.

1. For extensive analysis of this and related questions, see Tommy Lott, "A No-Theory Theory of Contemporary Black Cinema," *Black American Literature Forum* 25, no. 2 (Summer 1991): 221–36.

2. For more on duplexing and other issues of representation, see Clyde Taylor, *The Mask of Art: Breaking the Aesthetic Contract in Film and Literature* (Bloomington: Indiana University Press, 1998).

3. A feature-length documentary has been made about Belafonte, who surely ranks as an outstanding leader for African Americans: a thinker, rebel, hero, and artist. But, alas, the film is Cuban-made and seldom seen in the U.S.

4. A case in point is the outcome of a stunning conference held in Boston at WGBH-TV in 1992. At the African American Television Programming Summit, over a hundred action-oriented people were present, including film directors, film historians, television programmers, studio executives, station managers, foundation officers, bankers, students, community activists, journalists, museum curators, fiction writers, and academics in the field of communications. The group held a fair representation of the best and the brightest black minds associated with the issue. In two days this group completed an amazing piece of work. It traced the history of the problem, recalling the evolution of PBS and its original mandate to serve the television needs of communities like black America—a commitment which it has dramatically abandoned. The group worked out a masterful series of strategies for influencing television programming in the interests of black people.

The report that emerged from this gathering captures some of the vividness of the meetings themselves. (I recall this clearly since I had a small role in co-editing the report with Jacqueline Lindsay.) The moment looked like one of the best opportunities to turn things around that has come along in some time. The recommendations in this report have not been advanced because of the absence of appropriate black institutions or institutional power. Whether or not those of us implicated in its vision recover its findings, the report reflects the clear sense that only a collective effort will move us toward wider exposure and more responsive programming. Decisive black institutions may remain a long-range goal in a post–civil rights climate that is witnessing the dissolution of black solidarity. But in the near term, we can do more to harness the power within existing institutions, or to influence them from outside. If this work of collective empowerment is undertaken by the thousands of individuals who are directly involved in sparking and sustaining black creativity in film and other media, we can build on the achievements of today's documentaries on black leadership, and ensure that tomorrow's films will be even more powerful.

Write to WGBH Educational Foundation, Alston, MA, for a copy of the report, called "The Re-invention of Black Television Programming: A Story of Vision and Community—A Report to Participants of the African American Television Programming Summit."

6

Rewritten on Film
Documenting the Artist

JANET K. CUTLER

> "THE HISTORY MOST PEOPLE WILL BELIEVE IN IS THE HISTORY
> THEY SEE ON THE SILVER SCREEN. HISTORY IS NOT WHAT ACTUALLY
> HAPPENED—EVEN IF IT IS WRITTEN IN A BOOK . . . I WANTED TO BE
> WHERE HISTORY WAS MADE, WHERE IT IS REWRITTEN ON FILM."
>
> —MIGNON DUPREE, IN JULIE DASH'S *Illusions* (1983)

The films and videos that take as their subject the lives and works of black artists play a special role in the history of African American documentary production. They celebrate extraordinary lives and careers, while explicating the process of artistic production and affirming the contributions of African Americans to the cultural life of this country. Perhaps more importantly, African American art documentaries link art-making to self-definition and collective expression. If the desire to make works of art is part of a longing to make one's presence felt in the world,[1] this desire is heightened for African American artists whose works counter the invisibility and distortion of black images and concerns in mainstream American culture.

In Julie Dash's film *Illusions,* Mignon Dupree, a fictional entertainment industry executive who passes for white, yearns to see Hollywood produce films in which black characters are more than just "props in their stories—musical props, dancing props, or comic relief." Although clearly not mainstream productions, African American art documentaries fulfill Mignon Dupree's vision: they powerfully assert the integrity of black experience, while representing and reclaiming black history. Thus, these films and videos respond to Toni Cade Bambara's desire "to see myself, hear myself,"[2] while bringing black art and artists to public view. In these and other ways, African American art documentaries serve as counter-narratives of black experience. They can be viewed as what Manthia Diawara calls "performances" in which "an individual or group of people interpret an existing tradition—reinventing themselves in front of an audience."[3]

In the historical context of absence and distortion, such reinvention is a political act. African American documentaries lend voice and visibility to black artists, examining their dynamic position within and beyond black communities. In these works, which offer artists a forum for their concerns, discourses of race and representation inevitably intersect with discourses of race and oppression: these documentaries articulate the ways in which art can express the richness and multiplicity of black experience, and at the same time they suggest that art can address social injustice.

African American art documentaries extend the achievements of their artist-subjects: they document and disseminate views of accomplished, otherwise under-represented artwork. Further, as works of media art, these documentaries add to the growing body of provocative African American creative productions. Grounded in concrete depictions of the work of African American painters and sculptors, writers and musicians, dancers and performers, and photographers and film / videomakers, the best African American art documentaries interrogate assumptions about the role of black artists and redefine the function of black art.

This chapter surveys more than fifty surviving films and videos produced over the last thirty years by African Americans, a body of work that celebrates a diverse group of black artists, including singer Betty Carter, photographer Roy DeCarava, filmmaker Oscar Micheaux, writer James Baldwin, and performance artist Barbara McCullough. Among the artists documented are well-known figures like Langston Hughes and Paul Robeson, and individuals whose behind-the-scenes creative work inspired others, like librarian-turned-poet Miss Fluci Moses and dance teacher Thelma Hill. There are documentaries linking groups of artists to each other and to their communities, such as *Big City Blues* (1981), as well as films that trace the history of a particular art form, such as *The Black Theater Movement* (1978). Finally, there are hybrid works born of collaborations between documentarians and performing artists, such as *Praise House* (1991).

The films and videos considered here were financed, produced, distributed and exhibited under a wide range of circumstances and conditions. Some are rough-hewn student or apprentice works; in fact, producing a personal art documentary on a shoestring about one's mentor is a common "rite of passage" for many media artists who, like Alile Sharon Larkin and Ayoka Chenzira, later go on to independent narrative feature production. At the other end of the spectrum are polished documentary productions that cleared many hurdles before securing private and public funding and gaining relatively wide exposure. Thus, this body of work includes a range of material: home-movie-like, low budget productions financed by the filmmaker and seen by community audiences; mid-level documentaries supported by government grants or progressive foundations, shown at festivals, and seen by university, public library, and cultural center audiences; and high-end productions co-produced by the Corporation for Public Broadcasting or by consortia of international television stations, aired before vast audiences here and abroad, and made available to home video users.

The film/videomakers in this study do not limit themselves to a single site or approach; even those who at one time held staff positions within the broadcasting industry are "independents" who work primarily outside the commercial mainstream, moving between film and video productions, narrative and documentary projects, traditional and experimental modes of representation. Their works reflect the various "conventions of reality" employed by nonfiction film/videomakers. Many productions are classical, well-made, "education films"; others employ the more improvisatory *cinéma vérité* style introduced in the early 1960s, in which the use of lightweight, portable camera and sound equipment allows an intimate relationship between filmmaker and subject.[4] The most recent works are even more personal; they treat the experiences and responses of the film/videomaker as viable subjects. In addition, today's documentarians often blur the line between nonfiction and fiction, between documentary and narrative, and create hybrid forms. In *Blurred Boundaries*, Bill Nichols identifies an alternative mode of representation, "performative documentary," to account for works like Marlon Riggs's *Tongues Untied* (1989) which mix expressive, poetic, and rhetorical elements and stress subjectivities rather than historical materials.[5]

Many documentarians exhibit a strong identification with their artist-subjects. Like the artists they celebrate, these film/videomakers make works that preserve and extend cultural tradition, and they devise alternative networks to promote and exhibit their work. Identification between film/videomakers and their subjects is strongest in works which feature artists who are family members or beloved teachers. In other cases the identification is sparked by a sense of shared struggle, especially when both documentarian and artist see themselves as "storytellers" intent on illuminating previously neglected aspects of black experience. This becomes especially clear when documentary subjects offer accounts of how they have drawn on black history and culture, while recognizing the fragmentary nature of that material. Interviewed in Yvonne Welbon's *The Cinematic Jazz of Julie Dash* (1992), Julie Dash discusses the need for black cinema to capture fleeting moments and fragmentary documents: "As black people we're dealing with 'scraps of memories,' I think W. E. B. Du Bois said, and we cannot trace our history so easily." In this way, the viewer is reminded that the making of documentary film and video, no less than the arts documented in those works, involves constructing narratives from "scraps of memory."

The urgency behind these documentaries is prompted by several factors: on the one hand, African Americans have been forcibly cut off from their ancient history and heritage; on the other hand, African American cultural contributions in this country have for centuries been marginalized—largely undervalued and unrecorded. Documentary film / videomakers must assume the role of cultural historians, filling in gaps and creating significant, sometimes imaginative connections to the past and to collective experience,[6] countering misrepresentations perpetuated by the dominant culture, and constructing more telling narratives of black experience. As a kind of media storyteller, film / video counteracts the ephemeral quality of the oral tradition, while taking on something like the role of the African griots, elders in the community who mentally record, then verbally recount, local and familial tales. As self-referential works, these documentaries elegantly weave two strands: the power of the arts to reflect and extend the images, language and customs of black life in all its diversity; and the power of film to record and elaborate on the achievements of African American artists. In so doing, they place the media arts' possibilities for creative personal and collective expression in a broader cultural context.

Thus, black art documentary employs diverse, sometimes overlapping modes: the authoritative, "educational"; the direct, "*cinéma vérité*"; the personal, "autobiographical"; the dramatization, "psycho-drama"; the mixed mode, "performative." As well, this work addresses a range of themes: the intersection of the various arts; cultural links between events and people; the need to produce counter-histories in the face of misrepresentation; art as a social or political act of community; the importance of memory when so much has been lost or suppressed by official institutions; the relationship between family and work, between individual and collective identity.

Since many of these works are not described anywhere in film literature, this chapter considers in some detail both the most complex, fully realized works and those that are more fragmentary. The essay is organized into sections that deal with documentary makers/subjects/ genres. The first two sections call attention to significant makers of art documentaries—St. Clair Bourne and Michelle Parkerson. The next two sections stress connections between filmmakers and their artist-subjects; many documentarians pay homage to artist-mentors, while others depict like-minded artist-activists. Finally, the chapter addresses two important subgenres of the art documentary—survey films and performance documentaries.

Questions of competing realities, multiple truths and fictions, and objectivity and subjectivity find fertile ground in documentary, particularly in works about artists; in these films and videos, the creative depiction of black experience by artists overlaps with issues of documentary mode and practice. Like all histories and indeed like narrative films, documentaries are constructions or what John Grierson called "creative treatments of actuality,"[7] employing an array of formal strategies to shape and structure material. But the powerful impulse to tell one's own story, in fact or fiction, to define and re-define one's own identity through the performing, fine/visual, and literary arts, is an enduring strand that runs through African American art documentaries. These films bear witness to the struggles and pleasures of artists who have contributed so palpably to the cultural life of this nation and the world.

THE ARTIST AS ACTIVIST: ST. CLAIR BOURNE

One of the most accomplished black documentarians to have emerged from the social and political crucible of the 1960s is filmmaker St. Clair Bourne, whose training ground was *Black Journal*, that period's pioneering African American television series. A Columbia University student-activist, Bourne was arrested and "kicked out of film school . . . three days later I had an interview and three days later after that I received a call that I was an associate producer for this national television documentary series. And so, within a week after being in jail, for taking over Columbia University, I became the youngest person on the team."[8]

Bourne soon became a guiding force on *Black Journal* and, later, he independently produced a number of engaging portraits of major black artists and art forms. While at *Black Journal* (1968–1971), Bourne produced a piece on Paul Robeson that mixed live action and animation, as well as *Afro-Dance* (1969–1970), a comparative study of African and

African American dance forms. *Soul, Sounds, and Money* (1969) is a look at the music industry that features Smokey Robinson, Gladys Knight and the Pips, and Isaac Hayes, performing in Hollywood, New York City, and Memphis. Other television work followed: Bourne's *Langston Hughes: The Dream Keeper* (1988), produced for public television's *Voices and Visions* series, is a reconstruction and contextualization of the life of a major artist, employing performance pieces that dramatize important moments in Hughes's personal and professional life; *New Orleans Brass* (1994), a film produced for the National Geographic *Explorer* television series, examines the tradition of the brass band.

As an independent producer, Bourne established Chamba, a company that has created more than fifty works, including documentaries about artists. Works directed by Bourne include *Big City Blues,* a profile of contemporary musicians who reinterpret traditional Chicago blues; *In Motion: Amiri Baraka* (1982), a portrait of a complex living artist-activist structured to reflect the rhythms of its subject's life; and *Making "Do the Right Thing"* (1989) an account of the production of Spike Lee's movie that focuses on the Bedford-Stuyvesant community in which it was shot.[9]

Bourne's art documentaries span the range of subgenres and thematic concerns considered in this study: *Afro-Dance,* for example, is a performance piece; *Big City Blues,* a survey film; *In Motion: Amiri Baraka,* a work that adopts the performative style of its subject; *Langston Hughes: The Dream Keeper,* a more conventionally structured, biographical work. A close examination of these works demonstrates Bourne's mastery of diverse styles and subjects.

Bourne's nine-minute *Afro-Dance* focuses on the culturally significant links between traditional African dance and late 1960s African American choreography and popular dance. At the beginning of *Afro-Dance,* Bourne cuts between shots of traditional dancers in Africa and contemporary American dancers. Bourne then introduces dance historian and instructor Percival Board who speaks about the connection between past and present before instructing his students to begin their exercise in the style of "an old African ritual" and then overlay the style of "the modern jazz of the black man today." Board also points out that "as African dance migrated to other parts of the world, it evolved into new forms," citing West Indian calypso dance, Brazilian Macumba ritual dance, and the Lindy Hop as dances in which black males strike defiant poses to protest oppressive social conditions.[10]

The social function of dance in black communities is also explored: thus, dancing is seen not just as "enjoyment," but as a meaningful form of expression to mark births, engagements, marriages, and deaths. At the same time dance is a form of social protest. The film features a modern dance performance choreographed by Elio Pomari, whose concert pieces draw inspiration from urban experience, including popular social dance forms. Performed by dancer Diana Ramos, the piece echoes what Pomari calls "the African tradition of conveying messages through dance that tell of our view of the world." In a rubble-filled, urban back lot, Ramos moves to a spoken text that describes the black woman's journey from slavery to the rural South to life in the city. Sometimes stumbling across broken concrete, Ramos's movements interpret words such as "I am laughter, half-smiles, stifled screams."

Production still from St. Clair Bourne's *Big City Blues*.
Courtesy of Chamba Productions.

In *Big City Blues* (also called *New Blues*), Bourne again examines the links between the past and the present: the old-time blues singer Jim Brewer is presented alongside contemporary practitioners Billy Branch, Son Seals, and Queen Sylvia Embry. The connection between generations is a theme sounded in a number of documentaries about artists, but here the emphasis is on emerging blues musicians who both inherit the tradition of their predecessors and need to break new ground, to create forms that are both personal and accessible to contemporary audiences.

Bourne's interest in establishing context is clear from the opening: Chicago is called "the urban birthplace of the blues" over a high angle zoom out from the Loop. Voice-over reminiscences about the old days accompany the montage of Chicago street scenes that follows. Bourne relies heavily on a narrator in these opening scenes, but soon shifts the burden of explaining the blues to interviews with the musicians, often accompanied by lyrical performance footage. For example, a hand-held camera circles "harpist" Billy Branch, zooming in and out as he plays for students in a school auditorium, while on the soundtrack he talks about how he had aspired to become a lawyer before he became inspired by the blues. Bourne cuts to a scene in which Branch talks about his role as "spreader of the word," then cuts back to the auditorium where Branch tells his audience that pop music began with the blues, which began with slave music. He sings examples of blues that show how slaves' songs worked on several levels and included coded messages: to the initiated, a phrase like "I want to go down that long lonesome road" expressed the clandestine desire to escape. Branch's belief in the importance of conveying history—both in performance of his music and in discussions with young people—resonates with the work of other African American artists.

Having established the roots of the blues, Bourne examines its contemporary forms. Son Seals, a proponent of change whose lively blues performances attract cross-over audiences, is shown being interviewed on a Chicago radio program about his childhood and his growth as a musician. Bourne cuts between the interview and *cinéma vérité* footage of one of Seals's performances. In these sequences, Bourne's rough-hewn, vital filmmaking style echoes Seals's music, which replaces the melancholy blues of the past with a new style of blues that "livens it up."

Increasingly playful, Bourne introduces delightful visual surprises in the next sequence, which focuses on bandleader Queen Sylvia, a woman working in a male-dominated industry who introduces her performance by saying, "We're going to have some music for ladies for a while." Bourne cuts away from the concert to a beauty salon where a woman is getting a haircut. He bridges the two spaces with voice-over commentary in which Queen Sylvia encourages ladies to do what they want, then zooms back to reveal that Queen Sylvia is the beautician speaking to her customer. In another sequence, Queen Sylvia tells the story of being broke and working her way back to Chicago and illustrates it by singing "Travel All Over This Land." Bourne has her begin the song in her living room, then cuts to her continuing it onstage.

Big City Blues is typical of Bourne's style: he links material in inventive ways, creating elegant transitions between interview and performance footage. He mixes edgy *cinéma vérité* footage—utilizing hand-held cameras, zooming in and out, and rapid editing—with more conventional voice-over narration and talking head interviews. The film also takes up themes that dominate Bourne's art documentaries—including the importance of keeping alive traditional art forms, often by reinvigorating them through contemporary elaborations. When the film ends by circling back to its opening image, an aerial view of the Chicago Loop, the narrator reports that the blues has changed but the beat continues: "These songs are about more than pain, they're songs of survivors that touch all kinds of people."

In Motion: Amiri Baraka eloquently articulates Baraka's interlocking artistic and political concerns. This videotape ostensibly focuses on a limited time period—the two weeks prior to Baraka's sentencing for resisting arrest—yet opens out to encompass multiple narrative threads. There is the *cinéma vérité* story of Baraka's attempt to "fight the system," beginning with consultations with lawyers and ending with an account of the final resolution of his case. There is episodic material that depicts a multi-faceted Baraka "in motion," writing at home, doing poetry readings, exhorting crowds at political demonstrations, hosting a radio

Amiri *(left)* and Amina Baraka.
Courtesy of Chamba Productions.

show, teaching a class, etc. And finally, there is the contextualizing story of Baraka's evolution as an artist-activist, recounted by those who know him best—family members and fellow writers—and illustrated by archival footage and recurring excerpts from the 1967 film version of his play, *Dutchman*.

In Bourne's words,

> My Baraka . . . videotape [is] . . . chronological, but I take leaps into nonlinear thought process, mainly through Baraka's poetry, so I felt that I had to be true to him. . . . But still if you look at it structurally there's a storyline there. He gets up in the morning, he goes to his press conference. You find out at the press conference who he is, what happened in flashbacks, then he goes to his political rally at night. . . . I mean you can see there's a story, and then he finished up, he goes to the court trial.[11]

In Motion: Amiri Baraka offers a vivid portrait of the artist as poet, family man, cultural activist, and political organizer—an extraordinary individual enmeshed in diverse communities.[12]

Bourne shapes this videotape by organizing it into richly detailed sequences. One such section called "Notes" opens in a WBAI radio station control room with Baraka seated and wearing headphones, ready to begin his program. Music fills the soundtrack before he speaks, and as he starts his introduction, there is a cut to footage of a crowd on the street. A sinuous lateral camera movement reveals that they are demonstrating against South African Airways. The next shot returns to the control room, where Baraka defines his program (and his central concerns): "Notes! Musical notes, aesthetic notes, social notes." Bourne cuts back to the demonstration, where Baraka is telling the crowd that the struggle in South Africa is not about apartheid, but about political power—who will rule in South Africa.

The sounds of jazz fade in over the street sounds and the film cuts back to Baraka in the studio commenting on the music he's playing, recommending Arthur Blythe's *Blythe Spirit* album and commending Columbia Records for trying to "do some good in its old age." This recommendation is followed by another: Baraka mentions that he'll be at the New Federal Theatre at the Henry Street Settlement House with his new play *Boy and Tarzan Appear in a Clearing*. The film then cuts to a long excerpt from the production, followed by a sequence in which students in a classroom debate points raised by *Boy and Tarzan* with its author, followed by another excerpt from the production. The jazz fades back in and there is cut back to Baraka saying that he will be featuring the *Blythe Spirit* album all evening, then reminding his listeners that he will be reading at St. Mark's Church in-the-Bowery in the East Village.

A shot of the outside of the church gives way to close-ups of Baraka's face, as he rocks to the rhythm of his words, ending with a freeze frame as the poem ends. Baraka's voice on the radio saying, "I have a date with the state," returns as the jazz music fades in: "I'll be back two Wednesdays from now . . . hopefully." Though unified by the radio show, this section of the film is dizzying in its tracing of Baraka's exhaustive activities as radio show host, music critic, social activist, dramatist, teacher, and poet.

Bourne portrays Baraka as a highly visible public figure, but also a private individual cared for by an affectionate family. Interviews with his parents are especially important in this regard. Early in the film his mother says, "I think he's a genius," but later worries about what will happen to him in jail. To the mother's dismay, Baraka's father suggests that his son might well organize the whole prison and start a riot. Baraka's wife recalls their courtship, their professional collaborations, and their tumultuous domestic life. Baraka is shown at home, typing as his son plays the drum, talking with his daughter about the pitfalls of dog ownership. Baraka's evolution as a literary and political figure is traced by his peers: Allen Ginsberg reminisces about "Lee's" Greenwich Village literary salon frequented by Cecil Taylor, Don Cherry, and Ornette Coleman, where Ginsberg first met Langston Hughes. A. B. Spellman cites events that transformed Baraka, like his travel to Cuba at a time when "we all had a romance with the Cuban Revolution." Joel Oppenheimer recalls his difficulty accepting Baraka's steady conversion to poet-activist, and mourns the fact that he and Baraka stopped talking. In a rooftop interview in Harlem, Ted Wilson and Askia M. Toure recall the period of Baraka's radicalization, especially his attempts to establish the National Black Arts Movement uptown, and the way he was finally "run out" of Harlem.

Bourne's use of interview material provides not only information but also a syncopation that shapes the work: "Stylistically, it was different from anything else I've done," Bourne explains.

> It had a rhythm inside, the way the people talked . . . from Allen Ginsberg, to Baraka, to A. B. Spellman, to his mother—they all had a musical flow, and I was able to actually edit it so that it was really a fluid piece. It is like music to me. It tells a narrative story, but there are flashbacks, and the flashbacks are the story of Baraka's life, and the main story is his attempt to defend himself against these charges that the police beat him up for when they said he beat up his wife. In that film all the elements that I wanted to do come together. Baraka was a person who I could learn from and get deeper into what he was thinking. The style of his poetry demanded a comparable film style, and I think it worked.[13]

At the end of the video, the audience learns that Baraka indeed ended up serving "ninety days for so-called resisting arrest." Comparing his situation to that of Paul Robeson (who told the House Un-American Activities Committee, "there are only two things that the state doesn't like about me—my nationality and my opinion"), Baraka protests the severity of the sentence. He points to the grand jury's dismissal of the charges against him and its indictment of the police for harassment, the recommendation for probation and non-custodial sentence, as well as five days of grand jury testimony and twenty-eight months of courtroom proceedings. In conveying Baraka's view of American justice, *In Motion* functions as its own act of political protest.

In *Langston Hughes: The Dream Keeper,* Bourne adopts an expansive yet linear approach, chronologically tracing Hughes's life and literary achievements against a vivid historical backdrop. Using titles with dates to note the crucial periods in Hughes's life and their relationship to world events, Bourne tries to give the audience "parallel events of the times in which we're talking, so if I talk of Langston Hughes in 1921, then I'll show you what was going on then, so when he says what he says, you'll see, hopefully, 'Oh, he said this, but he said it a time when blacks couldn't go into the Army.' . . . So, the context is everything."[14] Bourne calls *Langston Hughes* "my 'Broadway' documentary, and the reason I call it that is it's big and shot all over the country, and in Paris and Senegal. We didn't have any money problems. It doesn't have the cutting-edge, small, driving aesthetic that a lot of independent films have. It doesn't look hungry. In a way I like it because I think it captures Langston, but I always say, 'That's my Broadway documentary.'"[15]

Bourne contextualizes Hughes's personal and professional development with archival films, audiotapes, and television footage of Hughes, as well as interviews with Hughes's biographers Arnold Rampersad and Faith Berry, writers James Baldwin and Amiri Baraka, and President Leopold Senghor of Senegal who calls Hughes "the greatest influence on the Negritude movement." *Langston Hughes: The Dream Keeper* also features expressionistic reenactments of Hughes's life and writing, often involving reading in voice-over. In Bourne's words, "In *Langston* . . . I had to use docudrama with actors, animation, musical performances to tell a story. So now what I'm interested in most is the narrative docudrama, where number one it's a real event and you try to re-create it."[16]

Bourne's use of docudrama is evident in a reflexive sequence in which a child, experiencing the power of a masterful storyteller, recognizes the role of storytelling as personal history. A boy runs across a field to a house as the narrator reads:

Aunt Sue had a head full of stories. Aunt Sue had a whole heart full of stories. Summer nights on the front porch Aunt Sue cuddles a brown-faced child to her bosom and tells him stories. And the dark-faced child listening knows that Aunt Sue's stories are real stories, he knows that she never got her stories out of any book at all, but that they came out of her own life. The dark-faced child is quiet of a summer night listening to Aunt Sue's stories.

More typical are sequences set in bars and nightclubs featuring actors and dancers reciting and dramatizing Hughes's poems and prose. In one such sequence the poem "When Susanna Jones Wears Red" is heard on the soundtrack, while a woman in a red dress dances to trumpet music in a set that represents the Lenox Lounge and in a set with an abstract white background. In another sequence, Hughes's Simple character holds forth in a barroom setting. These settings for dramatizations recur throughout the film: at times, the fictional characters appear in the deep background as Louise Patterson and Amiri Baraka speak of Hughes in the foreground. Bourne also includes scenes that dramatize Hughes's personal experience, although no character specifically represents Hughes. When dealing with Hughes's first trip to Paris, for example, Bourne inserts shots of three young people wandering through the streets of that city; and when recounting how Hughes's father withheld tuition money for a second year at Columbia University, Bourne inserts a shot of books being thrown into a river.

Bourne shows how Hughes absorbed and incorporated elements of black culture in his literary works. In the film, Hughes talks of being deeply influenced by Kansas City blues and of introducing the blues to literature, to create a "new form of poetry": Hughes's blues-influenced "Sweet Girls" is then read and performed. Later, over footage of a church choir, Hughes talks about the influence of the Negro spiritual in his stories. And Hughes claims that he included the syncopated rhythms of jazz in his poetry. In the poem, "Note on Commercial Theatre," which is read on the soundtrack, Hughes describes the misappropriation of black cultural forms that may have prompted him to attempt a more authentic incorporation of those forms in his work:

> You've taken my blues and gone—
> You sing 'em on Broadway
> And you sing 'em in the Hollywood Bowl,
> And you mixed 'em up with symphonies
> And you fixed 'em
> So they don't sound like me.
> Yep, you done taken my blues and gone.

* * *

But someday somebody'll
Stand up and talk about me,
And write about me—
Black and beautiful—
And sing about me,
And put on plays about me!
I reckon it'll be
Me myself!
Yes, it'll be me.

The misappropriation of black culture by white artists is a theme sounded by other art documentaries, particularly those that deal with music. In Gil Noble's *Jazz, the American Art Form* (1970), Eubie Blake cites the influence of Pete Johnson and Willie "the Lion" Smith on George Gershwin's work, and recalls that Lucky Roberts, Fats Waller, and William Grant Still taught Gershwin to play ragtime. Orlando Bagwell's *New Worlds, New Forms* (1993) also argues this point: "We couldn't let them take our dance—they had taken everything else—we couldn't let them take the Lindy Hop." Perhaps the most positive answer to Langston Hughes's question of who is best qualified to convey the richness of black cultural forms to mainstream audiences lies in the body of films and videotapes under consideration here. St. Clair Bourne and others have turned their cameras on black artists not only to praise their accomplishments but to make two related political points: blacks have been systematically stripped of their African heritage, and their cultural production in America has too often been co-opted by the mainstream entertainment industry.

BREAKING NEW GROUND: MICHELLE PARKERSON

If St. Clair Bourne's work best represents the range of black art documentary practice, Michelle Parkerson's work is important for its intense treatment of a focused subject—black women artists. Parkerson has modestly argued that her stature as a leading media artist owes less to her skills as a film/videomaker than to her perceptive choice of subjects: "I think that what's gotten [my films] attention is who the films are about. These women are truly outstanding. Their artistic expressions are totally unique and totally innovative in whatever forms or field they're working in . . . not that the documentary style of my work is that. I have really heavy and pressing and constantly nagging concerns about style: how to do that, what it is and what styles are appropriate to what subjects." [17] In fact, appropriate style is one of Parkerson's great strengths. Her ability to adopt diverse formal constructs, each of which matches the "unique and innovative artistic expressions of [the] outstanding women," characterizes four accomplished works: *But Then She's Betty Carter* (1980), *Gotta Make This Journey: Sweet Honey in the Rock* (1983), *Stormé: The Lady of the Jewel Box* (1987), and *A Litany for Survival: The Life and Work of Audre Lorde* (1995, with Ada Gay Griffin).

The *cinéma vérité* approach to *But Then She's Betty Carter* is informed by what Parkerson calls "an improvisational, jazz pacing." Moving freely between interviews with jazz vocalist Betty Carter (alone or with her long-time friend Lionel Hampton), performance footage of Carter in concert, and stills that illustrate the trajectory of her career, Parkerson creates a profile that is both lively and reflective. At the opening of the film we are introduced to Carter through photographs and music, then by hand-held camera footage that follows her from the dressing room to the stage of a crowded university auditorium. As she sings, footage of Carter's performance gives way to an interview at home in which she talks about learning to sing in church and her desire to go beyond such traditional music: "Church music, that old stuff, has quality but who wants it anymore?" As she talks about her desire to "improve, improvise, and stimulate this instrument," the viewer is led to understand something about Carter's rigorous dedication to innovation, all the while being treated to her polished, mature singing style. "Gotta redo it," she says, underlining her desire to move beyond what she has already achieved.

The idea that art extends tradition is especially clear in this film. Carter's devotion to jazz takes the form of pushing the limits of what has come before, including her own contributions to the field. Interview footage with Lionel Hampton adds to the tracing of roots. Sitting with Carter backstage, Hampton delivers a kind of oral history characteristic of documentaries about musicians, explaining that "our music came from slavery" and evolved to jazz through the efforts of John Coltrane and others. However, as Hampton and Carter reminisce about her coronation as Betty "Bebop" Carter and life on the road, the film's relaxed didacticism gives way to affectionate exchanges about how times have changed, including the use of new language—what was "hep" is now "hip"—in the jazz world. In such moments of anecdotal banter, Parkerson's film reveals itself to be the antithesis of the illustrated lecture in jazz history. The relaxed, improvisatory quality of Carter's interaction with Hampton is infectious, extending even to the editing room: Parkerson ends the Carter-Hampton sequence not with a succinct concluding point but rather with a shot in which her subjects playfully ask to be excused in order to go look for a bite to eat.

What follows is a much more intricate weaving of Betty Carter's songs and the interview material. As she sings "I Don't Know Where My Man Is" and "Most Gentlemen Can't Take Love," Carter's speaking voice is superimposed over the performance footage, talking about how hard it is for the men in her life to understand what she does and how much she cares for her work. In interview footage that continues the discussion, Carter notes that her professional life has largely eclipsed her personal life. Performance footage of Carter's devastating rendition of "I Was Telling Him about You" prompts similar treatment: Carter's speaking voice once again comments over the performance footage, providing a transition to interview footage in which the singer discusses her desire to become a better musician and her commitment to educating her sons. This leads to footage of one son's high school graduation, followed by performance footage of Carter scat-singing "My Favorite Things": its lyrics describe simple, domestic pleasures and serve as a soundtrack for images of Carter alone at home, working in her garden and at her Singer sewing machine.

Returning repeatedly to performance footage that showcases Carter's extraordinary vocal work, Parkerson intercuts words and images that underline the price paid for this accomplishment: early sections of the film are peppered with Carter's terse statements about her inability to find an understanding man, her infrequent visits with far-flung friends, and her helping her children obtain a good education only to have them leave home after graduation. Like other Parkerson heroines, Carter is revealed in interview footage and in the lyrics of her most poignant songs to be a woman whose dedication to her career has cut her off from domestic life and even from the company of loved ones. But what at first appears simply to be a life of personal deprivation and loneliness is shown over the course of the film to be something richer and stronger: Parkerson makes clear in scenes like Carter's giddy get-together with Hampton that the singer has passed up a conventional life in favor of membership in a loosely knit, specialized community of artistic innovators. In this regard, Parkerson steadfastly refuses to sentimentalize her subject: Carter's ostensible isolation, her rare enjoyment of limited, occasional contact with kindred spirits, and her alienation from the music establishment are presented matter-of-factly as natural outgrowths of her fierce independence.

This is not a standard biographical film that strings together archival photographs and footage of the subject's life and career, or a socially engaged documentary filled with testimony about how the artist overcame obstacles. Instead, this profile of the extraordinary, charismatic vocalist is grounded in the dynamic quality of her performances in the present, and in conversations that touch on the ways her music and her life evolved. Through the dynamic pace of the editing, the hand-held camera movements, and juxtapositions of concert and interview material, Parkerson finds a cinematic form that evokes the rhythms of jazz and the spirit of her subject. Parkerson ends this powerful film with Carter's contention that children need to hear and appreciate the work of important blues and jazz musicians.

Gotta Make This Journey: Sweet Honey in the Rock is a monument to the celebrated women's *a cappella* vocal group. Parkerson adopts a relatively standard broadcast style to depict the individual members of a musical ensemble whose longevity has made it a cultural institution. Twenty-two different women have sung in the five-person group over the years, all of them committed to composing and/or performing songs that speak to social and political issues. Its founder Bernice Johnson Reagon explains, "People on-stage have the burden of political action." For Sweet Honey in the Rock, artistic considerations and social/political considerations are virtually the same: their lively repertoire includes songs that take on wide-ranging topics, including the plight of blacks in South Africa, but the group is primarily committed to songs that address the lives and experiences of African American women.

Like the protagonists of Parkerson's other documentaries, the women of *Gotta Make This Journey* preserve and advance the artistic forms they practice. In the opening moments of the film, as the women arrive at the Gallaudet College auditorium for their ninth annual concert, a voice on the soundtrack informs viewers that, "As black artists, if you function within a context of black culture, you have to do more than pass on what has been passed on to you. You have to in fact document your living experience as part of the chain of black existence." And like Parkerson's other protagonists, members of the Sweet Honey ensemble forsake more conventional personal lives in favor of membership in a community of like-minded artistic innovators. What sets these women apart from other Parkerson subjects is their joyful acceptance of lives dedicated to art. The most doctrinaire and least melancholy of Parkerson's works, *Gotta Make This Journey* examines solidarity rather than isolation, collective empowerment rather than sacrifice. Sweet Honey is itself a community: the women are linked to each other and to members who came before them (one member notes that "we stand on the voices of all the others").

Parkerson gives each woman—Yasmeen Williams, Evelyn Harris, Aisha Kahil, Ysaye Barnwell, and Bernice Johnson Reagon—an opportunity to speak about herself as an individual, after which each is shown as a member of the ensemble through Parkerson's use of photographs, testimonials, and performance footage. The concert footage not only demonstrates their talents as soloists and ensemble performers, but also their musical range: Sweet Honey's repertoire includes jazz, blues, reggae, gospel, spirituals, rap, and African songs. Parkerson also intercuts interviews with Alice Walker, Ben Chavis, and Angela Davis that acknowledge the group's vital role in the cultural life of the black community.

In *Stormé: The Lady of the Jewel Box*, Parkerson addresses performance-related issues of race and gender by profiling Stormé DeLarverie, the male impersonator who worked at the Jewel Box, a popular Harlem nightclub featuring drag performers. From 1955 to 1969, Stormé essentially "ran the show." Brian Rogers, a former Jewel Box Revue female impersonator and according to Stormé, "one of my first born," says to his mentor: "You were the overseer." Sixty-six years old when the film was made, Stormé is a repository of information about the past, having "been in the business since 1939," initially as a big band singer. She recalls witnessing, from the wings, the first appearance of the Supremes at the Apollo.

The challenges Parkerson took on in this film are considerably different from those of *But Then She's Betty Carter* and *Gotta Make This Journey*. Not only is Parkerson introducing viewers to a fascinating person; she is unlocking a part of the past that was invisible to most of mainstream culture. There is no performance footage from the revues; many of the performers, including Stormé's favorite star, Mr. Lynn Carter, have died; and Stormé, at the time of the filming, had retired from performing and was working as a security guard at another club. The film opts for the privileged opportunity to spend time with Stormé as she relaxes at home at the Chelsea Hotel or, wandering backstage and opening a trunk full of memorabilia, recovers eight-by-ten-inch glossies of past Jewel Box Revue stars (Stormé points herself out in old photos, the only "male" among "female" performers). The cumulative effect of the film derives primarily from spending time alone with Stormé, listening to her stories about the past—her problems "growing up hard" as a child of "mixed blood" in New Orleans, her triumphs as a Jewel Box headliner, her close friendships with fellow performers, and her contention that she has always been the same person, whether dressed as a man or a woman.

Parkerson employs situations to "open out" the interview format, including interview footage of Stormé and Brian Rogers affectionately discussing their careers, claiming that the Jewel Box was a precursor of "La Cage [aux Folles]," and asserting more than once that, "We are family." There is footage of Stormé rousting gawkers outside the club

Still from Michelle Parkerson's
Stormé: The Lady of the Jewel Box.
Courtesy of Women Make Movies.

where she acts as bouncer, and at the end of the film there is a sequence
in which Stormé (in the present) sings several verses of "There Will
Never Be Another You" before an appreciative club audience.

Throughout, Parkerson maintains a confidential, self-conscious
tone, even allowing her subject to acknowledge several times that a film
is being made. Stormé talks about "this project," tells loiterers in front
of the club to move on with the words, "Honey, they're making a film,
do you want to get in it?" and answers questions we can hear posed by
the off-camera interviewer. At one point, overwhelmed by emotion, the
otherwise steely Stormé suggests that Parkerson turn off the camera
since she is about to cry. Black and white photographs of Jewel Box
Revue stars dissolve into tinted hues, seemingly coming to life, a strategy that implies that, despite Parkerson's skills as a documentarian, she
can never quite recapture the glamour of the Jewel Box's colorful ex-
travaganzas.

Stormé never entertains the issues of cross-dressing as performance
and its relationship to identity. Succinct and dignified, she insists, "I
always kept a touch of class . . . All I had to do was just be me and let
people use their imaginations." Parkerson instead refers the question
of cross-dressing and its challenge to social constructions of gender to

Joan Nestle, director of the Museum of Lesbian Herstory, who distinguishes between cross-dressing as a long-standing theatrical tradition
(she lists Sarah Bernhardt, Katherine Hepburn, Marlene Dietrich and
Grace Jones) and less visible cross-dressing as a way of life (she speaks
of women who neighbors assume are men until their deaths produce
"surprise discoveries"). Like Parkerson's other protagonists, Stormé is
fiercely independent and self-reliant. Asserting that she is very much
her own creation, Stormé says "I model myself after me." Her words
echo those of the protagonist of Parkerson's next film, Audre Lorde,
who calls herself "the architect of who I am."

Seven years after the completion of her celebrated trilogy of documentaries on women artists, Parkerson released a fourth film, her most
accomplished work to date in this area. Co-directed with Ada Gay
Griffin, and edited by Holly Fisher, *A Litany for Survival: The Life and
Work of Audre Lorde* is an insightful, elegantly structured, detailed portrait of the celebrated black lesbian poet and political activist. A feature-
length, award-winning documentary that required eight years of research, filming and post-production work, *A Litany for Survival* captures
the intricately interwoven strands of Lorde's professional and personal
life, as well as the evolution of her literary and political pursuits.

Parkerson's doubts about her ability to depict fictional characters
led her to become a documentary rather than narrative filmmaker:

> Coming out of school, I felt that characterization was something I had yet to
> fully learn, so that I felt I would find characters in real life heroes, real life
> role models. That has led me on to a *sequence* of films because there are so
> many of them. The artists were a conscious decision. *Betty Carter, Sweet
> Honey in the Rock,* and *Stormé . . .* were part of a trilogy that I had envisioned
> a long time ago. These were three really different kinds of art, artistic ex-
> pressions and African American women with different political visions
> about why they do what they do. *Audre Lorde* came later."[18]

With *A Litany for Survival,* Parkerson's concerns should be laid to rest:
Audre Lorde emerges as a protagonist every bit as complex and compelling as her counterparts in fiction film.

Unlike her trilogy, the Audre Lorde project was not initiated by
Parkerson; in fact, she rejected the idea as unfilmable until convinced
otherwise by Griffin:

> It was a film I was invited into. Ada Griffin came up with the idea. I always
> thought [Lorde] would be a very worthy subject for a documentary, but I
> thought that she was so expansive that I couldn't think of a format that could
> contain Audre Lorde into an hour or even a feature-length program. There

are so many tangents of Audre's work. But Ada had a vision about encapsulating all these different elements of her work, her life, her impact under
one umbrella.[19]

The first few sequences of *A Litany for Survival* deserve a detailed
look. They exhibit strategies employed by the filmmaker throughout
the work to implicate the viewer in a reading of Lorde's life as a tapestry of complexities and contradictions resolved in unconventional and
ultimately deeply satisfying ways. The film's brief prologue consists of
three close-ups of Lorde's face. In the first, she is ill, her head resting on
a pillow as she reads from a journal in a strained voice, "What I leave
behind me has a life of its own. I've said that about poetry. I've said it
about children. Well, in a sense I'm saying it about the very artifact of
who I have been." In the next shot, she is strong and collected: in what
the viewer assumes to be a public reading of her work, Lorde speaks in
measured tones of "those of us who live at the shoreline / standing on
the constant edge of decision." In the third shot, the camera pulls away
from a close-up of Lorde peering through the viewfinder of a video
camera to a somewhat wider shot of her standing, relaxed and smiling, in a tropical setting: she talks to no one in particular saying, "The
mornings here are so intense, and I wanted to capture it, and I wanted
to have it in my mind's eye." At this point, West Indian drumming and
chanting fill the soundtrack and the title appears over an image of a
handwritten copy of Lorde's poem "October." The head credits then appear between shots of tropical seascapes.

The three tightly framed shots that introduce Lorde largely with-
hold her location in time and space: without the usual visual coordi-
nates, the viewer is plunged into an intimate, uncharted relationship
with the poet. The filmmaker's strategy of creating intimacy and imbalance makes watching *A Litany for Survival* an especially intense experience. The film actively engages the attention and intelligence of viewers
by employing editing that reverses the usual cause-and-effect patterns
of conventional cinema; the significance of sensuous details is only
retroactively explained, prompting viewers to solve the film's mysteries, puzzles which run parallel to those of Lorde's life.

After the credits, the image of the sea, which served as a backdrop,
is identified in an additional title: "St. Croix, U.S. Virgin Islands." This
begins the film's intricately edited second sequence, which juxtaposes
hauntingly beautiful turn-of-the-century archival footage of people
disembarking from ships in the West Indies, color images of Lorde
standing on cliffs looking out to sea, Lorde's voice reading a poem about
the lives of Caribbean women "who saw their men off on the sailing

vessels," and Lorde's description of encountering "a point here where the Atlantic meets the Caribbean . . . standing there as an African Caribbean American woman, I could feel flowing through me Africa, the horrors of the Middle Crossing, those fathers and mothers of mine who survived that, who came to these shores here, who came to Grenada, Barbados, the connection there with the indigenous people of these islands, and who I am as I sit in this place. It felt as if there was a total consciousness for one moment of all of these threads."

Audre Lorde *(left)*, seen with her daughter in a still from Ada Gay Griffin and Michelle Parkerson's *A Litany for Survival: The Life and Work of Audre Lorde.* Courtesy of Third World Newsreel. Photo by Blanche Wiesen Cook.

The film's third sequence again throws the viewer into the middle of an activity: former New York governor Mario Cuomo's voice announces Lorde's appointment as the State Poet from 1991–1993 over a loosely framed shot of Lorde and Norman Mailer wandering onto an auditorium stage, followed by a carefully composed shot of the formal proceedings. In an excerpt from Lorde's acceptance speech, the poet addresses the considerable contradictions in her appointment, cataloguing those aspects of her identity that make her an unconventional choice: "What does it mean that a black, lesbian, feminist, warrior, poet, mother is named State Poet of New York?" She goes on to talk about the work of a poet in bridging those contradictions, and "the work of the poet in all of us to achieve what has not yet been," concerns traced throughout *A Litany for Survival*.

St. Croix is not identified until minutes after it is depicted. Even then, the full significance of the West Indies in Lorde's life is not apparent until the film's fourth sequence during which, after evocative archival images of Harlem, Lorde notes that "I grew up in Manhattan ... my parents were West Indian ... and we always were told when we were growing up that 'home' was somewhere else. No matter how bad it got here, that was not 'our home,' you see. And somewhere there was this magical place that if we really did right, someday we'd go back to." The contrapuntal structure of this opening sequence quickly establishes a sense of Lorde's writing, her voice, and the visual imagery that is important to her, but it makes its points in a non-didactic way. *A Litany for Survival* is constructed out of many such brief sections, each edited to convey the interwoven nature of Lorde's past and present, and her personal and professional life, returning often to archival footage to establish a historical context. In a sense, the film succeeds in depicting Lorde's identity as something akin to the glistening coral reefs of her beloved St. Croix. Shaped in part by the tides of social change, it is nevertheless powerfully of its own making, constructed of layer upon layer of experience, intricate in its structure, solid to its core.

The elegance of the film's construction and the intelligence of Lorde's words make *A Litany for Survival* a particularly expressive and evocative work. This is a film that takes the time to detail its subject's life and the evolution of her career, to see her alongside friends, family members, and students and other women engaged in artistic and political struggles. What holds the film together, however, is Lorde herself and her self-defined warrior persona. Early on she talks to her daughter about the importance of being a warrior in the world; her son says he was raised to fight. The fighter image is linked throughout to civil rights and to feminist causes and finally to Lorde's struggle with cancer. Even that, however, is placed in a larger context: imagining a war going on in her body in which white corpuscles are white South Africans, she reads a poem dedicated to black liberation as images of riots in South Africa appear on the screen. This strategy of linking Lorde's poetry and her personal experience to historical events and to the experience of others echoes the goals of many of the women artists and filmmakers in this study.[20] Ultimately, *A Litany for Survival* conveys the vibrancy of Lorde's life, a testimony to her fierce determination "to speak/ remembering/ we were never meant to survive."

MEDIA AND MEMORY: WOMEN ARTISTS
AND THE TRANSMISSION OF CULTURE

Michelle Parkerson is one of many women documentarians whose works focus on the accomplishments of black women artists. In fact, of the more than fifty extant art documentaries by African Americans, a surprising number—approximately twenty—are works by women film/videomakers who pay homage to influential women artists who have inspired them, and in many cases served as mentors. These films and videos stand as powerful testimony to women's crucial role as keepers of the past and transmitters of tradition and culture. In "Reading the Signs, Empowering the Eye: *Daughters of the Dust* and the Independent Cinema Movement," Toni Cade Bambara presents a "roll call" of more than seventy women film/videomakers whose narrative and documentary works redefine images of black women. Their documentaries are almost without exception devoted to the achievements of women artists. [21]

Yvonne Welbon's *The Cinematic Jazz of Julie Dash* articulates many of the themes central to documentaries by and about black women. Welbon presents interview footage of Dash recalling the experiences that prompted her to become a filmmaker: her early realization of the discrepancy between her life in public housing projects and what she saw on television (her neighbors were much more complex and fascinating than the characters she found in mainstream media) [22]; her attraction to the works of writers Alice Walker, Toni Cade Bambara, and Toni Morrison that showed her "I do exist"; and her decision to take on the task of presenting previously unseen images of black women onscreen. Dash explains, "I don't want to just do things that have to do with race . . . with this obstacle or that obstacle . . . but about black women relating to one another, what we do, what we say, how we enjoy each other, what our plans are." Welbon intercuts this interview material with film clips that illustrate Dash's points, including excerpts from *Four Women* (1977), *Diary of an African Nun* (1977), *Illusions* (1983), and *Daughters of the Dust* (1992).

Dash's interview comments about the driving impulse behind her fiction films have direct application to an understanding of her performance documentaries, and by extension to the larger field of art documentaries by African Americans. Dash articulates in concrete and poetic ways the urge to commit black cultural tradition to film, to keep it from being forgotten or destroyed, and to prevent it from being superceded by conventional forms employed by the mainstream film industry. She mourns the absence of family photos and recounts how, in their place, black women treasure a button from a grandfather's shirt, keeping it safe for years before handing it down to the next generation. Dash sees her filmmaking as equivalent to this process: her works visually collect and pass on memories.

The maker of *Cinematic Jazz*, Welbon also uses fragmentary materials, the scattered bits and pieces out of which she creates impressionistic histories: "I'm relying on memories and respecting them as history. . . . I'm not going to be able to find too many documents. What I did was record oral histories and recreate them. There are fragments of writing . . . very few photographs . . . but there is enough you can take and reconstruct, so for me the documentary isn't necessarily what is traditionally formal documentary."[23] This sentiment is echoed by many African American documentarians who aspire to make films about the artists who influenced them. Ayoka Chenzira, the director of *Syvilla: They Danced to Her Drum* (1979), notes that

> Syvilla was dying when I was making the film—[I remember] wanting desperately to say so much about her and not being able to find anything about her hardly in the Schomburg Center for Research in Black Culture, but finding a lot of people who knew about her through the oral tradition. . . . Of course, in our culture, the visual proof doesn't always exist, or what happens is you get the PBS documentaries that show during Black History Month and they all have the same photographs in them. . . . Now much of my work focuses on the function of memory and why people choose to remember or not to remember.[24]

The desire to reconstruct cultural history—a motivating force behind many art documentaries by African American women—is tempered by keen awareness of the film industry's historic resistance to "oppositional" works that critique the very social and aesthetic conventions that underpin mainstream cinema. The film industry's dismissal of works perceived to be unconventional and non-commercial results in large part from its mandate to produce conventional, broadly commercial "product" in a profit-driven arena. In *Cinematic Jazz*, Julie Dash catalogues the forces against which she struggles to produce, publicize, distribute, and exhibit her narrative and documentary films, including *Daughters of the Dust*. Of Hollywood she says, "It's very difficult for women and more than difficult for black women. It's a miracle that any black woman could survive there, and most don't survive very long." Echoing Dash's concerns, Yvonne Welbon notes that most people don't know the name of a single black woman filmmaker, adding that as a student at the Art Institute of Chicago, the only such name she knew was that of Julie Dash: "If I looked around me, there was no evidence that there were any other black women filmmakers and that was very disturbing."[25]

In part, Dash feels her problems producing films, getting them seen in festivals, and finding distributors result from the unconventional nature of her works: her female protagonists are fully rounded human beings rather than stereotypes, and her plots focus on the texture and quality of women's lives rather than tales of racial conflict. Speaking in *Cinematic Jazz* of white distributors' opposition to *Daughters of the Dust*, Dash says, "It's not the type of black woman they're used to looking at, it's not the kind of story they're used to seeing." Dash also implicates her fellow male independent film/videomakers: "Our work is definitely being suppressed on every level—with the help of the male filmmakers by their silence."[26]

O. Funmilayo Makarah's *Creating a Different Image: Portrait of Alile Sharon Larkin* (1989) is, like Welbon's *Cinematic Jazz*, designed to grant greater visibility to the work of a sister media artist. Makarah shares Welbon's impulse to forge a connection with her subject, to learn and convey crucial facts about the life and experience of black women film/videomakers. Makarah begins her profile with Larkin's assertion that "I am an independent filmmaker," then cuts from an extreme close-up of Larkin's eyes to a similar close-up of the eyes of the African mother in Larkin's 1979 film *Your Children Come Back to You*. Later, Makarah implies a connection between herself and her subject by including interview material that articulates the dream of many women to become media artists: "quoting" from Larkin's 1982 film *A Different Image*, Makarah focuses on a photograph of Larkin's mother from that film, as Larkin says, "I always thought of college as something I did for my mom, but film school, that was for me . . . This was my dream, to make films. . . . This was the dream that we had—little colored girls, as we say—to be able to create films." But Larkin had always been told that the arts were not for poor folks, that artists were eccentric misfits.

The desire of young media artists to lend cinematic immortality to their mentors characterizes many art documentaries by African American women. Larkin's beloved mentor was poet Fluci Moses (the pen name of Louise Jane Moses), the subject of Larkin's simply titled videotape *Miss Fluci Moses* (1987). As is so often the case, such film/videomakers make documentaries to share their enthusiasm for figures they view as extraordinary. In Larkin's words on the soundtrack, "Once [Moses] took me under her wing and told me the story of her life, I just knew someone has to put this on tape." As Makarah documents Larkin and Larkin documents Moses, they create a chain of influence that links women artists across generations.

Larkin's videotape preserves and extends African American cultural history by documenting and sharing Moses's story and poetry. While including a few still photographs from Moses's past titled "European Traveler," "World War II Service Club Director," "Poet," "Friend," and "Mentor" and some footage of others reading Moses's poetry, Larkin allows contemporary footage of Moses herself to dominate the proceedings. Larkin features Moses's reading of "Let's Tab This Moment for the Record," one suspects, to convey to the viewer something of the shared sensibility of herself and her subject: both videomaker and poet use their craft to establish connections between the present and the past, document significant moments, and create a living history. Moreover Larkin's chronicling in her videotape of Moses's career is matched by Moses's chronicling in her poems of her ancestors: reading from her poem "Black Hands," Moses presents a litany of her forebears' contributions to this country which include laying rails, canoeing streams, smelting iron, digging coal, baking biscuits, and tidying homes. Again, reading from "Africa, I Hear the Sound of a Distant Drum," Moses addresses a theme that runs through the work of almost all those artists appearing in these film/video works—the connection with ancestors and an ancestral homeland.

Moses's poems lend elegant shape to her memories, but her more free-form reminiscences are equally compelling: Larkin's videotape captures Moses's account of her childhood as the tenth of eleven children, as well as family tales that predate her birth, such as Booker T. Washington's visit to her family's Alabama home. She explains her early understanding of the best ways to handle sexist and racist confrontations, lovingly describes her first car (a Jeep with a convertible top), and provides details of her work life.

Most of all, Moses speaks of her desire to be part of history in terms that echo Larkin's desire to "put things down on tape": "I've been thinking that Negroes or black people should make a record of their living here, and I've been jotting these little poems down for years. And so that in order to keep a record of just my family and what I thought and the ways I felt during the years I was living, I thought that writing a book would be just the thing." The sentiment she expresses—the desire to "make a record of my family being present, especially since they had done so much for humanity"—is the center of the videotape's thematic interest and concern. If Moses's poems are, as she describes them, "shadow castings . . . that reflect my presence in the world," so too are Larkin's video images that preserve Moses on screen: Moses died just two weeks after attending the premiere screening of *Miss Fluci Moses*.

Larkin is one of a number of young black women who have come of age as film/video artists by casting more mature artists—often beloved teachers—as the subject of their apprentice works. Others include Ayoka Chenzira and Kathe Sandler who, as New York University filmmaking students, produced films that passed on the teachings of their dance instructors. Chenzira's *Syvilla: They Dance to Her Drum* and Sandler's *Remembering Thelma* (1981) combine archival stills and footage, voice-over narration, and interviews with students and professionals to introduce their subjects' careers as dancers, choreographers, and teachers, and speak to their accomplishments. What is touching and at times unsettling about these works is the discrepancy between their ambition to be "well-made" documentaries and their reliance on fragmentary source materials. The films that have emerged from these efforts are little valentines painstakingly patched together out of bits and pieces of disparate footage, cinematic scrapbooks that convey above all the intensely personal commitment of student filmmakers to teachers who have touched them and enriched their community, and who must not be forgotten.

Chenzira explains the impetus behind *Syvilla* by saying that, "While I was at NYU I was also dancing professionally and Syvilla meant a lot to me. I lived in her studio, it became my second home. When she was sick and dying, I really went into a panic. This was the first—aside from my mother—major role model for me. . . . In class you had to pitch what you wanted to do and then try to pull a crew together. Well, nobody wanted to do a film on an old black woman who was dying. . . . But George [Stoney, a renowned documentary filmmaker and then-Chair of NYU's Undergraduate Filmmaking Department] was so supportive." Chenzira notes that today she would feel less constrained in making *Syvilla*: "I found the documentary format as it was being taught and displayed 20 years ago, when I was training, to be very confining . . . there were many more things that I wanted to say about Syvilla Fort. Had I known what I know now, they would have been said."[27]

Even so, *Syvilla* lovingly conveys a poignant portrait of its subject. Though suffering from cancer, Fort is shown nurturing the talents of students of all ages, talking about her career as dancer and teacher, and finally conducting her last class and closing her dance studio. Footage of Fort's early, incandescent performances was apparently unavailable to the filmmaker, who instead arranged to have dancer Dyane Harvey recreate the works that had catapulted Fort to stardom: John Cage's *Bacchanale*, his first composition for prepared piano, written specifically for Fort's choreography, and *Danza*, a piece that fuses Fort's interests in classical ballet, modern dance, and African, Caribbean, and South

American dance forms. Chenzira's film is particularly interested, however, in tracing the distinctive trajectory of Fort's life—how she traded her career as a modern dancer-choreographer for one as a teacher of professional dancers, and then of non-professional community members, increasingly using her studio as her home and as a home-away-from-home for young people suddenly homeless because of their parents' disapproval of their pursuit of an artistic career.

Kathe Sandler describes her first film, *Remembering Thelma*, as "a form of documenting my teacher who died in a tragic accident in 1977. I was studying film at NYU and I was interested in it, through all the influences. . . . Bob Van Lierop, Ousmane Sembène, thinking about this unwritten history and then starting this film on Thelma Hill."[28] Sandler introduces Hill, emphasizing the same themes sounded in *Syvilla*: "Teacher, dancer, and mentor to several generations of dancers and choreographers, her unrecorded work behind the scenes touched countless lives and had an immeasurable influence on American dance." As in *Syvilla*, Hill's dancing is itself linked to the issue of "passing on" traditions: she is described as someone who learned the Horton technique and then trained others, just as Fort is "the vital link between the Katherine Dunham and Alvin Ailey schools." One of the pleasures of Sandler's film is the way it incorporates television footage of the Alvin Ailey troupe in performance, allowing the audience to experience Hill's dancing in that context as well as in the context of her later work with students.

A special case in films about mentors is Cheryl Fabio Bradford's study of her mother titled *Rainbow Black: Poet Sarah W. Fabio* (1976). In its opening sequence, Bradford is shown traversing the Oakland, California mud flats and handling pieces of driftwood while on the soundtrack Fabio reads a poem that equates driftwood with the weathered, long-journeying spirit of African Americans. The film further links Fabio's growth as a poet with the evolving political climate. Claiming roots in the tradition of Langston Hughes and the Harlem Renaissance, Fabio traces her radicalization to contact with the Black Power movement and Stokely Carmichael, and to her travels to Europe during which she first experienced traces of the Holocaust. Fabio's artistic development was also affected by her becoming a spokesperson for her community, and by her transformation from an artist who wrote "first for the page" to one who combined poetry and performance. The film returns at several points to footage of Fabio in a recording studio producing Folkways Records albums in which her chanted poems are accompanied by flute, guitar, and conga drum music.

Like others featured in these works, Fabio discusses her struggles as a black artist and teacher. As a writer, she started a small press in the 1960s because mainstream publishers at that time were uninterested in works by black women authors; as a teacher on an unnamed predominately white campus of 20,000 students, she sees herself as "in effect a one-room black schoolhouse" for the 300 African Americans enrolled in her Black Studies program.

Rainbow Black is distinguished by its privileged perspective on its artist-subject: Bradford sometimes documents the poet in institutional settings, but more often places her in the context of home and family, her daily workplace. One memorable scene finds Fabio discussing and reading aloud from her poetry while sitting cross-legged on the floor of her bedroom, surrounded by dozens of books and manuscripts through which she leafs to find excerpts, a cup of coffee nearby on the carpet. Such informal, domestic views characterize this portrait. With her infant grandchild sprawled across her lap as she delivers classroom lectures, Fabio is a teacher who views her students as extended family members. She teaches them poetry writing, but also serves as "the sole influence pulling them away from the major culture that was destroying their identity." Answering a question posed by her daughter-filmmaker in the classroom, Fabio lists poems she has written about black women—historical figures (Rosa Parks; Phillis Wheatley, the first African American woman poet) and family members (her grandmother; her daughter)—and adds a statement that echoes those of Julie Dash, Syvilla Fort, Thelma Hill, Alile Sharon Larkin, Miss Fluci Moses, and others committed to celebrating a continuity between generations of African American women: "Certainly I have been interested in what were the things that my grandmother presented to me in word and image that I must present to my daughters, and my granddaughters and through them to other black women that I come in contact with, students and friends."

The complex bond between generations of women is an important issue for a number of the film / videomakers and their artist-subjects. Not surprisingly, the impulse to establish connections with previous generations of women is often expressed in depictions of the family: the relationship between daughters, mothers and grandmothers. According to Marianne Hirsch:

> There can be no systematic and theoretical study of women in patriarchal culture, there can be no theory of women's oppression, that does not take into account woman's role as a mother of daughters and as a daughter of mothers, that does not study female identity in relation to previous and subsequent generations of women, and that does not study that relationship

in the wider context in which it takes place: the emotional, political, economic, and symbolic structures of family and society." [29]

Many of the African American women media artists examined here make documentaries that contest racism and patriarchy, while valuing black women's wisdom and power. In addition, these works assert the positive aspects of families shattered by slavery, oppression and poverty.

O. Funmilayo Makarah ends *Creating a Different Image* with the title, "This production is dedicated to my mother, my grandmother, and the women before me who have worked to create a different image." Yvonne Welbon's grandmother is a significant inspiration for her filmmaking. In her autobiographical, experimental documentary, *Remembering Wei Yi-fang, Remembering Myself* (1995), Welbon parallels her grandmother's movements from Honduras to North America at the age of twenty-two and her own movement from the United States to Taiwan at the same age. In Welbon's words, "My grandmother's memories are so vivid you can see everything she says very clearly and so it's not hard to illustrate these memories. . . . We have a lot of people who can tell us these stories and we can re-create the pictures, so that's part of my style."[30] In all of her work, Welbon always considers, "Is this something my grandmother can sit and watch and enjoy?" Kathe Sandler says much the same thing: "I wanted to make films that were accessible to the African American community from various walks of life . . . media that would be as identifiable to my grandmother and aunts as it would be to my godmothers who are writers."[31]

There are many other art documentaries by women about women who have directly or indirectly influenced their lives.[32] Monica Freeman's *Valerie, A Woman! An Artist! A Philosophy of Life!* (1975) is a short film that introduces audiences to sculptor Valerie Maynard in her studio and on the streets of Harlem. Carroll Blue's *Varnette's World: A Study of the Young Artist* (1979) juxtaposes Varnette Honeywood's paintings with live-action street scenes designed to illustrate the idea that art has a direct relationship to its community. Demetria Royals's *Mama's Pushcart* (1988) celebrates the achievements of Ellen Stewart, the driving force behind the La Mama Theater; Royals marshals an impressive amount of archival material, stills from productions, and interviews with artists to chronicle Stewart's work shepherding the company though the triumphs and tribulations of La Mama's quarter century as an internationally known outpost of innovative dramatic productions. Elena Featherstone's *Visions of the Spirit: A Portrait of Alice Walker* (1989) offers audiences the opportunity to hear Walker talk about her childhood and her career and especially to see her with her family in the context of her rural home. In Debra Robinson's *I Be Done Been Was Is* (1984), four comediennes talk about their unconventional women's work in the context of women comics who came before, while Demetria Royals's *Conjure Women* (1995) suggests connections between women whose artistic work in different media can be seen as having magical, transformative powers.

In her *Trumpetistically, Clora Bryant* (1989), Zeinabu irene Davis profiles a pioneering artist with whose efforts she identifies: "I felt she was taking an unconventional path as a woman trumpeter, and that I too was taking an unconventional path as a filmmaker." Davis sums up her own work and that of others in this study: "It's an impulse among black women filmmakers in particular to pay tribute to someone else who's inspired them."[33]

A LIFE IN THE ARTS: THE ARTIST AS A SOCIAL FORCE

Many black documentarians focus on and identify with the political commitment of their artist-subjects. Carroll Blue, William Miles, and Gil Noble among others have all produced documentaries that celebrate the socially engaged work of internationally known artists, such as author James Baldwin, photographer Roy DeCarava, and singer/actor Paul Robeson. In so doing these film/videomakers "join the struggle," producing works that extend both the aesthetic and social concerns of the artists they document. When author Alice Walker says, "If I didn't write, I'd throw bombs,"[34] and when photographer Gordon Parks titles his autobiography *A Choice of Weapons*,[35] they underline the fact that one role the artist can play—including the media artist—is that of an urgent, incendiary force for social change.

In *Paul Robeson: The Tallest Tree in Our Forest* (1977), Gil Noble extends his work of reportage as producer/on-camera interviewer of the long-running television series *Like It Is* to create a full-length documentary that "tells the extraordinary story of an extraordinary man." Noble is not alone in wanting to set the record straight about Paul Robeson's place in American history; William Miles and William Greaves also worked on projects that celebrate Robeson, the premier artist-activist of his generation, while noting the difficulties of documenting his life.[36]

Noble's documentary relies on materials from archival collections—especially from the Paul Robeson Archive, overseen by Paul Robeson, Jr.—including photographs, recordings of Robeson singing, speaking, and acting, excerpts from films, and newsreel footage of his concert appearances abroad. To call attention to the challenge of assembling an account of Robeson's life from necessarily limited fragments, Noble begins with shots of the Robeson Archive, full of stacks of books, cans of film, and a reel-to-reel tape recorder on which we hear Robeson's rendition of "We Are Climbing Jacob's Ladder," as the title for the film appears on screen. The image of the tape recorder as Robeson's stand-in recurs throughout the film, making clear the difficulties of documenting a person whose career was first destroyed, then eradicated from American history. In a recent interview, Noble explains, "The Robeson story is very significant because he never appeared on American television. And that's to this nation's shame. And he was blacklisted in this country, and that's to this country's shame. Not only that, but he was perhaps the most gifted man who ever lived, regardless of race and nationality. And yet our educational systems don't tell his story."[37]

In Noble's view, Robeson's is a story of uncompromising principle —the dramatic tale of a man who had prodigious talents as a singer, a film star, an athlete, and a scholar, and who was willing to sacrifice his lucrative career for his convictions. Noble's film outlines the major events in Robeson's life, linking them to historical moments, while chronicling Robeson's gifts in the voice-over narration: he was "one of the greatest football players of all time." He showed that "the black man had his own unique and potent culture." He was "black, beautiful, and brilliant." What emerges is a portrait of a man who not only wanted "to sing the folk songs of my people," but who wanted to know where the music came from, as well as the "relationship between Negro music and all the nations of the world." Indeed, the film presents Robeson as a teacher/scholar who examined the links between African music and Moravian and Bach chorales and concluded that "all men are brothers because of their music." The film's many commentators, especially Harry Belafonte and Dizzy Gillespie, note Robeson's desire to pass on the traditions of African music and to assert the relationship between Africa and other parts of the black diaspora, his knowledge of more than 30 languages, his identification with the working class at home and abroad, his support for trade unions, his work on behalf of world peace, his outspoken attacks on fascism and racism, and his friendship with the Russian people. The film thus offers a litany of Robeson's convictions while it celebrates his intellect, his voice, his physique, his acting, and his integrity and dignity.

Noble's narration presents Robeson as a colossal yet tragic figure who secured international fame—"Paul Robeson became the most well-known man in the world"—only to be discredited, isolated, and denied the opportunity to work during the McCarthy era: his passport was revoked, he was refused television and theater appearances, his bookings were canceled, and he was ostracized. Noble explains the importance of pursuing the Robeson story: "He was painted as a Communist, he was painted as an anarchist, he was painted as a disappointment, he was painted as somebody who was bitter, you know, he was misrepresented. The little that we heard about him was there was something wrong with him . . . he had this malignancy called Communism, that he was some evil person. . . . I think his story needed to be told and put in a better perspective."[38]

The film also reminds audiences of those who did not abandon Robeson: fellow progressive artists, the community churches that allowed him to perform, the tens of thousands who gathered at the Canadian border to hear him (a concert that "went unreported"), the South Wales miners who protested the U.S. State Department's denying Robeson the right to travel and sing to them (their only solution was to listen to a radio broadcast he prepared especially for them), the British Members of Parliament who petitioned for the return of Robeson's passport. And through the words of Paul Robeson, Jr., the film takes the position that Robeson was in some ways simply ahead of his time. He lived to see many of his ideas come to pass: the travel of American leaders to China, the admittance of blacks to major league baseball, the independence of African nations.

Noble's film attempts to define heroism, even to create an image of Robeson as a mythic figure. As an alternative narrative, the film is meant to answer the vicious attacks on Paul Robeson—from the mass physical violence that broke out at his Peekskill, New York performance to the more personal assaults on his life and integrity. And the film raises significant questions about storytelling and its relationship to documentary filmmaking: Who will tell the story? Will children hear about the kinds of heroes who will give them a sense of dignity and pride?

Two voices dominate this film: the voice of Robeson, whose renditions of "Old Man River" and "Ballad for Americans" seem like irreplaceable parts of American culture and history; the voice of narrator Gil Noble, who sees connections between Robeson's career and his own as a documentarian committed to social justice. Reflecting on his career, Noble explains the ways he has learned from his chosen documentary subjects: "So doing these documentaries has really been a quest for myself, a quest to understand myself, to take on a value system that makes me a better person."[39] Noble's *Paul Robeson* is therefore personal, if not explicitly so; it provides a transition between more conventional, authoritative documentaries and intensely autobiographical works. When Noble appears at the end of the film, standing in the cemetery where Robeson is buried, he provides what is clearly labeled as the film's commentary, valorizing his subject in terms unlike those used by any other filmmaker in this study:

> The physical remains of Paul Robeson end here. But what about the man's story? Surely, it represents a major chapter in America's history. The tragedy is that story has hardly been told. Mass media has in fact suppressed large amounts of information about this man. Despite exhaustive research we were unable to come up with precious little news film that was shot of this man here in this country. You undoubtedly noticed how much still photographs we had to use. And what little motion picture that we did include in this documentary came from overseas. Not even the Library of Congress has much to offer in film on this man, Paul Robeson. Where is that film, we ask? We also ask why has his name not been listed in our books? Books about our history, America's history, the history of the civil rights movement, the American arts. We also ask why his name has not been listed on the Football Hall of Fame. Maybe now, in death, his name will rise up again and claim its proper place in our history. Certainly our children should know that story. It is a story of strength and gentleness, commitment and unbending principle.

For documentarians, the opportunity to chronicle the life of a fellow filmmaker has special resonance.[40] Several documentaries have focused on "race films"—films featuring all-black casts made by black filmmakers for black audiences in this country. Pearl Bowser's *Midnight Ramble: Oscar Micheaux and the Story of Race Movies* (1994) is an extremely well-researched, illustrated lecture that includes voice-over narration spoken by James Avery and expert testimony from archivist Bowser, author Toni Cade Bambara, filmmaker Carlton Moss, historian Robert Hall, journalist St. Clair Bourne, Sr., illustrator Elton Fax, and Micheaux's actors Frances Williams, Herb Jefferies, Edna Mae Harris, and Shingzi McKay. Co-directed with Bestor Cram and with a script by film scholar Clyde Taylor, *Midnight Ramble* contains archival footage and stills from the period, as well as extensive excerpts from extant "race films." These excerpts provide the film's fundamental pleasures—images from a tradition of black filmmaking in which black audiences could view recognizable images of themselves on movie screens.

Midnight Ramble carefully places "race movies" in historical context. It traces their development relative to the racial violence that swept this country between 1890 and 1920, including the "Red Summer of 1919," and it gives particular attention to the disillusionment of black soldiers returning from World War I only to face racism at home. It follows the parallel lines of Hollywood and "race movies" into the period when new, racially integrated movie theaters, together with entertainment industry co-opting of African American popular cultural forms, effectively ended the production of "race movies." *Midnight Ramble* demonstrates the ways in which "race movies" provided alternatives to the demeaning and dehumanizing images of blacks in mainstream culture, including those in the various versions of *The Clansman*—book, play, pageants, parades, and D. W. Griffith's film *The Birth of a Nation* (1915). One of the excerpts in *Midnight Ramble* is from Micheaux's *Within Our Gates* (1926), described as the first film to tell the story of a lynching from a black point of view. Commenting on a scene showing the attempted rape of a black woman by a lecherous white man, Toni Cade Bambara makes a case for the way Micheaux's controversial film parodies *The Birth of a Nation*, reversing its stereotypes and "setting the record straight about who rapes who."

The sense of a lost past dominates *Midnight Ramble*, as it does so many documentaries about artists. The film abounds with references to lost footage and concludes with the words, "Today only a few fragments of these films survive, reminders of a time when movie makers struggled to fill the hunger black Americans had to see themselves portrayed with dignity, affection, and pride." The problem of locating film excerpts also makes it difficult to appreciate fully the contribution of Oscar Micheaux, here remembered as the great entrepreneur: the rancher-turned-writer who singlehandedly published his own books, sold them door to door, and finally insisted on directing the 1919 film version of his novel *The Homesteader*, which became the first feature-length "race movie."

Midnight Ramble traces recurring elements in Micheaux's films—particularly his obsessive concern with miscegenation and the "drop of black blood" theme—and the reception his films received. Micheaux is also presented as an *auteur* who did many jobs: as author-screenwriter, fundraiser, actor, director, editor, publicist, and distributor of his films Micheaux was "an inspiration to the independent black cinema movement which has grown up in his shadow." While it includes a few telling anecdotes—Micheaux "borrowing" a squirrel coat from a visitor and using it for a scene before its owner knew it was missing—*Midnight Ramble* focuses instead on the social significance of Micheaux's work and of "race films" in general. Elton Fax says that Micheaux, while concerned with making a profit, believed he was "helping to elevate our people"; he wanted "to teach that the colored man can be anything." These values are summarized by Toni Cade Bambara, who says, "the existence of a body of films from that period is proof that we were there, that certain kinds of assaults, such as *The Birth of a Nation*, did not go unanswered, that the . . . industry was challenged and that there was a movement in those days to try to do justice to black character and to black community life. It gives us memories, a sense of the past, and it puts a bone in the back."

Oscar Micheaux, Film Pioneer (1981), written and produced by Carol Munday Lawrence, provides a less ambitious, more human-scale approach to the subject. Neither definitive nor scholarly, Lawrence's film is nevertheless enormously endearing, relying as it does on a series of charming stories recounted by Lorenzo Tucker and Ethel Moses, two actors who worked with Micheaux, and lively docudrama material featuring Danny Glover in the role of filmmaker Micheaux. As Tucker and Moses reminisce about how Micheaux got the actors and the shots he wanted—and especially the way he succeeded in getting his films distributed—the film illustrates those moments. It opens with a dramatization of Micheaux shooting a scene from one of his films; a later dramatization shows him building his one-man distribution network by driving through rural areas and talking with a small-town movie theater manager about booking Micheaux productions. When Tucker and Moses recall that Micheaux used beautiful chorus girls in scenes set in the Cotton Club because "those poor guys from the South need to see pretty legs," Lawrence's dramatization features a young woman singing the erotically charged "If You've Never Been Vamped by a Brown Skin Before, You've Never Been Vamped at All."

As moments are recalled and then pictured, a relatively intimate, anecdotal portrait of Micheaux emerges. He suffered from intense abdominal pain and often directed scenes while reclining on a couch and eating handfuls of starch to settle his stomach. He was a resourceful filmmaker who knew how best to exploit existing situations, sometimes filming from a telephone booth on a busy downtown intersection when he needed a "crowd scene." He was a shrewd businessman who plowed all of his earnings back into new films, and was deeply hurt whenever those films were not successful. He treated his cast and crew like family members, often serving as a father figure to his co-workers. The film is propelled by such anecdotes, which are delivered with profound respect and admiration. Micheaux is called a "decent, clean type of fella who thought his movies would uplift the blacks of the South." His plots might have seemed corny but his films were beloved: they engendered the unique "excitement of seeing a colored cast not picking cotton or not playing comedy parts, really dressed up, really living, talking like real people talk." Micheaux's depiction of blacks as attractive people enjoying a good life fueled the dreams and ambitions of thousands of African Americans.

Like other films about socially engaged artists, Carroll Parrott Blue's Conversations with Roy DeCarava (1983), made for television and co-directed with David Schwartz, communicates photographer DeCarava's dedication to creating images that contradict the idea that African Americans are not worthy of depiction, images that stand in opposition to the depictions of African Americans as caricatures or "a problem." Combining DeCarava's extraordinary images with commentary about his life and his art, the film seamlessly collages Alex Haley's voice-over narration, interview material with DeCarava, and jazz background music, to accompany both DeCarava's still photographs and footage of him shooting pictures. In fact, the film directly links jazz and photography, saying that jazz "approaches the visual experience of photography at the precise moment when things come together." The filming of the photographs is varied—employing zooms, a range of camera movements, and dissolves as well as cuts between the still images.

The formal elegance of DeCarava's photographs makes an arresting counterpoint to his informal anecdotes. DeCarava is explicit about being the only black student at Cooper Union where the atmosphere was "chilly"; about losing out to a white student who "of course got the scholarship" though DeCarava had the best record; and about having his portfolio rejected as "too Negro" by the many art directors and publishers to whom he showed his work. He also acknowledges the important influences on his life: the Harlem Art Center that encouraged ordinary people to get involved in the arts, the artists Vincent Van Gogh and Charles White, and the photographers Edward Steichen, who included DeCarava's work in the celebrated *The Family of Man* publication, and Ansel Adams, who speaks about the significance of DeCarava's work. Like the artist-subjects of many of the documentaries discussed here, DeCarava talks about the need to create one's own mechanisms for getting work to the public. The film notes that DeCarava opened a short-lived photo gallery in the 1950s dedicated to representing the work of black photographers who portray blacks with dignity. The film juxtaposes a positive *New York Times* review of a show at DeCarava's gallery with his comments on historical invisibility. DeCarava explains that the influential gallery "fell into a black hole" and remains unmentioned in all official accounts of photographic history in this country.

Carlton Moss's *Paul Laurence Dunbar: America's First Black Poet* (1973) begins with Dunbar's lines, "We wear the mask that grins and lies," as the screen fills with images of African masks. Illustrating the poetry is a strategy employed throughout by Moss, who uses dramatizations and background music to "bring to life" both readings of Dunbar's work and significant moments in his biography. For example, a first-person narrator tells stories of Dunbar's childhood, accompanied by images of a child playing with blocks. Dunbar's rejection from a job ("We don't hire niggers") prompts an image of a hand crushing a piece of paper. Docudrama footage takes us into the world of the elevator operator, Dunbar's first job and the one he held when he began writing seriously. The short story "Blood Guilty," which describes the lynching of an innocent black man told from the point of view of a vengeful, then shamed, white man, is pictured in a series of still photographs and, briefly, in live action footage that conveys the terrors of Southern rural justice.

James Baldwin: The Price of the Ticket (1989), co-produced by William Miles and Karen Thorsen, is a thoroughly researched, yet fluid work that captures the complexities of the writer, while maintaining a deeply emotional commitment toward its subject. The film begins and ends with Baldwin's funeral at the Cathedral of St. John the Divine in Manhattan on December 8, 1987; the body of the film interweaves the strands of Baldwin's personal life and his literary activities, using archival interviews with the writer, footage from a 1984 television dramatization of his autobiographical novel *Go Tell It on the Mountain* and from the Broadway production of his play *Blues for Mister Charlie*, and readings from his writings by Maya Angelou.

The film's "witnesses" include family members, friends, fellow artists, biographers, and students, all of whom were deeply affected by Baldwin. The soundtrack is full of songs that have specific application to moments in Baldwin's life, including Odetta's rendition of "Motherless Child," Fats Waller's "Why Do I Lie to Myself about You," The Freedom Singers' "We Shall Not Be Moved," Bobby Short's and David Baldwin's arrangement of "Have a Little Talk with Jesus," and Baldwin's own rendition of "Precious Lord, Take My Hand."

The Price of the Ticket benefits from extensive television interview material in which Baldwin talks about his stern father, his years as a preacher and their influence on his writing, the public reception of his work, his years as an expatriate in Europe, his travels to Istanbul, his return to the United States during the civil rights era, his anger about racism in America, and his hopes for the future. The question of what it means to be an artist—and particularly a socially engaged public figure —is given extensive analysis here. Baldwin's need to find a place to work is a central issue. Driven out of the country by his barely controllable rage in the face of racism (dramatized in the image of a glass of water thrown against a mirror), Baldwin moved to Paris because "he wanted to be a writer and couldn't be a writer in America." Baldwin's need to find a private, secure working environment took him to a small village in Switzerland; it was there that he listened to Bessie Smith and

Fats Waller, whose music "gave me the key" to the language with which to write *Go Tell It on the Mountain*. The problems of finding publishers for one's writings are also examined: the former Knopf editor William Cole recalls championing the publication of *Go Tell It on the Mountain* in the late 1940s, and regrets the fact that he was away at the time Knopf editors rejected the manuscript for Baldwin's second novel, *Giovanni's Room* (1956), scared off by its homosexual theme.

The role of the artist as a social and political activist is also explored in *The Price of the Ticket*. Baldwin's life and art flourished while he was abroad, but he felt compelled to come back to America to be part of the civil rights movement of the 1960s. Over footage of demonstrations, Baldwin says, "I came home to see . . . to do whatever I could do." James Briggs Murray says Baldwin was "one of the first to articulate what we were feeling—what we would feel." Continually questioned about the relationship between his art and his politics, Baldwin is shown appearing in many public forums, including *The Dick Cavett Show*, where he speaks eloquently about the ways racism is institutionalized in America. In another interview, he asserts that race continues to be a defining issue: "As long as you think you're white, I'm going to be forced to think I'm black."

Baldwin further makes clear that his writing will engage issues central to the social upheaval of the period, a decision Baraka notes in the film made Baldwin "too radical" after *Blues for Mister Charlie*— no longer granted his marginal status "on the edge of the Pantheon marked 'Colored.'" Baraka takes on the question of Baldwin's politically charged works, saying: "James Baldwin was in the tradition. People are always saying to me, 'Why is your work so political?' That is our tradition—whether you're talking about Frederick Douglass, or W. E. B. Du Bois, or Zora Neale Hurston, or Toni Morrison, or Alice Walker. And why is that our tradition? Because not only is our tradition to include society as the focus for art—you see as its principal focus the development of society—but as an oppressed people we have no other choice but to fight."

No other African American art documentary better conveys the impact of the assassination of Malcolm X and Dr. Martin Luther King, Jr. than *James Baldwin: The Price of the Ticket*. The film focuses on the crushing sadness and disillusionment Baldwin experienced, then articulated in his writings and interviews. Having seen him in footage of demonstrations, and having heard his tale of buying a suit to attend a demonstration with Dr. King only to find himself wearing the suit to King's funeral, the viewer is not surprised when Baldwin bitterly accounts for the slowing of his literary output by reminding an interviewer that he is "writing between assassinations."

At the heart of the film is the notion of Baldwin as an outsider on several levels—the black homosexual expatriate who was celebrated and attacked by blacks and whites at various points in his career. As Baldwin says, "There are days, and this is one of them, when you wonder what your role is in this society and what your future is." Baldwin, found to be "too political" and "too angry" by whites, was also ostracized by blacks who found him "not revolutionary enough" because he was unwilling to embrace the revolutionary politics of the black power movement. Baldwin's hatred of violence and firm commitment to the idea that "all men are brothers" caused *Soul on Ice* author Eldridge Cleaver (and other black leaders) to dismiss Baldwin for "hating his own race."[41] Yet Baldwin remained the inspiration for many writers, including those writers like Ishmael Reed and Amiri Baraka, who attacked Baldwin during his lifetime. As Baraka points out in the film, "He brought that cry into the cocktail parties as well as to the universities as well as to the streets. All of us interested in black liberation, interested in human progress, and interested in writing owe him a great debt."

The end of the film is particularly poignant: it deals with a dying Baldwin and the question of his legacy. Students talk about the ways he encouraged their creativity. Baldwin biographer David Leeming notes that "everybody who came into contact with Jimmy had his or her life changed. That's the mark of a real teacher, a real preacher, and a real prophet. Jimmy was in many ways a prophet." Bobby Short points out that a person of Baldwin's talent and commitment to human rights shouldn't "go in and out of vogue like a tie or a hat." Baldwin's brother David emotionally relates Baldwin's hope for his own legacy: "I pray I've done my work so that when I've gone from here . . . and when someone finds himself digging through the ruins . . . somewhere in that wreckage, they'll find me. Somewhere in that wreckage they'll use something that I left behind. And if I've done that, then I can feel I accomplished something in life." Baldwin is heard saying, "A day will come when you will trust you more than you do now. And a day will come when you will trust me more than you do now. We can trust each other. I really do believe in the New Jerusalem. I really do believe that we can all become better than we are. I know we can. But the price is enormous and people are not yet willing to pay." By the film's last sequence, when it returns to the footage of the funeral with which its began, one's response to the images has necessarily deepened. The film has created an intimate connection to the person we see carried in the coffin. It is to us that Baldwin seems to be waving in the photograph that closes the film.

TRACING THE EVOLUTION OF BLACK ARTS: THE SURVEY FILM

Documentaries in this section survey artists working within a single tradition and trace the history of a particular art form. While few films focus on the fine arts—e.g., Carlton Moss's *Two Centuries of Black American Art* (1977)—several of these films and videos explore musical traditions, and especially the notion of African origins and the connections between African traditional music and music of the black diaspora. Gil Noble's first feature-length documentary, *Jazz, the American Art Form*, cited by its director as "the first African American–produced documentary shown on WABC-TV during prime time,"[42] exemplifies these works. Himself a jazz musician and at one time leader of the Gil Noble Trio, Noble invites audiences to see the similarities among various forms of music in various countries; as the film's narrator, he argues that African tribal dance and music "merged with harmonies all over the world." In this way the film provides links between African music, work songs of plantation workers and prisoners in U.S. chain gangs, the samba in Latin America, and calypso music of the Caribbean. To explain the origins of jazz, Noble interviews key musicians about their understanding of the history of blues and gospel, about cool and hot jazz, bebop and ragtime. Noble also presents extraordinary footage of artists in performance, including Louis Armstrong, Count Basie, Nat Cole, Billy Eckstine, Duke Ellington, Erroll Garner, Dizzy Gillespie, Billie Holiday, Thelonius Monk, Charlie Parker, Paul Robeson, Art Tatum, and Sarah Vaughan.

Two musicians articulate the film's central issues. Dizzy Gillespie claims that his music is compatible with black music world-wide, then travels to New Orleans and Jamaica to demonstrate links between modern jazz, Dixieland, and calypso music. Sequences featuring Gillespie support the film's conclusion that "it all works—mutuality is there." Eubie Blake, who both opens and closes the film and is its chief spokesperson, expresses the film's larger point of view—that the story of jazz has not yet been told, that the significant contributions of black artists have not yet been acknowledged. The opening sequence with Blake sitting at a piano sets the tone: ever the voice of authority, he offers the viewer history "from the horse's mouth"; Blake playfully raises the issue of how history is recorded by suggesting that the real story of Paul

Revere's ride has not been told, since no one asked the horse. He happily corrects a number of misconceptions. For example, "Paul Whiteman
was not the king of the big band era—James Reese Europe was the
king," and the cakewalk was not demeaning to blacks, it was a put-
down of whites.

A more modest, but related work, Billy Jackson's *Didn't We Ramble
On* (1984) traces the ancient African origins of present-day football
marching bands and New Orleans jazz funeral processions, invoking a
spirit that is passed on over many generations. Dizzy Gillespie serves as
the historian/storyteller, charting the links between African drummers
and the celebrated Florida A&M marching band ("the modern fulfillment of a 700 year old ideal"). Gillespie's illustrated lecture employs
maps, engravings, and photographs to trace a musical tradition that is
said to have traveled from Africa to seventeenth century Europe, where
Turkish bands prompted Napoleon's desire for a military band, to the
American colonies where black participation in the Revolutionary
Army's fife and drum corps and in military bands in World War I helped
to keep up troop morale. There is a commitment to demystification in
this film which lends special historical and cultural meaning to a form
that might otherwise be taken as simply half-time entertainment. As the
film points out, it is important to value how "the old teach the young
how to remember."

Orlando Bagwell's *New Worlds, New Forms* is a positive, future-
oriented work that also traces the evolution of African music in the
black diaspora, showing how such music reinvented itself, fusing with
the music of diverse cultures to create new, invigorated forms. Bagwell's polished, international co-production includes interviews with
anthropologist Sheila Walker who points out that despite "having been
stripped of nearly all we had," blacks created new cultural forms connected to African heritage, and musicologist Bernice Johnson Reagon
who notes that in the process of cultural adaptation, materials are not
so much "confiscated" as put together to create something new that
nonetheless "is ours." The film has the quality of an illustrated lecture
on the merging of cultures: how Jamaicans created reggae, maintaining an African form in English; how people stamped their feet and
clapped their hands when drums were taken away; how religious feeling expresses itself in music, providing a transition from the human
to the spiritual, from the past to the present. Thus, the film expands
some of the concepts central to St. Clair Bourne's earlier and far briefer
Afro-Dance.

Bagwell's film suggests that the collective unconscious is most clearly expressed through dance, and that each region adopts a dance form

through which to express its African roots. For example, one section of the film characterizes present-day college fraternity step-dancing as a modern ritual of solidarity, then compares it to traditional African rituals involving stamping and clapping. Another section focuses on the fusion of African and European cultural traditions in the samba, the national dance of Brazil: Joao Jorge Santos Rodrigues, president of Grupo Olodum, explains that through the ring samba "each generation tells the next its own part of the African story." The film also addresses other African cultural forms that survived in altered ways. In the section on Brazil, Bagwell details how enslaved Africans hid deities and dance rituals behind the rituals of Catholicism, how they continued to practice African blessing rituals under the guise of Christian baptism, and how their religious rituals merged over time with those of Catholicism to produce distinctive Afro-Brazilian forms. In Bagwell's words, "When we sing and dance, we reveal who we've been, who we are, and who we can be."

Other films that survey an art form take "race films" and black theater as their subject. William Greaves's *That's Black Entertainment* (1985), unlike the documentaries that concentrate on the contributions of Oscar Micheaux, traces the history of "race films" by focusing attention on available film footage. Sadly, this relatively recent body of work is already largely lost due to film deterioration and scholarly inattention. Greaves sets out to address this situation, bringing to public view many "missing bits of American film history." *That's Black Entertainment* opens with images of director/narrator Greaves in a film vault, introducing the subject and discussing an excerpt from *Souls of Sin* (1949), in which he appeared as an actor. As he looks through stills from all-black productions, Greaves explains that these films were made for a fraction of the budget available for comparable commercial features, and were "more honest and respectful of black life." Greaves traces the history of these works, asserting that they were not simply made in reaction against D. W. Griffith's 1915 *The Birth of a Nation* (some were made five years earlier). Rather, the Griffith film stimulated black producers to make films that told the truth about African American life. Greaves then presents clips from 29 surviving "race films," narrating and commenting on their social and historical importance. He also provides samples of the stereotypic images of blacks featured in mainstream cinema, including animations like *All This and Rabbit Stew* (1941), which prompted African Americans to press for more accurate cinematic representation.

That's Black Entertainment celebrates the range of all-black cast films —dramas, romances, mysteries, and westerns—and presents treasured clips: Bessie Smith's only screen performance, singing in *The St. Louis Blues* (1929); Sammy Davis, Jr., as an eight-year-old child dancing in *Rufus Jones for President* (1933) while his mother, a young Ethel Waters, looks on; and Lena Horne in *Boogie Woogie Dream* (1942). Greaves also shows black filmmakers appearing as actors in their own "race films," including William Alexander (*Souls of Sin,* 1949), Oscar Micheaux (*Murder in Harlem,* 1935), and Spencer Williams (*Juke Joint,* 1947). In Greaves's view, these precious documents will offer insight into what life was like "as long as film and tape can hold an image."

Woodie King, Jr.'s *The Black Theater Movement* is a feature-length documentary that traces the evolution of black theater from the late 1950s to the late 1970s, beginning with Lorraine Hansberry's *A Raisin in the Sun* (1959), which occasioned Lloyd Richards's debut as Broadway's first black theater director. The film details the rise of the burgeoning black theater movement, calling attention to the artists-activists whose creative efforts and social / political commitment were most crucial to its development. Playwright and poet Amiri Baraka, a co-founder of the Black Arts Movement, talks about the need for theater to be a revolutionary forum for protest that reflects the values of black liberation. Robert Hooks, founder of the D.C. Repertory Company and co-founder of the Negro Ensemble Company, analyzes the particular struggles of those production companies.

King includes interviews with many influential performers, writers and directors, including Roscoe Lee Browne, Ed Bullins, Ossie Davis, Ruby Dee, Lonne Elder III, Al Freeman, Jr., Lorraine Hansberry, Ysef Iman, James Earl Jones, Robert MacBeth, Ron Milner, Ntozake Shange, and Glynn Turman. Joseph Papp, producer of New York's Public Theater, discusses production of works like Ntozake Shange's *For Colored Girls Who Have Considered Suicide/ When the Rainbow Is Enuf.* King intercuts these interviews with footage of various television crews and independent filmmakers documenting black theater productions. In addition, King presents original footage of 1970s black theater companies across the country, including excerpts of their plays in production.

Woodie King's years in the black theater, especially his tenure as the director of Henry Street Settlement's New Federal Theater, make him the ideal spokesperson and historian for a populist theater movement that reflected and to some extent sparked the political turmoil of the times, including those internal divisions that split progressive forces within the black community. The film is concerned with dispelling myths—particularly the notion that black theater has no past. King makes clear that black theater experienced a long period of struggle and growth marked by severe financial difficulty and great artistic achievement. *The Black Theater Movement* celebrates the survival of black theater in this country, crediting its longevity to vital links between the theater and the lives of African Americans.

Street scene during the
First World Festival of Negro Arts,
Dakar, Senegal, 1966.
Photo courtesy of William Greaves Productions.

In a film that links all the arts, Williams Greaves's *First World Festival of Negro Arts* (1966) is a poetic treatment of the relationship between traditional African arts and those of the African diaspora. One of the earliest and best such surveys, *First World* is the official documentary film of the event of the same name, held in Dakar, Senegal. More than two thousand writers, artists, and performers from 30 nations in Africa and the African diaspora participated in this gathering designed to celebrate traditional and contemporary black culture. Greaves, who produced, wrote, directed, and narrated the film, has a particular gift for capturing what it is like to have traveled an enormous distance and to have found oneself in bustling streets and concert halls in the company of huge and wildly diverse crowds of people, all of whom are enthusiastic witnesses and performers in an exhausting series of extraordinary cultural events.

Early in *First World Festival*, Greaves offers viewers footage of Emperor Haile Selassie of Ethiopia and others arriving by plane and motorcading through the streets of Dakar applauded by thousands of onlookers. Greaves cuts from views of dignitaries to shots of people lining the streets, his hand-held camera conveying the excitement of those on the sidelines. Performance sequences are electrifying: the most exciting feature "roll calls" of performers from one country after another, demonstrating traditional musical forms, culminating in a montage of drummers and dancers in rapid succession—representatives of Trinidad, Togo, Sierra Leone, Burunde, Ghana, Liberia, Gabon, Mali, the Ivory Coast, Haiti, and Nigeria. By the time the film is over, the audience has seen and heard President Léopold Senghor of Senegal articulating the goals of the festival; intellectuals like Aimé Césaire of Martinique, and Alioune Diop of Senegal debating the concept of Negritude; and artists like Duke Ellington, Langston Hughes, and Alvin Ailey performing and viewing exhibitions of painting and sculptures.

What focuses the film's images is a poetic narration that personifies the spirit of creativity of the African diaspora. "Who am I?" Greaves asks on the soundtrack: "My name is Duke Ellington . . . three thousand miles and four hundred years separate you from Africa, yet you are here. . . . My name is Ethiopia. . . . My name is Africa. . . . These are the gates through which you must pass if you are to know me. . . . I am the American Negro spiritual, the dancers of Alvin Ailey. . . . Search for me in their movement. . . . I am the dancers of Chad." Greaves's narration is so eloquent, dignified and serene that it conveys something of the ancient spirit of the African continent, where art flourished three thousand years ago: "The dance is an old friend of Africa—it is a river that flows from soul to soul—it is a river that brings life and joy and love."

The utopian nature of the event, the conviction that "art has always led the way," and the celebratory narration combine to lend a sense of mission to the event—of transcending geographic distance and linking cultural past and present. As in many of the films in this study there is a strong conviction, expressed through the voice-over narration, that "often you draw inspiration from the art of your ancestors, an art rich in symbol and function. To them, art was never an end in itself, but a means by which the human spirit is lifted to ever higher planes of consciousness." Greaves's voice-over narration further connects art with the "desire to be free" at a crucial historic moment when many of the African nations were beginning to succeed in their quest for liberation.

Art "serves many causes—but none more than human dignity." It is not only the art that needs to be cherished and preserved, but the relationship between the black people, who can know one another through art: "We have many moments of history and creativity to share."

REINVENTING PERSONAL AND COLLECTIVE IDENTITY: PERFORMANCE DOCUMENTARIES

One advantage of film/video over text-based documentation is its ability to present moving images of artists at work and in conversation. This is especially true of documentaries about artists whose work is not static but time-based: musicians, poets in readings, dancers, theater companies, and performance artists. All such documentaries strike a balance between performance footage and contextualizing materials, but not all strike the same balance: the amount of performance footage included can vary widely from documentary to documentary, depending on the inclination of the film/videomaker and the availability of such footage.

The roots of performance documentaries can be found in early films like the Edison Company's series of *Annabelle Dances* (1895–1897), in which Edison invited Manhattan's premiere vaudeville performers to his New Jersey film studio, produced 30-second documents of their star turns, and exhibited those short films in peep show kinetoscopes and later in life-size Vitascope projections.[43] Contemporary works—in which performance footage dominates and contextual materials are minimal or nonexistent—include Stan Lathan's *Alvin Ailey: Memories and Visions* (1974), which features a brief scene in which Ailey lists his artistic goals while strolling past dancers poised to begin a performance, plus lengthy excerpts of Ailey's troupe performing his dances, each prefaced by a very brief voice-over introduction by Ailey.

Other performance documentaries are less documents of artists than collaborations between media artists and performers. Their origins may have been in films like *Choreography for the Camera* (1945), produced by American avant-gardist Maya Deren. This film—a collaboration between filmmaker and dancer-subject—began a new genre that merged the strengths of cinema and choreography. Contemporary proponents of performance documentary include Julie Dash, whose *Four Women* is designed to communicate through a combination of dance movement and film techniques, and Barbara McCullough, who has produced both conventional and experimental performance work. McCullough's rough-hewn *World Saxophone Quartet* (1980) is a document consisting of fixed-position, long-take concert footage intercut with brief interview material recorded backstage on the same evening, while her *Fragments of Barbara McCullough* (1980) features the ritualized performance of McCullough and her fellow artists.

A consideration of performance's social/political/cultural function converges with themes central to documentaries about artists: both can link the present to the past, especially through rituals that recall cultural traditions; can provide an opportunity for subject-speakers to transcend more passive, objectified roles; can serve as an arena for expressing emerging identities and transforming cultural images. As bell hooks explains, "For African-Americans, performance has been a place where we have reclaimed subjugated knowledge and historical memory. Along with this, it has also been a space of transgression where new identities and radicalized black subjectivities emerge, illuminating our place in history in ways that challenge and interrogate, that highlight the shifting nature of black experience. African American performance has been a site for the imagination of future possibilities."[44]

The issue of performance is complicated by a number of factors which Coco Fusco and other scholars have pointed out: the fact that many cultural performance practices were outlawed and forced to go underground, sometimes emerging as synthesized, cross-cultural forms; the removal of drums, a primary performance tool, by slave owners; the commodification of black performance as a white form of entertainment, including the codification of blacks as exotics and as victims/problems.[45] Author and theorist bell hooks makes a distinction between performance as art and as a survival technique, calling attention to the notion of "wearing the mask," in Paul Laurence Dunbar's words, as a fundamental tool of disguise for blacks in their "performance" mode before whites.[46] Nonetheless, blacks throughout the diaspora have viewed performance as a potential site not only for building community, but for expressing oppositional stances. Feminist scholars have identified a similar impulse in women's performance—replacing traditionally passive, commodified objectification with transgressive, assertive roles as subject-speakers.[47]

In *Four Women* and *Praise House*, Julie Dash documents performance pieces conceived for the camera, using expressive film techniques and stylized dance in ways that extend the possibilities of both forms. The performance aspect of Dash's narrative and documentary work is linked to her interest in cultural tradition, especially in collective experience; in her films, performance often expresses group experience rather than personal or individual subjectivity. At other times, characters enact their identities and dramatize their internal experience through dance. Thus, Dash's performance documentaries imaginatively reframe and recode women's identities, suggesting both diversity and interconnection, especially across generations.

Designed as a collaborative work directed by Dash and choreographed and performed by Linda Young, *Four Women* utilizes Nina Simone's song of the same title as a "script" to be visualized by Dash and Young. Dash employs a variety of film techniques—including dissolves, freeze frames, and superimpositions—to interpret a dance performance dedicated to representing the experience of black women struggling to survive in America from the time of the slave trade to the present. The film's opening sequence is its most abstract, and each successive section is increasingly representational: these four sequences correspond to the four verses of the Simone song. As Simone begins to sing "My skin is black / My arms are long / My hair is woolly / My back is strong," the experiences of four different women are enacted: Aunt Sarah, the plantation "mammy"; Saphronia, the tragic victim of rape; Sweet Thing, the prostitute; and Peaches, the modern, politically assertive woman. Each character/verse is given a distinct cinematic treatment. In the opening sequence, fabric fills the frame, and a figure draped in veils emerges—stretches and poses—while sounds of whips, water, and chanting recall the slave trade that brought her to America. In contrast, sensuous close-ups of hands, mouth, and feet introduce Sweet Thing, a sexual object who seduces the camera. Dash's varied film styles provide a cinematic equivalent for each character, each lyric.

Praise House, produced for the *Alive from Off Center* public television series, is a collaboration between Dash and the Urban Bush Women performance troupe. Like *Four Women, Praise House* features multiple female protagonists, each representing a distinct facet of African American life. But whereas *Four Women's* heroines are presented sequentially (and, by implication, in different time periods), the protagonists of *Praise House* are presented simultaneously and their experience is intricately interwoven. Alternately representing separate members of a multigenerational family and a single character in childhood, youth, and old age, *Praise House* juxtaposes the experiences of three characters: Hannah, the child visionary who makes chalk drawings of angels; an unnamed young woman—presumably her mother—who rides buses and performs domestic chores; and Granny Louise, a dying old woman whose "life is a dream" and whose "teacher is the angel that stands by me." Dash cuts between a variety of spaces—interior and exterior, naturalistic and stylized, real and imagined—that include a domestic kitchen, living room and bedroom, a bus, a cemetery, and an outdoor environmental sculpture area, weaving the threads of three characters' lives in those settings to create a tapestry of their workaday and spiritual lives. That experience is alternately painful and ecstatic: visions overtake Hannah, death claims Granny Louise, and domestic chores consume the young woman.

Praise House privileges women's experience—domestic spaces, women's work, and an imaginative spiritual terrain characterized by what the grandmother describes as beautiful light and many colors. The images that dominate the frame—an electric fan's blades spinning, a woman wearing lace, fans on the wall, family photographs on a table —are accompanied by gospel songs, ritualistic dancing, and African rhythms. In the spirit dance sequences, visionary figures / spirits / angels fill the screen, swirl past the camera, and circle the main characters. There is a sense of continuum between the African American characters and ancient African culture and between the generations—both Granny Louise and Hannah are seers who "Draw or Die" (a motto embedded in one of Granny Louise's drawings that echoes Dash's strong commitment to the production and distribution of her idiosyncratic films). As in Orlando Bagwell's *New Worlds, New Forms,* dance is presented in *Praise House* as a way of communicating with spirits; the spirits are called by drums and dance, take hold of the human beings as they dance, destabilize and transform the human body. The function of music as a release from work and a spiritual force is addressed here. Most importantly, *Praise House* evokes the idea that African culture remains a vital force in the memories and activities of present-day African Americans, sustained through transcendent dance, music, and ritual.

In *Fragments of Barbara McCullough,* McCullough documents her own and others' performance pieces in a straightforward style enlivened at times by layered superimpositions and solarized images. The most provocative and fully developed piece in this video compilation reel is its first "fragment," titled *Water Ritual #1: An Urban Rite of Purification.* McCullough prefaces the piece with a statement about how being raised as a Catholic led her to feel "as if I had an affinity for ritual," a sentiment that informs her complementary desire to create neopagan performances and to "create rituals with one camera . . . to create cathartic experiences for [video] viewers." McCullough as a performance artist places herself at the center of *Water Ritual #1:* she sits outdoors in the middle of a circle of rocks, while on the soundtrack she talks about a childhood of lighting candles and saying prayers. The final gesture of the piece—a solarized image of McCullough squatting and urinating in the field—invokes elemental powers. The second "fragment" features a double, superimposed image of McCullough standing in the field, dressed in rags, thrashing and tugging on a rope constructed of wrapped and twisted fabric that protrudes from her midsection like an umbilical cord, stretching across the field toward and beyond the camera position, evoking primitive birth rituals.

The title "And other Bits" continues McCullough's imagistic linking of art and the natural world. The first "bit," photographed in a more conventional manner than the "fragments" that preceded it, documents artist David Hammons rummaging through a pile of industrial rubble accompanied by a jazz soundtrack. He pulls out broken chunks of concrete and wire and places them on his head and chest, forming a "hat" and "vest." The second "bit" features N'Senga Nevgudi who informs us in a voice-over statement that she works with discarded nylon stockings "because they are the closest material I can find to the body." Nevgudi sits surrounded by photographs of her stocking sculptures, her face hidden beneath a layered stocking mask festooned with nylon dreadlocks. She strips away the mask layer by layer, and her performance ends when her smiling face is finally revealed. In the two "fragments," McCullough documents her performance art in ways that provide entry to uninitiated viewers, and in her two "bits" she documents fellow artists who share her concern with creating rituals that incorporate the application of cast-off materials to the human body. McCullough has structured each performance/documentation so that it ends with a sly, visual "punch line."

Saundra Sharp's *Life Is a Saxophone* (1985), co-directed with Orlando Bagwell, is an especially articulate performance documentary which adopts multiple strategies to film poetry readings by Kamau Daáood, the artist called "the word musician" in the credits. The dynamic approach is apparent in the opening shots of city streets and a car breaking down in traffic; as Daáood runs from the car, racing into the background and away from the camera, the credits for the film come up, along with the sound of his voice reading a poem invoking the spirit of Martin Luther King, Jr. The following sequence, in which Daáood is filmed at a public reading of that poem, cuts to diverse views of Daáood and the bass player who accompanies him, punching through the rhythms of the words he speaks.

The filmmakers' ability to find a distinct cinematic "voice" that approximates the mood and rhythm of each particular poem under consideration is impressive. For example, the filmmakers use jagged, MTV-style associative editing to depict a poem set on the streets of Los Angeles: as Daáood walks across an empty lot, the film cuts from the poet to details mentioned in the poem, including a graffiti-covered concrete wall, a chain link fence, a pinball arcade (as Daáood reads the line "I don't read, I don't write"), and young men carrying large stereo speakers across a street (as Daáood repeatedly chants "I love my speakers"). In contrast, the filmmakers use an austere long take, with a slow zoom in at the end, to show Daáood alone on a hillside overlooking Los Angeles reading a poem in honor of reggae musician Bob Marley. During one public performance, the filmmakers occasionally cut to a woman seated in the audience, sketching Daáood's face; when the poem is finished, the drawing is also complete. Back in the hilltop park, the filmmakers superimpose the ghostly image of a woman dancing near Daáood in time to his words, then cut seamlessly between the last line of one stanza and the first line of the next to show Daáood continuing his reading before an audience, accompanied by a more flesh-and-blood version of the same interpretive dancer.

There are also opportunities to see Daáood at work. At the Watts Towers Creative Arts Center, where Daáood is both artist-in-residence and featured performer, there is a wordless sequence in which he plays the piano. Starting with a shot of the poet which zooms back to reveal that we have been watching his reflection in a mirror, the filmmakers employ a series of cuts and camera movements that focus on Daáood's hands and his face, conveying a sense of his mind at work on his improvised composition, an illustration of his earlier statement that he has to be in a certain state of mind to create his art. In another sequence Daáood expresses a theory, then the filmmakers illustrate it: Daáood is seen laying down tape-recorded tracks of verse after discussing his desire to create "word music" compositions mixing many elements, including solo and accompanying voices. He discusses—and we see— how a poem is put together in pieces, built up over time.

Toward the end of the film, back on the hillside, Daáood comments on the fact that "there are very few symbols for our culture." Saying that African Americans need a symbol—like the Irish shamrock, but not like the watermelon—he suggests the saxophone: "the image for what we have done here as an art form. . . . Europe carted the reed instrument out of Africa, but we snatched it back. . . . Our contribution is what I call 'African American classical music': jazz." What follows is a performance at the Watts Towers Creative Arts Center of "Life Is a Saxophone" in which Daáood reads while rocking his body like a musician playing a saxophone, accompanied by a variety of performers, including a martial arts expert who moves in time to the poem's rhythm. The poem catalogues the accomplishments of a number of African American artists and as each is named, there is rapid drumming, accompanied by brief shots of that person's face.

This is not a didactic film so much as it is a performance piece that employs a variety of film techniques in combination with the poet reading. As in the works of Julie Dash, this film's cinematography not only documents but also interprets and extends the performance, in this case to show the multifaceted qualities of its subject's work, always discovering fresh film techniques appropriate to conveying the spirit and rhythms of his words.

"SONGS OF SURVIVORS"

Not surprisingly, black filmmakers early on staked out documentary as an arena in which truth-telling, especially regarding social injustices, could thrive. Most often produced, distributed, and exhibited outside mainstream channels, most documentary film and video remains a commercially marginalized form. Only a handful of such work finds large audiences through theatrical release or public television airing, while most must find a place in niche markets like public libraries, university media study collections, or community-based film/video centers. This very "invisibility" allows independently produced, alternative documentaries to remain remarkably unencumbered in their ability to challenge conventional media versions of reality, especially in areas like the representation of race.

If documentaries about artists seem at first an apolitical subgenre of black nonfiction film and video,[48] the works in this chapter quickly dispel that view. In fact, the assumption that African American art documentaries focus on charismatic musicians or uplifting tales of overcoming obstacles belies the subversive edge that characterizes these works. What is at stake in these film and videos is the important role artists play in questioning the authority of mainstream media and asserting a counternarrative of black experience and achievement. Through their poems, novels, plays, and music, African American artists speak to the realities and complexities of life in America, offering truths that challenge the limited paradigm of black experience perpetuated in American culture.

In *Creating a Different Image*, filmmaker Alile Sharon Larkin says, "I consider myself a storyteller. I am attempting to create affirmations and celebrations of my culture." Theorists such as Kimberlé Crenshaw call storytelling an important socio-political tool for the disenfranchised, since "storytelling aims at challenging versions of reality put forward by the dominant culture."[49] In her view, such stories may be based on personal or individual experience or anecdote as readily as on conventional historical documents. The slave narratives are certainly an example of the kind of storytelling that was not initially deemed trustworthy, but ultimately accepted as primary historical documents.

To assail the authority and accuracy of African American images and concerns in mainstream culture, documentarians use conventions like expert testimony and archival footage, at the same time they employ alternative sources of evidence like personal narratives and performance. In art documentaries, issues of truth, historical accuracy, and authenticity involve validating subjective experience and connecting the individual to the collective. Like other art forms, documentaries create imaginative links between individuals and communities, rekindling racial memory and dramatizing spiritual connections to Africa and the experience of slavery.

The recognition that documentary film/video asserts the real, while engaging in alternative storytelling and impressionistic historiography, creates a link between film/videomakers and the artists they celebrate.[50] As Ayoka Chenzira points out, "I think that most black filmmakers will acknowledge, even if they don't take on the term 'documentary filmmaker,' that in all of our filmmaking, we are giving witness to either the history or the psychology or the emotions of a people. Whether you've a larger social context to look at, or whether you're looking at a small narrative piece that focuses on a family using certain people to tell the story, that's a form of documenting."[51] Like the creative works they document, art documentaries demonstrate the relationship between the expressive and social/political functions of art. In their photographs, stories, poetry, and music, African American artists strive to tell the untold stories of African American struggles and achievements. As photographer Carrie Mae Weems says in *Conjure Women*: "How do you begin to construct a reality that's not so much 'positive' as deeply true and meaningful about black experience?" Taken together, the documentaries in this study constitute an eloquent answer to that question.

NOTES

1. In *The Nation*, Langdon Hammer describes the artist's desire to make things as "a general longing for embodiment, a desire we all feel to manifest ourselves in the world." "Poetry and Embodiment," November 24, 1997, 32.

2. From the film *Midnight Ramble: Oscar Micheaux and the Story of Race Movies* (1994).

3. Manthia Diawara argues for an approach to black American studies that engages and elaborates on the values of black British cultural studies. "Black performance studies would mean study of the ways in which black people, through communicative action, created and continue to create themselves within the American experience. . . . Such a 'performance' is both political and theoretical: it refers to and draws on existing traditions; represents the actor as occupying a different position in society; and interpolates the audience's

response to emerging images of black people." Diawara proposes "performance studies" as an alternative to "oppression studies," a particularly useful approach to documentaries about artists since it is through the arts—literature, music, dance, etc.—that African Americans have asserted the integrity of their experience and created an image of what Diawara refers to as "black good life . . . the object of interest and even envy of Americans of different origins and races." "Performative Acts: Black Studies, Cultural Studies," *AfterImage*, October 1992, 7. Documentary films and videos—cultural artifacts for such performance study—also represent the kind of applied multi-disciplinary scholarship Diawara suggests; he himself has made a documentary about the life and work of *cinéma vérité* filmmaker Jean Rouch, using "reverse anthropology" to examine visual ethnography from the position of its subjects. Diawara's *Rouch in Reverse* (1996) depicts "new African images and voices, ones that defy stereotype and primitivism."

4. Clyde Taylor points out that black documentary filmmakers like St. Clair Bourne "reacted against the way white nonfiction films portrayed blacks": citing the voice-of-God narration, the feigned objectivity, and authoritarian vision of those works, Taylor contends that African Americans were more attracted to the *cinéma vérité* mode which allowed them to stress the complexity of their subjects. (See Clyde Taylor's Whitney Museum of American Art curatorial notes for a February 1988 exhibition featuring the work of St. Clair Bourne.)

5. Bill Nichols, "Performing Documentary," in *Blurred Boundaries* (Bloomington: Indiana University Press, 1994), 92–106.

6. As Henry Louis Gates points out, "Our histories may be irretrievable, but they invite imaginative reconstruction. In this spirit, diasporic feminist critics like Hazel Carby have made the call for a 'usable past.' This call for cultural retrieval—tempered by a sense of its lability, its contingency, its constructedness—has sponsored a remarkable time of black creativity." Henry Louis Gates, Jr., "The Black Man's Burden," in *Black Popular Culture: A Project by Michele Wallace*, ed. Gina Dent (Seattle: Bay Press, 1992), 77.

7. John Grierson, *Grierson on Documentary*, ed. Forsyth Hardy (Berkeley: University of California Press, 1966), 13.

8. Interview with St. Clair Bourne, conducted by Phyllis Klotman, July 1992.

9. "Basically it is really the story of what happens to a small section of the Bedford-Stuyvesant community which get inundated with this major Hollywood production that's being directed by a Black guy. . . . The community has always been the source and strength of what I do . . . what was beginning to happen was that there were these Black Hollywood films, not the Blaxploitation films, but the new ones that were beginning to emerge, and I couldn't figure out why these brothers were collaborating with Hollywood. In my generation that was bad. You sold out and here these cats were running to do it. Spike said, 'I'm going to do this film, and I'm going to keep control.' I said, 'Get out of here. You are not going to be able to do that.'" Interview with St. Clair Bourne, conducted by Clyde Taylor, *Artist and Influence 1996*, vol. 15, ed. James V. Hatch, Leo Hamalian, and Judy Blum (New York: Hatch-Billops Collection, 1996), 60.

10. Warrington Hudlin's film *Capoeira of Brazil* (1980) features a performance of *capoeira*, a blend of dance and self-defense, in which men dance on their hands and use their feet as weapons, which also evolved as a way of disguising a form that had been outlawed by Portuguese slave owners. Ella Shohat and Robert Stam describe attacks on indigenous cultures which sometimes led to new hybrid forms and to oppositional aesthetic practices: "The religions of the

colonized were institutionally denounced as superstition and 'devil-worship.' Thus the 'spirit dances' of the Native Americans were forbidden, and African diasporic religions such as Santeria and Candomblé were suppressed, partly because medicine men and women, prophets, and visionary-priests—the *papaloi* of the Haitrian revolution, the *obeahs* of the Caribbean rebellions—often played key roles in resistance. Colonialist institutions attempted to denude peoples of the richly textured cultural attributes that shaped communal identity and belonging, leaving a legacy of both trauma and resistance." *Unthinking Eurocentricism: Multiculturalism and the Media* (New York: Routledge, 1994), 17.

11. Interview with Bourne, conducted by Klotman.

12. "I characterize my films basically as personalized narrative documentaries.... My *Baraka* film is that.... One film that I thought was good was Marlon's [Riggs] film *Tongues Untied*. I thought that was very good, although I'll tell you something, I think that... and this may be ego speaking... I think I did the same thing structurally with *Baraka*, but he did it better than I did with *Tongues Untied*. I think he did it much better. . . . I told him 'Listen, I thought my film *Baraka* was the best of this genre but that [*Tongues Untied*] was much better' and I told him that." Ibid.

13. Interview with Bourne, conducted by Taylor, 57.

14. Interview with Bourne, conducted by Klotman.

15. Interview with Bourne, conducted by Taylor, 59.

16. Interview with Bourne, conducted by Klotman.

17. Interview with Michelle Parkerson, conducted by Phyllis Klotman, July 1992.

18. Ibid.

19. Ibid.

20. Ada Gay Griffin addresses the role of black women documentarians: "I think it's no coincidence that so many films by African American women are portraits of other women or are historical portraits, or are autobiographical. We need to have our history and our lives, our experiences available to each other and future generations who are yet to be. Pat Aufderheide, "A Praise Poem: Filming the Life of Audre Lorde, Interview with Ada Gay Griffin," *Black Film Review* 8, no. 3 (1996): 22–24..

21. Toni Cade Bambara's essay in *Black American Cinema* lists women film / videomakers who can be said to answer the question posed by Abbey Lincoln in the September 1966 issue of *Negro Digest:* "Who Will Revere the Black Woman?" Bambara credits Zeinabu Davis with the insight that black women documentarians make homage films to their mentors. "Reading the Signs, Empowering the Eye: *Daughters of the Dust* and the Independent Cinema Movement," in *Black American Cinema,* ed. Manthia Diawara (New York: Routledge, 1993), 118–44.

22. Marlon Riggs, whose 1991 videotape *Color Adjustment* traces the depictions of blacks on television—from their total exclusion to their growing representation in prime time—claims "television is the primary vehicle by which we tell stories about ourselves." Riggs objects to television's perpetuation of the "oppressive and repressive myth of the American family" and asks viewer to consider the price of inclusion.

23. Interview with Yvonne Welbon, conducted by Phyllis Klotman, May 1997.

24. "Most of my information for *Syvilla* really came through interviewing other people. There was a lot of pressure on me to make Syvilla seem super famous. She was famous, but in a kind of underground way, and I made the

decision—and I'm still glad I did—not to bring in people like Marlon Brando to say how wonderful she was, even though he had studied with Syvilla and there were all these photographs of Marlon Brando and Syvilla. Somehow I felt it was the regular, ordinary people that she touched, whose families didn't want them to be dancers or artists and Syvilla gave them a home that was more important than saying 'Well, Harry Belafonte went there and this is what he thinks of Syvilla.'" Interview with Ayoka Chenzira, conducted by Phyllis Klotman and Janet Cutler, March 1994.

25. Interview with Welbon, conducted by Klotman.

26. This is not to say that Dash is without allies in her efforts: she sees herself as part of a community of women film/videomakers who regularly pool their talents, working cooperatively and interchangeably on each other's productions. Dash's efforts recall those of Barbara Ann Teer, director of the National Black Theater who, in the 1960s and '70s, "eliminated the negative dog-eat-dog aspect of Western theater" by extending the concept of the black family unit to the members of her company: "as members of the same family, . . . [actors] build sets. Lighting people dance. There is total cooperation in all phases of her theater." Jessica B. Harris, "The National Black Theatre," *The Drama Review* 16, no. 4 (December 1972): 40.

27. Interview with Chenzira, conducted by Klotman and Cutler.

28. Interview with Kathe Sandler, conducted by Phyllis Klotman, April 1995.

29. Marianne Hirsch, "Mothers and Daughters: A Review Essay," *Signs* 7 (Autumn 1981): 202.

30. Interview with Yvonne Welbon, conducted by Phyllis Klotman, May 1997.

31. Interview with Sandler, conducted by Klotman.

32. While it is primarily women film/videomakers who document the work and lives of women artists, it is important to note Abiyi Ford's *Lois Mailou Jones: Fifty Years of Painting* (1983) as a significant exception. Ford took over the project which had been abandoned by another filmmaker—a documentary based on a retrospective exhibition of Jones's work. Using some of that footage, but relying primarily on his own, Ford creates a film that is less a record of Jones's career than a dynamic interaction between the camera and her paintings. Interview with Abiyi Ford, conducted by Phyllis Klotman, December 1993. Nor are all mentors female: Carroll Blue's *Conversations with Roy DeCarava* is a clear nod to the photographer with whom she most identifies and, in her interview with Phyllis Klotman, Kathe Sandler says, "St. Clair Bourne was probably the greatest influence on me in terms of directing me into the film business, I ended up working for him."

33. Telephone interview with Zeinabu irene Davis, conducted by Janet Cutler, December 1997.

34. From the film *Visions of the Spirit: A Portrait of Alice Walker*, 1989.

35. More than one film is dedicated to tracing the prodigious career of Gordon Parks, whose work as a photographer, filmmaker, author, and musician make him the Renaissance artist of this group—and the only African American artist to have directed a full-length documentary about his own life. His *Gordon Parks: Visions—The Images, Words, and Music of Gordon Parks* (1986) is in some ways a remake of an earlier film made by Warren Forma, *The Weapons of Gordon Parks* (1966–1967). Forma's film draws heavily on Parks's autobiography *A Choice of Weapons* and employs his musical compositions as background music.

36. In 1987 William Miles directed the "wrap-around" for WNET's *Paul Robeson: Man of Conscience*, in which Paul Robeson, Jr. answers questions from an audience before and after a screening of Saul Turell's *Tribute to an Artist*, which forms the central part of the broadcast. The Turell film, narrated by Sidney Poitier, demonstrates some of the problems of missing footage: it repeatedly uses excerpts from Robeson's films to illustrate his life and his work and glosses over the issue of Robeson's politics. The problematic task of documenting Robeson's career is approached in another way by William Greaves in *Resurrections: A Moment in the Life of Paul Robeson* (1990), which Greaves considers an unfinished work-in-progress. The centerpiece of this film is a performance by actor Moses Gunn in the role of Robeson: in its current form, *Resurrections* consists primarily of Gunn delivering Robeson's essay "The Negro Artist Looks Ahead." The film also offers a concise and clear account of Robeson's career, while relying on stills of Robeson's All-American days at Rutgers, his stint at Columbia Law, his concert performances, and his starring role in the 1933 movie version of the Eugene O'Neill play, *The Emperor Jones*, and Broadway production of *Othello*. Greaves's narration provides a coherent explanation of Robeson's life as artist and activist, detailing his various public campaigns against fascism in Spain, colonialism in Africa, and racism in America.

37. Interview with Gil Noble, conducted by Janet Cutler, August 1997.

38. Ibid.

39. Ibid.

40. This is especially true of trailblazing figures like Oscar Micheaux, many of whose works, like much of early cinema—have deteriorated or disappeared. As Stephen Gong points out, "Early cinema was seen as a disposable product by its creators and audiences . . . more than half of the theatrical films produced in this country before 1951 have been lost forever." Stephen Gong, "Saving Early Cinema," in *Before Hollywood: Turn-of-the-Century Film from American Archives*, ed. Jay Leyda and Charles Musser (New York: The American Federation of Arts Film Program, 1986), 11.

41. Henry Louis Gates, Jr. describes Baldwin's fall from favor in the late 1960s: "Baldwin was 'Joan of Arc of the cocktail party,' according to the new star of the Black Arts movement, Amiri Baraka. His 'spavined whine and plea' was 'sickening beyond belief.' He was—according to a youthful Ishmael Reed—'a hustler who came on like Job.'" Henry Louis Gates, Jr., "The Welcome Table," in *Thirteen Ways of Looking at a Black Man* (New York: Random House, 1997), 12. Gates goes on to analyze the public treatment of black intellectuals: "If someone has anointed a black intellectual, rest assured that others are busily constructing his tumbrel" (p. 18). Later Baldwin was embraced by even his greatest critics, and Gates concludes, "Like everyone else, I guess, we like our heroes dead" (p. 20).

42. Gil Noble, *Black Is the Color of My TV Tube* (Secaucus: Lyle Stuart, 1981), 103. As producer of *Like It Is*, Gil Noble has made numerous short documentaries—five to fifteen minutes in length—many of which have artists, such as Erroll Garner and Charlie Parker, as their subject.

43. "Delegated to find subjects for the 50-foot loops that ran through the Edison Company's peep show kinetoscopes, [cinematographer] W. K. L. Dickson turned to New York music halls, burlesque, traveling shows, and vaudeville to supply bits of self-contained performance. Each subject had only to be autonomous enough to support its tiny, animated fragment: Annie Oakley taking potshots at clay targets, Sandow flexing his deltoids, 'Madam Rita'

dancing, Indians from Buffalo Bill's Wild West Show, which had just closed in Brooklyn, reenacting *War Council* and a *Ghost Dance*." John L. Fell, "Cellulose Nitrate Roots: Popular Entertainments and the Birth of Film Narrative," in *Before Hollywood*, 39.

44. bell hooks, "Performance Practice as a Site of Opposition," in *Let's Get It On: The Politics of Black Performance*, ed. Catherine Ugwu (Seattle: Bay Press, 1995), 220.

45. In her discussion of performance, Coco Fusco calls attention to the ways that artists re-work stereotypes, which she describes as "a very different objective from that of the imaginative retrieval of 'original cultural forms,' or that of creating entirely new paradigms devoid of historical traces." "Performance and the Power of the Popular," in *Let's Get It On: The Politics of Black Performance*, 158–75.

46. hooks in *Let's Get It On: The Politics of Black Performance*, 210.

47. Martha Gever, for example, comments: "Since the connotations of femininity and images of the mute compliant female body go hand in hand in Western culture, the female performer who presents herself simultaneously as speaker and subject has afforded feminism a metaphor for opposition to such sexist representations as well as a foundation for alternative modes of representation." Martha Gever, "The Feminism Factor: Video and Its Relation to Feminism," in *Illuminating Video: An Essential Guide to Video Art*, ed. Doug Hall and Sally Jo Fife (Berkeley: Aperture/Bay Area Video Collective, 1990), 234.

48. Clyde Taylor suggests that funders may be partial to art documentaries because they assume that they will be supporting works with "acceptable" subjects. Taylor, Whitney Museum curatorial notes.

49. Kimberlé Crenshaw, quoted in Neil A. Lewis, "For Black Scholars Wedded to Prism of Race, New and Separate Goals," *New York Times*, May 5, 1997, B9.

50. Film scholars Valerie Smith and Manthia Diawara point to a coincidental emphasis on "the real" in African American narrative film—a response to the inauthenticity of images of blacks in entertainment industry movies and television—and James Snead writes about independent filmmakers' efforts to produce works that offer alternatives to the kinds of roles, images, and narrative representations encoded in Hollywood film. For further discussion of these issues, see the following: Valerie Smith, "The Documentary Impulse in Contemporary U.S. African-American Film," in *Black Popular Culture: A Project of Michele Wallace*, ed. Gina Dent (Seattle: Bay Press, 1992), 56–65; Manthia Diawara, "Black American Cinema: The New Realism," in *Black American Cinema*, ed. Manthia Diawara, 3–25; James A. Snead, "Images of Blacks in Black Independent Films: A Brief Survey," in *Blackframes: Critical Perspectives on Black Independent Cinema*, ed. Mbye Cham and Claire Andrade-Watkins (Cambridge: MIT Press, 1988), 16–25. For international perspectives on this issue, see Kobena Mercer, "Diaspora Culture and the Dialogic Imagination: The Aesthetics of Black Independent Film in Britain," also in *Blackframes*, as well as Ella Shohat and Robert Stam's *Unthinking Eurocentrism*.

51. Interview with Chenzira, conducted by Klotman and Cutler.

7

Uptown Where We Belong
Space, Captivity, and the Documentary of Black Community

MARK FREDERICK BAKER AND HOUSTON A. BAKER, JR.

"I WILL TELL YOU. JUSTICE CAN BE A CHARACTERISTIC
OF AN INDIVIDUAL OR OF A COMMUNITY, CAN IT NOT?"
"YES."
"AND A COMMUNITY IS LARGER THAN AN INDIVIDUAL?"
"IT IS."
"WE MAY THEREFORE FIND JUSTICE ON A LARGER SCALE IN THE LARGER ENTITY,
AND SO EASIER TO RECOGNIZE. I ACCORDINGLY PROPOSE THAT WE START
OUR INQUIRY WITH THE COMMUNITY, AND THEN PROCEED TO THE INDIVIDUAL
AND SEE IF WE CAN FIND IN THE CONFORMATION OF THE SMALLER ENTITY
ANYTHING SIMILAR TO WHAT WE HAVE FOUND IN THE LARGER."
"THAT SEEMS A GOOD SUGGESTION," HE AGREED.
"WELL THEN," SAID I, "IF WE WERE TO LOOK AT A COMMUNITY COMING INTO EXISTENCE,
WE MIGHT BE ABLE TO SEE HOW JUSTICE AND INJUSTICE ORIGINATE IN IT."
"WE MIGHT."
"THIS WOULD, WE MAY HOPE, MAKE IT EASIER TO FIND WHAT WE ARE LOOKING FOR."
"MUCH EASIER."
"DO YOU THINK, THEN, THAT WE SHOULD ATTEMPT SUCH A SURVEY?
FOR, IT IS, I ASSURE YOU, TOO BIG A TASK TO UNDERTAKE WITHOUT THOUGHT."
"WE KNOW WHAT WE ARE IN FOR," RETURNED ADEIMANTUS; "GO ON."

—PLATO, "FIRST PRINCIPLES OF SOCIAL ORGANIZATION," IN *The Republic*

I

The post and privilege of documentation is financed by power. It is
maintained at sites of professional enunciation. From the beginning,
organized human societies have included a priestly or scholarly caste of
documentarians. Whether scribes, griots, or shamans, these scholar/
priests have always been comfortably positioned and unequivocally
charged with documenting the genealogy and legitimacy of power.
Documentarians of this first order may seem little more than well-

financed propagandists. Yet, their ubiquity and equivalent structural function across cultures serve as historical reminders of the wisdom of Nietzsche's insight that all knowledge is but the metaphorically costumed appearance of power.

In recent years, the writings of French theorist Michel Foucault have built on this Nietzschean proposition, carrying poststructuralist investigations of knowledge and power to such sites as medicine (the clinic), law (prisons), mind or rationality (the asylum), and the body (sexuality). For Foucault, the "order of things" is determined by knowledge formation and its asymmetrical and uneven development in human societies. Epistemology is destiny. This is Foucault's insight for a postmodern world. And where documents are concerned, Foucault suggests they exist, qua documents, only when they are certified by ruling power and professional enunciators. Only the original, official, legal seal of professionalism—whether inscribed or merely implied by the overall process of production—creates a document. Conventionally defined, a document is a function of writing or mechanical forms of print reproduction. Hence, documents are always functions of an apparatus of literacy. Their purpose is to provide original evidence and official information. By inference, what we designate as history and news are professionally dependent upon documents. Correlatively professional historians and journalists are always literate dependents of power.

For Afro-American intellectual history a key question has always been: "Can an Afro-American document exist?" Afro-American culture has traditionally been, in the famous phrase of James Baldwin, a "bastard of the West." Baldwin's phrase signals—albeit if not entirely—a tragic Afro-American illiteracy vis-à-vis a supposedly original American national conversation. The author of *Notes of a Native Son* writes as follows in that collection's final essay titled "Stranger in the Village":

> I am told that there are Haitians able to trace their ancestry back to African kings, but any American Negro wishing to go back so far will find his journey through time abruptly arrested by the signature on the bill of sale which served as the entrance paper for his ancestor. At the time—to say nothing of the circumstances—of the enslavement of the captive black man who was to become the American Negro, there was not the remotest possibility that he would ever take power from his master's hands. There was no reason to suppose that his situation would ever change, nor was there, shortly, anything to indicate that his situation had ever been different.[1]

Baldwin here suggests a concise history of Afro-American documentary. Removed from history and genealogy by white power and its documentary entitlements (signatures, bills of sale), Afro-Americans were systematically undocumented. In the dreadful transatlantic trade from Africa to America, a society evolved in which "there was no reason to suppose that . . . [the Afro-American's documentary] situation would ever change . . . nor . . . that it had ever been different."

American documentary, in all its fullness, has been coextensive with a no-exit silencing of black voices—a literate denuding of African personhood. Hence the condition of the "Negro" in the New World with respect to documents has been far less one of empowerment than shock. Witness Ralph Ellison's protagonist in the novel *Invisible Man*. Finding himself at the scene of an eviction in Harlem, the invisible man is astonished and unnerved by found contents of a wardrobe drawer belonging to the evictees:

> I turned away, bending and searching the dirty snow for anything missed by my eyes, and my fingers closed upon something resting in a frozen footstep: a fragile paper, coming apart with age, written in black ink grown yellow. I read: Free Papers: Be it known to all men that my negro, Primus Provo, has been freed by me this sixth day of August, 1859. Signed: John Samuel. Macon. I folded it quickly, blotting out the single drop of melted snow which glistened on the yellowed page, and dropped it back into the drawer. My hands were trembling, my breath rasping as if I had run a long distance or come upon a coiled serpent in a busy street. It has been longer than that, farther removed in time, I told myself.[2]

But the invisible man has only himself "to tell." His report is uttered in a private language of shock and bafflement. Samuel's document stands in a clearly teleological relationship to the bill of sale profoundly imagined by Baldwin. Black "freedom" like black servitude itself is a function of white documentation. Those who bear the "mark of oppression" can only read in disbelief. Provided, of course, they can read.

The critical race theorizing of Patricia Williams brings documentary considerations of Baldwin and Ellison into the perspective of "rights." In *The Alchemy of Race and Rights*, Williams describes a parallel quest for apartments in Manhattan that she and a colleague made. Her white male colleague enters an informal, handshake agreement with his sublessors and feels quite comfortable. Williams by contrast understands the terrors of Afro-American documentary shock—a state of baffled uncertainty when literacy, power, and law are all on someone else's side. She signs an elaborate contractual agreement with her landlord. Explaining the difference between her and her colleague, she carries readers to the documentary (bill of sale) history of female ancestors. Those who have been shocked (rather than made wealthy) by white documentary power respect, admire, and adhere to its contractual conditions.

Ironically, literate contractual documentation becomes the only possible black rock in a weary land without rights. If documents like bills of sale ensured slavery, it was nonetheless a written constitution, free papers such as those discovered by Ellison's hero, an Emancipation Proclamation, and post–Civil War amendments that fostered an articulation of Afro-American documentary history. This "free" history seems unimaginable in the primal scene etched by Baldwin. Williams writes as follows: "The problem with rights discourse is not that the discourse is itself constricting but that it exists in a constricted referential universe. The body of private laws epitomized by contract, including slave contract, is problematic because it denies the object of contract any rights at all."[3] However when rights are conferred on blacks a shift of existential horizons occurs: "For the historically disempowered, the conferring of rights is symbolic of all the denied aspects of their humanity: rights imply a respect that places one in the referential range of self and others, that elevates one's status from human body to social being. For blacks, then, the attainment of rights signifies the respectful behavior, the collective responsibility, properly owed by society to one of its own."[4] Artists and scholars such as Baldwin, Ellison, and Williams agree that their own acts of documentation—whether novel, essay, or critical race theory—depend upon a referential universe that they both half create and imbue with shadowy, contestatory substance. Black documentary history is less a traditional archive than an extended psychological case history of collective documentary shock. Recorders like Williams, Baldwin, and Ellison are always compelled to reconfigure official disciplinary lines. When we speak of the black community, those aware of black documentary shock will always infer heroic disciplinary efforts to move from shadow to act.

II

In the field of history it was only in 1972 that a monograph appeared, bearing the title *The Slave Community*, in which the author John Blassingame writes: "By concentrating solely on the planter, historians have, in effect, been listening to only one side of a complicated debate. The distorted view of the plantation which emerges from planter records is that of an all-powerful, monolithic institution which strips the slave of any meaningful and distinctive culture, family life, religion, or manhood [sic]. The clearest portrait the planter has drawn of the slave is the stereotype of Sambo, a submissive half-man, half-child."[5] As a corrective for this "distorted view," Blassingame proposes methodological concentration on traditionally ignored or discredited sources of what might be called black voicings: "an investigator of the personality development of slaves must depend largely on the personal records left by the slave, especially autobiographies."[6] The prerequisite for this methodological shift is black documentary faith in an alternative historical vision. Blassingame's faith posits an independent black communal development nowhere credited by an "official" white historical line. In a practical sense, the existence of a black community—like the existence of any community—is an epiphenomenon of such an historical faith or will to documentation. Someone has first to act. Working against notions of a black "Sambo" personality conditioned solely by mind-numbing labor, Blassingame asserts: "The social organization of the quarters was the slave's primary environment which gave him his ethical rules and fostered cooperation, mutual assistance, and black solidarity. The work experiences which most often brought the slave in contact with whites represented his secondary environment and was far less important in determining his personality than his primary environment."[7] What Baldwin projects as silence and amnesia for the captured African, Blassingame documents as the primacy and voicing of the "quarters"—the slave "community." Further, the black historian regards the emergence of "community" as a product of a contest between white hegemonic desire and the black will for unique cultural preservation and development: "The more his [the slave's] cultural forms differed from those of his master and the more they were immune from control of whites, the more the slave gained in personal autonomy and positive self-concepts."[8] In the wardrobe drawer, Ellison's protagonist found not only a white-signed manumission paper, but also knocking bones for black music set beside other genealogical reminders of a distinct black cultural lineage. And when Williams rolls out the scroll of her family history, she finds not only evidence of her white male ancestor's occupational grandeur, but clear testimony, at the site of the black woman's body, of an almost incomprehensible strength of survival and perseverance in the face of white "child molestation."

A "community" is always a construct, a product of a collective will to documentary power. For the black community, such a purchase has meant an enduring ability to transcend the shock of documentary misrecognition (e.g., Sambo) in imaginative acts (folksongs, shouts, hollers, autobiographies) that constitute declarations of cultural independence. The methodological alchemy of the black essayist, artist, scholar, or historian is to convert such implicit declarations of freedom to disciplinary capital.

In his influential monograph *Imagined Communities*, Benedict Anderson writes:

The idea of a sociological organism moving calendrically through homogeneous, empty time is a precise analogue of the idea of the nation, which also is conceived as a solid community moving steadily down (or up) history. An American will never meet, or even know the names of more than a handful of his 240,000,000-odd fellow-Americans. He has no idea of what they are up to at any one time. But he has complete confidence in their steady, anonymous, simultaneous activity.[9]

According to Anderson, the document that produces this American "community" is the newspaper. With its calendrical date at the top of the page and mass-market circulation in a language shared across classes, it is possible for the newspaper to assume the role of a communal ceremony: "The significance of this mass ceremony—Hegel observed that newspapers serve modern man as a substitute for morning prayers—is paradoxical. It is performed in silent privacy, in the lair of the skull. Yet each communicant is well aware that the ceremony he performs is being replicated simultaneously by thousands (or millions) of others of whose existence he is confident, yet of whose identity he has not the slightest notion."[10] Documentary "media" thus allows each reader to imagine his or her own community membership. In an age of fiber optics, the Internet, and trans-spatial satellite transmission, the reach of mediatized communitarianism is virtually unlimited. He whose mergers are vast enough is he who defines the world and word "community." At our turn of the millennium, stakes are vastly higher than Anderson's "print capitalism" or Blassingame's historian's will to contestation can imagine. Professor Richard Ford writes about recent communitarian impulses in the United States as follows:

Communitarianism is (in practice, if not in theory) the identity politics of moderate and liberal white America. Its appeal is to those who cannot unite around a unifying history of subordination and who do not embrace the explicitly reactionary politics of the nationalist new right or the anti-social extremes of white supremacy. In a self-fashioned Greek epic, the communitarian seeks to reestablish order at home and thereby to secure his own identity, while confronted by implacable enemies.[11]

Ford emphasizes the exclusive cast of comunitarianism, its paradoxical late-capitalist desire to expend resources only on private white middle-class interests. He also notes that present-day "community" interests often commence with a nostalgic call for a return to golden days of a communal past in which differences were amalgamated through public-spiritedness and civic finance. In a word, Ford alerts us that the sign "community"—in the discourse of a new globally mass-circulated communitarianism—has lost all normative, civic, and actional value, becoming merely an identifying sign of a white politics of gated "communities" and other-phobic policing and surveillance. Black documentary strives preeminently to avoid entrapment in such late-capitalist economies of community as an empty racist sign. And black documentarians are cautious to avoid an essentialist, in contrast to an imagined, concept of the black community. Naive essentialism merely springs the trap of the empty racist sign, augmenting an identity politics that is sometimes as unattractive in blackface as the most disingenuous forms of white communitarianism. Overcoming the shock of seeing oneself and one's community misrecognized by print, telecommunal, virtual economies of white media desire requires imaginative acts of redefinition. Redefinition demands a thoughtful elevation to documentary status of previously neglected cultural production.

First, then, let us say the definite article in the phrase *the* black community is an inexact and inadequate modifier in the context of our present-day United States. The singularity suggested by *the* has always been problematic. *The* represents a dream of solidarity and consensus across a wide field of investigation and an elaborate social taxonomy. There were as many types of slave "communities," for example, as there were locations of slaveholding in the United States. Similarly, there are —and always have been—as many variations on communal black life in the United States as there are locations, arrangements, class alignments, social and economic configurations of black American life in general. Arguably—given the vast and tragic number of black citizens under the impress of the American criminal justice system—the black community might signify a community of prisoners. This is an exaggeration, but one that captures, we think, a necessary modification of *the* in any invocation of black community.

The relational aspect of community—its always imagined cast— directs our methodological gaze away from an emotionally satisfying definiteness of articles. We can, of course, observe this scholarly caution and at the same time enact a useful black documentary project. We have only to imagine ourselves part of that community of imaginative investigators that includes Baldwin, Williams, Ellison, Blassingame, and others who offer guidance and examples for our work.

Tentatively, then, black community signifies the imagined and "alternatively documented" cultural, material, intellectual, and spiritual life and history of Africans and their descendants in the United States. African American community is an extension of the mental, physical, and spiritual history of African (i.e., always marked by "color") personhood in the United States. Methodological concern focuses not on African survivals or romantic, cultic, essentialist reconstructions of the

Nile Valley, but on the ceaseless transmutations of African material and expressive cultural productivity through various moments of American historical life. If one seeks to escape essentialism, as well as any claim to a purity of black "factual" presentation, one might suggest the definition of *black documentary film* that follows:

Black documentary is any film or video (whether made by a black director or not, whether "fiction" or "nonfiction" under traditional academic definitions) dealing specifically with the situation of African personhood in America in its myriad transmutations. Black documentary seeks not only to record and interpret the obvious surface oppression of African Americans (Ellison's eviction scene), but also to uncover the underlying politics and forces of the system ("rightlessness" as signified by manumission papers and bills of sale) that has brought about and sustains African American oppression. This is the necessary "sobriety"—a characterization drawn from the work of the scholar Bill Nichols—that black film or video must possess in order to earn the title *black documentary.* Under this definition what traditional academic scholarship designates as *non-documentary* or *fiction* may be included as *black documentary.* A film like *Menace II Society*, for example, may, in Nichols's phrasing, "call . . . [for] public rather than private response" and stand more accurately as a "documentary" for that reason. In part, the desideratum is which "public" is referenced; whose "reality" is verified in the participatory moment of spectatorship. Expanding our definition, we assert that the use of "fictive" technique—scripting, characters, staging, and editing—does not disqualify a film like *Menace II Society* from black documentary recognition. The employment of actors and staging in many well-respected—indeed "classic"—documentary films such as Robert Flaherty's *Nanook of the North* and Pare Lorentz's *The River* is precisely what helps such films sustain their rating as "classics." Cinema studies scholar Michael Renov persuasively reveals why any characterization of documentary that suggests an absence of fictive analogues or technical mediation is suspect. "Our attempts to 'fix' on celluloid what lies before the camera—ourselves or members of other cultures—are fragile if not altogether insincere efforts. Always issues of selection intrude (which angle, take, camera, stock will best serve); the results are indeed mediated, the result of multiple interventions that necessarily come between the cinematic sign (what we see on the screen) and its referent (what existed in the world)."[12]

The British filmmaker John Grierson, who is traditionally credited with inventing the term *documentary,* makes solid allowance for art and fiction when he distinguishes between "lower" (newsreels, travelogues) and "higher" (*Night Mail*) forms of documentary. Beyond the lower forms, Grierson states, "one begins to wander into the world of documentary proper, into the only world in which documentary can hope to achieve the ordinary virtues of an art. Here we pass from the plain (or fancy) descriptions of natural material, to arrangements, rearrangements, and creative shapings of it."[13] "Creative shapings" and "mediation" carry us well beyond scientific or strictly factual recordings of the object as in itself it really is. We move from naturalism to, at least, creative realism. Assuming a provisional definition of black documentary film—even one as broad as we have stated—leaves the task of providing illustrative examples that can sustain the burden of black community representation as it can be inferred from our initial discussion. For it is precisely at the site of representation that we discover the self-reflexivity of any projected conceptualization, production, critique, or viewing of black documentary film. Articulateness of representation sets in motion the process of, as it were, coming into history.

If we take Baldwin and Blassingame at their word, it is a literateness of self-representation (i.e., the oxymoronically "collective" autobiographical voice) that begins the process of black communal legitimation beyond the bill of sale. One might say, in fact, that it is subversive readings of the bill of sale as the end (i.e., *purpose* as well as *telos*) of history that conduce toward the unique, black expressive cultural and material production which leads to a sense of community. Black documentary subversion produces a concentrated spell-binding close-up on black voicings—on the subject or purveyor of a literate, black, mass-certified, public self-representation. These voicings constitute the core of black documentary. In their public representativeness they become metonymic for community.

It is impossible, though, to claim such metonymy in the absence of spatial considerations. To be representative of community the voice must not only issue from a mass-certified source. It must also signify a potential for black motion. The voice (re)claims black space. It demands public spatial arrangements that enhance black American citizenship. The issue of space grows increasingly critical for black documentary in an era where white privatization shamelessly masquerades as communitarianism. Ford, whom we earlier cited, writes: "By avoiding or suppressing the social conflict [produced by an expanded rather than a contracted public sphere] that actually brings a spirit of community into existence and which gives it life, an easy communitarianism, based on the fiction of the repressed community of shared values, produces its practical antithesis."[14] Two films are especially adept in their illustration of a black community documentation based on the spatialized black voicings of a representative self: *I Remember Harlem* by William Miles and *Menace II Society* by Albert and Allen Hughes. We shall survey Miles's documentation of Harlem, then focus analysis on the black urban west.

III

Produced in 1980, *I Remember Harlem* is a four-part film tracing the history of Harlem from 1600 to 1980. Clayton Riley wrote the script; it is narrated by Adolph Caesar. William Miles, the director, says of his project: "I wanted to make a film about Harlem. Not only about how I remembered Harlem. But about how other people remembered Harlem. And to hear what Harlem meant to them. So I decided to go back as far as possible to find out what made Harlem Harlem." These words are spoken by Miles in the first part of *I Remember Harlem*. We are thus alerted that his film is not simply personal or autobiographical, but an act meant to encompass a vast historical tract through the agency of popular memory. This citing of agency means that vernacular, quotidian, everyday realities of myriad interviewees will serve as a collective authority on "what made Harlem Harlem." The array of faces and voices brought before the camera in single-person close-ups dur-

Lenox Avenue and 125th Street, 1937.
Still from William Miles's *I Remember Harlem*.
Miles Educational Film Productions.

ing the film is, indeed, multilingual, intergenerational, cross-class, gender-mixed, interracial, and occupationally varied. Perspectives range from the long view of a white man of Dutch ancestry whose great-great-great-great-grandfather was one of Harlem's original settlers, to the haunting voices of Omar St. John and Conrad S. Peter describing the destiny of blacks in the New World. There are stories of Finns and Irish and Italian and Jewish youths passed in Harlem. They mix with energetic, self-conscious descriptions like that of Isabel Mendez who tells of the arrival of Puerto Ricans.

Miles succeeds in summoning voices of "other people" in the office of filmic explanation. A truth of storytelling in all its ethnic variety seems to arise. In one sense, this truth may be categorized in a way suggested by Professor Farah Griffin's *Who Set You Flowin'?* Griffin analyzes what she calls a "migration narrative"—a tale of uprooting and movement in search of more promising futures. In *I Remember Harlem,* the migration narrative is not only one of movement from Europe to the United States or from the rural South and agrarian Midwest to the urban North. Miles's interviewees are aware of such empowering tales of mere place change, but their principal concerns are always more on-the-ground and practical where migration is concerned. Almost all of them recall Harlem as preeminently a space that offered their families better and more comfortable housing. Arthur P. Davis captures this habitational desire for decent "quarters" when he tells of his family's departure from the railroad-flat, outdoor-toilet, cold-water facilities of Hell's Kitchen to join the ranks of blacks headed for Harlem's steam-heated apartments located on 134th and 135th Streets. Maintained in splendid white luxury through most of the nineteenth century, Harlem reluctantly yielded space during the first decades of the twentieth century for black occupancy. Already immigrants from Ireland, Scandinavia, Italy, and elsewhere had found in the commodious housing and spacious boulevards of Harlem better accommodations than they left behind. There is great attractiveness in this tale of a change of houses; it is the essence of American signification, replete with Horatio Alger resonances, luxurious quarters opening up for respectable aspirants to a better American life.

What does not appear in Miles's film or Riley's script, however, is an emphasis on the presence of Africans in Harlem from its very Dutch beginnings. There is only one line in Adolph Caesar's narration about the importation of "slaves" to build Harlem for European colonists. Moreover, colonists themselves are depicted as altogether honorable men in their transactions with the Lenape, the Native Americans on-site when the colonists arrived. The historical clean-up job of part one of *I*

Remember Harlem allows various scenes of Harlem's earliest historical development to unfold as a tale of urban progress, white enlightenment and taste, and peaceful (for the most part) white immigrant co-habitation and sharing. "What," we ask ourselves, "happened to those African slaves imported to build Broadway?" What does it signify that the urcondition of Africans in Harlem was captivity?

These questions haunt—but do not seem unduly to trouble—*I Remember Harlem's* unflagging assertions of a black communal creativity and style that have been freely self-sustaining. Part one announces Harlem as a place "Where trouble blends into hope and joy into style." And Wilbur Mitchell, one of the film's most compelling interviewees, asserts that people ask: "Which way is Harlem going, backward or forward?" Mitchell responds that Harlem just is. There is no before or after. Harlem has always been strong; it shall forever flourish.

I Remember Harlem's script and narrator continuously reassure us that no matter how bruised and battered Harlem and its black residents have been or may be in the future, Harlem remains invincible to time and crime's dreadful erosions. One might call this durative claim for Harlem a legendary filmic voice. The narrator says: "If there is a broken heart for every light on Broadway, there is surely a storyteller for every lamppost in Harlem." But if Harlem is many-storied, there are tight cinematic reins on how far any of *I Remember Harlem's* stories seem to go in narrating what might be called a counter-legendary narrative of New York "uptown" existence. The "Capital of the Black World," site of the Harlem Renaissance, steam-heated refuge from the habitational horrors of Hell's Kitchen and San Juan Hill, the Harlem we are seduced to embrace in *I Remember Harlem* is a fabled dream that all blacks—everywhere—and all whites—everywhere, including royalty, Popes, celebrities, and Cuban heads of state—long to inhabit.

The spatial dimensions limned by what we have called the legendary voice of the film are full of sweet music, fashionable dress, stable housing, neighborhood camaraderie, glorious entertainment, unlimited ability to make ends harmoniously and satisfyingly meet. The film's extraordinary archive of photographs and vintage footage bids fair to convince us that Harlem streets have always been filled with energetic black citizens making a fine show . . . and on their way to one or another fine show of "Negro talent" at Harlem's innumerable theaters. Behind such still photos and old footage, there is always the sound of music: ragtime, jazz, big band, bebop: slow clarinets, tripping piano runs, moody saxes making the point. Only rarely is this panorama of fabled and legendary spectacle interrogated by alternative scenes —counter-legendary scenes that reveal, for example, rodent-infested,

Harlem wedding photo, 1915. Still from
William Miles's *I Remember Harlem*.
Courtesy of Velma Green Hopkins.

substandard, garbage-laden stairways of decaying tenements that, surely, motivated Harlem's black citizenry to take to the streets. Seldom do
we encounter head-on—or, better, in full view—the agonies of ritual
black unemployment and the dehumanizing effects produced by inadequate social, health, and public municipal services.

Music trips happily on, accompanying interviewees who talk of
"Golden Twenties" or bright theaters in which Dusty Fletcher gave
birth to comedy skits like "Open the Door, Richard." The reason this
legendary foregrounding—even in its refusal of Harlem's ur-moment
of African captivity—does not completely overwhelm Miles's sincere
desire for a "historical" Harlem is because legends are always inextricably bound to legendary men. And when such men (we use the gendered
"men" advisedly here, because *I Remember Harlem* is indisputably a
male history) make an appearance in the film, they set in operation all
the anxieties of presence and absence that orbit the question: "What
happened to those African slaves imported to build Broadway?"

In one sense, the charismatic leaders documented by Miles fit per-
fectly the definition of black, mass-certified representativeness we earlier discussed. Marcus Garvey, for example, is presaged by Yosef Ben-

Jochannan's description of Paul Robeson as "another Marcus Garvey." Garvey appears most eloquently in his own voice as it was recorded at the first convention of the United Negro Improvement Association. In the film, the West Indian leader's sonorous voice constitutes an amazing vocal moment: resonant over a still photograph of the old Madison Square Garden where the UNIA convention was convened, and announced by the eloquent lead-in of the Garveyite Captain James H. Thornhill. Thornhill, who is one of the film's most interesting interviewees, tells us that 80,000 people were in attendance for Garvey's speech.

"Africa for the Africans, both at home and abroad!" This sounds cultic and romantic to a 1990s hearing. But as Thornhill and Leonard C. Randolph (also an interviewee for Miles) describe Garvey's project, we know that a legendary and almost completely fictive Africa was for Garvey the equivalent of a spectacular sign. It announced a program of black self-empowerment. Thornhill and Randolph believe Garvey confronted—head-on—death threats and other intimidation from respectable black folks and Ku Klux Klansmen alike. He unflinchingly articulated the necessity—gleaned from the programs of Booker T. Washington at Tuskegee—for black folk to seize independent economic stakes in spaces where they live. The pomp and ceremony of Garvey's many "legions" were a masquerade for his project. They were required attractions for a program to mobilize the masses, to motivate the black majority to make a leap of economic faith. Garvey meant to move millions of men and women toward not only black self-esteem, but also business development and black communal economic self-sufficiency.

Garvey came to the United States, Thornhill tells us, only after he had traveled and surveyed the world and discovered economic dependency and dreadful daily living conditions as global norms for black folks. We are alerted to what Marxists call the "base" of uptown existence as Garvey found it. Black folks owned nothing; they were discriminated against (even in those theaters they patronized with uncritical praise) at every turn. Mental colonization caused them to take pride in a Cotton Club where only the bodies of helpers, servants, and spectacular entertainers were black. Black pleasure and patronage were not reasons for the Cotton Club's existence. How different, then, was the club from a southern economy where pleasures of cotton were reserved for whites only, while blacks did the dirty work?

The symbolic significance of Garvey as *I Remember Harlem*'s first counter-legendary spokesperson is magnificently captured by Thornhill as he recites names of ships in Garvey's Black Star Line: Yarmouth, Booker T. Washington, Phillis Wheatley, Shady Side. These names signify economic enterprise, counter-hegemony, a business-like black eloquence, and independence. Garvey found Harlem an economic disaster and worked successfully to do something about it. He was deported on charges of "using the mails to defraud" because black middle-class "legends" such as Du Bois and white Federal authorities were terrified of his success. His total success would have shifted dramatically spatio-economic arrangements of Harlem as a black sign. Arthur P. Davis (to whom we shall return) points out in *I Remember Harlem* that Hell's Kitchen did not contain room for black families "to expand." Garvey believed a carefully thought, industrious, mass-certified black economics could provide unlimited global space for black expansion. The affective counter-hegemonic success of Garvey's vision is attested by the enduring loyalty of Thornhill and Randolph. It is confirmed by the very fact of the Jamaican leader's deportation.

I Remember Harlem's studious and, we think, self-conscious attempt to avoid a confrontational economics of captivity are paradoxically undone by the film's romantic quest to preserve the legendary status of Harlem's historical discourse. This discourse, as we have stated, is impossible without legendary men. Legendary men are not easily assimilable to romanticism. Their very mass-certified appeal demands from them analytical and brutally honest assessments of actual on-the-ground conditions of the black majority.

In the United States, such black majority conditions have almost never been attractively romantic. An absence of community and the articulation of a critical project for its attainment (as an expansive spatio-economic zone of black independence and productivity) are normally the first announcements of counter-legendary voicings. Hence, the appearance of representative black spokespersons in *I Remember Harlem* breaks what might be called the film's "continuity of complacency": its myths of eternal endurance, happy musical masterpieces, and prodigal repetitions of the black body entertaining. The film's counter-legendary articulations tell a discomfiting story about the actual state of space where a black urban majority lives. Representative black voices seek to map and institute a program of daily needs for the masses: space for expansion, dignified employment for hand and body, food for sustenance, self-esteem for the spirit.

Although plumes, parades, and showmanship are aspects of an apparatus of representativeness and critique, daily bread is vastly more important than gaudy circuses. Projects that come to fruition in breaking the complacency of black "world myth" ("Harlem, Capital of the Black World") are less occupied with kente cloth than with serious, analytical implications of African servitude in the building of Broadway.

The figures in *I Remember Harlem* who assume the representativeness of mass needs are almost all male. They include, in addition to Garvey: Father Divine, Adam Clayton Powell, Jr., Willie Bryant, and Malcolm X. Father Divine combines a self-mystifying account of his own godhead—his own "spontaneous combustion" into life at the corner of 135th and Lennox Avenue—with the provision of food, jobs, coal, shelter, and hope for Harlem blacks during the Great Depression. Powell lambasts infamous Harlem housing inspectors who for ten dollars sign off on properties creaking with hundreds of code violations. Powell also solicits responsible policing for Harlem. Bryant, holding forth in glory as the Mayor of Harlem, is handsomely characterized by the journalist James Hicks. Hicks describes Bryant's magnanimity on the journalist's arrival "uptown" after migrating from Ohio. Hicks also provides the voice-over for stunning footage of Malcolm X—especially *I Remember Harlem*'s account of the famous twenty-eighth precinct incident in which Malcolm commanded the allegiance of four thousand men and women from the Nation of Islam.

Followers of the Nation converged on the twenty-eighth after one of their members was beaten and jailed. Malcolm is summoned by authorities to disperse the crowd. Calmly, he demands to see the jailed Muslim in order to determine his condition. When his demand is granted and the jailed man is dispatched for medical care, Malcolm calmly walks outside the precinct's door and waves his arm to signal all is under control. Four thousand men and women fade into the night, producing the well-known response from white authorities: "That's too much power for any one man."

In combination with Miles's depiction of the Hell's Kitchen 1935, 1943, and 1964 race riots, the appearance and work of representative men like Father Divine and Malcolm imply an unseen, systematic force of spatial confinement. From an intra-communal perspective, we infer the absence (save for Cora Ford and, perhaps, Mary Bruce and her dancing school) of representative black women. Madame C. J. Walker does not make a showing; nor does Jessie Fauset, nor Mary McLeod Bethune, nor heroic legions of "church women" and "women's auxiliaries" who we know provided mainstays, political, cultural, economic, and social leadership for Harlem. Further, there is no hint of gay or lesbian life in Harlem—during the renaissance or at other times.

However, if gender representation is skewed, the same can not be said of class. The vernacular energies of *I Remember Harlem* in combination with the film's rich array of notables—from Joe Louis to Adam Powell—give it fine demographic breadth. Though their physical space may be confined, the variety of Miles's interviewees is virtually unlimited. In fact, the film's omniscient voice-over is seriously challenged at points by the magisterial presence of a figure like Wilbur Mitchell, who appears in all four parts of the film. Seated like a griot in his dark recliner—and graced with flawlessly groomed gray hair and unwrinkled skin of a man who has been prudent, but not unadventurous—Mitchell is a storehouse of Harlem wisdom.

But there are literally scores of "ordinary" black citizens who come before the camera's eye in *I Remember Harlem*. Their storytelling is effortlessly believable. If Harlem is, in fact, marked by an unseen menace and systematic confinement, it also is the site of a compelling human variety and energy.

What moves this mass of humanity is a notion of style and excellence that *I Remember Harlem* embodies in footage, narration, and photographs of Joe Louis. Louis's fabled reticence is more than compensated by his dazzling pugilistic mastery. In *I Remember Harlem*, the boxer and other black athletes like Jackie Robinson, Willie Mays, and Sugar Ray Robinson imply a community appreciation for what can only be called a distinctive black kinesthesia—a unique style of black bodies in motion. This peculiar motion-sense—though its triumphs are reported from outside through a crackle and static of radio waves—provides an objective correlative for a cherished community value.

Black sports heroism becomes a symbolic in-motion space for psychological expansion. Whites, while enjoying profits reaped from ex-

Still from William Miles's *I Remember Harlem*.
Brown Brothers, Sterling, Pa.

ploiting the physical skills of black athletes, remain paranoid about the ramifications of black athletic dominance. White anxiety peaked with Jack Johnson's 1910 defeat of the white Jim Jeffries for the heavyweight title. Victory for a black man over a white—documented on film for public viewing—raised Federal eyebrows and prompted Congress to pass a law banning films of live fights.[15] The system's attempt, following the Johnson–Jeffries fight, to undocument Afro-American victory, became an ironic mark in the historical win column for blacks. If whites were so agitated by the threat of African American victory, then blacks couldn't help but think they must be onto something big. This, combined with Johnson's empowering accomplishment, symbolized the collective movement of all black bodies forward—another sign of possibility for a black good life in America.

Of course, the black majority was not materially richer, even on mornings after a black athlete's grandest triumphs. And interviewees in *I Remember Harlem* who tell stories of boycotts, demonstrations, and marches to secure dignified treatment in Harlem stores, and respectable jobs in largely white-owned businesses, should probably be seen as more practically useful than black athletic victories. But the menacing economic segregation of Harlem is not represented in its enormity. We are told that black women can not work (or try on hats) in local emporiums, and we hear of a struggle to secure jobs through a "Harlem Compact." But the exclusive economics of uptown remain less threatening in Miles's work than the danger of a groggy, disoriented white man named Max Schmeling stumbling around a boxing ring in his second fight with Louis.

How does one represent the labyrinthine economic desire and aberrant racial dynamics of the founding (and enduring) moment of African labor in Harlem? Discussing her brilliant novel *Beloved*, Toni Morrison says her investigation of race and slavery in America left her asking: "Why are so many things left unsaid?" She concludes: "They are unsaid because they are unspeakable." Perhaps the dynamics of those first (unseen) Africans is unrepresentable by *I Remember Harlem* because a legendary voice can never speak them. Spectators can articulate them only by indirection—by reading Miles's film against the grain. *I Remember Harlem*, then, reveals not simply a story of ennobling legendary remembrance, but also a repressed story of black confinement and circumscription.

Nostalgia works myopically and romantically to sustain a portrait of "safe" and liberated Harlem spaces that once existed. Yosef Ben-Jochannan invokes a time when it was possible to bicycle to Central

Park uptown, enjoy a black picnic, fall asleep on the grass on your stomach with wallet in plain view and awaken with all goods and person in fine order. Dr. Hyacinth Davis recalls a Harlem whose doors were never locked, where young adults promenaded safe boulevards on Sundays, stopping for ice cream at attractive parlors along the way. The force of such nostalgia is revealed when even vernacular interviewees like Al Henry and Emmanuel Kennedy compulsively repeat a legend of blankets and free air.

Henry and Kennedy, former Harlem gang members, talk of a time when black youth ascended to tenement roofs, spread blankets at sunset, and relaxed into early morning hours. The version of urban pastoral emerging from such accounts is coextensive with *I Remember Harlem's* legendary intentions. Pastoral works to avoid realities of rigidly segregated 125th Street stores where blacks were unwelcomed, except, of course, as subservient consumers, poorly paid janitors, and "colonized others." But the stories of Kennedy and Henry also include narrations of gang warfare that dissolve into Ben-Jochannan's lament that uptown community was "breaking down" in the late 1950s: "No one cared. And then, it was impossible to go into the park anymore with your blankets."

Slowly—from blurred visual fields and melancholic jazz—a gallery of horrors displaces pastoral in *I Remember Harlem*. One after another,

William Miles *(left)* interviews James Baldwin
for his film *I Remember Harlem*.
Miles Educational Film Productions.

victims of a drug trade appear in still photographs. Heroin has come to Harlem; black residents try unsuccessfully to enlist support from New York municipal authorities. The filmic narrative becomes almost entirely pictorial, showing bleak death on sidewalks—the integrity of the black urban body wounded by full syringes. We witness a criminal economy of death flowing over a black Harlem population as powerless to control its source and intricacies as it is to control broadcast waves of Joe Louis fights or Jackie Robinson home runs.

James Baldwin is an eloquent interviewee in *I Remember Harlem*. He captures a dark undertext of economics and control symbolized by the heroin trade. His clipped, sonorous, and gestural expressivity recounts a tale in which Baldwin's southern family makes its way to the promised land of Harlem. With studious irony, Baldwin calls Harlem an "African" village, suggesting that uptown was once a place where "everybody's child belonged to the community."

This, we think, is a wry pastoral return upon seventeenth-century black bodies captured to serve the Dutch. But Baldwin puts aside pastoral and talks of his own personal discovery of an "undocumented" black state of being. He says that no black greats or notables were presented in the official histories of his schools. So, he recalls: "I read my way through two libraries—the Schomburg and the 124th Street library. I read everything. I know this because when I wanted more books I was sent downtown." On his trip "downtown" to the New York Public Library at 42nd Street, Baldwin becomes aware of the real economics—social and fiscal—of Harlem.

A white policeman seeing the young boy crossing the street viciously shouts: "Why don't you niggers stay uptown where you belong?" Baldwin realizes: "We [in Harlem] were menaced. And the aim of whites was to make a captive population know it was a captive population." Space contracts; public "services" becomes a misnomer with respect to Harlem. The young Baldwin is suddenly aware that: "We [Baldwin's family and, metonymically, the entire black population of Harlem] were captive and could not move." And, indeed, a sense of incarceration and lost possibilities marks the penultimate moments of Miles's film. The gang and drug narratives of the vernacular segue into the middle-class achiever Gordon Parks's story of Red Jackson— "toughest gang leader in all of Harlem."

On assignment from *Life* magazine, Parks encounters Jackson at the 115th Street precinct; the gang leader is giving the desk sergeant hell because the police have failed to protect one of Red's boys. One of Red's fellow gang members has been found floating in the East River. Why?

The answer is "police betrayal": a failure of the municipality's public servants and services to aid a black Harlem citizenry. Red has been trying to break up his gang—to be free of the horrors of black internecine violence. New York City police have agreed to serve and protect. But no one has protected the boy whose body has been discovered in the East River.

Parks points out that Red was a "natural leader," a young man who with proper nurturing, education, and care could have become a great force for community empowerment. *I Remember Harlem* implies, however, that under hostile policing and municipal malign neglect, Jackson could only become a victim of the American criminal justice system. Significantly, the origin of each of the riots chronicled in Miles's film is a conflict between municipal police and a black community male. In a final scene with Gordon Parks, the camera captures a saddened man who says that the one redeeming quality that existed when he was growing up under horrible domestic conditions in Harlem was "hope." "That's gone now," says Parks. An economics of captivity is inscribed by *I Remember Harlem*. The devastation occasioned by these economics is most depressingly felt in the loss of hope and youthful leadership. A dramatically narrowed sense of spatial possibilities is a consequence of this loss. The state of black community is documented, therefore, by an implicit narrative of incarceration.

Gallantly, Miles resists such a conclusion. Stirring lyrics of the spiritual "Soon I Will Be Done with the Troubles of This World" rise up as we are treated to a montage of spires, turrets, stonework facades, stars and crescents, Hebraic talesmen, and churchgoing Christians. Otherworldliness and religion are presented as antidotes (spatial fillers) for death and blight occasioned by drugs and municipal neglect. One congregation and its minister have purchased neighborhood buildings and are engaged in a project to make these buildings livable. Hence, the concerted attempt of *I Remember Harlem* to resist an implicit narrative of captivity proceeds by dissolving heroin addiction, lost leadership, economic segregation, and human tragedy into a narrative of religion and "redevelopment."

Heavy equipment levels historic Harlem buildings as architectural models and drawings meet the camera's eye. Attorneys, black businessmen, public officials talk of economic self-help, renovation, renewal: black capitalism driven by an independent community. But the fate of the Apollo Theater, shown in the glory of its reopening under "black management," is emblematic of this narrative's vulnerability. A last shot of the Apollo in *I Remember Harlem* reveals a battered, closed building.

Adolph Caesar informs us that the Apollo's reopening proved but a faint burst of black idealism. Though the last scenes of Miles's film show airplanes, construction machinery in motion and bricklayers at work on the new Schomburg Research Center, there are everywhere blank buildings, bombed-out structures, blighted lots, vast empty tracts that seem unlikely to be filled. The leveling of "redevelopment" has merely opened a way for cold sunshine, an endless winter of black hope.

There is a scene of carnival near the close of *I Remember Harlem*. Perhaps it is meant to signify the topsy-turvydom of all black life in America striving for community. The scene is full of Bakhtinian excess. However, this inversive jollity seems out of keeping in the presence of the ironically self-reflexive policing of Miles's "captivity" narrative. One of the film's best services in the office of black community is its implicit recognition and chronicling of the counter-legendary effects of mass-certified spokespersons such as Marcus Garvey, Malcolm X, and Father Divine. Added to this is *I Remember Harlem*'s marvelous archival preservation of vintage film footage and classic photographic records. Finally, there is the stunning excess of interviewees who eventually compel us to read against the grain.

"Outside" refusals of municipal aid produce "inside" effects of drugs, economic deprivation, and police "nightstick justice." Perhaps the most symbolic apparel in *I Remember Harlem* is the formal get-up of black tie and top hats. This seemingly contradictory "black formality" is seen in the film's representations of interracial gatherings of artists and writers during the Harlem Renaissance and also in the scenes of black men outfitted in tuxedos who shine the shoes of whites during the Great Depression. Finally, there is a stunning portrait of three ragamuffin black boys who obviously have looted their formals during a Harlem riot. In a sense, one might read these representations of black formal outfitting as symbolic for the work of black documentary in America. Trappings of the traditional, formal academic documentary may well cover a body of complex black evidence just beneath.

But it is, of course, the ragamuffin boys themselves who have appropriated the formals. Only when they tell their stories—beyond constraints of shoe-shine interracialism—will there be an opportunity for us to grasp what black community can truly mean for our United States. Judge Bruce Wright best captures the incumbencies of the formal when he says of Harlem's relationship to policing—and hence to space: "The police are in Harlem to guard [white] property. They are here to watch us." When the community knows it is militaristically watched, formal attire surely masks what Richard Wright and William Miles realize as black counter-legendary "things unknown."

IV

Baldwin's discovery of the captivity narrative running through annals of daily life in Harlem is at once a revelation of willful white spatial constraints and a recognition of an urgent need for black counter-literacy. Significantly, Baldwin's discovery occurs in the very context of libraries and reading—as counters to the historical absence he feels from texts that portray him and his family as savages. Both Baldwin and the film *I Remember Harlem* realize that while blacks may be patronized for their "legendary" production of ragtime, jazz, home runs, and graceful fisticuffs, they are not likely to be granted public services, livable housing, and real opportunities for spatial expansion. "Why don't you niggers stay uptown where you belong?"

In effect, Miles's film creates expressive cultural space for rethinking a prevalent white American myth that tourists shall eternally take the "A" Train to an ever-enduring Harlem and eternally be entertained by exotic African bodies in motion. Like the World War I and World War II footage and photographs, which form backdrops for Miles's project, there is an ongoing and globally significant war in progress in Harlem. This conflict, as we have suggested, is one between captors and captives, municipal policing and black Harlem bodies in motion. To speak of war within the community as a colonial contest between American white institutional and individual racism and black colonized subjects has been a recurrent strategy of American black nationalist politics. *I Remember Harlem*'s documentary energies reveal the devastating effects that a ringed apparatus of policing, surveillance, and neglect maintains to keep blacks "uptown where they belong." Beyond this documentary revelation, however, are *I Remember Harlem*'s weaving of visuals, voices, and melodies that suggest economic and political alternatives to colonization and containment.

The topsy-turvydom of carnival, the leadership potential of young charismatic figures like Red Jackson, economic redevelopment, expressive culture that drives counter-legendary signification from one black generation's critical memory to the repertoire of the next: These are liberatory alternatives. What we earlier referred to as disciplinary revision can be seen, at a vernacular level, in the reconfiguration of values instanced by Ben Sidran as he describes African slave Christianity: "The preacher took the role of lead singer, the group actionality was generated by the vocal and rhythmic response of the congregation (they were all lead singers, group singers and rhythm players), and the musical-religious ritual became the most important single experience in the daily life of the slave, much as it had in preslavery Africa."[16] Through oral culture and music which contained coded messages of deep-seated, oppression-induced pain, Africans transformed Christianity from a Western to an anti-Western institution. Sidran's observation, of course, confirms Blassingame's notion of the primacy and empowering value of the "quarters." Miles's film, at first blush, can be viewed merely as a well-crafted and utterly traditional documentary confirming Faulkner's assessment: "These others were Negroes. They endured." At a level of "quarters" specifying, however, *I Remember Harlem* represents a counter-legendary impulse that is relentlessly critical, anti-colonial, counter-hegemonic.

Young black artists in our own era have "stepped" like *I Remember Harlem*'s legendary men vocally to the establishment downtown. These young artists' restructuring of Western modes of musical production—like a black shifting of Western Christianity's boundaries—has resulted in a form highly critical of, if not downright antagonistic toward, the dominant white culture in which it was created. Rap music by contemporary inner-city youth projects "secular values of by-all-means necessary" (Nelson George) and proves that black culture always evolves toward collective, conscious spaces located as far from Western thought as possible.

In *Politics among Nations*, Hans Morgenthau defines political power as the "psychological control over the minds of men." One can not begin to discuss black documentary film without first blocking or warding off the "attempt by the oppressor to have his definitions, his historical descriptions, accepted by the oppressed." In the nationalist classic *Black Power*, Stokely Carmichael (later Kwame Toure) states: "When we begin to define our own image . . . the black community will have a positive image of itself that it has created." Toure's injunction surely suggests that when we analyze filmic documentation of black community, we must work with the same transformative canniness that has been displayed by black expressive cultural artists and political spokespersons such as Baldwin, Ellison, and Williams. In a humorous sense, we might say we must be as adept in redefining documentary as stereotypical white southern racists were in employing their thick oral-cultural drawls to distort the pronunciation of Negro to *nigre*.

We know that despite kudos, hoopla, and vigorous announcements of a new day in black film, blacks in the United States still do not possess the same means of oral and visual representation as whites. Thus, while well-respected documentary theorists like Bill Nichols (to whose work we earlier referred and which we heartily respect) are obligated to make a distinction between fiction and documentary film, their official line is necessarily blurred when analyzing black films. For, in their fictional form black films often manifest the very elements of documentary film that Nichols argues must be absent:

> . . . fiction attends to unconscious desires and latent meanings. It operates where the id lives. Documentary, on the other hand, attends to social issues of which we are consciously aware. It operates where the reality-attentive ego and superego live. Fiction harbors echoes of dreams and daydreams, sharing structures of fantasy with them, whereas documentary mimics the canons of expository argument, the making of a case, the call to public rather than private response.[17]

If *I Remember Harlem*'s legendary narrative is driven largely by the "reality-attentive ego and superego," nonetheless the film shows a strong propensity for representing a nightmarish dreamscape of captivity—as well as those representative spokespersons and black stories laboring to provide imaginative "fictions" of community empowerment: wake-up calls to community.

A captive spatial condition (i.e., documentary "illegitimacy") has demanded that black American filmmakers compensate for a lack of attention to their specific plight. Thus "fiction" film (as well as the dreamy, fictional undertexts of a film like *I Remember Harlem*) becomes for many black filmmakers a funded medium through which to document a dying community—"to make a case" against white racism and call for public action to right injustices against a black majority. Issues of space, communitarianism, representation, policing, and surveillance converge in such labors.

We return to Harlemite and interviewee Arthur P. Davis and his memories of Hell's Kitchen. Hell's Kitchen—spanning 37th to 51st Streets and 8th Avenue to 11th or 12th Avenues—received its name because on Saturday nights all hell broke loose between families of different ethnicities, forcing police to ride their paddy wagons "up and down the street at all hours of the night." Davis recounts the story of a white officer confronting a black woman he suspects of soliciting on 41st Street between 9th and 10th Avenues. The woman is actually waiting for her husband to return from work. When her husband exits the trolley just in time to see the detective grabbing his wife, a fight ensues. The fight between the black man and the detective sets off a three-day riot. Davis touts: "The biggest riot in New York."

I Remember Harlem proves that Hell's Kitchen—known today as Times Square with 42nd as its most prominent street—is no stranger to the thwarting of strong, effective leadership within the black community. In a sense, it seems as though the fate of young black men like Red Jackson was sealed even before Davis and his family accompanied other blacks to steam heated apartments uptown.

V

The 42nd Street Development Project, Inc., "the largest development effort ever undertaken by the State and City of New York, and one of the largest renewal programs launched in the country," was approved in 1984. Under the original plan, four office buildings were to be built on the eastern tip of Times Square, nine historic theaters renovated in the mini-block, and a hotel and merchandise mart constructed at the western site on 42nd Street and Eighth Avenue. With $241 million provided by the project's office developer, Prudential Insurance Company of America, the State took title to nine of thirteen acres. These sites included eight theaters, three mid-block parcels and four office sites. Though the sites were cleared of tenants, theaters stabilized and maintenance and security vastly improved, New York City's steadily declining real estate market called for a revised strategy to insure the success of the overall plan. In September of 1993, a plan was unveiled for the Project called "42nd Street Now!" to be carried out by major lighting consultants, architectural and graphic design firms. The plan involved potential developers in the form of corporations and media moguls like Sony, MTV, and the Walt Disney Company. In Howard Muschamp's *New York Times* article hailing "42nd Street Now!" he confirms Neil Smith's claim that "the inner-city is suddenly valuable again, perversely profitable": "Multiculturalism may be the bane of the academy, but in the marketplace it's a boom. Dr. Dre sells records, Amy Tan sells books, and Tibor Kalman wasn't hired by Benetton because they hoped his multi-cult-graphics would put the company out of business." Thus, Muschamp suggests that if blacks were not valued by city governments and white corporate America as commodities (like the endless parade of black entertainers and athletes in Miles's films) they would be considered useless as a race. The Project's proposed "clean-up" of 42nd Street, a block "with a reputation as perhaps the nation's sleaziest, is a smoothly choreographed step in exactly the right direction" for suburban whites who are quick to reclaim any public space claimed by blacks as a cultural meeting place.

In articles justifying "42nd Street Now!" the predominantly black and Hispanic populations that define the area are consistently described as a group involved in the real "decay, crime, drugs, pornography, and prostitution," to which the street has fallen victim. Such a vilifying justification for privatization of public space is no more than an underhanded claim that wherever inner-city black cultural values come to rest, the evils of society follow. While feeling empowered enough to manipulate the public's image of blacks in general, a white American power structure also rejects what Trevor Boddy calls "the messy vitality of the metropolitan condition, with its unpredictable intermingling of classes, races, and social and cultural forms," for a "filtered, prettified, homogenous substitute." Just as the Rockefeller Center, which houses many underground shops and restaurants, was considered the "model of homogeneity" in its heyday, white New Yorkers today are seeking safety behind the corporate battlements of privatization called "42nd Street Now!" In doing so, they are "imposing a middle-class tyranny on the last significant urban realm of refuge for other modes of life, other values."

VI

It is, however, far to the geographical west of 42nd Street—to Los Angeles, in fact—that we turn to observe how a new generation of black filmmakers has answered vilification, "clean-up," surveillance, and public space issues surrounding the project of documenting black community. A new wave of post-blaxploitation socially conscious filmmakers such as Spike Lee (*Do the Right Thing, Malcolm X, Clockers*), John Singleton (*Boyz N the Hood*), and Albert and Allen Hughes (*Menace II Society, Dead Presidents*), make "fiction" films that cause us to, in Nichols's words, "prepare ourselves not to comprehend a story but to grasp an argument."[18] *Menace II Society* presents the most compelling argument of all these films about the black filmmaker's documenting—through fictive means—the community.

Though not considered "documentary" under accepted definitions, *Menace* proves that a theorist like Nichols is misguided if he holds black documentary to the strict scrutiny of his own definitions. For *Menace*, the Hughes brothers' 1993 debut film, ironically fulfills many of the essential requirements for what Nichols considers "true" documentary film. Though categorized as fictional, *Menace* does not "harbor echoes of dreams and daydreams."[19] Under Nichols's own definition, the Hughes brothers' premiere effort successfully "mimics the canons of expository argument, the making of a case, and the call to public rather than private response."[20] *Menace* mirrors the lives of real people in real situations and provides insights to induce a necessary, consciousness-altering argument for the emancipation of blacks from a damaging institutional captivity. It is, at the same time, a film about surveillance and the power which the gaze affords those who own the means of its strategic operation. *Menace II Society*, though labeled "fiction," successfully documents the poverty-plagued police state that is the black Los Angeles community of Watts—its inhabitants and/or prisoners.

The film opens with news footage of the 1965 Watts Riots. A police officer rams the double barrel of his shotgun against the head of an unarmed black man during a round-up; another officer viciously beats a rioter with his billy club while his partner joins in the brutality; black rebellers are handcuffed and slammed against police cars—dead bodies are counted. Simultaneously, white news anchors create the enemy with anxious broadcasts about the impending threat of "roving bands of rampaging Negroes." Two scenes later we are propelled to post-riot Watts, 1994. The menacing sound of helicopter blades slicing through smoggy Los Angeles skies emerges from darkness. It is accompanied by the equally ominous presence of heavy bass filling the theater's aisles and alcoves until it seems the entire auditorium is ready to explode. The scene fades up, affording spectators an aerial view of Watts from the cockpit of an LAPD helicopter. As the instrumental version of Ice Cube's "Ghetto Bird"—a rap attacking the LAPD's use of military helicopters to police the "hood"—crescendos, one witnesses the dystopia of urban sprawl, reminiscent of shanty towns in South Africa under apartheid. Black dwellings are uniform, almost generic in their construction, crammed together like cages in a kennel.

Chief William Parker is the man responsible for transforming the Los Angeles Municipal Police Department during the 1950s from an all-American white-washed Hollywood ideal of flatfoot and mounted officers to the ubiquitous military force it is today. It was Parker—a man obsessed with the elitism and technical proficiency of the Marines—who in the 1950s reformed the LAPD, and in so doing proclaimed war on the Big Bad Wolf of Los Angeles, the Black Man.[21] Parker's successors followed in his militant footsteps. Eduard M. Davis was appointed chief of the LAPD in August 1969.[22] A brave officer who "on at least one occasion risked his life to prevent the death by police gunfire of an armed and dangerous criminal," Davis is heralded for having remarked: "It was better to save a life than to kill one." Davis's ferocious term as police chief, however, was spotted with the "continuing inappropriate use of deadly force." After four years in office, Davis could count only 366 black officers, "or five percent of strength, although the city was then about seventeen percent black."[23]

Chief Daryl Gates (in office during the release of *Menace II Society*) was next in line to head the LAPD's armed squadrons. In 1980, Gates—a seven-year driver, aide, adjutant and executive officer to Chief Parker during the 1950s[24]—flexed his strategic muscle and offered his own SWAT team to President Jimmy Carter to aid in freeing the Tehran hostages. Mindful of a militaristic agenda, Gates struck muscular poses for the home crowd: "This is war," he exclaimed. "We're exceedingly angry. . . . We want to get the message out to the cowards out there, and that's what they are, rotten little cowards—we want the message to go out that we're going to come and get them." The chief of Gates's drug unit stepped up and added: "This is Vietnam here."[25]

In the early 1960s, Gates used problematic crime statistics to create an image of the inner city as a literal "concrete jungle." He had the audacity to testify before a United States Commission on Civil Rights about an "embattled minority." Since the Watts riots of 1965, the LAPD has increased helicopter surveillance of the "hood" by keeping an average nineteen-hour per day watch over the Los Angeles inner city. The division responsible for this improved aerial security has been appropriately named the LAPD "Astro" program. To facilitate policing of the "hood" by the department's myriad Aerospatiable helicopters—complete with infrared cameras, thirty-million-candlepower "Nightsun" spotlights and radio contact with ground patrol-car forces—the LAPD has turned Watts and surrounding inner-city districts into a three-dimensional surveillance map. The department has painted the tops of carefully selected homes with street numbers for quick identification of neighborhoods from the air. In addition, a fleet of Bell Jet Rangers has been added to the Astro program. These military copters are used to transport SWAT personnel to any "high crime areas" throughout the inner city. LAPD's response to the proposed threat of "embattled minorities" was on such an extreme scale that white Westwood and Bel Air homeowners were compelled to invest in high-tech, armed-response security systems. While their white enemies dug fortified trenches some thirty miles off, blacks in Watts became confined under the omniscient eye—the gaze—of the LAPD.

After the 1965 riots, the few large retailers who operated in South Central Los Angeles fled to greener pastures. Smaller, privately owned businesses were left to suffocate under the heavy hand of discriminatory bank practices. Thus, half a million black and Latino consumers were driven out of their inner-city neighborhoods and forced to commute to malls and supermarkets on the outskirts of white communities. Alexander Haagen, a city developer, recognized the profit potential for a retailer who was willing to set up business in the neglected South Central area. Businesses were skeptical. Haagen's rationale seemed realistic enough, but some questioned his common sense upon realizing that his proposal required the return of white-owned retailers into what many saw as a simmering pot of black anger and resentment. Haagen, sensing the growing skepticism of larger retailers, devised a plan for the design of "security-oriented" malls. These security designs, which won Haagen national acclaim, were no more than plagiarized versions of Jeremy Bentham's eighteenth-century Panopticon prison.

Bentham's design consisted of a circular building which was to house any deviant who required heavy surveillance. In the central courtyard was to be a watch tower whose vantage allowed armed guards to keep constant watch over inmates as well as fellow security workers. Haagen set out to apply the Panopticon model to his inner-city shopping malls. In each instance, Haagen's malls came complete with gated entrances and a central surveillance tower to house the headquarters of the shopping center's manager as well as an LAPD substation. A surveillance operator monitors the mall's audio and video units and maintains twenty-four-hour communication with police and fire units, as well as other "Panopticon" malls hooked into the overall security system.

One horrible consequence of Haagen's profit-driven determination to "reinvest" in the "hood," is that the idea of a twenty-four-hour, high-security, Benthamian gaze over shopping malls proved too valuable to the dominant white power structure to use on shoppers alone. Haagen's design has migrated from a shopping mall project to the inner-city housing projects of South Central. The Imperial Courts housing project, for example, has been fortified with a substation of the LAPD, perimeter fencing, and required identity passes.[26]

In *Menace* there is the ever-looming suggestion that, as Mike Davis states, "the social perception of threat [has become] a function of the security mobilization itself."[27] The constant presence of the LAPD in Watts, in effect, brainwashes black and Latino residents, prisoner-of-war style, to believe the proverbial hype that they are, in fact, a bestial threat. Today, with the enemy too far off and greatly outnumbering them, they have nowhere to turn their brainwashed, stereotypical criminal behavior but on themselves. In his book *The Miseducation of the Negro*, Carter G. Woodson explains the problem that arises when a people is subjected to a false, yet dominant ideology: "The difficulty is that the 'educated Negro' is compelled to live and move among his own people whom he has been taught to despise."[28]

VII

In 1988, a Hollywood-informed (or a Hollywood "informing") LAPD and the subordinate black oral sector braced for one of the fiercest and most widely underrated battles in the history of war. Chief Gates implemented his HAMMER program—which involved full sweeps of potential gang members in LA's black communities—and "raided a group of apartments in the 3900 block of Dalton Avenue near Exposition Park."[29] Property was systematically destroyed, innocent people brutalized and still others wantonly slain for "two minor drug busts." While "thirty-two terrified captives were forced to whistle the theme from the 1960s Andy Griffith TV show,"[30] (ironically, the last fossilized remains of any notion of a kind and caring sheriff's department), the rap ensemble Niggaz With Attitude (N.W.A.) caught the overall spirit behind the tenor of the times and sang "Fuck Tha Police!" in response.

In 1988, N.W.A.'s second album *Straight Outta Compton*, dropped like an atomic bomb of injustice documentation on Chief Gates's sadistic party. The controversial "Fuck Tha Police" became an empowering street anthem for much of black America. MC Ren's lyrics: "Lights start flashin' behind me / but they scared of a nigga so they mace me to blind me," became a rallying cry for the victimized residents of South Central to stand up and take action. Ice Cube's lyrics "Fuckin' with me 'cause I'm a teenager / with a little bit of gold and a pager / searchin' my car / lookin' for the product / thinkin' every nigga is sellin' narcotics" stood as a warning to Gates and the larger white power structure that blacks had caught on to genocidal plans for Los Angeles' black community. Eazy E's lyrics—arguably the hardest on the cut: "Without a gun and a badge what do you got? / A sucker in a uniform waitin' to get shot," stepped blacks into the societal "ring" as the number one contender challenging the Rambo version of Jim Jeffries to the social / cultural equivalent of a fifteen-round death match. The militant rhetoric of N.W.A. rap attracted the attention of the FBI, who called for the ban of "Fuck Tha Police" and kept the ensemble's five members under close surveillance. For the first time, the once distant war was no longer amusing to white parents of "trendy" children. Suburban homes, protected by expensive alarm systems, were raided by the blatantly antagonistic music of N.W.A. White children flooded record stores by the millions to purchase and take home a copy of Cube, Ren, Eazy, Dre, and Yella's angry lyrical flows. Similarly, the Hughes brothers' first film became necessary viewing for all white American children who truly wanted to be "kids." The counter-legendary was in full effect.

VIII

In *Menace's* prologue, the two protagonists, O-Dog and Caine, enter a Korean market in Watts to buy a bottle of beer. The ever-paranoid O-Dog, labeled by Caine in a voice-over as "America's worst nightmare," catches the watchful eye of the Korean woman who runs the store along with her husband. He informs her: "You ain't got to be creepin'!" He selects a beer and walks to the counter for a confrontation with the woman's husband who forgets to give O-Dog his change. A game of interracial "dozens"[31] ensues. After several exchanges between O-Dog and the Korean man, the store owner informs O-Dog, "I feel sorry for your mother" (thus committing dozens' *faux pas* number one). O-Dog murders the man, then drags his wife to the back of the store and forces her to give him the videotape which has recorded the murder from a surveillance camera above the counter. He obtains the tape, and then murders her.

What is evident from the opening of *Menace* is that the LAPD's efforts to contain blacks through bellicose support of the "massive privatization of public space and the subsidization of new, racist enclaves"[32] has transformed Watts into a large-scale "Panopticon prison." With the economics of captivity firmly rooted, every black inner-city youth has been enrolled unknowingly in a lifelong Berlitz immersion course in surveillance. O-Dog knows the store owner's gaze is on him. Similarly, he is aware that the video camera has recorded his murderous actions. For he has developed fluency in the language of the powerful "policing eye" that even Chief Parker would be wont to admire. He knows that acquiring the tape means acquiring the power of what Michel Foucault calls the "dominating, overseeing gaze."[33]

"I'm gonna be larger than that nigger, Sagall!" brags O-Dog to Caine and A-Wax after mentioning the murder video. Possession of the surveillance tape has propelled O-Dog's aspirations above the "hood." In his mind, and the minds of his comrades, he is no longer subordinate-black-male. Having successfully infiltrated lower levels of the LAPD's "Panopticon" tower of aerial and ground-based surveillance units, O-Dog has lived N.W.A.'s lyrics and progressed from subordinate ghetto-dweller to omnipotent hero. He has violently earned a vantage point from the other side of LAPD's two-way mirror of inner-city surveillance. His point of advantage is as rare to O-Dog and his friends as the aerial view of Watts in *Menace*'s earlier moments. That they watch the tape repeatedly is testament to their empowered fascination. Surely, O-Dog feels it is only a matter of time before he infiltrates the chief command base of the LAPD itself, parting with a full bag of tapes documenting his single-handed annihilation of the entire force.

Another sequence which illustrates the detrimental effects of security mobilization in Watts begins when Caine and his cousin Harold are carjacked after a party while driving to a local fast-food restaurant. The film's directors foreshadow Caine and Harold's impending doom with a close-up of a traffic light at Crenshaw Boulevard. The sound of the light changing from green to yellow to red, which is usually inaudible, is increased tenfold, stressing not only the violence that is about to occur, but on a more literal level, the desolateness of the inner-city street. A bird's-eye view of Harold's car coming to a stop at the light confirms this assumption; his is the sole car on the dimly lit street. Mike Davis suggests that even in the private sector, the success of what he calls "Westside pleasure domes" is dependent on "the social imprisonment of the third-world service proletariat who live in increasingly repressive ghettos and barrios. In a city of several million yearning immigrants, public amenities are radically shrinking, parks are becoming derelict . . . youth congregations of ordinary kinds are banned and the streets are becoming more desolate and dangerous."[34] Thus Harold and Caine become ironic victims of the "well-policed" streets of Watts.

In *Power/Knowledge*, Foucault discusses the role of the eighteenth-century doctor. He explains that, "doctors were, along with the military, the first managers of collective space." Their job was to police public spaces for local conditions, peaceful human co-existence, residences, the migration of men and the propagation of diseases.[35] The demand of A-Wax—the O.G. (Original Gangster) of the group—for "a mother-fuckin' doctor" upon entering the emergency room with the injured Caine suggests a medieval yearning for a doctor of old, one who would not only tend to Caine's shoulder, but also to the root of the injury itself—the diseased, inhumane, urban apartheid that is Watts.

Caine is admitted to the hospital on two separate occasions during the course of the film. The first time he is admitted as a result of black-on-black crime, the second, as a result of police brutality. The role of the doctor has shifted since the eighteenth century, however—he now tends only to literal wounds. Foucault stresses that the eighteenth century "military" were chiefly concerned to think the space of campaigns (and thus of "passages") and that of "fortresses."[36] While the role of the doctor in society has been reduced to mere clinical work, the LAPD has taken up the slack and added to its list of duties policing the spaces of habitations and towns. Leaving the LAPD in charge of human co-existence, local conditions, and residences, however, is equivalent to leaving a newborn in the hands of a clumsy Sasquatch. Caine is treated and released on each of his visits to the hospital. His ultimate fate at the hands of black gangbangers suggests that what the Los Angeles inner city needs is not military mobilization, but rather, "a motherfuckin' doctor."

In an effort to combat the effects of the imposed hardship on black inner-city neighborhoods, black-underground expressive forms—among which we would number both *Straight Outta Compton* and *Menace II Society*—have emerged like culturally conscious antibodies, prepared for combat. As a function of the LAPD's new policing responsibilities, the psyche of the black-male ghetto dweller has been reprogrammed. Nowhere is this more evident than in the slang used by Watts youth in *Menace II Society*. "You down for a 187?" (a number referring to LAPD's penal code for first-degree murder) rolls off O-Dog's lips as effortlessly as the word "nigger." As if responding to some unspoken canonical power, the young men in *Menace* translate the cryptic language of the LAPD and allow it to form the foundation of their vernacular. The insurgent opportunity that the interpretation of these codes offers O-Dog and friends manifests itself as black military instruction rather than avoidable deviant behavior. In *Menace,* it is clear that the LAPD is not respected by inner-city youth as a protection department. (And here we recall Red Jackson's comrade and the East River.) Were they asked what the letters LAPD stand for, Caine and O-Dog would answer, "the Los Angeles Plantation Department." Thus, the revenge of Caine on the two men who murdered his cousin can be viewed as a tragic breaking of the symbolic hoe of law in refutation of police plantation overseers.

One scene in particular draws attention to both the irony and ultimate success of the LAPD's multi-million dollar inner-city surveillance program. The scene takes place in A-Wax's car. As O-Dog "pumps" Caine's adrenaline for the impending battle with the two men who murdered his cousin, A-Wax, in frame's foreground, surveys the "hood" with the precision of an electronic motion-detector. In this moment, he is using the power of the gaze in his surveillance-imprisoned neighborhood, and turning it against his own people. Foucault, no doubt, would view A-Wax's actions as a direct result of the LAPD's larger surveillance of the same collective space: "There is no need for arms, physical violence, material constraints. Just a gaze. An inspecting gaze, a gaze which each individual under its weight will end by interiorising to the point that he is his own overseer, each individual thus exercising this surveillance over, and against, himself. A superb formula: power exercised continuously and at what turns out to be a minimal cost."[37] Foucault's theory is ironic in that the LAPD's surveillance efforts are anything but inexpensive. Simultaneously, the scene is testament to the success of the police department's efforts because black inner-city youth have, as A-Wax demonstrates, internalized and subsequently turned a policing gaze on themselves.

When they're not seeking revenge or inside watching O-Dog's murder tape, the male characters in *Menace* are "hanging" on the streets or in the trash-strewn dirt lots behind the Watts's projects. Hundreds of unemployed and derelict black males play the "dozens" and "shoot the shit" while tipping 40-ounce bottles of malt liquor that could not be found in any Westwood liquor store. While the pluralistic downtown crowd has been erased from existence by the addition of interior shopping areas for use by Los Angeles's financial and cultural elite, blacks and Latinos are forced to outlying areas to shop amongst themselves.[38] This pushing-out of people of color from L.A.'s Downtown streets is only part of the larger plan to move blacks southward, toward Watts, and hold them captive there. William Whyte, in his 1985 study *The Social Life of Small Spaces,* states, "the quality of any urban environment can be measured, first of all, by whether there are convenient, comfortable places for pedestrians to sit."[39] In *Menace,* O-Dog and others sit atop uneven concrete walls, while many are forced to stand. It is as if the city is engaged in a plot to make public spaces even in the "hood" as unlivable as possible. There are few convenient (and certainly no comfortable) places for groups of young black men who gather outside their homes in *Menace* to sit. (A car ride through 1995 South Central confirms this state.) The nonexistence of resting places suggests that Los Angeles, fueled by the success of its downtown exiling of lower and working-class blacks and Latinos, believes that if it makes living conditions in the inner-city inconvenient and uncomfortable enough, blacks will have no choice but to pick up and return to Africa. The huge ghetto crowds legitimize, in more ways than one, Gordon Gecko's prophetic pronouncement in Oliver Stone's *Wall Street:* "If you're not inside, you're outside!" For immediately outside cramped interiors of their homes is as far as the jobless blacks of *Menace* venture. They are, at the same time, outside the privileged, white-mainstream Los Angeles lifestyle.

Whether it was the 1921 arrest of Upton Sinclair for his public reading of the Declaration of Independence or the breaking up of 1960s family picnics and public love-ins, the LAPD has a history of class warfare and the dispersal of public gatherings.[40] The low-angle close-up of a police car driving in slow motion toward a gathering of black men outside the projects in *Menace* captures this history with alarming clarity. A-Wax, who spots the car first, alerts his fellow men, who drop their 40s and take off with the panic of wanted fugitives. As the police car rattles and pings up the dirt lot, it appears as powerful as a cruising juggernaut. The car personifies Foucault's mechanism: "It's a machine in which everyone is caught, those who exercise power just as much as those over whom it is exercised. . . . Power is no longer substantially identified with an individual who possesses or exercises it by right of birth; it becomes a machinery that no one owns."[41]

When Caine and Shariff are pulled over by police and harassed on

Dayton Avenue, the sound of a helicopter validates Foucault's statement. Surveillance, in this scene, is operative on at least three levels: the surveillance-detecting black males, the ground-patrol police who pull them over, and the LAPD helicopter with its infrared beam trained on them all. That Caine and Shariff are pulled over because of the expressive chrome Dayton rims that ornament the tires of Caine's recently acquired 5.0 Ford Mustang, suggests that he and Shariff are suspect because of their formal trappings. In this, they are reminiscent of their Great Depression ragamuffin counterparts in Miles's film. To reiterate Judge Bruce Wright's statement: "The police are in Harlem to guard [white] property. They are here to watch us." The call of Chief Gates's HAMMER program to suspect blacks of gang affiliation based on fashion sense alone, suggests that the formal trappings of Caine's car make the police in *Menace* paranoid of those counter-legendary "things unknown" that lurk beneath the surface of black style and motion.

In a later scene where Caine is interrogated by an LAPD detective, played by Bill Duke, the camera circles the table where they sit. This camera movement, like a point of view shot from the perspective of some robotic surveillance device, trains a watchful eye on both Caine and the detective. Caine and Duke are black men tragically caught on different sides of a system in which no one is free from the "dominating overseeing gaze." *Menace*'s co-director, Allen Hughes, in an interview with Henry Louis Gates, Jr., expresses what he feels is the film's driving force: "*Menace* was made with a historical perspective. That's how we did it, starting with the Watts riots. We're telling the audience that this is not our fault. That there's history here. The '65 riots, right. This is where this art came from. The despair, and the bloodshed, the whole thing."[42]

The film's strikingly human characters, graphically real violence, and humanistic storyline arise like a tarnished Black Phoenix from the fiery urban history forged by the personal interests of power- and money-hungry whites like Chief Parker and Alexander Haagen. These men had no idea their quests for personal notoriety and the improved safety of Los Angeles through use of heavy surveillance could backfire. In *Menace*, as in the real world of South Central Los Angeles, surveillance has somehow escaped its origins, loosed its ties to the high-tech, space-age laboratories where its power was harnessed in the form of video cameras, infrared beams and Nightsun, and become an enveloping entity. It has embedded itself firmly in the mind state that is the LAPD and simultaneously become part of what cultural critic Nelson George calls the "ghettocentric" mentality of the "hood": "If Professor Molefi Asante's philosophy of Afrocentricity means placing Africa at the center of one's thinking, then ghettocentricity means making the values and lifestyles of America's poverty-stricken urban homelands central to one's being."[43] This is the aspect of ghetto life that *Menace* documents for an audience that is either too naive or too close to the inner city to see clearly the overall dynamic of the "system" in operation. We are all susceptible to and carriers of that omniscient disease called the "gaze." But counter-legendary documentary refigurations like N.W.A. rap and the Hughes brothers' signifying *Menace* can appropriate even the "gaze" and turn it to a profitable and liberating spectatorship.

CONCLUSION

The truth of our black situation in the United States is that we have been relegated to shadows. We have been held captive like Platonic prisoners, guided over a white power structure's cliff of false "whole truths." The architect Corbusier said that an effective public space for the erection of any building contains ample amounts of the natural elements: sunlight, earth, and sky, in that order. Like New York City's elevated subway, which explodes above ground somewhere around 125th Street blocking sunlight from predominantly black and Hispanic neighborhoods, black Americans have traditionally sustained an underground existence. This "authentic" existence has always been equivalent to the undertext of a film such as *I Remember Harlem* or *Menace II Society:* counter-legendary, though economically hard pressed. Above ground, blacks have been continuously deprived of an essential element of the societal building block, imprisoned by shadows in a white-run system. This system, however, has always been suspected by the black mind as one of duplicitous communitarianism and disingenuous projections of hope. Under such conditions and their damaging psychological consequences black documenting creative forms like "underground" rap have been forged. Such forms have broadcast, from the "inside" to the outside, lyrical knowledge bordering sometimes on the morbid or nihilistic about black-urban survival under white-imposed hardship. Emergent black documenting forms are like the elevated train breaking into the fierce light of a New York uptown summer day. When black documentary successfully resists traditional disciplinary imperatives and moves out of shadows to act, then possibilities of mass-certified motion are born. Emergent forms provide representative voice for uptown longings for a black good life in America. Black documentary films like *I Remember Harlem* and *Menace II Society* effectively recuperate and transmogrify the surveilling gaze of white spatial confinement. They release counter-legendary energies of collective black voicings and allow uptown to enter official economies of community in America. Black documentary thus foregrounds and recodes what is indisputably ours in uptown existence. Its expressive, filmic, scholarly, lyrical reconfigurations offer a sense of black community that can be obtained only in America uptown—whether a remembered Harlem or an LAPD-menaced South Central, Los Angeles.

"DO YOU THINK, THEN, THAT WE SHOULD ATTEMPT SUCH A SURVEY?
FOR, IT IS, I ASSURE YOU, TOO BIG A TASK TO UNDERTAKE WITHOUT THOUGHT."
"WE KNOW WHAT WE ARE IN FOR. GO ON."

NOTES

1. James Baldwin, "Stranger in the Village," in *Notes of a Native Son* (Boston: Beacon Press, 1955), 144.
2. Ralph Ellison, *Invisible Man* (New York: Random House, 1952), 272.
3. Patricia Williams, *The Alchemy of Race and Rights* (Cambridge: Harvard University Press, 1991), 159.
4. Ibid., 153.
5. John Blassingame, *The Slave Community* (New York: Oxford University Press, 1979), vii.
6. Ibid.
7. Ibid., 41.
8. Ibid.
9. Benedict Anderson, *Imagined Communities* (New York: Routledge, 1991), 26.
10. Ibid., 35.
11. Richard T. Ford, "The Repressed Community: Locating the New Communitarianism," *Transition* 65 (1995): 101.
12. Michael Renov, "Toward a Poetics of Documentary," in Michael Renov, ed., *Theorizing Documentary* (New York: Routledge, 1993), 26.
13. Philip Rosen, "Document and Documentary: On the Persistence of Historical Concepts," in Renov, *Theorizing Documentary*, 64.
14. Ford, 110.
15. Daniel J. Leab, *From Sambo to Superspade: The Black Experience in Motion Pictures* (Boston: Houghton Mifflin, 1976), 1.
16. Ben Sidran, *Black Talk* (New York: Holt, Rinehart, and Winston, 1971), 19.
17. Bill Nichols, *Representing Reality: Issues and Concepts in Documentary* (Bloomington: Indiana University Press, 1991), 4.
18. Ibid., 5.
19. Ibid., 4.
20. Ibid.
21. Mike Davis, *City of Quartz: Excavating the Future in Los Angeles* (New York: Verso, 1990; reprint, New York: Vintage Books, 1992), 251.

22. Gerald Woods, *The Police in Los Angeles: Reform and Professionalization* (New York: Garland Publishers, 1993), 248.

23. Ibid., 251.

24. Ibid., 257.

25. Davis, 268.

26. Ibid., 241–44.

27. Ibid. 224.

28. Carter G. Woodson, *The Miseducation of the Negro* (Trenton, N.J.: Africa World Press, 1993), xiii.

29. Davis, 275.

30. Davis, 276.

31. "Dozens" is a traditional black, inner-city game, usually played by two people, in which each person tries to make the most original insult on the other's character, lifestyle, clothing, etc. There is an unspoken rule in "dozens" that prohibits insults of any kind on one's family members (especially one's mother!). If this rule is broken, violence may ensue and the person who broke the rule automatically loses the game for having to resort to such an underhanded tactic.

32. Davis, 227.

33. Michel Foucault, *Power/Knowledge: Selected Interviews and Other Writings 1972–1977* (New York: Pantheon Books, 1980), 152.

34. Davis, 227.

35. Foucault, 150–51.

36. Ibid., 151.

37. Ibid., 155.

38. Davis, 231.

39. Ibid., 232.

40. Ibid., p. 258.

41. Foucault, 156.

42. Henry Louis Gates, Jr., "Blood Brothers: Albert and Allen Hughes in the Belly of the Hollywood Beast," in *Transition: An International Review* XX (1993): 63.

43. Nelson George, *Buppies, B-Boys, Baps & Bohos: Notes on Post-Soul Black Culture* (New York: Harper Collins Publishers, 1992), 25.

8

Discourses of Family in Black Documentary Film

VALERIE SMITH

To mention ideas of family in late twentieth-century United States culture is to enter a universe of euphemism, allusion, and displacement. Invoked by politicians, pundits, and policy makers, the notion of family has come to mean more than simply the institution that "[nurtures and socializes] the young, [regularizes] some form of domestic life, [and supports] individuals drawn together in collectivities by virtue of kinship *or* by voluntary emotional bonds—without any particular privileging of genders and / or sexual inclinations."[1] Rather, in a political context largely shaped by, or in response to, the resurgence of conservatism, Newt Gingrich's Contract With America, and the Christian Coalition, to talk about family, or family values, has become code for policies that, among other things, are anti-immigrant, anti-choice, heteronormative, anti–child care, anti–single-parent household, anti–welfare reform, and pro-censorship. In other words, the cluster of principles invoked by the category of family values a specific conception of family while it works to undermine others: families that are poor, immigrant, headed by one person or by two people of the same sex, or that are in other ways minoritized or non-normative.

If the notion of family is loaded in mainstream culture, it is at least as vexed when modified by the adjective "black." Throughout the history of urban and black sociology and policy, the "Negro" or "black" family has been the juncture at which responsibility for social and economic injustice has been shifted from racist and inequitable institutions to the ostensible deficiencies of blacks themselves.[2] Of course, Daniel Patrick Moynihan's 1965 report *The Negro Family: The Case for National*

Action provides the most familiar, but by no means the only example of this tendency. (E. Franklin Frazier before him, and William Julius Wilson afterwards, to name but two, have made and elaborated similar claims.) Although Moynihan begins by acknowledging that major political, administrative, and legal developments have failed to yield equality of opportunity, thereby implying that further measures are necessary, he asserts nevertheless that poverty derives largely from the "deterioration of the Negro family."[3] That same disintegrating structure is, to his mind, "the principal source of most of the aberrant, inadequate, or antisocial behavior that did not establish, but now serves to perpetuate the cycle of poverty and deprivation." [4]

As Michele Wallace, Hortense Spillers, Deborah E. McDowell, Wahneema Lubiano, and many others have argued, not only is Moynihan guilty of blaming the victims of racism and socio-economic inequality, but more specifically, he rests the burden for the decline of "the Negro family" disproportionately on the shoulders of black women.[5] He assaults black women from at least three distinct but interrelated directions. First, at the time the *Report* was published, black women were reported to divorce or separate from their husbands more frequently, and bear more children (within and outside of the institution of marriage) than their white counterparts. As a result, he argues, they are more likely to depend upon welfare, a sure sign of family disintegration. Second, he implicates black women indirectly in the apparent emasculation of black men when he argues that Jim Crow and unemployment historically humiliated men more deeply than women. And third, he blames the perceived predominance of households headed by women for the rates of crime and educational underachievement among young black men.

If, as Stephen Steinberg argues, the discourse surrounding "the black family" marks the liberal turn away from race-based politics and public policy to either a rhetoric of self-help or emergent neoconservatism, it also marks a place where conservatives (of all races) and black nationalists find common ground.[6] Popular and scholarly language and research about the black male as endangered species, as well as church- and community-based programs nationwide designed to rescue and empower black boys and men may be inspired, at least in part, by sincere desires to protect the future of the race. But they are motivated as well by the same heterosexist and heteronormative assumptions that undergird the mainstream discourse. Patriarchal ideas of family, in other words, are as crucial to ideas of racial authenticity as they are to neoconservativism.[7] From the nationalist perspective, as Rhonda M. Williams has written,

families are *the* sanctioned site for the reproduction of authentic racial ethnic culture. Healthy families are monogamous, dedicated to masculine authority, and affirm traditional gender roles.... dysfunctional families spawn
a crisis-ridden racial community populated by carriers of a disabled masculinity.[8]

Or, as Paul Gilroy puts it:

Representations of the family in contemporary black nationalisms appear
to mark the site of what can minimally be called an ambivalent relationship
to America. The newly invented criteria for judging racial authenticity are
... disproportionately defined by ideas about nurturance, about family,
about fixed gender roles and generational responsibilities.[9]

In this essay I examine a group of documentary films and videos by
African American directors that problematize constructions and narratives of black family from a variety of perspectives: Camille Billops
and James V. Hatch's *Suzanne Suzanne* (1982) and *Finding Christa* (1991),
Marco Williams's *In Search of Our Fathers* (1992), Thomas Allen Harris's
Vintage: Families of Value (1995), and June Cross's *Secret Daughter* (1996).
I consider how these films position themselves in relation to prevailing
discourses of family as well as their strategies for complicating and re-
cuperating ideas of and the work of black families.

THE MYTH OF THE IDEAL NUCLEAR FAMILY:
SUZANNE SUZANNE AND *FINDING CHRISTA*

Among black documentary filmmakers, Camille Billops has created the most sustained body of films about black family. In different
ways, each of her four films engages questions concerning the meaning of family, practices of representing family, and the consequences of
keeping family secrets. *Suzanne Suzanne* and *Finding Christa* most directly address how ideologies of family are maintained and interrogated
through strategies of representation.

A 16mm black-and-white documentary shot mostly in 1977 and released in 1982, *Suzanne Suzanne* locates an account of physical and drug
abuse in a specific family within a more expansive critique of the nuclear family. The demystification both of this family and of the idea of
the middle-class nuclear family is achieved within the context of a nonfiction film that destabilizes the very status of the truth itself.

Billops and Hatch undertook this film intending it to be the story of
Billops's niece Suzanne Browning's battle against drug addiction. During the course of their interviews with Suzanne and other relatives, the

Still from Camille Billops and James Hatch's *Suzanne Suzanne*.
Photo courtesy of Hatch-Billops Collection.

story of Suzanne's and her mother's (Billops's sister Billie's) experiences of abuse emerged. The film that was to situate Suzanne as a recovered drug addict thus became additionally, if not instead, an exploration of the suffering to which women are vulnerable in the nuclear family. The filmmakers then constructed an implicit narrative forged from sequencing, cross-cutting, and the interpolation of still photographs and footage from home movies that identifies domestic violence as a major factor in Suzanne's addiction.

In an interview with playwright/director George C. Wolfe, Billops says that she and Hatch "could not arrive at what the film was about until [she] told their editor . . . about Mr. Dotson's [her stepfather's] home movies." She continues: "These were the missing pieces that gave the film its focus. . . . [The home movies] gave the family a history."[10] The footage and photographs certainly place the characters within a generational, class, and regional context. They also produce much of the narrative tension in the film, for they prompt questions about how the beaming young girl shown at age eight becomes the adult addict, how the seemingly stable family becomes fractured.

What is perhaps most striking about these interpolated images is their familiarity. Several fix moments that have become ritualized within the construction of the nuclear family. They establish the family in the recognizable terms of middle-class respectability. They thus memorialize a picture-perfect family whose history might be reconstructed out of the photographic record of public events: holiday celebrations, deaths, births, and so forth.

And yet, it is precisely the familiarity of these images that the film contests. The silent record of the still photographs and the home movies encodes a subtext of family stability and safety that viewers recognize and interpret, and that Billops and Hatch's film challenges. By juxtaposing Suzanne's and Billie's stories with images from family albums and archives, Billops and Hatch prompt viewers to question both the process by which we attribute meanings to images and the overdetermined, explanatory power of certain rituals. Perhaps more important, the use of these materials enables the film to address at once the pathology of this particular family and the nature of the oppressive cultural weight that the image of the nuclear family bears.

Mr. Dotson's Bell and Howell home movies dramatize the commodification of women and children that Billops and Hatch's film critiques. Virtually all of the footage from these films centers on women and children, under the proprietary, controlling gaze of the male—the absent father—behind the camera. Displayed in Easter finery or in scenes of domestic bliss, they are signs of the family's, particularly the father's, achievement.

Suzanne Suzanne, in contrast, is the product not of the father behind the camera, but of a daughter with her partner / co-director and cinematographer. Here, women and children are not silent collaborators within a family romance. Rather, they speak in response to questions that Billops poses or that they pose themselves. Moreover, while cinematographer Dion Hatch, like Mr. Dotson, is invisible within this film, Billops is both audible and visible. The sight of Billops on camera reminds the viewer of the constructedness of the film and the cinematic process. It is also a figure for the black feminist intervention within received family narratives. Simultaneously director and subject, relative and observer, insider and outsider, she occupies the position from which the multiple manipulations of parents, sons, and daughters can be made visible.

Through juxtapositions and the multiple interrogations of its material, *Suzanne Suzanne* problematizes the potentially destructive nature of the middle-class nuclear family; the film's discourses work to dismantle the image of the ideal family created by the photographs and home movies. Indeed, the inclusion of these materials in the film challenges their status as evidence. However much one might wish to read photographic images as denotative—signs of what really existed—they too are fictive constructs; like the techniques of cinematic or literary realism, they represent a body of conventions that privileges particular ideological positions. The shot of Alma (Billops's mother) and her granddaughters going off to church—the one in an elegant suit, the others in dresses with crinoline slips—memorializes a 1950s vision of family harmony. Given the subtext of domestic violence, this Bell and Howell moment points to the central role of performance and imitation in the construction of familial and individual identities.

Still from Camille Billops and James Hatch's *Finding Christa*.
Photo courtesy of Hatch-Billops Collection.

By addressing the subject of domestic violence, *Suzanne Suzanne* takes on a topic that has only recently become speakable in representations of families. *Finding Christa* is even more daring, for, as Barbara Lekatsas has written, "a mother who gives up her child is considered even lower on the scale of civilization than a brutal father."[11]

The account of Billops's relationship to her own daughter, Christa Victoria, lurks on the periphery of the first film. Christa appears as an infant and toddler in photographs and clips from home movies; Billops and Christa sing the title song together. In *Finding Christa*, Billops and Hatch bridge the gap between the wistful image captured on screen and the haunting voice heard at the beginning and end of *Suzanne Suzanne*.

Finding Christa opens with a photograph of the four-year-old Christa as she appeared shortly before Billops gave her up for adoption. In the voice-over, the adult Christa speaks in a plaintive voice that reveals her sense of longing and betrayal: "My last memory of you is when you drove off and left me at the Children's Home Society. I didn't understand why you left me. I felt so alone. Why did you leave me? It's been so long since I felt complete." The first portion of the film seeks to answer Christa's question.

The narrative present begins in Billops and Hatch's loft in New York, where Billops plays for her friend, photographer Coreen Simpson, the tape she received from Christa after a separation of more than twenty years. Billops explains the decision to put Christa up for adoption calmly and directly, saying: "I was trying to give her something else, because I felt she needed a mother and a father. I'm sorry about the pain it caused Christa as a young child, but I'm not sorry about the act."

The film then takes viewers back to the community in Los Angeles where Billops and her family lived and where she made her choice. As they do in *Suzanne Suzanne*, photographs and footage from home movies here too re-create the apparent joys of this family's life in the late 1950s. Clips from Billops's baby shower and still pictures of Christa being bathed and playing under the Christmas tree conjure up a picture-perfect family. Yet interviews with friends and relatives confirm Billops's account of the limited options available to single mothers at the time. In one striking moment, Billops reflects upon the fact that although those close to her did not want her to give up the child, no one offered to keep Christa or was able to help her in meaningful ways.

While the first section of the film focuses on Billops's story, the second centers more fully on Christa's, describing her life after she was left at the Children's Home Society. Through interviews with Christa, her adoptive siblings, and mother Margaret Liebig, we learn that she found what appears to be a nurturing, loving family. Margaret's dreams for herself had long included adoption. After having had four children of her own, she adopted Christa to "satisfy this aching that was in [her] heart."

Also a singer, Margaret encouraged Christa's love of music. Despite this support, Christa is still haunted by deep-seated frustrations dramatized in pantomimed home video sequences. Margaret says she prompted Christa to find her biological mother in hopes that this experience would bring her some contentment.

Billops and Christa's reunion is played out in several scenes, including the filmed first meeting at Newark Airport (with the taped first phone conversation playing in the voice-over); a filmed party in the New York loft; and reenactments of crucial moments spent together. The decision to work with reenactments was at least partly circumstantial: the filmmakers decided to make the movie several years after the initial reunion when Christa and Billops had had a chance to adjust to each other.

Finding Christa does not idealize the reconnection of mother and daughter, for Billops and Christa continue to have radically different needs. Billops ran away from the narrative consolidated by the family pictures. She continues, as Marianne Hirsch has written, "to voice women's need for adventure and their exclusion from what she refers to as 'the news.'"[12] Yet Christa is desperately in need of the very relations Billops seeks to escape. As Margaret puts it, Christa missed "somebody to identify with," and by that, Hirsch rightly argues, "she means baby pictures and family photographs. . . . The implication is that Christa will not recover until she, too, can read her history and constitute herself through such pictures; until . . . she can connect her present self to a past image of herself."

The film is full of still photographs and home movies that reconstruct Christa's personal and familial past. The series of reenactments and interludes are the places where past and present tensions threaten to bleed through the orderly veneer. For instance, in a stylized scene that follows shortly after a dramatic re-enactment, Christa and Billops exchange memories and look at photographs as if they are playing cards or involved in a tarot reading. This sequence juxtaposes Christa's need to know and belong with Billops's need to draw and maintain boundaries. It establishes rivalries between mother and daughter, and hints even at a competition between the two mothers.

As in *Suzanne Suzanne*, the visual style of *Finding Christa* thus complements its thematic and ideological concerns. The interweaving of interviews and archival footage presents one set of facts, but truths too intimate for direct testimony and too private for the spectatorial gaze are encoded in the hallucinatory interludes. In both films, stagey sequences question and contest the truth claims of still photographs and home movies, the stock in trade of the documentary mode. The very presence of the interludes reminds us that the more familiar representations adhere to certain conventions and are thus constructions in their own right. While they may point to the way things might have been, and invoke the dreams that the past holds dear, they can never fix a vision of the way things used to be.

THE MYTH OF THE PATHOLOGICAL BLACK FAMILY: *IN SEARCH OF OUR FATHERS*

Marco Williams's *In Search of Our Fathers* tells the story of the director's nine-year search to find his father. In the film, Williams situates his personal history in relation to widely circulating myths of absent African American fathers and the dysfunctional families they leave be-

Marco Williams, in a still from his *In Search of Our Fathers*.
Copyright Julie Nestingen/FRONTLINE.

hind. Such myths and the studies that undergird them fail to acknowledge not only the impact of broader social and economic factors upon African American lives but also the misogyny of their assumptions. They fail to recognize, in other words, the complex interconnections among constructions and realities of race, gender, and class.

In *In Search of Our Fathers*, Williams critiques the relentless masculinism of these narratives about the crisis of black manhood. Without romanticizing single-parent households, he challenges the assumption that matrifocal families are pathological. Through interviews and the voice-over we return with Williams to the home of his extended family in Philadelphia, where successive generations of women have raised children without husbands. Perhaps because of the network of nurturing relatives, as one of his cousins says, their family is "proof that women raising children without fathers doesn't breed delinquents."

Indeed, Williams would seem to offer his own and his mother's story as a powerful counterexample to familiar mainstream representations of black single-parent households. Although Winnie, his mother, dropped out of college to give birth to her son, she does not seem to have sacrificed much in the way of mobility and independence: she went on to a career in banking in New York before moving to Paris to become a chef. When we meet up with her near the end of the film, she is living in Cambridge, Massachusetts. Williams himself is also ambitious. A Harvard alumnus, he is enrolled in the film school at UCLA by the time he completes *Fathers*.

Williams prompts those to whom he speaks to discuss issues that have long been shrouded in silence. Moreover, the film at first seems set up to offer a corrective to popular cultural representations. In an early voice-over that accompanies a *cinéma vérité* sequence, for example, he alludes to sociological reports commonly understood to be true that pathologize the black family. Most of the film is given over to fairly conventional uses of interviews and still photographs that establish the objectivity of the directorial perspective. The film might thus appear merely to replace popular "negative" images with "positive" ones.

However, Williams incorporates a variety of self-reflexive gestures in the film that undercut his authority and allow him to avoid this kind of binary logic. These reminders call attention to the artificiality of mainstream and oppositional representations alike. While these inclusions may be read as disingenuous markers of the filmmaker's humility before the power of his medium, they might also be seen to undermine the illusion of cinematic transparency that naturalizes and authenticates partial truths.

The most fascinating interviews in the film are those Williams conducts with his father and mother. They compel us not only because of what they suggest about gender and parenting, but also because of what they reveal about the process and ethics of documentary filmmaking. The film begins with a taped phone conversation between Williams and his father, James Berry, during Williams's senior year at Harvard. During this conversation, Williams attempts to set up a meeting with the reluctant Berry and announces to him both that he wants to make a film about their relationship and that he is recording their exchange. Clearly annoyed by these revelations, Berry refuses to consent to a process he considers "surreptitious" and "counterproductive."

By beginning the film in this manner, Williams opens up for scrutiny the complex power relations between documentary filmmaker and subject. He is both participant in and observer of this narrative; while the investments that attend each position sometimes run in tandem, they also sometimes oppose each other. Williams the private citizen may need to meet his father to gain information and satisfy some personal longing, but Williams the filmmaker knows that he is sitting on a timely and marketable narrative. The private citizen may wish to interrogate his father in order to punish him, but the filmmaker needs to maintain cordial relations. The filmmaker may seem merely to turn his camera upon an experience in order to make it available to the viewing audience. But the transparency and apparent objectivity of his position are belied by the editing techniques and use of sound that inflect each position emotionally and politically. In this sequence, Williams's use of a poignant soundtrack emphasizes his feeling of abandonment. However, he also signifies on his father's obvious class aspirations by including his halting use of multisyllabic words.

The conversation we overhear is both a private and a public event, although at the time the exchange occurs, only one participant is aware of that fact. Berry's anger at this revelation exposes Williams's position as intermediary: we cannot escape the fact that his search for the "real" story implicates us in a voyeuristic relationship with his father. From this opening sequence, we cannot avoid recognizing the questionable ethics both of documentary looking and making. The authenticity of this cinematic practice is thus challenged by the construction not only of the subject, but of the director as well.

Throughout *Fathers*, Williams makes futile attempts to speak with and visit Berry; finally, nine years after the film begins, the two men meet at Berry's home in Ohio. So much has led up to this meeting that this scene clearly constitutes the film's climactic encounter. As Williams acknowledges after the conversation, meeting his father is disappointing and has no real effect upon him: whatever his expectations, the encounter hasn't "changed his life" or "made him whole." Although Berry eventually warms to Williams, his remarks about his relationship with Williams's mother are unmistakably crude and insensitive; in retrospect, Williams is relieved that he did not have to sustain an ongoing relationship with him. The meeting certainly challenges the masculinist assertion made earlier in the film that boys need "a man image" in the family while they're growing up.

Although the film centers on the search for Berry, Williams's conversations with Winnie, his mother, reveal much about the director himself; they too comment upon the subtleties of the documentary process. During the course of the film, Williams travels first to Paris, then to Cambridge to visit and talk with his mother. These conversations are skillfully edited to reveal how mother and son work through their discomfort with both the subject of Williams's conception and the presence of the camera. In the initial exchanges with his mother, Williams rarely appears on camera. His is a disembodied voice that asks intrusive questions that, in turn, she tries to avoid. By the end of the film, they appear on camera together and each questions and responds to the other. The evolution of their on-screen relationship suggests the depth of the bond that connects them and subtly overturns the presumptively masculinist narrative of black men in crisis.

Moments of self-reflexivity interrupt his exchanges with Winnie. Twice while he visits her he includes slates (places that mark the synchronicity of soundtrack and visuals) to call attention to the presence of the camera. These moments disrupt the illusory seamlessness of the cinematic practice and highlight the awkwardness of the structure and content of the interview. Viewers may feel more sympathy for Winnie than we do for Berry; nevertheless, we stand in an equally voyeuristic relation to her as we do to him.

Later in the film, on two separate occasions, first the tape recorder malfunctions, then the film runs out. The tape recorder breaks as Winnie describes a fantasy she had while pregnant of falling down a flight of stairs and losing her baby. Williams runs out of film during the final moments of his last conversation with her. Clearly, he could have chosen to edit both of these moments out of the film. But by leaving them in, he demystifies his role and power as director. He acknowledges the partial nature of the counter-argument to which the film points. Perhaps most significantly, he allows Winnie room to exceed the limiting gaze of the spectator.

THE MYTH OF THE HETERONORMATIVE FAMILY:
VINTAGE: FAMILIES OF VALUE

Vintage: Families of Value, the first feature-length film by Thomas Allen Harris, is an experimental documentary, released in 1995, that

Anita's back, still from Thomas Allen Harris's
Vintage: Families of Value (1995).
Printed with permission of Thomas Allen Harris.

looks at three African American families from the perspective of lesbian and gay siblings, including the filmmaker and his younger brother, the artist Lyle Ashton Harris. The subtitle inverts and complicates the conservative catch phrase, thereby conveying something of the project of the film. For *Vintage* undermines the tendency on the part of conservatives and nationalists alike to set constructions of family and homosexuality in opposition to each other.

The film focuses on three different kinds of configurations: three sisters, Adrian and Anita Jones and Anni Cammett; a brother and a sister, Paul and Vanessa Eaddy; and the two Harris brothers. Rather than centering his own perspective and voice as interlocutor, Harris invited the three groups of siblings to record their own stories using video cameras over the course of five years. Although the extent of the subjects' technical skill and innovativeness varies, this charge corresponds with the film's commitment to providing something of the diversity of gay and lesbian experiences of family. By interweaving personal disclosure with documentary and archival footage and audio-visual montage, this film creates what Harris considers a form of family album. It looks at some of the ways gay and lesbian siblings see family, thus articulating the multiplicity of narratives that operate within the category of family.

The film explores these issues in a variety of ways. The subjects consider their relationships with parents and other siblings; they reflect upon their connections and rivalries with each other; and they lay claim to the sorts of rituals and practices by which family is traditionally defined. For example, the Jones sisters and Harris brothers tentatively draw connections between their sexuality and their relationships to their parents. The Jones sisters suggest that their sexuality may result from their experience of having been abused or having witnessed abuse as children, and the Harris brothers suggest that their sexuality may have been determined by their identification with their mother in opposition to their violent father. But even as the Joneses and Harrises challenge these trajectories themselves, the absence of such moments in the Eaddy family narrative calls into question too-easy generalizations that would construct homosexuality as the logical consequence of domestic violence.

Although the siblings clearly take comfort in each other, these relationships are not free of competitiveness, projections, and disappointments. For instance, class differences inflect the bond between the Eaddys. The only one of his siblings to finish college, Paul expresses the hope that Vanessa will "make something of herself." For her part, Vanessa knows that Paul is ashamed of her, and wonders to what extent his response results from educational differences, how much of it has to do with the way class and sexuality converge in her "butch" style.

And the Harrises and the Joneses alike express frustration with the ways in which their siblings carry the burden of their history of familial hurt and betrayal. The younger Jones sisters, Anita and Anni, accuse Adrian of wallowing in the victimization she suffered as a child. Anita wants her to try to forgive her stepfather for abusing her; Anni wants her to work on healing herself. Adrian's discomfort before the camera reveals how far she is from hearing what they have to say; in an interview conducted by the filmmaker, Anni complains about being required to mediate her sisters' disputes, even as her own concerns go unacknowledged.

While all three groups of brothers and sisters submit conventional ideas of family to critical scrutiny, all seem finally to celebrate its value and to position themselves in relation to the conventions of American family life. That they pay homage to their memories, to networks of kin both present and remembered, and to their shared future makes space for redefinitions of family, and detaches ideas of black family from the presumption of homophobia.

THE MYTH OF THE RESPECTABLE WHITE FAMILY: *SECRET DAUGHTER*

Aired on November 26, 1996, as part of the PBS documentary series *Frontline, Secret Daughter* by June Cross is the story of a mixed-race woman raised by black parents after her biological parents—Norma, her white mother, and Jimmy, her black father—separated. Although she has regularly visited her mother and stepfather, the actor Larry Storch (known to most of us as Corporal Agarn on the sitcom *F Troop*), June has participated in a series of subterfuges about her identity throughout her life. Some people believed that she was the biological child of an abusive black couple, adopted by Norma and Larry. Even Norma's best friend believed for a long time that June was the child of Larry Storch and Pearl Bailey. Now a *Frontline* producer in her mid-forties, June has decided to ask her mother to acknowledge their relationship publicly. Doing so requires Norma to confront her own shame at having had a black lover and to risk the disapproval of her more conservative friends, those upon whom her status depends, as historian Larry May, June's half-brother, puts it.

This film invokes several narratives that reflect American anxieties about family and culture: it involves secrets surrounding adoption and race; concerns about the impact of absent fathers, especially absent black fathers; critiques of the "family values" platform. And it even explores the personal consequences of President Clinton's National Conversations about race.

Adoption narratives generally involve revealing to a child raised as if she were a biological offspring that she is adopted. The child then decides whether to uncover the secret of the concealed biological relation. *Secret Daughter* puts rather a different spin on that familiar situation. June never believes that the Bushes, the middle-class black couple in Atlantic City in whose home she grows up, are her biological parents, although they raise her and love her as if she is their own. She is taken to live with them when she is four and regularly visits her biological mother. Rather, she is required to pretend to be her biological mother's adopted daughter in order to protect her mother's social position. In this case, adoption becomes the fiction that covers over the secret of the biological relation; June bears the burden not of locating her mother, but of trying to get her to own the nature of their real connection.

Norma comes from a working-class Midwestern Mormon family, but is raised primarily by her mother and Nazi-sympathizer stepfather in Long Beach, California. Shortly after graduating from high school, she gives birth to her first child, Larry May. But Norma dreams of being a movie star, so she leaves Larry with her mother, and then in a series of foster homes, in order to pursue her career.

Norma never finds the fame she seeks, but through her relationships with men in entertainment she achieves some visibility in that world. Through her association with Larry Storch, the man to whom she has been married for the last thirty-five years, she met Jimmy Cross, the black man with whom she lived for several years and who fathered June. Perceived by many of his contemporaries as a genius in his own right, Jimmy Cross was known as Stumpy in the team Stump and Stumpy. With various partners he performed in nightclubs and on screen as a singer, dancer, and comic, often invoking the expressions and movements of the minstrel tradition.

In the course of making *Secret Daughter,* June comes to understand and partially to recuperate her absent black father. As a result of her investigations, he becomes more than simply the man who left her and her mother to fend for themselves. Rather, she uncovers the connection between his professional and personal failures. She both grows to appreciate and take pride in his talent, and to understand the nature and consequences of the exploitation he endured. As Storch himself and Jerry Lewis both admit on camera, like other white entertainers, they went to Harlem to catch the acts of performers like Cross. They would then incorporate their timing, jokes, and gimmicks into the shows they put on downtown before white audiences. But while Cross's routines made Lewis famous, Cross's own career fell into decline. In the face of his own failures, he began to drink heavily and became increasingly abusive of Norma. When she left him, she cut him out of her life and out of June's as well.

On her own, Norma became increasingly troubled by what it meant to have a child who is visibly black. She justifies having given her daughter over to the care of a black family by arguing that June needed to be raised in a loving environment rather than being subjected to the humiliations of white racism. But she also admits that her male friends could not accept her black child, and that after she and Storch married, she feared that his association with June might ruin his career.

Apart from these circumstantial explanations, the film suggests repeatedly that Norma is repelled by the body of her daughter as a sign and site of miscegenation. And June yearns for that connection and identification as fiercely as Norma wishes to hold it at bay. Norma consistently rebuffs June's efforts to read their resemblances despite the differences of skin color. For example, in a sequence immediately following the opening titles, Cross juxtaposes still photographs of herself and her mother, thus inviting the viewer to consider the similarities of features and expression. In the voice-over, she describes herself as a child staring at pictures of her mother, and spending hours gazing at her own face in the mirror, "trying to find her likeness in my face. . . . I wanted her to acknowledge that evidence of our kinship, but she saw no likeness. Even as I grew older she insisted I looked nothing like her." Later, Norma asks June on camera when she came to see herself as black, since she had been raised initially among white people. In a moment of uncharacteristic directness, June replies that she actually realized that she was black during a visit to Norma's home, when Norma looked at her in the bathtub and said, "if only you weren't so dark, we could be together."

In one of the most poignant sequences, occasioned by June's failure to turn on the sound when videotaping an interview with her mother, June supplies the voice-over for one of Norma's stories while Norma's lips move. It is at that moment, when June fully expects Norma to refuse to appear on camera again, that June seems to achieve that connection with the mother's body and story that has proved so elusive in the past.

These moments in the film raise important questions about the way discourses of racial difference disrupt and transform the process of identification and illuminate the impact of racial hierarchy upon miscegenous domestic relations. Moreover, June's situation—coming of age both in the shadow of Hollywood during the 1960s and 1970s and against the backdrop of rapidly changing race politics—suggests how history and representational practices alike impinge upon the development and enactment of identities.

For my purposes here, what seems most striking about this film is the way in which it exposes the lies and secrets upon which the myth of the respectable white family depends and against which the aberrant black family is defined. Not only does the film position Norma in a line of "wild" white women, thus raising the problematic of the reproduction of bad white mothering, but it establishes as well the existence of a respectable black middle-class extended family that is at least partly responsible for saving June. This is not to say that *Secret Daughter* leaves us with a convenient reversal—the good black family versus the bad white one. The film actually leaves many questions about June's relation to the Bushes unanswered. But in its refusal to separate constructions of blackness and whiteness, it offers its own response to discourses around black pathology. By turning the gaze on the secrets white families keep, it introduces new terms into both private and public conversations about race.

NOTES

1. Wahneema Lubiano, "Black Nationalism and Black Common Sense: Policing Ourselves and Others," in *The House That Race Built: Black Americans, U.S. Terrain,* ed. Wahneema Lubiano (New York: Pantheon Books, 1997), 245–46.

2. For a detailed and persuasively argued discussion of the place of family discourse in post–Civil Rights policy and sociology debates, see Stephen Steinberg, "The Liberal Retreat from Race during the Post-Civil Rights Era," in *The House That Race Built,* 13–47.

3. Daniel Patrick Moynihan, *The Negro Family: The Case for National Action* (Washington, D.C.: Department of Labor, Office of Policy, Planning and Research, 1965), 5.

4. Ibid., p. 30.

5. See Michele Wallace, *Black Macho and the Myth of the Superwoman* (New York: Dial Press, 1978; rpt. New York: Verso, 1990); Hortense Spillers, "Mama's Baby, Papa's Maybe: An American Grammar Book," *Diacritics* 17, no. 2 (Summer 1987): 65–81; Deborah E. McDowell, "Reading Family Matters," in *Changing Our Own Words: Essays on Criticism, Theory, and Writing by Black Women,* ed. Cheryl A. Wall (New Brunswick, N.J.: Rutgers University Press, 1989), 75–97; Wahneema Lubiano, "Black Ladies, Welfare Queens, and State Minstrels: Ideological War by Narrative Means," in *Race-ing Justice, En-gendering Power: Essays on Anita Hill, Clarence Thomas, and the Construction of Social Reality,* ed. Toni Morrison (New York: Pantheon Books, 1992), 323–63.

6. Here I borrow Lubiano's use of black nationalism. As she writes, "black nationalism as a cultural narrative that explains many black Americans' under-

standing of themselves—a kind of common sense even for black people who don't think of themselves as nationalist." See "Black Nationalism and Common Sense," 245.

7. Reflecting upon this kind of convergence, Kobena Mercer remarks: "Welcome to the jungle, welcome to the politics of indeterminacy at the twilight of modernity." See his *Welcome to the Jungle: New Positions in Black Cultural Studies* (New York: Routledge, 1994), 265.

8. Rhonda F. Williams, "Living at the Crossroads: Explorations in Race, Nationality, Sexuality, and Gender," in *The House That Race Built*, 144.

9. Paul Gilroy, *Small Acts* (London: Serpent's Tail, 1993), 197.

10. George C. Wolfe, "Camille Billops," *A Journal for the Artist* 6 (Spring 1986): 27.

11. Barbara Lekatsas, "Encounters: The Film Odyssey of Camille Billops," *Black American Literature Forum* 25 (Summer 1991): 398.

12. Marianne Hirsch, *Family Frames: Photography, Narrative and Postmemory* (Cambridge: Harvard University Press, 1997), 181.

9

Springing Tired Chains
Experimental Film and Video

PAUL ARTHUR

FACING DOWN, THE GROUND SPRINGS TIRED CHAINS. VOICES SPRING FROM
THE EYE THERE, AT CORNERS-SLEEP. HOARSENESS BECOMES RHETORIC
SEASONED/AS FIRST DISTINCT WORDS LACERATE GRIM OPPRESSION
REALITY A BEHIND VISION TOMB WIDOWED ENFEOFFMENT JETTISONED.

—CECIL TAYLOR, "SOUND STRUCTURE OF SUBCULTURE
BECOMING MAJOR BREATH/NAKED FIRE GESTURE"

EXTENDING THE BOUNDARIES

On the face of it, the idea of an African American avant-garde cinema
sounds dubious if not faintly dismissive. There is little in the extensive
history of post–World War II filmic experimentation that would seem
conducive to a black presence. It is not that the movement's aesthetic
foundations, institutional structures, or political agendas barred inclusion; it is simply that until recently the domain of avant-garde concerns
and practices appeared culturally irrelevant—and often economically
prohibitive—to black artists. Further, while there were many examples
of black involvement in cutting-edge American literature, painting, and
especially music, no comparable models existed for non-mainstream
film during the period of major expansion in avant-garde production
and public visibility.[1] Indeed, despite the utopian rhetoric and intermittent social activism associated with alternative film groups of the 1960s,
the avant-garde's egalitarian aspirations, in terms of both organization
and representation, were rarely extended to people of color. By the end
of that decade, as a less overtly politicized "countercultural" ethos attained prominence, the prospect of an interracial avant-garde all but

disappeared. Thus the recent surge of non-mainstream work by black film- and videomakers, at once imbricated in yet separate from current ideologies and practices of white avant-garde cinema, could be regarded as an autonomous development. Nonetheless, for reasons that I hope to make clear, understanding the motives and strategies of black experimentalism requires a mapping of substantial exchanges and intersections with, as well as divergences from, the wider historical field of avant-garde activity.

Among the most telling obstacles to earlier black participation was the often contentious historical relationship between black aesthetics and the tenets of European modernism, in particular the imperative of medium-specific formal exploration adopted by successive generations of experimental filmmakers. Alain Locke, the tireless promoter of the Harlem Renaissance, called for a fusion of modernist literary techniques with black vernacular idioms, a fusion manifest in the visual arts by Romare Bearden, among other painters. By the late 1960s, this stance had been repeatedly discredited as counterproductive to black cultural self-determination, its most strident repudiation voiced by advocates of the Black Arts Movement.[2] Conversely, independent film had by that time abandoned its previous critical engagement with aspects of racism, conformism, and militarism—admittedly couched in narrative hybrids such as Cassavetes's *Shadows* (1959) and Mekas's *Guns of the Trees* (1961)—in favor of more subjectivized, reflexive approaches to the critique of dominant values. Thus the handful of black actors, writers, and directors who were fellow travelers during the underground, Beat phase of the movement drifted into other spheres.[3] For the next twenty years, with the singular exception of the L.A. Rebellion of the 1970s,[4] the vision of an indigenous black cinema was entirely bracketed on the one hand by the limits of traditional documentary and, on the other, by the popular allure of Hollywood.

It is only in the last decade or so that grassroots pressures for greater inclusion of non-white cultural perspectives have furnished conditions for a black presence in the landscape of avant-garde cinema. Heightened sensitivity to perceptions of racial exclusion has prompted a long-delayed broadening of focus by funding agencies, museums, exhibitions venues, academic media departments, and public television. At the same time, avant-garde cinema's revision of formal paradigms in tandem with a renewed interest in the treatment of social issues has created an aperture for artists of color. Even with a dramatic increase in opportunity and accomplishment, it is too early to consolidate black experimentalism under the rubric of a movement. Its visual styles are too varied and unstable, the profile of its practitioners too heterogeneous and geographically dispersed. Moreover, it is evident that the recent flurry of film and video production is underwritten less by self-conscious adoption or endorsement of existing avant-garde practices than by the overall failure of conventional documentary and fiction film to realize the imaginative scope of African American identity. In this sense, the affinities and linkages located in the following discussions are heuristic; they are not dependent on familiarity by black artists with either the white avant-garde canon or its theoretical justifications (although expanding enrollment of African Americans in film and art schools makes such familiarity more likely).

The initial evidence of an interweaving of non-mainstream sectors is institutional, and there is little doubt that black experimentation has claimed a place within prevailing channels of avant-garde funding, distribution, and exhibition.[5] Where once the published rosters of grants, screening schedules, artists in residence, and the like consisted entirely of white film- and videomakers, they have become increasingly diverse. Further, as (mostly) young black media artists attempt to define alternative methods of visualizing their personal and social experience, deployment of themes, materials, and formal strategies analogous to those already ensconced in avant-garde practice encourages a process of mutual accommodation. Black artists are afforded access to organs of publicity and a ready-made audience attuned to both the problematics of self-representation and the challenges of unconventional form. The avant-garde's willing incorporation of minority perspectives helps to validate an informal multicultural agenda, inoculating the established movement against charges of aesthetic stagnation and ideological complicity. To be sure, the idea of an alliance founded on explicit organizational goals and policies is improbable, yet the advantages to both parties are relatively obvious and largely pragmatic.[6]

Devoid of a legacy of experimental achievement within their own community, black artists operate outside the web of intergenerational competition that continues to encumber not only poetic or imagistic styles but feminist and queer initiatives as well. In this sense, de facto exclusion has resulted in a greater freedom to revisit older experimental styles and meld elements from disparate mainstream genres. However, if their position as avant-garde neophytes exempts black artists from certain burdens of modernist succession, it can also impose limitations not encountered by the white avant-garde. For instance, the aesthetic postures of alienation or parodic detachment, which have provided other factions with markers of personal authenticity, are anathema to African American experimental work. In consequence, the rich comedic traditions of both avant-garde cinema and black culture remain largely untapped. Validation of black avant-garde production seems integrally connected to its "seriousness" of engagement with conditions of racial oppression. An invidious spirit of exemplification binds artists to a vexed standard of political responsiveness. And as is generally the case in marginal cinema, the impulse toward cultural resistance is vitiated by suggestions of art world elitism. Although manifest in myriad forms of personal and social signification, a version of DuBoisian double consciousness haunts the trajectory of black experimental cinema. Marlon Riggs, in a deft commentary on the contradictions between popular accessibility and formal innovation, argued for a "new wave of media activism" that could merge realist prerogatives of social documentary with avant-garde subjectivity.[7] The crux of Riggs's proposal is the subversion of essential or exclusive components of social identity in representation, a balance of individual difference and commonality obviating the twin traps of reductivism and solipsism.

The avant-garde canon has frequently been chided by feminists and postmodernists as a bastion of socially conservative idealist discourse.[8] What this line of criticism tends to mask is a deeply embedded identitarian impulse which can stand as a precursor to contemporary multicultural energies. Over several decades, avant-garde film's insistence on self-representation, and on the ancillary documentation of subcultural activities and charismatic figures, resulted in the timely projection of Beat, hippie, punk, and queer oppositional styles.[9] Without repeating or appropriating previous micro-political paradigms, black experimentalists have addressed omissions and distortions perpetrated by both Hollywood cinema and social documentary through formulas which parallel the free-wheeling bricolage of post-1960s avant-garde groups. At the risk of over-generalizing a varied and complex field, a frequent vehicle for the notion of individual identity as fragmented and multiple—at once socially constructed and subjectively autonomous—consists of assembling disjunct materials in a nonlinear, essayistic treatment of autobiographical themes. Recurrent elements include archival footage and recorded speech, talking-head interviews and pseudo-interviews, pop music, spontaneous scenes of quotidian domestic or street life, and sync-sound interludes of dramatic or abstractly expressive performance. As distinct from practices in documentary and independent narrative, this discursive format is grounded in a first-person "voice" or source of knowledge that asserts the power of personal imagination as it subverts the illusion of a unified subject position. Although constituent features of this loose description are employed in a variety of patterns and combinations, the basic outline is applicable to a number of works discussed below.

Two points need to be made about the relationship between a segmented, collage approach and documentary practices. First, the avant-garde has in one sense edged closer to traditional documentary via its renewed interest in historical retrieval, the analysis and/or celebration of discarded episodes in the history of cinema or, alternatively, the examination of subjectivities suppressed by historical representation.[10] Second, the conventions of mainstream documentary have also shifted in the last decade or so—Michael Moore's *Roger and Me* (1989) is a convenient touchstone—to permit more personal, subjective interventions by filmmakers, in the form of voice-over narration, home movies, on-screen appearances, and so on. Given these convergences, what are the grounds for continuing to make critical distinctions between the two camps; indeed, why shouldn't black experimentalism be considered a branch of the personal or essayistic documentary? An initial justification for inclusion in the avant-garde domain is, as I have suggested, institutional. Documentaries are funded, distributed, and exhibited to the public through different channels than experimental work. For instance, most documentaries are feature length (one hour or more) and are shown as single programs; the work considered here is, with several exceptions, less than feature length and is normally programmed in heterogeneous group shows.

Despite the recent revision in standards of objectivity, documentaries are nonetheless understood or "indexed" by viewers through conceptual frameworks which emphasize informational or pedagogical functions rather than expressive modalities.[11] The distinction is less a matter of theme or content than of *enunciation*. Irrespective of any shared commitment to a critique of social inequality or the redress of historical amnesia, experimental work differs from documentary in the nature and degree of its insistence on direct, self-conscious participation in the events or situations represented. Further, the autobiographical impulse in the work considered here implies an enunciative presence at once embodied in and mediated by the play of formal signifiers. While documentaries often cast the representation of marginal subjects as exemplary, as individual cases intended to illustrate a general condition, the avant-garde tends to problematize broader social truths as inextricable from individual consciousness. Refusing to posit an authoritative knowledge separate from that of personal experience, avant-garde film and video operates under an injunction to create aesthetic templates adequate to the presentation of inner, as well external, realities. Its formal practices therefore constitute a rejection of the realist tropes of visual transparency, linearity, and closure—effects which even the recent "personal" documentaries of, say, Ross McElwee and Nick

Broomfield are at pains to jettison. Not only is the documentary regarded by experimentalists, including Marlon Riggs, as complicit in the propagation of bourgeois values, its conventional rhetorics of evidence, argument, and univocal explanation are deemed incommensurate with the exploration of identity as a bundle of multiple, overdetermined, and contradictory strands.[12]

A central, nearly ubiquitous feature of post-1960s avant-garde *and* documentary styles is found footage (including still photos, sound, and other artifacts). Here again, the recruitment of extant materials by black experimentalists has a stronger affinity with avant-garde usage than it does with documentary's inscription of archival images, usually a visual accompaniment to and illustration of past events referenced by interview subjects or by a voice-over narrator. In both sets of practices, found footage may be assigned either a negative or a positive valence depending on a work's thematic orientation. It can become the target of either an ideological unpacking or comic inversion of its original contextual meaning—usually the case with material gleaned from entertainment industry sources or state-produced propaganda (e.g., instructions to schoolchildren on how to avoid an atomic bomb attack)—or serve as an instrument of remedial historical memory, evidence of something ignored or suppressed because it calls into question a dominant social narrative (e.g., the existence of black cowboys).

In mainstream documentaries, regardless of political stance or method of selection and composition, found materials are adduced as direct, formally transparent signifiers of the Real. Footage may be edited into montage sequences juxtaposing disparate sources or production contexts—for instance, snippets from a Hollywood drama spliced to a newsreel scene—but such formal liberties rarely emphasize or substantially modify visual aspects of the original scenes. Their primary function is to advance an expository or argumentative process. In the avant-garde, however, found footage is frequently denatured by optical printing, looping, changes in speed and other techniques which can themselves be thematized by an overarching critique (e.g., looping of TV ads as a visual correlative of stultifying cultural repetition). When combined in complex montage patterns, recycled materials are made to yield not just a set of image contents but stylistic qualities and a mode of production pointedly at odds with that of the work in which they are contained. An additional effect of found images and speech, integral to postmodern concepts of fragmented subjectivity, involves the splitting or deflection of creative authority, the recognition that every text is in some sense a fabric of quotation. The underlying motives, as well as the tactics, of appropriation adopted by black experimentalists are hence more closely aligned with avant-garde practices than they are with documentary's "evidentiary" approach.

The ability to locate, duplicate, edit, and compositionally alter found footage has been considerably enhanced by recent video technologies. While 16mm film—despite escalating production costs—remains the standard gauge for feature-length documentaries, video is clearly the primary format for non-mainstream black artists, a choice governed as much by aesthetic and social prerogatives as by economic criteria.[13] The combination of comparatively lower budgets, enhancing video's potential for public funding, and near-universal access to playback equipment allows for less rigid, localized strategies of circulation and reception. Lacking the mass appeal of Hollywood products, black experimental shorts are nonetheless more easily assimilated into alternative settings such as college classrooms, clubs, and community organizations. The desultory promise of wider exposure through public television and cable outlets has prompted some artists to adhere to broadcast requirements for length, image quality, and acceptable content, but just as often an engagement with video elicits a self-conscious resistance to the middlebrow "public service" ethos of PBS. As the history of avant-garde film has demonstrated, and the commodification of hip hop and rap music confirms, the flaunting of technical crudity or aesthetic alterity does not insure an oppositional cachet as "outsider art." As is the case in the contemporary avant-garde, critical contestation by black artists of TV's dissemination of bourgeois ideology—in particular its racist, sexist, and homophobic underpinnings—is always in danger of being co-opted by the parodic instincts of mass culture itself.

The urgent dialogue conducted by black experimentalists with televisual languages, with news and other nonfiction discourses as well as dramatic spectacle, is the obverse of an equally persistent desire to mobilize more "organic," indigenous, or Afrocentric cultural idioms. As David James has suggested, micropolitical cinemas can validate their own sense of mission by transposing forms of art with which the producing group has a background of prior achievement. Just as earlier avant-garde coteries borrowed tropes from poetry and painting, black film and video adapts expressive and syntactic elements from jazz, blues, and other musics, as well as from dance, black poetry, and theater. According to James, non-mainstream minority movements "initially shape themselves by documenting practices in the earlier medium, and in the process develop ways of internalizing its aesthetic principles *filmically*, in their own form."[14] This insight helps clarify the distinction between black experimentalism and an adjacent mode of "performance documentary," ostensibly neutral transcriptions of performances or portraits of performing artists. Indeed, the quiddity of the work in question is at least partly defined through the interpenetration of vernacular, socially rooted aesthetic patterns and the modernist (or postmodernist) imperative to recontextualize artifacts of mass culture.

SPEAKING IN TONGUES

Having argued for certain axes of connection to avant-garde cinema while acknowledging salient points of divergence from documentary, it is necessary to further annotate the formal and thematic vectors in which black experimentation parts company with other non-mainstream initiatives. This task is best realized through detailed descriptions and analyses of specific works. There is one area, however, that requires a bit of preliminary qualification. Despite a shared reliance on recycled materials as pretext and object of ideological critique, and despite the use of analogous formal devices, the recontextualizing impulse in black film and video proceeds from a rather different stance or body of rhetorical assumptions than those associated with avant-garde film. Simply stated, the relation of black artists to mass media representations indicates a level of disenfranchised hostility in which appropriated images are not just deceptive or alien but constitute part of an armature of determinate subjugation.

Both avant-garde and black practitioners tend to yoke claims for political efficacy to the exposure and interrogation of hegemonic visual discourses, especially those discourses which construct normative attitudes toward race, gender, and sexuality. Beginning with the work of Bruce Conner in the late 1950s, the avant-garde has doggedly pursued a strategy of mocking inversion of media images. As filmmaker Abigail Child describes her method, "I'm trying to dislodge, unearth, and subvert the image, exploring the limits of representation, asking how I can bring forward the contradictions in the image."[15] Similarly, Craig Baldwin asserts, "There's a political edge to it when you take the images of the corporate media and turn them against themselves."[16] Despite the palpable separation inscribed between original context and critical reordering of found materials, there is frequently a subtext of secret pleasure in the selection and handling of such images, a hovering ambivalence stemming perhaps from a prior moment of (childhood or adolescent) appreciation. Even as it registers the malign effects of mass cultural ideologies, the avant-garde's approach to found footage harbors a tenuous identification with the system, or social formation, which produced the artifacts. This mixture of disdain and desire is evident as far back as Conner's landmark *A Movie* (1958), in which cinema's propensity for violent spectacle is paralleled with our century's trajectory of mechanized disaster. Cinema is recognized as a public arbiter, as well as recording instrument, of violent action; as such, neither the maker nor the viewer is entirely exempt from complicity in the cycle of destruction and spectatorship.

In a eulogy for Marlon Riggs, Isaac Julien reminds us of the difficulty faced by black artists of "how to name yourself in a language that has named you as other."[17] The title of Riggs's best-known work, *Tongues Untied* (1989), hints at the double burden imposed by silence—the historical exclusion of black media artists from articulating their own histories, and the accumulation of repressive languages by which the entertainment industries "speak" for and to the social experience of minorities. The deployment of found materials by black experimentalists is underwritten by affirmative as well as nullifying impulses, an intersection of remedial historical representation with the intended creation of a new historical subject equipped its own discursive logics. Operating beyond the limits of textual pastiche, the contestation of past images becomes inseparable from the struggle to directly integrate art into the praxis of everyday life. British artist and theorist Kobena Mercer encapsulates the importance of found imagery as follows: "At a micro-level, the textual work of creolising appropriation activated in new forms of black cultural practice awakens the thought that such strategies . . . may be capable of transforming the 'democratic imaginary' at a macro-level."[18] What counts as historical evidence and the means by which evidentiary fragments are fashioned into personal or collective counter-narratives are issues that suffuse contemporary culture. In the recent work of black film- and videomakers, the "evidence" of mass media representation is entwined with and finally sublated by vernacular elements of voice, music, and visual movement.

The practice of recombining extant images into compilation films is nearly as old as the cinema itself. Jay Leyda recounts how in 1898 Lumière cameraman Francis Doublier constructed a version of the Dreyfus affair by connecting a series of generic shots—an army parade, a street scene, a government building, and so on—none of which actually referred to the "depicted" events.[19] It is possible to extrapolate from this story that manipulation of found footage originates in a perceived absence, in the attempt to make visible an *idea* or meaning latent in the original material but to which it is necessarily blind. A particular kind of absence, the socially conscious reception of black viewers, is crucial to the compilation pieces of Tony Cokes. *Black Celebration* (1988) brings together news clips of police and National Guard troops suppressing the 1967 uprisings in black urban ghettos. The visual text for this video —derived from an earlier gallery installation—is stripped of its familiar rhetoric by the use of repetition, slow-motion, and the superimposition of politically militant speeches. Following the corporate logo for "Universal Pictures," a matrix of shots of burning stores, soldiers on patrol, arrests, and confrontations between angry residents and occupying forces are shuttled into various configurations as printed titles and disjunctive voice-overs address the events as "A Rebellion against Commodity." Statements about the social effects of consumerism by Morrisey, Barbara Kruger, and Martin L. Gore, among others, initially suggest spontaneous voices of ghetto rebels, but as the tape proceeds they emerge as a highly diverse chorus challenging the unvoiced, official explanations of urban unrest.

The looping of scenes destabilized by the counter-authority of speeches (and music) has a dual purpose. It demands that we "look again," re-viewing the media spectacle of "rioters" and "peace-keepers." It also summons an aesthetic awareness of the grim beauty of compositions and human movements in a rich patina of dark tones and ominous gestures. In addition, the formal rigor of repetition is freighted with a larger thematic of historical redundancy, an accumulating weight of racially exploitative images, as well as physical acts, and the simmering resistance they provoke. *Black Celebration* has a superficial resemblance to the avant-garde style known as *structural film*; however, its affect of barely suppressed rage against both social and image-making systems creates a marked separation from the latter's reflexive investigations.

In *Fade to Black* (1991), Cokes again reworks scenes taken from mass media representations of African Americans through an overlay of printed statements, music, and speech. A chronological parade of demeaning Hollywood stereotypes and revisionist portrayals starts with *Uncle Tom's Cabin* (1903) and concludes with a swipe at Spike Lee's *Do the Right Thing* (1989) (juxtaposed with the subtitle "I do not see the strong black women who raised me anywhere in this film"). Hollywood's record of "framing" black characters is evoked and called into question in a tripartite visual field: shots seemingly recorded off a television screen are sandwiched between titles and dates at the top of the frame and printed first-person comments at the bottom. For example, brief prologue images from *Vertigo* are underscored by the question, "What does this mean to me?" Later, a scene from *To Kill a Mockingbird* (1962) elicits the indictment "Chained? Framed? You know what I

Still from Tony Cokes and Donald Trammel's *Fade to Black*.
Printed with the permission of Video Data Bank, Chicago, Ill.

mean?" Cokes plays off cinema's capacity for multiple, discordant sources of knowledge—sound/image and text/images collisions —to "talk back" to mass cultural representations of race.

On the densely textured soundtrack, music by N.W.A., Byrne-Eno, The Last Poets, and other groups is interspersed with excerpts from Jesse Jackson, Malcolm X, and Marxist philosopher Louis Althusser, who elucidates his concept of "hailing" or ideological interpellation. A summary statement of Cokes's polemic against the deceptions of Hollywood cinema, by black as well as white directors, appears near the end: "I ask why the discourse of my enemies should dictate my actions and perceptions." By including a postscript from Malcolm, "You'll be a slave as long as you're responsible and respectable," the videomaker challenges the usefulness of polite, distanced cultural analysis. His visual technique is insistently crude, a low-tech history lesson which refuses the cloak of disinterested critique, substituting instead the perspective of an active, outraged subject of Althusser's "state ideological apparatus."

A more elliptical handling of found materials is offered by Lawrence Andrews in *An I for an I* (1987). Several shots from *Rambo: First Blood II* (1985) and a Leon Kennedy prison movie are wedged into a diverse orchestration of enacted scenes, interviews, diary-like shots of domestic routines, and an assortment of sync-sound and contrapuntal sound units. Andrews makes a personal descent into the social mythology and pathology of male action, with the role of black masculinity highlighted as simultaneous paradigm and demonized other.[20] Icons of media violence are adduced as agents in an internalized regime of black machismo and internecine hostility. A jarring yet thematically coherent stream of vignettes assays linkages between the mass cultural landscape of brutality, self-defeating standards of phallic toughness among black men, and the seepage of physical domination into erotic encounters. The most powerful image is a closeup of a man being repeatedly punched in the stomach over the spoken refrain, "Again. Harder." Whether this sequence is mechanically looped or performed in real time is somewhat ambiguous. A metaphor for inner-directed feelings of frustration and anger, meshed with a homoerotic attraction to physical pain, this image is posed rhythmically against looped shots of Rambo wielding a machine gun followed by shots of an explosion.

In another closeup, a kitchen knife is slapped again and again on a bare hand, displacing the punching episode into a grisly symbol of sexual intercourse. Here as elsewhere, a pulsing exchange of diegetic movements and found footage expresses the distorted process of internalizing cultural definitions of self. Sensationalized models of male potency, through which and against which all men in our society define their attitudes, are addressed in their specific impact on African Americans. Andrews charts his own immersion in a realm of coded masculine images yet refrains from the fervid condemnations delivered by Cokes. As an antidote, his elusive polyrhythmic editing of visual materials counters the dull thud of media bravado with brief moments of domestic and creative activity, including shots of cooking and a hand playing an African thumb piano. It is in such gestures, positioned as outside the limits of prior representation, that we glimpse the potential for individual resistance.

Subtitled "a personal journey through black identity," Marlon Riggs's *Black Is . . . Black Ain't* (1995) was shot and partially edited toward the end of his long battle with AIDS and was completed posthumously. Riggs's early films were relatively straightforward documentaries and even after his formal breakthrough in *Tongues Untied*, he continued to alternate between mainstream (e.g., *Color Adjustment*, 1991) and more experimental projects (*Non, Je Regrette Rien*, 1992). *Black Is* is something of a hybrid, a documentary essay with avant-garde leanings, comparable in certain respects to Yvonne Rainer's feminist collage narratives. As is the case with Lawrence Andrews and other artists, Riggs gathers an array of disparate elements and stylistic tropes in exploring multiple, at times antithetical, views of African American subjectivity. Making common cause with an anti-essentialist slant in recent cultural theory, he interrogates the notion of Blackness as a transcendent, replete signifier of selfhood.[21] Through pointed juxtaposition of interviews, found footage, and dramatic or performative interludes, Riggs develops the position that even as an historically specific response to racism, there can be no single "authentic" version or marker of black identity. He surveys a spectrum of individual components, from gender and sexual orientation to physical attributes (e.g., skin tone and hair texture), class divisions, and the cultural imperative of Afrocentrism—none of which, he maintains, deserves a privileged or integral status in the calculus of identity. The argument is not solely or specifically with dominant social constructions but focuses on myopic exclusions and divisive myths within the black community.

Production still from Marlon Rigg's *Black Is . . . Black Ain't*;
Marlon Riggs *(left)* and Bill T. Jones.
Signifyin' Works.

In *Tongues Untied* (1989), Riggs laments the secondary marginalization of gay men by the reactionary rhetoric of fundamentalist churches and the stand-up comedy of performers such as Eddie Murphy. Where *Tongues Untied* employs a simple counterpoint of repressive stereotype and queer self-assertion—provocation answered by artistic solidarity —*Black Is* engages in a complex and nuanced dialectic. For instance,

Riggs rehashes the European tradition of depicting blackness as moral negation, then situates a response in the 1960s slogan "Black Is Beautiful." He goes on to demonstrate how despite its emancipatory appeal, Black Power served to marginalize women, as Angela Davis maintains, through "the rehabilitation of black patriarchy." Employing a similar tactic of admitting positive effects of liberatory movements then exposing their limitations, Riggs applauds the black church as instrumental in civil rights organizing but decries its homophobic policies, citing activist Bayard Rustin's concealment of his sexuality as cogent illustration. This line of inquiry is then capped by a joyful gospel congregation in Los Angeles which welcomes homosexual parishioners, resolving in a historical montage the apparent contradiction between black religion and gay liberation.

In each mini-essayistic sequence, Riggs is intent on creating connections between past and present that are grounded in the poetic retelling of his own life history. A schoolboy says in an interview that knowledge of history is overrated, that what counts are contemporary models of success. In its validation of historical continuity within diversity, *Black Is* rebuts the hedonism encountered in several street-hardened kids. As the title suggests, the dilemma of defining black identity—tied to but not synonymous with political empowerment—is rooted in discursive practices. If the problem of hierarchical conceptions of identity is compounded by divisive or exclusionary language (and visual representations), the solution is to forge a more heterogeneous, inclusive racial discourse. In *Tongues Untied*, the process of articulating twin markers of blackness and homosexuality was emblematized by the subcultural idioms of vogueing and "Snap!" Here the master trope adopted by Riggs is the *gumbo*, a favorite childhood dish cooked up in brief segments across the length of the work. In form as well as theme, *Black Is* embraces a host of different stylistic ingredients, economic and social as well as personal signifiers of identity. The gumbo metaphor embodies in a single, slowly evolving image a framework for the goal of "communal selfhood" advocated by Riggs. In this mirroring of form and function, the familiar strategy of postmodern pastiche is invigorated, redeemed by a didactically lucid and celebratory urgency.

What distinguishes *Black Is* from other recent personal documentaries—the films of Ross McElwee come to mind—is the profusion of cinematic roles Riggs is able to embody. Befitting his conception of fluid identity, Riggs switches from interviewer to interviewee, from performer (e.g., a wonderful, painful songfest of African American music) to commentator, anchoring individual sections with voice-over introductions and transitions. He casts himself as various literal and symbolic characters: artist, child, friend, scholar, PWA (person with AIDS). We see him in and out of the hospital and in and out of chronological time, gravely ill in one shot and then cavorting in the woods. Thus a personal horizon of mortality, and of autobiographical closure, haunts but also empowers the convergence of personal with social-historical themes. *Black Is* acquires a singular poignancy both in the recognition that its maker will not live to complete the work and that his continuing creative labors are helping to keep him alive. Broached as an experimental investigation of the variables of self-naming, it stands as a last will and testament, a literal bequest whose generosity and communal spirit is, at the least, inspirational.

PERFORMING THE SELF:
ALLEGORIES AND PSYCHODRAMAS

For artists such as Riggs and Lawrence Andrews, the use of visual and aural quotation and the dialogic splitting of sound/image unity is not, or not simply, a plank in a (post)modernist aesthetic agenda of fragmentation. Rather, quotation, repetition, and the preeminence of human speech in rhythmic structures are etched with affinities to non-European and indigenous black performance traditions. In a discussion of formal techniques in African American literature, James Snead points to the use of "circulative" iteration as derivative of African music and dance more than to modernist practices of repetition.[22] One can draw a similar inference from recurrent image patterns in experimental film and video, where the emphasis is not on progressive development of phrases leading to a structural or thematic resolution but on a continuous texture of differing beats that together map a sequence of choral changes. Alternatively, visual systems governed by parallel editing can evoke an antiphonic call-and-response familiar to blues stomps and gospel music.

In the same vein, re-worked quotations of found imagery can suggest culturally specific improvisational techniques having little to do with the aims of modernist collage—for example, the jazz soloist's treatment of standard melodies in a way that disrupts their original flow and, hence, their identification with sentimental platitudes. Leah Gilliam deploys clusters of jazz-like visual riffs in *Sapphire and the Slave Girl* (1995), a vibrant contribution to the emerging cinematic paradigm of intertextual polyphony. Acted, spontaneously recorded, and recycled scenes are layered around a double exercise in urban detection. The crux of the enigma invoked by Gilliam is how women subjectively navigate a tough Chicago neighborhood and the liberating potential of female disguise. Brief excepts from a 1959 British mystery film, *Sapphire*—about the murder of a young black woman passing for white in elite society—sets off an intricate play of naming and concealment. "Sapphire" was a common appellation for mulatto women that figures obliquely in Willa Cather's 1940 novel, *Sapphira and the Slave Girl*, a romantic story with lesbian overtones about a jealous wife (Sapphira) and a light-skinned servant. Both the British film and American novel turn on problems of assimilation and the scandal of interracial coupling.

Gilliam inverts and prismatically filters the allegory of "passing" in white society to encompass transgendered as well as transracial social confusions. Variables of personal identity are thematized, displaced onto urban architectures—three sections are ambiguously labeled "Networks," "Buildings," and "Open Spaces"—and mirrored in the formal design. As a TV voice-over complains, "Just tell me the name of the genre so I know the rules." The composite identity of "Sapphire" is assumed by five very different-looking women; she is at once an "undercover" agent gathering clues and the object of (self-)investigation. This elusive heroine oscillates in her relationship with the outside world between being an alienated loner stuck inside a drab apartment and a member of a secretive cadre of streetwise women.

At one point in her decentered trek through the inner-city neighborhood, she switches clothing in a narrow alley, assuming the costume of a businessman or 1940s private eye. The adoption of wigs and fashions from several decades, from Black Panther leather to call girl to bohemian, is animated by a soundtrack blending original jazz with samples of Latin American and other ethnic musics. In a telling insertion of found footage, a white reporter tries to interview a black girl at a bus stop during the attempted integration of Little Rock Central High School. Her mixture of fear and defiance, positioned against the contemporary dilemma of women in a hostile environment, acts as both historical contrast and reminder of the power of silence as a form of masking. The uncertain focus of pursuit in Gilliam's video, coupled with its views of a deracinated urban landscape, hints at a feminist re-reading of Poe's "A Man of the Crowd." It is as if Sapphire, the woman in the B-movie mystery whose romantic life (and death) hinged on a slippage in racial perception, had been transformed into a proactive version of the outcast woman.

Sapphire and the Slave Girl is one of the few experimental works which does not feature a strong vocal performance. In Gilliam's muted rite of female passage, musical improvisation and rhythmic movements of walking bear the subjective weight frequently accorded to speech. The significance of the artist's direct voice, or the voice of a surrogate figure, in black film and video cannot be overestimated. Although the technical properties of video recording are clearly important, the centrality of spoken performance is rooted as well in populist oral traditions, in an aesthetic realm that in contrast to image composition appears less overdetermined by conditions of mass culture. In this sense, voice, and sound in general, is posed in virtual opposition to the cult of image "purity" maintained by earlier avant-garde idioms—and still in vogue in some circles. Thus the ideals of a silent cinema dedicated to exclusively visual rhythms and affective qualities, the greatest exponent of which is Stan Brakhage, are largely irrelevant to black experimentalists. Silence, or for that matter subordinate musical accompaniment, is not a viable option to the extent that it limits the expressive range and cultural specificity of self-inscription as realized in performative tropes.[23]

Black film and video's invocation of role-playing, verbal storytelling, song, and poetic recitation is grounded in an autobiographical impulse, the desire to re-create one's own story rather than the stories of others. Just as the stress on vocalization in black cinema stipulates an embodied rather than an optical arena of subjectivity, an insistence on first-person narrative separates this work from the avant-garde's parodic engagement with Hollywood performance styles—exemplified in the films of Andy Warhol and George Kuchar. The prerogatives of autobiographical performance, especially its ability to juggle inner and external histories, are most clearly defined in a group of videos that re-enact or allegorically portray childhood traumas of identity. In *Flag* (1989), Linda Gibson revisits the disturbance produced by her early fascination with patriotic symbols and rituals. She assembles a patchwork of scenes around discrepancies between democratic rhetoric and the reality of racial division, mingling a child's diary entries, stills and home movies, printed texts, street interviews with people trying to designate the meaning of the American flag, and a medley of physical routines in which idiosyncratic dance movements collide with stylized variations on saluting. *Flag* flickers with the uncertainties of memory, the evocation of a child's credulous view of equality etched with an adult's knowledge of social hierarchy. As in *Black Is*, Gibson formally enunciates the principle of collective correspondence within diversity, reclaiming the youthful vitality of tolerance as a function of creative arrangement.

An adolescent's dawning awareness of class boundaries is rendered in Cheryl Dunye's wry memento, *Janine* (1990), about the videomaker's crush on a private school classmate. The tangled desires of same-sex interracial romance are verbally recalled as catalysts of transformation, at once cause and effect of a crisis of identity (a similar dilemma is probed from a male perspective in *Tongues Untied*). Dunye's anecdote unfolds in a playfully self-deprecating voice reinforced by stills, printed texts, and isolated shots of fetishistic objects such as candles and a carnival keepsake. As in *Flag*, subjective enunciation flickers between the emotional orientation of childhood and a more cautious, reflective framework of social knowledge. What Dunye describes as a painful awakening is couched by her mother as a "problem" requiring medical intervention. Refusing to wallow in accusation or guilt, Dunye manages to at once lament the loss of naive trust and reproach the exercise of class privilege.

The erotic psychodrama, in which the filmmaker, or an obvious stand-in, enacts a liberatory quest for sexual self-recognition, is among the earliest and most durable genres in American avant-garde cinema, connecting the groundbreaking films of Maya Deren and Kenneth Anger in the 1940s to contemporary practitioners such as Sadie Benning and Peggy Ahwesh.[24] Several formal and thematic aspects of the psychodramatic legacy have been revitalized in black experimental cinema as conduits for the statement and symbolic resolution of sexual anxieties as they intersect the social reckoning of otherness. Typically, a film- or videomaker's revelatory self-exposure in front of the camera incites a double-edged confrontation with a prior moment of sexual confusion. Declarations of erotic longing are frequently visualized in metaphors of death and rebirth, in oneiric condensations of action, or the magical display of threatening or benevolent supernatural figures.

Wet Dream #4, video still from Thomas Allen Harris's *Splash* (1991).
Printed with permission of Thomas Allen Harris.

286 | PAUL ARTHUR

Thomas Allen Harris's *Heaven, Earth and Hell* (1994), for example, embellishes an oracular journey of first love, rejection, and bereavement with costumed figures taken from African and Native American cosmologies. Harris himself assumes several mythic roles in a narrative poised between autobiographical detail and dreamlike ambiguity. *Splash* (1991) has an even stronger affinity to the psychodrama's allegorical search for sexual meaning. Here Harris erects a fantasy of sadomasochistic frustration through a trope of entrapped desire, with the protagonist emoting from a literal cage. This externalized mechanism of sexual repression is traced by the speaker to society's compulsory standards of whiteness and heterosexuality.[25]

Although hardly the exclusive terrain of women and gay men, the psychodrama has proven an especially useful forum for the questioning of forbidden, or merely ideologically devalued, frameworks of social bonding. Zeinabu irene Davis's *Cycles* (1989) and Julie Dash's *Praise House* (1991) share a similar regard for the significance of spiritual customs as consolation for the uncertainties and degradations of menial labor and domesticity. Davis draws from Caribbean folklore to inflect her protagonist's anxious anticipation of menses, an event made more acute by the inferred abandonment of a romantic partner. The editing scheme juxtaposes talismanic objects with prosaic tasks of housecleaning and bathing, imbuing the female body's cyclical evacuation and regeneration with an aura of ancient fertility rites. Through the rhythmic alternation of enacted scenes of female isolation and solidarity, a secularized ordeal of ritual seclusion from the outside world is superimposed onto the modern subject's demand for change and self-definition.

Praise House, a collaboration with the performance group Urban Bush Women, lends a sinuous visionary cast to an intergenerational parable of familial conflict, rebellion, and spiritual reconciliation. Abstracted movements of women's everyday work, shown in factory as well as domestic caretaking situations, are elaborated as the premise and processual backbone of creative expression. As women of various ages and attitudes filter in and out of a single communal dwelling, their brief exchanges of nurture and hostility are invested with wider significance by allusions to African and Southern ceremonial beliefs: corporeal inhabitation by spirits, the gift of "second sight," ecstatic gestures of flight and bodily yearning. The central relationship concerns a young girl's attachment to her dying grandmother and her refusal to accept the authority of a haggard woman, either an older sister or her mother. A fusion of dance, musical speech, and dramatic mime, *Praise House* unearths a rarely addressed internecine struggle for a balance between connexity and individual freedom.

Stylized performance as a natural product of female interaction is treated in a context devoid of unconscious or spiritual imagery in Cheryl Dunye's *She Don't Fade* (1991). In this reflexive gloss on how to filmically stage an explicit sexual encounter from a non-pornographic angle, the psychodrama's ambivalent tracking of identity is transmuted into a playful round of personal confession, storytelling, and the mechanics of lesbian lovemaking. The actors, including Dunye herself, are understandably self-conscious about performing in semi-scripted sexual scenes. The director does not try to hide but rather foregrounds this discomfort, exposing the mutual reticence that pervades any dynamic of sexual compliance and resistance, encompassing all those gnarly protocols and shifts of dominance otherwise known as seduction. The byplay between what is enacted on screen and how it is perceived, the slippage between "actor" and "spectator," mirrors as it displaces the gropings of on-screen couples. The result is an incisive commentary on our multiple, attenuated expectations for sexual completion.[26]

Working once again in the gap between psychodrama and in-group documentation, Dunye rehearses the issue of performance as vehicle of self-validation in *The Potluck and the Passion* (1993). Her explicit theme is group tensions and the personal disclosures unleashed by social role-playing. During a dinner party celebrating the anniversary of a lesbian couple, female guests improvise a series of conversations exposing unexamined attitudes toward friendship, jealousy, work, and cross-cultural identification. Romantic cliches and blind spots concerning lesbian relationships, prompted by a character's visual appearance or speech, are undercut by various instances of petty dissimulations. The dinner party begins to feel more like a skirmish than a Sapphic idyll and, of course, that's the point. Held together by a series of comic vignettes featuring the entire party or pairs of guests, *Potluck* trips lightly through a minefield of submerged prejudice. By the end, this multiracial microcosm of assertive women have dredged quite a bit of surprising psychic baggage. Direct talking-head interviews further annotate an individual character's possessiveness, diffidence, or smug assumptions of cultural solidarity. The interplay of fictive roles and fake *vérité* recording is further complicated by the insertion of found footage fragments of a cartoon mammy and Josephine Baker in performance—two disparate and problematic versions of black female roles, sites of both potential identification and disavowal.

Cauleen Smith activates a very different approach to performance in *Sapphire Tape #1: The Message* (1994), a dramatized critique of ghetto-centric images of black masculinity ("The Message" is also the title of an influential early hip hop record). A bare-chested man stalks around

an apartment drinking and smoking, looking every inch the prototypical "gangsta." A woman's off-screen voice is attempting to direct and
control, or perhaps simply describe, his movements as it speculates on
the theatricalization of male power and threat. The question of whether
the man is "acting" or being recorded spontaneously is never fully resolved, but in either case the voice-over seems to emanate from a space
outside the action. Hand-held camera movements caress the man's
body, creating a dance of mutual attraction and withdrawal. However,
a looped repetition of shots, poses, and glances undercuts both the ostensible unity of performance and the viewer's ability to sort out the formal masks of dominance and submission.

In the distinct splitting of voice and image, of language and bodily
performance, Smith inverts and destabilizes a common division in gendered authority: the male agent of knowledge against the female object
of scrutiny. However, in the context of black experimental cinema, her
critical gesture of dis-articulation also underscores the degree to which
vocalization figures as an index of subjective presence. Frequently, the
voice is presented as an instrument of abstract, rhythmic sound as well
as semantic content, a necessary synthesis of body movement and language. The imagination of an aesthetic discourse in which speech, song,
and musical sounds can alternate and overlap has been a focus of black
American culture at least since the Harlem Renaissance, as demonstrated in the career of Langston Hughes. More recent, and perhaps
more cogent, precedents for the use of musical speech in black cinema
are the fusions of jazz and poetry promoted by the Black Arts Movement in the late 1960s and the related surge of singing and chanting in
the cutting-edge music of John Coltrane, Sun Ra, and Cecil Taylor. This
legacy is particularly evident in the sound structures composed by
Riggs, Cokes, Gilliam, and Lawrence Andrews.

In the loosely diaristic patterning of *and they came riding into town
on BLACK AND SILVER HORSES* (1992), Andrews immerses the rhythmic qualities of African American vernacular speech in an ambivalent
process of personal witnessing. A collection of what he refers to as "interchangeable verses" spirals outward from the testimony of a man
who, by his own account, was wrongly convicted of a vicious mugging.
Bracketing emotional verbal descriptions of crime with an officious talk
on handgun safety, polemics on justice with poetic images of apocalypse, *BLACK AND SILVER HORSES* reminds us of the twin functions
of testifying as personal expression and public evidence. The act of witnessing, removed from stock religious connotations of spiritual healing, dissolves into a tissue of negotiated truths in which the poisoned
stream of commercial television simultaneously submerges and galva-

nizes memories of racial injustice (including dreams and textual citations from Aimé Césaire's "Notebook"). As Andrews bears witness to the unending conflation of black male experience with criminality, he transforms TV's public "record" by fragmenting, collaging, and condensing its repetitive messages; for instance, "Verse 12" delivers a skittering two-minute visual riff of "unedited" footage covering forty-eight hours of nonstop banality.

There is one final entry to be made in the catalogue of performance techniques and musical tropes employed by black experimentalists. The advent of hip hop culture in the early 1980s has furnished a major impetus for the structuring of sound—and to a lesser extent, visuals—in recent videos. The low-tech, improvised mixture of beats, street language, and sampling pioneered by Grandmaster Flash anticipates some of the effects of abrupt rhythmic and tonal shifts in the work of Riggs, Cokes, and especially Art Jones. In addition, the electronic sound mixing executed by rappers can be roughly analogized to graphic manipulations of video images by color solarization, split screen, and other denaturing devices. Jones's *Know Your Enemy* (1990) and *Knowledge Reigns Supreme* (1991) are, for lack of a better term, deconstructive music videos celebrating the second, politically militant phase of rap music. In *Enemy*, whose title makes a play on the overtly racist army indoctrination films of World War II and the Vietnam invasion, Public Enemy members Chuck D and Harry Allen are interviewed using a PixelVision toy camera answering charges of anti-Semitic lyrics in their record "Welcome to the Terrordome." Jones studs their remarks with short excerpts from Malcolm X, Huey P. Newton, Eldridge Cleaver, and Angela Davis, suggesting a historical continuity between 1960s activists and current rap groups. The persistent question, "Who is the enemy?" is framed within a dynamics of media distortion of black cultural politics. *Knowledge* is essentially a portrait of rapper KRS-One (Chris Parker) as he inveighs against the Eurocentric educational system and racist news reporting. In both tapes, Jones employs an aggressively coarse visual style that undermines the polished look of commercial music videos. Reviving and totally subverting the tenets of spontaneous *vérité* documentary recording, he extends the arena of personal performance to embrace the gritty textures and jarring movements of a defiantly untutored camera style.

CODA: RE-TAKING THE PAST

By any standard, the cinematic career of William Greaves is remarkable, and it has been remarkably undervalued. He began as a stage actor

Production still
from William Greave's
Symbiopsychotaxiplasm: Take One.
Photo courtesy of
William Greaves Productions.

and was featured in several films made by black directors in the late 1940s; in addition, he has a starring role in "March of Time" producer Louis de Rochemont's Hollywood "problem film," *Lost Boundaries* (1949). Spurred by the postwar social realism of semi-documentary productions—and his disgust with entertainment industry's exclusionary practices—Greaves moved to Canada where, from 1952 to 1960, he worked in several creative capacities at the National Film Board on nearly eighty films, including the first North American *cinéma vérité* documentaries. Upon returning to the United States, he undertook an impressive series of nonfiction projects for various government agencies and public television. These include biographies of Frederick Douglass, Booker T. Washington, and Ida B. Wells. From 1968 to 1970, Greaves served as executive producer and co-host of NET's seminal *Black Journal*. He has gone on to direct the controversial portrait, *Ali, the Fighter* (1971), and features.

In 1968, with money obtained from a private patron, he shot nearly seventy hours of footage for a projected five-part series of experimental narratives revolving around a single directorial provocation: the heated argument of a married couple over the husband's infidelity and the prospect of having children. Five different couples, recruited from the ranks of New York stage actors, improvised their way through repeated takes of the same basic scene staged at different locations in Central Park. The premise was that not only the dramatic scenes but the filming process itself, complete with off-camera instructions and creative discussions, would be recorded and woven into the finished work. What emerged from this adventure in reflexivity and demystification was *Symbiopsychotaxiplasm: Take One*. Greaves screened an initial cut of the film for potential distributors, who were thoroughly mystified, after which it was shelved. *Take One* was finally dusted off in 1991 for a retrospective of Greaves's work at the Brooklyn Museum of Art and has since played to receptive audiences and admiring reviews at film festivals and private screenings. In 1995, Greaves recut several sections, adding footage from other "takes."[27]

This brief note on the genesis of *Take One* omits two absolutely crucial details. Having assembled a racially diverse, mixed-gender crew of veteran documentary technicians, Greaves encouraged their collective creative input, an opening which resulted in what the director refers to as a "palace revolt." Frustrated over the progress of shooting and what they felt was a lack of coherent structure, the crew met privately to voice their discontent ("we're just sitting around here and are gonna just rap about the film"). A filmed record of several meetings was shown to Greaves, who then happily inserted them into the emerging design via parallel editing or split-screen effects. In addition to these sidebars, which nearly swamp the dramatic core, the crew shot spontaneous vignettes with assorted intruders and passersby, of which the most telling are a subdued confrontation with a cop demanding to see a city filming permit and the scatological ramblings of a homeless denizen of Central Park. In a continuous series of slippages and outright abdications of creative authority, it is this figure, the thoroughly addled "Victor," who assumes a role as tertiary chorus, providing sly metacommentary on both the film's method of production and its dramatized battle of the sexes. In retrospect, the exchange of power is pure artifice, a function of discursive self-reference; as Greaves puts it, "The film had to be chaos, but chaos of a very special character, *intelligible* chaos."[28]

As a summary restatement of the political and aesthetic ambitions of 1960s alternative cinema and street theater, *Take One* taps into the utopian energies manifest in Happenings, the ritualistic improvisations of the Living Theater rituals, and the theatricalized spectacles of antiwar demonstrations (e.g., the attempted "levitation" of the Pentagon during the November 1967 March on Washington). There is as well a critical engagement with traditional theater, grounded in a closet domestic drama worthy of Ibsen or Chekhov, played out against the backdrop of a countercultural imperative to critically reanimate the focus of spectacle. *Take One* touches, and makes important contributions to, many of the period's cultural obsessions: the philosophical dialogue between theater and cinema, scripted and spontaneous behavior; the relationship of new forms of realism to stylized convention; the interdetermining processes of individual and collective liberation. As in other late-sixties revisions of *cinéma vérité*-as-performance, including *David Holzman's Diary* (1968) and *Gimme Shelter* (1971), Greaves ruptures the simple fiction/nonfiction dichotomy of means and terms of address. His scattershot yet rationalized dismantling of aesthetic boundaries inserts *Take One* into the cauldron of generalized cultural critique of power and repressive control; it deserves a place on the decade's roster of revisionist cinema alongside the work of Warhol, Godard, Jack Smith, Rivette, Chris Marker, and Dusan Makavejev. Interestingly, Greaves refers to his overall procedure as a "screen test" (the same term exploited by Warhol), regarding the offhand/directed ambiguity of this approach as encapsulating the era's rebellious attitudes toward authority.[29]

If *Take One* partakes of its historical moment in a clarifying jolt of invention, it also sparks a connection with a double trajectory more pertinent to the concerns of this essay. Greaves's project can be construed as a bridge between the independent directorial tradition of Spencer Williams and Oscar Micheaux—often revered for their visual and narrative infractions of commercial codes—and a current generation of black experimentalists. By the same token, *Take One* underscores affinities between earlier modes of avant-garde cinema—spanning the meta-documentary excursions of Jonas Mekas and the self-destructing spectacles of Smith, Ron Rice, and George Kuchar—and the work of Riggs, Dunye, Andrews, and their cohort.[30]

Greaves's unheralded accomplishment is clearly prescient in its organization and production methods, but what makes *Take One* all the more remarkable is the way in which its core of social issues prefigures the current identitarian cultural landscape. One of the first lines delivered by the character "Freddy," following a short pre-credit sequence, ignites an underlying tension: "You're telling me the name of the game is sexuality?" His wife, "Alice," accuses him of being a "faggot" because he won't fuck her in a "normal" fashion. Her comment sets in motion an intermittent series of accusations, confessions, and equivocations about sexual stereotypes that exfoliates from dramatic scenes to conversations between the actors and then director, then resurfaces in the crew's pri-

vate gripe sessions. This seemingly impromptu theme is finally recon-
figured in the lewd axioms of the interloper Victor. A crew member expresses his disgust with what he views as the contrived nature of the
enacted argument: "This isn't Edward Albee. . . . This dialogue [about
the nature of gender roles] is prescribed from birth." Reiterating the
contention that sexuality is a function of nature rather than a social construction, another crew member blatantly reveals his homophobia during an exchange about whether Freddy could possibly be gay. Victor's
final word on the topic of romantic attraction has a convoluted logic befitting the sexual ambiguity of his own outrageous performance: "Love
is the feeling of a penis for a cunt."

Take One is organized like a hall of mirrors ("You know Alice, you're
really talking in circles") with one level of filmic reality refracting and
intensifying the cracks and contradictions in another level. As Victor
puts it, "What is this thing? Oh, it's a *movie* . . . so who's moving whom?"
Power relations masked by personal prescriptions of gender difference,
sexuality, and race are framed by psychodramatic excesses inherent in
the original scripted scene. The film's thematic sinew is gathered around
acknowledgment, dismissal, or casual denigration of human diversity.
Without ever acquiring the clang of didactic exposition, this problem
keeps pulsing near the center of every benignly corrective or irreducibly
hostile confrontation. If the film as text maps an undulating terrain of
social inquiry enlivened by pressing controversies in our own social
climate, its unanticipated rescue from the coils of obscurity should re-
mind us of the many tasks left to complete in our efforts to historicize
and conceptualize the important body of work in black experimental
cinema.

NOTES

1. Frequently lauded for their poetic imagery and infractions of narrative
convention, the "race movies" of Oscar Micheaux and, especially, Spencer
Williams's 1941 *Blood of Jesus* were rediscovered in the late 1960s, receiving
regular screenings at avant-garde showcases such as the Collective For Living Cinema in New York, along with other "suppressed" examples of ethnic
filmmaking. However, to the extent that they were appropriated by the white
avant-garde as part of a program of historical retrieval of non-commercial
artifacts, these works were still largely unknown by the first wave of African
American filmmakers. The best account of the politics of 1960s underground
film is in David James, *Allegories of Cinema* (Princeton: Princeton University
Press, 1989), esp. 85–119.

2. For Locke's assessment of modernism, see *The New Negro* (New York: Atheneum, 1968). See also Ralph Ellison, "The Art of Romare Bearden," in *Going to the Territory* (New York: Random House, 1986), 227–38. The irrevocable split between modernist tendencies and 1960s black radicalism is amply documented in Addison Gayle, ed., *The Black Aesthetic* (Garden City, N.Y.: Doubleday, 1971). Essays in this volume by Hoyt W. Fuller, Ron Karenga, and Larry Neal are especially cogent in their rejections of "European" aesthetic programs. As Neal puts it, "the Black Arts Movement is radically opposed to any concept of the artist that alienates him from his community" (p. 273).

3. The New American Cinema Group, formed in 1960 as a loose alliance for the production and publicity of independent features and documentaries, included several black members. The first "catalogue" of the Film-Makers' Cooperative, an artist-run distribution collective with a policy of open admissions, lists a half dozen films made by or with black artists.

4. The L.A. Rebellion was grounded in a curious hybrid of realist energies and experimental impulses. Although its adherents produced perhaps a half-dozen films reasonably classified as avant-garde, their primary aim, as I understand it, was the revision of narrative structures and social protagonists under the aegis of the European New Wave and Latin American Third Cinema; see Clyde Taylor, "The LA Rebellion: New Spirit in American Film," *Black Film Review* 2, no. 2 (1986): 9–16; also Ntongela Masilela, "The Los Angeles School of Black Filmmakers," in *Black American Cinema*, ed. Manthia Diawara (New York: Routledge, 1993), 107–17. With a few exceptions, the aesthetic orientation and institutional parameters of the L.A. School are markedly different from those of the work considered in this essay. Although their points of convergence are of interest, I must reserve fuller discussion for another occasion.

5. The degree to which black experimental media have been incorporated within avant-garde circles is evident in, for example, the catalogue listings of distributors such as Film-Makers' Cooperative, Electronic Arts Intermix, Frameline, and Women Make Movies. Of course, other criteria for institutional inclusion such as gender or sexual orientation are also relevant here. There is a comparable crossover effect found in the broadcast schedules of the PBS series "Independents" and the screening schedules of major venues, including the San Francisco Cinematheque, various gay and lesbian festivals, and the Whitney Museum of American Art's influential Biennial selections of film and video. For instance, in the 1997 Biennial, five of twenty-five chosen media artists (or collective groups) were black, more than the total for all previous exhibitions combined. Unfortunately, critical journals specializing in avant-garde cinema, *Millennium Film Journal* for instance, have yet to acknowledge the burgeoning significance of African American work. Nor has this lacuna been filled by publications dedicated to minority artists—*Black Film Review* and *Visions* are two examples. *Black Face*, an organ of the Black Filmmaker Foundation, has provided more extensive coverage.

6. The relationship between black British and African American experimentalists, with Isaac Julien as a pivotal figure, is instructive if somewhat peripheral to the concerns of this essay. It is sufficient to note that the emergence of the Black Audio, Sankofa, and Ceddo collectives was underwritten by both a level of political activism and a theoretical sophistication unknown in the U.S. In addition, governmental and communal structures of organizational and financial support encouraged black artists to form semi-autonomous channels of production and distribution rather than be assimilated into the—admittedly small and desultory—system of British avant-gardism. For an overview of the

black British movement in film and video, see Jim Pines, "The Cultural Context of Black British Cinema," in *Blackframes: Critical Perspectives on Black Independent Cinema*, ed. Mbye B. Cham and Claire Andrade-Watkins (Cambridge: MIT Press, 1988), 26–36.

7. "A Snap! Queen Deliberates: 'Reading' the Media," *Video*, November–December 1991, 8. Not surprisingly, the debate around audience expectations and the institutionalization of black experimental film and video has received a more intensive and theoretical exploration in England; see for example Judith Williamson, "Two Kinds of Otherness—Black Film and the Avant-Garde," *Screen* 29, no. 4 (Autumn 1988): 106–13.

8. One of the earliest attacks is by Constance Penley and Janet Bergstrom: "The Avant-Garde: History and Theories," reprinted in *Movies and Methods, Volume II*, ed. Bill Nichols (Berkeley: University of California Press, 1985), 287–300.

9. For a recent re-reading of 1960s Underground Cinema through a grid of gay subcultural identification, see Juan A. Suarez, *Bike Boys, Drag Queens, and Superstars* (Bloomington: Indiana University Press, 1996).

10. On the resurgence of historical discourse in the avant-garde, see my "The Appearance of History in Recent Avant-Garde Film," *Frame/Work* 2, no. 3 (1989): 39–45.

11. Noël Carroll has a useful discussion of "indexing" as a categorical tool bypassing questions of style or theme: "From Real to Reel: Entangled in Nonfiction Film," *Philosophical Exchange* 14 (1983): 22–26.

12. The post-1960s brief against documentary's rhetorical structures comprises diverse charges leveled by disparate creative and theoretical factions, including feminists, post-structuralists, community activists, and minority artists. Riggs cites the "disempowering" effects of "non-participant" documentaries in "A Snap! Queen Deliberates," 8. For a collection of broadsides by academic commentators, see the essays by Brian Winston, Bill Nichols, Jay Ruby, and E. Ann Kaplan in Part One of *New Challenges for Documentary*, ed. Alan Rosenthal (Berkeley: University of California Press, 1988). For an analysis of how the traditional documentary constrains minority perspectives, see Trinh T. Minh-ha, "Documentary Is/Not a Name," *October* 52 (Spring 1990): 87–94; also Kobena Mercer, "Diaspora Culture and the Dialogic Imagination," in *Blackframes*, 50–61.

13. Although cognizant of significant divergences in the historical development and formal properties of video and film, I conflate the two formats in the following discussions since previous institutional and productive dichotomies have been largely eroded, and the video practices of black artists are roughly compatible with those of a dominant faction in avant-garde film. The high modernist reflexivity of the movement referred to as "video art," pioneered by Nam June Paik, Peter Campus, and others, has had no real counterpart in black experimentalism.

14. David James, "The Most Typical Avant-Garde: Film in Los Angeles/Los Angeles in Film," unpublished manuscript, 3–4.

15. Cited in William C. Wees, *Recycled Images* (New York: Anthology Film Archives, 1993), 74.

16. Ibid., 81.

17. "Black Is . . . Black Ain't," *Sight and Sound* 4, no. 7 (July 1994): 22.

18. "Diaspora Culture and the Dialogic Imagination," in *Blackframes*, 59. In a similar vein, Pratiba Parmar concludes that "It is these politicized appropriations of dominant codes and signifying systems which give us powerful

weapons in the struggle for empowerment," in *Queer Looks: Perspectives on Lesbian and Gay Film and Video,* ed. Martha Gever, John Greyson, and Pratiba Parmar (New York: Routledge, 1993), 11. Although no one working in American experimental cinema has offered such cogent and sweeping claims for the effectivity of found materials, much of the work discussed here would seem to implicitly support this position.

19. Jay Leyda, *Films Beget Films* (New York: Hill and Wang, 1964), 12.

20. A ghettocentric encoding of African American men as an "endangered species" has surfaced recently in a variety of cultural contexts, including the controversial 1994 "Black Male" exhibition at the Whitney Museum of American Art. Inexplicably, neither the work of Cokes nor Andrews, nor that of Ulysses Jenkins, Thomas Allen Harris, or Cauleen Smith was included in the exhibition's four separate film and video series.

21. The perspective elaborated by Riggs echoes that of other black cultural commentators; see for example the essay by Henry Louis Gates, Jr., "The Blackness of Blackness: A Critique of the Sign and the Signifying Monkey," in *Black Literature and Literary Theory,* ed. Henry Louis Gates, Jr. (New York: Methuen, 1984), esp. 285–93.

22. "Repetition as a Figure of Black Culture," in *Black Literature and Literary Theory,* 67–68.

23. In *Tongues Untied,* Riggs renounces the dire historical consequences of silence, as summarized in this anthem by the late poet Essex Hemphill: "Silence is my shield / Silence is my sword / Let's end the silence." The interweaving of disparate modalities of black speech is a prominent feature of not only Riggs's work but that of Andrews and other artists.

24. P. Adams Sitney provides the most lucid account of psychodrama in his seminal history of the American avant-garde, *Visionary Film* (New York: Oxford University, 1974), esp. 3–19 and 93–102. Although he tends to periodize the form as a stepping stone in the development of the post–World War II generation of makers, a wider perspective suggests that the psychodrama has served as an initial vehicle by which various emerging artistic cadres—Beats, women, gays, Asian-Americans—assert the primacy of subjective discourse in cinema.

25. Isaac Julien's *Looking for Langston,* a seminal film in the development of black experimental cinema, is quite explicit in its debt to the psychodramatic trance films of Deren and Anger. Not only does its elliptical structure recall the earlier works' subjective shattering of time, individual shots and techniques pay tribute to the liberatory promise of the postwar avant-garde. Manthia Diawara's grudging acknowledgment of Julien's relation to American avant-garde traditions is tendered in "The Absent One: The Avant-Garde and the Black Imaginary in *Looking for Langston,*" *Wide Angle* 13, nos. 3/4 (July–October 1991): 96–109. Regrettably, Diawara oversimplifies the history of this movement as "concerned solely with the process of filmic production itself" (101), failing to recognize the avant-garde's persistent mobilization of outcast sexualities. This leads to a muddled opposition of "avant-garde" and "blackness." I see no merit to his claim that *Langston* and other films "parody the avant-garde in order to reveal its racism . . . " (103). My preference for de-marginalizing black experimentalism, positioning it in a broader film-historical flow, is arguably less condescending to both the white avant-garde and to the political and aesthetic goals of black media artists.

26. Alexandra Juhasz discusses Dunye's video, along with the work of Sadie Benning and others, as an example of a new wave of feminist art that challenges the outmoded prohibition against exhibiting the female body: "Our

Auto-Bodies, Ourselves: Representing Real Women in Feminist Video," *Afterimage* 21, no. 7 (February 1994): 10–14.

27. As of this writing, Greaves is still anticipating a much-belated theatrical release and is beginning to put together funding to complete a second chapter, "Take Two." I wish to acknowledge his generosity in allowing me access to a revised print and for answering my assorted questions with great good humor and enough spicy anecdotes to fill a separate essay.

28. Quoted in Scott MacDonald, "Sunday in the Park with Bill," *The Independent* 15, no. 4 (May 1992): 28. A selection of Greaves's notes, before and during production, and a transcription of a brief scene from *Take One* have been published in MacDonald's *Screen Writings: Scripts and Texts by Independent Filmmakers* (Berkeley: University of California, 1995), 31–48.

29. See McDonald, *Screen Writings*, 32, 34.

30. As a footnote, the avant-garde filmmaker Peggy Ahwesh programmed *Take One* as part of a 1997 retrospective of her work at the Whitney Museum of American Art, implicitly claiming Greaves's film as a precedent for the recent re-emergence of reflexive performance in majority avant-garde practice.

10

Black High-Tech Documents

ERIKA MUHAMMAD

Technology is changing at a more rapid pace than our society has ever experienced. Digital tools enable artists to produce work that is more conducive to collaborative art processes. Consequently, artists encounter new challenges and opportunities as they work to build and define what are proposed to be the most sophisticated and powerful communication networks our culture has encountered. Issues of media access and empowerment are integral to the work of African American artists as they examine how digital and electronic culture influences the production of knowledge as it relates to theories of race and nation. In effect, their work explores the nature of identity formation as our understanding of communal exchange evolves. Though techno-muse Lynn Hershman Leeson asserts that "communities once delineated by physical space and geographic territories are now located by connectivity, access, and linkage,"[1] our increasingly electronic culture has led at the same time to more solitary activity. This chapter will offer examples of work by African American artists who build digital habitats and lay political foundations in spirit and space, employing new media tools in creative and progressive ways.

Artists Pamela Jennings, Philip Mallory Jones, and Reginald Woolery use computers and other digital and electronic technologies to create "High-Tech Documents."[2] I treat "High-Tech Documents" as a deliberately resilient designation that reflects the continual change of technology. As artists have always employed "new media" to comment on the character of society, their dexterity with the new forms has encouraged and inspired ideas and propositions about the nature of cultural production. This inherently reciprocal exchange creates dialogue and work that constitute a sense of the contemporary. The artists discussed herein not only use digital media to comment on digital culture, but they also employ digital tools to comment on the chronicling of history and to anticipate future realities. When we discuss the effect of new media technologies on the production of black documentary texts, the direct reference is to a larger discussion of document standards. Our memory of and familiarity with old technologies allow us to navigate this new terrain. Consequently, critics with the technological know-how and theoretical savvy pose provocative questions about the effects of new media on the dynamics of cultural hegemony. Overall, this chapter will explore the application of new media technologies that, in essence, document the history and social culture of diaspora life.

Screen shot from "the book of melancholy," part of the
CD-ROM *Solitaire: dream journal* by Pamela Jennings.

PAMELA JENNINGS

Pamela Jennings is an electronic media artist whose work explores narrative structures for new media. In her essay "Narrative Structure for New Media: Towards a New Definition,"[3] Jennings suggests that the narrative structures of non-Western cultures offer languages compatible with the sophistication of new Western technologies. Specifically, she articulates the idea that the theories and processes of African oral literature provide a suitable foundation for such a narrative model. "With the advent of computer-based interactive art and information systems, many issues arise concerning the use of alternative engines through which narrative information may be created,"[4] she says. "Our culture is presently experiencing a shift in the organization of knowledge away from the linear motif."[5] Jennings's work challenges both the notion of the traditional book in this century and the notion of narrative theory. She asserts that nuance, indeterminacy, and polyventiality are major players in her work.

Jennings's CD-ROM project *Solitaire: dream journal* (1996) mixes the metaphor of the game board and the book. *Solitaire* takes the user through what its designer describes as "a haunting journey in quest of peace with oneself and connection with others."[6] A three-dimensional solitaire game is the engine that moves the player through the journal.

The solitaire board is designed as a tetrahedron (a three-faced pyramid), whose triangular sides correspond to the themes of melancholy, flight, and balance. A move made on one side of the tetrahedron randomly opens up a chapter of the three corresponding "books": "the book of melancholy," "the book of flight," or "the book of balance." The idea is to see how many pages you can access. The better your strategy, the more chapters you will be able to enter and explore. These chapters (windows) make it possible for *Solitaire* to place you in several contexts at the same time. In the game, your identity is the sum of your distributed presence. *Solitaire* is a document of self-discovery—the documentation of Jennings's narrative with a player's credits creates an aesthetic of recovery that unfolds dense layers of heterogeneous material culled from personal and popular memory. Mathematical and statistical "facts" are presented not objectively or subjectively, but rather conceptually, so that the player becomes involved in a thick discursive text.

A compelling idea that arises in Jennings's piece is the idea of magic, which can be understood as a space of possibility. An exercise more than a game, *Solitaire* awards the user not with points, but with beautiful, visceral images akin to the soothing elements of yoga or meditation. It's an exercise in patience—a sleight of hand at the mouse invokes a mystical charm that is enchanting. The feeling of "What happens next?" that is reminiscent of a good mystery novel is at the core of Jennings's piece. The player participates in the construction of the narrative as he or she surrenders to the collaborative task of delivering the story. *Solitaire* is a prime example of the success of the elliptical nature of digital documentation: it is a demonstration of both the nature of CD-ROM interactivity and the nature of the person who plays the game.

Like Philip Mallory Jones, who will be discussed later in this chapter, Jennings is also heavily influenced by the tropes of art cinema. With a background in experimental video and installation, her move into new media is simply another vehicle through which she can articulate her cultural obsessions. Attention to audio resonances in visual images is her main interest. "Music is universal," she says. "I like to think of my work as opuses to make an analogy with the structure of classical music."[7] *Solitaire* is a composite of graphic synching, animation, music, and the principles of checkers. "I lay a lot of my personal stuff out in my development process, and I like the idea of transferring this 'personal quest' to the user,"[8] explains Jennings. Her work is "open" in the sense that she allows players to explore her psyche, and consequently the game is very difficult. She confesses, "If I'm inviting you to come and view what's going on inside my head, you will have to work for it."[9]

Image from Pamela Jennings's CD–ROM *Solitaire: dream journal*.
Screen shots from "the book of flight," part of the CD-ROM
Solitaire: dream journal by Pamela Jennings.

Sound is a crucial element in *Solitaire: dream journal*. To create nuanced layers of tone, Jennings used combinations of her voice, sampled sounds, and algorithmically controlled serial interludes. Jennings's influences come more from performance and dance critical theory or computer games"that gouge your eyes out and defeat your imagery stuff. I think the intensity of many of the action computer games is detrimental, not only to words, but it creates a more violent being and awkward social environments." Accordingly, *Solitaire* relies much more on concepts of music and sound as a binding force—there is a continuous line of sound that runs throughout the piece.

Solitaire led to Jennings's next computer-book project, *the book of ruins and desire* (1996), in which she created a kinetic, interactive, mixed-media sculpture that explores issues of desire and communication. The reader stands before a table on which rests a sculptural object with hinged metal leaves (pages). From inside the surface of the case, a voice whispers "Touch me." The sound piques the reader's interest, aurally conveying permission to interact with the book. As you turn the book's metal pages, you begin an exploration into its multiple layers, composing your own collage of Jennings's imagery and text. Jennings admits that *the book of ruins and desire* was a product of her consideration of the word "book." A lot of the research that she was doing on the concept of the artist's book was quite fascinating to her. With an artist's book, the reader can actually handle—finger, stroke, rub, and manipulate—the story or narrative that is contained within the binding. In this way Jennings's book is about the body and offers an example of how we can make our digital experiences corporeal.

"For the past ten years, artists have been pondering how to do an electronic book—they were being very literal, but were not succeeding with the physical execution of the idea,"[10] explains Jennings. She was hugely influenced by Peter Greenaway's film *Prospero's Books*, which is his version of *The Tempest*. Greenaway created very elaborate prototypes (animations) of the books that Prospero took along with him on his voyages. For example, "The Book of Motion" stood on a podium that wouldn't stop shaking. "When I saw Greenaway's rendition of an electronic book, I decided that I really wanted to make [construct] that type of concept," she adds excitedly. "But not with movie magic."[11]

The degree of a turned page and its velocity are calculated in a fuzzy logic inference engine programmed into a microprocessor. The fuzzy logic component of *the book of ruins and desire* creates the numerous experiences (or stories) a person can read. In traditional logic, there are zeros and ones—on and off—true and false. Fuzzy logic looks at and considers the gray points between zero and one. If you want to look at it objectively, it offers more possibilities because it processes information not in terms of on and off, but in terms of the *degree* of on and off; and on that basis, it will provide a unique experience.

This information (the result of the degree at which the reader turns a page) is fed to a Macintosh computer running the MIDI programming language Opcode MAX. MIDI (Musical Instrument Digital Interface) is the standard communications protocol between musical instruments and computers.[12] Programmed as a video and audio switching device, MAX determines which images and sounds are played back (which the reader sees and hears via a small LCD monitor and embedded speakers). MAX also regulates the qualitative dynamics of the media such as volume, video direction, and playback speed. In addition, MAX is programmed to create MIDI interludes (background music when the book isn't being read) via freeware serial music libraries. As a sculptural artist and digital musician, Jennings is akin to the underground MIDI musicians who hold jam sessions on-line; they lay down MIDI tracks providing a framework for various types of music to be made. In the same vein, Jennings's installation piece allows players to "make music" (or "perform data") improvisationally.

Jennings says that the metaphors of "ruin" and "desire" relate to her psychological state of mind at the time she designed the pieces. "For instance, with ruins, I find actual architectural ruins quite beautiful, and I like to stand in the middle of them and imagine the energy that once inhabited those environments. It's like I can look at the structures and imagine the desire that was there before."[13]

Jennings creates some of the more progressive works in the canon of new interactive art by artists of color. Her use of iteration, serialism, open structures, fuzzy logic, language, desire, and interactive media proves to be a potent combination.

The development of new tools—or a rethinking of how we use the tools we already have—will be crucial to the development of interactive designs that push the horizon of storytelling and image-making in new media. As Jennings maintains, "It is a waste of energy and resources to make applications that merely imitate media that exist in other forms, such as print, television, and film. The early television industry, for example, quickly learned that radio plays don't work on TV."[14] But just as photography prepared the ground for the moving image, today's digital tools are the forebears of a new age of interactive communications.

Pamela Jennings is a graduate of The School of Visual Arts, NYC and works in Silicon Valley. She is interested in defining narrative media and the mapping of ethnography in digital space. Jennings is currently a MPhil/Ph.D. candidate at The Center for Advanced Inquiry in Interactive Arts (CAiiA) at The University of Wales.

PHILIP MALLORY JONES

Having worked in video as an art medium since 1969 and incorporated digital tools since 1990, Philip Mallory Jones is one of the most prolific and transnational black video artists working today. In the late 1960s he was drawn to video because of an attraction to machines and gadgets, as well as the appeal of working in what he describes as a "videomatic" medium he could help define. Jones was profoundly affected by Jean Cocteau's film *Beauty and the Beast,* which is reflected in his use of surreal and abstract imagery in such works as the interactive CD-ROM *First World Order* (1994), *Paradigm Shift* (1992), *Mask* (1991) and *Dreamkeeper* (1989). These films exhibit the dense yet comprehensible complexity that is his trademark.

Image from Philip Mallory Jones's CD-ROM
First World Order.
Image by Philip Mallory Jones, 1994.

Jones's body of work explores "the development of codes, based on emotional progressions and an African sensorium, without dependence on specific language comprehension."[15] Using video and digital interactive media, he experiments with the development and composition of a technological language derived from ancient and surviving African symbolic conventions and codes. *First World Order Project Development* (1997) is a CD-ROM and Web site that explores the cultures of the African diaspora and communicates their common, often encoded knowledge in a way that traverses cultural barriers. The project illuminates a complex global diaspora, originating in Africa but transcending race and ethnicity, which is defined in terms of modes of expression, paradigms of perception, and systems of symbolic communication. "Integral to my work is the notion that communication happens vertically and horizontally. Horizontal communication represents linear, spoken language that we normally use; vertical communication is related to instinct and intuition—a way to knowledge and understanding that I feel is more powerful than intellect."[16]

As local and national identities diversify and villages grow smaller as a result of the advances of new media technologies, Jones's work creates a new kind of language that redefines the diasporic cultural landscape. Like Reggie Woolery's work, which will be discussed shortly, Jones's work probes the reconfiguration of social and political identity formations. Both artists' work raises questions about the types of cultural borders that are crossed and the production of knowledge created at the intersection of the digital and the real. As a scholar of iconography, Jones is sensitive to the underlying non-verbal connections between societies scattered across many continents and separated by diverse histories and languages: "As a digital media practitioner and instructor, I am ideally equipped to create a means of cultural communication that transcends these differences. My works address the problem of appreciating and understanding world cultures by rewriting world history."[17]

"Digital technology," he notes, "is capable of expressions which are outside of the conventions of Euro-American media."[18] Jones finds that multimedia allows him to "create pieces which incorporate the ancient and surviving codes to tell stories, without verbal language dependence, which are interpretable in various African cultures."[19] As Jones manipulates video, sound recordings, and computer technologies, he realizes that the uncovering of cultural identity is not an essentialist practice. Rather, he states, "It is a way to communicate the stories of the past and imagine the narratives of the future."[20]

"The perception, or assumption, that 'narrative' and 'documentary' are somehow more relevant is part of larger issues affecting artists of color," says Jones.

> We are generally expected to speak about people of color in terms of sociopolitical issues or problems. This limits the scope of our discourse. Representation of African and diaspora peoples and cultures is not necessarily the *raison d'être* of a work by an artist of color. Portrait artists working in paint

and photography, for example, will sometimes use these subjects as a vehicle for exploring the characteristics of the medium. Hopefully, an artist's work expresses truth, which need not be the same as objective reality. People of color and our culture are well served by the mature and well-crafted work of media artists producing in the full spectrum of genres.[21]

His work shows that all aspects of life and experiences of people of color are relevant subjects for expressive considerations; so too is the full spectrum of approaches valid. People of color are vastly varied, and not everyone's story can be told the same way.

Jones's 1992 video *Paradigm Shift*, a prime example of the artist's pioneering work, employed the latest in digital video technology—morphing, layering, rotoscoping, composition—to form a sequence that is complex, subtle, dense, and non-linear. Special effects allow Jones to neutralize "documentary truth" by emphasizing the inconstancy of the "real." Because Jones uses representational imagery in an approach that is not narrative, his work often gets lumped into a "documentary bag" by critics. But conventional documentary is not what Jones practices, for he feels that no media can offer an objective reality. What Jones feels he can process is a greater understanding of how digital media works, and he thereby has also come to an understanding of his own self. Jones refers to his works as essays, poems, or portraits, for he wants the audience to come to their own truth.

Paradigm Shift was broadcast internationally on venues such as MTV and Canal+ in France. Because his audience was international and multilingual, Jones used the opportunity to create a computer-modified video that would communicate complex global cultural connections and ideas non-verbally. He wanted the piece, which lasts only a minute, to have the same level of impact as an effective television commercial. In a 1995 interview, Jones admitted that his challenge with this video was to "grab [the audience's attention], so that the piece will mean something to somebody, even though they won't have any idea of what it is while it's happening—it's going to happen and then it's going to be over." Communicating subliminal visual information, Jones saw, was a definite capability of video that could be further enhanced with artistic computer animation.[22] Through the use of morphing, Jones performs what Ella Shohat and Robert Stam refer to in *Unthinking Eurocentrism* as anthropophagy. That is, he "assumes the inevitability of cultural interchange between 'center' and 'periphery,' and the consequent impossibility of any nostalgic return to an ordinary purity. Since there can be no unproblematic recovery of national origins undefiled by alien influences, artists in the dominated culture should not ignore the foreign presence but must swallow it, carnivalize it, recycle it, for national ends, always from a position of self-confidence."[23]

The sequences in *Paradigm Shift* are not just an idle jumbling of imagery. Every pictorial selection is entirely intentional—and the intention is that by composite, morph, juxtaposition, association, and sequence, a relationship between the images can be uncovered, discovered, and recognized. For example, in the video we see iconography symbolic of a mother and child from several different cultures and historical periods "morph" into each other. Morphing allows a transmutation (surface manipulation) of the mother and child figure, as the software provides a cross-dissolve allowing the key features—nose, eyes, and ears—to stay in place as the transformation takes place. In conceptualizing the video, Jones used a theoretical model based on the hieroglyphic system, in that he rationalized the images as symbols. He points out that the hieroglyphic system is the oldest symbolic system in the world, and that it was never a spoken language. It was an entirely visual language, in which meaning was evoked from the way the icons were organized. "The ancient icons of Russia are another symbolic language," argues Jones. "They are in fact a transmutation of the hieroglyphic system—that is, you don't have to explain the images to know what they are."[24]

If the spectator can identify one of the symbols in *Paradigm Shift* through the benefits of morphing, he or she will eventually know the whole. In essence, the audience will recognize one image and see that it is analogous, or that it relates something about the other images. Jones insists, "If you know one, you know all of them. It's right there. They look the same, it's the same postures—an organized posture. But it's also more than that—it's about how people express and see. They are all talking about a principle as well. So someone may not have encountered images from the Nile Valley or natives cultures in this hemisphere, but they have seen an African icon of a woman and her child. What I want to evoke is a community of ideas that can open up other doors of recognition, embracement, understanding—if that can happen on some level, then the exercise has been successful."[25]

Writers Robin King and John Lansdown have looked at how computer technology can be categorized within the visual arts and design and their studies provide a useful model through which we can further understand Jones's video work.[26] King provides a model that suggests four stages of application: *mimetic, derivative, innovative,* and *emergent. Paradigm Shift* is mimetic because the images Jones uses are replications of images produced in other media—in the case of *Paradigm Shift,* photography. The derivative stage is recognizable in Jones's work as he is trying to establish his own stylistic conceptions of the computer-generated work. For example, although Jones works within a hybridized genre that necessarily preserves its discontinuities and multivocalities,

Paradigm Shift reveals that history and memory are not contingently constructed, that they are produced through a concrete system of codes with an absolute foundation. *Paradigm Shift* is emergent in that the video is characterized by the unique properties of the morphing software, embodying simulation and intelligence. The fluid nature of the video reveals an ideology that suggests a need for united political action without asserting a belief in a transcendent aesthetic. Instead, Jones offers us a selected modification that realizes that the construction of history and memory is malleable and particular. Artists such as Jones are involved in the "repudiation of both naively 'democratic' and cynically eclectic strains of postmodern pluralism, [while] at the same time they retain a postmodern suspicion of modernist master narratives and claims to aesthetic transcendence."[27]

Jones uses the computer as a tool to continue what he has already been doing but enhances the efficiency, reliability, speed, and accuracy of his work. He asserts that he works with what is available to him in terms of tools, materials, and skills, as his quest is to manifest his vision. As an artist, he asks certain kinds of questions that he endeavors to answer through media—whether writing novels, making sculpture in plexiglas, creating 16mm animated films, or working in the darkroom or in the digital realm. Making media for Jones is about exploring the nature of the medium and bringing something new into the world. From the beginning of his work in media in 1969, he was attracted by the possibility of "invention" afforded by a medium (video) that, for the first time, allowed a synthesis of many artistic forms. There were very few rules, and those who worked in the field defined the medium through their work. Consequently, because of the constant and rapid changes in technology, this frontier still exists.

A consultant to various art museums, foundations and universities, Philip Mallory Jones serves as a Senior Lecturer in the College of Fine Arts at Arizona State University.

REGINALD WOOLERY

Reginald Woolery's *Keep Your Handsa Off the Park: A Role-Playing Game in Real and Virtual Worlds* (1997) is tri-elemental in nature and can be played as a board game and/or on the Internet. In the game, the mayor of New York City has decided to privatize the maintenance of Tompkins Square Park. Three groups express interest in the job, and game players decide if they want to be members of big business, small business, or the community (local residents and the homeless). There are also two variables involved, government and the press, who act as information facilitators and sources. For four weeks, using a game board, the Internet, and physical spaces in the local community, the members of each group role-play and strategize to come up with an ultimate narrative of why their team should control the park. At the end of the four weeks, each group presents a proposal before an impartial tribunal at a public hearing—sort of a "High-Tech" town meeting. The challenge for the players is to pose the best case to a planning board so that their team can gain control of the park.

The game brings community land issues down to a level where individuals, business leaders, and politicians can learn from one another. It offers an opportunity to reinfuse our democratic public sphere with unbiased participation, suggesting an end to both corporate special interests and community apathy. The game is framed within the circumnavigation of urban spaces, which in this instance is Tompkins Square Park—the largest public square in Manhattan, which is now infamous as a result of the Tompkins Square Police Riot in 1988. Located on the Lower East Side of Manhattan, it is the neighborhood where immigrants have settled in tenements for 150 years. The poverty and decay notwithstanding, for decades it quartered an extraordinary conglomeration of ethnic groups, including Slavs, Poles, Ukrainians, Chinese, Puerto Ricans, Jews, and several generations of bohemians. These were all communities within themselves that lived side by side but did not mix. In the 1940s, when small industry moved out and veterans of the war left, thousands of Puerto Rican immigrants arrived. However, with no major industry or business to employ its people, the neighborhood began to deteriorate. In the late 1960s, groups such as the Black Panthers and Young Lords roamed the area, and in the 1970s, hundreds of neighborhood buildings were abandoned, an example of how the lack of social mobility leads to geographic immobility. In the late 1980s, wealthy harbingers of change came together to gentrify the neighborhood. With no rent control standards, ethnic restaurants and small businesses were forced out, and the homeless took to the park, sharing its space with the neighborhood folk who refused to go.

There are many different people with various needs who congregate in Tompkins Square Park: homeless, multicultural ethnic groups, skinheads. Middle-class families live in overpriced homes overlooking the park, and students and working-class professionals rent apartments from landlords who would love the chance to evict them and triple the rent. In the summer of 1988, New York mayor Ed Koch imposed a curfew on the park, forcing the homeless out and into the streets nightly at the stroke of twelve. The ensuing tension erupted on August 6 after a riot squad evicted dozens of homeless in a brutal battle. On May 31,

1991, another violent outbreak occurred when Mayor David Dinkins sent police troops in full riot gear to roust the homeless from the park and barricade its entrances during a concert. In the aftermath, various community groups representing different constituencies have been battling among themselves for control of the park.

Interested in issues of urban economics and democracy playing out on the World Wide Web, Woolery was attempting to merge his interests in access, urban renewal policy, and digital multimedia spaces to create an exercise about democracy. The long history of Tompkins Square Park, as a social and political space in transformation through internal and external pressure (i.e., privatization of community gardens), provided the perfect context for his needs. In 1992, Woolery saw a documentary on public television that profoundly inspired him, entitled *The Betrayal of Democracy*. Produced and narrated by journalist William Grieder, the film traveled through the heartland of America while its host interviewed citizens about the deep sense of betrayal they felt toward elected officials and the political process. Mindful that Grieder did not resort to stereotypical analysis of this country's woes (by pinning them on the underclass and minorities) but rather suggested that the distance between elected officials and the population was a result of the increased relocation of governmental offices outside communities (and the delegation of critical oversight on issues to the media), Woolery saw the opportunity to play with the idea of electoral and visual representation through a role-playing game.

Keep Your Handsa Off the Park came together conceptually while Woolery was a student in a race and urban renewal policy class taught by Stephen Gregory, assistant professor of Africana studies at New York University. There, at Woolery's urging, Gregory decided to transform the last weeks of his course into a role-playing performance with Tompkins Square Park as the focus. "In a game design course, I focused on strategies that made people engage with computers beyond just browsing the Web. I learned how to create digital/real environments [which] people want to go to and have an investment in. My utopian aim is to translate this investment into 'real world' activism."[28]

By allocating bonus points for application of the game's strategies to real-world spaces, Woolery allowed players an opportunity to realize that their efforts in cyberspace could translate into cultural and political change in the "real" world. In American society, public space and citizens' participation in politics continue to decline dramatically because the industries that employ (and consequently lay off) citizens represent the labor-displacing technologies of the post-industrial era that have led to the annihilation of reform-based social contracts. *Handsa* is informed by an understanding and a rendering visible of how political knowledge is secluded within institutional structures that both privilege and exclude particular bodies, voices, aesthetics, and forms of authority. Woolery problematizes this practice and history of social alienation in New York and visually develops a participatory ethical and political discourse.

Woolery describes *Keep Your Handsa Off the Park* as a mixture of *Sym City* and *Dungeons and Dragons*. Yet the latter reflects an interesting dynamic of the African American community. "We are not a homogeneous group," says Woolery.

> And in regards to imaginary worlds, there are cultural things we consider before we get involved. In designing this game, I realized that it's easier for folks to play role games than to play a fantasy-driven game like *Dungeons and Dragons*. However, we are used to the shedding of identity in our culture. For example, children tag a person 'it' and you can shed this identity. The whole medieval stance of *Dungeons and Dragons* invalidates something cultural about us. To be candid, folks of color don't necessarily play around with the devil. But I like to use the example of gangsta rap and the use of techno-turntables as a form of role-playing similar to that in cyberspace. The reason I think gangsta rap was an important form is because people responded to it cross-geographically. Furthermore, performance on the net is really an exercise in signifying and personas.[29]

Owing to the political realities of "haves" and "have-nots" (of phone lines, on-line services, and computers), Woolery is quick to admit that the creation of "Black High-Tech Documents" will be successful if artists and producers continue to find innovative ways for cyberspace and virtual reality to extend into real life. *Handsa* is based on the assumption that participants care about the outcome of the game. "We need some sort of consumer appeal that will allow all players involved to accept the outcome of the game," he says. "It has to be something that they want to participate in, so they'll be willing to take the time. The same thing that attracts people to play lotto every week—having a stake."[30]

A precursor of these new developments in digital media is black video. Initially it was critiqued as a body of work that seemed doubly marginalized—not only was it black, but it had been forced to build its audience in ever more diverse venues with little institutional support. In this era of decreasing congressional support for the NEA and a continually diminishing pool of arts and media funding, many critics, riding the hype of new media, have ironically abandoned the study of video because they perceive it as a dying art form. However, it is important to define video and cinema's interface with digital/interactive

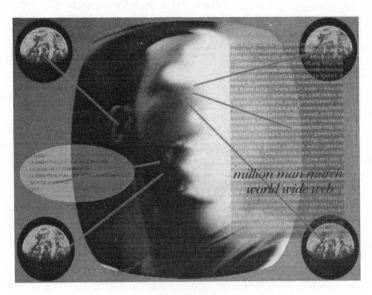

Screen grab from Reggie Woolery's CD-ROM
World Wide Web/Million Man March.
Reggie Woolery, producer/designer.

media as worthy of continued practice and critical consumption. For example, Woolery makes a definite connection between his work and activist video, with many of the formulations of *Keep Your Hands a Off the Park* being contextualized in activist media, whose topics concentrate specifically on the social, political, and cultural issues facing communities of color in America.

Woolery's CD-ROM *World Wide Web/Million Man March* (*WWW/ MMM*) (1997) juxtaposes two identity/community formations: (1) the backlash against black male masculinity centered around the 1995 Million Man March in Washington, D.C., and the first O.J. Simpson verdict, and (2) the vocal opposition to the Internet due to issues of pornography. Woolery witnessed a sense of paranoia and utopia around these two identity formations and wanted to place them in tandem. Having come back from the March and realizing that the popular media had defined the critical space within which he could talk about his experience, Woolery attempted to speak to that experience through the voices of others, refusing to present a closure or solitary definition. "I don't describe this work as a CD-ROM because a CD-ROM is basically a storage device. This is a non-linear piece which allows me to work out a number of ideas. All my work has probed the possibility or the impossibility of identity, in particular constructions of whiteness and blackness, femininity and masculinity." Woolery said that the topic of *WWW*

IMMM provided an opportunity for him to examine questions of spectatorship and what an audience brings to a work.

Reginald Woolery, a writer and digital artist, is a 1998–99 fellow at the Society of the Humanities at Cornell University in Ithaca, New York, exploring the theme of the virtual, old and new.

* * *

Discussing the works of Pamela Jennings, Philip Mallory Jones, and Reginald Woolery sheds an interesting light on the policy implications of current demographic patterns of Internet access and usage. The aforementioned artists are highly privileged individuals because of their access to the tools and resources of the institutions that they are affiliated with. In *Bridging the Digital Divide: The Impact of Race on Computer Access and Internet Use,* Vanderbilt University professors Thomas P. Novak and Donna L. Hoffman affirm that "the Internet is expected to do no less than virtually transform society, [and] key demographics variables like income and education drive the questions surrounding the Internet."[31] Artists working in the digital realm like Jennings, Jones, and Woolery "cross" the "digital divide," and their work reflects the information of a growing number of "haves" usually viewed as "have-nots." In their 1997 study, Novak and Hoffman found that "Over 5 million African-Americans have ever used the Web in the United States as of January 1997"[32]—a number, they point out, that is considerably larger than the current popular estimate of 1 million (at this writing) frequently reported in the press. "While income certainly matters, education is what counts." They state that increasing levels of education positively influence both computer access and Web use. "Access translates into usage. . . . Access to a computer at home, work, or school is currently the dominant mechanism by which individuals gain access to the internet."[33] Consequently, they concede, the policy implication is obvious: to ensure the participation of all Americans in the communication revolution, it is critical to improve the educational opportunities of African Americans.

NOTES

1. Lynn Hershman Leeson, ed., *Clicking In: Hot Links to a Digital Culture* (Seattle: Bay Press, 1996), vii.
2. The term I use to define Jennings's, Jones's, and Woolery's work, "High-Tech," has what Woolery refers to as "boy toy" connotations, which is

indeed a legitimate critique. The female and black perspectives are increasingly marginalized in these discussions.

3. Pamela Jennings, "Narrative Structures for New Media: Towards a New Definition," *LEONARDO* 29, no. 5: 345–350.

4. Interview with Pamela Jennings, conducted by Erika Muhammad, September 5, 1997.

5. Ibid.

6. Jennings, "Narrative Structures for New Media," 345.

7. Interview with Jennings.

8. Ibid.

9. Ibid.

10. Ibid.

11. Ibid.

12. In "Narrative Structures for New Media," Jennings provides a definition of MIDI adapted from Christopher Yavelow's *Macworld Music and Sound Bible* (San Mateo, Calif.: IDG Books Worldwide, 1992), 34. Developed in 1982, MIDI is an international specification used by musical instruments that contain microprocessors to communicate with other microprocessor-controlled instruments or devices. MIDI communicates *performance data*, not actual sound.

13. Interview with Jennings.

14. Ibid.

15. Interview with Philip Mallory Jones, conducted by Erika Muhammad, April 15, 1997.

16. Ibid.

17. Ibid.

18. Ibid.

19. Ibid.

20. Ibid.

21. Ibid.

22. "State of the Arts: Artist Uses Technology to Tackle the World," *College of Fine Arts Newsletter*, Arizona State University, 1994–95, 2–3.

23. As articulated by Ella Shohat and Robert Stam in *Unthinking Eurocentrism: Multiculturalism and the Media* (New York: Routledge, 1994), 307.

24. Interview with Jones, conducted by Muhammad.

25. Ibid.

26. As cited by Robin Baker in "Computer Technology and Special Effects in Contemporary Cinema," in *Future Visions: New Technologies of the Screen*, ed. Philip Hayward and Tana Wollen (London: British Film Institute, 1994), 32.

27. As articulated by Judith Wilson in her discussion of contemporary visual artists and global histories in "New (Art) Histories: Global Shifts, Uneasy Exchanges," from the exhibition catalogue for *New Histories* (Boston: The Institute of Contemporary Art, 1995), 15.

28. Interview with Reginald Woolery, conducted by Erika Muhammad, May 15, 1997.

29. Ibid.

30. Ibid.

31. Thomas P. Novak and Donna L. Hoffman, "Bridging the Digital Divide: The Impact of Race on Computer Access and Internet Use," can be found on the Web at <http://www2000.ogsm.vanderbilt.edu/>. Novak and Hoffman co-direct Project 2000 at Vanderbilt University.

32. Ibid.

33. Ibid.

11

The "I" Narrator in Black Diaspora Documentary

MANTHIA DIAWARA

It is customary to define *diaspora* as the voluntary or involuntary dispersion of a social or ethnic group. Diaspora studies therefore look for the stability or discontinuity of the identity of individuals or groups from their origins to their present location. In thinking about the black diaspora and its representation, some of the issues of retention of African cultures or rupture with origins and traditions commonly come into play. However, identity politics notwithstanding, the quest for modernity for the group and the individual in the diaspora also constitutes the main motivation of the people who insisted upon the concept. Diaspora subjects such as W. E. B. Du Bois, Aimé Césaire, Langston Hughes, Patrice Lumumba, and Kwame Nkrumah were interested in removing obstacles from their people's path toward modernization, in opening access to the tools of Enlightenment, and in valorizing their people's contribution to universal civilization.

The representation of these figures on film by Louis Massiah, Raoul Peck, and John Akomfrah has resulted in different subjective strategies in the documentary genre. One can even say that these filmmakers have reshaped the documentary genre in their attempt to reconcile identity politics with the universal message of modernity in their films. To film the African diaspora is to represent that which is African about the subjects in the first place; on the other hand, it is also about the depiction of what is modern and liberating about the diaspora subjects.

The intersection between the two poles of diaspora thematics, identity politics and modernist liberating aesthetics, has resulted in first-person documentary narratives by Raoul Peck, John Akomfrah, and Louis Massiah. The first-person point of view enables these directors to build and validate their own identity through the identities of the diasporic subjects of their films. Another measure of the merit of first-person narratives lies in their ability to demonstrate, through such poetic devices as irony, realism, or allegory, the significance of the life of the diasporic subject to present conditions. It is therefore possible to define the first-person narrative in diasporic cinema as the filmmaker's revisionist construction of history in which the narrator is as central to the film as the film's object, or what I call the diasporic subject. In fact, there is a blurring between the identities of the filmmakers and/or narrators and the diasporic subjects which transcends the different poetic languages of the films to constitute a thematic cluster in diasporic documentary.

THE ALLEGORICAL MODE: RAOUL PECK'S *LUMUMBA*

In Raoul Peck's *Lumumba: The Death of a Prophet,* an allegorical film about the myth of Lumumba, the director-turned-first-person-narrator poses as the ghost of Lumumba to haunt the streets of Brussels and its high society. The allegorical narrative is imposed on the documentary genre from the beginning, when we learn that the director cannot go to Zaire (present-day Democratic Republic of Congo) to make his film. To produce the documentary, he had therefore to rely on home-movie

Patrice Lumumba at Ndjili Airport in Leopoldville,
December 2, 1960, the day after his arrest.
AP/WIDE WORLD.

footage, archival material in Europe, interviews with journalists, Belgian colonial officials, and family and former collaborators of Lumumba. It is allegory that provides this film with its magic, inasmuch as it constitutes the power in the voice-over poetry that makes the viewer believe that Brussels is Kinshasa (formerly Leopoldville and the capital of Congo).

Lumumba: The Death of a Prophet is a challenging documentary not only because the director was unable to go to Zaire and film the "real" places Lumumba inhabited and the people he died for. The challenge also comes from the voice-over, which is poetic and mythical instead of objective and balanced in the tradition of the classical documentary. In fact, Peck's Lumumba can be seen as an indictment of the objective documentary style in the way it debunks so-called "facts" about Lumumba's character. This is most effectively executed in the film through Peck's juxtaposition of Lumumba to Mobutu (the former dictator of Zaire) and the past to the present. Peck uses newsreel footage and newspapers to show how Lumumba was depicted as a communist, a devil, and a harbinger of violence. Mobutu, on the other hand, was called a hero who saved the nation and promoted peace. The Belgians, meanwhile, are portrayed as saints whose only task was to educate the Congolese and prepare them for independence. We soon learn that these images are no more objective than the action-packed films that we see on the television screen in the director's hotel room. From a new perspective imposed by the end of the Cold War, we now see Lumumba as the hero and Mobutu as a traitor to the Pan-African revolution and as an evil dictator-president. As for the Belgians, they liked their Africans as long as "they remained stupid." At the time of the independence of the Congo in 1960, "there was one bishop for the country and no one with a bachelor's degree." So much for the objective documentary.

In Peck's Lumumba, images mean nothing without the words that define them. To paraphrase Jean-Luc Godard, a good documentary for Peck does not depend on just the right image, but on the mot juste, a poetic language with the power to invent meaning for the images. In fact, it is a measure of Peck's genius in this subjective documentary to have succeeded without the "real" images of the Congo, to have created a documentary account of the life and myth of Lumumba out of what Peck himself calls "ces trous noirs"—these black holes—which are "images in our heads. Forbidden and harmless images." Mobutu is afraid of these forbidden images: could it be, the narrator asks himself, that these "black holes are more corrosive than the images that they hide?"

The documentary pleasure—by which I mean the desire to know who Lumumba is—is inextricably linked to our desire to know what the black holes in the narrator's head are hiding. We want to know who Raoul Peck is, what his class position is, and why he is making this documentary on Lumumba. We learn at the beginning of the film that Peck's parents are expatriates from Haiti who came to the Congo at the time of independence to replace Belgian colonial technocrats where there were few university-trained Africans. His mother worked as a secretary in different transitional governments, from revolutionary leaders to *coup d'état* organizers to dictators. We see Peck's class position from the home movies of his childhood. He grew up privileged in a country where the majority was exploited and kept illiterate and where Lumumba was killed for trying to bring a revolution. Peck himself explains his position in the home movies as ambivalent: "We were *Mundele*—white people—when it was convenient, and Africans when it was convenient."

Making a film on Lumumba is therefore a process of self-examination for Peck. Even though we learn about Mobutu's betrayal of Lumumba and Belgian racism toward the people of Congo, what concerns us most in the film is how Peck feels about Lumumba. We identify with Peck's guilt for growing up privileged in Congo at a time when it would have been better to have been a revolutionary like Lumumba. We empathize with him for wishing that his parents had left Congo before the betrayals and the coups. Why did they stay in Congo for so long? So that they could be among the first black bourgeois to take vacations in Europe? And why didn't Lumumba leave before he was assassinated?

The film takes on additional importance when the viewer realizes that Peck holds him or her responsible as well for Lumumba's death. He compares the massacre in Congo to other crimes against humanity such as the Holocaust and the A-bomb dropped on Hiroshima, in order to reveal to us that our neutral position vis-à-vis these horrendous crimes is a form of guilt. To drive this point home, the narrator takes his camera to a black-tie party in Brussels. As he passes by people drinking cocktails, the voice-over states that the ghost of Lumumba was everywhere in the room, and that the destinies of the people at the party are forever linked to his.

It is remarkable that *Lumumba: The Death of a Prophet* begins in a street in Brussels called *"Place des martyrs."* Peck is searching for Lumumba in a place dedicated to the martyrs of the two great wars. This scene is soon followed by archival footage of a jungle; the voice-over reads a poem by Henri Lopes entitled *"Du Côté du Katanga,"* which goes as follows: "Near Katanga, they said that a giant had fallen during the night." The same poem is recited toward the end of the film over images of deserted Brussels streets. As Peck interchanges images of Africa and

Europe while reading the same poem, one gets the sense that the myth of Lumumba is everywhere—everywhere there is oppression. One understands finally that Peck did not need to go to Zaire to make his film on Lumumba.

By linking his destiny and ours to Lumumba's quest for freedom, Peck creates an original space for black diasporic expression through the documentary genre. His allegorical style is well-suited to describing the dispersion and transfiguration of African identity and motifs in the modern world. The presence of both Peck and Lumumba as diasporic subjects in the film, or the blurring of the identities of the filmmaker and the object of the film, underlines the important role of identification in the documentary genre. This subjective relation between subject–object, Peck–Lumumba, which is taken for granted in diaspora studies, is often ignored in the classical documentary in favor of objectivity, "realness," and impartiality. In diaspora studies, identification with the hero is therapeutic and a function of the cultural worker or researcher coming into consciousness from a liminal space or a space of indeterminacy. That is why Peck rejects objectivity earlier in the film and borrows from the techniques of experimental filmmakers. One can read *Lumumba: The Death of a Prophet* sometimes as a video-diary, sometimes as a surrealist film in which the images and the sound enter into conflict, and sometimes as a historical documentary.

THE IRONIC MODE: JOHN AKOMFRAH'S *TESTAMENT*

I would like to turn now to *Testament* by John Akomfrah (Black Audio Film Collective) to address another style in first-person narratives in black diasporic cinema. Narratologically speaking, *Testament* is more complex than *Lumumba*. The voice-over commentator is a woman who also refers to herself as another character in the film. She uses the narrating "I" to comment on the documentary, and yet she is treated in the story/history as "Abena" or "she" instead of "I." These confusions of characters are further complicated by the use of time in the film. For Abena, the "I" narrator, time is static; the *coup d'état* that overthrew Kwame Nkrumah in 1966 is at the origin of her trauma. On the other hand, Abena, the character in the film, has to count time. She has returned to Ghana twenty years later on assignment as a reporter for British television. She has to produce reportage on a film that Werner Herzog is making on slavery in Ghana, and is therefore bound by time.

Whereas I describe the poetical style of *Lumumba* as allegorical, I would call *Testament* an ironic or deconstructivist documentary. As I will show, the film derives its poetics of irony from the way history is *mise en abîme* by the loss of memory. Abena the narrator is traumatized by the 1966 coup; history no longer has a meaning for her. On the other hand, Abena the character in the film is forced to make sense of history; not only does she have to make her report before Herzog finishes shooting his film with Ghana as a backdrop, but she has also to piece together her own identity and to remember history as a critical assessment of the present.

The film draws its poetic irony from these embedded and contradictory narratives. Herzog's film within the film is the first sign of narrative irony. The narrator exposes Herzog's film as historically inaccurate and obsessed with images of cannibalism and violence. As Herzog ignores the slave castle of Almina and builds his own setting, stereotypes and clichés take the place of history. Abena's reportage is a document which ironizes Herzog's setting as fake history and an inauthentic testament. The irony in Abena's reportage is reminiscent of the ending of Chinua Achebe's classic novel *Things Fall Apart*, where a colonial administrator turned African historian (like Herzog turned African filmmaker) pushes aside the history of the Africans in order to emphasize the civilizing mission of the British. The director of *Testament* deconstructs Herzog's film just as Achebe reveals the naivete of the colonial administrator in his novel.

Another ironic language in the film concerns Abena's relation to her former comrades from Nkrumah's ideological school. After the coup, the soldiers destroyed the school and burned the books. Nkrumah and his regime were soon demonized as the enemies of the people, while the coup leaders were transfigured as the saviors of the nation. Abena herself left the country "like a thief in the night," while her comrades stayed to face the consequences. Rashid, Danzo, and Mr. Park now consider Abena an outsider. Rashid believes that the conditions in Ghana are too hard for Abena and that she should move into a hotel where it is more comfortable. He dismisses Abena's criticism of the coup as "exile talk." Danzo, for her part, refuses to talk to Abena. She is seen throughout the film as either turning her back, rolling her eyes, or pursing her lips at Abena's questions. As for Mr. Park, he has embraced numerology as a way of coping with reality. He explains the different coups in Ghana as determined by the coincidence between the first names of the coup leaders and the day of the week they were born. "They were all born on a Sunday: Kwasi Acheampong (coup of 1966), Kwasi Akuffo (1972), and Kwasi Rawlings (1981)." Abena's reliance on Rashid, Danzo, and Mr. Park to document the past ironizes the film's claim to truth, or, for that matter, the claim to truth in any documentary film.

In *Testament*, Akomfrah realizes the ultimate dream for every diaspora subject: the return home. We have seen that part of the frustration of the narrator in *Lumumba* was not to have been able to return to Congo. It is always desirable in the diaspora experience to visit the home that one was forced to leave. This kind of return operates as a guarantee for the diasporic subject's identity. That's why Peck talks about black holes in his mind that needed to be filled with the repressed images of Lumumba. The camera represents the mind of the first-person narrator in diasporic films, and the images that the camera takes are images of "home" that fill the black hole in the narrator's mind.

In *Testament*, the return narrative is complicated by two factors, one experiential and historical and the other mythological and psychological. To find Ghana and the Nkrumah revolution again, Abena has to find her comrades Danzo, Rashid, and Mr. Park. But as I have already shown, Abena's comrades have changed, and they no longer believe in the ideals of the past. When we see flashbacks of Nkrumah addressing a jubilant crowd, or of students at the ideological school, we know that only Abena is interested in these images. Her friends do not even share with her the memories of torture and rape at the hands of the soldiers during the coup. Unlike Abena, who wants to go back to 1966, they have erased everything from their minds except for the challenges that they have to face daily.

Abena is a theoretical character in the film who wants to find a synthesis between the past and the present, between tradition and modernity. Like Peck in *Lumumba*, she prefers the images in her mind to reality. She tries to find Ghana in traditional folk songs, in the ideological writings of Nkrumah's party, and in poetry. For example, she is often distracted from her reportage or from interacting with her friends and into flashbacks or subjective images of women dressed in traditional clothes and singing revolutionary songs. One such song calls upon the gods and the ancestors to help Ghana free herself from foreign control. Another song summons the people to rise up and punish those responsible for the crimes committed against Ghana. At the end of the film, Abena recites a revolutionary poem which goes as follows: "There is victory for us in this struggle for the Convention People's Party. Sons of Ghana, rise and fight. Daughters of Ghana, rise and shine. . . ."

One realizes at the end that Abena has brought the traditional songs up to date and inserted them in the larger cause of the Ghana revolution. The film reclaims Nkrumah as the true hero and the soldiers as those who have committed a terrible crime. The transfiguration of traditional songs into modern revolutionary poetry reminds one of Richard Wright's *Black Power*, a classic diasporic return narrative. *Black Power* is also about the Ghana revolution. In the book, Wright shows his impatience with reactionary traditional customs, and he urges Nkrumah to modernize them and use them in his revolution.

Finally, one must also look at the psychological impact of return in *Testament*. I call this the trauma of diasporic subjects. We have seen Abena's struggle to recapture the past and to belong to the present of Ghana. But her former comrades treat her as an outsider and a tourist. We also know that Abena left Ghana "like a thief in the night." She feels guilty for abdicating her responsibility to her country, in the same manner that Peck feels guilty towards Lumumba and the Congo. In fact, the search for identity in diaspora films is as much an expression of guilt as it is an exercise in self-empowerment. Both Peck and Abena feel guilty for siding with the victimizers by abandoning African shores.

Testament goes deeper in exploring the trauma caused by the separation of the diasporic subject from Africa. The film begins with Siamese twins on an operating table: "I've always thought that two bodies could be one, live together, believe in the same thing, live for life." But later in the film, after the operation is completed, one of the twins survives and the other dies. By taking us from the unitary moment, the moment of the Lacanian imaginary where everything is fluid, amorphous, and connected like the Siamese twins, to a symbolic moment and a transition to identity formation, the film delineates the diasporic trauma. The Atlantic slave trade which took Africans away to distant shores, and the coups during the Cold War which caused new dispersions and genocides, are like the surgical "splitting" of the twins. The return narrative, insofar as it enables Abena to revisit this original moment of splitting, is important to the discourse of the diaspora. They are the ones through which the diasporic subject discovers her identity and difference. Abena cannot go back home again, but she can build a new relationship with Rashid, Danzo, and Mr. Park.

At another level of the film, Abena's trauma is more personal and precedes diasporic return narratives. When she was a child, she used to be afraid of a ditch in her parents' yard. She imagined wolves coming out of it and taking her away. She had dreams of being covered in a blanket of leeches. She therefore had to fill the ditch with bricks and rocks to prevent the little beasts from coming out. Of course, Abena associates this form of death with Nkrumah's death and the political death of Ghana. To survive the trauma and to exorcise her fear of empty holes, Abena has to face her childhood memories. She has to follow the traces of her father, who blamed his political failures on the river gods and turned his back on his family and society. Abena too spends much of her time on the river when she cannot find answers to her questions in society. She and Danzo revisit their elementary school, hoping to find out where things went wrong. Abena sees flashbacks of soldiers destroying effigies of Nkrumah, of open graves in the cemetery. She sees images of folk dances and mobs burning books. It is only then that she is able to look without fear at the empty holes, the diasporic holes born in violence. She can now give Nkrumah a proper burial and continue the struggle begun by him and other diasporic subjects.

THE SYMBOLIST MODE:
THE FILMS OF LOUIS MASSIAH

Louis Massiah's films *The Bombing of Osage Avenue* (1986) and *W. E. B. Du Bois: A Biography in Four Voices* (1996) are special because they provide a historical explication of the past through the voices of ordinary people and artists, incorporating poetic and subjective diction as parts of the historical documents, hence my reference to them as symbolic films. We have seen that in *Testament* Akomfrah uses a woman as first-person narrator, but also to take his own place as filmmaker in the diaspora. Massiah too uses voice-over or on-screen narrators as mediators between himself and the diasporic subjects of his films (the MOVE people and W. E. B. Du Bois). Insofar as these narrators stand in sometimes as the voice of Massiah, and sometimes as the voice of his diasporic subjects, they become the symbols simultaneously of the subject and the object of the diaspora.

The Bombing of Osage Avenue is unusual as a documentary because it is less about the actual bombing of the MOVE house or the assignment of blame than it is about community and identity. The film opens with a definition of Cobbs Creek Park community through images. There are kids riding bikes, the elderly talking in familiar spots; everybody knows everyone else. As Toni Cade Bambara puts it in her poetic voice-over, "people are at home in the rituals and rhythms of the place." Everybody belongs and "You don't have to know that you are on the margins of the community." One of the ordinary voices says that the neighborhood was self-sufficient before the bombing; "you didn't have to go to Center City for your shopping." Other people, black and white, come to repeat more of less the same vision of Cobbs Creek Park neighborhood. In fact for Louis Massiah, repetition is a narrative style which becomes as effective for the documentary genre as it is for fiction. For example, we are told several times that Mother's Day is a family tradition that started in Philadelphia, that the seige of the MOVE compound began on Mother's Day, and that the bombing violated the aesthetic contract which is symbolized by Mother's Day.

The MOVE family is a post–civil rights social movement which settled on Osage Avenue after being forced out of different neighborhoods in Philadelphia. Clearly, therefore, the MOVE people's struggle is

Neighbors react to the police siege on MOVE
headquarters in Philadelphia, May 13, 1985.
AP/WIDE WORLD.

a struggle for belonging, citizenship, and justice. The film documents
the MOVE family's relation to their neighbors in the predominantly
black working and middle-class community in order to bring out the
shortcomings of each side. For example, the presence of the MOVE
family in the community reveals that the civil rights gains have not
borne fruit for everybody to gain access to citizenship and economic
emancipation. As the conflict between some of the community members, who are concerned about their image and the market value of their
houses, and the MOVE family reveals, the black middle class has constructed the lower class as a different race to be avoided at all cost. The
film also shows that the MOVE people, with their barricades, obscene
language, and foul odors, may have been stuck in the resistance politics
of the 1960s, without any recourse to modern strategies and dialogue
with the community. In fact, the MOVE Family was using the community as hostage in their struggles against the police and City Hall. The
film shows that, when the final confrontation takes place between the
police and MOVE, it is really the community that loses. The people realize their helplessness against MOVE and the fire bombs of the police;
their neighborhood is transformed into a war zone; things will never be

A bomb is dropped from a Philadelphia
police helicopter on MOVE headquarters,
as captured by WCAU-TV on May 14, 1985.
AP/WIDE WORLD.

the same again. *The Bombing of Osage Avenue* reveals the psychological
loss and the political disempowerment of a community that is unable
to take care of its own. Massiah brings out the best in Toni Cade Bambara, who comments on the images of Cobbs Creek Park and its community. The collaborative work between Massiah and Bambara forces
the filmmaker to occupy the place of the writer and vice versa, producing a result that is nothing less than a re-articulation of the documentary genre in a poetics of symbolism.

   W. E. B. Du Bois: A Biography in Four Voices is Louis Massiah's latest
collaborative work with four major writers—Wesley Brown, Thulani
Davis, Toni Cade Bambara, and Amiri Baraka—who are used as both
characters and voice-over narrators of the film. The first part of this
four-part documentary is told from the point of view of Wesley Brown.
It deals with Du Bois's formative years at Harvard and in Germany,
discusses the publication of *The Souls of Black Folk* in 1903, and culmi-
nates with the creation of the Niagara Movement in 1905, and the
NAACP, the first civil rights organization, in 1909. Brown's narrative
highlights Du Bois's clash with Booker T. Washington, whom Du Bois
accused of neglecting the full civil rights of black people through his
emphasis on technical training at the expense of the liberal arts. Du
Bois was committed to the intellectual as well as the physical freedom
of black people; it was for this reason that he and other black leaders

such as Monroe Trotter and Ida B. Wells formed an alliance called the Talented Tenth to lead the race into modernity, and to fiercely oppose Washington's attempt to only channel the energies of black people into manual work. In these early years, Du Bois also published a book entitled *The Philadelphia Negro*, in which he interviewed more than 3,000 people in an attempt to document the new types of black workers emerging out of the industrial revolution. Most people see in this book, which resembles the European physiologies of the 19th Century, the cardinal elements of the discipline of sociology in American.

Thulani Davis, the second narrator, picks up the thread of Du Bois's life from 1919 to 1929, date of the Stock Market crash, and possibly of the end of the Harlem Renaissance. Davis focuses on Du Bois's activities as a full time leader of the NAACP, the creation of *Crisis*, the most important journal on race in America, and the challenge created by Marcus Garvey, a black nationalist with a separatist and populist agenda. At this time, Du Bois was enjoying a bourgeois cultural existence, having married his daughter to Countee Cullen, a well-known poet of the Harlem Renaissance and son of a prominent family in Harlem. However the marriage did not last, because Countee Cullen was also gay, a fact to which Du Bois was oblivious. Davis's narrative is most attentive to culture as it reveals Harlem as the capital of the black world, where people were free to participate in the cosmopolitanism and modernism of jazz

W. E. B. Du Bois addressing the Congress of Partisans
of Peace at the Salle Pleyel in Paris, April 22, 1949.
AP/WIDE WORLD.

music and the other arts of the Harlem Renaissance movement. This moving part also shows Du Bois's puritanism toward the more extrovert members of the Harlem Renaissance, and his vulnerability against the populism of the race pride advocate and nationalist Marcus Garvey.

Toni Cade Bambara, in the third section of the film, 1934–1948, rationalizes Du Bois's attempts to broaden the basis of the NAACP among black people and to create a relief organization as a reaction to Garvey's criticism. But Du Bois's interest in black economic self determination is seen by the elitist members of the NAACP as an exercise in self-segregation and Garveyism. Walter White emerged as the new Leader of the NAACP causing Du Bois to resign from the organization and to return to Atlanta University as professor. Other fascinating moments of this section include Du Bois's publication of *Black Reconstruction* which is Marxist in its approach and instrumentality; the creation of *Phylon*, a journal of race and culture, at Atlanta University; the beginning of a major project entitled *Encyclopedia of the Negro*; and the Manchester Congress of 1945, which was attended by many Africans determined to take their destinies into their own hands.

Amiri Baraka's narrative occupies the fourth and last part of *W. E. B. Du Bois*. It is mainly concerned with Du Bois's efforts to internationalize the black struggle, his relation to the Communist Party, and his indictment by the U.S. government. Baraka is pained by the number of times Du Bois is betrayed by his friends, the NAACP, and McCarthyism. But there were also moments of victories, such as the speech Du Bois delivered at the Waldorf Peace Conference, his decision to join the Communist Party after the indictment, and—the most celebrated of all the return narratives—the trip in 1961 to Ghana, where he lived until his death in 1963.

Louis Massiah's skill as a director is apparent through his ability to work with four very different writers in the Du Bois project, and to keep all of them focused on the theme of the film. His skill as a filmmaker is manifest in the plot structure, which never ceases to intrigue the spectator. The narrative is built around tensions which oppose Du Bois to Booker T. Washington, Marcus Garvey, Walter White and the NAACP, and finally the McCarthyites. In each case Du Bois learned from his opponent and grew stronger. For example, he organized the Niagara Movement to fight Washington, and he steered the NAACP toward a broader economic and cultural base as a result of Garvey's criticism of the assimilationist position of the Talented Tenth.

W. E. B. Du Bois: A Biography in Four Voices is a *tour de force* of documentary filmmaking, presenting evidence and maintaining a self-reflexive film style at the same time. From Grierson to Leacock and Rouch, objectivity has dominated the packaging of information and evidence in the documentary genre. As a reaction to this logocentrism, postmodern documentarians such as Trinh T. Minh-Ha have deployed a fragmentary film language in order to put into question the validity of information in documentary films. Massiah's strategy is different because he does not challenge the fact that documentary films are capable of conveying verifiable information. But he redefines the documentary genre by presenting the evidence on a subjective grid. He places other artists and / or characters between himself and the evidence presented. By effacing himself in this manner, Massiah is able to show the evidence from different points of view. In other words, in Massiah's films the evidence is built intersubjectively.

This is not to say that Massiah's work is without any echo in the documentary world. On the contrary, the reflexive and repetitive narrative style of *The Bombing of Osage Avenue* reminds the viewer of *Handsworth Songs*, a film about the riots of Handsworth (U.K.; 1985) by John Akomfrah and the Black Audio Collective. Massiah's films are part of an international diasporic documentary emergence about major black leaders which includes: *Lumumba: The Death of a Prophet* by Raoul Peck, *Testament* by John Akomfrah, *Looking for Langston* and *Frantz Fanon: Black Skin and White Mask* by Isaac Julien, and *Langston Hughes: The Dream Keeper* by St. Clair Bourne. Louis Massiah should be recognized for being, more than anyone else, the connecting thread for this movement. *W. E. B. Du Bois: A Biography in Four Voices* is the most important film in scope and artistic achievement so far in the movement.

INTERVIEWS

Over the course of the last five years co-editors Phyllis Klotman and Janet Cutler conducted interviews with many documentary film / videomakers who have played a vital role in shaping the direction of African American documentary film and video. While the interviews evolved in different ways in response to the film / videomakers' specific interests and concerns, the same core questions were posed to each of the documentarians. All were asked, for example, to comment on the place of documentary work in their careers, to offer a personal perspective on the nature and function of documentary filmmaking, and to describe the production circumstances and funding environment in which they worked.

The interviews with film / videomakers have been used in two ways. They have served as an important resource tool for the scholar / authors, providing a source for quoted material within the chapters. In addition, the interviews have been excerpted in the following appendix to the book. These excerpts are necessarily fragmentary, having been taken from much longer interview material. Not official artists' statements, they nonetheless provide insight into the careers of very different individuals with diverse experiences and views of the forces that shaped their work in documentary. Full transcripts of the interviews are available for study at the Black Film Center / Archive at Indiana University.

CARROLL PARROTT BLUE

My background is in still photography. I managed to do a summer workshop at MIT guided by Minor White back around 1967. And I started doing street photography during that time. I had seen the work of Roy DeCarava beforehand. His approach to photography was a guiding light for me in terms of what could be done around making images of African American people. He practiced a Black aesthetic—a way of viewing Blacks with pride—that I've incorporated. In 1967, I started walking the Boston streets, taking photographs and keeping what I had seen in Roy's work in the back of my mind.

My documentary photography ended up being published in a wonderful book series called *The Black Photographers Annual*. There were four volumes published. I was very proud to be in volumes three and four. Joe Crawford was one of the original organizers. He took money that he made from an engineering job and poured the money into publishing these books. The series used Black photographers from everywhere. It featured historic sections highlighting pioneers from the early part of this century—P. H. Polk, official photographer for Tuskegee Institute; Harlem's James Van Der Zee; Addison Scurlock, Howard University's official photographer; and Hamilton Smith, from Boston. So you had a sense of the longevity of this tradition's aesthetic. It also included the work of the Kamoinge ("Group Effort") Workshop. Roy DeCarava co-founded this group in New York in the '60s. Kamoinge was part of the public protest against the Metropolitan Museum of Art's "Harlem on My Mind" 1969 exhibition. The group disapproved of the art this museum brought to us as a people. The exhibition contradicted what our aesthetic really was. I am still firmly entrenched in this Black aesthetic. These books honor a positive, beautiful image of the Black people in terms of family, in terms of work, in terms of entertainment and pleasure.

I went to Boston University from 1960 to 1964, graduating in English Literature. I specialized in the English Renaissance period. I wanted to write. Yet, I ended up moving to Los Angeles after graduating and becoming a probation officer. Working on this job, I kept wondering how I was going to do something creative with my life. Soon I quit writing. And I pondered how I was going to get back into it. It was then that I made a decision to go into still photography. I demoted myself from being a probation officer to become a night attendant at Central Juvenile Hall. I worked there from ten at night to six in the morning. Then from nine to five daily, I went to Los Angeles Trade–Technical College, where I majored in still photography. That was my beginning. In Los Angeles at the time, there was another photographer who came from the same tradition as Roy DeCarava. His name was Leonard Taylor. He made incredibly beautiful images. Leonard and Roy were the most influential in terms of helping me to develop my own style and personal expression. After publishing my photographs in *The Black Photographers Annual*, I made a trip back to New York and was introduced to Roy. After he looked at my portfolio, he asked me to go and photograph a smile. That was my hardest assignment.

In L.A. I also met Robert Nakamura, a Japanese American photographer and filmmaker. Bob had just graduated from UCLA Film School. He, with other UCLA Asian American filmmakers, had started a media arts organization called Visual Communications. Today this is the premiere Asian American media arts center. He said, "Well, you're doing photography so you might as well be doing film. Why don't you do film and photography together?" By this time I was working for Professor Harold Zirin, the NASA solar weatherman, at the California Institute of Technology's Solar Astronomy Laboratory. I was a darkroom technician. They would film the sun every day. They threw me into this lab and had me print and process both 16mm and 35mm film. And so I got a chance to work with a contact printer and optical printing in the development of 16mm and 35mm film. I got a chance to see how film worked on a technical level. Around this time, Bob asked me if I would be interested in going to UCLA Film School. So I went to UCLA Film School with this base as a still photographer and a film lab technician. I ended up with an East Coast education from Boston University from 1960 to 1964 and a West Coast education from UCLA from 1976 to 1980.

At UCLA I was influenced by a lot of the Black student filmmakers: Haile Gerima, Larry Clark, Charles Burnett, Ben Caldwell, John Reir, Pam Jones, Billy Woodberry—all who had come in before me. Now my class had several very good Black students as well—Julie Dash, Sharon Larkin, Barbara McCullough, Bernard Nichols and me. We came in together around 1976. Some other classmates were Ramon Melendez (*Stand and Deliver*); Alex Cox (*Repo Man*); Michael Miner (*Robocop*); and Neal Jimenez (*The River's Edge* and *Waterdance*). During this time I was also influenced by the work of Topper Carew's *Say Brother*, of Ellis Haizlip's *Soul!*, of William Greaves's *Black Journal* and New York–style filmmakers such as St. Clair Bourne, Stan Lathan, Gil Noble, Charles Hobson, and Kathleen Collins. Johnny Simmons, then a USC film student, introduced me to Carlton Moss. Carlton Moss introduced me to Frances Williams. Both major film pioneers, Frances and Carlton were the most important mentors for me in this early independent Black film community.

Meanwhile, Robert Nakamura had come back to teach at UCLA Film School. He asked me to be his graduate teaching assistant. During my first teaching experience, my students included Melvonna Ballinger and John Esaki. Bob was really instrumental in encouraging me to combine still photography and documentary filmmaking with teaching. During this time I continued working with Visual Communications. Through them I learned about the idea of taking people's archival photographs and using them to tell stories. I also worked on Bob's film, the first Asian American feature film, *Hito Hata*. And so I was being influenced by African American still photographers and filmmakers while working with Asian American filmmakers as they built an Asian American media community by making documentary and later, feature films.

The first film I made at UCLA in 1976 was a Super–8 film called *Two Women*. I had worked on other films and had done smaller things by myself, but this was the first film that I did that I sent out to film festivals after finishing it. Johnny Simmons, who has turned into a wonderful cinematographer and very fine artist, worked with me on this film. The film was a story of a young girl who was eighteen years old and my aunt, Mrs. Lillie Skannal, an older woman who was almost in her eighties. Both women talked about their approach to life. The older woman spoke of her need to turn to a God, or something spiritual to guide her. And the young girl talked about how she used her own will. Before, I had been doing portraiture, still photographs of people so now I translated that style of working into film. *Two Women* was very good for me because I won second place in the 1976 Virgin Islands Film Festival and first place in the 1977 Los Angeles International Film Festival. It was also as a sample portfolio piece used to secure a grant from the American Film Institute to make my next film, *Varnette's World: A Study of a Young Artist*.

Varnette's World won a Gold Hugo, the top award at the 1979 Chicago International Film Festival. It got a lot of play in Europe—everybody was asking for UCLA Black filmmakers' work on the festival circuit. And it turned out that Mark Weiss was producing a local show about independent filmmakers on New York City's PBS station, WNET-TV. He used my film for that program. David Loxton and Kathy Klein saw it and asked if it could be picked up for national broadcast on their program. That's how *Varnette's World* was shown on groundbreaking WNET-TV's series, *Non-Fiction Television*. When I came up with the idea to do a film on Roy DeCarava, I turned to David, who had previously done a film on photographer Henri Cartier Bresson. Immediately he understood my goals and was sympathetic towards what I wanted to do. That's how I got the chance to make *Conversations with Roy DeCarava*.

I went through a lot of trouble to make it to a national broadcast of *Conversations*. David Loxton took my film proposal with Jesus Trevino's proposal to the Corporation for Public Broadcasting and said, "These people deserve money, give it to them with the minority producers set-asides funds." So we got money to make our films. After I finished the film, one PBS executive hated it and blocked it from national prime time broadcast. So I became aware of the "soft feed" system. We made dubs of the video, sent it to several programming people at various stations to get it on air. Although *Conversations* won first place, the Blue Ribbon, at the 1980 American Film Festival, it was still a difficult film to get validated. Today, it's considered a classic. Also, I was able to experiment with some of the formal elements in this film.

Film sound has constantly intrigued me. Especially because as an African American my culture's music is so rich and varied. I like to design sound in film to create dynamic and dramatic atmospheres. In *Conversations with Roy DeCarava,* there's a scene where Roy goes to a subway. As he moves through the subway, I show his subway photographs with the sound of the subway car coming and leaving the station. The design is used as a way of building tension as Roy begins to talk about being a Black photographer encountering prejudice in the 1960 advertising world. The sound emphasizes what that emotional stress and pressure meant to him. The sound, like his life, reached a certain high point. I use this approach to sound the same way in *Varnette's World* and in *Nigerian Art: Kindred Spirits.* Sound is a separate means of telling a story. As a matter of fact, Walter Murch, who got an Academy Award for doing the sound design of *Apocalypse Now,* is my primary sound teacher. He says sound goes straight to the subconscious because your conscious brain can't filter pure sound out. You hear a cry . . . .or, a loud noise. Boom! It goes straight through your brain just as it is, without your thoughts being able to stop it.

Conversations was made during a very heady period for independent documentaries. We're talking between the early '70s and mid-'80s. Films like *Men's Lives, Rosie the Riveter, Babies and Banners, Seeing Red,* and *Harlan County, U.S.A.* dominated. In 1981–83, I worked for Jane Fonda on three of her feature films—*Rollover, On Golden Pond,* and *Nine to Five.* I also worked on her film for television, *The Dollmaker.* So I got a sense of what Hollywood is like. After this Hollywood experience I made a conscious decision to make personal films out of documentaries.

In the late '80s, I trained with Henry Hampton. I worked on *Eyes on the Prize, Part II.* This was on the *Malcolm X* story and the *Harold Washington* story. Some of the other Black producers on that series included Louis Massiah, Judy Richardson, Sam Pollard, Jackie Shearer. I also trained under Adrian Malone, who did *Cosmos* and *The Ascent of Man,* while Adrian was the executive producer at Smithsonian World. I made *Nigerian Art: Kindred Spirits* under his direction.

Michele Parkerson and I are pretty much contemporaries in terms of what we are doing. Constantly, I look at newer documentary filmmakers. One that I've been really just touched by, beyond belief, is the genius Marlon Riggs. Recently I looked at another avant-garde filmmaker, Tony Cokes, who did *Fade to Black.* I see that many documentary filmmakers are moving more into video, avant-garde, and synthesizing all of the materials into personal expressions. It's almost like jazz. Improvisation, polyrhythms, strange ways of editing and cutting, using strips, moving text—that sort of thing. So I think that technology has a lot to do with how we develop as filmmakers. I have also been influenced by the Black Audio Collective in England. They are working on how to use sound, visuals, and theory in ways that are different, encapsulating all of the stuff I'm talking about.

My biographical life story contains the way I understand the world. I was born on August 23, 1943, in Houston, Texas. I went to elementary school, junior high school, and high school right there in Houston. I remember we had this library contest at Jack Yates High School. The principal said that whoever read the most books would win. I won hands down because I was a kid that read all of the time. So the librarian took the list of books I had read and she said, "Everything on your list is a biography." And up until that time I didn't realize how fascinated I am—even today—with people's lives. Biographies inform me of what my society is about. So that's really what I am doing with documentary film and video. It's not so much me detailing a person's biography. It's me using documentary to get a handle on what my society is by reflecting a person's life on film. How do people get through this society successfully? How do they maintain humanity in a society that doesn't want us to be humane? So that's the essence of what I'm doing. I'm using documentary to comprehend who we are and to leave tracks for people to see and say, "Oh, this is how that person did it. Well, maybe I can do it as well."

My target audience is everybody, or whoever wants to check my work out. Timothy Leary once said, "There are only two kinds of people in the world. There are those who want to evolve and those who don't. And both kinds are at war with each other." I'm with the group that wants to evolve.

JANUARY 1992
LOS ANGELES, CALIFORNIA

ST. CLAIR BOURNE

There is an African American tradition in documentary filmmaking, and I am probably the third generation. Bill Greaves is the second, maybe the first, but before him there were erratic attempts by different people, people like Bud Outlaw in Philadelphia. Bud Outlaw was just a free-lance shooter, a cameraman who carried his camera in the trunk of his car and drove around and shot, and gave it to news shows. And there were people like Jimmy Manas, who was making films in Brooklyn two to four years before *Black Journal* started in the '60s. He's still around.

And there are a bunch of people like LeRoy Lucas, who was a camera-person. Most of them were filmmakers in the classic sense, people who filmed and shot and edited little pieces.

I actually came to documentary film through political work. I saw the representation, misrepresentation and confusion of the civil rights movement in the major media by white male spokespeople who attempted to tell white America what "those people" were doing, and usually what they said was wrong, or distorted, for their own psychic needs. And I knew that I had a better handle on that. . . . So, basically, my thing was to tell the story that I thought was happening, and to do it in a way that everybody could see it, and TV was the way.

I was in Columbia University Film School in 1967–68, and I was a student activist, and as you know in '68 we took over the university. I was one of those arrested, and I was kicked out of film school. And Arthur Barron, who was my documentary teacher, saw me and said, "Look, I think you're really talented. It's a shame that you got kicked out of school, but there's a new series that I'm gonna recommend you to, and there's a guy named Bill Greaves, the executive producer." . . . And then he told me about this series called *Black Journal*, which was about to start. Three days later I had an interview, and about three days after that I received a call that I was an associate producer for this national television documentary series. And, so, within a week after being in jail for taking over Columbia University, I became the youngest producer on the team.

Black Journal for years was a major influence on all documentarians—black documentarians, but even white documentarians. For example, the magazine format as we know it really didn't come from *60 Minutes*, it came from us. We had done it two years before [because] we only had one hour every month, and the only way to really jump around the country was to do segments, and then we had to figure a way to smoothly make a transition from one to the other. We used . . . visuals and African drums, and Bill Greaves and Wali Sadik making those verbal transitions. That essentially became the magazine format. *Black Journal* did that, then *NET Journal*, which was the white counterpart, then *American Dream Machine*, and then CBS and NBC picked it up.

If you look at black filmmaking as an inverted pyramid, he's [Bill Greaves is] the base which everything else comes out of, because it was he who set up the three-point dictum that we were supposed to work by: one, to define the reality, the black reality, which in those days, as now, was usually problem/struggle; two, to define why the struggle/problem/situation evolved; but most important, he said—and if you didn't do this, then you were really derelict in your duty, and three, to suggest a way out. It did not have to be *the* way out, but you had to show people trying to attempt to resolve the difference. And that's what he said really would distinguish our films from the do-good, well-intentioned white filmmakers, that we could actually get inside and show a direction out. And maybe this is a generational thing, but I find the third element sorely lacking in the current wave of black filmmakers.

The primary influence for me was Bill Greaves's style, but there are a couple others. Bill Jersey's film, *A Time for Burning*, influenced me quite a bit, because it was *vérité*, personal, and had a sense of drama, social issues, conflict, resolution. . . . And then he did *Welcome Home, Brother Charles*, about a Vietnam guy coming back . . . And then John Cassavetes's work, even though he was structured.

I don't go in with an idea of what I want out of [my subjects] right away. I let that evolve. If they're black subjects, I try to evaluate the level of political awareness, and go in on that, because what people really want, white or black but especially black people, they really want a chance to say stuff that they can't say. And, if you give them that opportunity, and if they trust that you will not basically fuck over them in the process, then—to the extent of their ability—they'll try to structure it in a way that you want it done. Then you tell them, "Look, the way I want it done is the way you do it," and they can really relax and they can just come out.

I don't see myself as a presence. I never have put my own questions in. I've never been in a film that I've made. I try to capture the reality and the texture surrounding the reality, so that people will see my version, but also get the nuance of how the people live, so that *they* can make an evaluation on not just the person, but the background. The context, that's very, very important, and that's how I use archival footage, too. [In] the *Langston Hughes* film, what I do is try to give you parallel events of the times in which we're talking.

I try to tell a story which is interesting. The first couple of pieces that I made were sort of film essays, like thought pieces on film. But then, as I began to get more comfortable with the equipment and the technique, rather than make an essay, I would try to find people who represented the sentiment, and then follow them. Even if in a limited way, a day or one hour, or they go into a meeting, they talk, they come out. At least I've got a chronological thing there.

The target audience tends to be African American. Now, what Bill taught me was that you can target an African American audience, and that does not eliminate anybody else. In fact, the purer the African American taste, the more interesting it is to other people. Because the more specific the better—the purer—so people can lock into it, and say,

"Oh, I didn't know this." That's the idea. If somebody goes, "I didn't know that," and doesn't feel threatened, then I know that I've done it. Even if they feel threatened, that's still all right. But they have to really be given the purest version of the person or the subject matter. That's the job of a documentarian. The whole issue of universality is basically something concocted to prevent people of color from getting access to the tools of self-definition.

JULY 1992
INDIANAPOLIS, INDIANA

AYOKA CHENZIRA

I haven't thought about myself as a documentary filmmaker for a long time. In fact the first production of mine that went into distribution, *Syvilla: They Dance to Her Drums* was strictly a documentary piece. [Since then] the closest thing that I've done to a straight documentary would be *Secret Sounds Screaming: The Sexual Abuse of Children*, and even that pulls in experimental and narrative elements. I use the experiences of people, and specifically of Black history, as resource material now to do experimental and narrative work. Part of the shift was that I found the documentary format, as it was being taught and displayed 20 years ago when I was training, to be very confining. There were many more things that I wanted to say about Syvilla Fort. Had I known what I know now, they would have been said. There is this thinking that documentaries are objective. Nothing is objective. Narrative pieces aren't, and certainly documentaries aren't. Not even *60 Minutes* is objective. Everything is quite skillfully shaped, and some people shape better than others, but they're not objective in any way. *Zajota and the Boogie Spirit* is very much a documentary kind of film in that it uses the actual experiences of Black people around the world to play itself out, but it's in animation and there is a mythical character in it (which implies a personal vision for me), and then there is the notion of myth, magic, dance, and survival issues within the historical context it deals with. Looking at documenting that way is much more exciting and interesting to me than being locked into the traditional documentary format. The other problem is that most of Black culture resides in the oral tradition and our institutions are people, as opposed to papers and buildings. So when the people die it's devastating.

I remember when I made *Syvilla*—Syvilla was dying when I was making the film—wanting desperately to say so much about her and not being able to find hardly anything about her in the Schomburg Center for Research in Black Culture, but finding a lot of people who knew about her through the oral tradition. Now much of my work focuses on the function of memory and why people choose to remember or not to remember. *Zajota* is all about how once you reclaim your memory, for example, there are these things that happen to you, these very empowering things. So I've gotten excited about documentary work again as I see other people doing it because it is becoming much more personal documentary, which I find much more exciting than the old way where you had to have, as a way to maintain this rubric of journalistic integrity, the visual proof. Of course in our culture, the visual proof doesn't always exist, or what happens is you get the PBS documentaries that show during Black History Month, and they have all the same photographs in them.

[Filmmakers] are no longer confined to how the documentary has been traditionally presented, which is: You have an interview with the subject; you justify that subject with people who are scholars and speak very eloquently about the subject as justification that the subject is important; then you bring in historical photographs (the more scratched they are, the better) that give you a sense of time and place, and you come up with a list of ten questions.

What we were taught, as I remember, were things like the use of the memorabilia, the photographs, kind of living with your subject, the kind of questions you would ask them, but most of my information for *Syvilla* really came through interviewing other people. There was a lot of pressure on me to make Syvilla seem super famous. She was famous, but she was famous in a kind of underground way, and I made the decision—and I'm still glad I did—not to bring in people like Marlon Brando to say how wonderful she was. I didn't want her used in that way, which of course made the documentary unexciting to my colleagues. Then of course when it was time for distribution, there can be 200 films about Martha Graham, but nobody knew who Syvilla was. People were like, "See, I told you, you should have put those famous people in there," but it was okay because for years I was on the road with *Syvilla* doing dance classes, lecturing, and showing the film, and was able to support myself totally off of that film for a long time.

I looked at *Schindler's List* . . . and the film reminded me of how much we've lost in Black culture. There were few people who put our pictures under floor boards to hide them; there were few recorders going up to the slave and saying, "How do you feel on this cotton picking day?" It has been left up to some of the slave narrators, of course, . . . so you don't really have the visual information that would allow you to organize and to have the world be sympathetic to your cause because the things that the world is used to seeing, the evidence, does not exist in the way that it exists with more contemporary atrocities, like the atrocities of World War II, like certainly Sarajevo. And of course Black women are so left out. Women are really not included in the documentation process in terms of what's available, in terms of narrative, in terms of photographs. They're there, but not in a way that would help me form a complete picture. So [now I am] using history as resource material to jump off into what I want to say within a more narrative context.

There is so much embarrassment around the issue of slavery, which is the exact opposite of the Holocaust and the Jewish experience. The Jewish people have said, "This happened, you're responsible, you did nothing about this for a long period of time. We have lost 6 million people and we are never going to let you forget it and we are never going to let any of our people forget it." In the African American experience, it has been, "Could we not talk about this, could we not show this to people, could you stop embarrassing us?" . . . Instead of assigning the role of offender to where it belongs, we have wrapped ourselves up with, "Somehow it's our fault and we were really terrible and we didn't photograph well." I think with the documentary opening up stylistically, there are ways to begin to make vital, valuable information available to young people who, if you get the right formula, will sit and look.

I think it's critical that people document. I am so happy that the cost of video cameras keeps going down, and I am hoping that more people will just pick up a camera and turn it on their grandmother, turn it on their grandfather—as opposed to just documenting birthday parties—but to really begin to consciously think about all the holes that we have, again because so much of the history is in the oral tradition and because we need the proof. In Hollywood narrative work we go from *Guess Who's Coming to Dinner* to the Spike Lee films so there's this whole period where Black people have not grown up on the screen, and it's devastating because it looks like we've gone from *To Sir With Love* to *Boyz N the Hood*. It's like, "What the hell happened?"

Narrative work is a way of documenting too. It just does it differently. You take an idea and you pull the story through characters so that you can talk about documenting by using the narrative format.

Most Black filmmakers will acknowledge, even if they don't take on the term "documentary filmmaker," that in all of our filmmaking we are giving witness to either the history or the psychology or the emotions of a people, whether you're [looking at] a larger social context, or . . . at a small narrative piece that focuses on a family. Because you are making films that are of a specific time and place and using certain people to tell the story. That's a form of documenting, and I would certainly put myself in that category.

MARCH 1994
NEW YORK, NEW YORK

ALONZO CRAWFORD

I'm so focused on what's happening in my neighborhood, in Washington, D.C., I don't spend time thinking about a career in Hollywood. I like to think of myself not as a Hollywood filmmaker, but as a neighborhood filmmaker.

Crowded is a film that came about as a result of legal action against the state of Maryland and the city of Baltimore. It was commissioned by the Legal Aid Services of Baltimore, Maryland, on behalf of the inmates in the Baltimore city jail. The inmates were suing the governor, the mayor, the warden . . . to force the reduction of the population in the jail. At the time they contacted me to film the conditions inside the jail (1977–1978), there were 2,100 inmates warehoused there. The city jail of Baltimore was designed to house 900. Before the inmates contacted me, they had done research on overcrowding in the nation's jail system, and they discovered that animals in a zoo in the United States, by law, were required to have more space than the inmates in the Baltimore city jail.

So, when the Legal Aid Services of Baltimore contacted me, they asked if I could document the conditions inside the jail on film to use in litigation of their case, for a budget of $400. They called me because they had heard about this guy around Washington, D.C., who had this reputation for doing films on low budgets. I said, "Do a film for $400? I don't know if I can do that. I mean I can do some things, but nobody can do that." I thought about it for a while and said, "Okay, we'll try."

I took on this project because I thought the film had to be done. I put some of my own money in the project. That was how much I believed in the case of the inmates. But, I had one condition, that I would be allowed to make a total film, rather than randomly shooting some footage on the conditions that the Legal Aid Services wanted to show. They agreed, as long as the judge and the defense agreed the film was admissible as evidence in the case. This forced me to think about this documentary in a way that was different from the way I had ever thought about documentary film before. My question to myself was "How can I make this film appear objective and make a statement about the entire penal system in the United States, as I see it?" I felt the penal system stripped its people of all dignity and humanity. My opinion was formed based on research I had done about the incarceration of African American males. . . .which I felt was closely linked to the racial attitude of white America toward black America. I felt something had to be said about it that would represent a collective voice of how we [black Americans] feel. I decided on a pedagogical approach in which the method of application is an educational process for the collective. *Crowded* was to be a teaching tool which was very much in keeping with the way I like to approach film.

We shot the film in two days . . . and it was not easy. We learned the hard way to expect the unexpected. All of the crews on my films are made up of my students in the film program at Howard University's School of Communication, Radio, Television, and Film Department. On the first day of shooting we had this beautiful Howard University film student with us on the crew. The inmates were, you know, lusting after her, acting out their emotions in a very silly way. This didn't look good for the film if I was going to make any statement about the system. I knew I had to effect a change in their behavior. It took a lot of nerve on my part to step up in the midst of this crowd of hard-core men that were coming back from lunch and talk to them. I said, "Look, we are here because we understand and believe in your lawsuit against the government, and we want to help." I asked them, "Don't you think your behavior will have a negative impact on your case and what we are trying to capture on film? I am sure that you don't want it to look like this is a nice place to be, that you are all happy-go-lucky about being here. So, why don't we try to calm down and go about business as if this was just another ordinary day—as if you don't see us and the camera here. If there is any one of you who disagree with that, we will pack up the camera and leave right now. So, let us know." Within an hour after that —I don't know how it happened—through their own communication system the entire population knew what I had said and why we were there. From that point on each block was expecting us and knew what behavior we expected of them. I was able to head off a situation that potentially could have gotten out of hand because the word about this beautiful woman working with the crew was traveling equally as fast throughout the jail. Instead, the inmates became really supportive. They cooperated with the crew and assisted with the moving and setting up of equipment, lights, tripod, etc.

So, we finished the film and it was accepted by the prosecution, the defense attorney and the judge. The inmates won their case. . . . The administration was ordered to reduce the inmate population and to cut the maximum number back to 900.

I am a graduate of Columbia [University]. I went there because I wanted at the time to be a documentary filmmaker, because I believed it to be the film of truth . . . and I went to Columbia because they were willing to give me a scholarship . . . and because Arthur Barron, the documentary filmmaker for ABC network was there. I wanted to study under Arthur Barron, and Erik Barnouw, the authority on documentary film history, who was also there. Barron produced and directed documentaries for ABC, *Birth and Death, 16 in Webster Groves,* and *Return to Webster Groves.*

I wanted to make documentary film, because I came out of an experience of racial prejudice and I thought skills in documentary filmmaking would be helpful in my efforts to expose it to my audience . . . [and] the whole point in going to Columbia graduate film school was to study documentary filmmaking. But, when I got there, I quickly realized to my dismay the curriculum was not really about documentary film at all. Instead, it was about making film in the Hollywood mainstream. Arthur Barron and Professor Erik Barnouw were on the faculty but their courses represented a very small portion of the film program's curriculum. Most of my training at Columbia focused on Hollywood and European filmmaking. Under the department chairman, Professor [Stefan] Sharff, I studied the film classics. He taught a course in film analysis where we analyzed the works of Eisenstein, Hitchcock, Howard Hawks, John Ford, and others. I became fascinated with the analysis of film and the use of film language by the various great directors from Europe and the United States. Professor Sharff taught us to look at film analysis as purely a technical skill. Our task was to look objectively at the film language and to dissect it into its elements of film grammar. Though I was not learning skills in documentary film [my idea of film truth and my weapon to fight racial prejudice], I found that I could use the skills of film analysis to attack racial prejudice. I took the concepts of film analysis one step further—to interpret the meaning of the elements of film language into the socio-political terms of narrative film.

Film language is an expression of the cultural values of the society in which it is produced. However, the filmmaker must have a clear understanding of cultural values and know how to express those values in cinematic terms, in order to accurately represent them for the screen. The filmmaker must also be free from outside cultural influences that strive to exploit her/his culture, in its own interest. An oppressed filmmaker will produce an oppressive film. The Hollywood filmmaker does not face this dilemma, she/he is left untethered to discover unique cinematic expressions consistent with her/his world view. For example, in Western society individual rights and freedom are among the highest expression of cultural values. The cultural fabric of the nation is woven from the threads of inalienable individual rights. Hollywood films express this cultural value of the importance of the individual through their use of the close-up shot, which separates the individual from the rest of society. How can they do it? Nothing in nature exists by itself, alone. Everything has to exist in harmony or in opposition to that which surrounds it—above it, below it, and beside it. But it seems that in Hollywood the idea is to portray the individual in isolation to the rest of the world. Of course this is for a reason, which is political in nature, and has racial overtones. The concept of individualism is uplifted in the consciousness of society for social, political, and economic reasons. Everyone in society can't be powerful and rich. Most of us must be weak and poor in order for the few to be powerful and rich. Implanting the ideal of the individual in social consciousness is achieved in cinema and literature by portraying the individual as a hero, someone for ordinary people to look up to. In cinema the close-up separates the individual from others. The individual is portrayed as possessing special abilities, overcoming odds, and accomplishing things ordinary people feel they could not. This has led the audience to accept and believe in the premise of the superhuman, someone to admire and idolize. Even when ordinary people consciously attempt to resist this idea, we are captivated by the elements of the language in the film's narrative. "Resistance is futile."

As a black filmmaker faced with a different reality, I am forced to use the grammar of film in a different context. Yes, I use the close-up in my grammar of film, but in a different socio-political context. In Hollywood, the story of life is told primarily from the point of view of the medium shot and the close-up. On the surface, the utilitarian value of the medium shot and close-up is to present narrative story and to reveal inner character. However, the socio-political subtext is to isolate while raising the individual to the status of hero or heroine, in the mind of the audience. As a black filmmaker, I have a different social, political, and economic history. Therefore, it makes sense that I would use the language of film differently. On a utilitarian level, the close-up has the same purpose, there is a certain universality to human perception. Human beings receive and process certain types of visual stimuli in ways that are universal. But, how these visual stimuli are used in cinematic context is the cultural expression of the filmmaker. What I have done for myself is read between the lines of the critical theories in film grammar. I decided to use the close-up to expose individual behavior that is contradictory to the collective consciousness. Life in my films is told from a collective point of view—the group shot. Used in this social context, heroism is removed from the equation; contradictory individual behavior is characterized as negative to collective cultural consciousness. The Western notion of the use of close-up is now turned on its head. The definition of individualism is refocused and redefined in terms the political necessities of the collective.

I believe the collective independent approach to be vital to the nurturing development of black America's culture. This is true in day-to-day life of the black community, as well as the black artist. I am a black independent filmmaker, whose struggle is inextricably tied to the day-to-day struggle of the community against the forces of racial and cultural prejudice. The independent struggle is strengthened when joined with collective movement. In my opinion, independence is defined by the method used when going about the work of filmmaking free of outside influences from forces that wish to oppress you. It also means to work collectively for empowerment and social awareness.

The power of film to teach, to effect change in cultural awareness, is more effectively achieved by involving the community in the film production process. In other words, I don't believe we [black filmmakers] can afford to wait for the traditional consumption of the film product to affect the social consciousness of our community. No one has ever been changed by a single film unless they were ready for change before seeing it. No one goes to a movie and leaves changed—no matter how progressive it might to be—if they are not ready for change.

In 1978, I was trying to make a film titled *Dirt, Ground, Earth, and Land*, using the collective independent approach. It took two years of planning before we started shooting because it took that long for the community to fully trust and believe in us. It was literally a war we were involved in. We went to war under the banner of "pedagogy in cinema," with the motion picture camera as our weapon. The film was about housing and the rights of poor people. Part of our work as filmmakers was to inform them of their rights. This is the difference between Hollywood production and neighborhood production and the use of the motion picture camera. The camera can become a powerful magnet when used as a pedagogical tool.

When a film crew enters an oppressed neighborhood the community is immediately attracted to the camera. This is a pivotal moment when the choice is made to galvanize the community to a higher consciousness or reduce it down to a standard of social, political, and economic dependence. It is a natural curiosity for people to want to know what is going on in their community, and to be included. With the Hollywood production, you are forced away. The Hollywood producer will say, "Step back, get out of my way. I need to make this movie about you, and this is the way I see it. This is my view of you." The pedagogical approach to filmmaking encourages you to say, "This film is about you, about us. This is how we speak to each other. Now what do you have to say?" The filmmaker and the community talk to each other, people start to see, and say, "Oh, wow! The landlord is going to take my neighborhood? Yes! We all have the same problem!"

This is the strategy, and everyone decides, "Hey! Let's make a fight of it." During the production process we came up with innovative ways of dramatizing the issue. We put on a mock demonstration which really got the community involved, to the point that they took their landlord to court, and sued him. My student crew and I were subpoenaed to appear at the trial, the judge subpoenaed our film—the film was not even finished—and the community won their case.

This is the power in the pedagogical film process. The power of film to raise social consciousness is in getting people involved in role-playing, thereby engaging them in a process of critical self-analysis. They may not immediately know that they are analyzing their reality, but eventually the reality catches up to the art.

It is said, "When one watches a film, they are witnessing the transformation of reality." Well, what about when the spectator is watching their own participation in the transformation of that reality?

That is the real power in film: to effect change in reality.

JULY 1992
INDIANAPOLIS, INDIANA

ABRAHAM (ABIYI) FORD

I was very much affected by images when I was a kid. I used to be fascinated by pictures of the nativity and other stories of the Bible used by missionaries who came to Ethiopia to preach. They used to cut out the pictures from felt material and paste them, or stick them onto display boards while they told the stories. I was attracted to colorful pictures even before that from the books that my mother had around the house. I became visually oriented and had a rough time learning how to read. I just wanted to look at more and more pictures. Words simply didn't carry the same weight for me. It was not until American comic books came on the scene that I unconsciously picked up on my reading. My need to follow the story driven by the pictures, in effect, forced me to read. The way the stories progressed in the panel paintings interested me because it was almost like going to the cinema. I did not know it at the time but, of course, like every other youngster of the day in Addis, I was very much part and parcel of the madness of going to the movies. Our favorites were the serials that would leave us in suspense about what would happen, from week to week. I remember some of them, *The Scarlet Rider, The Lone Ranger, Flash Gordon,* and many others. These were some of the American films that helped orient us toward the fantasies of Western culture.

By the time I came to this country, I was already being driven by certain forces that affected me as a consequence of my attraction to the power of the moving image. For instance, I wanted to become a pilot very much not because I knew anything about being a pilot but because of the images that I remembered of the fighter and bomber pilots of World War II in the movies. I visualized myself in the cockpits of those planes, and I always wondered about how Hollywood shot those wonderful and exciting scenes on film. These things attracted me to the Air Force so when I graduated from Junior College, I immediately volunteered and enlisted in the US Air Force. My status as an immigrant to the US was one of a permanent resident at that time. To become a pilot in the US Air Force one had to be a commissioned officer, and to get a commission one had to be a US citizen. My dreams of becoming a dashing pilot were thus scuttled. I did, however, toward the end of my enlistment, get to fly single engine propeller driven aircraft through the Aero-Activity program that was open to enlisted men. The results, however, from the battery of aptitude test I took indicated that I had a propensity for the visual and photographic arts. My first training assignment, therefore, was as a camouflage specialist. Once assigned to permanent duty, I became very much involved, during my free time, in the design of such things as library window displays, Halloween horror houses, and set designs for staged musical and theatrical performances. For my imagination and creativity in doing these things I drew heavily from the ideas I picked up from the movies I was so impressed with during my childhood. Eventually I was honorably discharged from the Air Force and I moved to New York where I enrolled at Columbia University. As an undergraduate, I tried many disciplines for a concentration and did not find one until I was exposed to film while working as a staff assistant in the technical center of the Film Department. There I was fortunate enough to have the run of the facility, so I took advantage and learned as much as I could about the technical equipment in film production.

I completed my undergraduate and graduate work at Columbia University, and served as the Technical Director of the Graduate Program in Film Studies in the School of Fine Arts, also at Columbia University. Eventually I was appointed as an Associate in Film and taught technical production courses on the graduate level. While at Columbia, I was instrumental in organizing the Community Film Board. This was an open door program at the university that provided free lectures and some hands-on experience in film production to members of the Harlem community who were not registered students. Professor Erik Barnouw who was sensitive to the needs of the community, encouraged the program. The program's significance was that it exposed the university to the Harlem community in a positive and constructive way. There were some ups and downs, though. As might be expected, there were some bad apples among those who came to the program. In fact, a case did occur where two brothers came in and walked off with nearly fifteen thousand dollars' worth of university equipment, claiming that they had liberated the stuff. Efforts to recover the equipment were all in vain. In spite of the setback, we continued with the program, but of course, with less exposure to expensive equipment.

William Greaves is really the backbone of the tradition of African American documentary film. He knew his art well, and was very efficient in raising the necessary funds to write, produce, direct, and distribute his films. Quite a bit of African American documentary material on television was credited to Bill Greaves. He was on the cutting edge of the tradition of the black documentary. And I suspect he is probably responsible for a great deal of the documentary film activities that took place during the civil rights movements. He was, in fact, the progenitor of the television program *Black Journal.*

There were quite a few people involved in bringing the African American image to the television screen in the form of the documentary. Offhand, I remember people like Roland Mitchell, camera and sound person; Peggy Pinn, producer, coordinator of production training; Madeline Anderson, producer and director; Jim Brown, independent filmmaker; and many others who I cannot remember now. Most of these people continued working with *Black Journal* after Tony Brown began hosting the program. Most, in fact all of these activities, were associated with WNET, Channel 13 of New York. Peggy Pinn was responsible for organizing and administering the WNET training program in the nuts and bolts operation of actual cinematography in documentary field production.

All of this was during the period of the civil rights movement and quite a lot of film was shot on the events of those days. The Selma-to-Montgomery March attracted filmmakers from all over. Except for the

WNET African American group, very few African Americans were active in documentary filmmaking in those days. None of the production firms used black technicians in those days.

On *Lois Mailou Jones:* While I was preparing to shoot the documentary on Lois and her paintings, I discovered that there was a major documentary film festival—The Great Art Fest—being held on the mall between the Capitol building and the Washington Monument. The focus of the festival was on classical painters from all over the world. The Art Fest consisted of twelve projectors projecting simultaneously onto twelve screens arranged in a large circle. I went to the Mall and spent nearly five hours walking about from screen to screen looking at film on art. The result is that I decided that my approach to filming Lois would have to be different from anything I saw at the Mall. Most of the films I saw presented the work of the artist through the eyes of friends and or critics. Others were painstakingly crafted with a great deal of details for the eyes of the art student. None were, in my opinion, of the kind that would hold the attention of a random, non-captive audience. I decided, therefore, that my approach would be one that would capture and retain the attention of a broad audience from beginning to end. For these reasons, I elected not to use the standard approach to the documentary. I chose, instead, a non-standard treatment of the subject on film.

At first there was quite a good deal of resistance from Lois Jones because she expected me to do a traditional documentary on her. I finally convinced her to trust me with the project. I was quite certain that film was not the proper medium to show her art for its own sake. The proper way to display art like hers is in a well-lit art gallery. In this way, I also argued that duration and direction of eye movements in appreciating art should be driven entirely by the viewer and not by the subjective movements of the camera as directed by the filmmaker. Showing her art through my camera directions would eclipse that personal experience and diminish the viewer's relation to the art. I, therefore, chose not to make a film about her paintings per se, or about her as a person. Instead the film I made was a combination of the interaction between two artists—the painter and the filmmaker—and how the cross-fertilization of their skills is used to interpret the art work and convey the historical and contemporary significance of Lois Mailou Jones and her work.

On *Burkina Faso: Land of the People of Dignity:* To shoot the film on Burkina Faso, I took two graduate students from our department with me, Ellen Sumter and Steven Cobb. This was going to be a collaborative production between INAFEC (The African Institute for Cinematography Studies) at the University of Ouagadougou, and the Department of Radio, Television, and Film of the School of Communications of Howard University. There were eighteen film students and four faculty members from INAFEC. Two of the faculty members were French. At our very first pre-production meeting one of the French teachers asked: "In America the way you respond to whites is different from the way Africans respond to whites here in Africa; how do you black Americans feel about working with whites like us on such a project?" I immediately knew where that question was taking us so, I replied: "In America, we as blacks do not tolerate any expressed or implied signs of racism or bigotry. If such things are absent while we work together here, then we shall have no problems at all. It is not the biological whiteness that bothers us; it is the notion of supremacy that claims whiteness as its form that we categorically reject. Additionally, if in the course of our working together, you do not betray the revolution of Burkina Faso, then we should have nothing to worry about. If any of these things surface, we will put a screeching halt to our operation. It is as simple as that." That settled matters once and for all. It was a good exchange.

By our first meeting, they had already worked out an approach to shooting the film, which was to be a promotional film on Burkina Faso. A student director had been assigned, and the plot consisted of a standard tourist scheme. Two tourists visiting Burkina Faso were to be filmed as they went from village to village. Little children would come and hold their hands as they guided them through their villages saying, "This is where my mother lives, and this is where my daddy works, etc. . . ." We found the idea to be quite boring, to say the least. Not only that, we were told by one of the French teachers that they had already identified the ideal couple for the film—"They're friends of ours, and they are neither white nor black; they are half-castes." It became clear to us then that we were on totally different tracks. After a lengthy debate, we came up with the idea that we should give the word to the Burkinabe (the people). The new idea that would allow us to drive the film with the words of a griot replaced the initial approach. We also insisted that we (from the U.S.) should not make decisions about where and how to shoot, because we were, after all, outsiders and guests of the Burkinabe. Instead, they were to help guide us through the entire filming process. We would merely provide the technical skills, and become their students as we learned about their country and culture during the course of the production. Eventually a fascinating griot was found in the village of Ouahabou, and we used him to set the direction of the narrative for the entire film. Since there were so many last-minute changes in the entire approach to the shoot, we decided to turn it into a full-blown workshop, which included location scouting and mise-en-scène planning before each shooting sequence. The singular student director was eliminated in favor of a rotating director so that all the students would get a chance to work and make decisions in all key positions. In this sense, the film is not my film. It is the collective work of all the students and that fact is evident in the end product.

Deep down, I truly do not believe in the dichotomy between documentary and fiction film as far as being a filmmaker. One is simply a filmmaker period, and that's what I consider myself to be. I do not favor one over the other. I have worked on both types and on occasion some experimental films as well, like the two films I made without the use of a camera by scratching and painting on black and clear leader. Some people have attempted to pigeonhole me as an animator because of the experimental films. I am not an animator. I will try anything. I will shoot images to match music and vice versa. Whatever appeals to me and whatever is feasible at the time, as long as I have the skills to use the equipment, I will produce something. Like all independent filmmakers I strive to make a film whenever possible. For example, I have a proposal to make a film on the subject of Ethiopians and the African diaspora. Such a film could be done dramatically, or in documentary fashion. If I got enough money, I would do it in a dramatic format. As I said before, this does not mean that I favor the dramatic over the documentary. The documentary requires as much imagination as the feature film. It is, after all, the manipulation of reality in the final analysis. A good manipulator of reality will produce a good documentary film.

I have done both film and video. With video, I am not too much concerned with achieving high standards in aesthetics because the quality of lighting, and things of that nature, do not lend themselves well to the medium unless it is carrying film. In film, on the other hand, I am more sensitive to those aspects. The very nature of the medium and the technical requirements plus the cost differential will determine the attention you give to film. Not being able to immediately see the results of a film shoot forces one to be a lot more careful during production than would be the case in video production. It is all in the technical nature of the two mediums. The argument over video or film is, I think, a pseudo argument. The nature of video lends itself to certain phenomena that do not require that much tedious attention when the image obtained is not less effective than one shot on film. On the other hand, because of its flexibility and greater latitude in handling the image, film will allow more creative manipulation. In the end, it is not a question of one medium over the other but rather a question of the specific task before you. It is a matter of choosing the right medium for the job. I suspect there will continue to be a difference between the two mediums, and that's quite all right. More and more, we are beginning to see greater collaboration between the two mediums precisely because of their unique qualities. I think they are bound to grow symbiotically in the future. I do not believe that one will cancel out the other.

To me, film is the most powerful tool of social influence that man has ever known. I was so much influenced by the dominant motion pictures of Western culture, that, for a while and for all practical purposes, I lost my true cultural orientation and self-identity. For these reasons, I strongly feel the need to wield the power of film to help redress the awful damage done to the image of peoples of non-Western cultures. I hope to help reduce the asymmetry in the way we look at our world today. In my totality as an individual I shall try with whatever I can, and with whomever I can work, to share my life experience as an African through the process of my artistic expressions. I shall try to reach out to whomever in the audience for them to better understand me for what I am, who I am, and where I come from.

DECEMBER 1993
WASHINGTON, D.C.

HAILE GERIMA

When we did *The Wilmington 10*, I looked first, I studied the topography, I didn't care about the facts. Because I said, *60 Minutes* can do a film about guilt and innocence . . . but I wanted to know the cultural context of this whole debate. So we developed an amazing system for that—a way of interviewing. After a few journeys I took to North Carolina, I developed this thing of stoking the fire because I felt black people were like covered fire, and years of ashes has covered this amazing rage. . . . We just wanted the microphone to stare, to just stare at people, even if they didn't say anything that we felt was profound. . . . In telling stories to children, they just stare at you, so we said, "Let's just stare, let's not look like we know the facts. Let's not let these people say what we want them to say. Let them really feel they want to tell us something and it doesn't have to be about the Wilmington 10." Some of them started talking about history. . . . The old women, about 90 years old, on the porch, they were talking—"Oh, you're doing a movie about the Wilmington 10? I'm going to tell you a story about 1898." . . . So they will really throw you off, if you're a premeditated entrapper of the traditional, a conventional documentarian, [an approach] which actually peels away the cultural context. We didn't want to just have a premeditated form and content, and say "Now, fit the people within that context," ... so we had to train in advance how to ask, how to plead, how to stare, how to want more, how to not lead people to where we want them, but just to stare at them.

Those films [like *Child of Resistance* and *Bush Mama*]—when we shot them we didn't want them to look fiction. We felt they should look documentary.... Everything we have to do should be giving the texture of documentary so that people would believe us. Not play, Hollywood play. How does documentary negotiate with audiences, saying "I am not Hollywood, I'm real?" Because at that time Hollywood's slickness meant *unreal, artificial,* and it didn't change people.... There were many films done by Cuba and the liberation movements that were using films as an instrument of social change, so we felt fiction, even if it tried to throw things off, it always had this thing that it was artificial, plastic, unreal—and it's play, and the curtain will come down and everything will be okay. We said, "No, you want the film to be real." I don't know how much we succeeded, but that was our whole premise.

[When I started out to do *Child of Resistance* and *Bush Mama*,] I was disengaging. Having been the most colonized person by Hollywood films, my anger is also personal. I think it dislocated me. So when I hit UCLA I was a very angry man and defensive also, and very apprehensive. I knew that film was a weapon and this I think I got from Ousmane Sembene and the Latin American, the Cuban filmmakers. I didn't even think about audiences then, which was good because sometimes ... we make the prime criterion whether the audience liked the film. It begins to give you a formula slowly; sometimes unconsciously you start to incorporate, to reconsider.... I remember when I was cutting *Harvest: 3000 Years* I threw a split reel at a young French guy who stood by my editing room and said to me, "How long is your film?" I said, "I don't know, two or three hours." He said, "Haile, don't be a fool. If an owner wants to show two movies and your film alone is three hours, then your film is not commercially viable." I just picked up a split reel and threw it at him and we haven't talked since then. I felt violated to be informed of that fact because I didn't care about the audience.

Whatever has happened since the '70s has destroyed this whole idea of critical discussion, and without discussion nothing grows. We're isolated, all of us within the boundaries of our cave, and we make films, and I don't know how much of it is really transforming.

In the UCLA period criticism was in line with search, part of the obsessive search that we set in motion. We were challenging structure. ... There were many different things from different cultural dynamics— Iranians, African Americans, Latinos—and we said, "Why is the formula polluting film schools? . . . Can a structure be non-chronological? Why is Aristotelian always a guideline?" All these questions were making us imperfectly fool around with things. So if somebody is reviewing you [now] without understanding your motives and your goals, they never understood where we failed and where we succeeded. And that's what haunts me. While I'm carrying out what I set in motion and have grown from film to film, what is tragic is that I'm not being confronted from the very premise I depart from. Everyone is still judging my work from a formula or convention that I always wanted to divorce myself from. So that is the tragedy in the end. So while I know I will not change, it doesn't help me grow. During the UCLA period we [young filmmakers] hungered for criticism. That's something I know is the best tradition, but I don't see it now in my students, filmmakers, and film panels, everybody's a landlord, a nobility. There's a territory; everybody has a turf, so nobody is willing to debate and discuss.

Some kids come [to Howard University] and they want to be like Spike [Lee], so you have to work on them and say, "Well, Spike is already sitting on that chair, what is yours? And where are you, who are you? Find out who you are because Spike is already saying, 'No, it's not you, it's me.' You can't have two Spikes in the same place at the same time." But he influenced so many of them wanting to be filmmakers. That was the most positive thing. A lot of people have been seeing his work who have been inspired by him and have come here to film school, but our work is to say, "Who are you, what do you want to do in filmmaking? What are you obsessed by?". . . . Part of the teaching is to find the identity of the filmmaker and to deal with those issues, to say, "Well, for a second, forget about black people, just do it about your grandmother—she's black, so trust it's going to be a black story, but just make a film about your grandmother. . . . What you know completely is about your mother, your father, your grandparents, where you come from, those realities. You express them and then they will be claimed universally."

With [Spike Lee], you can see at least he craves to make films toward the liberation of African American culture. Now, the problem I think he has is how to mediate within the commercial context. He's like one of those jugglers, trying to juggle the social issues with commercialism. I can't be the judge of the success or the failure, but I can see the germ of what we're trying to do in his work. But with most of the other [young black filmmakers], I don't even know where they're coming from— their morality, their disregard of gender, of children, the graphic illustration of violence which is equal to bankruptcy in creative talent. . . . This whole claim of changing society by violating the sanctity of human life . . . Showing anything is easy, but showing without showing is the hardest thing in film work. Showing people fornicating, showing people killing each other, can only violate us as spectators. It doesn't make us hate it, denounce it, or be sensitive to it. So I don't know where that comes from. I don't connect it to the early search of filmmakers who were saying, "Our films have to contribute, to be a part of social change. Society has to be confronted, challenged, within the cultural parameters."

One of the crimes of conventional cinema [is that] it addicted people to certain kinds of spectacle, large violations of the human body, large rape, spectacle. To show rape . . . to me, rape is the hardest thing to photograph—I hate the filming of intimate acts of people. To me, when the audience expects that from you, that's the lowest. At a given point, spectacle cinema has nurtured that side of people. They're so numb now. The worst example is to make a film of a woman getting raped and then to excite the men in the audience. This is the saddest thing that the audience is not walking out from. They continue to go. . . . Some days I'm tempted. I have scripts and letters I get from industry-oriented films, but I don't even go into them. . . . How many thousands of ways would you show a head exploding, and what is the objective: to make people hate violence? No, it doesn't work. I think the most important thing is to show things without violating people.

OCTOBER 1993
WASHINGTON, D.C.

WILLIAM GREAVES

It was as an actor that I first became involved in film in the late 1940s. Actually, I had started out as a dancer and then went into acting. In the course of acting, I became progressively aware of the way in which the motion picture was used to misrepresent the African American. Despite the fact that I had become a featured actor on Broadway, in films and on the radio, white producers still periodically offered me stereotypical or demeaning roles, like "Rochester," and I routinely turned down those kinds of roles. . . . The final straw came when I was cast in a Broadway play with Gloria Swanson, which Jose Ferrer was directing. I hadn't read the play, but I heard the part was that of a Pullman porter. So I said, "All right. I'll play a Pullman porter. Pullman porters are as dignified as other people, sometimes even more so." But then they wanted me to hoke up the part, shuffle and act like Stepin Fetchit, and I quit the show after the second day of rehearsal.

I was very interested in political issues of the time, and I also was studying African history. Understandably, I was in no mood to play the buffoon or any other minstrel show character. Having worked for the black producer William Alexander as a featured actor in his black cast films, I began thinking about getting on the other side of the camera to do films on African and African American history. Right at that time, I was fortunate enough to read *Grierson on Documentary*, by John Grierson. It opened up new possibilities in terms of using film as an educational tool to change society. I was in my early twenties, and it was exciting to think that it would be possible to combine my theatrical skills and my interest in certain social and political issues through filmmaking.

Fortunately, right around that time, I had a featured role in the film *Lost Boundaries*, starring Mel Ferrer, which was produced by [Louis] de Rochement. In a way, he was the granddaddy of American documentary, even more than [Robert] Flaherty because de Rochement made documentary films for any number of non-theatrical organizations early in this century. He also made a number of Hollywood feature films in the '40s and '50s. I was very impressed with what de Rochement was doing and found terrific role models in both him and William Alexander. I decided to try my hand at film. De Rochement was wonderful to me, and allowed me to hang out in his editing room as an apprentice. At the same time, I studied filmmaking at City College here in New York in the evening, with people like Rohama Lee, Leo Seltzer, Arthur Knight and Lewis Jacobs. Hans Richter was then the head of the Film Institute at City College. Mike Roemer, who later on made *Nothing but a Man*, was a young assistant at de Rochement's, and we became friends and chatted about our aspirations to be filmmakers. I also became friends with a Canadian, Lou Applebaum, who did the music for *Lost Boundaries* . . . and talked to Lou about this wonderful place up in Canada called the National Film Board, that I had read about in Grierson's book. I told Lou that I would like to go to the NFB . . . since employment in the film industry in America was closed to me. Given America's hostile racial climate and its special form of apartheid at the time, there was no way that a person of color could work in the unions, could work with the studios, could work anywhere in the system, other than in the black cast films. . . . And there was the Cold War and the whole witch-hunting fever, too, led by [Sen. Joseph] McCarthy. It was a very obnoxious period in America because anyone who wanted America to become a democracy was automatically accused by McCarthy of working for the Soviet Union. Lou, who was on the Film Board's staff, said he would support my desire to go to the National Film Board to apprentice, and so

I applied to the John Hay Whitney Foundation for a fellowship. They turned me down but I went to Canada anyway, as an apprentice without pay at the NFB. I arrived in Ottawa without any money and, after about three or four months of cleaning floors and washing windows and stuff in the evenings, the NFB probably decided that I was really sincere and committed to becoming a filmmaker, and they took me on the staff. I worked at NFB as an assistant editor, a sound editor, an assistant director, an editor, a chief editor, and then a writer and a director. Over a period of eight years, I worked on something like 80 films at the Film Board. It was a fabulous experience. I was assigned to Unit B, and I found myself in this special production unit in the company of filmmaking geniuses like Norman McLaren, Tom Daly, Wolf Koenig, Roman Kroiter, Eldon Rathburn, and Stanley Jackson.

After eight years, I left the NFB to expand the Canadian Drama Studio, which I set up to train actors in the Method, the first time an Actors Studio-type organization was set up in Montreal. I also went to work with a United Nations specialized agency in Montreal, the International Civil Aviation Organization . . . as a public information officer. So in the daytime, I produced films, radio programs, and wrote articles for the agency's magazine. . . . I came back to America in 1963 to join the staff of the United Nations as a producer and director. . . . By then, I had been looking forward to coming back home. It was right around the beginning of the major phase of the civil rights revolution led by Martin Luther King and Malcolm X and all of the other significant leaders, and there were demonstrations and riots all over the place, and the promise of change in America.

There were barely a handful of black documentary filmmakers in America when I arrived in New York. Realistically speaking, it wasn't until 1968, when the television network series *Black Journal* was established, that the whole filmmaking field really began to move for African Americans. I was brought in as executive director and co-host of the series, which was transmitted by National Educational Television, the precursor of PBS, throughout the country. My extensive background in documentary film production was something of an asset to the producer/directors on the *Black Journal* staff, people like St. Clair Bourne, Madeline Anderson, Kent Garrett, Horace Jenkins, and a lot of other aspiring filmmakers who worked on the series.

Black Journal was a public affairs TV series set up by the Carnegie Endowment, the Ford Foundation, and later on, the Corporation for Public Broadcasting, to address one of the problems that the Kerner Commission on Civil Disorders had cited as a major factor in the urban disorders of the 1960s; basically, that the black community had no access to the media, and there was no outlet for it to express its needs and interests in the media. . . . Once *Black Journal* had established a track record as a major network series, other local stations started producing black shows all across the country patterned after the *Black Journal* format. We had four or five crews shooting at any one time all over the country, and even sent crews to Africa and Southeast Asia. Unfortunately, there has never been another black-controlled public affairs network series in the history of television since *Black Journal* that is concerned with the black experience in America. On the other hand, there have been thousands of "white" public affairs journals in network television since the dawn of TV.

We set up a *Black Journal* training school. Aspiring filmmakers from all over the city, largely Latinos and African Americans, studied the craft there and worked on the series as apprentices on our various crews. A number of these young people went on to become filmmakers. . . . The *Black Journal* Training School later became the National Education Television Film School.

We had to develop programming that would resonate within the black community, and one of the concepts that I used as a sounding board or "filter" in developing the monthly programs was that legendary cultural institution, the black barbershop. It seemed to me that the kinds of issues that are routinely discussed in a black barbershop provided excellent stimulation for our programming decisions. The producers and I would sit around . . . the table . . . and start kicking ideas around . . . and I would process them through my memories of the barbershop that I used to go to in Harlem as a kid, and that would help me to decide whether it was a "go" or a "no go" on a particular project the producers would propose to me.

From a black perspective, documentary films are films that agitate in the tradition of our leaders like Frederick Douglass. They investigate, expose and attempt to socially engineer change, and, of course, they provide positive role models. One could say they are usually activist, advocacy-oriented productions, weapons in the struggle for freedom, dignity, equality, liberation, self-expression, and human rights.

SEPTEMBER 1991
NEW YORK, NEW YORK

CHARLES HOBSON

I think one of the reasons that my name, and a few other names, don't come out quite as much in the "maker" discussion is because a lot of people don't understand the role of the producer. There are producers, writers, editors—very often documentary film editors are the major contributors because they take a lot material and sort of string it together. So very often the producer is seen as an entrepreneur and deal-maker. Unless, sometimes it's true, but when the documentary role is certainly non-profit, we all struggle. But the producers play a very important role in shaping the segment or program or series of programs.

I was born in Brooklyn, West Indian background, Jamaican parents, spent some time in Jamaica. My mother was actually raised in Cuba although born in Jamaica, so I had that kind of perspective. I was not a great student but I read Langston Hughes when I was in the sixth grade and from the sixth grade on, from that time on, I read every African American writer I could find. I used to make a pest of myself at the local library. As I went on to high school and college, again a rather mediocre student. . . . I studied for a master's in American studies. I knew a lot but not from a sense of a scholar but from the views of an enthusiast. I knew a lot about black literature, I was just fascinated. I then got to produce on WBAI Pacifica Radio and actually some other programs which were broadcast nationally.

I was riding around in my little red Porsche convertible and I used to listen to WBAI and they had a program on gospel. I wrote a letter to the program director saying, "This is the most uninteresting, mediocre gospel I've ever heard." I was Episcopalian, from the West Indies, I wasn't a Baptist, so I came to gospel in sort of an intellectual way. The program director at WBAI called me in and he said, "Do you have better ideas," so I said, "Yes." Then he said, "Why don't you do a pilot for us, a couple of them." So that went on for several years even though I just did these shows. In 1964 I was written up in *Variety*, I think his name was Bill Grealy and he is deceased now and meanwhile I never thought anybody listened to these programs except my mother and girlfriend; well, maybe just my girlfriend. Every year I did a "Black Christmas," holiday songs by black R & B artists. *Variety* did this huge write-up, I didn't even know who *Variety* was at the time.

I then got to produce on WBAI Pacifica Radio and actually some other programs that were broadcast nationally. In fact, one of the things that I produced during that time was a documentary on Paul Robeson —when at the whisper of Paul Robeson's name, people would leave the room. It's a program that Pacifica still runs although it was done almost 30 years ago. I was hired to be the writer of a new program being sponsored by Channel 5 here in New York at the time, Metro-Media, on the black community of Bedford-Stuyvesant. This was perhaps *the* first community television program produced by, for, and about African Americans. I was hired by Channel 5 to be the writer of this program largely because of the same reason I got the job at Pacifica, largely because of my knowledge at the time of African American issues. It wasn't because of my broadcast knowledge and for me it was great. I was a big Chester Himes fan, many of the others, Richard Wright, Langston Hughes, Walter White. I just read everything I could find.

I've been producing television programs and films for the last 25 years about the culture. I did the *Inside Bedford-Stuyvesant* and then I was called by WNET, NET at the time, to come in and be a part of this *Black Journal* program. I did a program on Pacifica radio for about a year, called *Review of the Black Press*. I would get maybe twenty, twenty-five of the major black papers and look for stories that you wouldn't find anyplace else or slants on stories that you wouldn't find anyplace else. I was then going to *Black Journal* to do a segment on the black press, so they hired me. I was going to do an on-camera segment. I think Bill [Greaves] was going to be the host. I was asked to write this segment about the black press and produce it. It was very exciting for me and I was also associate producer on the tape. I was having a great time because I liked television and traveling, doing things. But I did notice that the structure of the program made a number of people uncomfortable because basically all of the producers were white and the blacks on the staff were the assistants to the white producers and there was some discontent.

Al Perlmutter was the executive producer who really ran it. Al is still around. Don Dixon represented the station. The blacks wanted more involvement. They responded by making me a producer because then I was actually the producer of the black press segment. I should point out that when I got into this area, I always wanted to be a writer. I wanted to be like Langston Hughes and write short stories or a novel; then, of course, Chester Himes. At some point I learned that wasn't where my career was heading. So I refused—I said I'd rather not be on camera. I don't see how you can be a producer and be on camera. Some do it, but I felt that way because so much of what happens is behind the scenes. I'm a low-key kind of person. The relations got very difficult with the station and the group decided, "We're going to go on strike."

I didn't have any real reason, because they [WNET] were taking care of me, but I went out nevertheless with the strike for support. When we got to the press, I was somehow designated the spokesman. I guess I was maybe three, four years older than the others. There were intense negotiations with the station. I felt the station was hypocritical in its dealings with us—it didn't have a leg to stand on. There were some bitter exchanges. They were particularly mad at me, I felt, because I was the spokesperson, one, and secondly I was the producer. They had promoted me.

During this bitter confrontation I got a phone call from Hal Jackson. A very important black figure in radio, one of the first, if not the first black DJ, very interesting guy. Hal called . . . and said, "I think there's a job at ABC. They're looking for a black producer." So I came in for a meeting. Again, this was the '60s. I thought, "I'm smart, I'm the man." They approached me and I said, "Yeah, I'd be interested, I think I could do this with what I've done." So I became the producer of *Like It Is*, which is still on the air winning Emmys. I was producer/writer for that program. There was a settlement and the striking people went back.

The producer of *Like It Is* called it *The Way It Is* because, he said, "*Like It Is* isn't grammatically correct." So, he actually produced about three of the programs and then they brought me in and of course Gil Noble who was, again, very important. I said, "That's ridiculous," so I changed it to *Like It Is*. The shame of it is for me, ABC destroyed a lot of the *Like It Is* programs because they were cumbersome, too much videotape. A couple of them are at the Schomburg but I don't really have many of the programs. I went to *Like It Is* which is a part of ABC news. I was working within a conservative station and I was producing radical, really radical programming. It was just a local black program, but we were part of ABC news. What that gave me was access to local crews, editing facilities, so I had to work within a really literally racist, technical, white infrastructure. I heard racist remarks in the studio. Here I am bringing in Rap Brown, who is talking about "whiteys," "kill whitey dogs" and the director is asking the lighting guy, "Let's do that again because the sound wasn't right."

The four years that I produced it—I think I'm a very good producer—I was able to manipulate the bureaucracy, so I had excellent footage, I had crews . . . sometimes I would have six or seven documentaries going at the same time in production. We did everything. We did a piece on the black opera company, on young filmmakers. A guy I learned so much from—I think about this guy all the time—was an editor. An older, Lou Lapidus, conservative man from New Jersey, he was such a perfectionist with film, even though he said, "I don't agree with this garbage this guy is saying," but he would really care about it and his assistant editor Saul—I think Saul is still there—was also very, very diligent about what they did. [They were] very good at their jobs.

Every time I'd go into the studio I always wore my old Brooks Brothers suit, and I had a certain kind of manner, non-confrontational. I liked people. It was tough obviously to survive that. I think, 1968, both Gil and I won a New York Emmy. What happened was amazing. All of a sudden the technicians began to respect us. Although they didn't agree with the message, they respected the fact that we were producing this show, and it was one of the best shows coming out of that shop. There's always some disgruntled people, but generally they were very cooperative. Finally there was a working-class Italian guy, Dan Fanelli, and he came in and they assigned him to the show as a director. There were various directors. Dan became totally devoted to it. They interviewed me a couple of years ago for my contributions to *Like It Is* and ABC and about a series I did for the BBC called *The Africans,* and most of the people were still there.

I was actually Geraldo Rivera's producer. Not many people know this, but Geraldo Rivera went to Columbia Law School. After Law School he came to ABC as an intern in the news department and they had him do pieces. He did a piece about drugs in Harlem that was so controversial that they wouldn't put it on the air. I found out about it and I said, "Geraldo, I'll put it on *Like It Is.*" So we re-cut it . . . and it was so good that the news department then re-cut, and then after I ran it, they put it on. So I feel like I had something to do with the early stages of his career. Then management was trying to get back into *Like It Is* and tone it down or keep Gil in his place. They finally brought Geraldo on as the co-host of *Like It Is* for about six months.

Gil Noble was hosting it then. Geraldo wasn't very good on that program because he was more show business than the show required but they were the bosses. There were *Like It Is* programs I did, things that I was proud of: a one hour documentary on *Marcus Garvey,* the *Malcolm X* documentary which Gil and I had some dispute over.

Pioneer filmmaker Oscar Micheaux's work as an artist is very important, but how did he raise that money? The business is a business of entrepreneurs. It still is today so I know how hard it is to get projects off the ground. Getting the money meant coming in on budget and not using or abusing your expense account, adhering to all the basics and I had to learn on the job. We were doing a range of things and management trusted me, even though the police would call and screen our program on the Panthers. I had death threats in the mail: "These niggers are doing *Like It Is,* you're a dead producer, you're dead" kind of thing. As I said, they never had a picket sign, never had a group out there, and they knew it. They knew I was highly respected in the community even though I wouldn't wear a dashiki. I wore my round glasses, my Brooks Brothers, my Burberrys when I could afford it: you know, I wanted to be English. But my strongest interest was in black culture . . . not English culture, and this passion for Africa and black heritage helped to shape my life forever. Years later (1983–1986) I did get to live in the UK and work for the BBC. Making black programs, of course.

I decided I wanted to leave New York and I wanted to do some other things, I wanted to write. Tony Brown was brought in as the host of *Black Journal*. Tony was on the other side when he came in because he was this guy from Detroit and he came out of the blue. Tony Brown was an inspiration in a way. He was a producer of *Black Journal*, but he was also head of the School of Communications at Howard University, which had a major School of Communications. I kind of liked that idea—school, students. I was offered the job as head of the School of Communications at Clark/Atlanta University Center and my fiancée at the time was from Atlanta, an old Atlanta family, and we would have some links there. I was getting sick of New York even though I was born and raised here.

I love the feeling and the experience of talking about an idea, and one day you meet someone, and you do the research, and how many years later it becomes something you see on the screen. How you get through the politics and how you raise the money. The business side is very important, how to deal, how to find an option. I do follow the financial news. I'm interested in the markets and how they work, computers and making all those connections. I haven't done anything in my life as bold as Micheaux or probably as important, but that's a tradition that has be recognized.

I think to be a documentarian is a good answer. When I did the radio program for WBAI, I had basically three areas of music I explored: gospel music, especially the male quartet; rhythm and blues, again the quartets, the early do-wop groups; and calypso, which I think is a very important form of music, which still hasn't quite gotten recognized as a literary form. It's a brilliant form, but for cultural reasons hasn't gone as far as reggae, totally different music. Those are areas of music that even the hippest whites didn't know about at the time. I was interested in programs or subject matter about the black experience that whites in general, whites and some blacks, didn't get from reading the white press and that was really documenting them. Making film, that's what I tried to do.

MARCH 1995
NEW YORK, NEW YORK

WARRINGTON HUDLIN

In *cinéma vérité* documentaries there's nothing more exciting than going in and not knowing what you're going to get. Anything can happen. . . . And then it's just a matter of chipping away, the same way a sculptor would take a block of stone, with this mass of raw footage.

You chip away to find the story. [In *Street Corner Stories*] I was interested in drawing a parallel between blues as a musical form and blues as a mode of storytelling. So, I chose those stories that had blues values. By blues values I mean stories that showed the speaker's toughness of spirit and ability to transcend, not through any kind of happy ending or resolution or philosophy, but rather the will to persevere.

What really came out in *Street Corner Stories* is that people know what the importance and value of their lives are, and when the camera points to them, it's amazing how people immediately go to what's special about themselves.

[*Street Corner Stories*] ended up being broadcast, but it was very controversial. As I recall, there was an internal split [at WNET in New York]. And, as the legend goes, a black security guard who was peeking through the window and saw it, came in and said, "That's the best movie I've ever seen." Everybody said, "Really? You liked it?" "Yeah." And oftentimes I would show my film in very upscale circumstances, like at the Philadelphia Afro-American Museum. The people in the audience were all prim and proper, and did not really enjoy the movie, while the guy who was sweeping up or was in charge of security really thought it was very, very funny and engaging. So the movie can either clash with or confirm your sense of yourself.

I think that folklorists regard African Americans who make films as rabbits turned poacher—we're supposed to be in front of the camera and not behind it—and I've never found them to be friendly or hospitable.

At the time when I was trying to raise money through those [white controlled] sources, they were funding very alienated art about people who lived in homogeneous neighborhoods, who had no real community base for their films, but yet had a whole support infrastructure. They had places they could show the films regularly even though only ten people would come to see them. They had financing, they had exhibition, even though it was just alienated art with a very limited audience.

The best documentarians are those who go beyond getting the situation and the logical understanding of the people, and can get not only that but the emotional context in a *cinéma vérité* situation. Those are the people I really admire, people who can get people to act, not just to talk about it. That's easy to do, frankly, but what's hard is for them to act openly where exposure could be a possible embarrassment. And at this point, I think I really haven't seen too many Americans do that. I think it's because in America people are still scared. They're scared of emotion, anyhow, and also they're scared of putting out an emotional film which may, they think, scare the audience. Which in reality it probably wouldn't, and if it does, so what? That's what your job is.

JULY 1992
INDIANAPOLIS, INDIANA

ISAAC JULIEN

Basically the inception of *Looking for Langston* [1989] had to do with trying to document the past. It's a documentary of a different kind, call it a "film essay." The kind of filmmakers I was thinking of in relationship to *Looking for Langston* were, for example, Chris Marker who made *Sans Soleil* [1982]. Also I was thinking of other filmmakers such as Jean Cocteau [*Blood of a Poet*, 1930], Kenneth Anger, or Jean Genet [*Chant d'Amor*, 1950]. Pictorially, I was thinking of photographers who documented African American life such as [James] Van Der Zee. I didn't want to make a talking head documentary, but had wrestled with the idea for a long time of interviewing people, such as Camille Billops, who were witnesses and knew people from that period. They weren't actually in the end in the film because I really couldn't afford to shoot it in New York. We didn't have that kind of budget [$150,000].

Retrospectively it was a good thing that the budget was limited because that dictated the aesthetic strategy behind *Looking for Langston*, which was to create a "document" rather than a documentary. In a way the problem of trying to make *Looking for Langston* was a problem of documentary itself, which is that you couldn't rely on people giving you information ("talking heads" format) about certain moments because of questions of self-censorship around sexuality. During our research, we spoke to an ex-lover of Langston Hughes in Paris. We contacted friends of Langston Hughes in New York, and they were not interested in talking to us. If they did speak to us they certainly were not interested in being filmed. So one had to respect that. During this process you had to say to yourself, "Well, if I can't embark on that strategy, then really what I should try to do is to create an alternative way to document what my version of those historical moments would have been like." So we began research on archival material (found footage). A film like *Handsworth Songs* [1986] by the Black Audio Film Collective created a way of reusing archive, but in a slightly more transgressive way. I enjoyed the way archive is used in films like *Before Stonewall* [1985]. In a way those documentaries, *Handsworth Songs*, *Before Stonewall*, helped me find a cinematic language to express visually my experiences and thus helped me to document this imaginary '20s lifestyle in Harlem. The archive then became an extremely important visual strategy in making *Looking for*

Langston, whether it was photographic archive as a reference for the construction of visual iconography and mise-en-scène, [or] whether it was archive in terms of radio announcements, such as Langston Hughes's death. I had access to archival material from St. Clair Bourne's research-er, Minda Novak, which was an immense help, because after I saw St. Clair Bourne's *Langston Hughes: The Dreamkeeper* [1988], I thought, "Great, now I really don't have to do that kind of documentary." Instead, I could use archive in a different way.

During 1987 to 1988, my partner was teaching at NYU in Cinema Studies with Annette Michelson, and he undertook the main archival research. So we went to MoMA and we looked at all the films with Bill Sloan—jazz films, Bessie Smith's film [*The St. Louis Blues,* 1929]. We saw Pearl Bowser, and we looked at several films of Oscar Micheaux. We met Donna Van Der Zee and Roy DeCarava, and asked if their photographs could be in the film. That was a real task, sitting down talking to them. I tried to be as straightforward as possible about what I was doing, but I feared they wouldn't let me have access to their work if I described in detail the homoerotic aspect of the film. We figured they would prob-ably like the film, appreciate it aesthetically, but they wouldn't like it as a text. We looked at Van Der Zee photographs at the Schomburg. And then getting all the archive material, showing it to the cinematogra-pher [Nina Kellgren], to the production designer and art director [Derek Brown], I said, "This is what the film has to look like." Then to the cos-tume designer [Robert Woolery], and then all those things just got con-structed and the locations and interiors were treated in a similar fash-ion—everything had to be period as well. And with the art of black and white photography, it would marry all the elements together visually in terms of a period look.

The controversy began when we wrote a letter to the Hughes estate and we showed them the film. We knew that we were going to have to deal with this sometime. We had secured the rights for everything in the British Commonwealth, but not the United States Then we had various negotiations, and it was through those negotiations that we came up with the U.S. version of the film. They wanted every visual and textual reference to Hughes to be taken out. We in Sankofa really objected, but I thought, "Well, compromise," but we wanted to keep the Hughes foot-age in. I just thought, "It's not [the estate's] copyright because it's NBC footage." We had a contract from [David] Chertok, the archivist and he claimed we could use this. "It's public domain." That was the argument. But the poetry wasn't public domain—we found out later. So then the New York Film Festival decided to show the film and then we had Lin-coln Center lawyers behind us. They said the estate couldn't stop us from showing the film because you can quote lines from poems under fair usage, but you can only do that if you don't quote a whole poem. The problem was that the two clips of Hughes reciting his poem, "Ballad of a Fortune Teller," from the archive, used in the film constituted a whole poem. So they got us really, and all that transpired in between with me flying from London to New York for its festival screening—the Lincoln Center lawyer advised me to censor the sound at the point we would hear Hughes's poem the second time at the end of the film, which was really odd because I think they could have just actually shown the film in its entirety. They had the power to do it, and, in a sense it was strange that that never took place.

Essentially, this was a case of using copyright infringement as a form of censorship, but after the Lincoln Center screening, it just created more interest. Jackie Renal who then had the Bleeker Street Cinema in the Village wanted to show it and so it had a small run there, with only one screening a night, at 10 o'clock, for about two months. The point that it was shown at theater halls was important. I had several conversations with the late George Bass, executor of the Hughes estate, and he just kept saying, "Why Langston Hughes? Why not 'Looking for Jimmy'? [Baldwin]." The whole point to me was to give a picture or image of certain silences to visualize the "closet." Because James Baldwin was "out," it really would have contradicted my intentions.

Black and White and Color was another archival project, which was made in 1992 for the BBC and the British Film Institute coming out of a race and ethnicity research project. It basically grew out of five years of archival work conducted by BFI Television. The last time I made a documentary film was *The Darker Side of Black* [1994]. I've resisted the notion of wanting to make conventional documentaries, but *The Darker Side of Black* is the most conventional documentary I've ever made. But friends who are critics have said it's not *really* that conventional. It's not conventional by, I suppose, American PBS standards. People will still look at this documentary and think it's a bit unusual. It's got visual tableau motif scenes which are recurring. I'm very interested in the idea of mixing documentary and fiction, because I see documentary as fictional work anyway.

The Darker Side of Black is very visual, but it's not really as visual as I'd like it to be. That has to do with time to a certain degree, because *Looking for Langston* took up a lot of time doing research, and it was made under certain favorable conditions. The workshops in a way secured a certain way of working which has gone now; they were created by documentary filmmakers who were socialists and who had made films collectively in the '70s and '80s, and they wanted to work in a particular way. It was called an "integrated practice" which included ex-

hibitions, distribution of your work, and basically funding for a program of work, not just for the product—for Channel 4. So what that
meant was that you could submit a program of work and use funds for
three to four years because you had an agreement. Then you would start
your development one year, and then maybe get the budget for shooting it the next year, as well as being paid a wage. You had a whole year
to develop something, and that was really the main difference. Now, for
example, I was commissioned to make *The Darker Side of Black*, in August 1994. I finished it in February 1995, and it was broadcast in the same
month. So, you know, it was very different working conditions.

I think I have to find a way of doing it cheap. And I think that the way
you have to do it is to get something like a Rockefeller. Something that
can last so that you have space to write the script, go to different places
to research, and after all that work, do a very strong original script. Then
you can apply for the production money, and then you can shoot it. It
really is a question of development. What happens in the more conventional way is that the development period is squashed so that you don't
have the time to think of a different visual strategy.

* * *

Marlon Riggs's *Color Adjustment* showed with my film *Black and
White and Color* [in 1992] on the BBC in series together. That shows how
much his project works on a similar sort of terrain of inquiry. When
I first met Marlon, actually I'd heard there was a black gay filmmaker
and of course being someone who's gay myself and makes films around
racial representation, I was very interested. And the thing is, obviously
the function of knowledge, epistemologically speaking, is gossip. It's
very present among gay circles in the diaspora. And someone says to
me, "Marlon Riggs is gay. He made that other film about race on prime
time television, *Ethnic Notions*." I went, "Right, okay." And then I heard
through the black gay diasporian grapevine that he had seen *Looking for
Langston* and that he had been so influenced by it that he was going to
make a film about being black and gay himself.

The first controversy over *Tongues Untied* was an exchange of letters which took place in the *Gay Community News* over Marlon's having a white lover and whether this contradicted the message in his film.
So, Marlon had a screening of *Tongues Untied* and his mother, who was
based in Germany, traveled to meet him. The film was really very well
received. She was wonderful and really supportive of him. The audience were really pleased, because I think on one level that people
thought *Looking for Langston* was really very beautiful and aesthetic. But
Tongues Untied was in a way, sort of tougher, portraying the contemporary African American gay experience. It was always going to be a

compare-and-contrast, which I didn't mind because it was a tough film. I remember seeing it the first time and thinking, "Wow!" And in a way I suppose it's the only other film that I've ever seen which has reflected back to me my own experience and anxieties and predicaments, although it's different obviously because it's an African American experience. Mine is a black European experience. But I think at the same time it really spoke to me very directly. I was moved by the film, and I remember thinking, "Oh my god, yes, he's speaking a regime of truth here, the truth of our experiences as black gay men growing up and 'coming out' into white gay communities and the black communities."

I go to different film festivals around the world and, first of all, everybody knows about *Tongues Untied*. I just got back from South Africa, the first gay and lesbian film festival in South Africa, and I also was in Paris at the American Centre. Wherever I go people know of *Tongues Untied* and know of Marlon Riggs—his influence is phenomenal. Also one of the things which I'm glad to say is happening is that there's a whole new generation of black gay and lesbian filmmakers. Obviously filmmakers such as [Rose Troche] the director of *Go Fish* [1994], also Cheryl Dunye, Charles Lofton, Inge Blackman, and Tom Harris. From Chicago, Yvonne Welbon. There's a whole community of black lesbian filmmakers in Chicago. There's also a group of black gay filmmakers in Philadelphia as well. In England also there are younger black gay filmmakers. Obviously the question is, "How much access will they get to the means of production?" But even out of the mere existence of another generation there will always be a black gay and lesbian presence. The area of work where it's happening now is mainly in video; for example, Thomas Harris, it's very exciting, but marginalized because of the format. So that's why we don't maybe see it and hear about it in the same sort of way. But it's very alive and well. For example, if you go to the Gay and Lesbian Experimental Film Festival in New York, that's where you're going to see that work. So there's definitely a sort of legacy that Marlon has created. It will be very interesting to see how it develops into the late 90s.

* * *

Lord Scarman, who made an inquiry into the 1981 [race] riots in Britain [felt] there were really too many disenfranchised voices excluded from the mainstream institutions in British society. Channel 4 was actually created to represent those disenfranchised voices, and it was meant to be very different from the other broadcast institutions such as the BBC. It was for innovation and experimentation. And so I think that, combined with the policies of the Greater London Council, which actually encouraged the idea of a multi-cultural, multi-racial citizenship that London is, and for that to be reflected in the arts, you then had a second generation of black young people coming through various film schools, and universities, and art schools. In a way you met with the 1981 riots a second generation of young black people who sort of rose up against the prevailing conditions and the relations between police and the societal injustices. I think that situation created an institutional response and I think we were then able to respond. You had a certain amount of good will on the part of a number of black filmmakers who wanted to develop film and video workshops to create a space to make an intervention of a different kind. I think making that intervention meant that you wanted to make films which had some longevity and that would actually exist both in and outside of television.

So, the project was quite ambitious; it created a space for groups like Sankofa to come through, and the Black Audio Film Collective and other individual filmmakers like Pratibha Parmar. In New York you had people like Ruby Rich, who was head of the New York State Council on the Arts [Film Program], who is quite responsible for the new queer cinema. I mean she wrote a manifesto. She really pushed for lots of things. She funded a lot of new queer cinema. She funded the "Show the Right Thing" conference at NYU in 1991. She really initiated incredible things; with NYSCA you have another public funding source on the East Coast putting money into the arts, along with other art institutions. Also in the beginning of the '80s and the mid-'80s you see this whole explosion in gay culture taking place as well, obviously represented by [photographer Robert] Mapplethorpe—a whole shift. At the same time this is happening there's the AIDS crisis, and I think that crisis produced a political, artistic response. I think from all those different moments— the 1981 riots, the AIDS crisis, the explosion of cultural expression in response to those things—I think that's what created the fertile ground for the moment where you have different voices which come through in response to what's happening. I think also there are initiatives like Third World Newsreel, and Coco Fusco doing the *Young, British and Black* program, and that actually being seen by lots of people here in Soho, in New York. I think it was the first time that white avant-garde artists had thought about a consciousness around racism, race and representation, and avant-garde practices. And also it was in a form that was interested in challenging the idea of narrative cinema—it was experimental. And so I think that was postmodern. I remember the first screening of *Young, British, and Black.*

We had bell hooks, Cornel West, Barbara Kruger, Craig Owens, Simon Watney all in the same room, so you really had this sort of diasporian art world thing taking place. Of course, I think with work being available for people to hire, it was then made accessible to an American audience through the efforts of Coco Fusco and Third World Newsreel. You also had critics like Kobena Mercer finishing his Ph.D. and then getting a job to teach at [the University of California at] Santa Cruz, and then his meeting Marlon Riggs. I had also done quite a lot of work with Kobena Mercer for *Screen Magazine* [1988] prior to his leaving England. Things like that created a [black Atlantic] cultural exchange.

The number of people involved was extremely small. That's why Marlon's death is such a loss. That's the thing that's so depressing. To a certain extent one of the things I've been struck by very much, being in America is that obviously questions of class play a great deal in who gets to produce culture, work, and art. It does in Britain as well, but I think because of the '60s, because of the way the educational system is structured, you can go to art school. You have access to that as someone who comes from a black working-class background like myself. Obviously, Marlon would probably have to come from a certain background to be able to make the sort of intervention that he did. That's why I wonder a lot about him, because if I go out to gay clubs in New York, there's a very, very big black gay and lesbian subculture, but you don't see that in the cultural space. In America, the number of people who are in the business of making critical/political art, or making cultural work that is black and gay in content, is not that big. That's one of the things that I was struck by. In the British context, although there isn't a marketplace, although people are making things under very meager resources, it just feels that there's a lot of people doing that work. Also it probably has to do with the fact that it's Europe; it's London where you basically don't have things so defined by the marketplace only, although that's becoming less and less the case.

In Sankofa we were very highly aware of African American filmmakers. We knew Charles Burnett and Julie Dash's work. We'd seen their films. We invited Kathleen Collins to show her film *Losing Ground* [1982] at a film screening program we'd organized in Sankofa. We knew Haile Gerima. We'd met them because of the Third Eye Cinema Festival organized by June Giavanni and Pratibha Parmer, at the now defunct Greater London Council. We'd met Bill Gunn, Med Hondo and also seen their films.

We knew documentarians like Bill Greaves. We looked up to African American culture. And we looked to African American independent cinema for inspiration, particularly Charles Burnett and Julie Dash as the exemplars of the kind of work we'd like to do. I think it's about absence and "lack" of an authentic black independent British film practice. Actually in an odd sort of way, making *Black and White and Color*, we found out about a few black British independent filmmakers who came before us, such as Jamaican Lloyd Gardner who worked in Britain. But we very much looked toward African America cinema because that's where, to us, the exciting things were. I think I've got a more pragmatic, a more realistic view now, but I think then it was much more utopian.

SEPTEMBER 1994
NEW YORK, NEW YORK

WILLIAM MILES

It took 12 years to do *Men of Bronze.* That history was on a table [in the 369th Armory in Harlem], gathering dust. . . . The door was locked, and there were these photographs and manuscripts and captured weapons. I happened to be going up on the elevator one day, and the elevator stopped off on the second floor and the door opened up as a guy was coming out of this room. I looked over and I said, "Hey, what is that?" "It's the unit's library." I said, "How do you get in?" And, he said, "You don't," and he closed the door in my face and said, "They don't allow anybody in there. They don't want anybody to mess it up." . . .

I'm the curious type, and it bothered me that here I was in this outfit not knowing it had that type of history and it was locked up for safekeeping. So I said why don't I start the 369th historical committee, and maybe they'd give me access to the library? I had this young lieutenant named Nathaniel James, who wrote a letter to the commander, and then they said, "Yes, you can do that, but only on your own time, not while you're doing duty hours." The guy with the key was always missing during that time. So we got this other guy to talk to the commander. "You know, we're having these visitors come down from Albany and Washington; it would be nice if we could show them a display of the Unit's history, and these two guys here want to do it." So they gave us the key. So, we get in this room, and you see the folders curling up, the knotted up frames just scattered all over, scrapbooks and stuff. And after months and months of just looking through this stuff, I said to myself, what would happen if you took all that information and put it on the screen? Well, [support] seems to come in various ways. When I was doing *Men of Bronze*, there was a little lady in Arkansas. Now, you have to understand I was trying to produce that film during the bicentennial, where Americana was everywhere, right? So, I figured, this project is more American than America. I couldn't get a dime. Dick Adams, my old buddy . . . shot the entire thing with no money. . . . He happens to run into this lady, and told her the story about it, and she went to her bank to withdraw $30,000 out of the bank to loan me to do the film, and the president of the bank asked her, "Why are you doing this?" She told him the story, and he said, "No, no, we'll loan him the money." So, there was an article about this black guy in New York City who's doing a film about an all-black regiment in World War I, and this bank was supporting the effort. And, I said, "Now, isn't this wild? Arkansas."

You know, every time you see these Harlem films it is the same footage that seems to be shown, and there's a name, "Ed Lewis." So, like who's Ed Lewis? I found him, living in a little apartment with three television sets. He went bankrupt, and everybody assumed he had died. . . . This guy started when D. W. Griffith was doing his *The Birth of a Nation*. He said he had met Griffith in the elevator, and he said to him, "Mr. Griffith, I want to make films. Can you suggest something?" And, he said, "Well, I'm going up towards 57th Street and 7th Avenue, walk with me and I'll tell you." So, he was walking with [Griffith] and he said, "Look, make sure that you get wide shots, long shots, and extreme close-ups. That's the key to it." And, [Lewis] said, "Oh great," and he ran off and bought a camera. . . . He used to do something called "Negroes in Sports," and he covered some of the guys who became legends. Josh Gibson, the baseball player, who everybody claims, "Oh man, he would make Babe Ruth look like nothing." . . . He did Joe Louis. . . . Somehow he convinced the Loew's Victoria, which was on 125th Street, to let him play one of his shorts as an extra. And, more people went to see that extra than the main feature.

His stuff is all over the place. If you look at any Harlem documentary you'll find his material. . . . Everybody's got a little piece, but what happened to the rest of it? If he had not documented those things that he did, *I Remember Harlem* wouldn't have been possible, because I found out that it was his footage that was being utilized, and everybody laid claim to it. But then I found, in the Library of Congress, a list of the things that he had made, and boy, if anybody could find at least 50 percent of those titles, it's a gold mine, in a way, because it's the [Marcus] Garvey stuff.

Here's one for the books: I had been telling everybody about *Black Stars in Orbit* for two years. . . . At the last moment I was asked to change the title, and then I asked the question, "Why?" And, "Well, it sounds too confusing. Think about it." I thought about it and dismissed the whole idea. And then I get this call in which they're saying somebody from Washington, PBS, wanted the title changed. I asked who was it? Could I speak to him? They wouldn't give me the person's name, and that started to get to me. Now, I understand pressure. . . . I owe these bills, and they're holding the check. So, what do you do? Change the title and everybody would go away happy, except me. And so, I came back and they asked me again, had I changed it? And I said, "Okay, I'll change it." They jumped up and down, and then they said, "Get in touch with PI so they can come out with the press releases. And, by the way, what's the new title?" So I said, "Well, if you don't like *Black Stars in Orbit*, let's go for *From Slave Ship to Space Ship*," and they said, "no!" So they didn't change the title.

I think it isn't the camera person. I think its the person that's on camera, that's actually being seen, whether it's men or women who have these stories. To me their stories are more important than angles. I'm not into angles. People think you gotta do that type of thing, and some guys do. I think the story's coming out has to do it for me, and there's something about eyes. I'm always fascinated by eyes. It's telling tales out of your eyes.

JUNE 1992
NEW YORK, NEW YORK

CARLTON MOSS

I see myself coming out of the tradition of the Federal Theater, where it turned to the community and allowed people to do things that reflected their life without having to submit to their enemies to get approval. [Tom] Pounds—he's a student of Cripps—developed this thesis, that it's impossible for black films to express the black experience without relating to the oppression that blacks have been under, that's within the experience. And if you don't deal with that, then you don't have a story that reflects the life. And he's doing a thing on current films. We find now with all these kids that have gone to [film] school, it's very difficult to get them to make anything that deals with the community unless it's commercial. And the people who decide whether it's commercial are not community people. They would talk about justice, but they're not mature enough, developed enough to relate it to why there isn't justice, the social causes. And the one reason for that is that they're cut out of the planning. They have nothing to do with the planning. And they don't take advantage of what is there. And the other big thing is that they do not have any communication with other people who are doing that. See, when Magic Johnson plays basketball, he plays with [Larry] Bird. And they talk. And in talking, they talk basketball, but if you keep it outside of that, then you build up resistance to the other guy.

"Well, that white guy didn't want to tell me." You have the same sort of thing with these kids, they have as far as we can see, no identification with other people who are doing it.

When I first came out here, after making *The Negro Soldier*, in a genuine way all of the guys that I had been associated with said, "Look, we're going to get you a job." So I said "Well, all right." I couldn't turn this down. They arranged an interview with me to go see these guys who were making *Pinky*. Some of the guys who were in the army had come out of the Film and Photo League in New York. And they had an identification with the social progress of the country and that included this minority. So what they did, they made it easy that I had this contact with them. And one of them started, two of them started a documentary company, educational company. And they said, "Look, you can come and work with us." That's how it started.

JANUARY 1992
LOS ANGELES, CALIFORNIA

MICHELLE PARKERSON

My knowledge of . . . documentary filmmaking among African Americans dates back—you know I'm 39 years old—dates back to *Black Journal*, particularly the 1970–1972 seasons. I was an avid watcher of *Black Journal*, and I was just entering Temple University at the time. And, it was around that time that I was figuring that, "maybe I'll do film-making"—I was greatly impressed by *Black Journal*'s all-black production staff. Bill Greaves remains continually influential in my life, work and attitude about documentary filmmaking. Madeline Anderson, who was one of the first black woman producer/directors that I ever heard of, showed me that, obviously, it is possible for an African American woman to do this. Lou Potter, St. Clair Bourne. . . . I almost left Temple University to go to WNET Film School (*Black Journal*'s production train-ing program) . . . because I thought that was a more expeditious way to get at what I wanted to do, and I was overjoyed that the instructors were black. Jim Brown, who was an instructor with them, subsequently was the editor on the Betty Carter film, my first big film; Willette Coleman. All these folks were part of the *Black Journal* technical and administra-tive staff. . . .

Also, Monica Freeman's work was inspiring to me when I first saw her documentary work. All of this was a part of these black film festi-vals that were just beginning to blossom in the early '70s. . . . Seeing *Valerie, Hamilton Heights*—these were really inspiring films, and I knew that documentary was a really wonderful genre that hadn't been fully explored. There was room to grow, there was room to innovate. But I also was influenced by TV in the '60s, so I saw things like the NBC *White Paper,* the Prudential documentary series that Walter Cronkite used to narrate on CBS. I was like, 10, 11, 12, and these were really outstanding TV programs. My parents watched and they encouraged me to watch as a child. The Leacock/Drew documentaries of the '60s when J. F. Kennedy was president. So these also had another layer of influence on me, outside of the African American documentary filmmaking tradition. I also loved Fred Wiseman's work, the Maysles brothers—I loved their work. I particularly loved the narration-less style of their work, and these were things that influenced me.

Let's see, I think the TV docs of the '60s were also influential on me because they told of the civil rights movement that was then in process. They unraveled the personalities and took in-depth looks at what was happening on the social and political scene that I was growing into. My parents, also, were very active in the civil rights movement. So, I had another kind of respect for documentary as a political tool, beyond just entertainment, or beyond just the narrow division of it as ethnographic studies or as *Wild Kingdom* or *National Geographic* specials.

I'm learning. It's not that I've developed this directing style or this unique director's vision that my films are considered outstanding. I think that what's gotten them the attention is *who* the films are about. These women are truly outstanding. I tried to reach for that [her improvisational, i.e. jazz, pacing] in the Betty Carter film. *Sweet Honey* has another construct. *Stormé: The Lady of the Jewel Box* has another.

The definition [of documentary] that hangs in for me is John Grierson's "creative treatment of actuality," and that can mean a lot of things. That doesn't mean it's not docudrama and it's only narration. It's not that cut and dried. It's expansive. . . . This time in the early '90s is really exciting in documentary for me. Look at Marlon Riggs's work, Camille Billops's work, to name a few that are innovating format. Our preconceptions and our pretensions about documentary are all being messed with, and that's wonderful. The current generation of documentary filmmakers is meshing documentary, performance, autobiography, narration, stock footage compilation, all of it, in various combinations that give the meaning, the message of the film, the documentary, more impact. To me, that's what documentary is about. To me it's more, at this time and place, "experimental" than it is our narrow definitions of "documentary." What I do is, as I've said in other interviews, "docutainment." I have consciously selected black women artists to make documentary films about, but the entertainment component of their work is the impetus for and the drive for the documentary program structure, so in that sense it's a combination of both documentary construct and entertainment elements.

JULY 1992
INDIANAPOLIS, INDIANA

MARLON RIGGS

I was born February 3, 1957 in Fort Worth, Texas. I lived in Austin for a little bit, but I spent most of my time in Fort Worth. I lived there until I was about 11, and then moved around—my father and mother were in the military. We lived in Georgia, then Germany . . . for my high school years . . . and then I came back to the States to go to college.

Unfortunately, even now the American community [in Germany] is extremely insulated and isolated from the rest of the European experience. In fact, the United States was called "the world," so that anybody who lived in Germany was considered living in some strange, forbidden, and unknown land, where people kept referring to getting back to "the world," meaning the United States. I think all of us, the entire family, enjoyed living there, because in many ways—and then again, I was a young person, a typical teenager out with other peers. I think what it did in a way was to focus—because the community was very small there and relatively concentrated and people knew each other—a lot of dialogue and discussion, in a different way than a large community or urban setting where people don't know each other. Maybe those same discussions happen and action is taken, but it's usually within organizational contexts. [In Germany] because of the smallness of the community, a lot of things happened through the home, so black history month activities could be in people's homes; scholarship funds and drives for black students would come out of people knowing each other, rather than through an organization, per se.

I was seventeen when I returned to "the world." I had missed actually a lot in terms of what had been happening in the United States. This was 1970–1974. Of course, that was still a period of great turmoil in the country regarding civil rights, sort of post-civil rights but still, the aftermath of all of the turmoil during the sixties, anti–Vietnam War sentiment, Kent State, and Watergate, which was just starting to happen. But all this had been so removed from me because at that time in Germany there was no American television, no English television. So all of that information that came to people through television news or documentaries, I never saw. And the periodical we had at the time was the *Stars and Stripes*, which filtered everything, as it still does. So you got this very bland high school newspaper approach to journalism. It really was in some ways a culture shock when I returned because so much had happened in the States that I really had not been a part of.

I went to Harvard then, as an undergraduate. I had inklings of wanting to be an attorney, to go into law, perhaps into politics. But I really wasn't clear at the age of seventeen about what I wanted to do, except I knew that I wanted to do something that dealt with—and I couldn't put it in those words at the time—activism, a sort of social community activism. I think I had been very much bred with a sense of giving back to the community because of my mother and grandmother. It was in the way they lived. It wasn't so much because they kept telling me, "You have to do this," but it was more in the way my grandmother lived. She's still a very giving person . . . a very unselfish person. My mother in a much more conscious way inspired me in that the rhetoric of our home, especially with friends, was constantly about the require-ments for the black middle class, the requirements of social activism among the educated of the black community, of the informed, to con-tinue to work on behalf of the entire community and not just yourself. I just grew up with all those debates constantly happening in my home. I wasn't taking part, but I was listening. I was up 'til late at night hearing all of this, and I think in seeing the way my mother and grandmother lived—it just inbred in me to follow in that path. I felt, especially given the kinds of gifts that I had—I was always a good student in class, always leading this organization or that organization—that those gifts of leadership and writing should be used in the path of the uplift of our community.

So that it was clear to me by the time I went to college that I would do something, hopefully, that was helpful for the black community. Exactly what? Again I thought—teaching, maybe law, maybe politics. As I kept meeting more of the people who were going to law school, or the people who were actually attorneys, I realized that was not what I wanted to do. Most of what I saw in that profession, in fact, repulsed me. The same was happening in terms of my understanding of politics. I thought that it would be very difficult to try to maneuver in that kind of situation. And there was a certain kind of arrogance at Harvard, a de-tached casual arrogance, not the kind that you see caricatured in car-toons about Ivy League people. It was really unconscious and a kind of detachment from so much of what was happening in the world. A very distorted, narrow sense of priorities and of the importance of self and the world.

It was not just egocentrism but also class-centrism. They didn't see it, therefore, they didn't care about it. What they considered to be of importance did not include most of what was important to the majority of people across the world. Even what might be considered important to themselves if they were more in-touch human beings. So it wasn't really until I was in my last year there that I decided I wanted to do some form of work that really involved, at that time, television. To me it was television history, and I had already put them together in a very intellectual way. I wasn't going to film the same documentaries, but I said, "Well, I like history, I want to teach history, but I don't want to teach it in an Ivy League setting or just within a university setting, reaching perhaps a hundred or so students a year."

How do you communicate so much of what you're learning to vast numbers of people? To me it was television history, and I thought television history meant documentary. In some ways it was an intellectual, reasoned way of arriving at a career, rather than being inspired by the documentaries. I didn't go to movies, I didn't go to see documentaries, I didn't see feature films, I didn't watch television while I was in school. I didn't really know what I was getting into! I thought that this would be a way of doing the kind of thing I wanted to but didn't have any idea of how to do it. That was a really strange career path for anyone at Harvard to be taking at the time, and I still think so. Anyone going into the arts . . . I mean most people are moving into law, business, medical school . . .

I came back to Texas where I actually lived for another year with my grandmother and I went from television station to television station in the area, Dallas–Fort Worth and then Austin. I wrote to stations in other cities in Texas, asking them about how to move into this kind of work. I got nowhere. One, most stations weren't doing documentaries to speak of. They did television news specials but they weren't documentaries. Most of them were all-white, and when I talked to many of them on the phone—which I later recognized—they didn't realize I was black, would invite me in because I sounded enthusiastic, Harvard and so forth, looked at me walk through the door and you could tell by the look on their faces—this total shock. It was very clear the racism in Texas was very old-style, so that when you walked through the door and started to ask questions, you were regarded very clearly as an upstart, an affront. They didn't say that, but it was in the look on their faces, and in their refusal to give you any information or to suggest that there might be any possibility of your working with them at this station.

I talked to news director after news director. I ended up working at one television station as an administrative assistant (at the NBC affiliate in Fort Worth), so it was far from where I wanted to be, but it was a way in. At least I got my foot in the door, but realized after being there for two months that I wasn't going to go anywhere. People were afraid to talk to me, that is, the whites, because a rumor had gone out that this 20-year-old was out to take over the station, this black Harvard graduate. I mean I was very naive, innocent, and curious. I asked people what they did, how they got to do what they did. People took that as my "gathering information" so that I could plot their overthrow and take over the station. So people refused to talk to me. They would sort of look down and make excuses or give me no information. In some ways it was a heart-wrenching period. Again, I was very naive, I just assumed that since I was there, I could learn, and that wasn't the case. That's when I realized that I wasn't going to advance in the career I had chosen if I wanted to follow this path. I started applying then to graduate schools of journalism that had documentary programs, and came to the University of California at Berkeley out of that.

In some ways I felt that I finally had arrived at a place where I thought I could really start to do what I wanted to. I didn't want to stay on the east coast because I had been in Boston and I was sick of the east coast. And I had wanted to come to the west coast. It was stable, I had heard about California—it had this image. I was young, it seemed free, and I'm still I guess relatively young, but I was a child in many ways. It seemed free and easy and racially harmonious, though that was not the case. Once I got here, the work was challenging and I started to hone skills that in many ways still are benefiting me greatly in terms of writing and analysis, image-making, etc., through the program at Berkeley. I really didn't get much background in black history or black filmmaking, which I really eternally regret. And I would say that's truly the case for all of my years in school regarding African American history and culture. So much of what I'm learning now, I'm learning on my own, or by accident. It wasn't because I like Eurocentric or Anglo culture, or white history, if you will. It's just a matter of fact that these are the things you learn about the great painters and great political leaders. It's taken for granted that that's part of what one should know to be a civilized, educated human being in this country. None of that included the things that are now most critical to me and most inspiring within my own work and life.

My first documentary was *Long Train Running: The Story of the Oakland Blues*. It is a half hour documentary about the history of blues music in Oakland, California. Based on a song called "Long Train Running," but it was the continuation of a tradition from the '40s World War II period during which there was intensive migration of blacks, particularly from Louisiana and Texas, to the East Bay region. That was my graduate school thesis documentary. I co-produced it with another student. It was considered a professional project, so in fact it was shown on television. It won a number of film festival awards. It traveled different places, and it's still being shown. To my shock it was recently shown at a film festival at the Brooklyn Museum.

We didn't actually do any fund-raising. I had a fellowship to attend the school. We had equipment, the tapes, all of the technical services provided for, so it just required our own initiative. When I was finished, I was extremely happy with it. Now I'm okay with it; I mean, you learn a lot, obviously. You see things that you could do now that I didn't even know about then. But as a first work, I think that a large measure of it stands up still to time.

I completed *Ethnic Notions* after I left U.C. Berkeley. . . . I spent probably the next four, five years fund-raising, doing little bits and pieces, the route that many of us independent filmmakers have to go through to find the funding for the work and doing what I could until I ran out. Working for other people, primarily as an editor, and then returning to the project until I could finish it.

* * *

Recently, while *Tongues Untied* was showing at the Lesbian/Gay Film Festival, I did a presentation at the Whitney Museum of American Art which I entitled "Black Macho Revisited: Reflections of a Snap Queen." I dealt with what I considered pervasive homophobia in black independent filmmaking and black characterizations of supposedly black gay men within the rap music and popular music by black artists scene, and looked at not only just how black gay men are represented in music and films and TV by black artists, but also by black directors. Sometimes working for white directors reduces the black characters, as is true of Eddie Murphy. I hoped to provoke questions as to why these kinds of caricatures and stereotypes are represented over and over and over again, despite our all too intimate history as black people in general with destructiveness of stereotype and caricature as a model of dealing with the people and representing the people.

And I was looking particularly at black male artists who presented black gay characterizations in a way that was caricatured, that was demeaning. But beyond that they reflected for me a kind of psychic turmoil that black America is facing nationwide in terms of identity, particularly male identity in the black community and how the image, as I called it, of the "Negro faggot" becomes a reassuring icon that no matter how low we go, we're not *that*. Therefore, we're still men. I wanted to show that analysis in a number of different kinds of artistic venues in which black artists are now working.

I did it with humor as well, and I played off in some ways one of the prime features of a lot of these stereotypes of black gay men, which is that we're constantly snapping, and swishing. That's why I titled the paper what I titled it—it was in some ways a signifying that you see within the movies and the music—to redefine the meaning of the "snap" in the way that it has its diverse meanings within the black gay community. It is not just a sign of effeminacy, of weakness, of emasculation. It can be defiant, it can be witty, it can be a number of things; in other words, to reintroduce that much broader meaning into the debate, into the representation of black gay characterization.

So, it was working on a number of levels to try to undo the destructive arm of so much of the imagery that's out there and very popular now. At the same time, to question black macho in relation to a very anti-feminist stance, which I think is also related to homophobia, and also to question this way of trying to show up a very weakened and fragile and disintegrating identity that black people on the whole face in the country, which is why I see us sort of reaching so much for icons like Malcolm X that seem to provide a kind of certainty, a closure, around what it means to be black and a man, what it means to be empowered. So I wanted to deal with all those issues. I knew I was dealing with them in a forum where most people had not dealt with or heard this before. Most people within the forum had not dealt with a black gay man in a setting in which they did not have to do anything more than laugh, tease, or cajole. What I wanted to do was also to suck people in with those kinds of images, which I did with the first clip. I showed a bunch of bouncing queens on the screen—people were just laughing—then returned to some of those same images at the end of my presentation. By then, nobody was laughing, because that identity that they'd had with the dominant culture, and therefore with the *misconceptions* and even very *destructive* caricatures changed.

In some ways, what I did made them look at a different *kind* of identification—not with Eddie Murphy, but with me. Much in the way that when we see *The Birth of a Nation*, we black people don't identify with D. W. Griffith's Klansmen characters, and we can't at all with the black characters, and therefore we cheer when the white woman jumps off the cliff. In some ways, that's what I want to do, to redirect attention, so that when people see movies like *House Party*, or when they listen to Heavy D & The Boyz, or any of their favorite rap artists, or they see a new Spike Lee movie, that they don't just laugh. They may even see what this is doing to people, and how it fits a very historic pattern of stereotyping and marginalization of people, often of the entire black community, as well as communities within the black community, mainly women and gays and lesbians.

Homophobia's so taboo, people don't even want to talk about it. And as usual, the comments I got more often came from women. Even those who feel uncomfortable with the subject are more willing to articulate their discomfort, rather than the men, who will just sit there and stew. I find this at screenings of *Tongues Untied* when I'm doing it in mixed settings. The men sort of sit there, or if they do chance to speak, get hostile, defensive, and very threatened and angry.

I didn't look at it as bravery, I just looked at it as an imperative. I was just so sick of images, of words, of music, of history being written in which I was constantly written out—that is, my community. To me the parallel to what American culture has done to black people was so strong, and the need to break that pattern through voicing of our experience through declaring ourselves and therefore affirming our distance was the only way to break that pattern. I saw no other alternative. And partly because the time was right. It's not just me by myself, there is a community out there, as there has been a community from way back to Africa. That's something a lot of nationalists do not want in any way to entertain, that homosexuality was not a white creation. You can go to every culture and find homosexuality as well as bisexuality, and you will find it in Africa, as well as in India, as well as in Asia, as well as in America, as well as in South America. So it was in many ways breaking silence, it was taking the Act Up dictum "silence = death" and extending the meaning, so it's not just in relation to AIDS, but more in relation to the entire existence of the community and the historical legacy of the community.

Color Adjustment is the film I'm working on now. It's a history of black representation in prime time entertainment television from *Beulah* and *Amos 'n' Andy* to *The Cosby Show*. And looking at not so much what we have done in television as black people, but rather looking at what the representation of black people in prime time entertainment television has signified in terms of perceptions, of race relations, of racial attitudes, of the viewing public, the racial sensibilities of the producers and creators of these shows, who often wield the power, and not the actor. It's to show how there's been evolution, regression, or both in terms of the representation of black people in the media. It's very fascinating. I've talked with some people who created *I Spy* and *Julia*, to Stephen Bochco, to Norman Lear. I've talked with network entertainment people, as well as actors and producers like Tim and Daphne Reid, Denise Nicholas, and it's really interesting and provocative to see how very competing notions of what television entertainment should do or be about come into play when black people become a part of this medium in a very meaningful, more empowering way, as opposed to just figures to be exploited for their comic value. That's the tension that this documentary is exploring.

There's other black gay work that's in the making too, right now.

One's a short that I finished actually back in February called *Affirmations*. It's a ten-minute video work that explores black gay desire and dreams of political embrace by the larger African American community. There's a new work which is as yet untitled that deals with notions of black gays counterpoised against the anti-gay, anti-black, anti-feminist hysteria, in some ways unleashed and exploited by Jesse Helms.

It's surfacing in so many ways now, whether it's 2 Live Crew, or NEA, or Kid n' Play. It's not as if I defend all of these people and everything they do, but there's a general hysteria in terms of trying to impose a certain kind of social control and social values that's led to a very pervasive censorship. It goes beyond NEA and the country right now. [Jesse Helms] is in some ways the most salient, most horrific manifestation of this censorship hysteria, but he's definitely not it.

AUGUST 1990
OAKLAND, CALIFORNIA

KATHE SANDLER

For me, filmmaking is both storytelling and politics. It is about filling voids and vacuums of missing information, about who we are and how our stories are being told. I see my work as educating, entertaining, and, if it is fully realized—also healing.

I was always supposed to be a writer. My mother, an arts administrator—her name is Joan Sandler—has a special affinity for her friendships with writers. So growing up there were these women writer role models in my life: my godmothers Rosa Guy and Louise Meriwether, the late Audre Lorde, who was my mother's girlhood friend and our neighbor, Vertamae Grosvenor, Jayne Cortez, Paule Marshall, Maya Angelou, Marcia Gillespie and others. I also saw week after week the best black theater of the early 1970s; one of my mother's jobs was as a director of the now defunct Black Theater Alliance.

From the age of 10 until I was at least 21 years old, I wrote poetry, one-act plays, short stories, fiction, and some journalism. I was inspired by my teachers as a teenage member of the Frederick Douglass Creative Arts Center's writing workshops where I studied with Fred Hudson, Louise Meriwether, and Quincy Troupe.

I stumbled into filmmaking; my first film, *Remembering Thelma*, which I began in college at NYU, was a short documentary about the late dancer, teacher and mentor, Thelma Hill, whom I had studied dance with and who died in a tragic fire. But it was also a story of a behind-the-scenes African American woman in the arts who influenced many people, not unlike my own mother.

St. Clair Bourne was probably the greatest influence on me in terms of directing me into the film business and being my principal mentor. He gave me one of my first paying jobs in film on *In Motion: Amiri Baraka,* and he became the executive producer of my documentary, *A Question of Color;* Jackie Shearer was another important mentor to me, and was a godmother to *A Question of Color.* I have also been influenced a great deal by Haile Gerima, Michelle Parkerson, Bill Miles, the late Marlon Riggs, and Bill Greaves, as well as Gil Noble. I was also deeply influenced by the work of Richard Schmieken and Rob Epstein with their documentary, *The Life and Times of Harvey Milk,* as well as Lucy Winer and Kate Davis, two independent filmmakers who have also been my editors.

A Question of Color has been my most important and influential work to date, and I have screened it through the world. To make it I began a nearly decade long quest to explore in documentary film a burning issue which has had an impact on most black people, myself included —color consciousness and internalized racism around skin color, hair texture and facial features in the African American community. Knee deep in production, and years down the line, I gave in to some important advice and used my own voice and experience as a thread to telling this story which brought the entire film together in the most powerful way.

I've been lucky to have an intellectual collaborator on my documentary work for the past 15 years, my husband and co-writer Luke Charles Harris, who is an academic and an activist. He co-wrote *A Question of Color* and we are co-writing a new documentary, *Black Feminism,* with a close friend of ours who is an important black feminist, Kimberle Williams Crenshaw. This documentary will explore the impact of gender and race on black women and men, calling attention to the important tradition of progressive black feminism in our community. It will filmically buttress the groundbreaking work already done in academic, political and social arenas, and in the media by Angela Davis, Marcia Gillespie, Beverly Guy-Sheftall, the late Audre Lorde, Paula Giddings, Patricia Collins, Barbara Smith, Michele Wallace, and bell hooks, to name a few.

I think of myself as both a documentary and dramatic filmmaker. In the past, many people on the east coast thought of documentary film as being the only means available to them. Now people see narrative as a real option. The thing we want to watch out for is the tendency to denigrate the documentary—people who say, "Why don't you make a real film instead of a documentary?" We must challenge that idea because we need to have all these different mediums available to us to reconstruct African American identity.

APRIL 1995

BLOOMINGTON, INDIANA

JACQUELINE SHEARER

Regarding the tradition I see myself coming out of, right away, that makes me confront my own lack of historical understanding about filmmaking. Beginning with some film festivals that I went to overseas with Pearl Bowser, I was introduced to the likes of Oscar Micheaux, and understood that there were other black filmmakers before me. But, they tended to center on narrative more than on documentary. Madeline Anderson's film [*I Am Somebody*, 1970] was the first documentary I ever saw by a black woman, and that had a big impact on me, along with Bill Miles's *Men of Bronze*, and [William] Greaves's films. At the time I was centering myself in narrative filmmaking, so while I sort of noticed them there wasn't a direct relationship between me and them.

I began filmmaking in Boston Newsreel, a national New Left organization, in the '60s and '70s; it wasn't very good at production, but it was great at exhibition. The experience taught me that, more than anything else, film is something that's used, that's seen, and that sparks reactions in people. I'm grateful that that was how I came to it, along with a political understanding that filmmaking can socialize people to be more than unthinking cogs in the machine: logically it made sense to apply those same skills to another more liberating end. My own background in documentary has very much to do with film as a political tool, and with my being politically motivated. I didn't learn film in school. I studied history—I picked up film from friends—and I could have gone on be a history professor, or with different skills and inclinations, some kind of political organizer. But I hated meetings and I hated having to talk to strangers, and so I got into film. And then I remember reading a book about how documentary filmmaker John Grierson honed his craft doing industrials, and that appealed to me. I liked the notion of learning filmmaking by doing it. There was also a reverse snobbism in me that liked the idea of doing non-"art" films. You know, "I'm just an honest soul earning a living" kind of thing, and the way that I happened to do it was through this craft. I definitely saw it as a craft . . .

I worked at the ABC affiliate in Boston, not the public TV station, and I had to prove myself all the time, which is, I think, also part of being a documentarian. You wake up in the morning and say, "What's

God gonna throw at me today? How am I gonna interact with it to get my story?" There was something really sort of satisfying about that. My first concentrated productions happened after I had done *A Minor Altercation* with some friends on our own. Then Henry Hampton called me up and asked if I wanted to do films for *Blackside* (this was in the pre-*Eyes* days, when he was doing government-sponsored industrials). That made me think of the book I'd read on Grierson, and I thought this is great! I can hone my skills. By then I had decided that I wanted to do narrative because of the control issue. After doing a number of public affairs documentaries, where I learned to turn an idea into a product in a very short time, I really got tired of it and wanted more control. I wanted people to be saying what I scripted for them to say. I didn't want to dance around trying to get them to give me what I needed—I wanted to be in control. The films that Henry was doing for the Department of Labor and for Health and Human Services were scripted films for public education or staff training, in which people would want typical characters and prototypical situations. This was how I got experience in directing actors; I'd had a lot of experience directing crews and editors, but not performers, and this was a big step for me.

Then at a certain point I thought, to what end am I honing my craft? Am I going to be doing this kind of thing forever? I had gone to a couple of film festivals in Europe and met filmmakers from Third World countries with no resources, and I thought, "You have no excuse, Jackie. Hone your craft, but push it up to another level." That's when I ran up against the obstacle that I still confront every day, the reason why I had really taken refuge in being a craftsperson: I didn't know if I had anything to say of my own. Yet intellectually I realized that even though I thought I didn't have anything to say I probably did. So, I started the research project for what was intended to be a short documentary that I could distribute myself, and that, through rentals, would finance my first feature. But then I came to see that there was enough material in this little bit of film for a first feature, and that I might as well just lump it all together. And that's the project, the working title is *Addie and the Pink Carnation*, it's based on my research on black women domestic workers in the 1930s. There was one sentence in Gerda Lerner's book *Black Women in White America* that sent me off running, way back in the early '80s at a time when no one had written anything about this issue. I read master's theses that hadn't been taken out on interlibrary loan since the '40s and uncovered boxes of archival material in the Y headquarters on the East Side that no one had looked at for years. Even the domestic workers' union, an affiliate of the AFL-CIO, didn't know about it.

It's a huge project, and in the course of it I came up against a couple of things. One is the problem of working alone, and the other is the problem of my shying away from thinking that I had a voice. I wasted a lot of time and money. I did extensive fund-raising, and then just went through writers who weren't able to give me what I wanted. Finally I had to accept the fact that I'd have to write it myself. This was some of the most painful, but also the most gratifying work I'd ever done. And, then, there was a big fund-raising fiasco at NEH. I'd heard from friends that my project got the highest ranking by the panel; I was sure I would get the grant, and then they sent my project to outside reviewers, and somehow it wound up that I got a "no." It was very, very devastating, and I had to put the project away for a while.

I had just picked up the script again to go through it when I got the call from Henry about *Eyes,* so I put it aside again. Since then, working on *Eyes* and *The Massachusetts 54th Colored Infantry* (1991) and the latest stuff I've done, all documentaries, I've learned so much more about script writing and story telling, that in a funny way I feel more able today to deal with the *Addie* script. Before, like other socially conscious, first-time filmmakers, my script read like a political manifesto. I need to let Addie be a character who moves through life at her own pace because she needs to, not because I'm the puppeteer manipulating. I look at it now and I really understand how well-intentioned and emotionally flat it is. So, now, I'm gearing up to do that hard work.

I think that all of my training in narrative really helped when I came to do *Eyes on the Prize.* I was real nervous when Henry called me because I thought, "I haven't done documentaries in years. What if I don't know how to?" I had to look at a week's worth of videotapes, and read everything in a very short period of time. Then I became one of the producers and was paired with another producer, Paul Steckler. We were responsible for the fourth show—the one on Martin Luther King's last years, his death, and his Poor People's Campaign—and the seventh show—the one that looks at affirmative action in its various guises, especially at Boston school desegregation, and Atlanta, and the Baake case. We were all "salt and pepper" teams on *Eyes II.* We were gender mixed, too, until the only other black woman producer left. Her replacement was a black man, so there were two men on that team, black and white, but I was paired with a white man, Louie Massiah was paired with a white woman, Sam Pollard with a white woman, and so on.

It worked because Paul and I made it work. Luckily, we shared a certain temperament, we both worked with people in the same way, and we shared certain values. It was extremely painful, but I think that Henry is in some ways a genius. I worked with him in the old days when he was beginning the process of fundraising for *Eyes* so I know how long it took him and how persevering he was, but from my point of view, the "salt and pepper" stuff wasn't worth it. I understand that he wanted to shake us up and keep us from being too in-groupy and speaking only to the converted, and using in-language. I understand that those were problems, but there was such "ownership" of the history on the part of the black producers—there was no way you could have convinced us that the white producers had the same emotional stake. They certainly wanted to do their best. We all did. But you get a different shading from a supposed parity where it's not really parity. I think the mixing was good, but I wouldn't have done it in such a blanket, across-the-board way because it set us all up. . . . You have to spend a lot of energy fighting to get out of those boxes, getting the freedom to talk to each other. I think we did, and it was tremendous that we did, but it just took so much energy. . . . I think the story of the making of the film is as interesting as the film itself. It was a never-ending soap opera, and my friends in Boston will swear to that. They got so sick of "would you believe what he said today?" We were going crazy.

The other thing was the issue of universality. Henry was real concerned about making these shows accessible. I think that an *Eyes* done by an all-black team might not have seemed accessible at first glance, but I bet it would have given people another layer that we didn't quite get, another cultural-assumptive layer. We had a lot of fights, the fight to have a story on Malcolm for example. There was no way that the black producers were going to do the series without that, and we won. We also won the fight to cover the Black Panthers; some of the white producers really didn't get that. They said, "Well, but the Black Panthers didn't have as much membership as the NAACP," but that wasn't the point.

I've done so much historical documentary—it's funny since I was a history major it sort of comes full circle. But, there's such an issue about our history. One of the things for example, that I think Henry's contributed to a whole other way of understanding things is the "participant historian" idea in which you can't just be an expert, you have to be someone who's lived through it. Well, that's worth its weight in gold and it's an approach that's been used more and more in historical filmmaking. One of the things that I remember thinking when I first got into film was that if people who weren't used to thinking much of themselves saw that their lives were worthy enough to be up there on the silver screen, then that would help to prop up their self-esteem. [Shearer's short narrative film] *A Minor Altercation* was pretty much predicated on that idea.

I'd like to think you'd know that the seventh show [in the second series] was mine, especially because of the music. No one wanted to get stuck with the seventh show because it was the '70s, and the '70s was a boring decade. There was no music then, it was all disco. The working title of my show was "Legal Remedies," and everyone thought, oh, that's so boring—legal stuff. But I've always understood that music is a very important part of social history.

Music is a central way that we get over it. And so for the seventh show, the one on affirmative action and desegregation, I did a lot of research, because it seemed to me that there was more music than just disco in the '70s. I particularly wanted stuff by black women. Why not? That was one of my roles in the series since I was the only black woman producer. Also because of having grown up poor, I would always be the voice calling for attention to gender and class issues, in addition to race. You know they always intertwine. So, I did all this research and then just blanketed the show with music that would always be appropriate, that would fill the *Eyes* bill. It was always music that was current at the moment that the scene was happening. And, there were even a few disco numbers, but it just spans a range. A couple of professors have come up to me afterwards and thanked me specifically for the sound-track, which just thrills me no end.

I think the music is a signature. I've also gotten a lot of favorable comments on the soundtrack in *The Massachusetts 54th* for the *American Experience* series. The *American Experience* people were a little worried that I wasn't going to do a score, that I wanted to do the same thing I did with *Eyes* instead of doing wall-to-wall stuff. But I did do wall to wall stuff and the music was actually good. I mean, we liked it in the editing room; it wasn't just historically accurate, it was fun to play around with too.

We did the music research and got the pieces and had a music consultant from Wooster, Ohio, a woman who knew a lot about nine-teenth-century black music, make selections for us. And then we got two choirs, one from Howard University and one from U Mass, Am-herst, both led by choir directors who knew a lot about nineteenth-century black musical styles, to perform the pieces. So, I can see why the *American Experience* people were nervous because there were a lot of steps and it was complicated, but I think it worked out really well at the end. And I think, frankly, that another signature I'm less proud of—my mother always used to tell me—I always do things the hard way.

I think that I gravitate toward complex ideas, and I have finally been able to accept the fact that I'm an intellectual. For many, many, many years I didn't want to hear it, but I am, you know. And, so, I like taking a really dense, complex subject area and breaking it down. And one of the things that I like about filmmaking is that you have control over every atom. I mean, it's there because you wanted it to be there. So, it's perfect for those of us who love lists, and being compulsive, I can just do all these grids and think about things from all different points of view. But I worry about *The Massachusetts 54th;* I know that it's really useful in the classroom, and I know that motivated audiences really like it, but I think, frankly, that it's more dense than it should have been, because I was just too reluctant to surrender any of the purview that was mine. One of the pieces that I did for the Museum was a twelve-screen video wall, which I was really interested to do just formalistically. It was supposed to be on the fight for the right to vote in the 1960s, but once I did the research, I had to begin it in 1865 because I had to back up the story about reclaiming the right to vote. If, God forbid, some little kid should not understand that we used to have the right to vote, and then we lost it, and that's what the twentieth century was all about. So, it wound up being a nine-minute piece that scans a hundred years of history. That's what I mean about doing things the hard way; that's always the tension in me. I think it's much stronger history and much better politically, but it might have been a bit snazzier if I'd done a four-and-a-half-minute thing that went from 1963 to 1965. I hope that becomes less a signature of mine, but I have a feeling that's always going to be there.

For me it also gets back to that issue of having something to say, because to the degree that I see myself as a vehicle or a channel for higher truths, that's one agenda, which is totally different from the "starving artist in the garret" who may not have that kind of agenda, but who just wants to express him or herself. I'm less interested in expressing myself. I mean, I am, but it's ancillary to the main point of having something to say. I think that all films are constructions, including documentaries. So, this myth of objectivity is so ridiculous that I can't believe it still takes hold as much as it does. I like to think that I don't tell lies, but that's different from claiming to be objective, and that's different from saying that the world that I construct in my film is reality. I think that point of view is critical too, but I wish people understood point of view better. I always think of where you stand as you look out over your story. That's all it means. And, you have to stand somewhere.

If you are concerned about audience then TV makes sense as a place to get the message out, and I do care about audience. But if you care about image, then there's no question, film wins hands down. But I think television needs redemption—it needs saving—and with all of these channels, maybe the cable dream that I remember talking about twenty years ago is really going to come true. I really define myself as a filmmaker, but one who is learning about video just because of the industry and the audience.

I feel so isolated in my own experience that it makes me hesitant to generalize, but, for example, I remember in shooting *The Massachusetts 54th,* I felt that I was respectful of subjects in ways that didn't always serve me well as a filmmaker because I wound up shooting too much footage, but on a human-to-human basis, I remember a few interviews where I just felt it was real important not to fake things and make believe I was running when I wasn't, and not to interrupt, and to let people come at me in their own way. Sometimes I wonder how much that has to do with gender stuff. Like I've noticed that particularly with older women I'm extremely deferential. I think that some button gets pushed, you know, that has as much to do with my being a woman as a black woman. But, again, you know, I don't know because I'm trying to be a better and better filmmaker, and I have certain values and standards, and some of them are cultural, some of them are aesthetic, but I have a hard time making proscriptions from them.

So, see, that's part of the way that I'm trying to figure out how to get my own voice together, but I'm always going to have a bigger agenda, and I'm never going be someone who has something to say that's divorced from other stuff. So, I'm always going to need a hook to hang my two cents on. But, if I can come up with ideas that are mine, I think that the balance will be better than it's been during the last five or so years when I've been doing other people's visions.

JUNE 1992
NEW YORK, NEW YORK

YVONNE WELBON

I was very interested, when I started film school in 1991, in finding other black women filmmakers. . . . I only knew the name of one black woman filmmaker, Julie Dash, and it was a little disturbing to me at the time because I didn't think I was the only other black woman in the world who wanted to make film. . . . There had never been a black woman studying film at the School of the Art Institute of Chicago in the master's program, so there weren't any alumni for me to talk to. Our library did not own any work by black women and neither did the Video Data Bank at the Art Institute. If I looked around me, there was no evidence that there were other black women filmmakers, and that was very disturbing. . . . It took a lot of work to find out what I was a part of— who these other women were, where their work was.

It was very disturbing to me that I didn't know what . . . [Julie Dash] had gone through, what her schooling was like, where she found her inspiration, who her peers were, how Julie even came to the point where she was. I remember when she came to the Art Institute with her film *Daughters of the Dust.* . . . and there were all these children running around. . . . I don't think an average child—these were black children —would know what she looks like today, but they know who Spike Lee is. . . . In a sense black women filmmakers don't exist. People don't recognize them; they don't look at a black woman and go, "Oh, she's a filmmaker." So I was very interested in making sure there was some kind of document of her experience [*The Cinematic Jazz of Julie Dash*].

I did not make a conscious decision to become a documentary filmmaker, [but] I was just thinking recently that I've made five films and all five are documentaries in some shape, manner, or form. My work is experimental, and I've always employed narrative techniques within the documentary form. . . . Actually, four of the five films are autobiographical. *Sisters in the Life* is loosely autobiographical, a piece that came out of discussions with black lesbians in the community. Taking collective stories and making them into one piece was almost a community effort. Except for *Sisters in the Life,* there are no black lesbian films that document this coming of age, turning 13 and 14 and starting to be interested in sex and boys and love interests, and what happens when you're interested in your girlfriend instead of your boyfriend.

The other thing that I noticed is that all of my work has been cathartic—like some issue I'm working out. . . . And it made me think about looking back to not only African American art history but African art, early African art. A lot of it was purposeful. There was a reason why the art was made. It wasn't necessarily decorative. It could be utilitarian, useful, and I thought it was interesting because I was making these pieces to heal, as part of a healing process, and not really conscious of it. For example, I did a piece called *Missing Relations,* which is an autobiographical documentary, and it really focuses on my sisters. I have sisters who are twins, who were six months old and their father kidnapped them, and we never saw them again. Then they found my mother when they were 24, which was a couple of years ago. I wanted to deal with that, to look at what happened with that loss—that I had these little sisters for six months and then they were gone and how that affected me. I was very interested in how it affected them and the whole family, but I felt to be true to the story, I could only know what my own feelings were, and I couldn't do my mom and their father, and I couldn't do the whole story.

My whole interest in becoming a filmmaker had to do with my experience in Taiwan and the new Taiwan cinema which was happening in the 1980s, the decade that I was in Taiwan. There was a movement there called Xiang Tu, which meant "native soil." People were getting back to their roots. . . . First, there was a literary movement, and then it grew to a film movement where a lot of the works were adapted to film, and it was this "back to our roots filmmaking." . . . It had a lot of influence on me and the kind of work that I'm interested in doing.

I am definitely evolving a style, in which I employ experimental and narrative techniques in making my documentary work. For instance, in the last film I did, *Remembering Wei Yi-fang, Remembering Myself*, I tell this story of my experiences in Taiwan. I do a parallel story with my grandmother, because when I was 22 I left home and moved to Taiwan . . . . When my grandmother was 22, she left Honduras and immigrated to America. . . . Originally I had thought about using archival footage from the 1940s to document her experience, and I didn't in the end. I re-created her stories. . . . It personalizes the history. Instead of making it this larger social history, it is her history and in a sense it helps you see her more clearly.

What I did was record oral histories and found out again that to show that story is to re-create it. . . . So perhaps my work won't be seen as a documentary, because I've taken liberties that aren't standard. What am I going to do?

I've actually started producing, because I'm so business-minded, and have started developing projects. I don't want to direct, I'm not interested in narrative film. Directing is a very hard thing to do. But I like the business side. I like to deal with the money, figure out how to raise it, creating a plan. But I wanted to learn everything there was. I learned how to light, how to shoot, I took directing classes. . . . I was always the person who was the assistant director or the production manager or the coordinating producer. I'd be picked for the organizer. . . . But I also still want to make my own work, which is the documentary.

NOVEMBER 1992
BLOOMINGTON, INDIANA

FILMOGRAPHY

This filmography includes the most recent information we could obtain about the films, videos, and new electronic media listed. We did not include works when we could not find reliable information about dates and production credits. However, we did provide as much data as we could discover about works mentioned by the authors. To facilitate research, we created a more inclusive index of film/videomakers listed alphabetically; this index follows the filmography. The works of diasporic filmmakers, in addition to African Americans, are included in both the filmography and the index if they are referred to in the text. Distributors listed here are, of course, subject to change. Finally, we did not create separate entries for the newsreels and long-running television series that are listed at the end of the filmography, but there are separate entries for series-generated productions that are available as individual works.

Note: In the time between the start of this project and the publication of the book, there has been a great deal of exciting new documentary work. Whenever possible, we have included these recent titles in the filmography.

A Luta Continua
Other Titles: *The Struggle Continues*
> Year: 1973
> Credits: Produced, written, and directed by Robert Van Lierop
> Production Company: Tricontinental Film Center
> Distribution: Tricontinental Film Center

Adam Clayton Powell
Series: The American Experience
> Year: 1989
> Credits: Directed by Richard Kilberg; produced by Richard Kilberg and Yvonne Smith; co-produced by Barbara Margolis and Gary R. George; written by Richard Kilberg and Phyllis Garland

Production Company: R K B Productions
Distribution: Phoenix/BFA Films & Video

Adventures in Assimilation
Year: 1992
Credits: Directed by Richard Dean Moss
Production Company: Third World Newsreel
Distribution: Third World Newsreel

Affirmations
Year: 1990
Credits: Directed by Marlon T. Riggs
Production Company: Signifyin' Productions
Distribution: Frameline

Africans in America: Africa's Journey through Slavery
Year: 1998
Credits: Executive produced by Orlando Bagwell; produced by
Orlando Bagwell, Noland Walker, Jacquie Jones, Llewellyn
Smith, Susan Bellows; written by Steve Fayer
Production Company: WGBH-Boston
Distribution: PBS

Afrique, Je Te Plumerai
Other Titles: *Africa, I'm Going to Fleece You; Africa, I Will Fleece You*
Series: Library of African Cinema
Year: 1992
Credits: Written, produced and directed by Jean-Marie Teno
Production Company: Les Films du Raphia and Raphia Films
Productions
Distribution: California Newsreel

After Winter: Sterling Brown
Year: 1985
Credits: Directed by Haile Gerima
Production Company: Howard University School of Communi-
cations
Distribution: Mypheduh Films, Inc.

Aimé Césaire: A Voice for History. III, The Strength to Face Tomorrow
Year: 1994

Credits: Directed and conceived by Euzhan Palcy
Production Company: California Newsreel
Distribution: California Newsreel

Airmen and Adversity
Year: 1998
Credits: Produced, written, and directed by Steven Crump
Production Company: WTVI Charlotte Public Television

Ali, the Fighter
Other Titles: *The Fighters, Fight of Champions*
Year: 1971
Credits: Produced, directed and written by William Greaves
Production Company: William Greaves Productions, Inc.
Distribution: The Petersen Company

All Power to the People
Year: 1997
Credits: Produced and directed by Lee Lew-Lee

Allah Tantou, À La Grace de Dieu
Other Titles: *Allah Tantou, God's Will Be Done*
Year: 1991
Credits: Produced and directed by David Achkar
Production Company: Archibald Films
Distribution: California Newsreel

Alvin Ailey: Memories and Visions
Year: 1974
Credits: Directed by Stan Lathan
Production Company: WNET Television, New York
Distribution: Phoenix Films

amBUSHed
Year: 1992
Credits: Directed by Jared Katsiane
Distribution: Third World Newsreel

*America Becoming: A Look at the History of the Immigration and
Nationality Act from 1965–Present*
Year: 1991

Credits: Directed by Charles Burnett; executive producer/ producer: Dai Sil Kim-Gibson; written by Virginia Kassel and Dai Sil Kim-Gibson

Production Company: Greater Washington Educational Telecom. Assoc.

Distribution: PBS Home Video

America: Black and White
Series: NBC White Paper Series
Year: 1982
Credits: Produced and directed by St. Clair Bourne
Production Company: Chamba Mediaworks, Inc.
Distribution: NBC

America's War on Poverty (series)
Year: 1995
Credits: Executive produced by Henry Hampton
Production Company: PBS
Distribution: PBS Video

An I for an I
Year: 1987
Credits: Directed, written and produced by Lawrence Andrews
Distribution: Video Data Bank

"and they came riding into town on BLACK & SILVER HORSES"
Year: 1992
Credits: Directed by Lawrence Andrews
Distribution: Electronic Arts Intermix

Anthem
Year: 1991
Credits: Directed by Marlon T. Riggs
Production Company: Signifyin' Productions
Distribution: Frameline

Apollo
Year: 1976
Credits: Directed by Stan Lathan; produced by Fred L. Dukes and William Easley
Production Company: Perin Film Enterprises and Group W Productions

Being Me
> Year: 1975
> Credits: Directed by Madeline Anderson; produced by Lois
> Goodkind
> Production Company: Phoenix Films
> Distribution: Phoenix/BFA Films & Video

Bellevue Emergency
> Year: 1994–1995
> Credits: Senior produced by St. Clair Bourne
> Production Company: King Arthur Productions for ABC

The Best of Black Journal (compilation)
> Year: 1970
> Credits: Produced by Madeline Anderson, St. Clair Bourne, Kent
> Garrett, Horace Jenkins, and Robert Wagoner
> Production Company: William Greaves Productions

Beyond the Forest
> Year: 1985
> Credits: Directed, written and produced by William Greaves
> Production Company: William Greaves Productions, Inc.
> Distribution: William Greaves Productions, Inc.

Big City Blues
Other Titles: *New Blues*
> Year: 1981
> Credits: Produced and directed by St. Clair Bourne; written by
> Clayton Riley
> Production Company: Rhapsody Films
> Distribution: Chamba Mediaworks Film Library; Music Video
> Distributors; Rhapsody Films; Facets Multimedia, Inc.

Birth of a Nation 4*29*92
> Year: 1993
> Credits: Produced and directed by Matthew McDaniel
> Production Company: Guerilla Style Films and Rhythm Rock
> Live Video Film
> Distribution: Third World Newsreel

Black and Blue
> Year: 1987

Credits: Directed by Hugh King and Lamar Williams
Distribution: Third World Newsreel

The Black and the Green
Year: 1983
Credits: Produced and directed by St. Clair Bourne; written by
Lou Potter
Production Company: Chamba Organization
Distribution: Chamba Mediaworks Film Library; First Run/
Icarus Films

Black at Yale: A Film Diary
Year: 1974
Credits: Directed by Warrington Hudlin
Production Company: Black Filmmaker Foundation

Black Body: A Work in Progress
Year: 1992
Credits: Produced and directed by Thomas Allen Harris
Production Company: Evolution Productions
Distribution: Third World Newsreel

Black Celebration: A Rebellion against the Commodity
Year: 1988
Credits: Directed by Tony Cokes
Distribution: Video Data Bank

Black Champions
Year: 1986
Credits: Produced by William Miles
Production Company: Miles Educational Film Productions, Inc.
Distribution: Miles Educational Film Productions, Inc.

Black Cop
Year: 1968
Credits: Produced, directed and written by St. Clair Bourne
Production Company: KCET-TV

Black Is . . . Black Ain't
Year: 1995
Credits: Produced and directed by Marlon T. Riggs; co-produced

by Nicole Atkinson; co-directed by Christiane Badgley;
Carroll Parrott Blue and Valerie Grim as field producers
Production Company: Signifyin' Works
Distribution: California Newsreel

Black Nations/Queer Nations?
Year: 1995
Credits: Produced by Shari Frilot
Distribution: Third World Newsreel

Black Power in America: Myth or Reality
Year: 1988
Credits: Produced by William Greaves, Louise Archambault and
the Corp. for Public Broadcasting; directed by William
Greaves; written by William Greaves and Lou Potter
Production Company: William Greaves Productions
Distribution: Facets Multimedia, Inc; William Greaves
Productions, Inc.

Black Press, The: Soldiers without Swords
Year: 1998
Credits: Produced and directed by Stanley Nelson
Production Company: Half Nelson Productions
Distribution: Half Nelson Productions

Black Stars in Orbit
Year: 1989
Credits: Directed and produced by William Miles
Production Company: Miles Educational Film Productions, Inc.
Distribution: Direct Cinema Limited

The Black Theater Movement: From "A Raisin in the Sun" to the Present
Other Titles: *Black Theater: The Making of a Movement*
Year: 1978
Credits: Directed and produced by Woodie King, Jr.
Production Company: Black Filmmaker Foundation
Distribution: California Newsreel

The Black Unicorn
Year: 1996
Credits: Written, produced, and directed by Melba Boyd
Distribution: National Black Programming Consortium

Black, White and Married
Year: 1979
Credits: Produced, written, and directed by Philip Mallory Jones
and Gunilla Mallory Jones
Distribution: Ithaca Video Projects

Black Women, Sexual Politics and the Revolution
Year: 1991
Credits: Produced by Michele McKenzie and Cyrille Phipps
Production Company: Not Channel Zero; Black Planet
Productions
Distribution: Third World Newsreel

Bodily Functions
Year: 1995
Credits: Produced, written, and directed by Jocelyn Taylor
Distribution: Third World Newsreel

The Bombing of Osage Avenue
Year: 1986
Credits: Directed and produced by Louis J. Massiah; written by
Toni Cade Bambara
Production Company: WHYY Philadelphia
Distribution: Scribe Video Center

the book of ruins and desire (computer book project)
Year: 1996
Credits: Produced by Pamela Jennings
Distribution: Available through the artist

Booker T. Washington: The Life and Legacy
Year: 1982
Credits: Produced by William Greaves and Billy Jackson;
directed by William Greaves; written by Lou Potter and
William Greaves
Production Company: William Greaves Productions, Inc.
Distribution: Facets Multimedia, Inc.; William Greaves Produc-
tions, Inc.

Burkina Faso: Land of the People of Dignity
Year: 1988
Credits: Directed and written by Abraham (Abiyi) R. Ford
Distribution: Abraham (Abiyi) R. Ford

. . . But Then, She's Betty Carter
    Year: 1980
    Credits: Produced, directed and written by Michelle Parkerson
    Production Company: Eye of the Storm Productions, Inc.
    Distribution: Women Make Movies

Can't Jail the Revolution and Break the Walls Down
Other title: *Political Prisoners and Prisoners of War in the United States*
    Year: 1991
    Credits: Directed by Ada Griffin and Kenyatta Funderburke
    Production Company: Third World Newsreel
    Distribution: Third World Newsreel

Capoeira of Brazil
    Year: 1980
    Credits: Produced, written, and directed by Warrington Hudlin
    Production Company: WGBH/ Boston's New Television Work-
        shop in association with the Black Filmmaker Foundation

A Celebration of Life: A Tribute to the Life of Martin Luther King, Jr.
    Year: 1984
    Credits: Directed by Stan Lathan
    Production Company: Independent

Changing Images: Mirrors of Life, Molds of Reality
    Year: 1987
    Credits: Directed and produced by Marlon T. Riggs
    Production Company: Signifyin' Works
    Distribution: Signifyin' Works

Charles White: Drawing from Life
    Year: 1979
    Credits: Produced and directed by Carlton Moss
    Distribution: Pyramid Films

Chasing the Moon
    Year: 1991
    Credits: Directed by Dawn Suggs
    Distribution: Third World Newsreel

Children's Art Carnival — Learning through the Arts
    Year: 1979
    Credits: Directed by Monica J. Freeman

Choice of Destinies
    Year: 1970
    Credits: Produced, written, and directed by William Greaves
    Production Company: William Greaves Productions, Inc.
    Distribution: William Greaves Productions, Inc.

The Cinematic Jazz of Julie Dash
    Year: 1992
    Credits: Produced and written by Yvonne Welbon
    Production Company: Our Film Works
    Distribution: Third World Newsreel

Claiming Open Spaces
    Year: 1995
    Credits: Produced and directed by Austin Allen; written by
        Austin Allen and Gloria House
    Production Company: Urban Garden Films/WOSU TV
    Distribution: Urban Garden Films

Cleared for Takeoff
    Year: 1963
    Credits: Produced and directed by William Greaves

Color Adjustment
    Year: 1991
    Credits: Produced by Marlon T. Riggs and Vivian Kleiman;
        directed and written by Marlon T. Riggs
    Distribution: California Newsreel

Conjure Women
    Year: 1995
    Credits: Produced by Louise Diamond; directed by Demetria
        Royals
    Production Company: National Black Programming Consortium
    Distribution: Women Make Movies

Conversations with Roy DeCarava
    Year: 1983
    Credits: Produced, written, and directed by Carroll Parrott Blue
    Production Company: WNET-TV and Corporation for Public
        Broadcasting
    Distribution: First Run/Icarus Films

Creating a Different Image: Portrait of Alile Sharon Larkin
  Year: 1989
  Credits: Directed by O. Funmilayo Makarah

Crisis to Crisis: Voices of a Divided City
  Year: 1982
  Credits: Executive directed by Henry Hampton; series executive
    director, Alvin H Goldstein; produced and directed by Romas
    V. Slezas
  Production Company: Corporation for Public Broadcasting

Crowded
  Year: 1977
  Credits: Produced, written, and directed by Alonzo Crawford
  Production Company: Vigilant Cinema Productions
  Distribution: Vigilant Cinema Productions

Cycles
  Year: 1989
  Credits: Directed and produced by Zeinabu irene Davis; written
    by Doris Owanda
  Production Company: Mosaic Films
  Distribution: Women Make Movies

The Darker Side of Black
  Year: 1994
  Credits: Written and directed by Isaac Julien; produced by Lina
    Gopaul
  Production Company: Black Audio Film Collective in
    association with Normal Films for BBC Television and the
    Arts Council of Great Britain
  Distribution: Filmmakers Library, Inc.

The Deep North
Series: A World of Difference
  Year: 1988
  Credits: Produced, written, and directed by William Greaves
  Production Company: William Greaves Productions
  Distribution: Facets Multimedia, Inc.; William Greaves Produc-
    tions, Inc.

Deft Changes: An Improvised Experience
    Year: 1991
    Credits: Directed by Alonzo Speight
    Distribution: Third World Newsreel

Diary of a Harlem Family
Other Titles: *The Making of Life*
    Year: 1968
    Credits: Produced by Public Broadcasting Laboratories in
        cooperation with Life Magazine
    Production Company: WNET–13
    Distribution: Indiana University Instructional Support Services

Didn't We Ramble On
Other Titles: *Didn't We Ramble On, the Black Marching Band; Black
Marching Band*
    Year: 1989
    Credits: Produced by Billy Jackson
    Production Company: Nommo Productions
    Distribution: Filmmakers Library, Inc.

The Different Drummer: Blacks in the Military
    Year: 1983
    Credits: Produced by WNET New York
    Production Company: Miles Educational Film Productions, Inc.
    Distribution: Films, Inc.

Dirt, Ground, Earth and Land
    Year: 1983
    Credits: Directed, written and produced by Alonzo Crawford
    Production Company: Vigilant Cinema Productions

Doing What It Takes: Black Folks Getting and Staying Healthy
    Year: 1994
    Credits: Directed by Donna Golden
    Production Company: Not Channel Zero
    Distribution: Third World Newsreel

Doubles: Japan and America's Intercultural Children
    Year: 1995
    Credits: Produced and directed by Regge Life
    Distribution: Doubles Film Library

Dr. Martin Luther King, Jr.: An Amazing Grace
Series: Like It Is (television program)
>Year: 1978
>Credits: Produced and written by Gil Noble
>Production Company: WABC-TV
>Distribution: National Black Archives of Film and Broadcasting, Inc.

Dreamkeeper
>Year: 1989
>Credits: Directed and produced by Philip Mallory Jones
>Distribution: Electronic Arts Intermix

Drive By Shoot
>Year: 1994
>Credits: Directed by Portia Cobb
>Distribution: Third World Newsreel

EEOC Story
>Year: 1972
>Credits: Produced by William Greaves and the United States Equal Opportunity Commission. Written and directed by William Greaves
>Production Company: William Greaves Productions
>Distribution: William Greaves Productions, Inc.

Emergency Ward
>Year: 1958
>Credits: Directed by William Greaves
>Production Company: William Greaves Productions, Inc.
>Distribution: William Greaves Productions, Inc.

Ethnic Notions
>Year: 1987
>Credits: Produced, written, and directed by Marlon T. Riggs
>Production Company: Marlon T. Riggs in association with KQED
>Distribution: California Newsreel

The Exiles
Other Title: *Richard Kaplan's The Exiles*
>Year: 1989

Credits: Co-produced by Richard Kaplan and Lou Potter; directed by Richard Kaplan; written by Richard Kaplan and Lou Potter
Production Company: Richard Kaplan Productions
Distribution: Connoisseur Video Collection

Eyes on the Prize I: America's Civil Rights Years, 1954–1965
Year: 1986
Credits: Series creator: Henry Hampton; series writer: Steve Fayer; series producer: Jon Else; series senior producer: Judith Vecchione; executive producer: Henry Hampton
Production Company: Blackside, Inc.
Distribution: PBS Home Video; Signals; The Video Catalog
Awakenings (1954–56)
Produced and directed by Judith Vecchione; written by Julian Bond
Fighting Back (1957–62)
Produced and directed by Judith Vecchione
Ain't Scared of Your Jails (1960–61)
Produced by Orlando Bagwell
No Easy Walk (1962–66)
Directed by Callie Crossley
Mississippi: Is This America? (1962–64)
Produced by Orlando Bagwell
Bridge to Freedom (1965)
Produced, written, and directed by Callie Crossley and James A. DeVinney

Eyes on the Prize II: America at the Racial Crossroads, 1965–1985
Year: 1989
Credits: Executive produced by Henry Hampton; series writer: Steve Fayer; series associate producer: Judy Richardson
Production Company: Blackside, Inc.
Distribution: PBS Home Video; Facets Multimedia, Inc.; Cambridge Educational
The Time Has Come (1964–66)
Produced, written, and directed by James A. DeVinney and Madison Davis Lacy, Jr.; co-produced by Carroll Parrott Blue
Two Societies (1966–68)
Produced, written, and directed by Sheila Bernard and Sam Pollard

Power! (1967–68)
Produced, written, and directed by Louis Massiah and Terry
Kay Rockefeller
The Promised Land (1967–68)
Produced, written, and directed by Paul Stekler and
Jacqueline Shearer
Ain't Gonna Shuffle No More (1964–72)
Produced, written, and directed by Sam Pollard and Sheila
Bernard
A Nation of Law? (1968–71)
Produced by Louis J. Massiah, Terry K. Rockefeller, and
Thomas Ott; written by Louis J. Massiah and Thomas Ott;
directed by Thomas Ott
The Keys to the Kingdom (1974–80)
Produced, written, and directed by Paul Stekler and
Jacqueline Shearer
Back to the Movement (1979–mid 80's)
Produced, written, and directed by James A. DeVinney and
Madison Davis Lacy, Jr.; co-produced by Carroll Parrott
Blue

Facing the Facade
Year: 1994
Credits: Directed by Jerald Harkness
Distribution: Cinema Guild

Fade Out: The Erosion of Black Images in the Media
Year: 1984
Credits: Produced by Carol Munday Lawrence; directed by
Robert N. Zagone
Production Company: Nguzo Saba Films, Inc.

Fade to Black
Year: 1991
Credits: Written by Donald Bogle, Tony Cokes, and Donald
Trammel; directed by Tony Cokes and Donald Trammel;
produced by Tony Cokes
Distribution: Third World Newsreel

Fall River Legend
Year: 1980
Credits: Executive produced by Ruth Leon; directed by Stan
Lathan

Production Company: Canadian Broadcasting Corporation and the Zweites Deutsches Fernsehen

Fighter for Freedom: The Frederick Douglass Story
Year: 1987
Credits: Produced and directed by William Greaves; written by William Greaves and Lou Potter
Production Company: William Greaves Productions, Inc.
Distribution: National Audiovisual Center

Finding Christa
Year: 1991
Credits: Produced, written, and directed by Camille Billops and James Hatch
Production Company: Du Art Video
Distribution: Third World Newsreel

First World Festival of Negro Arts
Year: 1966
Credits: Produced, written, and directed by William Greaves
Production Company: William Greaves Productions, Inc.; U.S. Information Agency
Distribution: William Greaves Productions, Inc.

First World Order (CD-ROM)
Year: 1994
Credits: Produced by Philip Mallory Jones
Distribution: Available through the artist

First World Order Project Development (CD-ROM and web site)
Year: 1997
Credits: Produced by Philip Mallory Jones
Distribution: Available through the artist

Flag
Year: 1989
Credits: Directed by Linda Gibson
Distribution: Women Make Movies

Four Little Girls
Year: 1997

Credits: Directed by Spike Lee and Ellen Kuras; produced by
Spike Lee and Sam Pollard
Production Company: HBO

Four Women
Year: 1977
Credits: Designed and directed by Julie Dash
Production Company: Cineworks
Distribution: Women Make Movies

Fragments of Barbara McCullough
Includes *Water Ritual #1* and *And Other Bits*
Year: 1980
Credits: Produced, written, and directed by Barbara
McCullough
Distribution: Third World Newsreel

Frankie and Jocie
Year: 1994
Credits: Directed by Jocelyn Taylor
Distribution: Third World Newsreel

Frantz Fanon: Black Skin, White Mask
Year: 1995
Credits: Directed by Isaac Julien; written by Isaac Julien and
Mark Nash
Production Company: Normal Films Productions
Distribution: California Newsreel

Frederick Douglass: An American Life
Year: 1975
Credits: Produced, written, and directed by William Greaves;
written by Lou Potter and William Greaves
Production Company: William Greaves Productions
Distribution: Your World Video

Frederick Douglass: When the Lion Wrote History
Year: 1994
Credits: Produced and directed by Orlando Bagwell; executive
produced by Tamara E. Robinson; written by Steve Fayer
Production Company: Roja Productions and WETA-TV
Distribution: PBS Video

From Harlem to Harvard
Year: 1982
Credits: Produced by David Lewis, Marco Williams, David Gifford, and Carole Markin; directed by Marco Williams
Production Company: Foursquare Productions
Distribution: Third World Newsreel

From These Roots
Other title: *A Review of the Harlem Renaissance*
Year: 1974
Credits: Written, directed, and produced by William Greaves
Production Company: William Greaves Productions, Inc.
Distribution: William Greaves Productions, Inc.; Facets Multimedia, Inc.; Afro-Am Distributions Company

Fundi: The Story of Ella Baker
Year: 1981
Credits: Produced, written, and directed by Joanne Grant
Distribution: First Run/Icarus; New Day Films

Ghosts & Demons
Year: 1987
Credits: Produced and directed by Philip Mallory Jones
Distribution: Electronic Arts Intermix

Gift of the Black Folk
Other Titles: *Portraits in Black* (distributed on videocassette)
Year: 1974–75
Credits: Produced by William Hurtz; associate produced by David C. Driskell; written and directed by Carlton Moss
Production Company: Artisan Productions, under auspieces of Fisk University Department of Art
Distribution: Pyramid Film & Video

Goin' Back to T-Town
Series: The American Experience
Year: 1993
Credits: Produced by Sam Pollard and Joyce Vaughn
Distribution: PBS Video

Golden Goa
Year: 1985

Credits: Written, directed, and produced by William Greaves
Production Company: William Greaves Productions, Inc.
Distribution: William Greaves Productions, Inc.

Gordon Parks: Visions: The Images, Words and Music of Gordon Parks
Year: 1986
Credits: Produced by Shep Morgan and John Carter; directed by
Gordon Parks
Distribution: Xenon Home Video

Gotta Make This Journey: Sweet Honey in the Rock
Year: 1983
Credits: Produced by Michelle D. Parkerson; directed by Joseph
Camp
Production Company: Eye of the Storm Productions, Inc.
Distribution: Women Make Movies

The Great Depression
Year: 1993
Credits: Executive produced and series created by Henry
Hampton; series written by Steve Fayer; senior producer,
Terry Kay Rockefeller
Production Company: Blackside and BBC-2
Distribution: PBS Video
   A Job at Ford's
   Produced, written, and directed by Jon Else
   The Road to Rock Bottom
   Produced, written, and directed by Terry Kay Rockefeller
   New Deal/New York
   Produced by Dante J. James
   We Have a Plan
   Produced, written, and directed by Lyn Goldfarb
   Mean Things Happening
   Produced, written, and directed by Dante J. James
   To Be Somebody
   Produced, written, and directed by Stephen Stept
   Arsenal of Democracy
   Produced, written, and directed by Susan Bellows

Handsworth Songs
Year: 1985
Credits: Produced by Lina Gopaul; directed by John Akomfrah

Production Company: Black Audio Film Collective
Distribution: National Black Programming Consortium

The Hard Way
Year: 1974
Credits: Produced, written, and directed by William Greaves
Production Company: William Greaves Productions, Inc. and
National Heart and Lung Institute
Distribution: National Audiovisual Center

Heaven, Earth, and Hell
Year: 1994
Credits: Directed by Thomas Allen Harris
Production Company: Not Channel Zero
Distribution: Third World Newsreel

Heritage of the Black West
Year: 1995
Credits: Produced, written, and directed by St. Clair Bourne
Production Company: National Geographic Society Educational
Films
Distribution: National Geographic

Horace Tapscott
Year: 1984
Credits: Directed by Barbara McCullough
Production Company: Independent

I Am Somebody
Year: 1970
Credits: Produced and directed by Madeline Anderson
Production Company: Icarus Films
Distribution: First Run / Icarus Films

I Be Done Been Was Is
Year: 1984
Credits: Written by Terry L. McMillan; directed by Debra J.
Robinson; produced by Debra J. Robinson and Leslie Holder
Production Company: CBS, Movielab Video
Distribution: Women Make Movies

I Never Danced the Way Girls Were Supposed To
Year: 1992

Credits: Directed and written by Dawn Suggs
Production Company: Third World Newsreel Productions
Distribution: Third World Newsreel

I'll Make Me a World
   Year: 1999
   Credits: Series executive produced by Henry Hampton; co-
      executive produced by Sam Pollard; produced by Terry Kay
      Rockefeller; written by Sheila Curran Bernard
   Production Company: Blackside Inc. in association with WNET
   Distribution: PBS Video

I Remember Harlem
   Year: 1981
   Credits: Produced and directed by William Miles; written by
      Clayton Riley
   Production Company: Films for the Humanities
   Distribution: Films for the Humanities and Sciences

Ida B. Wells: A Passion for Justice
   Year: 1989
   Credits: Executive produced by Judy Crichton; produced by
      William Greaves and Louise Archambault; directed and
      written by William Greaves
   Production Company: William Greaves Productions and WGBH
      Educational Foundations
   Distribution: William Greaves Productions, Inc.

In Motion: Amiri Baraka
Other Title: *Amiri Baraka: In Motion*
   Year: 1982
   Credits: Produced and directed by St. Clair Bourne; written by
      Lou Potter
   Production Company: The Chamba Organization
   Distribution: Chamba Mediaworks Film Library; Facets Multi-
      media, Inc.; First Run/Icarus Films

In Search of Our Fathers
   Year: 1993
   Credits: Written, produced and directed by Marco Williams
   Production Company: Filmmakers Library
   Distribution: Filmmakers Library, Inc.

In Search of Pancho Villa
> Year: 1978
> Credits: Produced and directed by William Greaves

In the Company of Men
> Year: 1969
> Credits: Produced, directed and written by William Greaves
> Production Company: William Greaves Productions, Inc.;
>   Newsweek
> Distribution: William Greaves Productions, Inc.

Ina Mae Best
> Year: 1993
> Credits: Directed by Charlene Gilbert
> Distribution: Third World Newsreel

Inside Bedford-Stuyvesant (compilation)
> Year: 1968–1970
> Credits: Produced and written by Charles Hobson
> Production Company: Metro Media Television, Channel 5

Integration Report #1
> Year: 1960
> Credits: Produced and written by Madeline Anderson
> Distribution: Center for Mass Communications

Introduction to Cultural Skit-Zo-Frenia
> Year: 1993
> Credits: Produced and directed by Jamika Ajalon
> Distribution: Third World Newsreel

Jack Wilson, Musician
> Year: 1978
> Credits: Produced, written, and directed by St. Clair Bourne
> Production Company: Produced for KCET-TV
> Distribution: Chamba Mediaworks, Inc.

James Baldwin: The Price of the Ticket
> Year: 1989
> Credits: Directed by Karen Thorsen; produced by Karen Thorsen
>   and William Miles

Production Company: Karen Thorsen production in association
with Maysles Films, Inc. and WNET, New York; written by
Karen Thorsen and Douglas K. Dempsey
Distribution: California Newsreel

Janine
Year: 1990
Credits: Produced and directed by Cheryl Dunye
Production Company: Independent
Distribution: Third World Newsreel

Jazz, The American Art Form
Series: Like It Is
Year: 1970
Credits: Produced and written by Gil Noble
Production Company: WABC-TV
Distribution: National Black Archives of Film and Broadcasting,
Inc.

Jembe
Year: 1989
Credits: Directed by Philip Mallory Jones
Distribution: Electronic Arts Intermix

John Henrik Clarke: A Great and Mighty Walk
Year: 1996
Credits: Directed by St. Claire Bourne; produced by Kimiko
Jackson; written by Lou Potter; executive produced by Wesley
Snipes
Production Company: Chamba Mediaworks
Distribution: Chamba Mediaworks Film Library

Just Doin' It: A Tale of Two Barbershops
Year: 1976
Credits: Produced by William Greaves; written by Lou Potter
and William Greaves; associate produced by Lou Potter
Production Company: William Greaves Productions, Inc.
Distribution: William Greaves Productions, Inc.

The KKK Boutique Ain't Just Rednecks
Year: 1994
Credits: Directed by Camille Billops

Production Company: Hatch-Billops Production
Distribution: Third World Newsreel

Keep Your Handsa Off the Park: A Role-Playing Game in Real and Virtual Worlds
(CD-ROM/Board Game)
Year: 1997
Credits: Produced by Reginald Woolery
Distribution: Available through the artist

Kinfolks
Year: 1978
Credits: Produced and written by Henry Hampton; directed by
Dwight Williams
Production Company: Blackside, Inc.

The Kitchen Blues
Year: 1994
Credits: Directed by Charlene Gilbert
Distribution: Third World Newsreel

Know Your Enemy
Year: 1990
Credits: Directed by Art Jones
Distribution: Third World Newsreel

Knowledge Reigns Supreme
Year: 1991
Credits: Directed by Art Jones
Distribution: Third World Newsreel

Langston Hughes: The Dream Keeper
Series: Voices & Visions
Year: 1988
Credits: Directed by St. Clair Bourne; written by Leslie Lee
Production Company: New York Center for Visual History, Inc.
Distribution: Chamba Mediaworks Film Library; Carousel Films
& Video; Facets Multimedia, Inc.

"Let the Church Say Amen!"
Year: 1973
Credits: Produced, directed, and written by St. Clair Bourne

Production Company: Chamba Productions
Distribution: Chamba Mediaworks Film Library; First Run/
Icarus Films

Liberators: Fighting on Two Fronts in World War II
Series: The American Experience
Year: 1992
Credits: Produced by William Miles and Nina Rosenblum;
written by John Crowley, Daniel V. Allentuck, and Lou Potter
Production Company: Miles Educational Film Productions, Inc.
in association with Thirteen/WNET
Distribution: Direct Cinema Ltd

Life Is a Saxophone
Year: 1985
Credits: Directed by Saundra Sharp and Orlando Bagwell
Production Company: A Sharp Show

A Litany for Survival: The Life and Work of Audre Lorde
Year: 1995
Credits: Produced by Ada Gay Griffin; directed by Ada Gay
Griffin and Michelle Parkerson
Production Company: Third World Newsreel
Distribution: Third World Newsreel

Lois Mailou Jones: Fifty Years of Painting
Year: 1983
Credits: Directed by Alonzo Crawford and Abraham (Abiyi) R.
Ford; written and produced by Abraham (Abiyi) R. Ford
Distribution: Abraham (Abiyi) R. Ford

Long Train Running: A History of the Oakland Blues
Other Title: *History of the Oakland Blues*
Year: 1981
Credits: Produced, written, and directed by Marlon T. Riggs and
Peter Webster
Production Company: Regents of the University of California

Looking for Langston
Other Title: *Meditation on Langston Hughes (1902–1967) and the Harlem
Renaissance*
Year: 1989

Credits: Written and directed by Isaac Julien; produced by
   Nadine Marsh-Edwards
Production Company: Sankofa Film & Video
Distribution: Ingram International Films; Facets Multimedia,
   Inc; Water Bearer Films; Third World Newsreel

Lost Control
   Year: 1975
   Credits: Directed and produced by Edie Lynch
   Distribution: Phoenix Films

Lumumba: Death of a Prophet
Other Title: *Lumumba: La Mort du Prophète*
   Year: 1992
   Credits: Produced and directed by Raoul Peck
   Distribution: California Newsreel

The Lure and the Lore: A Day with Thomas Pinnock
   Year: 1988
   Credits: Produced and directed by Ayoka Chenzira
   Production Company: Crossgrain Pictures
   Distribution: Third World Newsreel

Making "Do the Right Thing"
   Year: 1989
   Credits: Produced, directed, and written by St. Clair Bourne
   Production Company: Chamba Organization and 40 Acres and a
      Mule Filmworks
   Distribution: Chamba Mediaworks Film Library; First Run/
      Icarus Films

Malcolm X: El Hajj Malik El Shabazz
Series: Like It Is
   Year: 1976
   Credits: Produced and written by Gil Noble
   Production Company: WABC-TV
   Distribution: National Black Archives of Film and Broadcasting,
      Inc.

Malcolm X: Make It Plain
Other title: *Make It Plain*
Series: The American Experience
   Year: 1995

Credits: Produced and directed by Orlando Bagwell;
co-produced by Judy Richardson; executive produced by
Henry Hampton
Production Company: Blackside, Inc. and Roja Productions
Distribution: MPI Home Video

Malcolm X: Nationalist or Humanist?
Year: 1969
Credits: Produced and directed by Madeline Anderson; executive produced by William Greaves
Distribution: William Greaves Productions, Inc.

Mama's Pushcart: Ellen Stewart and 25 Years of La Mama
Year: 1988
Credits: Produced by Louise Diamond; directed by Demetria
Royals
Distribution: Women Make Movies

Mask (CD-ROM)
Year: 1991
Credits: Directed by Philip Mallory Jones
Distribution: Available through the artist

The Massachusetts 54th Colored Infantry
Series: The American Experience
Year: 1991
Credits: Produced and directed by Jacqueline Shearer
Production Company: WGBH/Boston, WNET/New York and
KCET/Los Angeles
Distribution: PBS Home Video

Men of Bronze
Year: 1977
Credits: Produced, researched, and directed by William Miles
Production Company: William Miles and Killiam Shows, Inc.
Distribution: Films, Inc.; Proud to Be . . . A Black Video Collection; Facets Multimedia, Inc.

The Men of Montford Point: The First Black Marines
Year: 1997
Credits: Executive Produced by Christopher Duffy; produced
and written by Nora Hiatt; directed by Jerald Harkness

Production Company: Visionary Productions, Inc. with Wabash Valley Broadcasting

Midnight Ramble: Oscar Micheaux and the Story of Race Movies
Year: 1994
Credits: Directed by Pearl Bowser and Bestor Cram; produced by Pamela A. Thomas and Bestor Cram; written by Clyde Taylor
Production Company: WGBH-TV Boston
Distribution: Shanachie

Miss Fluci Moses
Year: 1987
Credits: Directed and produced by Alile Sharon Larkin
Production Company: Alile Productions
Distribution: Women Make Movies

Missing Pages
Year: 1972
Credits: Written, directed, and produced by Carlton Moss; associate produced by David C. Driskell
Production Company: Artisan Productions, under auspices of Fisk University Department of Art
Distribution: Pyramid Film & Video

Missing Relations
Year: 1994
Credits: Produced, written, and directed by Yvonne Welbon
Production Company: Our Film Works
Distribution: Third World Newsreel

Moments without Proper Names
Year: 1986
Credits: Directed by Gordon Parks

Monique
Year: 1991
Credits: Produced, written, and directed by Yvonne Welbon
Production Company: Our Film Works
Distribution: Third World Newsreel

Mother Tongue
Year: 1994

Credits: Directed by Patrice Mallard
Production Company: Third World Newsreel Workshop
Distribution: Third World Newsreel

Mrs. Fannie Lou Hamer
Year: 1983
Credits: Produced and written by Gil Noble
Production Company: WABC-TV
Distribution: National Black Archives of Film and Broadcasting, Inc.

My Grandmother Worked
Year: 1995
Credits: Directed by La Trice A. Dixon
Production Company: Independent
Distribution: Third World Newsreel

Mystery of the Senses: Vision
Year: 1994
Credits: Produced, written, and directed by Carroll Parrott Blue
Production Company: PBS
Distribution: PBS

Namibia Independence Now!
Year: 1985
Credits: Produced by Pearl Bowser
Distribution: Third World Newsreel

The Nation Erupts
Year: 1992
Credits: Executive directed by Caryn Rogoff; produced by Donna Golden, Thomas Poole, and Art Jones; written by George Sosa
Production Company: Black Planet Productions; Deep Dish TV Network and Not Channel Zero
Distribution: Third World Newsreel

Nationtime: Gary
Year: 1973
Credits: Produced, written, and directed by William Greaves
Production Company: William Greaves Productions, Inc.
Distribution: William Greaves Productions, Inc.; Facets Multimedia

The Negro Soldier
  Year: 1944
  Credits: Directed by Frank Capra; written by Carlton Moss
  Production Company: The War Department Special Services
    Division
  Distribution: Republic Pictures Home Video; Nostalgia Family
    Video; International Historic Films, Inc.

New Orleans Brass
  Year: 1994
  Credits: Produced and directed by St. Clair Bourne
  Production Company: Chamba Mediaworks, Inc.
  Distribution: National Geographic Society Educational Films

New Worlds, New Forms
  Year: 1993
  Credits: Written and directed by Orlando Bagwell; produced by
    Orlando Bagwell and Susan Bellows
  Production Company: Thirteen/WNET in association with RM
    Arts and BBC-TV
  Distribution: Public Media Incorporated

Nigerian Art: Kindred Spirits
Other title: *Nigerian Artists*
  Year: 1990
  Credits: Produced, written, and directed by Carroll Parrott Blue
  Production Company: Smithsonian World, PBS-TV
  Distribution: Smithsonian Video

No Crystal Stair
  Year: 1976
  Credits: Produced and directed by Philip Mallory Jones and
    Gunilla Mallory Jones
  Production Company: New York State Council on the Arts
  Distribution: Ithaca Video Projects

Non, Je Ne Regrette Rien (No Regrets)
  Year: 1992
  Credits: Directed and produced by Marlon T. Riggs; associate
    produced by Nicole Atkinson
  Production Company: Signifyin' Productions
  Distribution: Frameline

No Justice, No Peace: Black Males Immediate
>Year: 1994
>Credits: Directed by Portia Cobb
>Production Company: Third World Newsreel
>Distribution: Third World Newsreel

Not in Vain: A Tribute to Martin Luther King, Jr.
>Year: 1981
>Credits: Directed by Stan Lathan

Now Pretend
>Year: 1992
>Credits: Directed by Leah Gilliam
>Distribution: Third World Newsreel

O Povo Organizado (The People Organized)
>Year: 1976
>Credits: Produced, written, and directed by Robert Van Lierop
>Distribution: Tricontinental Film Center

Older Women and Love
>Year: 1987
>Credits: Directed and produced by Camille Billops and James Hatch
>Production Company: Hatch-Billops Production
>Distribution: Third World Newsreel

On Becoming a Woman: Mothers and Daughters Talking Together
>Year: 1987
>Credits: Executive produced by Byllye Avery; directed by Cheryl Chisholm
>Production Company: Independent
>Distribution: Women Make Movies

On Merit
>Year: 1972
>Credits: Produced, written, and directed by William Greaves
>Production Company: William Greaves Productions, Inc.
>Distribution: William Greaves Productions, Inc.

Opposite Camps
>Year: 1994

Credits: Executive Produced by St. Clair Bourne
Production Company: Other Films
Distribution: Chamba Mediaworks Film Library

Opportunities in Criminal Justice
   Year: 1978
   Credits: Written, produced, and directed by William Greaves
   Production Company: William Greaves Productions, Inc.
   Distribution: William Greaves Productions, Inc.

Oscar Micheaux, Film Pioneer
Series: Were You There? #5
   Year: 1981
   Credits: Produced and written by Carol Munday Lawrence;
      directed by Robert N. Zagone
   Production Company: Nguzo Saba Films
   Distribution: Beacon Films

Our House: Gays and Lesbians in the Hood
   Year: 1993
   Credits: Produced by Cyrille Phipps and Donna Golden
   Production Company: Not Channel Zero; Black Planet Produc-
      tions
   Distribution: Third World Newsreel

Paradigm Shift (CD-ROM)
   Year: 1992
   Credits: Directed by Philip Mallory Jones
   Distribution: Available through the artist

The Passion of Remembrance
   Year: 1994
   Credits: Written and directed by Maureen Blackwood and Isaac
      Julien; produced by Martina Attille
   Production Company: Sankofa Film/Video Collective
   Distribution: Women Make Movies

Paul Laurence Dunbar: America's First Black Poet
Other title: *Paul Laurence Dunbar; Portraits in Black* (distributed on
videocassette)
   Year: 1973

Credits: Written, directed, and produced by Carlton Moss;
associate produced by David C. Driskell
Production Company: Artisan Productions, under auspices of
Fisk University Department of Art
Distribution: Pyramid Film & Video

Paul Robeson: Here I Stand
Year: 1999
Credits: Directed by St. Clair Bourne; written by Lou Potter;
produced by Chiz Schultz and Susan Lacy
Production Company: WNET 13-TV and Menair Media International, Inc.
Distribution: WNET

Paul Robeson: Man of Conscience
Year: 1987
Credits: Produced by William Miles in conjunction with Saul
Turrell
Production Company: Miles Educational Film Production, Inc.
Distribution: Miles Educational Film Production, Inc.

Paul Robeson: The Tallest Tree in Our Forest
Year: 1977
Credits: Produced and written by Gil Noble
Production Company: WABC-TV
Distribution: National Black Archives of Film and Broadcasting,
Inc.

People of the Land
Year: 1970
Credits: Written, produced, and directed by Lou Potter
Production Company: NET

Perfect Image?
Year: 1988
Credits: Directed by Maureen Blackwood
Production Company: Sankofa
Distribution: Third World Newsreel

A Plan for All Seasons
Year: 1983

Credits: Written, directed, and produced by William Greaves
Production Company: William Greaves Productions, Inc.
Distribution: William Greaves Productions, Inc.

Porgy and Bess: An American Voice
Series: Great Performances
    Year: 1998
    Credits: Directed by Nigel Noble; executive produced by
        Charles Hobson; produced by James A. Standifer; written by
        Gloria Naylor and Ed Apfel
    Production Company: University of Michigan in conjunction
        with Vanguard Films, Mojo Working Productions, and
        WNET/New York

Portrait of Two Artists
    Year: 1982
    Credits: Produced and directed by Carol Munday Lawrence
    Production Company: Nguzo Saba Films
    Distribution: Beacon Films

Portraits in Black
Other titles: Video collection includes *Gift of the Black Folk, Paul
Laurence Dunbar: America's First Black Poet,* and *Two Centuries of Black
American Art*
    Year: 1978
    Credits: Written, directed, and produced by Carlton Moss,
        associate produced by David C. Driskell
    Production Company: Artisan Productions, under auspices of
        Fisk University Department of Art
    Distribution: Pyramid Film & Video

The Potluck and the Passion
    Year: 1993
    Credits: Directed by Cheryl Dunye
    Distribution: Third World Newsreel

Power vs. The People
    Year: 1974
    Credits: Produced, written, and directed by William Greaves
    Production Company: EEOC and William Greaves Productions,
        Inc.
    Distribution: William Greaves Productions, Inc.

Praise House
> Year: 1991
> Credits: Directed by Julie Dash
> Distribution: Third World Newsreel

Preaching the Word
> Year: 1987
> Credits: Produced by William Miles
> Production Company: Miles Educational Film Productions, Inc.
> Distribution: Miles Educational Film Productions, Inc.

A Question of Color
Series: African American Perspectives
> Year: 1992
> Credits: Executive produced by St. Clair Bourne; directed by
>   Kathe Sandler; written by Kathe Sandler and Luke Charles
>   Harris
> Production Company: Film Two Productions
> Distribution: California Newsreel

The Question of Equality (Series)
> Year: 1995
> Credits: Series senior produced by Isaac Julien; executive
>   produced by David Meieran
> Production Company: Testing the Limits in association with
>   Channel Four Television UK
> Distribution: KQED Video
>> *Out Rage '69*
>> Produced, directed, and written by Arthur Dong
>> *Culture Wars*
>> Produced, directed, and edited by Tina DiFeliciantonio and
>>   Jane C. Wagner
>> *Hollow Liberty*
>> Directed by Robyn Hutt; produced by Robyn Hutt and
>>   Bennett Singer
>> *Generation "Q"*
>> Produced and directed by Robert Byrd

Racism 101
> Year: 1988
> Credits: Written and produced by Thomas Lennon; co-produced

and directed by Orlando Bagwell; executive produced by David Fanning
Production Company: WGBH Educational Foundation; Frontline
Distribution: PBS Video

Rainbow Black: Poet Sarah W. Fabio
Other title: *Rainbow Black: Portrait of Sarah Webster Fabio*
    Year: 1976
    Credits: Directed and produced by Cheryl Fabio [Bradford]
    Distribution: Cheryl Fabio Bradford

Remembering Thelma
    Year: 1981
    Credits: Directed, written, and produced by Kathe Sandler
    Distribution: Women Make Movies

Remembering Wei Yi-Fang, Remembering Myself . . .
    Year: 1995
    Credits: Produced and directed by Yvonne Welbon
    Production Company: Our Film Works
    Distribution: Third World Newsreel; Women Make Movies

Resurrections: A Moment in the Life of Paul Robeson
    Year: 1990
    Credits: Directed, written, and produced by William Greaves
    Production Company: William Greaves Productions, Inc.
    Distribution: William Greaves Productions, Inc.

Richard Wright: Black Boy
    Year: 1994
    Credits: Produced by Dave Lacy; written by Richard Wright
    Production Company: Mississippi Educational Television and the BBC
    Distribution: California Newsreel

Roots of Resistance: A Story of the Underground Railroad
Series: The American Experience
    Year: 1989
    Credits: Produced by Orlando Bagwell and Susan Bellows; written by Theodore Thomas

Production Company: Roja Film Productions and WGBH/
Boston, WNET/New York and KCET/Los Angeles
Distribution: Filmic Archives

Running with Jesse
Series: Frontline
Year: 1989
Credits: Produced by Orlando Bagwell
Production Company: PBS
Distribution: PBS Home Video

Sapphire and the Slave Girl
Year: 1995
Credits: Produced and written by Leah Gilliam
Production Company: Independent

Sapphire Take #1: The Message
Year: 1994
Credits: Directed by Cauleen Smith

Secret Daughter
Series: Frontline
Year: 1996
Credits: Produced by June Cross
Production Company: PBS

Secret Sounds Screaming: The Sexual Abuse of Children
Year: 1986
Credits: Directed by Ayoka Chenzira
Production Company: Independent
Distribution: Women Make Movies; Third World Newsreel

Sense of Pride: Hamilton Heights
Year: 1977
Credits: Directed and produced by Monica J. Freeman
Distribution: Monica J. Freeman

Sentry at the Gate: The Comedy of Jane Galvin-Lewis
Year: 1995
Credits: Produced by Ayoka Chenzira and Barbara Chirinos
Production Company: Red Carnelian
Distribution: Red Carnelian Black Indie Classics Collection

Seven Songs for Malcolm X
Other Title: *The Story of Malcolm X*
    Year: 1993
    Credits: Directed by John Akomfrah; produced by Lina Gopaul
    Production Company: Black Audio Film Collective
    Distribution: First Run/Icarus Films

Shattering the Silence
    Year: 1997
    Credits: Directed, produced and written by Stanley Nelson;
        executive produced, produced, and directed by Gail Pellett
    Production Company: Gail Pellett Productions, Inc.

She Don't Fade
    Year: 1991
    Credits: Directed by Cheryl Dunye
    Distribution: Third World Newsreel

Shopping Bag Spirits
    Year: 1980
    Credits: Barbara McCullough
    Distribution: Third World Newsreel

The Show
    Year: 1997
    Credits: Executive produced by Stan Lathan and Rob Kenneally;
        produced by Robert A. Johnson and Mike Tollin; directed by
        Brian Robbins; co-produced by Carmen Ashhurst
    Production Company: Rysher Entertainment with Russell
        Simmons
    Distribution: Columbia/TriStar Home Video

Sisters in the Life: First Love
    Year: 1993
    Credits: Produced, written, and directed by Yvonne Welbon
    Production Company: Our Film Works
    Distribution: Third World Newsreel

Slowly, This
    Year: 1995

Credits: Produced by Gina Harrell; directed by Arthur Jafa;
    written by Arthur Jafa, Alexs Pate, and David Mura
Production Company: G.P.A. Films, Inc.
Distribution: Third World Newsreel

Solitaire: dream journal (CD-ROM)
    Year: 1996
    Credits: Produced by Pamela Jennings
    Distribution: Available through the artist

Something to Build On
    Year: 1971
    Credits: Produced by St. Claire Bourne
    Production Company: Chamba Productions
    Distribution: College Entrance Examinations Board

South African Diary
    Year: 1991
    Credits: Produced and written by Gil Noble
    Production Company: WABC-TV
    Distribution: National Black Archives of Film and Broadcasting,
        Inc.

Space for Women
    Year: 1981
    Credits: Produced, written, and directed by William Greaves
    Production Company: William Greaves Productions, Inc. and
        NASA
    Distribution: William Greaves Productions, Inc.

Spirit and Truth Music
    Year: 1987
    Credits: Directed and produced by Edward Timothy Lewis
    Distribution: Edward T. Lewis Film Library

Splash
    Year: 1991
    Credits: Directed, written and produced by Thomas Allen
        Harris
    Production Company: Evolution Productions
    Distribution: Third World Newsreel

Steppin'
> Year: 1992
> Credits: Directed by Jerald Harkness
> Distribution: Cinema Guild

Still a Brother: Inside the Negro Middle Class
> Year: 1968
> Credits: Produced, written, and directed by William Greaves;
> co-produced by William Branch
> Production Company: William Greaves Productions, Inc.

Stormé: The Lady of the Jewel Box
> Year: 1987
> Credits: Produced and directed by Michelle Parkerson
> Production Company: Eye of the Storm Productions, Inc.
> Distribution: Women Make Movies

Street Corner Stories
> Year: 1977
> Credits: Directed and produced by Warrington Hudlin

Struggle and Success: The African American Experience in Japan
> Year: 1993
> Credits: Produced and directed by Regge Life
> Distribution: Struggle and Success Film Library

Struggle for Los Trabajos
> Year: 1972
> Credits: Produced, written, and directed by William Greaves
> Distribution: William Greaves Productions, Inc.

Suzanne Suzanne
> Year: 1982
> Credits: Directed and produced by Camille Billops and James
> Hatch
> Production Company: Hatch-Billops Production
> Distribution: Third World Newsreel

Symbiopsychotaxiplasm: Take One
> Year: 1971
> Credits: Produced, written, and directed by William Greaves;
> co-produced by Manuel Melamed

Production Company: Take One Productions, Inc.
Distribution: William Greaves Productions, Inc.

Syvilla: They Dance to Her Drum
Year: 1979
Credits: Directed and produced by Ayoka Chenzira
Distribution: Third World Newsreel

Testament
Year: 1988
Credits: Directed by John Akomfrah
Distribution: National Black Programming Consortium

That's Black Entertainment
Year: 1985
Credits: Produced by Fred T. Kuehnert and G. William Jones;
directed by William Greaves and G. William Jones; written by
G. William Jones
Production Company: Skyline Entertainment
Distribution: VCI Home Video; Facets Multimedia, Inc.; Baker &
Taylor Video

To Free Their Minds
Year: 1974
Credits: Directed, written and produced by William Greaves
Production Company: William Greaves Productions, Inc.
Distribution: William Greaves Productions, Inc.

"Together We Can"
Year: 1985
Credits: Written by Carmelita Fitzgerald-Mills, Angela Noel and
Cheryl Fabio; directed by Cheryl Fabio
Production Company: FabioFitzgeraldNoel Communications
Distribution: MTI Film & Video

Tongues Untied
Year: 1989
Credits: Directed and produced by Marlon T. Riggs; produced
by Ron Simmons; written by Joseph Beam
Production Company: Signifyin' Productions
Distribution: Frameline

Touch of the Tar Brush
Year: 1991
Credits: Directed by John Akomfrah
Production Company: BAFC/BBC
Distribution: Third World Newsreel

Tribute to Jackie Robinson
Year: 1990
Credits: Directed and produced by William Greaves
Production Company: William Greaves Productions, Inc.
Distribution: Jackie Robinson Foundation

The Trouble I've Seen
Year: 1976
Credits: Produced and directed by Philip Mallory Jones and
Gunilla Mallory Jones
Production Company: American Film Institute in association
with the National Endowment for the Arts
Distribution: Ithaca Video Projects

Trumpetistically, Clora Bryant
Year: 1989
Credits: Directed and produced by Zeinabu irene Davis
Production Company: Wimmin with a Mission Productions

Two Centuries of Black American Art
Other Title: *Portraits in Black* (distributed on videocassette)
Year: 1976–77
Credits: Written, directed, and produced by Carlton Moss;
associate produced by David C. Driskell
Production Company: Artisan Productions, under auspices of
Fisk University Department of Art
Distribution: Pyramid Film & Video

Two Dollars and a Dream
Year: 1988
Credits: Produced and directed by Stanley Nelson; written by
Lou Potter
Production Company: Filmmakers Library, Inc.
Distribution: Filmmakers Library, Inc.

Two Women
> Year: 1976
> Credits: Produced and directed by Carroll Parrott Blue

Valerie: A Woman! An Artist! A Philosophy of Life!
> Year: 1975
> Credits: Produced and directed by Monica J. Freeman
> Production Company: Nafasi Productions Inc.
> Distribution: Phoenix/BFA Films & Video

Varnette's World: A Study of a Young Artist
> Year: 1979
> Credits: Produced, written, and directed by Carroll Parrott Blue
> Production Company: WNET-TV
> Distribution: Carroll Blue Film Library

Vintage: Families of Value
> Year: 1995
> Credits: Produced, written, and directed by Thomas Allen
> Harris
> Production Company: Chimpanzee Productions, Creative Time
> City Wide Productions
> Distribution: Third World Newsreel

Visions of the Spirit: A Portrait of Alice Walker
Series: America: A Cultural Mosaic
> Year: 1989
> Credits: Produced and directed by Elena Featherston
> Production Company: Raiden Productions; Reel Directions
> Distribution: Women Make Movies, Inc.

Voice of La Raza
> Year: 1972
> Credits: Produced, written, and directed by William Greaves
> Production Company: William Greaves Productions for the
> Equal Employment Opportunity Commission
> Distribution: William Greaves Productions

W. E. B. Du Bois: A Biography in Four Voices
> Year: 1996

Credits: Written by Toni Cade Bambara, Wesley Brown, Thulani
Davis and Imamu Amiri Baraka; directed by Louis J. Massiah.
Larry Banks, Arthur Jafa, and Michael Chin
Production Company: Scribe Video Center
Distribution: California Newsreel

The Walls Come Tumbling Down
Year: 1975
Credits: Produced and directed by Madeline Anderson
Production Company: Onyx Productions
Distribution: Phoenix Films

Wassa
Year: 1989
Credits: Directed by Philip Mallory Jones
Distribution: Electronic Arts Intermix

The Watermelon Woman
Year: 1996
Credits: Written and directed by Cheryl Dunye; produced by
Barry Swimar, Alexandra Juhasz, and Cate Wilson
Distribution: First Run/Icarus Films

We Are Universal
Year: 1971
Credits: Directed and produced by Billy Jackson
Production Company: Nommo Productions
Distribution: Nommo Productions

Wealth of a Nation
Year: 1964
Credits: Produced, written, and directed by William Greaves
Production Company: William Greaves Productions, Inc.
Distribution: William Greaves Productions, Inc.

What Is a Line?
Year: 1994
Credits: Produced, written, and directed by Shari Frilot
Distribution: Third World Newsreel

Where Dreams Come True
Year: 1979

Credits: Produced, written, and directed by William Greaves
Production Company: NASA
Distribution: William Greaves Productions, Inc.

Who Needs a Heart?
Year: 1991
Credits: Directed by John Akomfrah
Production Company: BAFC
Distribution: Third World Newsreel

Whose Standard English?
Year: 1974
Credits: Produced, written, and directed by William Greaves
Production Company: William Greaves Productions, Inc.
Distribution: William Greaves Productions, Inc.

The Wilmington 10—USA 10,000
Other title: *Project '98*
Year: 1978
Credits: Directed by Haile Gerima
Distribution: Mypheduh Films, Inc.

The World of Piri Thomas
Year: 1968
Credits: Produced by Dick McCutchen; directed by Gordon
Parks
Production Company: National Educational Television and
Radio Center
Distribution: Indiana University Audio-Visual Center

World Saxophone Quartet
Year: 1980
Credits: Produced and directed by Barbara McCullough in
conjunction with The Opened I, Inc.
Distributon: Third World Newsreel

World Wide Web/Million Man March (Web Site and CD-ROM)
Year: 1997
Credits: Produced by Reginald Woolery
Distribution: Available through the artist

Newsreels
>
> All American Newsreel (All-American; All-America)
> By-Line Newsreel

Television Series
>
> Black Journal
> Black Horizons
> Inside Bedford-Stuyvesant
> Like It Is
> Say Brother
> Tony Brown's Journal

FILM /
VIDEOMAKER INDEX

Achkar, David
  Allah Tantou, À La Grace de Dieu
Ajalon, Jamika
  Introduction to Cultural Skit-Zo-Frenia
Akomfrah, John
  Handsworth Songs
  Seven Songs for Malcolm X
  Testament
  Touch of the Tar Brush
  Who Needs a Heart?
Alexander, William
  All American (or All-American or All-America) Newsreel
  By-Line Newsreel (series)
  Call to Duty
  The Highest Tradition
  Village of Hope
Allen, Austin
  Claiming Open Spaces
Anderson, Madeline
  Being Me
  Black Journal
  I Am Somebody
  Integration Report #1
  Malcolm X: Nationalist or Humanist?
  The Walls Come Tumbling Down
Andrews, Lawrence
  An I for an I
  "and they came riding into town on BLACK AND SILVER HORSES"
Ashhurst, Carmen
  The Show

Atkinson, Nicole
  Black Is . . . Black Ain't
  Non, Je Ne Regrette Rien

Attille, Martina
  The Passion of Remembrance

Avery, Byllye
  On Becoming a Woman

Badgley, Christiane
  Black Is . . . Black Ain't

Bagwell, Orlando
  Africans in America: Africa's Journey through Slavery
  Ain't Scared of Your Jails (Eyes on the Prize I)
  Frederick Douglass: When the Lion Wrote History
  Life Is a Saxophone
  Malcolm X: Make It Plain
  Mississippi: Is This America? (Eyes on the Prize I)
  New Worlds, New Forms
  Racism 101
  Roots of Resistance: A Story of the Underground Railroad
  Running with Jesse

Bambara, Toni Cade
  The Bombing of Osage Avenue
  W. E. B. Du Bois: A Biography in Four Voices

Banks, Larry
  W. E. B. Du Bois: A Biography in Four Voices

Baraka, Imamu Amiri
  W. E. B. Du Bois: A Biography in Four Voices

Beam, Joseph
  Tongues Untied

Billops, Camille
  Finding Christa
  The KKK Boutique Ain't Just Rednecks
  Older Women and Love
  Suzanne Suzanne

Blackwood, Maureen
  The Passion of the Remembrance
  Perfect Image?

Blue, Carroll Parrott
  Back to the Movement (Eyes on the Prize II)
  Black Is . . . Black Ain't

Conversations with Roy DeCarava
Mystery of the Senses: Vision
Nigerian Art: Kindred Spirits
The Time Has Come (Eyes on the Prize II)
Two Women
Varnette's World: A Study of a Young Artist

Bogle, Donald
Fade to Black

Bond, Julian
Awakenings, 1954–56 (Eyes on the Prize II)

Bourne, St. Clair
America: Black and White
Bellevue Emergency
Big City Blues
The Black and the Green
Black Cop
Black Journal
Heritage of the Black West
In Motion: Amiri Baraka
Jack Wilson, Musician
John Henrik Clarke: A Great and Mighty Walk
Langston Hughes: The Dream Keeper
"Let the Church Say Amen!"
Making "Do the Right Thing"
New Orleans Brass
Opposite Camps
A Question of Color
Paul Robeson: Here I Stand
Something to Build On
Val Verde
Where Roots Endure

Bowser, Pearl
Midnight Ramble: Oscar Micheaux and the Story of Race Movies
Namibia Independence Now!

Boyd, Melba
The Black Unicorn

Bradford, Cheryl Fabio
Rainbow Black: Portrait of Sarah Webster Fabio

Branch, William
Still a Brother: Inside the Negro Middle Class

Brown, Tony
  Tony Brown's Journal

Brown, Wesley
  W. E. B. Du Bois: A Biography in Four Voices

Burnett, Charles
  *America Becoming: A Look at the History of the Immigration and
    Nationality Act from 1965–Present*

Chenzira, Ayoka
  The Lure and the Lore: A Day with Thomas Pinnock
  Secret Sounds Screaming: The Sexual Abuse of Children
  Sentry at the Gate: The Comedy of Jane Galvin-Lewis
  Syvilla: They Dance to Her Drum

Chirinos, Barbara
  Sentry at the Gate: The Comedy of Jane Galvin-Lewis

Chisholm, Cheryl
  On Becoming a Woman

Churchill, Joan
  Don't Believe the Hype: The Politics of Rap

Cobb, Portia
  Drive By Shoot
  No Justice, No Peace: Black Males Immediate

Cokes, Tony
  Black Celebration: A Rebellion against the Commodity
  Fade to Black

Cram, Bestor
  Midnight Ramble: Oscar Micheaux and the Story of Race Movies

Crawford, Alonzo
  Crowded
  Dirt, Ground, Earth and Land
  Lois Mailou Jones: Fifty Years of Painting

Crichton, Judy
  Ida B. Wells: A Passion for Justice

Cross, June
  Secret Daughter

Crossley, Callie
  Bridge to Freedom (Eyes on the Prize I)
  No Easy Walk (Eyes on the Prize I)

Crowley, John
  Liberators: Fighting on Two Fronts in World War II

Crump, Steven
  Airmen and Adversity

Dash, Julie
  Four Women
  Praise House

Davis, Thulani
  W. E. B. Du Bois: A Biography in Four Voices

Davis, Zeinabu irene
  Cycles
  Trumpetistically, Clora Bryant

DeVinney, James A.
  Back to the Movement (Eyes on the Prize II)
  Bridge to Freedom (Eyes on the Prize I)
  The Time Has Come (Eyes on the Prize II)

Diamond, Louise
  Conjure Women
  Mama's Pushcart

Dixon, La Trice A.
  My Grandmother Worked

Driskell, David C.
  Gift of the Black Folk
  Missing Pages
  Paul Laurence Dunbar: America's First Black Poet
  Portraits in Black
  Two Centuries of Black American Art

Dukes, Fred L.
  Apollo

Dunye, Cheryl
  Janine
  The Potluck and the Passion
  She Don't Fade
  The Watermelon Woman

Easley, William
  Apollo

Elliott, Dolores
  A Portrait of Max

Else, Jon
  Eyes on the Prize (Series)
  A Job at Ford's (The Great Depression)

Fabio (Bradford), Cheryl
Rainbow Black: Poet Sarah W. Fabio
"Together We Can"

Fanning, David
Racism 101

Featherston, Elena
Visions of the Spirit: A Portrait of Alice Walker

Fitzgerald-Mills, Carmelita
"Together We Can"

Ford, Abraham (Abiyi) R.
Burkina Faso: Land of the People of Dignity
Lois Mailou Jones: Fifty Years of Painting

Freeman, Monica J.
Children's Art Carnival—Learning through the Arts
Sense of Pride: Hamilton Heights
Valerie: A Woman! An Artist! A Philosophy of Life!

Frilot, Shari
Black Nations/Queer Nations?
What Is a Line?

Funderburke, Kenyatta
Can't Jail the Revolution and Break the Walls Down

Garrett, Kent
Black Journal (Series)

Gerima, Haile
After Winter: Sterling Brown
The Wilmington 10—USA 10,000

Gibson, Linda
Flag

Gifford, David
From Harlem to Harvard

Gilbert, Charlene
Ina Mae Best
The Kitchen Blues

Gilliam, Leah
Now Pretend
Sapphire and the Slave Girl

Golden, Donna
Doing What It Takes: Black Folks Getting and Staying Healthy

The Nation Erupts
Our House: Gays and Lesbians in the Hood

Goodkind, Lois
Being Me

Grant, Joanne
Fundi: The Story of Ella Baker

Greaves, William
Ali, The Fighter
Beyond the Forest
Black Journal (Series)
Black Power in America: Myth or Reality
Booker T. Washington: The Life and Legacy
Choice of Destinies
Cleared for Takeoff
The Deep North
EEOC Story
Emergency Ward
Fighter for Freedom: The Frederick Douglass Story
The First World Festival of Negro Arts
Frederick Douglass: An American Life
From These Roots
Golden Goa
The Hard Way
Ida B. Wells: A Passion for Justice
In Search of Pancho Villa
In the Company of Men
Just Doin' It: A Tale of Two Barbershops
Malcolm X: Nationalist or Humanist?
Nationtime: Gary
On Merit
Opportunities in Criminal Justice
A Plan for All Seasons
Power vs. the People
Resurrections: A Moment in the Life of Paul Robeson
Space for Women
Still a Brother: Inside the Negro Middle Class
Struggle for Los Trabajos
Symbiopsychotaxiplasm: Take One
That's Black Entertainment
To Free Their Minds
Tribute to Jackie Robinson

Voice of La Raza
Wealth of a Nation
Where Dreams Come True
Whose Standard English?

Griffin, Ada Gay
    Can't Jail the Revolution and Break the Walls Down
    A Litany for Survival: The Life and Work of Audre Lorde

Hampton, Henry
    Crisis to Crisis: Voices of a Divided City
    Eyes on the Prize (Series)
    Eyes on the Prize II (Series)
    The Great Depression (Series)
    I'll Make Me a World (Series)
    Kinfolks
    Malcolm X: Make It Plain

Harkness, Jerald
    Facing the Facade
    The Men of Montford Point: The First Black Marines
    Steppin'

Harrell, Gina
    Slowly, This

Harris, Luke Charles
    A Question of Color

Harris, Thomas Allen
    Black Body: A Work in Progress
    Heaven, Earth and Hell
    Splash
    Vintage: Families of Value

Hobson, Charles
    Black Journal (Series)
    Inside Beford-Stuyevesant (Series)
    Porgy and Bess: An American Voice

Holder, Leslie
    I Be Done Been Was Is

House, Gloria
    Claiming Open Spaces

Hudlin, Warrington
    Black at Yale: A Film Diary

Capoeira of Brazil
Street Corner Stories

Hutt, Robyn
Hollow Liberty (The Question of Equality)

Jackson, Billy
Booker T. Washington: The Life and the Legacy
Didn't We Ramble On: The Black Marching Band
We Are Universal

Jackson, Kimiko
John Henrik Clarke: A Great and Mighty Walk

Jafa, Arthur
Slowly, This
W. E. B. Du Bois: A Biography in Four Voices

James, Dante J.
Mean Things Happening (The Great Depression)
New Deal/New York (The Great Depression)

Jenkins, Horace
Black Journal (Series)

Jennings, Pamela
the book of ruins and desire
Solitaire: dream journal

Jones, Art
Know Your Enemy
Knowledge Reigns Supreme
The Nation Erupts

Jones, Jacquie
Africans in America: Africa's Journey through Slavery

Jones, Philip Mallory
Black, White and Married
Dreamkeeper
First World Order
Ghosts and Demons
Jembe
Mask
No Crystal Stair
Paradigm Shift
The Trouble I've Seen
Wassa

Julien, Isaac
  The Darker Side of Black
  Frantz Fanon: Black Skin, White Mask
  Looking for Langston
  The Passion of Remembrance
  The Question of Equality (Series)

Katsiane, Jared
  amBUSHed

King, Hugh
  Black and Blue

King, Woodie, Jr.
  Black Theater Movement: From "A Raisin in the Sun" to the Present

Lacy, Madison Davis, Jr.
  Back to the Movement (Eyes on the Prize II)
  The Time Has Come (Eyes on the Prize II)

Larkin, Alile Sharon
  Miss Fluci Moses

Lathan, Stan
  Alvin Ailey: Memories and Visions
  Apollo
  Black Journal
  A Celebration of Life: A Tribute to the Life of Martin Luther King, Jr.
  Fall River Legend
  Not in Vain: A Tribute to Martin Luther King, Jr.
  The Show

Lawrence, Carol Munday
  Fade Out: The Erosion of Black Images in the Media
  Oscar Micheaux, Film Pioneer
  Portrait of Two Artists

Lee, Leslie
  Langston Hughes: The Dream Keeper

Lee, Spike
  Four Little Girls

Lennon, Thomas
  Racism 101

Lew-Lee, Lee
  All Power to the People

Lewis, David
  From Harlem to Harvard

Lewis, Edward Timothy
  Spirit and Truth Music
Life, Regge
  Doubles: Japan and America's Intercultural Children
  Struggle and Success: The African American Experience in Japan
Lynch, Edie
  Lost Control
Makarah, O. Funmilayo
  Creating a Different Image: Portrait of Alile Sharon Larkin
Mallard, Patrice
  Mother Tongue
Markin, Carole
  From Harlem to Harvard
Marsh-Edwards, Nadine
  Looking for Langston
Massiah, Louis J.
  The Bombing of Osage Avenue
  A Nation of Law? (Eyes on the Prize II)
  Power! (Eyes on the Prize II)
  W. E. B. Du Bois: A Biography in Four Voices
McCullough, Barbara
  Fragments of Barbara McCullough
  Horace Tapscott
  Shopping Bag Spirits
  World Saxophone Quartet
McDaniel, Matthew
  *Birth of a Nation 4*29*92*
McKenzie, Michele
  Black Women, Sexual Politics and the Revolution
McMillan, Terry L.
  I Be Done Been Was Is
Miles, William
  Black Champions
  Black Stars in Orbit
  I Remember Harlem
  James Baldwin: The Price of the Ticket
  Liberators: Fighting on Two Fronts in World War II
  Men of Bronze
  Paul Robeson: Man of Conscience

Positively Black
Preaching the Word

Moss, Carlton
Charles White: Drawing from Life
Gift of the Black Folk
House on Cedar Hill: Frederick Douglass
Missing Pages
The Negro Soldier
Paul Laurence Dunbar: America's First Black Poet (distributed on video with title *Portraits in Black*)
Portraits in Black (video release of *Paul Laurence Dunbar*)
Two Centuries of Black American Art

Moss, Richard Dean
Adventures in Assimilation

Mura, David
Slowly, This

Nash, Mark
Frantz Fanon: Black Skin, White Mask

Naylor, Gloria
Porgy and Bess: An American Voice

Nelson, Stanley
The Black Press: Soldiers without Swords
Shattering the Silence
Two Dollars and a Dream

Noble, Gil
Dr. Martin Luther King, Jr.: An Amazing Grace
Jazz, The American Art Form
Like It Is (Series)
Malcolm X: El Hajj Malik El Shabazz
Mrs. Fannie Lou Hamer
Paul Robeson: The Tallest Tree in Our Forest
South African Diary

Noel, Angela
"Together We Can"

Ott, Thomas
A Nation of Law? (Eyes on the Prize II)

Owanda, Doris
Cycles

Palcy, Euzhan
   Aimé Césaire: A Voice for History. III, The Strength to Face Tomorrow
Parkerson, Michelle
   . . . But Then, She's Betty Carter
   Gotta Make This Journey: Sweet Honey in the Rock
   A Litany for Survival: The Life and Work of Audre Lorde
   Stormé: The Lady of the Jewel Box
Parks, Gordon
   Diary of a Harlem Family
   Moments without Proper Names
   Gordon Parks: Visions: The Images, Words and Music of Gordon Parks
   The World of Piri Thomas
Pate, Alexs
   Slowly, This
Peck, Raoul
   Lumumba: Death of a Prophet
Pellett, Gail
   Shattering the Silence
Phipps, Cyrille
   Black Women, Sexual Politics and the Revolution
   Our House: Gays and Lesbian in the Hood
Pollard, Sam
   Ain't Gonna Shuffle No More (Eyes on the Prize II)
   Four Little Girls
   Goin' Back to T-Town
   I'll Make Me a World
   Two Societies (Eyes on the Prize II)
Poole, Thomas
   The Nation Erupts
Potter, Lou
   The Black and the Green
   Black Journal (Series)
   Black Power in America: Myth or Reality
   Booker T. Washington: The Life and Legacy
   The Exiles
   Fighter for Freedom: The Frederick Douglass Story
   Frederick Douglass: An American Life
   In Motion: Amiri Baraka

John Henrik Clarke: A Great and Mighty Walk
Just Doin' It: A Tale of Two Barbershops
Liberators: Fighting on Two Fronts in World War II
Paul Robeson: Here I Stand
People of the Land
Two Dollars and a Dream

Richardson, Judy
   Eyes on the Prize II (Series)
   Malcolm X: Make It Plain

Riggs, Marlon T.
   Affirmations
   Anthem
   Black Is . . . Black Ain't
   Changing Images: Mirrors of Life, Molds of Reality
   Color Adjustment
   Ethnic Notions
   Long Train Running: A History of the Oakland Blues
   Non, Je Ne Regrette Rien (No Regrets)
   Tongues Untied
   Visions toward Tomorrow: Ida Louise Jackson

Riley, Clayton
   Big City Blues
   I Remember Harlem

Robinson, Debra J.
   I Be Done Been Was Is

Robinson, Tamara E.
   Frederick Douglass: When the Lion Wrote History

Royals, Demetria
   Conjure Women
   Mama's Pushcart

Sandler, Kathe
   A Question of Color
   Remembering Thelma

Sharp, Saundra
   Life Is a Saxophone

Shearer, Jacqueline
   The Keys to the Kingdom (Eyes on the Prize II)
   The Massachusetts 54th Colored Infantry
   The Promised Land (Eyes on the Prize II)

Simmons, Ron
  Tongues Untied

Singer, Bennett
  Hollow Liberty (The Question of Equality)

Smith, Cauleen
  Sapphire Take #1: The Message

Smith, Llewellyn
  Africans in America: Africa's Journey through Slavery

Smith, Yvonne
  Adam Clayton Powell

Snipes, Wesley
  John Henrik Clarke: A Great and Mighty Walk

Sosa, George
  The Nation Erupts

Speight, Alonzo
  Deft Changes: An Improvised Experience

Standifer, James A.
  Porgy and Bess: An American Voice

Suggs, Dawn
  Chasing the Moon
  I Never Danced the Way Girls Were Supposed To

Taylor, Clyde
  Midnight Ramble: Oscar Micheaux and the Story of Race Movies

Taylor, Jocelyn
  Bodily Functions
  Frankie and Jocie

Teno, Jean-Marie
  Afrique, Je Te Plumerai

Thomas, Pamela A.
  Midnight Ramble: Oscar Micheaux and the Story of Race Movies

Thomas, Theodore
  Roots of Resistance: A Story of the Underground Railroad

Tollin, Mike
  The Show

Trammel, Donald
  Fade to Black

Van Lierop, Robert
  A Luta Continua
  O Povo Organizado

Vaughn, Joyce
  Goin' Back to T-Town

Walker, Noland
  Africans in America: Africa's Journey through Slavery

Webster, Peter
  Long Train Running: A History of the Oakland Blues

Welbon, Yvonne
  The Cinematic Jazz of Julie Dash
  Missing Relations
  Monique
  Remembering Wei Yi-Fang, Remembering Myself . . .
  Sisters in the Life: First Love

Williams, Dwight
  Kinfolks

Williams, Lamar
  Black and Blue

Williams, Marco
  From Harlem to Harvard
  In Search of Our Fathers

Wood, Biddy
  By-Line Newsreel

Woolery, Reginald
  Keep Your Handsa Off the Park: A Role-playing Game in Real and Virtual Worlds
  World Wide Web/Million Man March

BIBLIOGRAPHY

Akomfrah, John, and Pervaiz Khan, eds. "Third Scenario: Theory and the Politics of Location." *Framework* 36 (1989).

Alexander, William. *Film on the Left: American Documentary from 1931 to 1942.* Princeton: Princeton University Press, 1981.

Allentuck, Daniel. "Official WWII History Doesn't Tell All." World Wide Web, http://members.aol.com/dignews/letoed2.htm, 24 June 1997. Originally published in *New York Post,* 9 February 1993.

Allentuck, Daniel, and Lou Potter. "To the editor." World Wide Web, http://members.aol.com/dignews/letoed1.htm, 24 June 1997. Originally published in *Newsday,* 7 January 1993.

Als, H. "Negro Faggotry." *Black Film Review* 5, no. 3 (1989): 18–19.

Anderson, Trezzvant W. *Come Out Fighting: The Epic Tale of the 761st Tank Battalion, 1942–1945.* Tiesendorf, Germany: Salzburger Druckerei und Verlag, 1945.

Arroyo, Jose. "Look Back and Talk Black: The Films of Isaac Julien." *Jump Cut,* no. 36 (May 1991): 98–107, 110.

Arthur, Paul. "The Appearance of History in Recent Avant-Garde Film." *Frame/Work* 2, no. 3 (1989): 39–45.

———. "The Last of the Last Machine? Avant-Garde Film since 1966." *Millennium Film Journal* 16/17/18 (Fall/Winter 1986–87): 69–94.

Ashe-Moutoussamy, Jeanne. *Viewfinders: Black Women Photographers.* New York: Dodd, Mead, 1986.

Baillou, Charles. "In Defense of *Liberators.*" *The Independent* 16, no. 3 (April 1993): 5.

———. "'*Liberators*' Filmmakers Defend Their World War II Documentary." *New York Amsterdam News,* 18 September 1993, 23.

———. "'PBS' Documentary, '*Liberators,*' Portrays History of Blacks in WWII." World Wide Web, http://members.aol.com/dignews/amsterdm.htm, 24 June 1997. Originally published in *New York Amsterdam News,* 14 November 1992.

Baker, Houston A., Jr. "Spike Lee and the Commerce of Culture." In *Black American Cinema,* edited by Manthia Diawara, New York: Routledge, 1993, 154–76.

Baker, Robin. "Computer Technology and Special Effects in Contemporary Cinema." In *Future Visions: New Technologies of the Screen,* edited by Philip Hayward and Tana Wollen. London: British Film Institute, 1994, 31–45.

Bambara, Toni Cade. "Reading the Signs, Empowering the Eye: *Daughters of the Dust* and the Independent Cinema Movement." In *Black American Cinema,* edited by Manthia Diawara. New York: Routledge, 1993, 118–44.

Barol, Bill. "A Struggle for the Prize." *Newsweek,* 22 August 1988, 63.

Becquer, Marcos. "Snap!thology and Other Discursive Practices in Tongues Untied." *Wide Angle* 13, no. 2 (April 1991): 6–17.

Bedford, Karen Everhart. "'Messy History': The Hardest Work." *Current,* 13 July 1993.

———. "Review finds factual flaws in '*Liberators.*'" World Wide Web, http://

www.current.org/hi317.html, 26 March 1997. Originally published in *Current*, 20 September 1993.

Bender, Benjamin. "Letter to the Editor." *New York Times*, 22 April 1985, A18.

Bernstein, Richard. "Doubts Mar PBS Film on Black Army Unit." *New York Times*, 1 March 1993, late edition, B1.

"The Black Side of Mass Media." *Black Enterprise* 10/11 (June 1980): 72.

Bobo, Jacqueline, ed. *Black Women Film and Video Artists*. New York: Routledge, 1998.

Borchert, James. "*Eyes on the Prize: America's Civil Rights Years.*" *Choice*, January 1988, 731.

Borden, Gail Frey. *Seven Six One*. Los Angeles: Burning Gate Press, 1991.

Bourne, St. Clair. "The African American Image in American Cinema." *The Black Scholar* 21, no. 2 (March/April/May 1990): 12–19.

———. "Bright Moments: The Black Journal Series." *The Independent* 11, no. 4 (May 1988): 10–13.

———. "The Continuing Drama of African American Images in American Cinema." In *Picturing Us*, edited by Deborah Willis. New York: The New Press, 1994, 145–52.

———. "The Development of the Contemporary Black Film Movement." In Gladstone L. Yearwood, *Black Cinema Aesthetics: Issues in Independent Black Filmmaking*. Athens: Ohio University Center for Afro-American Studies, 1982, 93–105.

Bowser, Pearl. "Homage to William Greaves." In *Independent Black American Cinema*, edited by Pearl Bowser and Valerie Harris. New York: Theater Program of Third World Newsreel, 1981.

Bradley, Jeff. "Black troops first to reach death camp." World Wide Web, http://members.aol.com/dignews/g-jacobs.htm, 24 June 1997. Originally published in *Denver Post*, 7 March 1993.

Brown, F., Jr. "Waiting for Langston." *Black Film Review* 5, no. 3 (1989): 12–13.

Butler, Alison. "The Half Open Door: Channel Four and Independent Production in the UK." *The Independent* 10, no. 8 (October 1987).

———. "Handsworth Songs: An Occasion for Hope for Britain's Third Cinema?" *International Documentary*, Winter/Spring 1988, 19–22.

Cham, Mbye, ed. *Exiles: Essays on Caribbean Cinema*. Trenton, N.J.: Africa World Press, 1992.

Channer, Colin. "Henry Hampton, Executive Producer, *Eyes on the Prize.*" *Millimeter*, January 1988, 58, 62.

Coleman, Stephen. "St. Clair Bourne: 20 Years Filming the Black Experience." *Black Masks*, October/November 1990, 4–5, 20.

Covert, Nadine. "Who's Who in Filmmaking: St. Clair Bourne." *Sightlines* 8, no. 3 (Spring 1975): 17–18, 31–32.

Cripps, Thomas. "*The Negro Soldier.*" In *Black Film as Genre*. Bloomington: Indiana University Press, 1978, 100–14.

———. "*The Making of The Negro Soldier.*" In *Making Movies Black*. New York: Oxford University Press, 1993, 102–25.

Crowdus, Gary, and Udayan Gupta. "*A Luta Continua*: An Interview with Robert Van Lierop." *Cineaste* 9, no.1 (November 1978): 26–31.

Cutler, Janet K. "Marlon Riggs: Identity and Ideology," *Persistence of Vision: The Journal of the Film Faculty of the City University of New York*, no. 11 (1995): 65–74.

Dastoor, Rhoda. "Black and Beautiful: Rhoda Dastoor Presents the View of Eminent Afro-American Directors and Actors on Film and Social Consciousness." *Saturday Statesman*, 11 February 1989, 1–5.

Dates, Jannette L., and William Barlow. *Split Image: African Americans in the Mass Media*. Washington, D.C.: Howard University Press, 1990.

Davis, Mike. *City of Quartz: Excavating the Future in Los Angeles*. New York: Verso, 1990.

Delgado, Richard, and Jean Stefancic. "#461 Critical Race Theory: An Annotated Bibliography." *Virginia Law Review*, March 1993, 1.

De Witt, Karen. "A Memory of Harlem." *American Film*, November 1978, 18–27.

Diawara, Manthia, "The Absent One: The Avant-Garde and the Black Imaginary in *Looking for Langston*." *Wide Angle* 13, nos. 3–4 (July/October 1991): 96–109.

———. *African Cinema: Politics and Culture*. Bloomington: Indiana University Press, 1992.

———, ed. *Black American Cinema*. New York: Routledge, 1993.

———. "Black British Cinema: Spectatorship and Identity Formation." *Territories, Public Culture* 3 (1990): 1.

———. "Black Spectatorship: Problems of Identification and Resistance." *Screen* 29, no. 4 (Winter 1988).

———. "New York and Ouagadougou: The Homes of African Cinema." *Sight and Sound* 3, no. 11 (November 1993): 26–28.

———. "Performative Acts: Black Studies, Cultural Studies." *AfterImage*, October 1992, 7.

Donovan, Livia. "Producers of PBS Fall Special, LIBERATORS, say: 'We're taking a stand against racism.'" *Volunteer Voice* 2, no. 1 (March 1992): 1, 6–7.

Douglas, Stanley. "Lecture of 1989." *Independent Eye* 10, no. 2 (Winter 1989): 36–40.

Dubner, Stephen J. "Massaging History." *New York*, 8 March 1993, 46.

Edelman, Rob. "Storyteller of Struggles: An Interview with Haile Gerima." *The Independent* 8, no. 8 (October 1985): 16–19.

Editorial Staff. "'The Liberators,' The American Jewish Committee, and a challenge to Channel 13." *New York Amsterdam News*, 18 September 1993, 12.

Ehrhart-Morrison, Dorothy. *No Mountain High Enough: Secrets of Successful African American Women*. Berkeley: Conari Press, 1997.

Ellis, Jack C. *The Documentary Idea: A Critical History of English Language Documentary Film and Video*. Englewood Cliffs: Prentice Hall, 1989.

Ellison, Ralph. "The Art of Romare Bearden." In *Going to the Territory*. New York: Random House, 1986, 227–38.

Euvrard, Janine. "William Greaves." In *Le Cinema Noir Americain*, edited by Mark Reid et al. Paris: CinemAction/Cerf, 1988.

Featherman, Mark. "Survivors Renew Ties with Black Liberators." *Forward*, 11 October 1991.

Flemming, Michael. "Abdul Jabbar's transition game is starting to score points." *Variety*, 4 May 1992, 12.

Ford, Richard T. "The Repressed Community: Locating the New Communitarianism." *Transition* 65 (1995): 96–117.

Forman, James. *The Making of Black Revolutionaries*. Seattle: Open Hand, 1985.

Foucault, Michel. *Power/Knowledge: Selected Interviews and Other Writings, 1972–1977*. New York: Pantheon Books, 1980.

Fusco, Coco. "Performance and the Power of the Popular." In *Let's Get It On: The Politics of Black Performance*. Seattle: Bay Press, 1995, 158–75.

———. *Young British and Black: The Work of Sankofa and Black Audio Film Collective*. Buffalo: Hallwalls/Contemporary Arts Center, 1988.

Gabriel, Teshome. *Third World Cinema in the New World*. Ann Arbor: University of Michigan Research Press, 1982.

Garafolo, Reebee. "Crossing Over: 1939–1990." In *Split Image: African Americans in the Mass Media,* edited by Jannette Dates and William Barlow. Washington, D.C.: Howard University Press, 1990.

Gates, Henry Louis, Jr. "The Blackness of Blackness: A Critique of the Sign and the Signifying Monkey." In *Black Literature and Literary Theory.* New York: Methuen, 1984, 285–93.

———. "Blood Brothers: Albert and Allen Hughes in the Belly of the Hollywood Beast." *Transition: An International Review* 63 (1994): 164–77.

———. "Hybridity Happens: Black Brit Bricolage Brings the Noise." *Voice Literary Supplement,* October 1992, 26–27.

———. "Looking for Modernism." In *Black American Cinema,* edited by Manthia Diawara. New York: Routledge, 1993, 200–207.

———. *"Race," Writing and Difference.* Chicago: University of Chicago Press, 1986.

———. *Thirteen Ways of Looking at a Black Man.* New York: Random House, 1997.

Gayle, Addison, ed. *The Black Aesthetic.* Garden City: Doubleday, 1971.

Georgakas, Dan, and Lenny Rubenstein, eds. *The Cineaste Interviews: On the Art and Politics of the Cinema.* Chicago: Lake View Press, 1983, 173–80.

George, Nelson. *Buppies, B-Boys, Baps & Bohos: Notes on Post-Soul Black Culture.* New York: Harper Collins, 1992.

———. "Wanted: Harlem Film Documentary Angel." *New York Amsterdam News,* 4 August 1979, 28.

———. "William Miles Films Harlem." *New York Amsterdam News,* 7 October 1978, D3.

Gever, Martha. "The Feminism Factor: Video and Its Relation to Feminism." In *Illuminating Video,* edited by Doug Hall and Sally Jo Fife. New York: Aperture, in association with the Bay Area Video Coalition, 1990, 226–41.

Gilroy, Paul. *Small Acts.* London: Serpent's Tail, 1993.

Goldberg, Jeffrey. "The Exaggerators: Black soldiers and Buchenwald." *New Republic,* 8 February 1993, 13.

Gordon, Asa R. "The Lesson of Buchenwald: A Death Camp of the Holocaust." World Wide Web, http://members.aol.com/asargordon/nazicamp.htm, 24 June 1997.

———. "'Liberators' under Fire." World Wide Web, http://members.aol.com/dignews/undrfire.htm, 24 June 1997.

Gray, Herman. *Watching Race: Television and the Struggle for "Blackness."* Minneapolis: University of Minnesota Press, 1995.

Greaves, William. "100 Madison Avenues Will Be of No Help." *New York Times,* 9 August 1970, 13.

Grundmann, Roy. "New Agendas in Black Filmmaking: An Interview with Marlon Riggs." *Cineaste* 19, nos. 2–3 (1993): 52–54.

Guerrero, Ed. *Framing Blackness.* Philadelphia: Temple University Press, 1993.

Hall, Stuart. "Cultural Identity and Cinematic Representation." *Framework* 36 (1989): 68–81.

———. "The Whites of their Eyes: Racist Ideologies and the Media." In *Silver Linings,* edited by George Bridges and Rosalind Brunt. London: Lawrence and Wishart, 1981, 28–52.

Hamilton, Charles V. "Blacks and Mass Media." In *Issues and Trends in Afro-American Journalism,* edited by James S. Tinney and Justine J. Rector. Washington. D.C.: University Press of America, 1980, 225–31.

Hampton, Henry, and Steve Fayer. *Voices of Freedom: An Oral History of the Civil Rights Movement from the 1950s through the 1980s.* New York: Bantam, 1990.

Haraway, Donna. "The Materiality of Information." In *Through the Looking Glass*, unpublished text.

Harris, Jessica B. "The National Black Theater." *The Drama Review* 16, no. 4 (December 1972): 40.

Harris, Lyle Ashton. "Cultural Healing: An Interview with Marlon Riggs." *AfterImage*, March 1991, 8–11.

Harris, Norma. "Documentary to Focus on Liberation of Jews by Black WW II Soldiers." *New York Amsterdam News*, 12 October 1991, 5.

Harris, Thomas Allen. "Searching the Diaspora: An Interview with John Akomfrah." *AfterImage*, April 1992, 10–13.

Hatch, James. "Interview with William Greaves." In *Artist and Influence*, edited by James Hatch and Leo Hamalian, vol. 9 (1990), 54–81.

———. "Interview with St. Clair Bourne." In *Artist and Influence*, edited by James Hatch, Leo Hamalian, and Judy Blum, vol. 15 (1996), 47–63.

Hemphil, Essex. "Brother to Brother." *Black Film Review* 5, no. 3 (1989): 14–17.

Hershman Leeson, Lynn. *Clicking In: Hot Links to a Digital Culture*. Seattle: Bay Press, 1996.

Hess, John, and Patricia R. Zimmerman. "Transnational Documentaries: A Manifesto." *AfterImage* 24, no. 4 (January–February 1997).

Higginson, Thomas. *Army Life in a Black Regiment*, edited and abridged by Genevieve S. Gray. New York: Grosset and Dunlap, 1970.

Hirsch, Marianne. *Family Frames: Photography, Narrative and Postmemory*. Cambridge: Harvard University Press, 1997).

———. "Mothers and Daughters: A Review Essay." *Signs* 7 (Autumn 1981): 200–22.

hooks, bell. "Performance Practice as a Site of Opposition." In *Let's Get It On: The Politics of Black Performance*, edited by Catherine Ugwu. Seattle: Bay Press, 1995, 210–21.

Howard, Steve. "A Cinema of Transformation: The Films of Haile Gerima." *Cineaste* 14, no. 1 (May 1985): 28–29, 39.

Hyatt, Marshall, comp. *The Afro-American Cinematic Experience: An Annotated Bibliography and Filmography*. Wilmington: Scholarly Resources, 1983.

Insdorf, Annette. "Liberating Subjectivity: More on the 'Liberators' Controversy." *New York Amsterdam News*, 9 October 1993, 12.

———. "Truths Lost in the Night and Fog." *Washington Post*, 26 September 1993, G4.

Jackson, Elizabeth. "Barbara McCullough, Independent Filmmaker, 'Know How to Do Something Different.'" *Jump Cut*, no. 36 (May 1991): 94–97.

Jacobs, Lewis, ed. *The Documentary Tradition*. New York: Norton, 1979.

Jamayane, Laleen, and Anne Rutherford. "Why a Fish Pond: An Interview with Trinh T. Minh-ha." *The Independent* 4, no. 10 (December 1991): 20–25.

James, David. *Allegories of Cinema: American Film in the Sixties*. Princeton: Princeton University Press, 1989.

James, George. "Nazi Survivors Reunite with Black Liberators." *New York Times*, 7 October 1991, B1.

Jameson, Frederic. *Signatures of the Visible*. New York: Routledge, 1992, 217–21.

Jimenez, Lillian. "Profile: William Greaves." *The Independent* 3, no. 10 (October 1980): 8–11.

Johnson, Thomas L., and Phillip C. Dunn, eds. *A True Likeness: The Black South of Richard Samuel Roberts, 1920–1936*. Columbia, S.C.: Bruccoli Clark; Chapel Hill: Algonquin Books of Chapel Hill, 1986.

Jones, G. William. *Black Cinema Treasures: Lost and Found*. Denton: University of North Texas, 1991.

Juhasz, Alexandra. "Our Auto-Bodies, Ourselves: Representing Real Women in Feminist Video." *AfterImage* 21, no. 7 (February 1994): 10–14.

Kamm, Henry. "No Mention of Jews at Buchenwald." *New York Times*, 25 March 1989, 8.

Katz, William Loren. *Eyewitness: The Negro in American History*. 10th ed. New York: Pitman Publishing Corp., 1967.

Kelly, Ernece B. "Where Are the Women Filmakers [sic]?" *Crisis* 98, no. 10 (December 1991): 8, 10.

Kendall, Steven D. *New Jack Cinema: Hollywood's African American Filmmakers*. Silver Spring: J. L. Denver, 1994.

Kennedy, L. "Soldiers' Stories." *Village Voice*, 17 November 1992, 65.

King, Sharon R. "Eyes on the Money." *Black Enterprise*, November 1988, 25.

Kleinhans, Chuck. "*Ethnic Notions, Tongues Untied*: Mainstreams and Margins." *Jump Cut*, no. 36 (1991): 108–26.

Kleinhans, Chuck and J. Lesage. "Listening to the Heartbeat: Interview with Marlon Riggs." *Jump Cut*, no. 36 (1991): 119–26.

Klotman, Phyllis R. "Conversation with Marlon Riggs, Oakland, California, August 1990." *Persistence of Vision: The Journal of the Film Faculty of the City University of New York*, no. 11 (1995): 75–85.

Klotman, Phyllis R., and Janet K. Cutler. "Keys to the Kingdom, A Final Interview with Jacqueline Shearer," *Black Film Review* 8, no. 2 (1995): 16–17, 32–33.

Klotman, Phyllis R., and Gloria J. Gibson. *Frame by Frame II: A Filmography of the African American Image, 1978–1994*. Bloomington: Indiana University Press, 1997.

Klotman, Phyllis Rauch. *Frame by Frame: A Black Filmography*. Bloomington: Indiana University Press, 1979; revised 1997.

———. "The Slave Narrative: One Hundred Years of Running." In *Another Man Gone: The Black Runner in Contemporary Afro-American Literature*. Port Washington, N.Y.: Kennikat Press, 1977, 10–22.

Knee, Adam, and Charles Musser. "William Greaves, Documentary Filmmaking, and the African-American Experience." *Film Quarterly* 45, no. 3 (Spring 1992).

Kotz, Liz. "Crises of Language and Difference." *AfterImage*, November 1989, 29–31.

Kresh, Paul. "Black Soldiers Gave the Gift of Life." World Wide Web, http://members.aol.com/dignews/jewishwk.htm, 1 January 1998. Originally published in *The Jewish Week*, 6–12 November 1992.

Lardeau, Yann. "Haile Gerima: Pour un mouvement de libération culturelle." *Le Monde Diplomatique* 364 (July 1984): 5.

Leab, Daniel, Jr. "Clement Price, *Liberators*, and Truth in History: A Comment." *Historical Journal of Film, Radio and Television* 14, no. 4 (1994): 475–78.

———. "Clement Price, *Liberators* (U.S., 1992), and Truth in History: Some Comments." In *World War II, Film, and History*, edited by John Whiteclay Chambers II and David Culbert. New York: Oxford University Press, 1996, 137–46.

———. *From Sambo to Superspade: The Black Experience in Motion Pictures*. Boston: Houghton Mifflin Co., 1976.

Lee, Rohama. "The Whirlwind World of William Greaves." *American Cinematographer*, August 1985, 68–72.

Lee, Ulysses. *United States Army in World War II, Special Studies: The Employment of Negro Troops*. Washington, D.C.: Office of the Chief of Military History, United States Army, 1966.

Lekatsas, Barbara. "Encounters: The Film Odyssey of Camille Billops." *Black American Literature Forum* 25, no. 2 (Summer 1991): 395–408.

Lemann, Nicholas. *The Promised Land: The Great Black Migration and How It Changed America.* New York: Knopf, 1991.

Leveritt, Annie, and Toni L. Armstrong. "Filmmaker, Activist, Writer: Michelle Parkerson." *Hot Wire,* July 1987, 26–28.

Lewis, David Levering. *W. E. B. Du Bois: Biography of a Race, 1868–1919.* New York: Henry Holt and Co., 1993.

Leyda, Jay, and Charles Musser, ed. *Before Hollywood: Turn-of-the-Century Film from American Archives.* New York: American Federation of Arts Film Program, 1986.

Little, Monroe. "Review: *Eyes on the Prize.*" *Journal of American History* 73 (1986): 837.

Locke, Alan. *The New Negro.* New York: Atheneum, 1968.

Lord, Lewis J., and Jeannye Thornton. "A Journey to Another Time and, to Many, Another World." *U.S. News & World Report,* 9 March 1987, 58.

Lott, Tommy. "A No-Theory Theory of Contemporary Black Cinema." *Black American Literature Forum* 25, no. 2 (Summer 1991): 221–36.

Lubiano, Wahneema. "Black Ladies, Welfare Queens, and State Nubstrels: Ideological War by Narrative Means." In *Race-ing Justice, En-gendering Power: Essays on Anita Hill, Clarence Thomas, and the Construction of Social Reality,* edited by Toni Morrison. New York: Pantheon Books, 1992, 323–63.

Lubiano, Wahneema, ed. *The House That Race Built: Black Americans, U.S. Terrain.* New York: Pantheon Books, 1997.

Lurie, Theodora. "Second Life for 'Eyes on the Prize.'" *Ford Foundation Letter* 22, no. 2 (Fall 1991): 1–5.

MacCann, Richard Dyer. *The People's Films: A Political History of U. S. Government Motion Pictures.* New York: Hastings House, 1973.

MacDonald, J. Fred. *Blacks in White TV: African Americans in TV since 1948.* 2nd ed. Chicago: Nelson-Hall Publishers, 1992.

MacDonald, Scott. "Sunday in the Park with Bill: William Greaves' *Symbiopsychotaxiplasm: Take One.*" *The Independent* 15, no. 4 (May 1992): 24–29.

———. "William Greaves." In *Screen Writings: Scripts and Texts by Independent Filmmakers.* Berkeley: University of California Press, 1995, 31–48.

Mankiewicz, Frank, and Joel L. Swerdlow. *Remote Control: Television and the Manipulation of American Life.* New York: Times Books, 1978.

Mapp, Edward. *Blacks in American Films: Today and Yesterday.* Metuchen, N.J.: Scarecrow Press, 1972.

Masilela, Ntongela. "Interconnections: The African and Afro American Cinema." *The Independent* 11, no. 1 (January/February 1988): 14.

Mattox, Michael. "St. Clair Bourne: Alternative Black Visions." *Black Creation* 4, no. 3 (Summer 1973): 32.

McDowell, Deborah E. "Reading Family Matters." In *Changing Our Own Words: Essays on Criticism, Theory, and Writing by Black Women,* edited by Cheryl A. Wall. New Brunswick: Rutgers University Press, 1989, 75–97.

Mercer, Kobena. *"Black Is . . . Black Ain't." Sight and Sound,* July 1994, 22–23.

———. "Diaspora Culture and the Dialogic Imagination." In *Blackframes: Critical Perspectives on Black Independent Cinema,* edited by Mbye B. Cham and Claire Andrade-Watkins. Cambridge: MIT Press, 1988, 50–61.

———. "Recoding Narratives of Race and Nation." *The Independent* 12, no. 1 (January/February 1989): 19–26.

———. *Welcome to the Jungle: New Positions in Black Cultural Studies.* New York: Routledge, 1994.

Miles, William, and Nina Rosenblum. "The Filmmakers' Response to Kenneth Stern's Report to the American Jewish Committee." 5 March 1993.

Miller, James. "Chained to Devil Pictures." In *The Year Left 2*, edited by Mike Davis, Manning Marable, Fred Pfeil, and Michael Speinker. London: Verso, 1987.

Milloy, Courtland. "Truths about Blacks, Jews in Another War." *Washington Post*, 29 May 1994, B1.

Minh-ha, Trinh T. "Outside In, Inside Out." In *Questions of Third Cinema*, edited by Jim Pines and Paul Willemen. London: British Film Institute, 1989, 133–49.

Mork, Christian. "What's Up, Docu? Handcuffed 'Liberators' Stirs Challenge to Oscar Nom Process." *Variety*, 22 February 1993, 5.

Motley, Mary Penick, ed. *The Invisible Soldier: The Experience of the Black Soldier, World War II*. Detroit: Wayne State University Press, 1975.

Moutousamy-Ashe, Jeanne. *Viewfinders: Black Women Photographers*. New York: Dodd, Mead, 1986.

Moynihan, Daniel Patrick. *The Negro Family: The Case for National Action*. Washington, D.C.: Department of Labor, Office of Policy, Planning and Research, 1965.

Muhammad, Erika. "Hi-Tech Histories." *Independent Film & Video Monthly* (July 1997): 32–37.

Murray, James P. "William Greaves: Documentaries Are Not Dead." *Black Creation* 4, no. 1 (Fall 1972): 10–11.

Nesteby, James. *Black Images in American Films, 1896–1954: The Interplay between Civil Rights and Film Culture*. New York: Lanham, 1982.

New American Cinema Group. In *Film Culture Reader*, edited by P. Adams Sitney. New York: Praeger, 1970, 70–83.

Nichols, Bill. *Blurred Boundaries: Questions of Meaning in Contemporary Culture*. Bloomington: Indiana University Press, 1994.

———. "'Getting to Know You . . . ': Knowledge, Power, and the Body." In *Theorizing Documentary*, edited by Michael Renov. New York: Routledge, 1993, 174–91.

———. *Ideology and the Image: Social Representation in the Cinema and Other Media*. Bloomington: Indiana University Press, 1981.

———. *Representing Reality: Issues and Concepts in Documentary*. Bloomington: Indiana University Press, 1991.

Noble, Gil. *Black Is the Color of My TV Tube*. Secaucus: Lyle Stuart, 1981.

O'Connor, John. "Three-Part Series on Blacks in the Military." *New York Times*, 18 May 1983, C27.

O'Grady, Lorraine. "Lorraine O'Grady on Black Women Directors." *Video, The Center for New Television*, March/April 1992, 1, 3.

Oulette, Laurie. "Too Little, Too Late? Miles and Rosenblum Defend *Liberators'* Accuracy." *The Independent* 16, no. 5 (June 1993): 4–6.

Parkerson, Michelle. "Answering the Void." *The Independent* 10, no. 3 (April 1987): 12–13.

Parks, Gordon. *A Choice of Weapons*. New York: Harper and Row, 1966.

Parmar, Pratibha. "That Moment of Emergence." In *Queer Looks: Perspectives on Lesbian and Gay Film and Video*, edited by Martha Gever, John Greyson, and Pratibha Parmar. New York: Routledge, 1993, 3–11.

Patton, George S., Jr. *War As I Knew It*. Boston: Houghton Mifflin Co., 1947.

Peretz, Martin. "Cambridge Diarist." *New Republic*, 8 March 1993, 42.

Petley, Julian, "Feature Films: *Testament*." *Monthly Film Bulletin* 56 (September 1989): 259–60.

Pfaff, Francoise. "Haile Gerima (1946–), Ethiopia." In *Twenty-five Black African Filmmakers*. New York: Greenwood Press, 1988, 137–55.

Pines, Jim. *Blacks in Film: A Study of Racial Themes and Images in the American Film*. London: Cassell and Collier Macmillan, 1975.

———. "The Cultural Context of Black British Cinema." In *Blackframes: Critical Perspectives on Black Independent Cinema*, edited by Mbye B. Cham and Claire Andrade-Watkins. Cambridge: MIT Press, 1988, 26–36.

Pines, Jim, and Paul Willemen, eds. *Questions of Third Cinema*. London: British Film Institute, 1989.

Pisar, Samuel. "Escape from Dachau: My Own, Private V-E Day." World Wide Web, http://members.aol.com/dignews/s-pisar.htm, 24 June 1997. Originally published in *Washington Post*, 7 May 1995.

Pochada, Elizabeth. "Another Military Liberation." World Wide Web, http://members.aol.com/dignews/nation.htm, 24 June 1997. Originally published in *Nation*, 22 February 1993.

Pogrebin, Letty Cottin. "Truth or Consequences: The 'Liberators' Controversy." *Tikkun* 8, no. 3 (May–June 1993): 55.

Pounds, Michael Charles. "Details in Black: A Case Study Investigation and Analysis of the Content of the United States War Department Non-fiction Motion Picture *The Negro Soldier*." Ph.D. diss., New York University, 1981.

Price, Clement Alexander. "Black American Soldiers in Two World Wars: *Men of Bronze* (1980) and *Liberators* (1992)." *Historical Journal of Film, Radio and Television* 14, no. 4 (1994): 467–74.

———. "*Men of Bronze* (U.S., 1980) and *Liberators* (U.S., 1992): Black American Soldiers in Two World Wars." In *World War II, Film, and History*, edited by John Whiteclay Chambers II and David Culbert. New York: Oxford University Press, 1996, 123–36.

Reid, Mark. *Redefining Black Film*. Berkeley: University of California Press, 1993.

Renov, Michael, ed. *Theorizing Documentary*. New York: Routledge, 1993.

Riggs, Marlon. "Black Macho Revisited: Reflections of a Snap! Queen." *The Independent* 14, no. 3 (April 1991): 32–34. Also appears in *Black American Literature Forum* 25, no. 2 (Summer 1991): 389–94; *Brother to Brother: New Writings by Black Gay Men*, edited by Essex Hemphill. Boston: Alison Publications, 1991.

———. "A Snap! Queen Deliberates: 'Reading' the Media." *Video*, November/December 1991, 6–8.

Riggs, Marlon, with Ron Simmons. "Sexuality, Television, and Death: A Black Gay Dialogue on Malcolm X." In *Malcolm X: In Our Own Image*, edited by Joe Wood. New York: St. Martin's Press, 1992, 135.

Riley, Clayton. "Snapshots of a Movement." *Christianity and Crisis* 16 March 1987, 97–98.

Rosen, Philip. "Document and Documentary: On the Persistence of Historical Concepts." In *Theorizing Documentary*, edited by Michael Renov. New York: Routledge, 1993, 58–59.

Rosenblum, Nina, and William Miles. "To ID readers:" *International Documentary*, March 1993, 11.

Ruddy, Christopher. "'Liberators' Took Liberties with the Facts." *Newsday*, 15 December 1992, 81.

———. "PBS Documentary Lies about Liberation of Concentration Camps." *New York Guardian*, December 1992, 1.

Rule, Sheila. "*The Making of Malcolm X*—The Documentary." *Ford Foundation Report*, Spring 1993, 21–24.

Rustin, Bayard. *Strategies for Freedom.* New York: Columbia University Press, 1976.

Saalfield, Catherine. "Overstepping the Bounds of Propriety: Film Offends Langston Hughes Estate." *The Independent* 13, no. 1 (January/February 1990): 5–8.

———. "Tongues Tied: Homophobia Hamstrings PBS." *The Independent* 14, no. 8 (October 1991): 4–6.

Sampson, Henry T. *Blacks in Black and White: A Source Book on Black Films.* Metuchen, N.J.: Scarecrow Press, 1977.

Sandler, Kathe. "Finding a Space for Myself in My Film about Color Consciousness." In *Picturing Us,* edited by Deborah Willis. New York: The New Press, 1994, 105–12.

Scarupa, Harriet Jackson. "Filmmakers at Howard." *New Directions* (April 1983): 4–10.

Scott, Tony. "*Liberators: Fighting on Two Fronts in World War II.*" *Variety,* 9 November 1992, 66.

Scott, William. "World War II Veteran Remembers the Horror of the Holocaust." Pamphlet, date unknown.

Seiter, Ellen, et al., eds. *Remote Control: Television, Audiences and Cultural Power.* New York: Routledge, 1989.

Shohat, Ella, and Robert Stam. *Unthinking Eurocentrism: Multiculturalism and the Media.* London: Routledge, 1994.

Sitney, P. Adams. *Visionary Film.* New York: Oxford University, 1974.

Smith, Valerie. "The Documentary Impulse in Contemporary U.S. African-American Film." In *Black Popular Culture,* a project of Michele Wallace, edited by Gina Dent. Seattle: Bay Press, 1992, 56–65.

Snead, James. "Images of Blacks in Black Independent Films: A Brief Survey." In *Blackframes,* edited by Mbye Cham and Claire Andrade-Watkins. Cambridge: MIT Press, 1988, 16–25.

———. "Repetition as a Figure of Black Culture." In *Black Literature and Literary Theory,* edited by Henry Louis Gates Jr. New York: Methuen, 1984, 59–79.

———. *White Screens Black Images: Hollywood from the Dark Side.* New York: Routledge, 1994.

Spillers, Hortense. Mama's Baby, Papa's Maybe: An American Grammar Book." *Diacritics* 17, no. 2 (Summer 1987): 65–81.

Stern, Kenneth S. "*Liberators:* A Background Report." Pamphlet, The American Jewish Committee, 10 February 1993.

Tajima, Renee. "Double Vision: Teamwork on *Eyes on the Prize II.*" *The Independent* 13, no.4 (April 1990): 21–23.

Tapley, Mel. "Bill Miles and Baruch Professor Make TV Documentary on Harlem." *New York Amsterdam News,* 24 January 1981, 33.

Tatum, Wilbert A. "A 'Liberator' from Harlem." *New York Amsterdam News,* 9 October 1993, 1.

———. "*Liberators: Fighting on Two Fronts in WWII*: Wins Coveted Prize." *New York Amsterdam News,* 16 October 1993, 12.

Taubin, Amy. "New Directors: From Upper Volta to Staten Island." *Village Voice,* 29 March 1983, 55.

Taylor, Clyde. "Black Films in Search of a Home." *Freedomways,* 4th quarter 1983, 226–33.

———. "The L.A. Rebellion: A Turning Point in Black Cinema." The New American Filmmakers: Selections from the Whitney Museum of American Art Film Program Series 26, Circular, 3–19 January 1986.

———. "Interview with St. Clair Bourne." In *Artist and Influence,* edited by James Hatch, Leo Hamalian, and Judy Blum, vol. 15 (1996), 47–63.

Temin, Christine. "Boston's Conscience Turns 100." *The Boston Globe,* 25 May 1997, N1.

Terkel, Studs. *"The Good War": An Oral History of World War Two.* New York: Pantheon Books, 1984.

Thelwell, Michael. "Pieces of the Dream." *Mother Jones,* February / March 1987, 58–59.

———. "TV Electronic Stimulus for Black Revolution." *Messenger* (Athens, Ohio), 27 December 1968, 4.

Treaster, Joseph B. "Film Blocked on Blacks Freeing Jews From Camps." *New York Times,* 12 February 1993, B3.

———. "WNET-TV Inquiry Finds No Proof Black Unit Freed 2 Camps." *New York Times,* 8 September 1993.

Turkle, Sherry. *Life on Screen: Identity in the Age of the Internet.* New York: Simon and Schuster, 1995.

United States Kerner Commission. *Report of the National Advisory Commission on Civil Disorders.* Toronto: Bantam Books, 1968.

Wali, Monona. *"Eyes on the Prize:* AFI Seminar Examines Black Participation in American Media." *The Independent* 10, no. 5 (June 1987): 8–9.

———. "Life Drawings: Charles Burnett's Realism." *The Independent* 11, no. 8 (October 1988): 16–22.

Wallace, Michele. *Black Macho and the Myth of the Superwoman.* New York: Dial Press, 1978. Reprinted New York: Verso, 1990.

Ward, Geoffrey C. "Matters of Fact: Up by the Bootstraps from Slavery." *American Heritage,* December 1986, 12, 14.

Warner, Virginia. *"The Negro Soldier:* A Challenge to Hollywood." In *The Documentary Tradition,* edited by Lewis Jacobs. New York: W. W. Norton, 1979, 224–25.

Waugh, Thomas. "Beyond Verite: Emile de Antonio and the New Documentary of the Seventies." In *Movies and Methods, Volume II,* edited by Bill Nichols. Berkeley: University of California Press, 1985, 233–57.

West, Cornel. "The New Politics of Cultural Difference." In *Out There: Marginalization and Contemporary Cultures,* edited by Russell Ferguson et al. Cambridge: MIT Press; New York: New Museum of Contemporary Art, 1990.

White, Keith. *"Glory* Short on Truth." Gannett News Service. 19 January 1990, 1–5.

Williams, David. *Eleanor Roosevelt's Niggers.* Davenport: Laura Books, 1976.

Williams, Jeanne. *"Eyes on the Prize: America's Civil Rights Years." Sightlines,* Winter 1987 / 88, 18–19.

Williams, John. "Black Filmmaking in the 1990s: A Pioneering Event." *The Independent* 11 (December 1988): 16–19.

Williams, Juan. *Eyes on the Prize: America's Civil Rights Years, 1954–1965.* New York: Penguin, 1987.

Williams, Patricia. *The Alchemy of Race and Rights.* Cambridge: Harvard University Press, 1991.

Williamson, Judith. "Two Kinds of Otherness: Black Film and the Avant Garde." *Screen* 29, no. 4 (Autumn 1988): 106–18.

Willis-Thomas, Deborah. *Black Photographers, 1884–1940: An Illustrated Biobibliography.* New York: Garland, 1985.

Winston, Michael R. "Racial Consciousness and the Evolution of Mass Communications in the United States." *Daedalus* 3, no. 4 (Fall 1982): 171–82.

Wolfe, George C. "Camille Billops." *A Journal for the Artist* 6 (Spring 1986): 27.

Wong, Herman. "Black Film Maker [Carlton Moss] Still Battling Stereotypes." *Los Angeles Times*, 30 May 1986, F 1.

Woods, Gerald. *The Police in Los Angeles: Reform and Professionalization*. New York: Garland Publishers, 1993.

Woodson, Carter G. *The Miseducation of the Negro*. Trenton: Africa World Press, 1993.

Yearwood, Gladstone L. "*Sweet Sweetback's Baadasssss Song* and the Development of the Contemporary Black Film Movement." In *Black Cinema Aesthetics: Issues in Independent Black Filmmaking*, edited by Gladstone L. Yearwood. Athens: Ohio University Center for Afro-American Studies, 1982, 53–66.

SELECTED REVIEWS

Allah Tantou

Chevallier, J. "*Allah Tantou.*" *Jeune Cinema* no. 288 (May/June 1991): 42.

Holden, Stephen. "Review/ Film Festival: Independence in Africa and Death in High Places." *New York Times*, 30 September 1992, C 18.

. . . But Then, She's Betty Carter

Daniel, Tina. Review of *But Then, She's Betty Carter. Variety*, 22 April 1981, 24.

Cycles

Willman, Chris. "Social Themes Dominate Film School's 'Women's Works.'" *Los Angeles Times*, 10 April 1989, F 2.

Eyes on the Prize

Covington, W. K. "*Eyes on the Prize: America's Civil Rights Years.*" *Sightlines* 21, no. 2 (1987/1988): 18–19.

Goodman, Walter. "'*Eyes on the Prize*,' Rights Struggle." *New York Times*, 19 November 1986, C 25.

Nonprint Editorial Staff. Review of *Eyes on the Prize. Booklist* 84, no. 10 (15 January 1988): 884.

Sitkoff, Harvard. "Film Review: *Eyes on the Prize.*" *Film and History*, May 1987, 43.

Eyes on the Prize II

Davis, Thulani. "A Sequel Due North." *Village Voice*, 30 January 1990, 57–58.

Goodman, W. "Recalling the Pursuit of the Still Elusive Prize." *New York Times*, 15 January 1990, C 11.

Hays, C. L. "Overcoming Obstacles to a Civil-Rights Chronicle." *New York Times*, 14 January 1990, 31–32.

Kantroqitz, Barbara. "Eyes Still on the Prize." *Newsweek*, 15 January 1993, 63.

Leonard, John. "Television: Divided We Fall." *New York*, 15 January 1990, 57.

Scott, T. Review of *Eyes on the Prize*—Second Season. *Variety*, 10 January 1990, 10.

Stahel, Thomas H. "A Potpourri of Genres." *America*, 17 February 1990, 153.

Weisbrot, Robert. Review of *Eyes on the Prize II. The Journal of American History* 77 (December 1990): 1128–29.

Zoglin, Richard. "When the Pot Overflowed." *Time*, 15 January 1990, 52.

Fade to Black

James, Caryn. "Critic's Notebook: Film as a Shaper of American Culture." *New York Times*, 19 April 1991, C 24.

Finding Christa

Canby, Vincent. "Documentary of Mother-Daughter Reconciliation." *New York Times,* 24 March 1992, C 15.

Moore, Darrell. "Movie Review: *Finding Christa.*" *AfterImage* 19, no. 9 (April 1992): 5.

Thomas, Kevin. "Movie Review; Los Angeles Festival, 'Home, Place, and Memory.'" *Los Angeles Times,* 11 September 1993, F 8.

Handsworth Songs

Auguste, R. "*Handsworth Songs:* Some Background Notes." *Framework* 35 (1988): 9–18.

Benson, Sheila. "Screenings in British Film Festival." *Los Angeles Times,* 18 February 1988, F 6.

Eisner, Ken. "Seven Songs for Malcolm X." *Daily Variety* 24 June 1993.

Petley, J. "Possessed by Memory." *Monthly Film Bulletin* 56 (September 1989): 260–61.

Williamson, J. "Cinema: To Haunt Us." *New Statesman,* 9 January 1987, 26–27.

In Motion: Amiri Baraka

Corry, J. "TV: Documentary Film Examines Amiri Baraka." *New York Times,* 28 June 1983, C 15.

I Remember Harlem

Clarke, G. "Television: Midwinter Night's Dream: 'I Remember Harlem.'" *Time,* 26 January 1981, 73.

Garisto, L. "Some Positive Thinking about Harlem." *New York Times,* 1 February 1981, 29.

Liberators

"Controversial Documentary." *Television Digest* 33, no. 39 (27 September 1993): 4.

Finkle, Lee. "*Liberators—Fighting on Two Fronts in World War II.*" *Journal of American History* 80, no. 3 (December 1993): 1192.

Greenberg, Melinda. "A Story of Liberation." *Baltimore Jewish Times,* 6 November 1992, 92.

O'Connor, J. J. "Review/ Television: America's Black Army and a Dual War Front." *New York Times,* 11 November 1992, C 24.

"PBS Film Voices Memories of Concentration Camp Liberators." *Jewish Advocate,* 29 October 1992, 18.

Review of *Liberators. Variety,* 9 November 1992, 66.

"The 761st Tank Battalion 'Black Panthers' on PBS." *New Pittsburg Courier,* 4 November 1992, B 1.

Looking for Langston

Gray, L. "Olympic Play." *New Statesman and Society,* 16 March 1990, 47.

Hoberman, J. "Young, Gifted, Black." *Village Voice,* 7 November 1989, 67+.

James, Caryn. "Film Festival: A Trip into the Middle Ages and a View of Langston Hughes." *New York Times,* 1 October 1989, 61.

Katzman, L. "Review." *Film Comment* 25, no. 6 (November/December 1989): 69.

Mercer, K. "*Looking for Langston.*" *Monthly Film Bulletin* 57 (February 1990): 45.

Thomas, Kevin. "'Langston' Dramatizes Black Gay Experience." *Los Angeles Times,* 26 January 1990, F 10.

Lumumba: Death of a Prophet

Holden, Stephen. "Review / Film Festival: Independence in Africa and Death in High Places." *New York Times*, 30 September 1992, C 18.

The Massachusetts 54th Colored Infantry

Holston, Noel. "Critic's Choice." *Minneapolis Star Tribune*, 14 October 1991, 8E.
Mink, Eric. "Public TV: Quality Now, Problems Later." *St. Louis Post-Dispatch*, 22 September 1991, 9G.
Stewart, Zan. "'Colored Infantry' Views Race in 1860s." *Los Angeles Times*, 14 October 1991, F11.

Men of Bronze

Howard, Juanita R. "Men of Bronze." *Film Library Quarterly* 12, no. 4 (1979): 44–46.
Millender, Dharathula H., and William Greaves. Review of *Men of Bronze*. *Film News* 36 (Spring 1980): 36.
Review of *Men of Bronze*. *Variety*, 28 September 1977, 22.

Midnight Ramble

Goodman, Walter. "Prewar Black Movies, Downside Up." *New York Times*, 25 October 1994, C 20.

No Regrets

Holden, Stephen. "The Self Stays Strong amid Shades of Prejudice." *New York Times*, 25 June 1993, C 15.

Suzanne Suzanne

Canby, Vincent. "Screen: 'Wend Kuuni.'" *New York Times*, 27 March 1983, 55.
Moore, Darrell. "Movie Review: *Suzanne Suzanne*." *AfterImage* 19, no. 9 (April 1992): 5.
Thomas, Kevin. "Movie Review; Los Angeles Festival, 'Home, Place, and Memory.'" *Los Angeles Times*, 11 September 1993, F 8.

Tongues Untied

Pincheon, B. S. "Invisible Men Made Visible." *Black Camera* 6, no. 1 (1991): 5–6.

CONTRIBUTORS

PAUL ARTHUR is Associate Professor of English at Montclair State University; he has published widely on avant-garde and nonfiction film, and writes regularly for *Film Comment* and *Cineaste*.

HOUSTON A. BAKER, JR., is Professor of English and Director of the Center for the Study of Black Literature and Culture at the University of Pennsylvania. His writing on African American representation in film, literature, and music includes: *Afro-American Poetics: Revisions of Harlem and the Black Aesthetic; Black Studies, Rap and the Academy; Modernism and the Harlem Renaissance; Workings of the Spirit: Poetics of Afro-American Women's Writings*.

MARK F. BAKER is a doctoral candidate in the Critical Studies Department at the University of Southern California and has worked in film production.

PEARL BOWSER is a historian, curator, and filmmaker; she is Founder / Executive Director of African Diaspora Images. Her writing has appeared in the anthology *Black Cinema Aesthetics, Black Scholar,* and *CineMaction*.

JANET K. CUTLER is Professor of English and Coordinator of the Film Program at Montclair State University. Her writing has appeared in *Black Film Review, Persistence of Vision,* and *Film Quarterly*.

MANTHIA DIAWARA is Professor and Chair of Africana Studies at New York University. He has published extensively on African and diasporic cinema and literature, including books such as *African Cinema* and *Black American Cinema*.

ELIZABETH AMELIA HADLEY is Associate Professor of African American Studies and Theater at Simmons College; she has worked in television and the theater. Her book *Bessie Coleman, The Brownskin Lady Bird,* has been optioned by Euzhan Palcy for a film based on the life of the famous flyer.

PHYLLIS R. KLOTMAN is Professor of Afro-American Studies and the Founder / Director of the Black Film Center / Archive at Indiana University. Her books on film include *Screenplays of the African American*

Experience, Frame by Frame: A Black Filmography, and *Frame by Frame II: A Filmography of the African American Image, 1978–1994* (with Gloria Gibson).

TOMMY LEE LOTT is Professor in the Department of Philosophy at the University of Missouri–St. Louis. He is editor of *Subjugation and Bondage: Critical Essays on Slavery and Social Philosophy* and *The Invention of Race: Black Culture and the Politics of Representation.*

ERIKA MUHAMMAD is a doctoral candidate in the Department of Cinema Studies at NewYork University; her dissertation, "Inside and Outside of the Box: Electronic Culture, the Popular, the Political," considers the relationship between digital culture and emerging artists.

VALERIE SMITH is Professor of English at the University of California at Los Angeles. She is editor of *Representing Blackness: Issues in Film and Video;* author of *Self-Discovery and Authority in Afro-American Narrative* and *Not Just Race, Not Just Gender: Black Feminist Readings.*

CLYDE TAYLOR is Professor of Film and Literature, Gallatin School and Africana Studies, New York University, and has published many articles about black cinema. His book *Breaking the Aesthetic Contract* was published by Indiana University Press in 1998.

INDEX

Italicized page numbers indicate illustrations.

abolitionist movement, 63n.5
Achebe, Chinua, 320
Addie and the Pink Carnation, 386
Affirmations, 383
African American community: access to technology by, 313; constructed through documents, 215–216; defining the, 216–220; diversity within, 311; documentation of, 211–214; of Harlem, *220*, 220–236; of Hell's Kitchen, 221, 222, 226, 235–236
African American documentation: concise history of, 212–214; on the 42nd Street Development Project, Inc., 236–237; as history of black community, 211–212; *I Remember Harlem* as, *220*, 220–236; *Menace II Society* as, 237–238, 240, 241–247; on slavery, 214–215; social issues and, 72–91; through documentaries, 247–248. *See also* High-Tech Documents
African American soldiers: contributions recorded by Miles, 40–55; controversy over liberator role of, 48–53, 57–62; early black documentaries on, 16–19, 23–25; in the Massachusetts 54th, 35–40; segregation/treatment of, 61, 70n.60; of the 761st Tank Battalion, 45–48, 53–55, 57, 67n.36, 69n.49; witnesses to liberation role of, 55–62; as World War II liberators, 45–48
African American women: bond between generations of, 180–181; culture transmitted by artists, 174–182; *The Different Drummer* on military, 45; *Gotta Make This Journey* on artistic, 167–168; *The Massachusetts 54th* on, 39–40; media representation of, 135; performance documentaries on, 199–204, 208n.32
African Americans: access to technology by, 313; chroniclers of, 7; gay

stereotypes of, 380–381; media stereotypes of, 73–74, 194, 210n.50, 277–278; race theaters catering to, 6–7, 31n.11, 194, 195–196; relationship between Jews and, 48–49, 62, 65n.24. *See also* black documentaries
African symbolic conventions/codes, 304–305
The Afro-American, 24
Afro-American Film Company, 15, 16
Afro-Dance, 155–156, 193
Aimé Césaire: A Voice for History, 140
Akomfrah, John, 319, 320–321
The Alchemy of Race and Rights, 63, 213–214
Alexander, William, 21, 22, *25*, 25–29, 27
Ali, the Fighter, 290
All American Newsreel Company, 27
All American Newsreels, 21
All This and Rabbit Stew, 194
allegories: in avant-garde productions, 282–289; used in *Lumumba*, 316–319
Allen, Alexander, 80
Allentuck, Daniel, 53
Alvin Ailey: Memories and Visions, 198
American Experience, 35, 48, 51
Amsterdam News, 8, 20
An I for an I, 278–279
"and they came riding into town on BLACK AND SILVER HORSES," 288–289
And We Still Survive, 86–87
Anderson, Benedict, 215–216
Anderson, Madeline, 40, *88*, 90, 93, 94, 109, 123, 138–139
Anderson, Trezzvant W., 54, 57
Anderson Watkins Film Company, 11
Andrews, Lawrence, 278, 279
Annabelle Dances, 198
Apollo Theater, 48, 231–233
art/artists. *See* black art documentaries
Associated Film Producers of Negro Motion Pictures, Inc., 27

Austen, Charles, 26
avant-garde productions: experimental extension of, 268–275; performance techniques used in, 287–289; relationship of black British/U.S., 294n.6; structural file style of, 277; unique approach of, 275–282; use of allegories/psychodramas in, 282–289, 293n.1, 296nn.24, 25. *See also* black documentaries

Bagwell, Orlando, 193–194
Baker, Ella, 135–136, *136*
Baldwin, Craig, 275
Baldwin, James, 112, 189–192, 209n.41, 212–213, 214, *229*, 230
Bambara, Tony Cade, 207n.21
Baraka, Amina, *159*
Baraka, Amiri, *159, 161*, 325, 327
Barnouw, Erik, 55
Barton, Haryette Miller, 28
Bass, Leon, 48
Battey, C. M., 3
BBC, 368–369
Before Stonewall, 364
Beloved, 228
Bender, Benjamin, *46, 46–47*, 52, 53, 56, 57–58
Bentham, Jeremy, 240
The Betrayal of Democracy, 310
Bibb, Leon, 87
Big City Blues, 152, *157*, 159
Billboard, 8
Billops, Camille, 252–253, 254, 255–257
biographical documentaries: compared to fictional films, 124–125, 140; difference in live/dead subjects of, 133–134; DuBoisean thought and, 145–147, 148–150; issues of, 127–130; paths of enlightenment through, 130–131, 140–149; possible new directions of, 148–149. *See also* black documentaries
The Birth of a Nation, 186, 194, 372, 381
Black and White and Color, 366–367, 370
black art documentaries: on artist as social force, 182–192; artist-subjects of, 153–154; cultural transmission/affirmation by, 174–182, 204–205; on evolution of black arts, 192–198; experimental extension of, 268–275; modes of, 154; origins of, 347; by Parkerson, Michelle, 164–173;

performance, 198–204; as response to media stereotype, 194, 210n.50; St. Clair Bourne on artists in, 155–164; special role of, 151–152. *See also* black documentaries
Black Arts Movement, 100, 269, 288
black athletes, 88–89
Black Celebration: A Rebellion against the Commodity, 276–277
black culture/identity: affirmed by *Black Journal*, 87–91; expressed by film language, 342–345; expressed through black documentaries, 124–127; influence on British film by, 370–371; misappropriation by white artists of, 164; music as expression of, 114–116; represented by artists of color, 305–306; Riggs on, 279–280; role of dance in, 156–157; separated from political documentary expression, 149; transmitted by art documentaries, 174–182, 204–205. *See also* African American documentation
black diaspora documentaries: allegorical mode of *Lumumba*, 316–319; films in symbolist mode of, 323–328; ironic mode of *Testament*, 319–323
black documentaries: avant-garde production of, 268–289, 293n.1, 294n.6, 296nn.24, 25; black culture/identity expressed through, 124–127; on the black family, 250–267; compared to fictional films, 124–125, 139–140, 350; compared to video, 350–351; during World War I/post-war years, 16–19; enunciation frameworks of, 272–273; expressing African American history, 119, 339–340; as generational bridge, 29–30; influence of *Black Journal* on, 91–95, 97n.41; inventing the contemporary, 75–78; legacy of, 62–63; on the Negro soldier, 23–25; performance, 198–204; researching early, 8; separation of culture from political, 149; of the silent era, 4–7; still photography and early, 3–4; William Alexander's short, 25–29. *See also* African Americans; biographical documentaries
black family: mainstream culture on, 250–251; myth of the heteronormative, 261–263; myth of ideal nuclear family and, 252–257; myth of

pathological, 257–261; myth of white family and, 263–266

Black Is . . . Black Ain't, 279–280, *280*, 281–282

Black Journal: achievements of, 75–78, 123–124, 356–357; black culture/identity affirmed by, 87–91; Charles Hobson's experience with, 359; influence on black filmmaking by, 91–95, 97n.41; nationalist–Marxist debate on, 82–87; origins/development of, 72, 73, 74; post-production on, *88*; production crew of, *78*; safety valve/stimulus functions of, 78–82; St. Clair Bourne on, 334–335

black movies, 185–187, 194–195. *See also* black documentaries

black nationalism, 76–77, 266n.6

Black Panther Party, 79, 80–82, 86, 89, 91

black performance documentaries, 198–204, 205n.3

black photographers: contributions of, 1–3; still photography/early film documentaries by, 3–4

The Black Photographers Annual, 329–330

Black Photographers, 1840–1940: An Illustrated Bio-bibliography, 2

black policemen, 81–82

Black Power, 77, 234

Black Power movement, 101

black production companies: during the 1910s/1920s, 15–16; Peter P. Jones Photoplay Ltd. as early, 11–15

Black Reconstruction, 327

Black Stars in Orbit, 372–373

black stereotypes, 73–74, 194, 210n.50, 277–278

The Black Theater Movement, 152, 195–196

black theaters, 6–7, 31n.11, 194, 195–196

Black Women in White America, 386

black world enlightenment: development of, 130–131; documenting role of Du Bois in, 131–133. *See also* biographical documentaries

Blackside, Inc., 100, 101–102, 103, *107*, 118, 120n.3, 137, 143–144

Blassingame, John, 214–215

"Bloody Sunday" protest, *99*

Blue, Carroll Parrott, 187, 329–334

Blue Nile Production Company, 28

The Bombing of Osage Avenue, 323–325, 328

Bond, Julian, 71, 101, 103

the book of ruins and desire, 302, 303

Borden, Gail Frey, 50

Boston Newsreel, 385

Bourne, St. Clair: on the artist as activist, 155–164; black life/culture documented by, 126; on future generations, 94; on *In Motion: Amiri Baraka*, 207n.12; influence of, 384; interview with, 334–337; mentored by Greaves, 109; as reporter/writer, 8, 21, 26; student protests documented by, 90, 92–93; on *The Making of Do the Right Thing*, 206n.9; use of interview material by, 161

Bradford, Cheryl Fabio, 179–180

Bridging the Digital Divide, 313

Bridgman, Jon, 50

Broome, George W., 9, 11, 18, 25

Broomfield, Nick, 272–273

Brown, Tony, 71, 109, 362

Brownsville raid, 10, 32n.19

Bryant, William, 26

Buchenwald death camp, 46–47, 50, 51, 52, 53, 56, 57–59

Burkina Faso: Land of the People of Dignity, 348–349

Bush, Anita, 14

Bush, George, 53

But Then, She's Betty Carter, 165–167, 374–375

The Butler, 16

Caesar, Adolph, 42, 221, 232

A Call to Duty, 22, 27

Carmichael, Stokely, 77, 92, 234

Carroll, Noël, xxi–xxii

Carter, Betty, 165–167

Cather, Willa, 283

Chamba, 156

Chenzira, Ayoka, 175, 178–179, 205, 337–340

Chicago code, 74–75

Chicago Defender, 8, 9, 12, 14, 16

Child, Abigail, 275

Choreography for the Camera, 198

Christianity, African slave, 233–234

The Cinematic Jazz of Julie Dash, 154, 174, 175, 176

civil rights movement: *Black Journal* discussion of, 79–80; role of music in, 112. See also *Eyes on the Prize;* race riots

Clarke, John Henrik, 141–142, 148

Clay, Cassius (Muhammad Ali), 114, 126, 138
Cleaver, Eldridge, 86, 92, 191
Cleaver, Kathleen, 79, 80, 82–83, 86
Clegg, Reverend, 92
Cokes, Tony, 276, 277, 278
Collins, Kathleen, 109
Color Adjustment, 367, 382
Colored America on Parade, 20
The Colored Champions of Sports, 20, 21
Colored Men to Arms!, 24
The Colored Soldiers Fighting in Mexico, 17
Conjure Women, 182
Connelly, Marc, 23
Conner, Bruce, 275
Conversations with Roy DeCarava, 187–188, 332–333
Cornell University incident, 89, 90
Du Côté du Katanga, 318
counter-enlightenment, 130–131
Crawford, Alonzo, 340–345
Crawford, Fred W., 58
Creating a Different Image: Portrait of Alile Sharon Larkin, 176, 181, 204
The Crisis, 4
Cross, Jimmy, 264–265
Cross, June, 263–266
cross-dressing performance, 169–170
Crowded, 340–341

Daáood, Kamau, 202–203
Dachau death camp, 50–51, 52, 59
dance, 156–157, 206n.10
Dash, Julie, 151, 154, 174–176, 199–201, 208n.26, 286, 391–392
Daughters of the Dust, 174, 175, 176, 392
David Holzman's Diary, 292
Davis, Angela, 281
Davis, Arthur P., 235
Davis, Benjamin O., 24
Davis, Eduard M., 238
Davis, Elmer, 26
Davis, Miles, 142
Davis, Thulani, 326–327
Davis, Zeinabu irene, 182, 208n.33
The Dawn of Truth, 12, 13, 14
A Day at Tuskegee, 8–11, 18, 32n.23
A Day in Birmingham, 7
A Day in the Magic City, 5
A Day with the Tenth Cavalry at Fort Huachaca, Arizona, 7, 19
DeCarava, Roy, 187–188

Delaney, Martin, 35–36
DeLarverie, Stormé, 168–170
Diary of a Harlem Family, 22, 123
diaspora, 315–316. See also black diaspora documentaries
Diawara, Manthia, 140, 152, 205n.3
Didn't We Ramble On, 193
The Different Drummer: Blacks in the Military, 44, 44–45, 62
Dirt, Ground, Earth, and Land, 344–345
Do the Right Thing, 277
Doing Their Bit, 17
Doublier, Francis, 276
Douglass, Frederick, 34, 35, 37
Douglass, Lewis Hayden, 38
"Dozens," 242, 249n.31
Dr. Martin Luther King, Jr.: An Amazing Grace, 129
Drea, Edward J., 60
Dreamkeeper, 304
Du Bois, W. E. B.: Black Reconstruction by, 327; documentary on, 118, 140, 323, 325–328; documenting enlightenment role of, 131–133; influence of DuBoisean thought by, 145–147, 148–149; The Philadelphia Negro by, 326; photograph of, 326; quoted, 113, 122; The Souls of Black Folk by, 10, 130, 132, 325; view on art, 100
Duffy, Christopher, 62
Dunbar Films, Monumental Pictures Corporation, 15
Dunbar, Paul Laurence, 16, 188–189
Dunye, Cheryl, 284–285, 287
Dutchman, 160

8th Illinois Regiment, 17
electronic books. See High-Tech Documents
Ellington, Bill, 60
Ellison, Ralph, 213, 214
The Employment of Negro Troops, 55
Encyclopedia of the Negro, 327
The End of the Holocaust, 50
Ethiopia, 28, 29
Europe, James Reese, 43
"An Examination of Liberators: Fighting on Two Fronts in World War II" report (1993), 52
Eyes on the Prize I: commitment to diversity by, 103–105; Jacqueline Shearer's work on, 387–388; legacy of,

119, 137–138; origins of, 100–101, 103; public television and, 105–110; role of music in, 110–117
Eyes on the Prize II, 35, 101, 103, 110, 111, 137–138, 387

Facts from Farm, Factory, and Fireside, 12
Fade to Black, 277–278, *278,* 333
family. *See* black family
FCC (Federal Communications Commission), 105–108
feminist video, 296n.26
15th New York National Guard, 41–42
Finding Christa, 255–257
First World Festival of Negro Arts, 196, 196–198
First World Order, 304
Fish, Hamilton, 41, 42
Flag, 284
Flavio, 22
For the Honor of the 8th Illinois Regiment, 13, 16, 17
Ford, Abraham (Abiyi), 208n.32, 345–351
Ford, Richard, 216–217
Forman, James, 85–86
Fort Wagner, 37, 40
42nd Street Development Project, Inc., 236–237
Foster Photoplay Company, 15
Foster, William, 14, 16
Foucault, Michel, 212
Four Women, 199–200
Fragments of Barbara McCullough, 199
Frantz Fanon: Black Skin, White Mask, 328
Frederick Douglass: An American Life, 25
The Freeman, 12, 13, 14
Freeman, Al, 134
Freeman, Monica, 374–375
Fundi: The Story of Ella Baker, 135, 136
Fusco, Coco, 369, 370

Gabriel, Teshome, 93
Gardelegen death camp, 52
Garrett, Kent, *88*
Garvey, Marcus, 7, 16, 145, 223–225
Gates, Daryl, 238–239, 240–241
Gates, Henry Louis, xxi, 206n.6, 209n.41
gay stereotypes, 380–382.
Gerima, Haile, 92, 93, 351–354
Gever, Martha, 210n.47
ghettocentricity, 246–247, 296n.20
Gibson, Linda, 284

Gift of the Black Folk, 25
Gilliam, Leah, 282–283
Gilroy, Paul, 252
Gimme Shelter, 292
Glory, 37, 38, 39, 40, 63n.6, 64nn.7, 8, 9
Godard, Jean-Luc, 317
God's Step Children, 6
Goode, Eslanda Cardoza, 128
Gordon, Asa, 51
Gorgeous Elks Parade, 12
Gotta Make This Journey: Sweet Honey in the Rock, 167–168
Grant, Harry, 16
Gray, Michael, 82
Greaves, William: accomplishments of, 108–110, 126, 347; cinematic career of, 289–293; *First World Festival of Negro Arts* by, 196–198; on history of race films, 194–195; as *Ida B. Wells* director, 137; interview with, 354–357; on place of black documentaries, 124; shown with Toni Morrison, *134;* work with *Black Journal* by, 75, 76, 77–78, *78,* 80, *88,* 89, 94
Green Pastures, 23
Greenaway, Peter, 302
Greider, William, 310
Grierson, John, 76, 218–219, 355
Grierson on Documentary, 355
Griffin, Ada Gay, 170, 172, 207n.30
Griffin, Farah, 221
Griffith, D. W., 372, 381
Guardian, 10

Haagen, Alexander, 246
Hamilton, Charles, 77, 79
HAMMER program (LADA), 241, 246
Hampton, Fred, 80, 81, 86, 92
Hampton, Henry, 94, 100, 101, 102–104, 108, 110, 119, 137
Handsworth Songs, 328, 364
Harkness, Jerald, 62
Harlem, *220,* 220–236
Harlem after Midnight, 23
Harlem Federal Theater, 23
Harlem Renaissance movement, 327
Harlem wedding photo, *223*
Harleston, Elise Forrest, 3
Harris, Thomas Allen, 261, 262, 286
Hatch, James, 252–253, 254, 256
Haynes Photoplay, 15, 16
Hayward, William, 42

Heaven, Earth, and Hell, 286
Hell's Kitchen, 221, 222, 226, 235–236
Heroic Negro Soldiers of the World War, 18
Hewitt, Masai, 80–81
The Highest Tradition, 27
High-Tech Documents: created by
    Pamela Jennings, 299–304; created by
    Philip Mallory Jones, 304–308; created
    by Reginald Woolery, 308–313;
    technology used to create, 298–299
Hill, Thelma, 179, 180, 383
Hirsch, Marianne, 180–181, 257
Historic Baptist Convention, 12
Hobbs, George, 62
Hobson, Charles, 93, 94, 357–362
Hoffman, Donna L., 313
Holocaust, 339. *See also* Buchenwald
    death camp; Dachau death camp
Holocaust revisionists, 60
The Homesteader, 7
hooks, bell, 199
Hooks, Benjamin L., 106–108
Horton, James, 39
House on Cedar Hill, 25
Howard, Juanita R., 44
Howard University black student
    movement, 113–114
Hudlin, Warrington, 206n.10, 362–364
Hughes brothers, 241, 247
Hughes, Langston, 162–164, 288
Huie, William Bradford, 29
Hutton, Bobby, 86

I Be Done Been Was Is, 182
I Remember Harlem, 220, 220–236, 227,
    233, 234, 235, 372
Ida B. Wells, 133, 136–137, 143
Illusions, 151
imagery: used in avant-garde produc-
    tions, 282, 287, 293n.1; used in High-
    Tech Documents, 302
In Motion: Amiri Baraka, 159–160, 162, 384
In Search of Our Fathers, 257–261
Indianapolis Freeman, 8
Insdorf, Annette, 61
Inside Bedford-Stuyvesant, 93
Integration Report #1, 123
Invisible Man, 213
The Invisible Soldier, 55

Jack Johnson, 142
Jackson, Billy, 193

Jackson, Jesse, 48, 71, *114*, 278
Jacobs, Gunther, 58–59
James Baldwin: The Price of the Ticket, 189–
    192
James, David, 274
Janine, 284–285
Jazz, the American Art Form, 164, 192
Jennings, Pamela, 299–304
Jewish/black relationship, 48–49, 62,
    65n.24
*John Henrik Clarke: A Great and Mighty
    Walk*, 141–142, 148
Johnson, George P., 15, 18
Johnson, Henry, 43
Johnson, Noble, 31n.12
Jones, Bill T., *280*
Jones, Lois Mailou, 348
Jones, Peter P., 3, 11–15, 25, 29
Jones, Philip Mallory, 304–308
Julien, Isaac, 276, 364–371

Keating, Kevin, *46*
"Keep Your Hand on the Plow," 111
*Keep Your Handsa Off the Park: A Role-
    Playing Game in Real and Virtual
    Worlds*, 308–312
Kelling, Douglas, 50
Kerner Commission mandate, 72–75, 79,
    91
Kerner Commission report, 71–72, 106
Kesting, Robert, 51
King, Coretta Scott, 112
King, Martin Luther, Jr.: biographical film
    on, 129–130; impact of assassination
    of, 76, 78, 83, 91, 93, 190–191; media
    strategies employed by, 101; photo-
    graph of, *99*; Poor Peoples' Campaign
    of, 83, 85, 387
King, Robin, 307
King, Woodie, Jr., 195–196
The Klansman, 29
Know Your Enemy, 289
Knowledge Reigns Supreme, 289
Kramm, Henry, 58

L.A. Rebellion, 294n.4
Langston Hughes: The Dream Keeper, 162–
    163, 328, 365–366
language: African symbolic conventions/
    code in, 304–305; cultural values
    expressed by film, 342–345; use of
    imagery, 282, 287, 302, 392n.1

Lansdown, John, 307
LAPD (Los Angeles Police Department), 238–239, 240–241, 242, 243–244, 246
Larkin, Alile Sharon, 176–178, 204
Lawson, Jennifer, 108
Lee, Spike, 124, 139, 140, 148, 237, 277, 353
Leeming, David, 191
Lerner, Gerda, 386
Lewis, Edward, 20–21
Leyda, Jay, 276
The Liberation of the Nazi Concentration Camps 1945, 50
Liberators: Fighting on Two Fronts in World War II, 47, 48–53, 56, 58, 60, 61. *See also* African American soldiers
Liberia, 28, 29
Life Is a Saxophone, 202–203
Life magazine, 22
The Life and Times of Harvey Milk, 384
Like It Is, 76, 360–361
Lincoln Jubilee, 12
Lincoln Motion Picture Company, 15–16, 17, 18, 19
A Litany for Survival: The Life and Work of Audre Lorde, 170–173
Lois Mailou Jones: Fifty Years of Painting, 348
Long, John, 55–56
Long Train Running, 379–380
Looking for Langston, 328, 364–365, 367
Lopes, Henri, 318
Lorde, Audre, 170–173, *172*
Lorentz, Pare, 218
Lost Boundaries, 290
Louis, Joe, 59, 60
Low, Seth, 9
Lumumba, 140, 316–319, 328
Lumumba, Patrice, *316*, 316–319

Macbeth, Arthur Laidler, 4, 31n.8
The Magic City, 7
Makarah, O. Funmilayo, 181
Malcolm X, 48, 85–86, 90, 115–116, *138*, 142, 148, 190, 226
Malcolm X, 124
Malcolm X: Make It Plain, 124, 137, 140
Malcolm X: Nationalist or Humanist, 138
Malcolm X: Struggle for Freedom, 138
Mama's Pushcart: Ellen Stewart and 25 Years of La Mama, 181
"The Man behind the Movie Shorts," 20

"Man with a Movie Camera," 15
Markbury, Donald L., 108
Mask, 304
The Massachusetts 54th Colored Infantry, 35–40, 64n.11, 387, 389, 390, 391
Massiah, Louis, 132, 133, 323–328
Maultsby, Portia, 111, 112, 114–117, 118
MAX technology, 303
McCarthyism, 327, 355
McConnell, E. G., *46*, 51, 56, 57
McCullough, Barbara, 198–199, 201–202
McElwee, Ross, 272
McKnight, Father Albert, 83, 84, 92
media: additional black-oriented TV news shows, 96n.15; avant-garde circles and black, 294n.5; *Black Journal* function as alternative, 89; black stereotypes in, 194, 210n.50, 277–278; coverage of African Americans by, 73–74; influence of entertainment, 346; narrative work of Hollywood, 339. *See also* television; video
Men Caught in the Middle, 81–82
Men of Bronze, 40–41, 43–44, 47, 56, 371
The Men of Montford Point, 62–63
Menace II Society, 237–238, 240, 241–247
Mercer, Kobena, xxi, 276
The Messenger, 4
Micheaux, Oscar, 6, 7, 25, 26, 185, 186–187, 361
Midnight Ramble, 185–187
Michelson, Annette, 365
MIDI (Musical Instrument Digital Interface), 303
Midnight Ramble, 185–187
Miles Educational Film Productions, Inc., 44
Miles, William: additions to historical record by, 40–45; *I Remember Harlem* directed by, 220, 221, 223, 226–227, 228, *229*, 231, 232; interview with, 371–373; *Liberators* controversy and, 48–53, 57–58; as *James Baldwin: The Price of the Ticket* co-producer, 189; on World War II liberators, 45–48, *46*, *49*
Millender, Dharathula H., 44
Miller, James, 91, 92
Miller, Melville "Doc," *41*, 42, 43, 56
Minnelli, Vincente, 24
The Miseducation of the Negro, 240
Miss Fluci Moses, 176, 177
Missing Relations, 392
Mitchell, Wilbur, 222

Mitgang, Herbert, 50
Moments without Proper Names, 22
Moore, Michael, 272
Moore, Richard, 83
Morrison, Toni, *134*, 174, 228
Moses, Fluci, 176, 177, 180
Moss, Carlton, 5, 21, 22, 23, 24, 54, 123, 141, 188, 192, 373–374
Moutoussamy-Ashe, Jeanne, 2
MOVE people, 323–324, *324*, *325*
Moynihan, Daniel Patrick, 250, 251
MS: A Negro City Built by a Former Slave, 12
Muhammad Ali (Cassius Clay), 114, 126, *138*
Muhammad, Elijah, 92, 145
The Murder of Fred Hampton, 82
Murphy, Carl, 16
Murphy, Eddie, 280
music: at funeral of Malcolm X, 115–116; civil rights movement use of, 112; exploration of blues, 157–159; as expression of black culture/identity, 114–116; *Eyes on the Prize* and role of, 110–117; Jacqueline Shearer on using, 389; MIDI technology used in, 303; misappropriation by white artists of, 164; rap, 234, 241, 289; used in *Fade to Black*, 278; used in *Massachusetts 54th Colored Infantry*, 38–39, 40, 64n.11
music videos, 289

NAACP, 325, 326
Nakamura, Robert, 330–331
Nanook of the North, 218
"Narrative Structure for New Media," 299
A Nation of Law? 1968–1971, 116
National Film Board (Canada), 76, 78
National Negro Business League (NNBL), 2–3, 4, 7, 9, 16
The Negro Family, 250–251
The Negro Soldier, 22, 23, 24, 25, 54, 123
Negro Soldiers Fighting for Uncle Sam, 12
The Negro World, 7
Neighbor-to-Neighbor program, 49
New Worlds, New Forms, 193–194
New York Age, 8, 11, 18–19
New York City Transit Union, 84
New York Daily News, 20
New York Times, 46, 48, 50
Newton, Huey, 78, 83, 86, 92, 94
Niagara Movement, 325

Nichols, Bill, xx, 153, 206n.5, 218, 234
Nigerian Art: Kindred Spirits, 333
Nixon, Richard, 84, 106
Noble, Gil, 127–129, 182–185, 192, 361
Norfolk Journal and Guide, 8
Notes of a Native Son, 212
Novak, Thomas P., 313
N.W.A. (Niggaz With Attitude) rap music, 241, 242, 247, 278

Of Blood and Hope, 59
On to Cuba, 13
183rd Engineers, 47
Opportunity Magazine, 4
Oscar Micheaux, Film Pioneer, 187
OWI (Office of War Information), 26–27

Paradigm Shift, 304, 306–308
Parker, William, 238, 242, 246
Parkerson, Michelle, 164–173, 374–376
Parks, Gordon, 21–22, 123, 208n.35, 230–231
Parks, Rosa, *102*
Patton, General George, 54–55, 68n.39
Paul Laurence Dunbar: America's First Black Poet, 188–189
Paul Robeson: Man of Conscience, 209n.36
Paul Robeson: The Tallest Tree in Our Forest, 127, 144, 147, 182–185
PBS (Public Broadcasting System): classic/high-profile subjects for, 125; *Eyes on the Prize* and, 105–110; nonfiction file format of, 137, 143–144; original mandate of, 150n.4. See also *Black Journal*
Peck, Raoul, 140, 316–319
performance documentaries, 198–204, 205n.3. *See also* avant-garde productions
Perlmutter, Alvin, 75
Peter P. Jones Photoplay Ltd., 11–15, 17
Peters, Brock, 142
The Phantom of Kenwood, 23
The Philadelphia Negro, 326
Phylon, 327
Pisar, Samuel, 59–60
Pittsburgh Courier, 16
Politics among Nations, 234
Poor Peoples' Campaign, 83, 85, 387
"Port Royal Experiment," 39–40
Portrait of Ethiopia, 28
The Potluck and the Passion, 287
Potter, Lou, 48, 49, 53, 76

Power/Knowledge, 243
Praise House, 152, 199, 200–201, 286
Prelude to Swing, 23
Progress of the Negro, 12
Prospero's Books, 302
psychodrama, 282–289, 293n.1, 296n.24,
  296n.25
The Pullman Porter, 16

Queen Sylvia, 158
A Question of Color, 384

race movies, 185–187, 194–195, 293n.1.
  See also black documentaries
race riots: *Black Journal* on, 76; following
  King's assassination, 83, 93; Kerner
  Commission mandate/report on, 71–
  75; strategy from television used in,
  95n.7; in Watts (1965), 238, 239. *See
  also* civil rights movement
race theaters, 6–7, 31n.11, 194, 195–196
racism: against black athletes, 88–89;
  against World War II black soldiers,
  57, 61, 70n.60; blaming the victim for,
  251; evident within film media, 123;
  popular discourse on, 122; within
  white-controlled unions, 84–85. *See
  also* social issues documentation
Rainbow Black: Poet Sarah W. Fabio, 179–
  180
Rambo, 278
Randolph, A. Philip, 4
rap music, 234, 241, 289
Reagon, Bernice Johnson, 111
Rebirth of a Nation, 13–14
Red Jackson, 230–231, 233, 236
Reeb, James, 100
Remembering Thelma, 178, 179, 383
*Remembering Wei Yi-fang, Remembering
  Myself*, 181, 393
Renov, Michael, xx, 218
*Resurrections: A Moment in the Life of Paul
  Robeson*, 209n.36
Richardson, Judy, 104, 105, 111
Ricks, Willie, 92
Riggs, Marlon, 153, 207n.22, 273, 276,
  279–280, *280*, 367, 368, 370; interview
  with, 376–383
Riley, B. F., 9
Riley, Clayton, 220, 221
The River, 218
Rivera, Geraldo, 361
Roberts, Richard Samuel, 15

Robeson, Paul, 127–129, 148, 155, 162,
  182–185, 209n.36
Robinson, Jackie, 125
Robinson, Renault, 81
Roger and Me, 272
Roosevelt, Theodore, 9, 10
Rosenblum, Nina, *46*, 47, 48, *49*, 58
Ruddy, Christopher, 51
Rushing, Byron, 36

Salem, Peter, 34
Sandler, Kathe, 178, 179, 383–385
Sapphira and the Slave Girl, 283
Sapphire and the Slave Girl, 282–283
Sapphire Tape #1, 287–288
Say Brother, 76, 106, 120n.17
Schindler's List, 338–339
Schmeling, Max, 59
Scott, Emmett J., 9, 11
Scott, William, 52–53, 58
Scurlock, Addison N., 4, 29
Seale, Bobby, 86, *114*
Secret Daughter, 263–266
Selznick Film Laboratories, 15
761st Tank Battalion, 45–48, 53–55, 57,
  67n.36, 69n.49
Seven Six One, 50
Shabazz, Betty, 48
Sharp, Saundra, 202
Shaw, Robert Gould, 37, 38, 63n.2
She Don't Fade, 287
Shearer, Jacqueline, 35, 37, 38, 40, 109,
  127, 385–391
Shohat, Ella, xx, 306
Short, Bobby, 191
Sidran, Ben, 233, 234
silent era black documentaries, 4–7
Sinclair, Upton, 245
Sisters in the Life, 392
Sixth Armored Division, 49–50
The Slacker, 15
The Slave Community, 214–215
slavery: Christianity and, 233–234;
  examination of, 214–215, 339
Sleigh, Alonzo, 93
Smith, Cauleen, 287–288
Smith, Leonard "Smitty," *46*, 56, 57
social issues documentation: to affirm
  black culture/identity, 87–91;
  contemporary black documentaries
  and, 75–78; Kerner Commission
  mandate and, 72–75; on nationalist–
  Marxist debate, 82–87; as revolution

safety valve/stimulus, 78–82. *See also* African American documentation; *Black Journal*; racism

The Social Life of Small Spaces, 245

Solitaire: dream journal, 299, 300, *301*, 301–302

Soul on Ice, 191

Soul, Sounds, and Money, 156

The Souls of Black Folk, 10, 130, 132, 325

sound/image splitting techniques, 282

Splash, 285, 286

Stam, Robert, xx, 306

The State Theater, 5, 6

Steckler, Paul, 387

Stein, Gertrude, 128

stereotypes: African American media, 73–74, 194, 210n.50, 277–278; gay, 380–381

Stern, Kenneth, 51, 53

Steward, Henry, *36*

still photography, 3–4

Storch, Larry, 263, 264, 265

Stormé: The Lady of the Jewel Box, 168–170, *169*, 375

Straight Outta Compton, 241

Street Corner Stories, 124, 363

structural film, 277

Suzanne Suzanne, 252–255, *253*

Swayle, Steven, 37

Sweet Honey in the Rock, 167–168

The Sweethearts of Rhythm, 27

Symbiopsychotaxiplasm: Take One, 290, 291–293

Syvilla: They Danced to Her Drum, 175, 178, 179, 207n.24, 337, 338

Talented Tenth, 326

Taylor, Cecil, 268

Taylor, Clyde, 206n.6, 210n.48

Teamwork, 25

technology: African American access to, 313; application in video work, 307–308; used in communication, 304–305; used in High-Tech Documents, 298–299

television: on audience and, 390; BBC, 368–369; black representation in prime time, 382; influence on Michelle Parkerson of, 375. *See also* media; PBS (Public Broadcasting System)

Testament, 319–323, 328

That's Black Entertainment, 194–195

Things Fall Apart, 320

Third World Newsreel, 369, 370

Thirteen/WNET review team, 50, 51–52, 53, 66n.30

This Is Our War, 16

Thomas, D. Irland, 8

Thorsen, Karen, 189

369th Colored Infantry, 17, 47

To Kill a Mockingbird, 277–278

Tongues Untied, 153, 276, 279, 280–281, 296n.23, 367–368, 380

Townsend, Robert, 124

Trammel, Donald, 278

Trinh, T. Minh-Ha, xxi, 328

Trooper of Company K, 17–18

Trotter, Monroe, 10

Trumpetistically, Clora Bryant, 182

Turpin Film Company, 15

Tuskegee and Its Builder, 12

Tuskegee Institute, 3, 10, 11

25th Texas Regiment, 10

Two Centuries of Black American Art, 25, 192

Two Dollars and a Dream, 135

Two Women, 332

United Federation of Teachers strike, 85

United Negro Improvement Association (UNIA), 7, 16

Unthinking Eurocentrism, 306

Valerie: A Woman! An Artist! A Philosophy of Life!, 181

Van Der Zee, James, 3, 7

Van Peebles, Melvin, 76, 92, 93

Varnette's World: A Study of a Young Artist, 332, 333

Victor George Galleries, 13

video: compared to documentaries, 350–351; computer technology applied to, 307–308; development of black, 311–312; feminist, 296n.26; MIDI technology used in, 303; music, 289. *See also* media

video art, 295n.13

Viewfinders, 2

The Village of Hope, 28

Vintage: Families of Value, *261*, 261–263

Visionary Productions, 62

Visions of the Spirit: A Portrait of Alice Walker, 181

vocal performance techniques, 283–284

Walker, Alice, 174, 181–182

Walker, C. J., 8, 136

Walker Manufacturing Company, 8
War As I Knew It, 54–55
War Department, 23–24, 26
Washington, Booker T., 7, 9, 10, 11, 16, 145, 325
Washington Post, 50, 61
Water Ritual #1, 201–202
Watts Riots (1965), 238, 239
Wealth in Wood, 28
W. E. B. Du Bois: A Biography in Four Voices, 118, 132, 140, 323, 325–328
Welbon, Yvonne, 174, 176, 391–393
Welcome, Ernest Toussaint, 17
Welcome, Jennie Louise Toussaint, 3, 4, 17, 29
Wells, Ida B., *133*, 133–135, 137, 143
When We Were Kings, 142, 144
Whipper's Reel Negro News, 15
Whyte, William, 245
Wiesel, Elie, 58
Williams, Frederick, 41, 42, 43, 56
Williams, Marco, 257–258, *258*, 259–261
Williams, Patricia, 63, 213, 214
Williams, Rhonda M., 251–252
Willis-Thomas, Deborah, 2
The Wilmington 10 — USA 10,000, 351–352

Winborn, Anna Mae, *27*
Wine, Alice, 111
WNET review team, 50, 51–52, 53, 66n.30
Wolfe, George C., 253
Woods, Meredith, 101–102
Woodson, Carter G., 240
Woolery, Reginald, 305, 308–313
World Saxophone Quartet, 198–199
World War I, 16–19
World War II: black newsreels/documentaries of, 21–22; Holocaust of, 339. *See also* African American soldiers
World Wide Web/Million Man March, 312, 312–313
Wright, Richard, 321

Xiang Tu movement, 392–393

Young, Andrew, 79
Young, British and Black, 369
Young, Linda, 200
Youth Pride and Achievement of Colored People of Atlanta, Georgia, 5
YWCA Parade, 16

Zajota and the Boogie Spirit, 337, 338